BISMARCK

BISMARCK

THE WHITE REVOLUTIONARY

VOLUME 1
1851–1871

Lothar Gall
translated from the German by
J. A. Underwood

London
UNWIN HYMAN
Boston   Sydney   Wellington

Published by the Academic Division of
Unwin Hyman Ltd
15-17 Broadwick Street, London W1V 1FP, UK

Unwin Hyman Inc.,
8 Winchester Place, Winchester, Mass. 01890, USA

Allen & Unwin (Australia) Ltd,
8 Napier Street, North Sydney, NSW 2060, Australia

Allen & Unwin (New Zealand) Ltd in association with the
Port Nicholson Press Ltd,
Compusales Building, 75 Ghuznee Street, Wellington 1, New Zealand

This translation first published in 1986
Originally published under the title
Lothar Gall, *Bismarck Der Weisse Revolutionär*,
© 1980 by Verlag Ullstein GmbH, Frankfurt am Main.
First paperback edition 1990

British Library Cataloguing in Publication Data

Gall, Lothar.
  Bismarck: the white revolutionary.
  1. Bismarck, Otto, Fürst von   2. Statesmen –
Germany – Biography
  I. Title
  943.08′092′4   DD218
  ISBN 0–04–943040–8 (hb) Volume 1
  ISBN 0–04–445778–2 (pb)
  ISBN 0–04–943053–X (hb) Volume 2
  ISBN 0–04–445779–0 (pb)

Library of Congress Cataloging-in-Publication Data

Gall, Lothar.
  Bismarck: the white revolutionary.
  Contents: v. 1. 1815–1871 – v. 2. 1871–1898.
  Translation of Bismarck.
  Bibliography: p.
  Includes index.
  1. Bismarck, Otto, Fürst von, 1815–1898.   2. Statesmen –
Germany – Biography.   3. Germany – Politics and
government – 1871–1888.   4. Prussia – Politics and
government – 1815–1870.   I. Title.
  DD218.G2213 1986   943.08′092′4 [B]   85–26658
  ISBN 0–04–943040–8 (hb) (v. 1)
  ISBN 0–04–445778–2 (pb)
  ISBN 0–04–943053–X (hb) (v. 2)
  ISBN 0–04–445779–0 (pb)

Set in 10 on 12 point Bembo by Oxford Print Associates Ltd
and printed in Great Britain at the University Press, Cambridge

for Claudia

'We cannot for one moment doubt
that he was a born revolutionary.
For revolutionaries are born
just as legitimists are born,
with a particular cast of mind,
whereas chance alone determines
whether the circumstances of his life
make of the same person
a White or a Red.'

Ludwig Bamberger,

Monsieur de Bismarck (1868)

CONTENTS

Contents

INTRODUCTION

The 'Circumstances of his Life':
Bismarck and his Time

'They are the great men in history', we read at one point in Hegel's *Lectures on the Philosophy of History*, written in 1830, 'whose own individual purposes embrace the substantial element that is the will of the World Spirit. This is where their true power lies.' They are great, that is to say, only in so far as they are able to recognize more surely and swiftly than other people the path from past to future marked out by a higher understanding, possibly doing so purely by chance or in the pursuit of some special interest. Though later generations were to interpret it quite differently, this represented a radical rejection of the idea that a great individual could decisively alter the course of history, for example by blocking 'what is due, what is necessary', or directing it along entirely new lines. In Hegel's view the greatness of a 'historically significant individual' lay purely in his or her becoming the 'agent of a purpose that forms a step in the advance of the universal spirit'.[1]

This quite decisive subordination of even what seemed to be the greatest and most powerful individuals to supra-individual historical forces of organization and development was not only specific to the Hegelian system. It was perfectly in tune with a general tendency of the period, although the popular view was already then a very different one. Among educated people of both right and left the prevailing opinion was that the organization and development of the life of history were above the arbitrariness of the individual, that higher forces were at work here and that these could be most clearly recognized through a correct view of and conception of the life of history itself. It thus appeared, in a deeper sense, as the great teacher. The tenet that possession of the past also ensured possession of the future and that a right understanding of the former rendered one capable of acting for the latter went largely unchallenged. This explains not only the extraordinary importance that historical discussions took on in the political life of the period between the fall of Napoleon in 1815 and the 1848 revolution, but also the powerful need for political action and political authority to be furnished with a historical legitimation.

It is no accident that both tendencies should have been reflected in the first public appearance of a man who was without question a 'historically significant individual' in Hegel's sense and who at the same time, unlike his uncritical admirers and admiring critics, retained throughout his life his generation's awareness of the supra-individual conditionality of political action and individual achievement – all his feeling for power and influence notwithstanding. When on 17 May 1847 the just 32-year-old 'estate-owner Otto von Bismarck-Schönhausen', only recently appointed deputy to one of the representatives of the Magdeburg knights, took the floor of the Prussian 'United Diet' for a 'justification' (*Berechtigung*), he argued in such terms from the start, in full awareness of what he was doing, seeking thus to legitimate his own position historically and supra-individually. In so doing he seized on one of the central issues of the great historical and political debate of the years immediately preceding the 1848 revolution, promptly making himself the talk of the capital, while at the same time he staked out positions that hardly anyone then suspected were going to have a decisive influence on the future.

His opportunity came with a speech by a representative of the traditionally liberal East Prussian knights, Ernst von Saucken-Tarputschen. Saucken had fought in the Wars of Liberation as a young man and was now one of the leaders of Prussian liberalism, which was just beginning to take shape as a political party. Like so many of the speeches to the assembly of delegates from the various provincial diets summoned to Berlin by the Prussian King Frederick William IV at the beginning of April 1847, Saucken's too had been a declaration of political principle. He had deplored the lack of trust currently prevailing between people and government and had pointed out how very different things had been in the period of major domestic reforms extending from 1806 to 1814 and clearly culminating in the Wars of Liberation, which they had all fought together. The view expressed was that it was only those domestic reforms and the expectations of freedom nourished by them that had enabled people to experience their outward situation – living under French rule – as being a constraint upon their freedom.

This view was not only common coin among the liberal historians of the period. It was the basis of the liberal belief that the external power and greatness of a state and the measure of freedom obtaining within it would in future be indissolubly interrelated. Indeed it was suggested that under the present leadership and given the continuing influence of the old ruling classes a second internal and external collapse of Prussia, as in 1806, would inevitably ensue. A fresh start must therefore be made, with fresh means and along fresh lines, from the point where the efforts of the reformers had petered out in 1815 under the Restoration.

All this was contested by the new and as yet completely unknown member who in striking contrast to his gigantic size had a curiously high-pitched, almost delicate voice and despite an often hesitant manner of speech evinced a quite remarkable degree of self-confidence. He dismissed the alleged connection between domestic reforms, demands for freedom at home and the successful struggle against foreign domination in the years 1813–14 as a thoroughly unhistorical construction. The Prussian people must be protected against such manipulations of history for transparently party-political ends: 'It seems to me that the national honour is ill-served', he stressed to 'repeated mutterings' from the majority of what despite its aristocratic composition was a predominantly liberal-minded body, 'by supposing that the maltreatment and humiliation that Prussians suffered at the hands of an alien oppressor were not sufficient to make their blood boil and cause all other feelings to be swamped by hatred of the foreigner.'[2]

When writing his memoirs almost two generations later, it was with evident relish that Bismarck recalled the storm unleashed by his remarks (which as spoken were probably even stronger – they will have been toned down in the minutes) saying that he calmly leafed through the pages of the *Spenersche Zeitung* until tempers had cooled somewhat. Not that the protests were confined to the liberal benches: 'A remark, framed with insufficient clarity, concerning the nature of the popular movement of 1813', as he wrote the following morning in a letter to his wife-to-be, had not only roused 'the whole opposition hullabaloo' against him but had also wounded 'the mistaken vanity of many members of my own party'.[3]

The young member's provocative contribution must indeed have rubbed a considerable number of conservatives up the wrong way, not only from 'mistaken vanity' or for reasons of political tactics. It was widely felt even in the conservative camp that the increasingly rigid and fossilized absolutist bureaucratic system was showing itself less and less equal to the new and pressing economic and social problems of the day. Here too it was appreciated that much was in need of reform and that, preparatory to this, a compromise must be reached with the middle classes, who particularly in Prussia's western provinces were becoming more and more powerful. This found expression not least in a tendency among conservatives to invoke the common heritage of the Wars of Liberation and thus – in a way – of the reform period too, however differently from the liberals they might place the individual emphases.

When Bismarck, in his brief 'justification', attacked this trend in the very sharpest terms, he was at the same time attacking the policy of conciliation and compromise with the forces of middle-class liberalism that was being pursued by a section of the government and a not inconsiderable number of members of his own party. He was openly taking up a position on the side of those – a relatively small group but one that was highly influential, especially at court – who, if they felt that Prussia's traditional aristocratic and monarchical order was in need of reform, did so because they wanted to see the principles that had allegedly underlain it given even greater effect. In foreign affairs this tendency accepted the spirit of the Congress of Vienna and of the Holy Alliance as a league against revolution in the interests of preserving the domestic order of the monarchies of central and eastern Europe; implicit in this stance was its verdict on the role of the people in the Wars of Liberation, as formulated by Bismarck. Its principal leaders in Prussia were the Magdeburg chief justice, Ernst Ludwig von Gerlach, then aged 52, and his brother Leopold, his senior by five years, who later became adjutant general to the king. Both were close friends of Frederick William IV and like him were given to political romanticism. From this point on Bismarck was generally regarded as being a particularly hot-headed and aggressive representative of this group in the public arena. It tallied with this general assessment of the situation that Frederick William IV, although officially – on the occasion of a reception for the members of the Diet – treating him for political reasons with marked indifference, nevertheless let him know in private shortly afterwards how much his courageous intervention had pleased him.

Bismarck noted this with great satisfaction. He had succeeded in what had unquestionably been his intention from the outset: the monarch himself and the circle of arch-conservative advisers around the throne now saw in him a young man who, though possibly still a little too hot-headed, even driven to what were perhaps rash extremes at times by his zeal and by his loyalty to his convictions, was absolutely reliable and would certainly have to be borne in mind in future when positions of trust were being allocated. And in Prussia, if one looked at the situation soberly and without contaminating reality with one's own expectations, the throne was still very much the seat of power, the law-giving authority and source of order in the land.

Without question, then, there was a good deal of opportunism involved in Bismarck's coming down so determinedly on the side of an arch-conservatism that was in many respects romantically obsolete, that in its whole outlook, governed as this was by the past, often appeared politically obdurate and out of touch, and that had few supporters left among the younger and more flexible members of the Prussian nobility. Yet it is precisely this element of opportunism that points to what makes it possible, in retrospect, to speak of opportunism, of a successful piece of calculation.

Hegel named as a key reason for the success of the great individual in history – thereby linking success and greatness in what is surely a not unobjectionable way – that individual's ability to recognize 'what is due, what is necessary', and to work towards it with 'passion', by which he meant in this instance a kind of cold obsession. In defining the course of history as inherently 'sensible' he avoided the question of the character and indeed the morality of this 'progress' that the occasional 'historically significant individual' substantially helped along. In other words, he refused to allow his judgement of the course of history and of the attitudes and actions of the people involved in it to be swayed by a hasty partiality; he did not wish his version of what the age was really driving out of itself to be distorted by his own desires, hopes, expectations and political opinions.

At the same time this was a call for a fundamental change in what both at the time and subsequently was often the usual perspective of biographical writing. And it does indeed give rise, even independently of the general philosophy of history that for Hegel was bound up with it, to a very radically altered approach. Seen from this viewpoint, the great individual appears in the guise not so much of an autonomous agent as – in relation to his historical success, which after all is the only reason why posterity is interested in him – of an embodiment of certain contemporary trends, offering a kind of seismograph of their strength and configuration at the time. On this reading his career will as it were trace the line of the forces, interests and opinions – constantly changing but nevertheless following one general direction – that determine the course of history.

Considered in this light, Bismarck's first public appearance and his decisive declaration of support for the extreme right implied a great deal more than can be covered by the usual purely biographical procedure. Both rested on an exceptionally ruthless analysis of the situation that at the same time evinced an extraordinary degree of independence with regard to all the common contemporary assessments. If we take as our starting-point the undoubted fact that for a long time Bismarck's most urgent desire had been for a full-scale public career, in other words that he was filled with burning political ambition, his assessment of the power question for one thing becomes of central importance. This is unmistakably revealed by the way in which he went about things. He saw the two crucial sources of power in Prussia as being – and for the immediate future remaining – the bureaucratic monarchical state and the land-owning nobility. In his view the existing order, which particularly in rural areas was still largely determined by patriarchal tradition, was scarcely at risk, the influence of liberalism was superficial and lacked any solid base as far as the interests of broad sections of the population were concerned, and the middle class was weak and in need of support, all its boastful words notwithstanding. For him the initiative lay clearly with the Crown and the nobility, the problem more in their weakness and indecision in the face of a supposedly ineluctable *Zeitgeist* than in any actual external threats.

The revolution that broke out in Prussia as it did almost everywhere in western and central Europe not ten months later seemed to invalidate this assessment in every particular. Admittedly, when we look at its course and outcome in the Hohenzollern monarchy we shall certainly not reach Bismarck's own verdict, which he continued to defend for decades, to the effect that it was only government weakness that had permitted things to go as far as they did and that in reality the revolution had no base among the people. But we shall be forced to admit that the revolutionary energy particularly of the peasant population was almost exclusively directed at the satisfaction of a small number of demands for material and institutional reforms immediately affecting their own lives and was thus very easy to channel. Nor could there be much talk, as far as large areas of Prussia were concerned, of a middle class marching confidently forward. Moreover, it can scarcely be denied that the power of the monarchical state, as of the nobility, turned out to be very much more solidly grounded than many even of that party had previously thought. And there is likewise no room for doubt about the part played by weakness and indecision, not least in the field of foreign policy.

Hand in hand with Bismarck's assessment of the power question was his assessment of what moved broad sections of the population to political action. In concrete terms, with regard to the role and the wishes of the Prussian people in the Wars of Liberation he was in complete agreement with his political friends on the conservative right wing. Granted, there was already latent in their criteria of judgement a deep-seated contradiction that was to come out into the open a few years later and to lead eventually to rupture and to a parting of the ways between them and Bismarck. Those criteria were in their case ideological; in Bismarck's they were naturalistic from the outset. In other words, the arch-conservatives, no less than the liberals, were convinced that at every level of the social scale human behaviour was governed by ideas and beliefs – ideas and beliefs that in the opinion of the former ultimately had their roots in tradition and religious revelation, while the latter saw them as stemming from a universal reason that embraced all things, binding them together, and that the individual was capable of grasping with his intellect. Bismarck, on the other hand, from an early stage in his career saw the decisive stimulus to political action – and not just among the wider population – as lying in self-interest and in pre-rational, as it were instinctive behaviour patterns. From this standpoint he always vigorously denied what the rationalists and the liberals liked to think of as the potentially scientific nature of politics. For him politics was always the 'theory of the possible',[4] the 'art of the possible' with the accent very much on the 'art', on the intuitive aspect, not excluding such demonic and dubious elements as might arise out of the material and out of the way in which it was handled.[5]

This naturalism, which occasionally went as far as open cynicism, characterized Bismarck's earliest steps on the political stage. It remained his most distinguishing characteristic through all the decades of his political career. It was a way of looking at things that inevitably and, as success after success appeared to prove it right, increasingly threw doubt on the credibility of the man who allowed it to govern not only his decisions but his whole way of going about things. Could someone, people inevitably wondered, who held so cynical a view of the world, who at least as far as politics was concerned saw power-seeking, the selfish protection of interests and essentially pre-rational modes of behaviour as being what mainly motivated people and the various kinds of human community, amount to anything more as a politician than an unadulterated power-merchant without any great aims or firm convictions, indeed ultimately without a conscience? Would not such a world view of necessity lead to a certain unscrupulousness with regard to means and even a kind of indifference with regard to ends? Was this not purely Machiavellism, unprincipled political banditry?

Such questions accompanied Bismarck's dealings throughout his life and have been asked incessantly ever since. The temporary triumph of a wholly unscrupulous political amoralism in the person of Hitler led to their being intensified, while at the same time revealing quite clearly the bounds that had in the one case been overstepped and in the other case not. The fact remains that the anti-idealist sobriety and often cynical scepticism that Bismarck exhibited in his politics very early on and continued to profess more and more outspokenly constituted an extraordinary challenge to his time. They cut him off from the various political groups and their respective ideals and convictions. They were responsible for creating that gap, that lack of credibility and consequently of trust around him that made his fall seem an immediate and not even particularly dramatic possibility at almost every stage of his career. It turned him, in other words, even in the years of his greatest success, into a lone wolf, with all a lone wolf's exacerbated mistrust but also with his heightened perceptions. It meant that in everything he did he stood for no one but himself, detached from all the programmes and beliefs, all the objectives and ideals of those around him, never subscribing to them, merely making use of them.

For himself – or did he also, in Hegel's sense, stand for his age, with all its ambivalences and contradictions, its laborious compromises and irreconcilabilities, its expectations and disappointments, and its achievements and weaknesses, that age of transition that historians – usually for somewhat superficial reasons but perhaps, deep down, quite rightly after all – have named after him? This brings us to the crux of the matter. To put it in extreme terms, were people right at the time and have they been right since to blame Bismarck for leading the nation down the wrong road and erecting, in the 1871 Reich, what was in many respects a bulwark against time, a structure anachronistic in its political as well as in its social foundations that subsequently and indeed with a certain inevitability furnished the basis for a calamitous development? Or are they positing an altogether disproportionate estimate of the potential of the individual and distorting the true historical context by losing sight of the extent to which Bismarck, like every successful man of action, embodied in his person and in his achievements the prevailing tendencies and forces of his day? In other words, is the 'wrong road' idea the most successful of all the legends surrounding the person and achievements of Bismarck, the one that at the same time, for all the apparent sobriety of its adherents, is capable of fostering the greatest illusions regarding the opportunities and potentialities inherent in the historical development of the German nation? The answer lies neither in the purely 'subjective' sphere – what did the man want; what were his intentions, his plans, his ultimate goals? Nor does it lie exclusively in the 'objective' sphere – what did he really achieve; what governmental and social order did he actually help to bring about? It lies in both, however much the emphasis must be on the objective elements. It lies in an analysis of what was possible for him and what was not, in the drawing-up of a balance-sheet of success and failure. In short, it lies in a sober examination of the scope that the historical situation and the supra-individual forces and tendencies governing that situation provided for himself, his actions and their effects.

PART ONE

In Search of a Way of Life

[1]

Between Two Worlds

Home, school and choice of profession – these are the three elements in a young person's life that we tend, with varying degrees of emphasis, to point to as actually shaping his character and in many respects providing him with his identity. As far as Bismarck's development is concerned, however, we can apply the rule in at best a negative sense. This gives us an initial insight into the personality of a man who remembered himself as having always been deeply solitary and thrown back on his own resources, seeking order and authority and needing them but taught by experience to expect neither from anywhere except within himself, a man whose existence was from an early age divided between searching for a way of life and playing a part.

'I became a stranger in my parents' house in earliest childhood and never again felt fully at home there', he wrote in the 'description of his inner life', the famous 'Werbebrief' or 'Letter of Proposal' addressed to his future father-in-law, Heinrich von Puttkamer, an arch-conservative and strictly religious Pomeranian country squire, six months before his entry into the political arena. 'The education I received at home was based on the viewpoint that everything was subordinate to the training of the intellect and the early acquisition of positive knowledge.'[1] 'At home' meant under the influence of his mother, who in this respect at least was completely dominant. Nor was that the only occasion on which Bismarck, looking back, associated his early inner alienation from his parental home closely with her. Eighteen years younger than her husband, she had found herself in 1806, when she was barely 17, placed by her marriage to Ferdinand von Bismarck, a landowner in the Brandenburg March, in a world she inwardly rejected and from which she sought with all her might to remove her two sons, Bernhard (b. 1810) and Otto, who was born on his father's Schönhausen estate near Magdeburg on 1 April 1815.

It was the world of the small Prussian landed nobility, of which it was the family's proudest boast to be one of the oldest resident representatives in the March. That world had seen many changes since the fourteenth century, when the family's ancestor, who came from a patrician merchant family in Stendal and was a partisan of Margrave Ludwig of Wittelsbach, was rewarded by the latter in the summer of 1345 with the estate of Burgstall. Most of those changes, however, had been undergone passively rather than

3

actively brought about: the rise of the sovereign state, the organization of a standing army and a central administration, and the 'transfer' from Burgstall to Schönhausen on the east bank of the Elbe in the sixteenth century, which had been 'extorted' from the Bismarcks with 'all manner of pressure and physical violence' by the Hohenzollerns 'purely because they coveted the hunting', as the family's youngest scion once resentfully remarked during the Franco-Prussian War.[2] From time to time, particularly in the seventeenth century, a stand had been made against the absolutism of the 'Swabian family' of the Hohenzollerns, of whom the Chancellor occasionally opined that in principle, leaving aside the concept of divine right, they were 'no better than my own'.[3] But that had been no more than obstruction. And even the energy with which, standing on custom and ancient right, they had set about it had scarcely been excessive. Eventually, if under protest at first, they had reconciled themselves to the new order and even become *fritzisch*: Ferdinand's grandfather, who of all the Bismarcks most resembled the future Chancellor, fell in 1742 as a colonel and an unreserved admirer of the king; his father fought at Kollin, Leuthen and Hochkirch until, severely wounded, he resigned his commission in 1758.

Against this world of dogged persistence, this long line of altogether rather bourgeois landed nobility, Wilhelmine Luise set her own family tradition, particularly the figure of her father, Anastasius Ludwig Mencken, whom she greatly admired and was always holding up to her sons as an example. Descended from an academic family from Leipzig and the son of a professor of law at the University of Helmstedt in Brunswick, Mencken had served as Cabinet secretary under Frederick the Great and subsequently as a member of the Cabinet under Frederick William II and Frederick William III. In the years preceding his death in 1801 he had eventually come to exercise a considerable influence on Prussian policy. A not uncritical supporter of enlightened absolutism, he represented the type of educated, sophisticated civil servant, experienced in office and in life, that absolute monarchy produced in its late period, principally in central Europe, and that laid the foundations of the prestige and influence enjoyed by the civil services of central Europe for a century to come. Such men saw the Old Prussian landed nobility, which often clung stubbornly to tradition, was intellectually as well as materially inflexible and tended to oppose on principle everything to do with centralized government and bureaucracy, as the major obstacle to any kind of reform in state, church and society as well as to enlightenment and sensible progress. It was in this spirit that the daughter had been educated. And Ferdinand von Bismarck, who to his monarch's great annoyance had resigned his commission early on and retired to his estate, was a by no means wholly untypical representative of that Old Prussian nobility, notwithstanding his personal qualities, his human kindness and amiability and his pronounced liberality in the way he lived his life and in his choice of friends. Here lay the seeds of a conflict that the children and above all the more sensitive younger son probably felt more keenly than the father, who had the protection of an unfailing self-confidence and the tolerance of the chivalrous patriarch and who,

4

moreover, largely fell in with his wife's opinions when it came to concrete decisions affecting their lives.

This applied, for example, to the question of the children's education. For Wilhelmine Luise von Bismarck it was a foregone conclusion that her sons should follow the new educational channel available as a result of the Prussian educational reforms carried out under Wilhelm von Humboldt after 1806. The primary aim of those reforms had been to provide the state in all spheres of its activity, including the army and the diplomatic corps, with a body of civil servants educated in a coherent spirit and to the same high standard. And civil servants, diplomats, possibly even ministers were what the sons were going to be, not lazy, complacent landed aristocrats with no ambition and no future. So there was no question of private tutors and a flexible transition to higher education, which was still the usual arrangement in rural areas at the time (in 1816 the family had left Schönhausen for Kniephof, near Naugard in Pomerania, to farm an estate inherited from a collateral branch). Instead in January 1822 the younger son, then aged 6, was sent to boarding-school in Berlin.

The school was the so-called 'Plamannsche Lehranstalt' or Plamann Institute, founded in the spirit of the great Swiss educational theorist Pestalozzi immediately prior to the Prussian reforms and chiefly attended by the sons of top Prussian civil servants. Of the objectives that had originally governed the school there was admittedly very little left in the 1820s, the period of intellectual and political reaction that followed the reform period and the Wars of Liberation. Here too, as was almost universal in Prussian education, deprived of its original content and context, much had become ossified in externals and mere formalities, in drill and hollow German pomposity, in an 'artificial Spartanism', as Bismarck himself put it.[4] He always looked back with deep distaste on the five years he had spent in that boarding-school in the Wilhelmstrasse. There was 'a great deal of coercion and method and unnatural training'; the teachers were 'demagogic gymnasts' and they 'hated the nobility'.[5] Moreover, the Institute had 'in the last years of its existence taken a direction' that 'favoured a kind of hothouse development of the intellect rather than the education of the heart and the preservation of youthful vigour'.[6]

This early separation from home, aggravated by the fact that for years his mother departed to take the waters in July and so made it impossible for him to go home for the summer holidays, inevitably struck him as the quite pointless outcome of an attitude to life that was prepared to sacrifice what was natural, the genuine possibilities of happiness that life offered, to mere illusions. 'My childhood was ruined for me at the Plamann Institute, which to me seemed like a prison', he once said with vivid emphasis. 'Whenever I looked out of the window and saw a team of oxen ploughing I had to weep with homesickness for Kniephof.'[7] It was probably here that he formed that bitter opinion of his mother expressed in a letter of 24 February 1847 to his future wife: 'My mother was a beautiful woman who loved outward show and had a bright and lively mind but little of what Berliners call *Gemüt* ['heart' or 'soul']. She wanted me to learn a lot and achieve a lot, and it often

5

seemed to me that she was hard and cold towards me. As a little child I hated her, and later I used to deceive her – successfully – with guile.'[8] Nor was that all. It would hardly be going too far to say that here, in the fact that the emotional shock of so early a separation from home was not countered by the experience of an inwardly accepted and meaningful order in the classroom and the dormitory, is the root of some of the underlying attitudes that were to characterize his entire life.

'I really loved my father', we read in a significant transitional passage a few lines farther on in the letter to Johanna von Puttkamer. His father was the world from which he felt so soon that he had been driven out; he was the good-humouredness of 'live and let live', the life of nature with its organic rhythms, the freedom and security of adulthood; he was *Gemüt* and individuality. On the other hand, cold and dismal, there were the city, strict discipline, a lifeless order, demands with nothing but platitudes to back them up, career-mindedness and a concept of education that called its own content into question. Here were undoubtedly set-pieces of normal human development, of the transition from the uncomplicated life of childhood to the increasing commitments of adulthood, commitments that are experienced as being harsher for the fact that the values, the future and the meaning that underlie them are not always immediately clear. But the additional factor here, which enormously aggravated the conflict, was the brutal accentuation of the problem by the special circumstances of Bismarck's life, the possibility, which literally thrust itself upon him, of assigning them to two different spheres and forms of existence, the one bourgeois, bureaucratic and urban, the other traditional, aristocratic and rural, and not least the fact that these principles were embodied in his parents – in a form, moreover, that contradicted every traditional conception of and distribution of parental roles, with the mother representing the pushing, demanding, intellectually oriented element.

The result of all this was that for Bismarck the normal adolescent conflict with the ways of the adult world very quickly broke the bounds of the purely private sphere. Bismarck's search for his own way of life took place in circumstances that were by nature supra-individual and of an eminently political kind. For *his* rejection of external demands, *his* failure to succeed in bourgeois terms at the same time took on a quality of loyalty to tradition and to the preservation of his patrimony.

Not that there was any question of this at first. Bismarck went through school – the Plamann Institute until the autumn of 1827, then the Frederick William Gymnasium until 1830 and finally, until he took his *Abitur* or school-leaving examination in April 1832, the famous 'Graue Kloster' (Grey Friary) in Berlin – without much demur but also with no great success or obvious intellectual or artistic interests. In all subjects equally he was a mediocre pupil about whom, even with the wisdom of hindsight, his teachers and fellow pupils were able to distinguish nothing particularly remarkable. And indeed he left school, as he put it in the famous sarcastic opening sentence of his memoirs, 'as a normal product of our state educational system' with superficial views and beliefs – whether or not they were the ones that, exploiting the appeal of contrast, he mentioned there –

and with no firm plans for the future or even ideas about what he wanted to study. Just one remark in the few sentences in which he reminisced about his schooldays more than sixty years later contains a clue, pointing yet again to the emotional core of the conflict that was to come out more and more strongly from now on: 'My historical sympathies', he said with regard to the national aspirations of the period, aspirations principally of the middle classes, and to the glorification of heroes of freedom in history, 'remained on the side of authority.'[9] Authority, however, meant the traditional order, the old Prussia, the primacy of Crown and nobility, of the country and rural relationships; in short, it meant his father's world.

For the time being, though, his actual career continued to follow the course plotted by his mother. At the beginning of the summer semester of 1832 he entered the University of Göttingen, then one of the leading universities in central Europe, to study law and so prepare himself – in a way that the eighteenth-century 'Fürstendienst' or 'Prince's Service' had hardly known – for the civil service and if at all possible for a diplomatic career. He had accepted this professional objective not from any particular interest but because it presented itself and because his mother persistently urged him in that direction. The only alternatives open to a Prussian Junker of the period, unless of course he developed special talents and interests at an early age, were service in the army or, as the eldest son or in the case of large, subdivided properties, the management of his father's estates. Bismarck very quickly rejected the former alternative, and it was not merely to please his mother that he did so. And there was no question of the second for the time being: Schönhausen was leased, and the father farmed the Pomeranian estates himself.

There was nothing unusual about a young student's choice of subject and of professional objective simply imposing themselves on him from outside through the wishes of his family, through his position in society and in the absence of any alternatives or impulses of his own. The great majority of Bismarck's fellow students, particularly those of his own circle, were in the same situation. University as a duty, as an extension of the school that by present-day standards most of them had hardly grown out of, was the usual thing, and the academic teaching took this into account to a great extent. Above all its principal component, the course of lectures, was essentially aimed at communicating knowledge that could be memorized, consisting of hours of recitation from a textbook together with voluminous collections of examples; the famous exceptions to this rule merely distort the overall impression.

It was they, however, that constituted the appeal of individual universities. They were the usually extra-curricular attractions that exerted the most powerful influence on the education, attitudes and opinions of the academic youth of the day and formed the basis of the outstanding importance of the universities in the nineteenth century, especially in central Europe. It was philosophers such as Fichte, Schelling and Hegel, theologians such as Schleiermacher (who confirmed Bismarck in Berlin in 1831), philologists such as the Grimm brothers, lawyers such as Thibaut and Savigny, historians such as Heeren, Rotteck and Dahlmann, literary historians such

7

as Gervinus – it was such men as these who turned the universities into those centres of intellectual, moral and often also political debate that released in the more receptive and intellectually more flexible section of the student population forces of self-examination and the desire for independent knowledge of the world, in short that set free an ideal of personality that perhaps determined the inner dynamics of the century more strongly than many other influences. This provided a counterweight to the more and more marked (and in the course of economic, social and political development undoubtedly inevitable and also indispensable) tendency towards specialists and professionals – a counterweight that held back the formation of a purely functional meritocracy and created essential preconditions for the development and spread of a specifically middle-class culture.

Bismarck's initial choice of lecture courses shows how a certain twin-track approach to university studies was very much taken for granted at the time: in addition to two courses in law to provide his 'bread-and-butter' training he attended, as it were for general guidance and education, courses in philosophy, the history of political science and mathematics. Of this broad choice, however, which in the following semesters in fact became steadily narrower, he made only very limited use, not only so far as his vocational courses but also so far as the other subjects were concerned. In the case of the former he soon fell back on mechanical preparation for examinations, and in the latter case his interest quickly waned – with one exception, on which he continued to lay emphasis as an old man. For at least two semesters he listened regularly and with growing interest to the historian Arnold Heeren (already 71 when Bismarck went up to university) and even from time to time sought to follow up what he heard with additional reading. The courses involved were one in general geography and ethnology, offering a sort of historical introduction to listeners from all faculties, and in the winter a course on 'Statistics and History of the European Countries'.

Heeren was the son of a Bremen merchant family and as such was particularly interested in questions of the economy and trade and their relationship to politics in general. After studying philosophy and history at Göttingen he had turned first to ancient history, and after extensive research he had published in 1793 and 1796 a voluminous two-volume work entitled *Thoughts on Politics, Communications, and Trade among the Principal Peoples of the Ancient World*. The book made a great impression on Heeren's contemporaries. Goethe called it one of the important books of the age, a work of lasting influence.[10] It earned its author a chair in history at Göttingen in 1801. In the book this disciple of Adam Smith showed the close connection between and interdependence of the production and exchange of goods and international relations. In other words, he was interested in the material foundations of the foreign policy of the peoples and states of the Ancient World. His procedure and intentions, typically of the Enlightenment, were generalizing. Like Montesquieu, by whom he was greatly influenced, he was concerned above all, while recognizing the historical contingency of all human activity, to bring out something akin to

8

general principles and guidelines as to what was permanent in and typical of that activity and of certain basic factors.

In the same spirit Heeren had gone on to look at recent history and particularly the *History of the European System of States and its Colonies*, as he called his likewise widely read second major work, which was written as a 'Handbuch', in other words rather in the manner of a textbook, and first published in 1809. In this he sought to show how out of the increasing interdependence of the individual countries and regions of the continent there had eventually, after a long struggle, emerged a working system of international relations. That system, he went on to explain, fixed the conditions for any kind of durably successful activity on the part of individual states. It made relations between states rational and calculable – always provided that the partners observed certain basic rules of play, including one forbidding attempts to break the system unilaterally. This last was the charge he levelled – secretly at first but in later editions openly – against Napoleon and his policies. Their failure appeared to him simply a logical confirmation of his theory that no policy could henceforth be successful outside and in opposition to the system, despite the fact that this was continually subject to radical change.

At his well-attended lectures Heeren expounded over and over again his insights regarding the material, principally economic and commercial foundations of foreign policy. What was particularly impressive was the way in which he sought with supreme impartiality to untangle the web of intersecting or overlapping, mutually complementary or mutually obstructive goals and interests of individual countries and in each case to interpret the whole picture, success as well as failure, in terms of the wider context. For someone who had been to school in Berlin in the 1820s this must have opened up an entirely novel, challenging and fascinating perspective. 'What I thought about foreign policy, for example', Bismarck said himself, looking back in his memoirs, '. . . was in terms of the Wars of Liberation seen from the standpoint of a Prussian officer.'[11] That was said of the student, but it was probably the student who first became critically aware of it. There is an almost complete absence of personal accounts of Bismarck from this period, but we can assume that what Heeren said about the foundations and laws of foreign policy made a considerable impression on him and did much to shape his own ideas and his own way of looking at things.

As witness the fact that Heeren's lectures were the only ones that succeeded in eliciting Bismarck's deeper interest. For the rest he increasingly wasted his time as a student, even after transferring in the autumn of 1833 to the University of Berlin, then just twenty years old and with some two-and-a-half thousand students already enrolled, more than a quarter of them budding lawyers. The importance of Berlin University as one of the new centres of intellectual life in Germany passed Bismarck by almost completely. Even the lectures of the world-famous Savigny, the head of the school of the history of law, managed to attract him on only two occasions, to say nothing of those of his academic antipode, Eduard Gans, the historian

Leopold von Ranke, the philosopher Friedrich Adolf Trendelenburg and the geographer Carl Ritter. When his wife said to him in later life, speaking of Berlin University, 'Ah, I expect you were there every day', his reply was a curt 'Never'.[12]

Much more important to him than study and the university – of which he even said, looking back, that one learned nothing in that 'hopeless institution' except how to 'ruin one's health and lead a good-for-nothing existence' – were other things: the fraternity life, his many friends and the pleasures of the carefree student life. Initially, on the basis of the ideas he had brought with him from school in Berlin, he joined the 'Göttinger Burschenschaft'. He left this loose fraternity even before the end of his first semester – whether because of the uncouth outward appearance of its members and the 'extravagance of their political views', as he later claimed,[13] or simply because he felt no real rapport with them and failed to find the happy-go-lucky attitude he was looking for, we do not know. Instead that same summer he joined the 'Landsmannschaft Hanovera', a duelling fraternity whose members came mainly from officer and civil servant families from Hanover and were heading for the same professions themselves. Like most of the associations of students from the same country or region, the 'Hanovera' was largely unpolitical in the sense that its members did not seriously question the existing state of affairs and indeed hardly even examined it seriously at all. For Bismarck the fraternity meant essentially the duelling-loft and the tavern together with the superficially hearty company of young men of his own age, out to enjoy their 'freedom' and have their fling between school and embarking on a career. He spent well beyond his allowance and accumulated substantial debts. He formed few lasting personal relationships, and there was little room in his life for anything but swaggering behaviour and student cant.

Both wants were supplied outside and indeed at the greatest possible distance from that world in the person of the American John Lothrop Motley, who later made a name for himself in the diplomatic service as his country's envoy in Vienna and subsequently in London, and also as a historian specializing in the Dutch Republic. Bismarck first met him in the summer of 1832 and spent all his student years with him; the two moved to Berlin together in the autumn of 1833 and even lived there together for a time. Their friendship ended only with Motley's relatively early death in 1877, at the age of 63. The American was one of the few real friends that Bismarck had in his life.

At first glance it must have seemed a somewhat curious relationship: on the one hand the slightly older, rather reserved New Englander, a Harvard student, very studious and with a highly romantic attitude to life, who had been drawn to Germany by the reputation of German scholarship and by his own literary and artistic interests; on the other hand the as yet very young – literally and figuratively – Prussian Junker 'from Pomerania', as he liked to sign himself, who was always involved in some quarrel or other and who in his wildly eccentric get-up, with his huge dog Ariel on the lead beside him, was soon a familiar figure in the little university town. What apart from a strong personal sympathy bound them together was put into words by

Motley in 1839 in an early novel entitled *Morton's Hope*, a romantic tale with unmistakably autobiographical elements. The friend whom his hero Morton, an American like himself, meets in Göttingen around 1770, one Otto von Rabenmark, is a born actor who for the benefit of those around him plays with verve and talent the part of the carefree young dare-devil, which goes down very well among his contemporaries. As soon as he and Morton are alone, however, he drops the part and 'talks sense': he reveals himself as a sensitive and well-read young man of many gifts who is fully aware of the theatricality of his behaviour and of its dependence on the company he happens to be in. Later in the story Rabenmark, viz. Bismarck in Berlin, conducts himself with the same facility and the same convincingness as an elegant and thoroughly proper nobleman.

Motley probably discovered Bismarck's sensitivity and gifts primarily in the field of literature, in other words where to judge from his behaviour one would least have suspected them. In Motley's enthusiasm for the world of Shakespeare, Goethe and Byron Bismarck evidently followed his friend, more soberly, to be sure, and also more critically so far as the tendency of such literary influences to swamp his own feeling for and understanding of life was concerned, but nevertheless, so it seems, with great intensity and growing discernment. The fact that Motley, far from being a bloodless romantic and abstract aesthete, was a man with a sense of humour who loved life's pleasures and plunged into amorous adventures with the same ease and abandon as Bismarck himself, obviously made it psychologically easier for the latter to gain access to that world. From the outset it made it seem richer and more relevant that it had hitherto struck him as being, either at school or at home.

And richness and relevance were qualities on which in his heart of hearts Bismarck was increasingly bent. His studies, such as they were, bored him. The excitement of playing different roles in different surroundings soon palled. And the prospect of working his way up step by step as a civil servant or diplomat, an existence in which the external stimuli would be slight and the internal motivation somewhat artificial, was slowly becoming more and more nightmarish. 'My life, looked at closely, is really rather pitiful', he wrote with unprecedented candour in a letter to a former student friend from Göttingen in June 1835. 'By day I pursue studies that do not interest me; my evenings I spend in the company of courtiers and civil servants, affecting a delight I am not Schulenburg enough to feel or to seek. I find it hard to believe that the most complete achievement of my chosen goal, the longest title and the largest medal in Germany, or the most stupendous distinction will indemnify me for the physically and spiritually shrunken breast that will be the product of this life. I am still frequently visited by the desire to swap the pen for the plough and the briefcase for the game bag; but that is something I can always still do.'[14]

At this point he had already, with the help of a tutor, passed his first law examination, if with hardly overwhelming success. He was now a *Referendar*, passing through the usual stages of such a candidate's training with the Royal Municipal Court in Berlin. At the same time he was preparing for the civil service entrance examination. This consisted of two

11

written works, one in philosophy and one in political science, and an oral examination in which the candidate had to show proof not only of specific specialized knowledge in the fields both of law and of 'cameralistics' (political and economic theory) but also, again in the spirit of the Prussian educational reforms, of his general level of knowledge and education. Bismarck passed this second examination in late June 1836, more successfully than the first but again strictly in terms of what was required, both his essays having clearly been written without any sense of commitment or wider interest beyond the matter in hand; his philosophy essay was 'On the Nature and Admissibility of the Oath', his political science essay 'On Thrift in the National Budget'.[15] These essays too, like his whole professional training until then, were no more than means to an end. The problem, however, was that he was finding even the end itself daily more questionable.

At the beginning of his Berlin semester even his mother appears to have had a moment's hesitation as to whether he was going to be able to meet the necessary requirements for a successful civil service career or whether it would not after all be better for him to give up his studies there and then and go into the army. As a result of this Bismarck took a somewhat closer look at his future career in the months that followed and did some hard thinking about its various stages. At any rate he spent those months gathering very detailed information regarding prospects in the different spheres of the diplomatic service, and he cultivated 'the company of courtiers and civil servants' to the same end. He reached the conclusion that, without influential connections and in view of the fact that for a long time the Prussian landed nobility had not exactly enjoyed preferential treatment in the allocation of important diplomatic posts, the best way to get on in this sphere was probably by training as a civil servant and then serving in the Zollverein or Customs Union administration, which meant specializing in economic and finance policy.

This was very soberly thought out. But Bismarck probably overestimated his own staying power from the outset, even taking into account the possibility of shortening the particularly unpleasant *Referendar* period from three to two years, as service in Prussia's Rhine Province allowed. He did more or less get through the first year at the Berlin municipal court, a year which was also occupied with preparing for the next examination, despite the fact that the courts themselves largely took advantage of the candidates as additional secretaries and clerks, with the result that there could be little question of any meaningful training. In his second year, however, which he began in the Aachen Regierungspräsidium or regional administration in June 1836, he soon fell victim to a severe crisis.

Direct entry into the diplomatic service was by way of the so-called diplomatic examination, a special examination at the level of the general *Assessor* examination (an *Assessor* being the next stage up the civil service training ladder from a *Referendar*). Admission to the examination was determined by the Foreign Ministry in accordance with requirements and on the basis of a candidate's educational background and an assessment of his special aptitudes. In this the connections and of course the person of the minister concerned played a not inconsiderable part. The then Foreign Minister, Friedrich Ancillon, a man of the stamp of Bismarck's grandfather Mencken, was known to have a low opinion of the Old Prussian nobility in the field of diplomacy. Furthermore it was he, as Bismarck himself related subsequently, who had put him on the roundabout path via civil service and Customs Union. In spite of this Bismarck got his elder brother, who was serving in the Potsdam regional administration at the time, to ask as early as the autumn of 1836 whether he might not be admitted to the diplomatic examination after all. Obviously in the mean time he had already begun to dread the idea of possibly having to spend many years working in general and economic administration. There was also the fact that his principal superior, whose patronage he had no doubt hoped for, the 33-year-old president of the Aachen administrative region and future Minister of the Interior Count Arnim-Boizenburg, was soon openly expressing doubts as to whether Bismarck would successfully complete the course by way of the Customs Union administration with its additional demands in terms of technical expertise. In short, inclination and ability seemed equally open to question and the prospects for the future pretty dim.

Bismarck did in fact make repeated attempts to reconcile himself to the civil service and to his work, which with his passage through the various departments was always changing quite rapidly. He can hardly be said to have been particularly successful, however, and the distractions of a spa town with an international, mainly English clientele further contributed towards continually curbing his zeal. As Arnim wrote to him with unconcealed irony a year later, he was delighted with his decision 'to transfer to one of the Royal Administrations in the old Prussian provinces in order to revert to a more strenuous performance of your official duties, which in the social circumstances obtaining in Aachen you strove for in vain'.[16]

Unlike in Göttingen or Berlin, the socializing in Aachen often represented an escape, a search for distraction; it was the expression of a feeling of dissatisfaction and inner emptiness. There was no more likely eventuality in such a situation than a kind of emotional *salto mortale*, the anticipation of and invocation of a great, all-embracing passion that would change everything. It was in the offing throughout his year in Aachen. There was soon talk of wedding plans, later postponed, of inclinations that, he said, lay much deeper than he had thought: 'Who knows whether I shall not come to rue what I now regard as good sense.'[17]

Finally, at the beginning of July 1837 he felt he had found his great love in the person of the daughter of an English clergyman. He followed her to Wiesbaden, where incidentally he lost a small fortune (more than 1,700 taler) at the gambling table, became well and truly betrothed to her, whether or not their engagement was official, and proceeded, his leave having meanwhile long expired, to accompany his 'family' all over Germany, clearly with no firm objective and with swiftly changing plans as far as the immediate future was concerned. He was hesitating 'whether to spend the winter with my relations in Naples or in Paris',[18] he wrote from Frankfurt at the end of August in a letter to Karl Friedrich von Savigny, the son of the great lawyer, who was preparing for the diplomatic service with him in Aachen and who did his best – successfully so far as this was possible – to keep his escapade from the authorities. A few days later Bismarck reported that 'because of circumstances arising' he would be going 'not to Geneva but to Munich for the time being'. He went on: 'I cannot say as yet how long we shall be staying there and where I shall be going next, whether to Paris or home for the time being.'[19]

As it happened, the journey to Munich came to nothing. His passport had expired, and the Bavarians would not let him in. Since on the other hand he could produce no written certificate of furlough, the Prussian legation in Stuttgart would only issue him with papers allowing him to return to Aachen. In spite of this he wrote to another friend from Strasbourg ten days later that he was 'travelling with the family to Switzerland at the moment and will be leaving them in Milan' in order to return home for the first time for two years. He had already mentioned his 'definite marriage' to Savigny at the end of August, saying that it 'will probably take place at Scarsdale in Leicestershire in late March'; in this letter, too, he speaks of his firm intention 'of entering the holy state etc. . . . with a fair-haired young British woman of uncommon beauty who to date understands not one word of German'.[20]

Nor did she need to learn any: Isabella Loraine-Smith, the daughter of an English country parson, disappeared from his life as swiftly as she had entered it. At the beginning of December, after a long silence, he wrote to Savigny from his father's estate at Kniephof that the 'projected alliance' was 'completely and irrevocably broken off . . . with the result that I am left with nothing but the memory of four very happy honeymoons [i.e. months] and a very substantial aes alienum [his Wiesbaden gambling losses]'.[21] The 'prize', as he laughingly remarked eight years later, had been stolen from him 'by a one-armed colonel of 50 years, 4 horses and an income of 15,000 rl'.[22]

His anguish at the break-up of this brief and curiously unreal relationship does not appear to have been very deep, which further confirms that it was more of an escape from what he was increasingly experiencing as an intolerable situation than a truly great passion – more occasion than cause. It solved nothing, of course, even if thanks to Arnim and Savigny the bridges for a return to his civil service training were still intact. On the contrary, on top of his own doubts he now had to deal with the reaction of his friends and family and the charge that he had failed to face up even to the very first demands of what was apparently his chosen profession.

In view of this Bismarck made one last attempt to play the part assigned to him. In mid-December 1837 he resumed his *Referendar* training with the Potsdam regional administration and outwardly at least professed great optimism. 'I am very glad now that I did not apply for the diplomatic examination immediately; for now that I have come so far the second state examination will in fact give me a much more solid footing; no matter what happens to me from now on, my career will always be secure', he wrote to his father at the end of January 1838,[23] though it was a time when his father, beset by major personal and economic worries, was in urgent need of some encouraging news; his wife was very ill, and the estate incomes were steadily declining. After a few weeks, however, Bismarck's new momentum was exhausted. He decided first of all to do his year's military service, and in late March 1838 he joined the *Gardejäger* or Fusiliers; fifty-two years later, and without another day's service behind him, he was to be appointed colonel general of cavalry with the rank of field marshal. As was usual in such cases, his superiors offered to let him continue his training in Potsdam on his days off, but Bismarck took no advantage of this, not even bothering to reply to the offer. Clearly he had made up his mind to discontinue his training and, following his military service, become a 'Landjunker' or country squire.

For this, however, he needed the consent and support of his parents. Whether under normal circumstances this would have been forthcoming is dubious to say the least. But in the mean time his mother's illness had turned out to be incurable: she had cancer. His father had to make arrangements for a quite different kind of life, particularly since he had relied on his wife a great deal in the management of his estates.

It is thoroughly typical of Bismarck's relationship with his mother that it was only her illness and her death – she died on 1 January 1839, aged only 49 – that made available to him a different life from the one she had always planned for him and been working towards. She certainly never approved his decision inwardly, and we do not know whether she even gave it her outward consent. In his crucial letter to the elder son Bernhard, Otto's father was silent on this point. 'While Otto was here', he wrote to him from Berlin, where for weeks his wife had been under medical treatment, on 19 July 1838, 'he really opened his heart to his mother. He not only told her how he loathed the whole business of public administration, that it was robbing him of all taste for life, and if he were to suffer almost his whole life long he might in the end become district president with an income of two thousand [taler] but could never hope to be happy. He besought his mother most urgently to give him another position; he offered, if we were to build another sugar factory, to go to Magdeburg and study the manufacturing process in practical terms and then run the factory in Kniephof. Because it distresses me very much that he should feel so unhappy and because when I was in Kniephof I saw with deep delight how very interested you are in agriculture and what excellent and fitting ideas you have for improving the estates there . . . I have decided to bequeath the estates there to you both as your property and derive my own livelihood from Schönhausen alone.'[24]

For Bismarck the way now lay open, the way into his father's world, into the life of the independent country squire of which he had such high hopes. Admittedly there had been some talk initially of his taking the second state examination and becoming an *Assessor* after all, just in case, but this came to nothing. In October 1839, after a certain amount of toing and froing, he asked for his discharge from the civil service. To begin with the brothers farmed the three Pomeranian estates – Külz, Jarchelin and Kniephof – together, using Kniephof as their base. In 1841, following Bernhard's election as Landrat or district administrator, they made a provisional partition, the elder brother receiving Jarchelin and the younger Kniephof

15

and Külz. In the final settlement following the father's death towards the end of 1845 these two went back to Bernhard while Otto received Schönhausen and returned to live there.

All of which looked like final decisions – for life, as it were. Estate-owner, possibly in addition Landrat and knights' representative on the provincial Diet – that was the sort of life, the sort of future that the 24-year-old Bismarck could now look forward to. Five years earlier, among his student friends, almost all of whom aspired to high public office, wanting to become judges, diplomats and top civil servants, such a life had in the last analysis seemed to him unthinkable, notwithstanding all his childhood home-sickness for life in the country and for the freedom and lack of constraint of natural surroundings. In a letter to his Göttingen student friend, Scharlach, referring to the fact that his leaving certificate from Göttingen had arrived six months late and so caused problems regarding his matriculation in Berlin, he had jokingly described the future that had thus been thrown off course: 'I shall therefore probably turn down the Foreign Affairs portfolio, amuse myself for a few years waving a sword at raw recruits, then take a wife, beget children, till the soil and undermine the morals of my peasantry by inordinate distillation of spirits. So if in ten years' time you should happen to find yourself in the neighbourhood [the letter was written from Kniephof], I invite you to commit adulterium with a young mulier facilis et formosa, to drink as much potato brandy as you fancy and to break your neck out hunting as often as you see fit. You will find here a well-fleshed home-guard officer, a moustache that curses and swears till the earth trembles, cultivates a proper repugnance to Jews and Frenchmen and thrashes his dogs and domestics with egregious brutality when bullied by his wife. I shall wear leather trousers, make a fool of myself at the Stettin wool market and when people address me as baron I shall stroke my moustache benignly and knock a bit off the price; I shall get tight on the king's birthday and cheer him vociferously, and the rest of the time I shall sound off regularly, and my every other word will be: Gad, what a splendid horse! In short, I shall be happy in the rustic circle of my family; car tel est mon plaisir.'[25]

This was at the same time a caricature of the average Prussian Junker that was entirely in line with the view he heard of the breed almost everywhere outside his own immediate circle. The fact that it was on the whole not the most gifted and industrious that clung to the soil was an opinion that was gaining ground even among the nobility itself. '"They eat not, neither do they drink", so what do they do? They number their ancestors', Bismarck jeered in a letter written when he was 18.[26] In other words, great social esteem no longer attached to such a way of life at the time; only in retrospect did it mysteriously become invested with this. It was significant that a man such as Ancillon, who both as a politician and as a political commentator stood for the old, pre-revolutionary order, at the same time had a fairly low opinion of the Prussian landed nobility and preferred to find his diplomatic staff elsewhere. In this he was following a long-standing tradition of the Prussian monarchy, a tradition that had led to the indigenous land-owning nobility being represented by only a relatively

16

small contingent in the gallery of Prussian political and military leaders of any importance. Men such as Schwerin, Bernstorff, Blücher, Derfflinger, Moltke and Prince Leopold I, known as the 'Old Dessauer', were all non-Prussians, to say nothing of the post-1806 reformers, Stein, Hardenberg, Scharnhorst, Gneisenau, Motz and Grolman.

So it was not particularly surprising that even within the family circle and among those who wished him well Bismarck's decision should have met with incomprehension and prompted anxious questions as to whether he had really given the whole thing his mature consideration. Others simply assumed he had not got what it took for anything else. In September 1838 Bismarck was induced by one of these inquiries to justify his decision in detail and draw up a kind of balance-sheet of his life hitherto. The inquiry was contained in a letter from a cousin by marriage, Countess Karoline von Bismarck-Bohlen, a woman of 40 whose house in Berlin he had regularly frequented. The original of Bismarck's reply is untraceable. All we have is the copy he made for his father of the rough draft, which, he wrote, was 'highly incomplete and disorganized'.[27] It is possible that he left things out, certain reasons and motives that it was all right for the cousin but not for the father to know about – for example, a reference to the 'truly enormous sum in debts . . . for the honourable settlement of which I saw no alternative but to acquire some means of my own', a reference that the editor of his letters still saw fit to suppress three generations later.[28] But on the whole the transcript probably contains all the crucial matter. For this reason Bismarck later also made it available to his wife-to-be as one of the key documents of his life.[29]

'That there was no need for me to become a country squire is an opinion I share with you', the crucial passage of the letter began. But if his reader was thereby led to expect a positive justification of his decision, she was to be disappointed. Instead Bismarck proceeds from an almost exclusively negative standpoint, setting out at length the reasons why he did not wish to become an 'administrative civil servant'. The narrowness and constraint of a bureaucratic existence, the pettiness and ineffectiveness of most of the decisions that had to be made, the subordination to a hierarchy and the authority of official status, in short the job of a small wheel in a large machine that struck him as in many respects resembling a perpetuum mobile – all these things amounted to an intolerable prospect for him. 'The Prussian civil servant is like one man in an orchestra; whether he is in the first violins or plays the triangle, with no overall view of or influence over the whole he has to play his little bit as set before him, regardless of how good or bad he considers it to be. I, however', this 23-year-old went on, 'want to make the kind of music I know to be good, or make none at all.'

The sentence has become famous as an expression of enormous self-confidence and quite exceptional determination, as a bold anticipation of the future. In reality it was more a grand gesture by one who was carried away by his own imagery. He was honestly addressing his own situation when he wrote 'that my ambition is more in the direction of not obeying than of giving orders'. What he feared above all, the idea that clearly obsessed him at this period, was that his own individuality, his own existence, however unsure he was of them as yet, might be overwhelmed by the outside world, by professional and social pressures. Never being able to become himself, forever having to play-act – that was the nightmare that haunted his inmost being.

It is not of course in this problem that we see revealed what was truly characteristic and decisive as far as the future was concerned but in the specific answer that Bismarck formulated, at least in outline. An escape into 'innerliness', into the purely private sphere, was not even considered as a possibility. Nor, if we look closely, was a more than purely external sense of fulfilment as a landowner and farmer, in other words in a chosen 'profession' in terms of the kind of middle-class professional morality that he had encountered among large sections of the civil service. The question on which his thinking on this matter was almost entirely focused was that of how to safeguard his own individuality in social and public life. The prospect of playing an outstanding public role was one that, as he unhesitatingly admitted, was capable of 'attracting me with a force that rules out all deliberation, as light attracts mosquitoes'. But only, he added, on condition that it was not paid for by a purely success-oriented adaptation to pre-existent convictions, arrangements and constellations of circumstances, in his own words 'by examinations, connections, examining of files, seniority and the goodwill of my superiors'. Precisely that was the case, however, in countries such as Prussia with its bureaucratic, absolutist system of government. Consequently public office and a public role were in his eyes not worth striving for there.

Not there – that was the point. Indeed he stated very clearly the conditions under which his decision would be a quite different one: 'In a state with a free constitution, anyone devoting himself to affairs of state can apply his whole energy to defending and putting into effect those measures and systems of whose justice and usefulness he is convinced', and he added that 'conviction is the only guiding rule of his conduct he need acknowledge in that he carries over into the public sphere the autonomy of private life'.

Here with remarkable clarity was an answer to the question that oppressed him regarding the preservation of personal individuality in public life and in a public function. He was determined to anchor that individuality in the way of life that from early youth had appeared to him as the counterpart of the one that school and his mother's educational aims sought to impose upon him. Its true fulfilment, however, he was convinced required a fundamental change in the political order that had shielded and preserved that way of life hitherto, despite all threats of disruption.

Here were the seeds of all the rest: the turning to the arch-conservatives, who wanted to overcome bureaucratic absolutism by reverting to the political order of the past, based on estates, and also the readiness to take up quite different forms of a 'free constitution'; the fundamental acceptance of differing views and convictions and the idea that all politics was based on conflict. At the same time here was evidence of a boundless subjectivism for which victory and defeat, triumph and humiliation always went to the root of the man's own existence, the man who 'in that he carrie[d] over into the public sphere the autonomy of private life', saw politics as a continual staking of his own self.

Not as unrestrainedly, though, as political passion and personal egotism have been associated in certain twentieth-century desperadoes. There was a further element present, an element the subjective importance of which was undeniable, however, it may be assessed from other points of view. For Bismarck it was the Archimedean point; it was what gave meaning to all his actions, particularly in the political sphere, a meaning that, so completely was he without any illusions, he was only rarely able to discover in those actions himself.

The need for this kind of support, the longing to believe in a supra-mundane power controlling the lives of individuals as of communities, is something that probably stirred in him at an early age. The second friend of his youth after Motley, a Balt named Count Alexander Keyserling, later to become curator of the University of Dorpat, with whom he spent his Berlin semesters, wrote to him twenty years later, looking back on that time: 'Do you not remember what in probably lucid moments you prophesied to me then: a constitution must come, that's the way to outward honours, at the same time one must be inwardly devout?'[30]

Undoubtedly this remark assumed in Keyserling's memory an importance it had not originally possessed. But even as a piece of day-dreaming about the future it is highly significant. Before any kind of positive belief the conviction evidently grew in Bismarck that without as it were an abutment in religion all action must lack inner force and so be doomed to failure. Were it not for his belief in immortality, he said on a subsequent occasion, life for him would be 'not worth getting dressed and undressed for'.[31] And from the other side we read in the 'Werbebrief' to Heinrich von Puttkamer: 'I spent many a hopelessly dejected hour with the thought that my existence and that of other men was pointless and unprofitable, perhaps no more than a by-product of Creation that appears and passes away like the dust from a turning wheel; eternity and the Resurrection lacked certainty for me, and yet I saw nothing in this life that seemed to me worth striving for with any seriousness or energy.'[32]

At what point the rational conviction turned into an existential need that changed his life we cannot say exactly. It happened during the period following the initial adjustment to his new surroundings, the period of increased inward and outward loneliness following the division of the estates and his brother's taking up residence at Jarchelin in 1841. This shows the function and the importance in biographical terms of the whole process that in speaking of Bismarck's 'conversion' we grasp only very imprecisely. In 1838 Bismarck had finally refused to go on playing the part that his home and his surroundings had cast him in. Abandoning this play-acting, predictable aspect of his existence, he sought the haven of a life based on tradition that was materially secure and yet still independent. Hidden beneath this, all his rational justifications notwithstanding, was a great deal of immaturity, an inner conflict and emptiness that must of necessity lead to a fresh and even more serious crisis as soon as the hopes he had associated with life as a country squire faded away. And the fact that those hopes had included more illusions and more romantic escapism than he was prepared to admit to himself, that a 'homecoming' to his father's world was just not possible and the fragmentation of his life hitherto was an aspect of his own nature, very quickly became clear to him. 'From illusions regarding the Arcadian happiness of a dyed-in-the-wool farmer with double-entry bookkeeping and chemical studies I have been retrieved by experience', he wrote to his wife-to-be nine years later. 'The profession was at the time still overlaid for me with the beautiful blue mist of distant mountains. Occasionally', he went on, 'when one of my old fellow students is making a rapid career for himself, I still feel slightly piqued by the thought that "I too could have had that", but then the conviction always asserts itself that man seeks his happiness in vain as long as he seeks it outside himself.'[33] This 'conviction' was dearly bought through those years, dearly in terms not of a subjective struggle – there can be little question of that – but of an objective suffering of an external situation that was increasingly experienced as deeply unsatisfying.

With virtually no previous training and despite a generally poor market, he and his brother had within a short time put the estates back on a profitable footing, although there was still an enormous burden of debt that for years, especially after his marriage, allowed him only an extremely modest life-style.[34] Only in the short term, however, did this success offer him a certain satisfaction, namely for as long as he had to struggle for it.

To achieve something and nevertheless remain free – that was what he had looked forward to. And in the first two years he seemed to find it, behaving almost as if he was a student all over again, bubbling over with life, off on every hunt, attending every party, involved in every diversion that offered itself, even if it meant riding 70 or 80 kilometres to be there, always holding his own and indeed outdoing everyone else – 'mad Bismarck' ('der tolle Bismarck'), as he was known in Pomerania ever afterwards. But when he had 'gone mad' in Göttingen, Berlin or Aachen there had always been someone at hand with whom he could 'talk sense': Motley, Keyserling, Savigny, or a casual acquaintance who was a cut above the average. Now it was quite different. Here there was hardly anyone who saw through the 'play-acting', who might have expected to find something else beneath the façade of the carefree dare-devil. One was what one was taken to be, and one prided oneself on it.

This was something Bismarck experienced very directly when he fell in love with Ottilie von Puttkamer in 1841 and her mother, a wealthy woman with estates in Pansin, turned him down flat with arguments that he felt to be expressive of a stuffy narrow-mindedness and shallow bigotry. He was deeply hurt, especially since the daughter bowed only too swiftly to her mother's will and the mother managed by no means only 'through scheming', as he tried to convince a friend later, 'to dictate to my intended a highly laconic farewell letter to me'.[35] It was a severe blow to his self-esteem; he himself spoke later of an overwhelming feeling of 'injured vanity at the fact that she did not love me enough to stand up to her mother'.[36] And he reacted with all the vehemence of a man who finds his very essence and quality being misjudged – and that by people with whom he had as it were cast in his lot, whose world he had entered of his own free will, without there having been any 'need' for him to do so, as he had stressed in the letter to his cousin Karoline. He had shared their pleasures, and now someone from their circle, because in the process he had harmlessly kicked over the traces a couple of times, believed she could look down on him and think less of him than of many of the 'more numerous than interesting clique of Pomeranian rustic squires, philistines and cavalry officers',[37] as he was to caricature his milieu with increasing frequency from now on; of him who more and more felt 'bored to death' among them, who after all simply did not fit into this society and into the limitations and restrictions of rural Pomerania. 'Ask a fellow how he is', he sneered once, 'and he'll tell you: "Very well, but I'm sorry to say I had a nasty bout of mange last winter."'

In 1842, in order 'if possible to blow away my troubles in foreign climes', he made a journey of several months through England, France and Italy. During this period he even briefly considered entering the English colonial service 'to play the Asian for a few years in order to give my act something of a change of scenery and smoke my cigars on the Ganges instead of on the Rega'.[38] Soon afterwards he mentioned that he was considering 'looking for another position, because as the Prussian civil servant is wont to say I crave a "higher motive and a broader outlook" on my profession'.[39]

On 7 April 1844 he did indeed apply to resume his civil service training. The regional administration in Potsdam gave its consent, though with a not exactly flattering rider. 'This is on condition, however', ran the reply, 'that you endeavour with strenuous industry to make up the ground lost since your resignation from the Civil Service and to combat the preconception that, as we cannot conceal from you, examination of your personal files shows to have arisen during your earlier employment here with respect to your eagerness to complete your training.'[40]

The trouble was, as he had written with regard to that 'eagerness' six months earlier, he could not make up his mind 'whether the routine of business in the Royal Civil Service would appeal to me in the long term'.[41] Well, on 3 May he re-entered that service; on 15 May he asked for a few days' leave as his brother's wife was fatally ill; and, just as in Aachen seven years before, he never returned from that leave. He had 'found the people and the work just as boring and unprofitable as before', as he told a friend two months later. Now he was drifting 'will-lessly on the stream of life with no other rudder than the whim of the moment, and it is a matter of some indifference to me where I am cast ashore'.[42] 'Since then I have been stuck here', he noted a further six months later, following a prolonged illness, 'unmarried, very lonely, twenty-nine years old, physically fit again but intellectually pretty unresponsive, running my business conscientiously but with no particular interest, seeking to make my subordinates' lives cosy according to their lights, and contemplating without irritation the way in which they cheat me for my pains. In the mornings I am peevish, after lunch amenable to every mild emotion. My company consists of dogs, horses and country squires, and among the latter I enjoy a certain esteem because I am able to read written matter with ease, I dress properly at all times, and yet I can still skin my game with the precision of a butcher, ride quietly and boldly, smoke great big cigars and cordially and cold-bloodedly drink my guests under the table.'[43]

For all the irony and self-mockery, here was also a quite fundamental disgust with his way of life and with his whole existence. He had reached a point at which almost anything might have come over him: total unscrupulousness in the choice of ends and means if only they promised to end this state of affairs, self-destruction and self-abandonment, amorality and the blind irresponsibility of the desperado – or a readiness for a kind of reorientation, an acceptance of self and of his own personality.

In those years of the gradual dissolution of all his hopes of basing an inner life on the externals of occupation and circumstances, Bismarck read a great deal, quite unsystematically and without any practical objective or educational interest in the usual sense, undoubtedly in many cases purely for entertainment and distraction, but also in search of elements capable of supporting such an inner life, of attitudes to existence and to the world that did not strike his over-acute eye as mere lies. Thanks to Motley and Keyserling he was already familiar with the works of Shakespeare, Goethe and Byron. He now also read Lenau, Chamisso, Uhland, Rückert, Béranger and above all Heine, whose ambiguous, fundamentally melancholy irony was so closely in tune with his own pose. Spinoza he had probably first come across in connection with his essay on the oath, and he now read more of his work – for 'reassurance', as he put it. He tried Hegel, there was mention of Voltaire, and the Young Hegelians he even studied with some enthusiasm. The conflict between rationalism and revelation, between history and the present that runs through their writings and the attempt at a reciprocal illumination of sense at first stirred a chord in him, though he was hardly convinced by their findings. After that there was never seriously any question of philosophy and the reading of philosophical works. Asked about Schopenhauer, with whom he had lived in the same city for almost a decade, he replied almost gruffly some forty years later that he did not know him: 'I never had the time or the inclination to concern myself with philosophy.'[44] Even the historical works of which he took in a great many at that time, Schlosser's *History of the Eighteenth Century*, Dahlmann's *Description of the French Revolution*, or Louis Blanc's committed treatment of the immediately contemporary history of the years 1830–40, he read with an almost unrelenting sense of inner opposition. It was all too neat for his liking, too artificial, idealistic, unlike real life.

None of all this seriously affected him. He drew from it an unparalleled profusion of images, quotations, comparisons and allusions that he then used with supreme assurance in his speeches and letters and even in many official papers, which they invested with a highly distinctive, not to say unmistakable character. But his reading matter always remained for him a kind of intellectual and literary quarry from which he extracted whatever happened to be important to him at the time with a complete disregard for context or the beliefs and opinions that lay behind it, melting everything down and merging it with his own outlook and way of thinking. He never was and never became a literary person, a person who draws his life and his identity from the world of the mind – which is not to say that he was unintellectual or indeed anti-intellectual. His life, his being, his whole approach were determined by other factors that were more immediately bound up with the world around him. He always needed the direct, external impulse, and his whole life long he remained deeply cut off from people who differed from him in this respect.

It was external impulses of this kind that helped him to surmount the crisis in which he found himself at the age of 30. In 1842 he had been introduced by a former fellow pupil at the Grey Friary, Moritz von Blankenburg, who followed in his footsteps in 1843 by resigning from the judicial service to manage his father's estates and who was later a leading figure among the Prussian conservatives for many years, to a group of Pomeranian Pietists that had formed around Adolf von Thadden-Trieglaff, the father of Blankenburg's fiancée Marie. The group's outlook, its prevailing spirit of meditative asceticism and austerity, its deliberately uncritical biblical fundamentalism and its outward forms of piety, which tended towards sectarianism and excess – to all of this his background had made him a stranger. That he frequented the group nevertheless was due to the growing intensity of his friendship with Moritz von Blankenburg, a man of supremely altruistic character who treated him with undeniable sympathy and a lively understanding, and not least to Marie von Thadden.

This relationship with his friend's fiancée has been the subject of much debate. Bismarck himself declared that she had become 'dear' to him 'as ever sister was to brother',[45] and there is no evidence, no hint that he felt for her any more or any differently than that. This proves nothing, of course. But we should beware of searching for an inner conflict that, if it ever existed, had no practical consequences.

What mattered was on another level. In Marie von Thadden Bismarck met a person with the kind of confidence and inner security that were what he longed for most for himself at this period of his life. In her Pietist missionary zeal Marie soon set about trying to persuade him that her composure was not the expression of a particular personality or an attitude to life that could be learned but the outcome of a strong Christian faith, an unswerving trust in a personal God.

She was successful only in so far as Bismarck allowed himself to become involved in a religious discussion at all. He clung, however, to a vague deism, to 'the hazy blue image of God he had formed for himself', as Marie von Thadden put it.[46] That 'confidence and peace' were the 'companions of faith' he did not doubt. But he implied that in his opinion even a misbelief could have this effect and that in the final analysis it was 'presumption on the part of believers . . . to regard their views as the right one'. The idea of omnipotence and the immeasurable greatness of God made it impossible, he thought, to believe in a personal God who was interested in the individual and in his needs, desires and expectations. 'It was borne in upon me', he went on in a letter written several years later, looking back on what he believed at this period, 'that God had denied man the possibility of knowledge, that it was presumption to claim to know the will and the plans of the Lord of the world, that man must wait in humility to see how his

Creator will dispose of him at his death, and that we on earth have no other means of knowing God's will than through conscience, which he has given us as a feeler with which to find our way through the darkness of the world.'[47] The rationalism of the Enlightenment and something of the pathos of the desperate man who feels abandoned and alone were both present here, but so was an instinctive rejection of the narrow and not infrequently bigoted self-assurance that he often encountered in this Pietist group.

Marie von Thadden was entirely free of this. Yet this could also be interpreted as meaning that everything did after all depend on the personality of the individual. And that is probably how Bismarck interpreted it. When Moritz von Blankenburg, obviously encouraged by some optimistic remarks that Marie had made, started to tackle the subject in a series of long letters, Bismarck went along with him at first but then soon let the correspondence drop. The need for something deeper on which to base a life that was now so open to question as far as he was concerned, that had indeed become almost a matter of indifference, remained clear and was increasing in intensity. But equally pronounced was his critical scepticism not only towards others but also towards himself. That a need is capable of producing its own fulfilment was something of which he was only too well aware. 'How can I believe when I have no faith to start with?' he protested to Marie von Thadden with some irritation during their first religious discussion in 1843. 'It either has to enter into me or it has without effort or will on my part to spring up inside me.'[48] Resistance and expectation got in each other's way, and seen purely from the outside it was in fact inevitable that the decisive breakthrough should have occurred at the moment when as a result of deep upheavals his resistance briefly broke down.

In the 'Werbebrief' Bismarck spoke in this context of 'events . . . in which I played no active part and which since they are other people's secrets I may not divulge, but which had a shattering effect on me'. We have no idea what he was alluding to; Bismarck never so much as touched on the subject again. One might therefore content oneself with assuming that the events in question must have been, for him, less important in themselves than in the 'practical result' that through them 'my awareness of the shallowness and unworthiness of my way of life became keener than ever, other people's good opinion of me oppressed me and put me to shame, and I bitterly repented of my life hitherto'. One is struck, however, by the fact that Bismarck here – and only here – uses Pietist forms of expression that in their general tone were in deep contradiction to his whole being and that also fitted ill within the whole context of what was in all honesty an extremely sober and self-analytical description of his 'inner life' to date. We may assume, therefore, that in his wisdom Bismarck slightly amended the reality of his 'inner life' at this point, perceiving that he must avoid giving any impression to the person to whom his letter was addressed that there might be a connection between his religious development and his relationship to the latter's daughter. For such an impression would no doubt have deeply alarmed a man for whom a sure faith was something one took

24

for granted and certainly an indispensable prerequisite for marriage. It would have aroused the suspicion that faith was here the somewhat dubious child of a thoroughly earthly love, if not a complete sham.

That there was such a connection is beyond question. And part of it was what, alienated under the pressure of circumstances and forced into stereotyped formulae, found expression in Bismarck's words concerning the crisis in his life, his 'awareness of the shallowness and unworthiness of my way of life': this was the heightened feeling of inner inadequacy that his encounter with Johanna von Puttkamer and his at first very hesitantly reciprocated love for her had aroused in him – a feeling that Bismarck in full awareness described as the precondition and initial expression of his religious transformation.

Johanna von Puttkamer was a close friend of Marie von Thadden. She too came from a Pietist home. She was the only child of a Pomeranian country squire who lived a secluded life on his Reinfeld estate in up-country Pomerania far to the east, farming the land himself and doing little as a member of the district and provincial Diets to alter the widespread view that politically as well as socially Pomerania was the most backward province in the entire kingdom. As heiress of her parents' estates, which comprised not only Reinfeld from her mother's family but also her father's Viartlum, Johanna von Puttkamer was a good match, though hardly a great one. The circle in which her home background, intellectually as well, had accustomed her to move was comparatively restricted, in political and social terms wholly bound up with tradition, in religious terms strictly fundamentalist and practising a very emotional kind of piety, virtually untouched by the intellectual currents of the time and in fact slightly more receptive only in the fields of literature and music. Shakespeare, the Romantics, particularly Jean Paul, Schumann as the great song composer, and Beethoven – these were the names with which she was familiar. Within that circle, however, she moved with great freedom and intellectual honesty, with sober, straightforward naturalness and with a great deal of common sense, her unquestioned piety being wholly realistic and relevant and 'free of religiosity', as Moritz von Blankenburg testified.

As early as the winter of 1843–4 he endorsed Marie von Thadden's idea that the 19-year-old Johanna might be the right woman for Bismarck. This implied a great deal. For however much they liked him they both knew him only too well: his 'mad spells', his restlessness, his need for change in all spheres of life, and not least his indifference to religion. Evidently they credited Johanna with the ability to deal with all this and to meet Bismarck as an equal on human terms – for Marie von Thadden was the last woman to see marriage as the blind subordination of female to male. They also believed Johanna would be able to give him an inner stability, possibly even to 'awaken' religion in him.

The first time Bismarck met Johanna was when his friends Marie von Thadden and Moritz von Blankenburg were married at the beginning of October 1844. The meeting failed to rouse a spontaneous passion in him, though he was neither unsusceptible nor inexperienced in this regard. They had already told him a great deal about her, doubtless making their intentions too clear for his taste as well as couching them in the emphatic style that was characteristic of the whole group and was hardly likely to have the desired effect on an outsider who favoured a more matter-of-fact approach. The two subsequently met several times at the home of their mutual friends – the Blankenburgs lived in Cardemin – in the period that followed, but without getting very much closer to each other. It was not until just under two years later, on a trip to the Harz Mountains with a wider group of friends organized – probably not without an ulterior motive – by Marie von Blankenburg, that he suddenly saw her with quite different eyes. 'After the trip we made together this summer', he wrote to her father a few months later, he had been 'in doubt only . . . as to whether the achievement of my desires will be compatible with your daughter's happiness and tranquility.'[49]

This last was no mere form of words calculated to counter any possible misgivings on her father's part. That with his character, his attitude to life and his unbelief he might destroy something that constituted the essence of the object of his affections, that the greatest obstacle to an alliance with her might lie within himself and that this might also, ultimately, be the reason for Johanna's reserve – these considerations must have preoccupied him very deeply in the weeks following the Harz trip. Prompted by this kind of self-doubt and probably also by a desire to get closer to the world she lived in, he spent much of his time during this period reading the Bible – 'more consistently and with a more determined suspension of my own judgement for the time being'. And when Moritz von Blankenburg, harking back to occasional conversations they had had on the Harz trip, wrote to him in a cautious attempt to revive their religious correspondence, Bismarck readily concurred.

While he was brooding thus, a constant prey to doubt, he heard in late October 1846 that Marie von Blankenburg was ill and her life in danger. The news shook him to the core, breaking down all his remaining resistance, all his scepticism and rational reservations. 'The thing that had been stirring in me', he wrote in the crucial lines of the letter to his prospective father-in-law, 'came to life when, with the news of the fatal illness of our late friend in Cardemin, the first fervent prayer, without my ruminating on its reasonableness, tore itself from my heart, accompanied by a keen feeling of grief at my own inability to pray and by tears such as I have been a stranger to since the days of my childhood. God did not hear my prayer at that time, but neither did he reject it, for I have never since lost the ability to ask things of him, and I feel within myself if not peace at least a confidence and optimism such as I no longer knew in my ordinary life. Steeped in the knowledge that I can never through my own efforts be free of sin and wrong-doing, I do not feel depressed and dejected in that knowledge, as I used to feel without it, because my doubts about eternal life have left me and because I am able to ask God daily with a contrite heart to be merciful to me for the sake of His Son and to awaken and strengthen my faith.'

The fact that under different circumstances his suit would have been virtually hopeless not only as far as the father but also as far as the daughter was concerned has fostered doubts since this letter came to light as to whether Bismarck was really being honest here or whether this was not primarily the future diplomat writing. Yet the wealth of such references to his personal life is quite unequivocal. From this point on belief in a personal God and in immortality were unquestionably among the basic components of his whole existence. 'I fail to understand', he wrote on a visit to Wiesbaden four-and-a-half years later, looking back on his life at that time, 'how a person who thinks about himself and yet neither knows nor wishes to know anything of God can endure his life for contempt and boredom, a life that passes away like a stream, like a sleep, or like a blade of grass that soon withers; we spend our years like a piece of idle gossip. I don't know how I used to stand it; were I to live now as I lived then, without God, without you, without children – I really would not know why I should not lay aside this life like a soiled shirt.'[50]

'Without God, without you, without children' – Bismarck was naming the pillars of his private life, the foundation of that 'autonomy of private life' that the 23-year-old had first hoped to 'carry over into the public sphere'. 'I thank God and I thank you', he telegraphed on their fortieth wedding anniversary, 'for forty years of steadfast love and loyalty. That's 14,610 days including 2,088 Sundays and ten 29 Februarys. Good and bad ones, but many, many more good.'[51] Sure of himself now, following his religious conversion and resultant acceptance of his own life, he had swept aside all remaining hesitation on Johanna's part and any further doubts and misgivings on the part of her parents. 'All right', he telegraphed to his sister from Reinfeld on 12 January 1847, laconic in his triumph. To his brother he reported that 'I found there a not unfavourable mood and a willingness to open far-reaching negotiations, and who knows what path these might have followed had I not greeted my intended with a determined accolade as soon as I saw her and so, to the speechless astonishment of her parents, moved matters forward to a different stage in which within five minutes everything had fallen into place.'[52] Not seven months later, on 28 July 1847, four weeks after the closure of the 'United Diet', the marriage took place at Reinfeld. As the letter to his brother went on to say, 'For the rest I believe I have secured a great and no longer looked-for piece of good fortune in that, to put it quite cold-bloodedly, I am marrying a woman of rare intelligence and rare nobility of mind who is at the same time extremely charming and facile à vivre like no female I have ever known.'

This was not simply the exalted opinion of a man in the first flush of love. It stood the test of decades, reflected and transmitted in hundred of letters that in their immediacy, intensity and unconditional devotion have few parallels even in the abundant literature of nineteenth-century correspondences. They show the extent to which the relationship governed him inwardly, giving security and meaning to his life, and how much he needed it in order to find himself and gain assurance and equilibrium, not just once but over and over again: 'You are my anchor on the good side of the river', as he put it himself on one occasion. 'If that drags, may God have mercy on my soul.'[53]

For however undeniably his religious experience and his love for Johanna von Puttkamer governed the very foundations of his future life, neither can we overlook the fact that the inner disintegration, debilitating scepticism and passionate unconditionality and egocentricity that were a part of his nature continued to have their effect. 'Things moving and impressive in earthly terms', he once wrote to Johanna with this in mind, 'such as can usually be portrayed with human resources always bear some relation to the fallen angel, who is beautiful but without peace, great in his plans and endeavours but without success, proud and sad.'[54]

His finding inner stability, a sure faith and a firm emotional tie did not mean that he became a different person. It did not mean that he now saw and assessed the world around him with quite different eyes or defined his place in it in quite different terms. On the contrary, his eye for its weaknesses, for the self-deceptions and illusions by which he was surrounded, and for the predictable aspects of human behaviour possibly became even sharper. In a character such as his the thought of his own and all existence being secure within a higher will released additional vigour and will-power as well as an attitude towards success in which the dominant features were a readiness to take risks, the temperament of the gambler and an unconcern that sometimes went as far as indifference. It was an element of what Goethe called the 'demonic', the kind of unconditional, passionate impulsiveness the roots of which, reaching deep down into the darkness, can perhaps be rationalized to some extent but are ultimately beyond any real explanation. And Bismarck was far too self-critical a person not to have discovered these traits within himself; as he put it once, there were in his soul 'whole provinces that I shall never let another person see inside'.[55] However – and this was to be the source of many problems – he now saw them as taken care of and in a certain sense even justified in the other-worldly governed-ness of all earthly and human order.

The apparently often unreflective pitching-in, the tremendous application, the abrupt tergiversations in full flight when one objective no longer seemed attainable and another suddenly beckoned – all these he explained over and over again were only to the superficial eye a matter of the individual's arbitrary and unconditional urge to have his way. In reality the individual was simply carrying out a higher will. The individual neither created the circumstances nor did he determine the course of history. His achievement consisted solely in recognizing what was in the historical air. 'History with its great events', he said once in conversation as an old man, 'does not roll on like a railway train at an even speed. No, it advances by fits and starts, but with irresistible force when it does. One must just be permanently on the look-out and, when one sees God striding through history, leap in and catch hold of his coat-tail and be dragged along as far as may be. It is dishonest folly and outmoded political wisdom to pretend that it is a question of weaving opportunities and stirring up troubled waters in order then to go fishing in them.'[56]

This was Hegel in Christian guise; this was the 'agent of the World Spirit'. And as with Hegel there was a great danger of glorifying one's own action, one's own cause, when one was successful, as the expression of a universal reason, the divine will, or providence and of disparaging and as it were morally condemning all that opposed it.

Here too, as in so many instances, Bismarck was on the border-line. He had far too sharp an eye for the spirit of Christian self-righteousness, as encountered in Pomerania and often subsequently among his political friends, for him really to have fallen a prey to it himself. When in the mid-1860s a Conservative Party colleague felt obliged to remind him of his duties as a 'Christian statesman', Bismarck brusquely interrupted him: no one had an exclusive right to decide what was politically responsible behaviour even in the Christian sense, and assiduous church-going and pious raising of the eyes to heaven meant nothing at all. 'Anyone who calls me an unscrupulous politician is doing me an injustice and should start by trying his own conscience in this particular arena . . . When I stake my life on a thing, I do so in the faith that I have fortified for myself in long and bitter struggle but also in sincere and humble prayer to God and that no word of man, not even that of a friend in the Lord and a servant of his Church, is going to overthrow for me.'[57]

The individual, in other words, stood in a direct relationship to God. But the pretension implicit in this also betokened the limitation: subjection to the ultimately inscrutable will and decree of a higher power. 'As God will', he wrote to his wife on 2 July 1859, following his recall as Prussia's envoy to the Federal Diet in Frankfurt and his transfer to St Petersburg, 'it is all merely a matter of time; nations and individuals, folly and wisdom, war and peace, they come and go like waves, and the sea remains. What are our states and their power and honour in God's eyes but ant-hills or bee-hives that the hoof of the bullock tramples flat or fate overtakes in the person of the bee-keeper come to collect the honey?'[58] And five years later, after what was possibly one of his greatest diplomatic and political successes in the Schleswig-Holstein conflict: the king 'thanked me at our farewell, much moved and giving me all the credit for what God's help has done for Prussia. May it please God to continue to lead us in mercy and not leave us to our own blindness. It is a lesson one learns well in this business, that one can be as wise as the wise ones of this world and yet at any point find oneself next moment walking like a child into the darkness.'[59] From an early age Bismarck had been accustomed to regard success, the implementation of one's own wishes and plans and the overcoming of one's political opponents, as at the same time corresponding in some way to a higher world order, and the temptations of power were only too familiar to him. For this reason the ties of religion were something he very consciously felt to be necessary, even prior to any direct religious experience; the 'at the same time one must be inwardly devout' of the not yet 20-year-old student to his friend Keyserling belongs in this context. For many years he carried about with him a devotional annual containing texts from the Bible for each day with accompanying commentaries by Luther, and under 27 September 1870, three weeks after Sedan and the victory over Napoleonic France, he found a sentence of Luther's that he underlined heavily in obvious agreement, even double-underlining the second part: 'No matter how just, how holy, how innocent, or how divine your business, it is necessary that you should go about it in fear and humility and that you should at all times fear God's judgements.'[60]

What he felt to be indispensable as far as he himself was concerned ought in his opinion to be true of society and of the state as well. 'How people who do not believe in a revealed religion, in a God of goodwill, in a higher judge and in a life to come can live together in an ordered manner – minding their own business and leaving others to mind theirs, is something I fail to understand', he declared next day to a small company at dinner.[61] Here the connection was clear and forceful: without religion, without belief, there was no real sense of duty, no deeper obligations, no supra-personal considerations and loyalties. 'Were it not for the wonderful footing I have in religion, I should have launched myself at the whole court bottom-first long ago.' What was left of true self-abnegation and dedication to the state and the monarchy was of religious origin, a residue of faith in secularized form, 'less clear and yet effective, no longer belief and yet still belief'. He did not wish to 'squander his strength under a master', as he had put it once thirteen years before with reference to Frederick William IV, 'whom one can obey only with the aid of religion'. If once these ties failed there was no further hold against selfishness, power hunger and naked self-interest. What in the last analysis was his own subordination and loyalty to the Crown but the expression of a metaphysical obligation: 'For why, if not by divine decree – why should I bow down to these Hohenzollerns? They are a Swabian family no better than my own and absolutely no concern of mine.'[62]

Here, expressed in exaggerated form, was a basic political conviction that in essence had emerged very early on in his career and subsequently took shape during his years in Pomerania, mainly in the conversations and discussions of the group around Adolf von Thadden-Trieglaff. In addition to Thadden the group comprised the Gerlach brothers and Ernst von Senfft-Pilsach, a brother-in-law of Thadden's who at that time held an important financial post in the Ministry of the Royal Household and from 1852 to 1866 was president of the province; another member was Ernst von Bülow-Cummerow, who in the 1840s acquired a name far beyond the frontiers of Pomerania as a conservative political commentator. A sort of intellectual mentor operating from a distance was the Berlin Professor of Legal Philosophy and Constitutional and Canon Law, Friedrich Julius Stahl, who though of Jewish parentage had been converted to Protestantism as a young man and who in those years was actually laying the foundations of a conservative-monarchical theory of constitutional law in Germany.

Outwardly and in terms of practical consequences Bismarck was at first in full agreement with these men as far as his basic political convictions were concerned. The core of their philosophy was that the existing political and social order was founded not on historically pragmatic but on metaphysical considerations. 'By the grace of God' applied not only to the position of the Crown but also to those of the nobility and the other estates as well as to their relationships with one another and above all to the function of each, the task it was required to perform in this world. That task was ultimately the 'realization of Christian doctrine', which was therefore the true 'purpose of the state' wherever its intervention was called for in the first place.

In other words, such a 'Christian state', which Bismarck explicitly professed in his speech in the 'United Diet' on 15 June 1847 against the political emancipation of members of the Jewish faith,[63] had as its first duty the protection and defence of the traditional social order. After all, the legitimacy of that order stemmed from the same source as its own. It would therefore be destroying its own foundations if it were to alter or even abandon society in the form it had taken hitherto.

The 'realization of Christian doctrine' thus meant keeping life on its traditional course as ordained by God and for the rest avoiding as far as possible keeping society in its traditional form in any kind of tutelage. So the political tendency was quite clear. Otherwise, however, the doctrine of the 'Christian state' was extremely abstract and general. Ludolf Camphausen, the Cologne banker and one of the Rhineland's leading liberals, who in the revolutionary period of nine months later became Minister-President of Prussia, was right in a way that went beyond mere political opposition when he said in the debate that in his opinion 'the concept of the Christian state ha[d] arisen not so much among practical statesmen as a result of real experiences and needs' – rather it was 'a discovery, possibly connected with external causes, of our modern-day political philosophy'.[64]

Bismarck himself did not feel wholly at ease as, outside his home circle and before far more critical ears, he ventured into the rarified atmosphere of such abstractions – however sure he might be, as on the occasion of his maiden speech, of the applause of his political friends and of the court. He therefore quickly fell back on a more robust and polemically exploitable line of argument that reflected his views as well as his political perspective in a much more immediate and concrete way. The state – and here, he said, he agreed with the liberals – was essentially a legal system. The crucial question, however, was where one saw the basis of that legal system, the source of all positive legislation: in this world or in a realm of revealed truth removed from the relativity and changeability of all things human, in other words in Christianity. 'If we remove this foundation from the state, we are left with a state that is nothing but a random aggregate of rights, a kind of bulwark against the war of each against each set up by the old philosophy. Its legislation will therefore no longer renew itself at the well-spring of eternal truth but at the vague and changeable concepts of humanity as they happen to form in the heads of those at the top. How, supposing they feel strong enough to do so, people in such states are going to combat the ideas of, for example, the Communists regarding the immorality of property, regarding the high moral value of theft as an attempt to establish man's inherent rights, the right to assert himself, is something I am not clear about', he went on, characteristically taking immediate advantage of what he assumed to be a dilemma for the opposition as representing the propertied middle classes. 'These ideas too are seen as human by those who hold them, in fact they are regarded as the proper flowering of humanity.'

Against the optimism of the Enlightenment and of liberalism, against the belief in the perfectibility of man and of human societies through their own doing by dint of reason, understanding and autonomous moral principles, Bismarck set, albeit in hidden form, the image of a sinful humanity in need of grace and redemption, the Lutheran conception of salvation by faith alone. The pretension to an absolute autonomy guided by an ethics standing on purely this-worldly foundations and on supposed laws of reason was equated with arbitrariness, with boundless subjectivism, indeed with the releasing of destructive forces, brutal interests and naked greed. Here he exhibited all the sceptical level-headedness with which he had regarded human behaviour, whether individual or social, from an early age; he himself stressed repeatedly that it was no doubt a defect in his eyesight that he saw the shortcomings of his fellow human beings so much more clearly than their merits. It seemed to him that on the basis of the unrestricted autonomy of the individual any kind of living together 'in an ordered manner' with people 'minding their own business and leaving others to mind theirs', as he put it in 1870, was unthinkable, and restraint and above all an inner meaning to life were not likely to result.

This did not prevent him from assuming for all practical purposes that the drives, goals and interests of the individual as well as of human societies were as a rule of a purely this-worldly nature and as such quite straightforwardly controllable and calculable. There appeared to be some contradiction here. For Bismarck, however, the contradiction was resolved or rather got rid of in the same way as the problem of the inner meaning of his personal life, if in both cases we disregard for the moment what was probably in the long run an indissoluble residue of doubt, uncertainty and sceptical despondency. Here again the idea of a higher and ultimately inscrutable meaning for earthly existence and the fact that all life was in need of grace as it were freed one from the obligation to hold the positive preconception of oneself and others that was imperative if one sought to derive an intellectual and moral meaning for life from life itself. There was no further need to fool oneself since nothing really crucial depended on it.

This did not of course mean that one should simply let things take their course, both as regarded one's own self and the world around one. But it did limit one's accountability in so far as it absolved the individual from responsibility for any system conceived as a whole, whatever form that system might take, and directed his actions towards individual decisions of conscience in the spirit of Christianity. The outcome in terms of concurrence with and opposition to other actions and what the whole thing added up to in the end were ultimately, together with its meaning, in the hands of God. The only permissible assumption in this regard was that what was feasible in any particular instance, precisely because it proved to be feasible, could not be in complete contradiction to God's purposes.

This Christian realism, not to say pragmatism, with which Bismarck entered political life and by which he always felt inwardly justified, for all his self-critical scepticism and even criticism with regard to his own actions and decisions, was as foreign as anything could be to all modern ideas about politico-social systems and to the criteria of judgement and action derived from them. However natural it has become for modern man to think in

these terms, it would be a great mistake to impute such thinking wholesale
to a man such as Bismarck, thus attributing to his actions from this point on
an inner logic that they simply did not possess. In this way Bismarck does
indeed become invested with wholly superhuman traits and becomes an
almost demonic hero-figure who in a process of negative reversal puts into
the shade everything that the exaggerated Bismarck-worship of the past
produced in this respect. 'That one can be as wise as the wise ones of this
world and yet at any point find oneself next moment walking like a child
into the darkness' – only a deeply sceptical pragmatist would say such a
thing, a man who was fully aware of the limitations of human planning and
action, not someone who regarded everything as foreseeable, feasible and
open to control.

The real problem of this Christian pragmatism, which Bismarck pursued
with the utmost consistency, lies in precisely the opposite direction: it is the
question of the limits of a man's responsibility for his own actions. In
Bismarck's case those limits have often been stretched much too wide both
by his admirers and by his critics, not only from the objective but also from
the subjective point of view. Bismarck himself, on the other hand, wanted
to have them drawn very tight in both respects.

Not so much in terms of looking back on and evaluating history – that
was something in which his interest remained minimal his whole life long.
His favourite complaint against the historians who dealt with himself, as it
had been against the historians he had occasionally read in his youth, was
that they construed things to their liking, they 'never [saw] anything except
through their own spectacles'.[65] No, the question of the limits of a man's
responsibility for his own actions was one that repeatedly concerned him in
immediate political terms and as a quite concrete human problem. At the
time of his entry into political life as a young member of the arch-
conservative faction around the Gerlach brothers, the problem culminated
in the question of the duties of a Christian politician, the reach of his
loyalties and the unconditionality of his principles. At the time, of course,
his entire political career, in so far as he looked for this to the political group
he had joined, depended on his answering this question 'correctly'.
Accordingly his answer, as for example in his profession of the 'Christian
state', remained extremely general and avoided all points that might
possibly have been controversial. Added to which the defensive battle
against the advancing political enemy represented by the liberal and
democratic forces soon took a dramatic turn, thrusting all other considerations
into the background for the time being. Such qualities as fighting spirit,
determination and staying-power now seemed more crucial than anything
else.

Bismarck was not short of these. Consequently he emerged from the
revolution of 1848–9 as one of the leading figures on what was now quite
clearly the dominant right wing of the Conservative Party. As one of the
leading figures not in theoretical terms, certainly, but in practical terms. As
a highly effective speaker before all sorts of bodies; as a skilful negotiator
and successful organizer; as a man who mastered the job of that newly
emergent figure, the modern party politician, with surprising assurance and

matter-of-factness, the job, in other words, of a politician whose dealings were no longer confined to the court, the bureaucracy, his peers and his subordinates. The concrete experience that Bismarck gathered here, the possibilities that opened up before him in the process and the practical insight he now received for the first time into what was and was not feasible – all this not only had a decisive bearing on his future political life. It also crucially influenced the answer he eventually gave to the question of the limits of responsibility of a Christian politician, a question that his arch-conservative friends had occasion to put to him with every emphasis.

[2]

The Way into Politics

'A constitution must come, that's the way to outward honours', he had told his friend Keyserling as a young man. And in the letter to his cousin justifying his decision to leave the Prussian civil service there was again mention of the 'state with a free constitution' that was the only kind in which, for a man such as himself, a political role was at all conceivable or desirable. As things turned out, he owed his political rise quite decisively to the introduction into Prussia of the constitutional, representative system of government – or more precisely to the crisis of that bureaucratic absolutism of which he had appeared to be a committed defender.

Only appeared to be. Because what he and his political associates had been after from the outset was not the re-entrenchment of bureaucratic absolutism. It was the re-introduction of the political and governmental role of the estates, principally of the nobility, for the purposes of safeguarding the existing social order against arbitrary encroachments from without or from above.

This was the direction in which, with his characteristically undogmatic candour with regard to the question of concretization and modification in detail, his thoughts and his political objectives ran throughout his life. Writing his memoirs, he remarked: 'The ideal I have always had before me is a monarchical power controlled by a representative body, independent and in my view based on estates or professional associations, to the extent that neither monarch nor parliament can alter the existing legal framework *unilaterally* but only communi consensu, with all governmental processes taking place in public and subject to public criticism by press and Diet.'[1]

But when he said in the same context that this basic attitude had actually brought him close to the liberal opposition and that the antagonism between them was ultimately due to their 'disagreeable manner' and windy dogmatism, his words concealed what were in fact quite fundamental differences of opinion. Particularly with regard to the role of the land-owning nobility, the share other social classes should have in political life and the need for reform of the still patriarchal agrarian structure, their views diverged widely. This was no less true so far as the role and function of the Crown were concerned and the right of majorities with respect to it.

In one only apparently formal point, however, he was right when he stressed his initial closeness to the liberal opposition. Both aimed, if only

35

one side said so openly, to bring about a radical change in the existing structure of the state. Both sought in this respect to realize their political objectives outside the context of the status quo. In other words, both were in this sense revolutionaries, and Bismarck, in a concealed form, was even the far more determined of the two. For even if it was the liberals' hesitant appeal to the principle of popular sovereignty in the revolution of 1848 that outwardly appeared to be the truly subversive element in that it radically called into question the position of the hitherto sovereign monarch, in effect it was no less subversive to seek to place the monarch under the tutelage of the professed champions of his absolute power and commit the Crown indefinitely to a particular political course and a particular political programme. Yet that is precisely what Bismarck and his closest political friends were aiming at. It was this that determined the direction and tactics of their policy, and it was this that first gave Bismarck his own concrete political standpoint, the position from which he argued and acted.

Ideally bureaucratic absolutism was based on the concept of an impartiality and justice, detached from all social ties and conflicts of interest, that found their place and their realization in the state. 'In the state' meant in a prince who in Christian responsibility and under divine guidance was committed solely to the common good and who in his actions was dispensed from observing the laws, in particular the common law evolved by and out of society, and was himself authorized to establish a better, higher and more universal law.

This theoretical justification of absolutism as taken up and developed further by many representatives of the Enlightenment placed the state above society as a matter of principle. It committed the state to ideal legal principles that allegedly arose out of the nature of things: to particular basic individual rights, to the concept of equality before the law, to the welfare of the community and the individual, and to their protection from outside and the guarantee of their freedom to develop. At the same time it favoured the reformist state that intervened in existing legal and social relationships, particularly since it was in these that the main resistance to increases in the power of the monarch and of the bureaucracy serving him and the new concept of the state was rooted.

However, reform and modernization of state and society not only took place at the expense of the beneficiaries of the old social order. In many cases they did not even correspond to the wishes and interests of those who were at a disadvantage under that order; this revealed the thoroughly ideological character of this concept of the state, by which the actual power interests involved were disguised. As a result, bureaucratic absolutism and its principles came increasingly under fire and were increasingly called into question from this quarter as well. Against the 'monarchical principle' there arose the principle of popular sovereignty and with it the demand for government by majority decision in a representative body or parliament.

In this situation, with the Crown threatened in its rights and in its position, support was forthcoming from forces that had hitherto steadily resisted its growing pretensions and now demanded, as the price for their support, at least a partial abdication of absolutism in their favour. This had happened once before in the years immediately preceding the great French Revolution of 1789, in the so-called 'aristocratic revolution' of the years 1787–8. On that occasion developments had overtaken it. This time, however, the prospects seemed a great deal more favourable.

The revolutionary rival from the middle-class liberal camp was much weaker. Moreover, the unrest of the rural population was easier to pacify; its immediate interests could be satisfied by the state. The traditional agrarian structure, which in the rural areas had been one of the main causes of the revolution of 1789, had very largely been done away with in Prussia decades before. What relics of the old feudal class system remained were regarded even by the immediate beneficiaries as bearing no comparison with what was to be feared if the rural peasantry were finally to go over to the middle-class liberal camp. The chief reason for this was that such relics were now of no more than formal significance, the social dominance of the rural upper classes having long since acquired an entirely different foundation.

Admittedly the more determinedly traditionalist members of the Gerlach circle did attempt before 1848 to reinforce those relics. In particular they sought to reform the institution of 'patrimonial jurisdiction' – jurisdiction by landowners in rural areas – along such lines and free it as far as possible from all state influence. Bismarck himself played a comprehensive part in these endeavours. But they were far more an expression of the traditionalist self-awareness of the old nobility and its attacking spirit than a desperate struggle to defend its own social dominance, which was what the liberal public, taking its cue from developments in western Europe, chose to interpret them as.

It was widely overlooked here – and the failure of the revolution stemmed in many respects from this self-deception – that the post-1806 reforms of which the liberals thought so highly had in reality produced results that were anything but helpful to their cause. Through them the traditional ruling class in rural Prussia had, almost without any disruption and with no significant forfeiture of its social and hence political power, become a class of generally well-established landowners who by 1848 had already very largely adapted themselves to the conditions of a market-oriented capitalist economy. The way in which Bismarck set about bringing the family's Pomeranian estates back into prosperity in the 1840s is a striking example of this. On the other hand the traditional middle class organized in guilds and corporations, which was in any case poorly represented in East Elbia – as the regions east of the Elbe were called – had if anything been weakened by the same reforms. For the new freedom of industry and commerce had created competition for it of a kind that the nobility had to fear only in isolated instances from the mobilization of land-ownership, in which an incomparably higher level of capital outlay was called for. Moreover, the few middle-class estate-owners were quickly absorbed into their aristocratic environment as far as their attitudes and life-style were concerned.

If in the country the new and as a rule solidly grounded order based on professional status almost completely replaced the traditional order based on birth, in the towns the opposite was often the case. The implementation of the liberal-capitalist economic system from above by the monarchical-absolutist state led not only to an entrenchment but even, so far as the top level was concerned, to a strengthening of the traditional social hierarchy. This was in fact true of the Crown as well, of the monarchical state as landowner and soon as entrepreneur too, although debts and mounting financial burdens soon cut back the effect here.

All this resulted in a growing self-assurance on the part of the landed upper class in Prussia. Only occasionally was this somewhat deflated by economic setbacks in the agrarian sector; for the rest – politically, too – it thrust more and more urgently towards fruition. At first, however, it very clearly took its bearings from two poles. One of these, concentrated mainly in the central provinces of the Prussian monarchy, was the circle around the Gerlach brothers, with Friedrich Julius Stahl as its chief spokesman in the press. The other was focused on a group of East Prussian and Westphalian nobles and landowners headed by Baron von Vincke (Bismarck's bitterest parliamentary opponent over the next few years), Ernst von Saucken and Alfred von Auerswald; it was by way of being the liberal counterpart to the first.

As against the Gerlachs' programme for the restoration of the old order based on the estates of the realm, this latter group put forward a development on the English model as a political objective worth pursuing. In England a modern aristocracy, moving with the times, had not only consistently held its own but had at the same time very often enjoyed commanding political influence. The members of the rural upper class in Prussia who inclined towards this view were not only very numerous; they could also pride themselves on finding numerous allies among the aristocracy of the rest of Germany, where something like a German Whig party was beginning to emerge. With representatives from virtually every state and province of Germany including Heinrich von Gagern from Hesse, Prince Karl zu Leinigen from the Rhineland Palatinate, the Austrian Anton von Schmerling, the Westphalian George von Vincke and the East Prussian Alfred von Auerswald, this played a considerable part in the revolution of 1848, though it was quite swept aside in the wake of further developments. Except in one or two south German states, the only milieu in which this liberal aristocracy made its presence felt in the period up to 1918 was the circle that formed around Freidrich, for many years Crown Prince of Prussia and Germany and subsequently the 'Emperor of Ninety-Nine Days'.

But before 1848 none of this could be foreseen. On the contrary, this liberal-minded aristocracy, self-confident, reformist, economically and socially powerful and at the same time receptive to the demands of other social groups, seemed to have everything in its favour. And when the 1848 revolution broke out there were probably many in this camp who believed in the possibility of a repetition of England's 'Glorious Revolution' of 1688–9. Then a large and self-assured noble class, acting in alliance with the aspiring middle class, had successfully opposed absolutism and established a political order that subsequently proved as durable as it was flexible and capable of evolving.

Nothing came of these hopes. On the one hand only a few monarchs were prepared genuinely to co-operate; the Prussian and Habsburg monarchies in particular soon felt they had sufficient support for a quite different policy. And on the other hand economic and social developments had already progressed so far beyond the situation that had obtained in England 160 years earlier that a proper integration of the lower orders in a liberal system dominated by the aristocracy and the middle class was clearly no longer possible.

The lesson of 1848 seemed in the last analysis to be that the conflicts of economic and social interests in society were now so sharply defined as no longer to admit of settlement through the parliamentary medium of discussion and compromise. A view that enjoyed wide currency was that in future other forms must be found that placed less emphasis on the idea of a possible consensus or balance of interests and more on the concept of the common good, which people now began to see once again in greater independence from such a balance of interests. In place of the political and social individualism that had hitherto dominated political thought a new collectivism was emerging, though it found a very different nucleus of crystallization and point of reference in the different political camps and social groups. On the one hand it was the social body divided into estates as hallowed by age and custom, on the other the unpropertied working population in town and country, the proletariat as the people proper. On the one hand it was the state in its traditional form, on the other the higher unity of the nation, which allegedly called for a re-examination by each individual of his existing loyalties and commitments.

It was in this profound change, which came about partly during the course of 1848 but above all in the wake of the failure of the revolution, that Bismarck finally found his specific position and with it, so to speak, achieved in public life as well the inner 'autonomy of private life' that was already his. His earliest parliamentary contributions in the United Diet of 1847, delivered with undoubted delight at the increasingly critical nature of the conflict and discussion as such, had all been professions of political faith. They identified him as a firmly principled supporter of the Crown and in particular of the Gerlach faction and its views. Leopold von Gerlach occasionally even gave him what almost amounted to hard and fast directives for his speeches. Bismarck's originality seemed to lie purely in the form he gave to his appearances, particularly in the way in which he would set up his political opponent in a debate, often quite regardless of the man's true opinion, in order subsequently to attack him.

In reality, however, there were already quite considerable differences between his basic political ideas and those of the group around the Gerlachs and Stahl, whose young man he was widely regarded as being. This is true not only of his speech about the Jewish question, in which a wholly materialistic, pragmatic concept of law shone through the mask of his equating custom with what was ordained by God. It is true also of many of his other utterances. These showed him as according a primacy to the standpoint of power and interests that, taken to its logical conclusion, could not even stop at his own position and that of his political friends. There is reason to doubt whether two projected speeches about manorial hunting rights and patrimonial jurisdiction, which promised to go several steps farther in this direction, would have met with the unqualified approval of his associates;[2] both questions, as it happened, failed to come up on the agenda of the United Diet. As a result – fortunately for his further political career – the pronounced naturalism of his approach was at first seen by his fellow conservatives in a purely formal light as being no more than an effective weapon with which to combat political opponents impervious to the kind of idealistic loyalty to conviction paraded in vain by many arch–conservatives, including Bismarck's future father–in–law.

This was also the view taken by the liberals and by public opinion, which was largely in sympathy with them. When the United Diet was dissolved at the end of June 1847, Bismarck left it with the reputation of being an arch-reactionary Junker, a man who for all his superficial eloquence and skill was almost a caricature of a wholly backward-looking, 'medieval' way of life. This misunderstanding on the part of both sides became even more marked during the ensuing revolutionary period. Nor can Bismarck be said to have done anything deliberately to counteract it. On the contrary, he took every opportunity to promote it, although he must have been clear in his own mind that, in the circumstances, with compromise and conciliation in one form or another apparently unavoidable, such an image was steadily reducing his chances of political office and of a major political role. It is obvious that at an early stage, hoping that in the end the counter-revolution would be completely victorious, he quite deliberately put all his eggs in one basket.

To some extent, however, it was external circumstances that determined his course and suggested this kind of personal all-or-nothing policy to him. To start with, the revolution barred his way as far as a political career in the traditional sense was concerned, namely as an adviser appointed by the Crown. And in the eyes of most conservatives this political agitator of recent weeks was quite out of the question as a political champion in the present situation. So in practical terms all he could do, short of executing a humiliating – and probably unsuccessful – about-turn, was to bet on confrontation and on there being a decisive battle between the two camps of 'royalists and liberals'. And that is exactly what, with brief interludes, he did for the next fifteen years – up until his appointment as Minister-President of Prussia in the autumn of 1862.

On his honeymoon, which from August until early October 1847 had taken him via Prague, Vienna, Salzburg, Berchtesgaden and Innsbruck to Venice and from there through Switzerland and back down the Rhine to Schönhausen, he had received an invitation at the beginning of September to dine with Frederick William IV in Venice, where the king was staying at the time. The invitation probably came through Major (as he then was) Albrecht von Roon, who was attached to one of the royal princes as his attendant and who knew Bismarck from Pomeranian circles. The king had taken the opportunity to tell Bismarck how greatly he valued his political stance and that of his circle. In doing so he had once again greatly nourished Bismarck's hopes of a political career in the service of the Crown. Six months later, however, in March 1848, the king yielded on the domestic front to the demands of the victorious revolution. At the same time he abandoned the old relationship of permanent consultation and peaceful co-operation with the Habsburg monarchy in a bid to place himself at the head of the national movement. That this had been an act of political shrewdness, enabling the king to avoid a bloody civil war and the complete breakdown of order as well as to save the Crown, was a claim that Bismarck rejected with great passion as mere titivation of the facts. For a moment, as he hurried to Berlin on 20 March, he believed the king to be under massive physical pressure tantamount to actual blackmail. In this belief he even considered freeing him by means of a bold *coup de main* carried out with the aid of his Schönhausen peasants, whose loyalty to the monarchy was allegedly unreserved. When he subsequently came to appreciate the true state of affairs, mainly as a result of information supplied by Roon, he was thoroughly contemptuous and resolved immediately to take part in every effort to save the traditional monarchical and aristocratic order – even in defiance of the current wearer of the crown.

Such efforts were being made almost from the outset. As early as 30 March 1848 Leopold von Gerlach noted in his diary: 'First attempt to set up a ministère occulte.'[3] A prerequisite for success was that there should be a member of the royal family behind such efforts as a potential regent or successor to the throne. So what Augusta, the wife of the brother of the then king and subsequently queen herself, committed to paper fourteen years later is not wholly improbable, particularly when taken in conjunction with immediately contemporary accounts, although the context in which she was writing was of course a precarious one. Bismarck – so Augusta, a granddaughter of Grand Duke Carl August of Saxe-Weimar, told her husband in July 1862 with the declared aim of preventing him from appointing the Pomeranian as chief minister in Prussia – had approached her on behalf of her brother-in-law Charles, Prince of Prussia, on 23 March 1848, in other words immediately after the successful breakthrough of the revolution, for authorization 'to use both the name of the absent heir to the throne [her husband had fled to England] and that of his son (who was still a minor) for a counter-revolution that was to disown the measures already carried through by the King and to question the latter's authority and soundness of mind'.[4] At any rate the alternative version that Bismarck later put forward several times, and for the last time in his memoirs, has little inherent credibility in view of the pliability of the reigning monarch at that time.[5] Added to which there was the fact that the liberal-minded queen continued throughout her life to stand up to him repeatedly and remained one of his most vehement opponents until her death in January 1890; she had caused him, Bismarck said as an old man, 'more problems than all the foreign powers and the opposition parties at home'.[6] Here, then, are even further grounds for scepticism with regard to Bismarck's retrospective claim that Augusta, egged on by a group of liberals around Georg von

Vincke, had been interested in the regency for herself. Rather we may assume that Bismarck did indeed take soundings at the time – albeit undoubtedly with extreme caution so far as the potential future queen was concerned – as to who might if necessary serve an aristocratic counter-revolution as monarchical head or even simply figure-head. On the other hand it is probably doubtful whether Prince Charles, a still very young and not particularly strong-willed man, seriously believed himself capable of playing a more successful version of the role of his French namesake Charles of Artois, the brother of Louis XVI who as mouthpiece of a counter-revolution had had to flee his country in a hurry on 14 July 1789 and who had come to grief again forty years later as Charles X.

Be that as it may, it is quite clear in which direction Bismarck's activities during these weeks were aimed. The free political jurisdiction of the Crown that he and his circle had so emphatically defended hitherto against demands from the left was now abruptly called into question. The monarch who although reluctantly and under pressure of circumstances used that jurisidiction to conclude an alliance with the middle-class liberal movement was not only accused of weakness and cowardice; he was also as a final consequence deprived of the legitimation for the throne. It now became apparent that for Bismarck and his friends that legitimation consisted above all else in the exercise of guardianship over the traditional social and hence also over the political order in so far as this was still anchored in the former.

Here the spirit of the sixteenth- and seventeenth-century Fronde asserted itself, that aristocratic opposition to absolutism that in order to achieve its goals had very soon allied itself with the middle class and become a champion of social reform. The political testament of Frederick William I had once named three noble families from the March who had always particularly distinguished themselves as 'wicked, insubordinate people' in opposition to the Crown and on whom therefore a constant eye must be kept; they included the Bismarcks.[7] It was a tradition that the youngest scion of the family continued conspicuously in 1848. What interested him, in other words, was not so much saving an independent throne; it was not so much the monarchy or even a state above parties. On the contrary, it was bringing that state back into society, as it were, which in Prussia meant a still essentially traditional society dominated by the aristocracy. And here, at the very beginning of his counter-revolutionary activities, a general problem arises that is of central importance not only so far as understanding Bismarck's future policy is concerned but also as regards assessing further developments as a whole.

It is the problem of the inner connection between the political order of the state and the socio-economic order. Here political value-judgements not infrequently come to light, albeit often quite spontaneously, that for their part bar the way to any understanding that goes beyond merely corroborating them. In relation to Bismarck and the attitude of his close political associates in 1848 this means that to say that what found expression in their policy was the narrow-mindedness, impercipience and selfishness of the East Elbian nobility is to brush aside the real problem and offer a pseudo-solution based on the idea of progress. After all, the political opponents of this extreme right-wing faction in Prussian politics themselves wanted nothing else but to bind the state to the interests, aims and ideals of society, harnessing it to their preservation and advancement – only they had quite another definition of society. No, the real difference lay not there but in the question of the warrant for the respective demands. And here the positions in 1848 were very sharply opposed, particularly so far as the criteria for the substantiation of and inner justification of those demands were concerned.

The fronts were not in fact drawn up as clearly as might have appeared at first. The democratic substantiation of the claim to political power and of demands for social reform was by no means paramount in the middle-class liberal camp. In fact many people had reservations regarding the pure majority principle. On the other hand representatives of the right felt they had more and more reason to suppose that, given the attitude of the rural population, democratic forms might possibly even serve their own political ends. Bismarck himself toyed with this idea in various contexts very early on and never lost sight of it again.

This meant, however, that the legitimation of one's own claim to power in the state and in society was ultimately governed by success. This was already implicit in Montesquieu, who was quoted by both sides: the constitution, laws and politics of a state were the expression of the relationships that had grown up historically within a people, of the internal and external circumstances under which it had evolved – in short, of the peculiarities of its social order, which for its part was understood as something natural.

That this naturalness, like everything in nature, obeyed objective laws and that the historical process itself could be apprehended in terms of natural law and the legitimacy of a claim to political power be substantiated scientifically was something that only the ostensibly positivist but in fact highly speculative social philosophy of a later age sought to prove. As opposed to this kind of bogus materialism, the widely prevalent conception in 1848 was still the 'idealist' one according to which political success was governed by a correct interpretation of social reality and of how it was going to evolve. Accordingly the acid test inevitably appeared to be the political struggle itself and the measure of agreement and active support that one's interpretation met with there. Seen from this viewpoint, it is not particularly surprising that conservatives and liberals used the same methods in 1848 and actually behaved in very similar ways. What they were after was confirmation – with its promise of success – of their basic political and social ideas and beliefs, proof of their doing justice to the facts. This goes some way towards explaining the deep crisis of identity into which liberalism was plunged by its failure.

The liberals undoubtedly went a step farther than the conservatives in their attempt at an ideal approximation to social reality. But the conservatives too, in their efforts through revolutionary counter-action to turn Crown and state into instruments of their endeavours, allowed themselves to be guided by a relatively self-contained social image of the world and of the future. Irrespective of all differences of material interest and well-founded claims to power on both sides, therefore, here was a quite fundamental ideological conflict, a conflict of world views that in 1848 flared up not so much between the middle-class liberal movement and the state and its representatives as between the liberal middle class and the conservative forces that were now beginning to take shape politically.

This obscured what would have been entirely possible areas of compromise. The triumph of the 'other side', however provisional, was felt to be intolerable. As Bismarck put it in extreme terms in the Prussian Lower House in March 1849, 'The battle of principle that has shaken Europe to its foundations in the past year is not of a kind that admits of mediation. The principles rest upon opposite foundations that inherently preclude each other. The one derives its legal authority ostensibly from the popular will but in reality from the club-law of the barricades. The other is based upon a decree ordained of God, a decree of God's grace, and seeks to evolve as an organic extension of the constitutionally established legal order.'[8]

Given these positions, a solution such as the one England arrived at in 1689 was a practical impossibility. It would have required a certain minimal consensus in terms of basic social and political ideas and objectives that did not obtain in Prussia in 1848 and was clearly not going to be achieved there. The inevitable consequence of this was that the two opposing sides, all protestations to the contrary notwithstanding, needed a powerful state in order to assert themselves unilaterally with its help. In Bismarck's martial language: 'The God who directs battles' must 'cast the iron dice of decision on this issue'. As a result, after 1848 the patronizing, authoritarian bureaucratic state gained further ground almost throughout continental Europe and thrust the political self-motion of society into the background once more.

These were constellations and trends of development that were wholly independent of the person and achievement of Bismarck. He did, however – and this was the basis of his success even at this stage – grasp them earlier and more soberly than most of his contemporaries and even the majority of his close political associates. At the outset there was a significant momentary vacillation. When Frederick William IV appointed the two leaders of the liberal opposition, Ludolf Camphausen and David Hansemann, both from the Rhineland, to head the Prussian government and promised far-reaching reforms and a modern constitution, it seemed that the Crown had finally decided upon an alliance not so much with the revolution, admittedly, as with the middle-class liberal movement that was still being carried along and indeed lent wing by it. The representatives of that movement were concerned for their part that the revolutionary upsurge might overshoot their own objectives both politically and socially – for the overwhelming majority of nineteenth-century liberals every revolution carried with it the terrible warning of what had happened in France after 1791. Consequently they were inclined from the outset to ally themselves with established authority and place all their hopes in reform. This was the tendency throughout Germany. It was particularly pronounced in Prussia, however, because especially in the districts east of the Elbe the middle class proper was decidedly weak and in the economically more developed regions it was badly in need of state assistance.

Initially, however, with the revolutionary movement almost universally triumphant even here, this inner weakness on the part of its middle-class liberal exponents remained largely concealed. It was the view of many even in the conservative camp that for the moment these were the only people capable of halting the plunge into chaos and anarchy, of 'guiding the state without serious convulsions over the abyss dividing the old system from the new', as they themselves defined their task.[9] 'Now with all our might into the new ship, even if it is with broken hearts' – this sentence in a letter written by Albrecht von Roon, at whose house in Potsdam Bismarck stayed during those crucial March days, reflects the mood of many conservatives.[10]

It was a mood that, at least for a moment, Bismarck himself came close to sharing. Early in April 1848 the United Diet was reconvened to act as an emergency transitional parliament, the problem being that otherwise absolutism would virtually have had to abolish itself and appoint the body that was to decide upon a new order, both by decree. Bismarck took the opportunity to acknowledge in what was his first public utterance since the outbreak of the revolution 'that this ministry is the only one that can lead us out of the present situation into an ordered and legally constituted state of affairs'.[11] The man who with reference to the present ministers had spoken less than a year before of the 'trite and tricked-out clichés of the politics of Rhine-wine salesmen'[12] now went on to say: 'The past is buried, and I regret more grievously than many of you that no human power is able to bring it back to life, now that the Crown itself has cast earth on the coffin.'

The Gerlachs took these remarks in very bad part, not so much because of the public attack on the king as because they saw in them the beginning of an unprincipled bowing to apparent success. Soon Bismarck himself was wishing he could have taken them back. He subsequently tried to excuse himself to the Gerlachs on the grounds that in a mood of resignation he had briefly come under the influence of the views and appraisals of others, 'some cleverer, some more cowardly'.[13] That was hardly the truth, however, and the Gerlachs' mistrust seemed from their point of view to be entirely justified. Bismarck was clear-sighted enough to see that the counter-revolution did not stand a chance at the moment. And he was sober enough to envisage other possibilities and other courses for himself as well. To what extent his speech represented an attempt to put out feelers in this respect we do not know. If it was, the reaction of the assembly certainly made it clear to him that for the moment at least he had been marked out as hardly 'ally material'. His retreat to a position of unconditional opposition and his attempt to justify himself to the Gerlachs were thus only logical. He saw that he was in danger otherwise of losing any kind of political base.

But there is something else that the speech brings out clearly. If – and this was obviously Bismarck's personal assessment, beyond all tactical consider-ations – the monarchical state and the middle-class liberal movement including its powerful liberal-aristocratic wing really did come together, then the past was indeed dead and an entirely new order in the offing. It was his belief, however, that such a development, if it was to be combated at all, was to be combated not by appealing to principles but only by appealing to interests. It was interests that divided the various social groups, particularly the rural population, the lower social orders and the propertied middle class, whereas at the moment at least shared convictions united them. This, therefore, was where one must start if one was looking for success. And success was what Bismarck was looking for above all else, then as later, without much scruple as to means.

Here it becomes clear how far he already was at this stage from the ideas of the politicians of principle of the old conservative school, notwithstanding the fact that verbally, in terms of the opinions and beliefs he represented, he was still entirely their man. The path he was following in this regard was indicated by the speech he made in the United Diet on 10 April 1848, the last day on which it sat.[14]

The new Finance Minister, David Hansemann, a herald of the modern industrial economy and the founder, soon after this, of the famous Discontogesellschaft, the largest private bank in Prussia in the 1850s and 1860s, had asked the Diet to approve the levy of an additional 40 million taler. Of these, 15 million were for a military contingency fund and 25 were to go 'towards the re-establishment of credit and towards the maintenance of industry'. The relevant committee of the Diet, in pleading for approval, spoke in specific terms of the 'creation and support of public utility enterprises aimed partly at alleviating temporary conditions of hardship, partly at maintaining and promoting commerce and industrial and economic interests'.

In his speech of rejection Bismarck first of all objected to the fact that anyone should come to what was a purely transitional parliament that was to be 'hurled into the ocean of oblivion' the very next day and ask for *carte blanche* on this kind of scale. Similar misgivings had been expressed by members of the committee. For Bismarck, however, they were more a point of departure as well as an opportunity for a passing shot at the Liberals, who, he reminded his hearers, were usually so meticulous about the formalities of constitutional practice. What he was really after was clarification of the 'question of need'. Here he thought he saw a chance of mounting a frontal attack on the new government and the new system and at the same time marking out a favourable battleground for a confrontation between conservatives and liberals.

'The latest files of the financial administration', he declared, gave him cause to 'fear . . . that the system guiding our finances sees the circumstances of our country more through the spectacles of industrialism than with the clear eye of the statesman, who surveys all interests in the country with equal impartiality; I fear, therefore, that the burden of this new imposition will be laid mainly upon the provinces and upon small towns and that the money raised will be used predominantly for the benefit of industry and money transactions in the larger towns.' If it was claimed that this and also the lowering of the milling tax were designed to counter revolutionary unrest in the big towns, such a policy would at best shift that unrest in the direction in which it was also shifting the burdens. The two things, he suggested, were connected. They revealed the true character of the new regime. Under the guise of various empty generalizations, in reality this served the highly selfish interests of a tiny class, the propertied middle class in the big towns. He must therefore cast his vote 'for decisive rejection' of this request for the 25 million, this 'panier percé of industry', as he called it in a private letter written two days later.[15] 'With this kind of support for industry, which is already suffering from overproduction because of lack of consumption', it would be difficult 'to ensure peace in the country in the long term'. All the government was interested in was 'taking away this or a lesser sum from the assets of taxpayers in order to pour it into the bottomless well of the needs of a faltering industry'.

What he was saying was that the liberalism that had now come to power was no more than the ideological trimming on the interests of a small and in itself unimportant stratum of society. It was the gear, so to speak, with which the stratum sought to harness to its carts other groups that numerically and in terms of their function in society were of far greater importance.

Which groups he had in mind here Bismarck subsequently made quite clear. To start with there were the craft tradesmen and small businessmen in the towns, particularly in the small and medium-sized towns. In election speeches and articles he repeatedly called upon them to think of their own interests and be quite clear in their minds what kind of a policy it was that in the same breath demanded protective tariffs for threatened industries and the complete abolition of all restrictions on competition as well as of the traditional, legally enshrined guarantees for the craft trades and for small business. When it was a question of 'filling the pockets of the manufacturers', he declared in the Lower House of the Prussian Diet in October 1849, for example, the state was soon on hand with protective measures to fend off unwelcome competition. When, however, it was a question of suitable measures 'to keep destitution and anarchy from the whole enormous trading and industrial class', people started citing the hallowed principles of liberalism. These had once, at the time of the Stein-Hardenberg reforms, concealed the 'propensity of a large part of the Prussian bureaucracy towards levelling and centralization'. Now, however, they concealed something far worse: the naked selfishness of the manufacturers and their political spokesmen.[16]

Considerably more important in Bismarck's eyes as potential allies in the struggle against liberalism were two other groups: the peasant population and the hitherto liberally inclined section of the land-owning nobility. He already had both groups in his sights when in his speech of 10 April 1848 he contrasted the big cities and the provinces. Liberalism, he declared repeatedly and in a variety of ways, was simply the political, economic and social programme of the urban propertied middle class. Anyone outside that circle who gave it his support was in effect giving that middle class a leg up. Worse, he was betraying his own interests in a quite irresponsible manner. For that kind of neglect of one's own interests would lead to distortions and biases in society as a whole from which in the long run everyone must suffer. This was also the main argument with which, as disappointment clearly spread among the rural population during 1848 with regard to the practical measures taken by the Berlin National Assembly, he confronted those who in the elections to this first freely elected parliament in Prussia had failed to vote him in – and that in his native Schönhausen, in the Jerichow district.

When Bismarck, to the delight of his opponents as well as of the caricaturists, frankly played the country squire, the farmer and the patriarchal employer by turns and when he repeatedly spoke of *the* aristocracy and of *the* estate-owners as of a unified class, he did so not only quite deliberately but in the long run also very successfully. Many differences of opinion persisted, of course. Yet there is no overlooking the fact that the efforts of Bismarck and his immediate political associates contributed decisively towards making the East Elbian estate-owners more clearly aware than they had been of the community of their economic and social interests and of the dangers threatening them. Prominent among those who stood in the front line with Bismarck here was the then Landrat Hans Hugo von Kleist-Retzow, a like-minded contemporary and a friend from Pomeranian circles whose home he shared during those months in Berlin and with whom he discussed every move in detail. Much stricter than Bismarck in ideological and religious matters, Kleist-Retzow was also the man who took over the job of reconciling the older and younger generations of conservative opinion and acted as their go-between; it was in this sense that Ludwig von Gerlach once described his relationship to Bismarck, in English, as that of a 'keeper of his conscience'.[17]

The chief tool of the efforts of Bismarck and his friends to bring the Prussian nobility back into a united front and if possible unite the peasant population behind it came to be the 'Association for the Protection of the Interests of Landed Property'. In essence this was based on an initiative of Bismarck, Kleist-Retzow and Alexander von Below-Hohendorf, another close political friend who in the 1850s became one of the principal spokesmen of Prussian conservatism. In persuading Ernst Gottfried von Bülow-Cummerow to take the chair of this association they acquired one of the leading members of the Pomeranian group centred on the Gerlachs. He was regarded as a man of the centre and enjoyed great and widespread respect as a conservative journalist.

A sort of trial meeting called by Bülow in Stettin at the end of July attracted a large number of east German estate-owners in consequence of the announcement four weeks before of the agrarian programme of the Camphausen-Hansemann government. According to that programme all remaining feudal rights were to be revoked without compensation and all land tax exemptions similarly abolished forthwith. In addition, as Bismarck had predicted in April, there was an appreciable increase in specifically agricultural taxation, notably in the levies on beet sugar and spirits.

The meeting protested against all this with great vehemence, Bismarck accordingly drafting a strongly worded petition to the king.[18] Finally it established itself formally as an association with an executive committee at its head charged with drawing up articles of association. This the committee immediately did. Just as the initiators of the enterprise had envisaged, it expanded the name of the association to include the words 'and for the Maintenance of the Prosperity of All Classes of the People', so setting its members' shared material interests at the centre of its concerns while relinquishing such distinctly feudal rights as patrimonial jurisdiction. On this basis it issued invitations on 11 August to a general assembly to be held in Berlin on 18 and 19 August. The chair of this 'Junker Parliament', which numbered some four hundred participants, was taken by Kleist-Retzow, one of the spiritual fathers of the whole enterprise, after an initial attempt had been made to find a rather more neutral figurehead.

Bismarck himself, while his wife lay in childbed – his eldest daughter Marie was born on 21 August – intervened in the proceedings several times, always for the purpose of drawing attention to the concrete shared interests of the nobility and of all landowners. 'These questions have to do', he wrote to a party colleague a few days later, explaining his position, 'not only quite literally with the livelihood of a large section of the Conservative Party but with whether King and government, faced with a crucial decision, are going to throw themselves into the arms of the revolution, announce that it is here to stay and seek to apply it to the social sphere.' In order to acquire any kind of base, he added, in order to be available to take part in public life to this effect, 'we do have to be so material as to defend our material interests'.[19]

This was at the same time a hit at Ludwig von Gerlach, for whom the whole enterprise went much too far in this respect. In his concern that conservative principles and ideals were becoming compromised by materialism, he had issued the watchword: 'Backs to the dung-heap, faces to the foe – such is the noble stance'.[20] But Gerlach was presupposing something that simply did not exist in this form as yet, namely the united front of those who stood with their 'backs to the dung-heap' and were aware of defending shared material interests. Such a front had first to be created. And here the younger members of the conservative right wing were much more down-to-earth and much more energetic than their political and intellectual leaders.

This was also true with regard to the nature and form of the conservatives' central organ, the *Neue Preussische Zeitung* or 'New Prussian Journal', which after lengthy preparations going back to the months of the United Diet was first published at the beginning of July 1848; it was soon known simply as the *Kreuzzeitung* from the Iron Cross of the Wars of Liberation that it featured on its front page. Established on a joint stock basis, the paper quickly gained considerable influence over public opinion in Prussia far beyond the narrow circle of its arch-conservative founding fathers and became the real nucleus of crystallization of a conservative party. The principal credit for this was due to its young editor-in-chief, Hermann Wagener. Formally a junior judge in the Magdeburg Consistory, Wagener had made a name for himself as a zealous champion of ecclesiastical orthodoxy and loyalty to the state against rationalism and theological as well as political liberalism. It was in Magdeburg that he had become familiar with the group around Ludwig von Gerlach, who then placed him in charge of the new paper that he had to a great extent initiated.

Wagener had the knack – which his patron, for example, lacked completely – of combining practice and theory, entertainment and political discussion, irony and earnest. As a result, he succeeded in creating a newspaper that was usually exceptionally well informed, reached its political opponents as well as its sympathizers and managed by means of effective attacks, alleged exposures and witty commentaries to get itself consistently talked about.

Bismarck's part in all this was considerable. He was a key member of the *Kreuzzeitung* staff from the outset and was always concerned to stay in direct contact with its editor-in-chief, a contemporary of his whom he had known since university. He encouraged Wagener in his efforts to increase the potential readership of the paper by taking advertisements, printing lists of foreign visitors and expanding the economic section. He urged the need for speedier and wider news coverage with a sure eye for the fact that a politically oriented newspaper gains greater influence the more indispensable it becomes as a news medium for friend and foe alike. But in particular he contributed large numbers of articles himself that did much to determine the style of the paper. Here as in his speeches he was almost without equal in his aggresiveness, drastic realism, often brutal mockery and delight in unmasking ostensibly idealistic motives. Indeed the change in the climate of discussion, its increasing bitterness and the tendency to suspect the motives of one's political opponent and to accuse him wherever possible of shallow materialism can be said to stem very substantially from him.

Here Bismarck evinced more and more strongly that anti-idealism, often grounded in cynicism, that was so much a part of his character. And for all their delight at the success of the paper it became increasingly clear to the arch-conservatives themselves that this could not remain without consequences as far as the credibility of their own principles and ideals was concerned and that treating the professed idealism of one's political opponent with irony threatened to drive a particular type of debate out of the political arena altogether. In this area too, as in the discussions about the tasks and objectives of the landowners' association, an element of dissent became visible that went far beyond questions of political tactics. It heralded a conflict of fundamental conceptions that was to split the newly emergent conservative camp as seriously as it did that of the liberals.

In both cases it was at the same time a conflict of generations, a change in the standards by which people were guided that clearly depended quite decisively on the different ways in which they had experienced the world in their youth. One crucial difference was probably in the first place the very obvious shift in the dynamics of the historical process from the political sphere in the narrower sense to the economic and social spheres in the decades of the restoration period after 1815. With this the importance of individual impulses to historical evolution diminished greatly as against that of supra-individual impulses that, being grounded in that evolution, were focused more on material considerations and interests.

This was reflected not least in the nonchalance with which such young conservatives as Bismarck, Kleist-Retzow and Wagener set about drumming up support among broad sections of the population. For the Gerlach generation, even if they saw the necessity for it, this was a leaf out of the revolutionary book, a playing with fire that they found most alarming. Outwardly, it was true, the whole attempt to attract to the newly emergent Conservative Party popular elements drawn particularly from the rural peasant population as well as from the craft trades and the urban lower middle class took the form of a spontaneous mobilization in defence of king and country along the lines of the Wars of Liberation. 'Patriotic societies' and 'associations for King and country' were founded and meetings and demonstrations organized to rally the 'loyalist' forces. It was obvious, however, that this time something quite different was afoot. Where before the conservatives had called upon a natural sense of allegiance, now they canvassed, they made promises, they held out to locally influential individuals certain personal prospects for the future, they appealed to interests, hopes and expectations. In short, they set about destroying with their own hands things – class distinction, subordination, feudal obligation – that they had only recently been demanding and that in terms of the way people thought were undoubtedly still very much present. Verbally they promoted the peasant, the craftsman, the small tradesman to partnership provided that he was prepared to share their political stance.

That this only happened verbally and that in reality the traditional hierarchical relationships of the old class structure had long since been transformed into and were now preserved in a system of material dependencies and limitations was something the younger conservatives took for granted. Accordingly they saw the whole exercise not as something giving cause for alarm, not as a questionable mortgaging of the future, but as an act of expediency and of political calculation. Not so the older ones. In their eyes these were concessions to the new age that undermined their own position and impaired its credibility. To them this emphasis on material interests, this openly paraded scorn with regard to idealistic positions and this canvassing for political allies among the lower orders seemed to be taking them a very long way from their original aims. They saw these things as the expression of a victory for revolution by the back door, as it were.

However, in this situation of a joint defensive operation against the forces of liberalism and democracy most of them put aside such misgivings for the time being. They did so not least because the new forms of political argument turned out to be extraordinarily successful. After the complete collapse of their parliamentary base in 1848, at the two elections to the House of Deputies that were held in 1849 the conservatives won a solid position here too. Even at the first of these, held in February under the old universal suffrage system, they had received fifty-three seats. In the July elections under the so-called 'three-class' electoral system they received 114, almost a third of the total of 352 seats, and that was with about seventy independents. Already in February a centre-right coalition had succeeded in getting its own candidate appointed Speaker, defeating the left.

The new political methods were generally felt to complement admirably those with which the older generation operated. It was almost as if a sort of division of political labour emerged as a result of the very different backgrounds of the two groups. On the one hand there were the older political notables of the school of the Gerlachs, Ernst von Senfft-Pilsach and General von Rauch, men who as officers and civil servants were firmly anchored in the existing hierarchy of state and society and who trod the traditional paths when it came to exerting political influence. As befitted their position they concerned themselves mainly with the king and with the top men in army, church and bureaucracy, seeking to win them over for their programme and for their objectives. And on the other hand there were the young men around Kleist-Retzow and Bismarck, the 'very vigorous and intelligent adjutant of our Camarilla headquarters', as Ludwig von Gerlach once called him around that time.[21] They battled in the press, in associations and before meetings, and subsequently again in parliament in the very front of the front line, so to speak, and in the process turned increasingly into professional politicians. After Bismarck had been elected to the House of Deputies to represent the Zauche-Belzig-Brandenburg constituency at the beginning of February 1849 and had his mandate confirmed in the fresh elections held in late July, he decided to let Schönhausen and bring the family to Berlin. There, in somewhat straitened circumstances, they lived in a tiny flat in the Behrenstrasse and later in the Dorotheenstrasse, and there his eldest son Herbert was born in late December 1849.

That a man should live in this way, as a member of parliament devoting his entire time to politics, was something quite new in Prussia; it arose out of the fundamental change that the revolution and the constitution had wrought in the situation. It was possible, therefore, to argue that the methods employed by the younger generation of defenders of the existing social order and the existing distribution of power were forced upon them by that situation and by their political opponents and did not in any way reflect a change in their basic political outlook leading to fresh principles and fresh objectives. Particularly in the case of Bismarck, who seemed on the face of it to go furthest in this respect, there was something else involved, too.

However clear-sightedly he recognized that in the circumstances abstract principles mattered far less than solid common interests and that it was only by mobilizing these that the onslaught of the new political and social forces could successfully be repulsed, people continued unquestioningly, disregarding his practical endeavours, to see him as an ideological extremist, a kind of Don Quixote of a feudal fantasy world, whom the caricaturists loved to depict as a knight in crayfish armour. That he of all people should make particularly skilful use of the liberals' and democrats' new methods and forms of party-political mustering through the press and through associations and meetings made this way of going about things look even more like a mere means to an end. It obscured the fact that behind it lay something completely new, a very much altered concept of the objectives of politics and of the real substance of the political struggle.

This represented a personal dilemma in which in the course of his parliamentary activities during the revolution Bismarck became more and more deeply entangled. In the public eye he was set firmly on the extreme right with no power base of his own and no solid electoral footing; 'we're Conservative, very much so, but not Bismarckian', was on Bismarck's own admission the position of many electors in July 1849.[22] However welcome he was as a fellow combatant, hardly anyone was prepared to come out openly in support of his position. His friends not infrequently besought him to take a back seat on this or that issue lest he jeopardize their success. So he was particularly dependent on the goodwill of his older political friends and patrons, above all the Gerlach brothers. And he repeatedly had to make express efforts to dispel the mistrust he aroused in them with occasional remarks he made and with his openly professed inclination to stress material and implicitly criticize ideological viewpoints.

This makes it rather difficult to distinguish what in his various utterances on concrete political problems in these years primarily served this end and what was the expression of his personal conviction. The disastrous tendency of even many critical biographers always to see their hero as the great original, in Droysen's words to attribute 'to genius too much and everything',[23] has led to many questionable findings here. It has brought to light alleged discontinuities in outlook and approach that largely disappear into thin air when we allow for Bismarck's outward dependence on his political patrons.

This is especially true of most of his declarations of principle on questions of domestic policy, in· particular on constitutional problems and the problem of the relationship of state and church. Here he followed very closely the line that the man who was really the theoretical brain behind the conservative right wing, Friedrich Julius Stahl, had traced in his writings and himself repeatedly emphasized and enlarged upon in newspaper articles and speeches in the Upper House, of which he was a member. Bismarck found this easier for the fact that Stahl's theories formed the ideological bridge between the older and younger generations of conservatives. On the one hand he emphasized with repeated reference to England and developments in England the traditional roots of constitutionalism in the estates of the realm. On the other hand he justified the adoption of modern political and parliamentary forms and methods by conservatives as well. On the one hand he underlined the importance of the 'monarchical principle', in other words the – as far as possible – unqualified preservation of royal sovereignty. On the other hand he took into account the desire to bind the Crown more strongly than hitherto to custom and the interests that were rooted in it, in other words to grant a special place in the state to the representatives of those interests. Finally, while committing the state to Christianity and consequently allotting a prominent political position to those who interpreted Christianity on earth, at the same time he made it perfectly clear that the alliance of throne and altar presupposed that the church should always follow the paths of orthodoxy and loyalty to the state.

This kind of reinterpretation and reinstrumentalization of liberal constitutional thinking into traditional conservative terms was something Bismarck accepted without reserve. In essence he was simply illustrating this concept in his public utterances, bringing it to life and filling it out with examples. But underlying this, however closely he stuck to the general line in principle, was a special element typical of his own political attitude and development. In relating Stahl's theories to the specifically Prussian situation, Bismarck robbed them of their abstract, universal character. State meant to him the Prussian state as it had evolved historically, aristocracy meant the Prussian land-owning nobility, army meant the royal army of Prussian absolutism, bureaucracy meant the enlightened civil service of the post-reform period, church meant the Prussian established church under the archiepiscopate of the Crown. Not that he failed to draw historical comparisons, particularly of the kind that Stahl drew with conditions in England. But what was decisive as far as he was concerned was always the political and social order obtaining in Prussia. In this respect too he was an 'out-and-out Prussian', as he liked to acknowledge his opponents' criticism.

He was very far, however, in both thought and deed, from the kind of Prussian nationalism that saw and judged everything outside Prussia through Prussian spectacles. On the contrary, putting Stahl's ideas into concrete terms relating almost exclusively to Prussia removed much of the dogmatic character of those ideas. It also qualified severely the element in them that was above nation, above state, together with the associated obligations and loyalties. And it left little room, even when this was not openly apparent, for the kind of supra-natural conservative principle, ideologically binding beyond the limits of the individual political community, that was so important to the Gerlachs. On the other hand the idea of power came out much more strongly than with Stahl himself in the emphasis on the historically evolved distribution of political weight in the Prussian state and in Prussian society. The crucial conclusion was always that this could not be altered arbitrarily unless the intention was to raise arbitrariness to the status of a political and legal principle – with all the consequences that that implied.

In pushing this aspect of the idea of power so far into the foreground, Bismarck was tying the law and the constitution to the current balance of power within the country in a way that could be called conservative only with regard to its tangible consequences in the situation obtaining at the time. In effect it was no less dynamic and materialistically pragmatic than were the views he developed during those years concerning the real driving forces behind social and political relations. As a result, he was very open with regard to changes and entirely new developments. This was also true of the sphere that was soon – and for many years to come – to constitute the real substance of his political life: international affairs and in particular the most burning international problems for Prussia at this time, namely relations with Austria and the so-called 'German question'.

What he called the 'standpoint of a Prussian officer' in the field of foreign policy he had already put behind him at Göttingen under the influence of Arnold Heeren. And that relations between large states in particular constituted an extremely delicate and tricky web that called for a maximum of skill, circumspection and knowledge as well as enormous discipline and self-control on the part of those whose job it was to deal with it – that was a fundamental insight that for all his emotional and unpredictable nature he had inherited from his background. Politics in the true sense, the manipulation and harnessing of all forces to great ends in the service of the community and the state, had for the circle of old-style Enlightenment bureaucrats from which his mother came, as well as for their royal masters, meant foreign policy, the assertion, protection and extension of the power of one's own state over against others.

This was something that was taken completely for granted in the so-called 'political testaments' of the Hohenzollerns. It was what the 'publicists', the political scientists of the day, taught the pupils they were training for public life. And it was the generally held opinion until well into the nineteenth century. Up until the threshold of the 1848 revolution, domestic policy usually came under the heading 'police' as the technical term for public welfare and the guarantee of internal security. Politics 'proper', that is, foreign affairs, was made to seem a sort of separate sphere requiring a degree of expertise and knowledge quite out of the ordinary, indeed almost a kind of superior wisdom regarding the special secrets of successful dominion, the *arcana imperii*.

Accordingly it had become the almost invariable practice among eighteenth-century monarchical states to draw their foreign affairs personnel not from within the country but from elsewhere. The purpose of this was to avoid as far as possible a domestic orientation and commitment and to ensure that the person concerned concentrated exclusively on the external power interests of the state and on assessing the possibilities and limitations of the international system. In the wake of the French Revolution and the accompanying nationalization and emotionalization of international relations that had reached its climax in the Wars of Liberation, all this had largely been swept away. On the other hand the connection between and indeed interdependence of domestic and foreign policy had become extremely clear. In the ensuing restoration period, however, there was an attempt to put the clock back in this respect as well and to return to the traditional techniques, the traditional ways of doing things.

How successful this attempt at a restoration of the pre-revolutionary state of affairs was as a whole can be seen not only from the fact that the renaissance of eighteenth-century ideas met with a wide response; apart from Heeren it was primarily the historian Leopold von Ranke who now helped them to break through on the academic front as well. It is also indicated by the fact that those who rose up in arms against it politically could for all their experience find nothing to set against it but Utopian claims that with the abolition of absolutism and the domestic suppression of peoples all international conflicts would automatically cease and foreign policy in the traditional sense become virtually unnecessary. 'Governments may cheat each other; political apparatuses may be set against each other until one destroys the other', wrote Johann Gottfried Herder in his *Letters for the Advancement of Humanity* (1793–7). 'Nations [*Vaterländer*] do not move against one another in this way; they lie quietly side by side and aid one another as families. Nations against nations in bloody battle is the worst barbarism in the language of man.'[24] And in 1819, after all the 'barbarisms' of the 'national wars' of the past twenty years, the French liberal Benjamin

Constant echoed him thus: 'Rulers may be at odds; peoples are as one.'[25] This remained the prevailing opinion until 1848: in Giuseppe Mazzini's 'Young Europe', in the liberal press and in parliamentary debates about the need for standing armies and about foreign policy budgets.

The consequence was that the field of foreign affairs, except where it was a matter of bold visions of and designs for the future, was left almost wholly to the political enemy on the domestic front. This was true, moreover, not only of the practical side, where it was inevitable in view of the distribution of power almost everywhere in central Europe, but also of the theoretical side. However lively the discussion of every important domestic policy issue in countries where conditions – the existence of a free press and a parliamentary body – made this possible in the first place, however energetically people strove for concrete counter-proposals and rival drafts, in foreign policy people were content with very general pronouncements. Even the liberals involved in the machinery of government hardly ever made a serious attempt to penetrate this sphere. It remained the preserve of conservative experts – with the accent on both terms, reinforcing the exclusivity.

It was a preserve that Bismarck himself had failed to penetrate by what might be called the normal route, and he had abandoned the roundabout way via the economic and Customs Union administration. This did not, however, turn him into a 'system critic' – unlike in the field of domestic affairs, where his experiences drove him very much in this direction. In foreign affairs he remained largely bound by the judgements imparted to him in his youth by his mother and by the ideas he had picked up in Heeren's lectures. The view that the self-affirmation of the state against other states, the preservation and if possible extension of its external power, constituted perhaps not the only but at any rate the first and most important object of all politics was one he never seriously questioned. In this he was much more a man of the eighteenth century than were most of his contemporaries. All his life he stressed very strongly the need for this whole sphere to be relatively autonomous.

Not that he was unaware of the repercussions of foreign on domestic affairs and of the way in which the two spheres were interdependent. This connection was so obvious in the restoration era and in the light of liberal questioning of the need for traditional foreign policy and power politics that only a case of severe blindness could have overlooked it. On the contrary, what he feared was that because of the increased threat from liberal and democratic forces that connection might come to be strained one-sidedly, namely from the side of domestic policy, by those who had hitherto had sole direction and control of foreign policy, namely the conservatives. Given their desire for unqualified preservation of the status quo, this could lead to a complete crippling of all foreign-policy activity, activity without which self-affirmation, let alone an extension of power under constantly changing conditions and in constantly changing circumstancs, was an impossibility.

For anyone who was not guided exclusively by the concept of

56

conservative solidarity and the ideas of the Holy Alliance of 1815 but still took a positive view of the seventeenth and eighteenth centuries, the time of the great Electors and of Frederick the Great, this was quite obviously the situation of Prussia in the decades before 1848. With one qualification, of course, which was nevertheless perfectly congruous since it was the outcome of activities that at this period left diplomacy largely in the hands of experts, most of whom came from the internal administration and were predominantly of middle-class origin.

That qualification had to do with economic and trade policy, in concrete terms the establishment and expansion of the Customs Union in the 1820s and 1830s. Prussia had assumed the initiative in this field almost from the outset, pursuing an aggressive policy based on self-interest. Seen from this angle, the lack of independence of Prussian foreign policy in all other spheres, both within the German Confederation and at the European level, inevitably stood out with especial clarity. It was a viewpoint with which Bismarck was familiar from early on, having tried to enter the diplomatic service by way of the Customs Union administration. It had once again, as he prepared inwardly for this course, emphatically steered his attention towards the material foundations and premises governing the relations between states and peoples, towards the rootedness of all foreign policy in self-interest that Bismarck had heard so forcefully argued in Heeren's lectures.

There was also the fact that in reaction to the historical images coloured by middle-class nationalism that had been his fare at school he had very quickly arrived at a kind of defiant identification with the image of a Prussia pursuing power with ruthless independence. Many of his remarks reveal this kind of crude glorification of the monarchical authoritarian state that Prussia had once been. When Prussia was invoked in his speeches it was the Prussia of the great Electors and of Frederick, never the backward-looking Utopia of the corporative state that put a curb on absolutism and on its claims to power, which was the ideal to which the Gerlachs subscribed.

Historians have often maintained that it was not until the 1850s, under the influence of the tangible confrontation with Austria during his time as Prussian envoy in Frankfurt, that Bismarck finally ceased to be a conservative ideologist and adherent of the ideologically based foreign policy of the Gerlachs and became a politician of power and interests. The truth of the matter is that in this instance too his position was established early on. He merely drew a veil over it occasionally in deference to the quite different views of his political patrons. Not that he needed to go to any great lengths in this regard, for at first the adherents of both standpoints almost always arrived at similar results.

Both sides promptly combated the national element in the 1848 revolution just as much as the liberal and democratic elements. The connection was quite clear: the national state was to be an instrument of change. Internally too it was to create entirely new conditions, radically restructuring the old political and social order in the individual states by way of a central constitution with binding norms. The 'entire national frenzy' was 'nothing else' but an 'expression of the freedom urge', the democrat Ludwig Bamberger once remarked laconically when the revolution was at its height.[26]

There were occasions when the Federal Diet invoked the idea of power in general terms, for example when it was a question of priority for Germans in the nationally mixed areas of eastern-central Europe, in what was then known as West Prussia, or in Bohemia. But to begin with no one gave any thought at all to how the existing European states would react to the question of a fresh major power being formed in central Europe and what limits this might place upon the formation of a national state, even so far as its external dimensions were concerned. With a remarkable blindness to the lessons that might have been learned from the fate of France after 1789, the liberals failed to see that they were literally driving together the forces that they ought to have been doing their utmost to keep apart: those who were in essence interested only in the protection of their own position and the preservation of an approximate balance of power in Europe; and those who were combating the revolution and the formation of a revolutionary national state out of profound political conviction. Whether it would in fact have been possible to keep those forces apart in the long run is not something we need go into here. It was highly characteristic and in many respects decisive as far as future developments were concerned that the revolution immediately antagonized both camps when with an almost reckless confidence in victory its representatives put forward a national programme as vague as it was ambitious.

The programme was based on the democratic concept of collective national self-determination. Its advocates started out from the liberal idea that, as in the relationships of individuals one to another, the concept of self-determination would lead not only to a natural solidarity but also to a sort of naturally determined, harmonic new order in the international sphere. This national 'idealism', which with the victory of the revolution achieved practical importance again for the first time since 1789, was decisively opposed by Bismarck in the very first statement on current foreign policy matters that he intended for public consumption. In it he simultaneously made his own position perfectly clear – a position that was 'anti-idealist' from the outset – in every conceivable direction.

The opportunity was provided by the release of those Prussian citizens of Polish nationality who had been convicted of treason in recent years on account of their Polish nationalist activities. In a manuscript sent to the *Magdeburgische Zeitung* from Schönhausen on 20 April 1848 – the paper did not print it, and it was not until thirty-eight years later that it was rediscovered and published – he painted a gloomy picture of the consequences that might arise from a practical realization of the 'visionary theory' that lay behind the whole process.[27] The fact that 'by way of thanks' for their release the men concerned had soon been leading 'bands that persecuted the German inhabitants of a Prussian province with plunder and murder, massacring and barbarically mutilating women and children', as he wrote in the heightened language of demagogy, was the most recent though in terms of scale comparatively least damaging consequence. What would be seen if this course were continued was 'German states deprived of the last of what German arms had procured for them in Poland and Italy over the centuries': 'This is what people are gaily prepared to throw away for the sake of the implementation of a visionary theory, a theory that must equally lead us to form a new Slav kingdom out of our south-eastern frontier districts in Styria and Illyria, give the Italian Tyrol back to the Venetians, and with Moravia and Bohemia create an independent Czech kingdom reaching right into the heart of Germany.'

The historical 'Germany', so the argument ran, would break up. Particularly in the east, with its mixture of nationalities, a Polish national state would constitute a power that even with the maximum concessions, namely full restoration of the pre-partition frontiers of 1772, would 'greedily' await 'every German predicament in order to gain East Prussia, Polish Silesia and the Polish districts of Pomerania for itself'. 'But how can a German', Bismarck solemnly demanded, 'for the sake of whining compassion and impracticable theories, dream of creating on the doorstep of the fatherland a relentless enemy who will always be trying to deflect his feverish domestic unrest by means of wars and who every time we are engaged in the west will attack us in the rear: who will and must be far more avid for conquest at our expense than the Russian Emperor, who is happy if he can hold his present giant together and would have to be very foolish to want to increase, by conquering German lands, the already large proportion of his subjects prepared to take up arms against him. *We do not, however, need Poland to protect us against Russia; we can protect ourselves.*'

As far as Poland and Russia were concerned, Bismarck stood by these judgements all his life, broadly speaking. Particularly this fear of any kind of political consolidation of Polish nationalism and the potential consequences of a restoration of the Polish state remained a crucial factor behind his policy vis-à-vis Russia as well as behind his foreign policy as a whole. 'Restoring the Kingdom of Poland in any shape or form', he wrote in a memorandum after the Polish revolt of 1863, 'is tantamount to creating an ally for any enemy that chooses to attack us.'[28] This consideration repeatedly prompted him to say things the brutality and icy unconditionality of which seem scarcely tolerable, especially in the light of what happened subsequently. An example is when, in a private letter to his sister written in March 1861, on the threshold of the Polish revolt, he fulminated: 'So smash those Poles till, losing all hope, they lie down and die; I have every sympathy for their situation, but if we wish to survive we have no choice but to wipe them out; the wolf can't help it either, that God created him the way he is, but we still kill him for it when we can.'[29] This was the sombre reverse side of unconditional devotion to the 'state egoism' that he was to describe just before embarking on his diplomatic career as 'the only sound basis' for the policies of a major state.

In opposition to the 'visionary theory' of the national party and the revolution, which in reality led 'once again to foreign chestnuts being hauled out of the fire to our own detriment', Bismarck's article of April 1848 invoked as a genuine 'national' objective – in which Prussian interests, necessarily directed against an independent Poland, were accomodated – the preservation of Germany as it had evolved historically. In so doing he tactily adopted very different approaches to those Prussian and Austrian territories that had not formed part of the German Confederation of 1815: whereas he included Posen (Poznan) and East and West Prussia as a matter of course, he drew a distinction between the Tyrol and Venetia, spoke of 'our south-eastern frontier districts in Styria and Illyria' and ignored the Hungarian problem altogether. Outwardly he thus aligned himself with the so-called 'Grossdeutschen', who advocatd a German national state incorporating all of Prussia but only the predominantly German-speaking areas of Austria and who were also, initially, to enjoy a clear majority in the Frankfurt National Assembly. In fact he had arrived at the same conclusion by accident, as it were, from entirely different premises.

His image of Germany was determined by three factors: a historical factor, a specifically Prussian factor and, inseparably bound up with the first two, a power-political factor. Only with regard to the first factor was he to some extent in touch with the main body of the 'Grossdeutschen'. Historically, Germany was for him the *Alte Reich*, that ultimately very loose association – though one sanctified by tradition and the trappings of empire – that had held the nations of central Europe together until 1806 and that had been renewed in 1815, albeit in a very much altered and even looser form. That that empire represented an ancient cultural entity and that this fact lent it extra cohesion were things he took for granted. But in his view, now and in years to come, it contained no truly definitive and certainly no physically delimiting element. When he wrote in that newspaper article that he 'would have found it understandable if the initial upsurge of German strength and unity had made room for itself by demanding Alsace from France and raising the German flag above Strasbourg Cathedral', it was the former *Reichsboden* that he had in mind, the actual territory, not a claim based on language and culture.

In fact he opposed such a claim most emphatically, arguing that it would destroy the political map as it had evolved historically and with it undermine any kind of order. Quite as a matter of course, he saw that order from the Prussian standpoint. The assumption he made was that the inhabitants of other countries, as long as they did not allow themselves to be guided by 'impracticable theories', conducted themselves no differently and that this and this alone was the source of calculability and hence of rationality in international relations. In terms of his image of Germany this meant that Germany must embrace and preserve both the territorial and political identity of Prussia; every Prussian had to be a German, without any distinction, and Prussia's political weight in Europe and its freedom of decision in matters of foreign policy must in no way be diminished by its German ties and obligations. A generation later Bismarck was to observe that he had 'found the word "Europe" constantly on the lips of those politicians who wanted from other powers something they dared not demand on their own behalf';[30] that was exactly how he viewed the use of the term 'Deutschland' by the representatives of the national party and of the revolution as well as by the advocates of Prussia's Union policy in the years 1848–50. In this, incidentally, he was already in full agreement with his future monarch, who in the summer of 1848 said in an open attack on his brother the king: 'Prussia must stand at the head of Germany as Prussia and not be incorporated in it as a province, in other words not become merged in it.'[31]

The demand that Germany must embrace the territorial and political identity of Prussia made it quite clear that Germany must not be allowed to become a suffocating burden on Prussia; that was the third factor that determined his image of Germany. A centralized constitution that, so to speak, mediatized Prussia was as unacceptable to him as an institutionalization of the primacy of the Habsburg monarchy that had been a *de facto* feature of the German Confederation since 1815, albeit in a very loose form.

For him, therefore, any extension of a future Germany beyond the frontiers of the German Confederation and the *Alte Reich* was, as far as Austria was concerned, ruled out in advance – quite apart from the fact that it had been his conviction from the outset that the remaining European powers would never allow that kind of empire to be formed in central and eastern-central Europe. Whether he assumed that Austria would behave differently from Prussia over the whole question and would sit on the fence geographically and as a European power with regard to a united Germany is very much open to doubt. If we analyse Bismarck's 1848 image of Germany more closely, if we examine the terms that from his Prussian and – in domestic affairs – arch-conservative standpoint he laid down for a future unification of Germany, it becomes clear that he neither saw nor aspired to a solution of this so-called 'German question'. 'We are Prussians, and Prussians we shall remain . . . We do not wish to see the Kingdom of Prussia obliterated in the putrid brew of cosy south-German sentimentality', he had told Hermann Wagener back at the beginning of June 1848.[32] All his efforts were initially directed at combating the revolution in this sphere as well. The bulwark on which he always fell back, every time, was Prussia, although for propaganda purposes he often spoke of 'Germany' and of German 'Einigkeit' ('oneness') and 'Einheit' ('unity'), occasionally playing the former off against the latter.

The individual foreign policy ideas or rather positions and basic attitudes that he developed in such a context were like theatrical set-pieces. They fitted into the most diverse patterns and designs including that of the nation state, provided that the 'idealism' was exorcized from it and the 'German' interest brought to the fore. Initially, however, what he wanted was that everything should stay the same – 'Alles beim Alten', as he wrote to his wife in March 1849[33] – because any kind of reorganization in this sphere would currently only benefit the revolution, in other words the middle-class liberal movement, and damage Prussia's political and power interests.

During these months Bismarck almost invariably mentioned both effects in the same breath – not merely for the ears of his arch-conservative friends but undoubtedly out of deep conviction. Yet here too there was a crucial difference. His political comrades-in-arms, at least the Gerlach brothers and Stahl, gave an essentially ideological account of the situation as a mirror-image of their own view of Prussia as stronghold and defender of the conservative ideal, which the enemy was out to weaken or even eliminate.

Bismarck on the other hand simply based his approach soberly on the current situation and the current balance of interests. The supreme national interest as far as Prussia was concerned – and in his eyes this was true of every state – must be to preserve and if possible extend its external power. Accordingly everyone was an enemy who, for whatever reason, stood in the way of that interest. This was what the national and liberal movement of the 'Frankfurters', as he disdainfully called them, was doing. They wanted to mediatize Prussia, Bismarck said; they wanted it to 'become merged' in Germany, as the king, who initially capitulated to them, had very rightly put it. Therefore the Prussian state and the Prussian Crown, if they allowed themselves to be guided by the Prussian national interest and not by romantic considerations of one kind or another, must resist the 'St Paul's Church fraud'.[34]

The left, as he declared in the Prussian Lower House on 21 April 1894, following the decision of the Frankfurt National Assembly to offer Frederick William IV the German imperial crown, were 'doing everything in their power' to force upon Prussia the kind of role in Germany that Sardinia had played in Italy, 'to bring us to the point where Carlo Alberto was before the battle of Novara [the defeat against the Austrian army under Radetzsky on 23 March 1849], where his victory must mean the downfall of the monarchy, his defeat an ignominious peace'.[35] 'The Frankfurt crown', he went on, 'may shine very brightly, but the gold that gives that shine its reality is to be obtained by first melting down the Prussian crown.' The national and liberal movement and the middle-class elements that supported it wanted by the roundabout way of a central constitution based on the principle of popular sovereignty and by way of the idea of unity to obtain as it were under false pretences a power they neither possessed nor were capable of achieving by direct means. In the circumstances he would prefer 'that Prussia remain Prussia'. And the proud Prussian patriot in him added, 'As such it will always be in a position to give Germany laws, not to receive them from others'.

Nevertheless, Bismarck tended at first to be somewhat circumspect in his public statements about the German question, often pointing out that 'everyone you ask wants German unity, as long as he speaks German'.[36] He did this mainly for reasons of practical politics, namely for the benefit of Frederick William IV, the then occupant of the Prussian throne. Frederick William had been a supporter of the national idea from his youth, admittedly in a romantically embellished form based on vague images of the past. This kind of viewpoint ignored most of the real problems and harmonized in hazy fantasies the political conflicts of power and interests in domestic affairs as in the relations between German states, particularly between Prussia and the Habsburg monarchy. Many people even from the conservative camp had followed the king along this road. They hoped, as did many liberals on the other side, that national unity would bestow a higher unity in the intellectual, social and political spheres as well and that it would prove to be a kind of panacea for all present conflicts and differences of opinion. Even the sobering experience of revolution, the impulses behind which Frederick William never managed to see in any other terms than those of vulgar presumption and the desecration of higher ideals, failed to destroy the fascination that flowed from the concept of German unity and the associated idea of Prussia's 'German mission'.

Back in December 1848 Frederick William IV had rejected in the sharpest possible terms the idea that a Prussian king should become German emperor by the grace of the people: 'Is this imaginary circlet baked from dirt and clay', he wrote disdainfully, 'to be accepted by a lawful king by God's grace, by no less than the King of Prussia, whose great blessing it is to wear what if not the oldest is certainly the noblest crown not stolen from anyone?'[37] Almost in the same breath, however, he indicated the way that he was prepared to go and that he might even himself help to pave: 'If the thousand-year-old crown of the German nation, which for forty-two years has been in abeyance, is to be awarded once again it is *I* and those such as I who will award it.' Hardly had he declined – on 3 April and finally on 28 April – the Frankfurt National Assembly's offer to make him imperial head of a Lesser German national state – a 'Kleindeutschland' not including Austria – before he embarked on an attempt to bring about the formation of such a national state on the basis of the so-called 'monarchical principle'. 'The free consent of the crowned heads, the princes and the Free Cities' – that was the crucial prerequisite, rather than a decision by representatives of the allegedly sovereign people, as was made clear even in the provisional answer given to the delegation from St Paul's Church.[38]

The spiritual father of and driving force behind this policy of Lesser German unification from above under the leadership of the Prussian Crown, a policy that was now set in motion and the consequences of which were to dictate Prussia's foreign policy stance and determine the possibilities of its policy for many years, was Joseph Maria von Radowitz. A Catholic of Hungarian origin, Radowitz had joined the army of King Jérôme of Westphalia at the age of 15; following a military career lasting almost ten years in the electorate of Hesse, he had entered the service of Prussia in 1823. After an initial period as military tutor to one of the royal princes, then as chief of staff of the artillery, in 1836 he was sent to the Federal Diet in Frankfurt as Prussia's military representative and in 1842 became Prussian envoy at the courts of Karlsruhe, Darmstadt and Nassau, which were served by a joint legation.

His origins and career placed Radowitz in quite different traditions and gave him quite different views from the majority of the Prussian land-owning nobility as also of the Prussian bureaucracy, which took its cue in part from the tradition of enlightened absolutism and in part from that of the Prussian authoritarian state. In many respects he was a man of the *Alte Reich*, a courtly aristocrat of the old school, a pendant in some ways to Baron vom Stein, except that in domestic affairs he was very much more conservative even than Stein and his imperial romanticism was more strongly oriented towards throne and altar. A close friend of Frederick William IV from early on, Radowitz above all found himself in sympathy with the latter over the idea of national unification on a conservative basis; Bismarck mocked him retrospectively as the 'clever wardrobe master' of his monarch's 'medieval fantasies'.[39]

It was the shared conviction of the king and his trusted adviser that the German princes must, by amalgamating and taking joint action, pave the way for a renewal of state and society in the spirit of Christianity and so overcome particularism, national selfishness and statism. As an opponent of bureaucratic absolutism and a supporter of the Christian ideal of a corporative state, Radowitz was a man very much after the heart of the Gerlach brothers and their associates. What he said and did during the revolution as leader of the extreme right in the Frankfurt National Assembly and as secret agent of the Prussian king almost invariably, however inconsistent and unclear it might appear on occasion, met with the approval of the Berlin Camarilla. This was initially true with regard to the German question as well.

Even before 1848 Radowitz had evolved concrete proposals for a closer relationship betwen the states of the German Confederation and a step-by-step approach to national unification. The path he wanted to see taken was that of reform of the Confederation and the creation of additional joint institutions; he also had in mind increased standardization in the sphere of law. However, in the memorandum that he presented to the Prussian king in November 1847 there was no mention of summoning a joint parliament, only of 'experts'.[40] Altogether the whole plan, for all its nationalist pathos, showed the only alternative to the liberal and democratic concept of unification to be a bureaucratic one. But at the same time the Radowitz plan, like the other, largely ignored all political conflicts of power and interest, for example in wanting to see the Customs Union extended to include Austria without regard for Prussian economic interests to the contrary.

This very point, in fact, reflected a specific 'idealism'. In the interests of a unification of Germany under conservative auspices, which was designed to give a decisive impulse towards re-establishing a Christian conservative order throughout Europe, Radowitz and in his wake Frederick William IV were prepared to make extraordinary sacrifices. This 'idealism', this primacy accorded to the goals of Christian conservatism in the supra-national sphere as well, even where particular interests of one's own country were affected, secured Radowitz the confidence of the Camarilla for a long time to come – even after he had begun to tread other paths.

This change of course was prompted, so far as Radowitz and so far as a section of the Pan-Germanist liberals and democrats in the Frankfurt National Assembly were concerned, by developments in Austria. Once the peasants in large areas of the monarchy had acquired almost unrestricted property rights over the land they farmed, a great many of them, as was to happen in slightly different circumstances in Prussia as well, lost interest in the revolution. In what was still an overwhelmingly agrarian country, this had resulted in the revolution losing much of its base. In late October 1848 Field Marshal Prince Alfred zu Windischgraetz, who was already in full control of Bohemia, had managed to march on and conquer Vienna. In so doing he had set the seal on the political victory of the old powers in state and society.

But instead of what was widely expected to be a simple restoration along the lines of the Metternich system, which was what the Prussian conservatives were counting on as well, things had begun to take a quite different course. The driving force behind this was Prince Felix zu Schwarzenberg. Descended from a wealthy family of Austrian magnates that had been raised to imperial princedom in the seventeenth century, after an eventful career as officer and diplomat he was appointed head of the government at the end of November 1848, well before his fiftieth birthday. It was his avowed intention to consolidate the monarchy into a firm unit, regardless of the specific traditions of its individual national territories, for which his predecessor Metternich had always shown great consideration. He wished to create a modern, bureaucratically organized, centralized state such as would be capable of concentrating the country's forces and bringing them to bear on the European scene as one. At his insistence the 18-year-old Archduke Francis Joseph, a nephew of the old monarch, was crowned emperor in early December 1848 in order to mark the new departure very sharply in dynastic terms as well. Three months later, following the dissolution of the revolutionary Imperial Diet, a uniform constitution was imposed on the country by decree. The chief purpose of that constitution, which in practice never came into force and was repealed two years later, was to promote a specifically Austrian national consciousness focused on Vienna. At the same time it was to lay the foundations for the process – now energetically pursued – of administrative, legal and not least economic standardization.

The importance of standardization, particularly in the economic sphere, was something that Schwarzenberg, unlike Metternich, saw very clearly. Furthermore, he was aware that economic and commercial policy was becoming more and more important in the field of international relations. This was particularly true of Austria's relations with the other German states. 'One of the most effective means that Your Majesty's government has at its disposal for maintaining and increasing its influence in the German-speaking world', Schwarzenberg wrote in a letter to Francis Joseph, 'is undoubtedly active participation by Austria in cultivating the shared material interests of Germany.'[41] For this reason Schwarzenberg, instead of appointing as minister an ordinary bureaucrat from the indigenous administration, chose a man who at first sight appeared to be quite out of place in his world and in the context of his policy, though he did as it were personify the extra dimension that that policy possessed from the outset.

The new man was Karl Ludwig Bruck, a businessman from Elberfeld. Originally a bookseller, he had set out to take part in the Greek struggle for independence, got stuck in Trieste and there built up a flourishing commercial and shipping business in the 1830s and 1840s. In 1848 Trieste had elected him to represent it in the Frankfurt National Assembly, where as subsequently in the Austrian Imperial Diet he had belonged to the 'Grossdeutschland' wing of the liberals. So his appointment as Minister of Trade and Public Works – the chief among these being the crucially important railway-building programme – was at the same time an indication of the fact that for all his concentration on the internal consolidation of the Habsburg monarchy it was never part of Schwarzenberg's intention to leave the rest of Germany to its own devices, so to speak.

Admittedly his government programme of 27 November 1848 declared that 'Austria's survival as a national entity is a German as well as a European requirement . . . Not until a rejuvenated Austria and a rejuvenated Germany have achieved new and solid forms will it be possible to determine their mutual relations governmentally.'[42] It was the death blow for the 'Grossdeutschland' programme: in Frankfurt a fortnight later the leader of the Greater Germans, the Austrian Anton von Schmerling, resigned as head of the central government and was replaced by Heinrich von Gagern, the leader of the 'Kleindeutschland' faction. For the rest, however, Schwarzenberg reserved every option. What the new Austrian Minister-President, who promptly proceeded to act in a highly dictatorial manner, understood by a 'rejuvenated Germany' in parallel to the 'rejuvenated Austria' he now set about creating – that was something he left people to imagine for themselves.

In Berlin, Schwarzenberg seems to have been misunderstood at first, probably quite deliberately. Certainly not, however, by Bismarck. His own disposition immediately told him that with Schwarzenberg there had arrived on the political scene a determined and coolly calculating representative of Austrian power interests who would never relinquish the German card in his hand unless forced to. It is fascinating to imagine the course events might have taken had these two men, who were in many ways so similar, ever had to deal directly with each other. Radowitz, however, obviously formed a totally false picture of Schwarzenberg. Blinded by his own views, in this case he vastly overestimated in particular the solidarity of opponents of the revolution beyond all national frontiers. In so doing he not only overlooked indirect indications, such as the appointment of Bruck, that contradicted this assumption; he also failed to see that Schwarzenberg's warning to the effect that the time was not yet ripe for decisions over the German question was by no means directed solely at the national party in Frankfurt.

This kind of misreading of the situation was, however, fostered by the fact that Austria was very soon, following a brief period of consolidation, largely incapacitated on the foreign affairs front by the Hungarian rebellion, which threatened to become the signal for the dissolution of Austria's multi-national empire. This strengthened the impression that Vienna would in its own well-understood interests accept a reorganization of relations in central Europe on a conservative basis.

Understandably, therefore, Radowitz felt the moment had now come for an independent initiative in the matter of the German question on the part of the Prussian Crown. Moreover, the idea of taking advantage of the present weakness of the Austrian Empire to make a bold thrust inevitably also appealed to those who, unlike Radowitz and Frederick William IV, started out not so much from national considerations and what was alleged to be Prussia's 'German mission' as from Prussia's own political and power interests. This led to Radowitz at first enjoying more support inside Prussia, even from within the conservative camp, than might have been the case had the circumstances been different. Bismarck, however, rejected him right from the outset, referring to him as a politician 'without an idea in his head', who was purely 'out for popularity and applause', a man 'whom nothing raised above the level of the ordinary save an astonishing memory'.[43]

As immediate adviser to the king, Radowitz was in practice the unofficial director of Prussian foreign policy from May 1849 onwards. The plan he sought to press forward in this capacity constituted, for all the wealth of ideas he often displayed in other contexts, a somewhat uninspired copy of Gagern's blueprint aiming at an 'inner' confederation of German states apart from Austria and a 'broader' link between this constitutionally governed federal state, headed by the Prussian king, and the Austrian Empire.[44] The crucial departure from Gagern's plans consisted in the fact that in place of a relevant resolution by a national constituent assembly there was to be a resolution by the German princes and Free Cities, in other words the principle of popular sovereignty was to be replaced by the so-called 'monarchical principle'. As Radowitz saw it, this was the direction in which the Frankfurt constitution, which could initially be adopted as a formal external framework, ought to be revised: by introducing a franchise based on tax liability, by setting up a special house of princes, by limiting parliamentary rights with regard to the budget and by strengthening the monarchical executive – exactly as, thanks to the conservatives, was happening in Prussia itself under the direction of Friedrich Julius Stahl and with the active collaboration of Bismarck.

Nevertheless, Radowitz hoped to be able without too much difficulty to win over the majority of the 'moderate' liberals who favoured the 'Kleindeutschland' solution. From his knowledge of the Frankfurt scene he assumed that they would now, following the failure of their own plans, give priority to the idea of unification and would accordingly be ready to make extensive compromises. The campaign launched by the left to force the constitution through further strengthened him in his hopes, adding as it did to the concern of the centre parties in Frankfurt that in a national state based on the idea of popular sovereignty they would swiftly be overrun from the left. In another respect the insurgent movement was likewise not inopportune as far as Radowitz was concerned, since in view of the situation in Austria the south German states too were thrown back on the military assistance of Prussia and were thus rendered more complacent with regard to Prussian plans.

In view of this Radowitz urged swift decisions. In late May 1849 the first major step was taken: Prussia concluded a preliminary alliance with the neighbouring kingdoms of Saxony and Hanover, calling upon the south German states in particular to accede to this venture;[45] the remaining states were regarded, as matters stood, as being voluntarily or involuntarily 'in the bag'. And when shortly afterwards, as had been hoped, a large proportion of the Lesser German liberals of the centre declared at a meeting in Gotha that they were ready to collaborate with and support the scheme, everything seemed to be going well. The reservation held out by Saxony and Hanover to the effect that their membership of the alliance was conditional upon the whole of non-Austrian Germany following their example initially gave Radowitz as little cause for concern as did the momentary hesitation of Württemberg and above all of Bavaria.

That the concept of national unity to which he appealed was seen in Dresden, Hanover, Stuttgart and Munich as a mere smoke-screen for Prussia's power interests and that these parties were manifestly only playing for time was something of which, unlike the coolly judicious Bismarck, he was clearly unaware. It further escaped his notice that other governments, in view of the experiences of the recent past, were a great deal more sceptical with regard to the chances of separating the demand for unity from the demand for freedom as advanced by the liberals and democrats.

The reproach was levelled against Prussia, covertly at first, that this was no policy directed towards the safeguarding of tradition and of the traditional order, even if the Prussian army did prove its worth in quelling the revolution. In terms of its consequences at least this was a revolutionary policy guided by Prussian power interests. As the Bavarian Minister-President von der Pfordten stated cautiously in the Bavarian parliament as early as June 1849, it must embolden all those who, like the insurgent Hungarians, sought to divide up central and eastern Europe into national states. On the other hand it gave encouragement to those who could imagine governmental organization only in terms of a dictatorially interventionist, centralized authoritarian state. In both respects there was the danger of a victory for the revolution through the back door, leading to the destruction of the historically evolved order in central Europe. Furthermore, the whole thing would constitute a positive challenge to the neighbouring powers, namely Russia and to an even greater extent France, to intervene.

Such arguments, however unmistakably they served individual national interests, particularly in the case of Bavaria, could not but impress even a Prussian conservative. They matched in many points what could be heard from the lips of the Russian ambassador in Berlin as the opinion of the tsar, who likewise observed the Radowitz venture with grave misgivings. But for the overwhelming majority of Prussian conservatives the Prussian-Russian connection was a corner-stone of all foreign policy, indeed a corner-stone of the whole status quo, the whole traditional order, at least in central and eastern Europe. Was it not therefore extraordinarily short-sighted to place that corner-stone at risk with a policy that clearly met with little favour among its initiator's own political friends in the other German states, that was therefore largely dependent for its success on the current balance of power, and that moreover imposed the necessity for unwelcome alliances, even if only with that section of the liberals that was most inclined to compromise?

Until August 1849, when the Hungarian rebellion was put down with the aid of Russian troops, the answer to this question, given the prospect of an extraordinary increase in Prussian power, remained open. Subsequently, however, as the chances of success for the Radowitz venture diminished as a result of the determined objections of Austria, now back in action once more, as well as of its rejection by Bavaria and eventually by Württemberg too and of ever-clearer warnings emerging from Russia, the chorus of fundamental criticism from the conservative camp began to swell in volume.

Bismarck became one of the critics' principal spokesmen. Outwardly he had kept very quiet until now; two biting articles by him in the *Kreuzzeitung* had appeared unsigned.[46] After all, the policy still enjoyed the support of the Prussian king, who was made extremely angry by the *Kreuzzeitung* articles – so much so that, according to Ludwig von Gerlach, had he known who had written them it would 'probably have made his engagement impossible'.[47] And it still had the support, albeit half-hearted in some instances, of the conservative Prussian government. He was of course neither capable nor desirous, any more than any of his political friends, of stabbing both of these publicly in the back.

Bismarck consequently found himself faced with a situation that was as unusual for him as it was for his listeners when on 6 September 1849 he stood up to address the Diet that had been newly elected in July. Instead of launching a frontal attack he had this time to choose his words carefully. He had to clothe his criticisms in language that offered no additional weapons to the enemy and that did not embarrass the government. This had the advantage that, pleading tactical considerations, he was given an early opportunity of setting up a position between the fronts, as it were – in fact it was probably here, in the field of foreign policy, that he first made the discovery that in certain circumstances total candour can do duty as skilful camouflage.[48]

The outward occasion for his intervention in the debate came with a motion put forward by the committee of the Diet, which had been asked by the plenum to prepare a statement about documents placed before it by the government concerning Prussia's Union policy. The motion gave express approval to every step taken by the government, stressing that the assumption was that the Prussian constitution would, when it came to it, be adapted to the projected Union constitution, in other words that this would not erect a different body of constitutional law. This in fact followed naturally from paragraph 111 of the current Prussian constitution, which referred explicitly to the case of 'a constitution to be established for Germany'. The liberals, however, wanted it made quite clear once again that the process of 'unification from above', that had now been launched would provide that minimum of inner homogeneity between the empire and the member states without which the liberals were convinced there could be no question of any real unity going beyond a mere confederation of states.

This was where Bismarck broke in. Behind all this, he said, lay yet another piece of political calculation aimed at turning the real power situation upside-down for the benefit of a particular party. Using the projected constitution of the empire to be set up by the non-Austrian German princes and the Free Cities, the liberals were making another attempt to push through what they had already failed to obtain in Prussia and ultimately – through the Prussian king's refusal to accept their offer of the imperial crown – in Frankfurt as well: namely to wrest for themselves a position of sovereignty over the individual states and hence over the monarchical and aristocratic order anchored in them. This was something to which the forces of conservatism must put a stop right away. They must make any recognition of the future constitution of the empire dependent on the proviso 'that a right of appeal and of assent are reserved to the Prussian parliament'.

In plain terms this was like saying: With its Union scheme the government is giving a leg up to the liberals and thereby furthering the domestic objectives of the revolution. Protect it from itself by not making the constitutional legislative process solely dependent on the resolutions of the central government of a future federal state but binding it to the consent of the individual state parliaments.

Looked at in this light, there could be no question of the speech representing – as Bismarck had stated at the outset – support for the government's policy, albeit accompanied by criticism of individual details. There could be even less question of the 'noble-mindedness', 'magnanimity' and 'resignation' with which the author of a leading article in the *Vossische Zeitung* of 8 September felt that Bismarck had cleared the way for a German policy for Prussia. Quite the opposite. In painting the dangers of that policy with regard to both domestic and foreign affairs in the gloomiest colours Bismarck was indirectly castigating it with extreme severity. While making tactical bows in the direction of the motives behind it, he made it appear irresponsible in conservative terms and incompetent into the bargain. The irresponsibility lay mainly in the fact that the policy continued to misjudge the true character of the 1848 movement and had fallen victim to the 'sickness induced by the St Paul's Church fraud', as he had put it in the *Kreuzzeitung* not four months before.[49] It was not the national element that had been the determining factor in that movement. 'The national movement', he stressed, 'would have remained confined to a few albeit outstanding men in restricted circles.' The tone had been set by the 'social element'. All concessions and all offers of compromise over the national question therefore fell wide of the real problems, indeed under certain circumstances made them worse.

By the 'social element' he did not of course mean the objective economic and social ills of the time: the poverty of large sections of the population to whom the much-invoked traditional social order was in no position to offer either protection or assistance; the position of the rural population, who under the terms of manorial relationships based on a quite different economic system were obliged to get rid of their produce on the newly emergent large-scale agricultural commodities market and were often barely able to scrape a living; the problem of unemployed small master-craftsmen, now beginning to despair of the future, and of a growing army of journeymen. What he was talking about was simply and solely the exploitation of such questions by small groups from what he alleged to be purely demagogic motives serving selfish power interests. Accordingly he defined the 'social element' of the revolution as follows: 'That the greed of the have-nots for other people's property and the envy of the less well-off towards those who are wealthy were aroused under false pretences, and the more long years of free-thinking, fostered from above, had undermined the moral ingredients of resistance in the hearts of men, the more easily those passions gained ground.'

Once again, then, he reduced everything to the question of power, although this time it was with a slightly different thrust: the centre of the picture was now, unlike in 1848, occupied by the 'radicals', the democrats – with whom, however, he lumped the majority of the liberals whenever opportunity offered. It was a question, he intimated once again, not of implementing tired ideas such as that of national unity or of enacting legal and constitutional principles that were allegedly above all party-political contention. As always in politics it was a question of a fierce competitive struggle among organized political groups. Anyone who failed to see this was a liability to the cause he represented, whatever he might try to do. For he was no longer capable of calculating the real consequences of his actions. He could only try 'to satisfy the insatiable demands of a phantom that under such assumed names as the spirit of the age or public opinion numbs the senses of princes and peoples with its din until everyone is afraid of everyone else's shadow and has forgotten that concealed beneath the lion's skin is a creature who, though noisy, is not so very terrible'.

Instead – so ran Bismarck's crucial conclusion – in the present situation a conservative must fall back on the reality of existing power positions, on the Prussian state and its internal order, now at least partially restored. Starting from there he must seek to pursue, both at home and abroad, a policy of which both the risks and the feasibility could be thoroughly calculated in advance. It was perfectly possible – and here he was addressing himself to those who had their eye primarily on the potential fruits of unification in terms of power gains – for such a policy to be one of power and expansion. The important thing was to ensure that one did not lose control of things and in the last analysis pursue a policy that was going to benefit others.

The implied quintessence of his speech was to point out that this was just what the present policy of unification did not ensure. In this it differed greatly from the policy of Frederick the Great, for example, whose name was always being invoked in this connection. Instead of tacking fearfully to and fro and taking into consideration forces of which he had no need, someone like Frederick, relying on the army and on the 'martial element' as the 'most prominent feature of the Prussian national character', would have sought an unequivocal decision. 'He would have had the choice', Bismarck went on, now proceeding very sharply to define his own political line as it were under cover of a critique of the government's unification policy and a defence of the ancient traditions of Prussia, 'of joining up with his old comrade-in-arms, Austria, following the break with Frankfurt, and there taking over the brilliant role that the Russian emperor had played in destroying, in alliance with Austria, their common enemy, the revolution. Or he would have been at liberty, with the same right as that with which he conquered Silesia, having declined Frankfurt's offer of the imperial crown, to tell the German people what consitution they were to have, under threat of his bringing the sword to bear. That would have been a national policy for Prussia. It would have placed Prussia, in the first case together with

71

Austria, in the second on its own, in the right position to help Germany to acquire the power that is its due in Europe.'

Here the whole man already stood revealed. Coolly he set the two options side by side: restoration of the policy of co-operation with Austria on the basis of conservative solidarity, albeit with a different distribution of political weight than before 1848, or an autonomous, Lesser German expansionist policy on Prussia's part, if necessary backed by force of arms. Which of the two possibilities deserved priority in his eyes he did not indicate. This may have looked like a tactical concession on the part of a member of an arch-conservative faction that meanwhile clearly favoured a policy of conservative solidarity with Austria. But in all probability Bismarck's own answer would have been: which of the two possibilities is to be preferred is something that only circumstances can decide.

He made it quite clear, though, that in his eyes there was no alternative to these two possibilities as guideline for a conservative and hence as far as he was concerned realistic and potentially successful foreign policy. Above all he once again dissociated himself – with a ferocity that, to judge from the sparse applause, went too far even for the right wing of his own party – from the idea that time had already passed a policy of Prussian national self-interest by. There could be no question, he said, of the majority of Prussian subjects, under the influence of the national idea, already feeling more German than Prussian. On the contrary, since 18 March 1848 Prussian soldiers had seen the black, red and gold flag as the 'banner of their enemy', and he had not yet 'heard [any of them] singing: "What is the German's fatherland?"'

This speech of 6 September 1849 wrought a major change in Bismarck's position within his own political grouping but also beyond it. Hitherto he had been regarded primarily as a home affairs firebrand who was if possible pulled back into the second line whenever it was a question of reaching compromises and forming majorities. 'To be used only when the bayonet rules unchecked', Frederick William IV had noted against his name the year before on a list of potential ministers for a conservative Cabinet.[50] Or as another source observed in even sharper terms: 'Red reactionary, smells of blood, to be used later.'[51] Now, however, he suddenly appeared as a man who knew how to marshal arguments against a particular policy in an attitude of sober realism in such a way as to appear not only to individuals of like mind but to whole groups, a man who thought in terms of alternatives and made room for different positions within his own camp, a man who held out to the government he was criticizing ways of changing course without losing face.

Underneath, of course, nothing had changed: in many of his utterances he remained a man of the extreme right. But the flexibility that he showed in this speech and the readiness to make allowances and not block possibilities for the first time made it conceivable, even within his own camp, that he might prove himself in some government office or even in the diplomatic field as something more than a party politician in the narrowest sense and one occupying extreme positions.

What may particularly have made people sit up and take notice in this respect was the formula he had hit upon in his speech for the foreign policy problem under discussion. The principal difficulty, he had explained, lay in 'how the federal state is to be encapsulated in the German Confederation, which is generally regarded as enjoying legal validity'. With this formula he rose above the stark alternatives of co-operation and confrontation with Austria while nevertheless leaving open the possibility of continuing to pursue the latter policy even within the outward forms of co-operation, in other words within a reconstituted German Confederation. In this way he built a bridge for those who feared that a settlement with Austria would close the door for the foreseeable future to an independent policy on Prussia's part, whether that policy lay in the direction of Lesser German unification or in that of an expansion of Prussian power or whether it represented a mixture of both. The decisive factors in each case could only be the interests of Prussia and the chances of serving that interest with some assurance of success.

Accordingly he again dissociated himself sharply from the left and from the national party in his capacity as a member of the so-called 'Union Parliament', which met in Erfurt to discuss and adopt the constitution of the new federal state. 'If it should after all come about that we clothe the body of German unity in the threadbare garments of a French constitution', he declared on 15 April 1850, proposing a motion that called for extensive revision of the Union constitution, this must on no account be allowed to lead to Prussia's henceforth being in tutelage to the small and medium-sized states and their peoples.[52] Under the current constitution, however, 'of the twenty-one million inhabitants of this federal state five million [would be] politically privileged and sixteen million politically under-privileged', namely sixteen million Prussians – 'and this at a time when the Prussian people is predominantly of the opinion that the efforts it has made to pull itself up out of the squalor of revolution and provide its neighbours with both material and moral support give it a special claim to political rights'. For a Prussian patriot, for a 'Prussian born and bred', a federal 'Kleindeutschland' was worth striving for only if Prussian hegemony within it was unambiguously assured, in other words if, rather than Prussia merging in Germany, the rest of Germany became part of a Greater Prussia.

The unconditional primacy of Prussia's power interest was here given further unambiguous emphasis: it appeared exclusively as a means to an end, as an instrument for the preservation of the traditional political and social order, which in Prussia itself had meanwhile been largely restored. If in his September speech Bismarck wanted the door left open for an expansionist Prussian power policy, if necessary even against a country such as Austria, it was evidently only on the premiss that such a policy did not undermine that traditional order. To all appearances it was a question merely of alternatives of conservative power and interest policy, of what might even be a purely tactical turning-away from a dogmatic narrowing of the spectrum of political possibilities such as could be observed among the arch-conservatives. There was no sign as yet that he would ever be prepared to go further in the pursuit of Prussian power interests. And even the now-famous speech of 3 December 1850 probably reveals its full significance only to us, looking back; for those immediately concerned it was undoubtedly the tactical elements and the objective verdict that commanded attention.

The occasion for this speech, which finally raised him to the position of foreign affairs spokesman of the conservative parliamentary group and consequently, in the altered political circumstances following the transition to a constitutional state, made available to him the highest offices in the Prussian diplomatic service, was the total collapse of the Union policy and Prussia's capitulation and retreat, which it managed to disguise only with difficulty, before massive pressure from Schwarzenberg. For months it had been becoming ever clearer that not only Austria but Russia too would never under any circumstances be prepared to accept the formation of a Lesser German national state under Prussian control. Prussia suffered an initial heavy defeat when at the insistence of the tsar it had finally to make peace with Denmark and to abandon the cause of Schleswig-Holstein. This cost Prussian policy a further enormous loss of prestige in the eyes of the German national movement. Particularly at the European level it showed Prussian independence and freedom of movement in a somewhat unflattering light. Schwarzenberg immediately pressed his advantage. Disregarding negotiations currently in hand for a settlement with Prussia, he invited the states of the German Confederation to resurrect the central institution of that confederation, the Frankfurt Diet. At the same time he tried to bind the Austrian-oriented small and medium-sized states in a joint-action alliance.

Both initiatives were not merely frontal assaults on the Union, which was already progressively falling apart. Beyond that they constituted an attempt largely to eliminate Prussia as a rival great power in central Europe and to establish a central European empire under Austrian control. This was of course not in the interests of St Petersburg. The Russians were prepared to lend vigorous support to Austrian policy as along as it was directed against Prussian expansionism. But they had no wish to aid and abet Schwarzenberg in his ambitious plans. Russia's sole concern was to restore the pre-1848 state of affairs with due allowance for the fact that its own political influence was now enormously enhanced. On this basis Berlin believed that despite the weakness of its own position it could continue to reject all offers of co-operation from Vienna. In fact Frederick William IV continued, for purely prestige reasons, to hold fast to his Union plan with no regard for its actual prospects of succeeding: towards the end of September 1850 he ostentatiously appointed Radowitz – the 'great imposter', as Bismarck now contemptuously called him[53] – to take charge of Prussia's foreign policy.

In so doing the Prussian monarch was at the same time reacting to a particular conflict that was finally to bring the whole question to a head. The source of this was the electorate of Hesse-Kassel, where the reactionary absolutism of the Elector and his hated minister Hassenpflug had come up against fierce opposition not only from the majority in the country's parliament, which was shortly afterwards dissolved, but also from a wider public including large sections of the army and the civil service. A particularly dramatic clash was in the offing. What lent the conflict a more-than-regional dimension was the fact that the Elector and his minister sought the backing of Vienna – Hesse-Kassel having for all practical purposes left the Union in May 1850 – while the opposition stood by the Union policy and accordingly looked to Prussia for at least indirect suport.

For Schwarzenberg, of course, the situation was as if tailor-made. But Prussia found itself faced with the somewhat delicate choice of either passively looking on, thereby completely robbing the Union of its internal cohesion, or in effect supporting opposition to a ruling monarch and so falling deeply into conflict with its own political principals at home.

The choice became impossible to evade when at the beginning of September 1850 the administration and – for the first and only time in a German state in the nineteenth century – the armed forces offered actual resistance to their sovereign and the Elector, after the country's supreme court had even pronounced his decisions unconstitutional, appealed to the Frankfurt Diet. This had meanwhile resumed operations at Austria's insistence, although initially without Prussia and the states that still supported Prussia. The Elector of Hesse-Kassel based his request for help on the treaties of 1815 and on its being the job of the German Confederation to safeguard the monarchical principle. In so doing he invoked the unbroken continuity of the Confederation in a way that Austria found highly undesirable. The legal foundation of the Elector's request was more than shaky: the constitution of the Confederation spoke only of cases in which the sovereign was acting within the terms of the constitution he had accepted. Yet in spite of this the Diet decided on 21 September, at the request of Austria, to intervene in the Elector's favour and if necessary even provide him with military assistance. This decision by a rump Diet completely dominated by Austria was immediately opposed by Prussia in the strongest possible terms – not only because implementation of it would have meant the end of all its Union efforts but because beyond that it directly affected Prussia's position as a great power. A successful intervention would have severed the lines of military communication between Prussia's eastern and western provinces. Quite apart from the political defeat involved, it would have placed the country in immediate jeopardy from federal troops under Austrian command.

Prussia therefore had to decide whether it was prepared, if necessary, to risk a military conflict of major proportions. There is no doubt that Schwarzenberg had deliberately engineered this situation, even though he had made Prussia repeated offers of reconciliation while doing so. Now too he pushed forward in a determined manner: in mid-October he engaged Bavaria and Württemberg under the banner of the old federal constitution to take joint action against Prussia, specifying that this was to include military action. Immediately afterwards the Frankfurt Diet gave Bavaria and Hanover the job of intervening in Hesse, and on 26 October it ordered a military invasion. The precise timing was left to the man who had meanwhile been appointed federal civil commissioner for Hesse-Kassel, the Austrian diplomat Count Rechberg.

Among those in leading positions in Berlin at this time, Radowitz alone was still absolutely determined to take up the challenge. Not only the Minister-President but also – chiefly for military reasons – the War Minister and the king himself were looking desperately for a way out, the king acting very much under the influence of the Gerlach brothers and their political associates, who decisively rejected the idea of a military confrontation with a fellow conservative power, namely Austria. They were prepared, if by no means unanimously, to make the sacrifices in terms of power and prestige that seemed in the circumstances to be inescapable if such a confrontation was to be avoided.

In view of the almost daily manifestations of Schwarzenberg's determination to provoke a conflict, nothing more could be expected from direct negotiations. Frederick William IV therefore turned to the tsar with the request that he mediate a settlement with Austria. Count Brandenburg, the Minister-President, took personal charge of this mission. The tsar readily agreed, and by means of scarcely veiled threats to the effect that otherwise he would take an active part in hostilities he forced the Austrians not only to come to the negotiating table but to conclude an interim agreement with Prussia. Showing great skill, however, Schwarzenberg managed to avoid tying his hands completely in that, once he was sure of Russian support, as in the Union question and in substance in the Hesse-Kassel question as well, he pushed his terms higher and higher and then insisted on an adjournment.

This meant that when immediately afterwards Count Rechber, the federal civil commissioner appointed by Hanover as executive power – an appointment with which Schwarzenberg had had nothing to do in formal terms – gave orders for the invasion of Hesse-Kassel, the Austrian Minister-President was able to declare that with a final agreement yet to be concluded a completely new situation had arisen. He did this quite without regard for the fact that the resignations on 2 November 1850 of von Radowitz as Foreign Minister and von der Heydt as Minister of Commerce had made clear to all the world how things stood in Berlin: the war party was definitely out and it was the turn of Radowitz's opponents; on hearing the news, Bismarck said, he 'rode round the table on my chair for joy'.[54] Nevertheless, Schwarzenberg demanded in the form of an ultimatum and as a prelude to any further negotiations the withdrawal of the Prussian troops that had meanwhile been marched into Hesse-Kassel as a precautionary measure to protect Prussia's lines of military communication. And not even Prussia's renunciation of the Union and the fact that military operations were confined strictly to securing those lines prevented him from repeating his withdrawal ultimatum on 24 November. He did this despite the fact that it was quite clear that the section of the Prussian government that was prepared to compromise had gone as far as it could hope to answer for at home and found itself facing an army that had suffered a major blow to its self-esteem. Schwarzenberg had now narrowed the choice to war or capitulation by Prussia. And for the purposes of his ambitious plans he would probably have preferred war, even though he knew that an unqualified victory would very likely have led to a subsequent confrontation with Russia and possibly with other powers as well.

In view of the military situation, in view of the lack of any future for its Union policy and not least in view of the attitude of the tsar, the Berlin government, after a certain amount of impotent shilly-shallying, finally

plumped for capitulation. The Prussian Minister-President Count Brandenburg having died suddenly at the beginning of November, the choice
was implemented by his initially only provisional successor, the former
Minister of the Interior Baron Otto von Manteuffel, who had at the same
time taken over from Radowitz at the Foreign Office, in direct negotiations
with Schwarzenberg on Austrian soil, at Olmütz in Moravia, on 28 and
29 November 1850.

Not that there was in fact any question of negotiations. It was a *Diktat* of
such severity that Manteuffel, the much-hated 'Minister of Reaction', had
to exceed the already very broad brief given him by his Cabinet in order to
obtain a settlement at all.

Essentially, Prussia had to give ground on all fronts. It recognized the
continued existence of the Confederation without its previously much-
invoked parity with Austria in the control of that organization. It agreed
that in Hesse-Kassel as in Holstein, where similar problems had arisen,
though in a less dramatic form, a 'legal state of affairs' should be created
such as 'accorded with the principles of the Confederation and made it
possible for Federal commitments to be met'. And it promised in a secret
rider to the 'punctation' or preliminary draft to demobilize its army
immediately as the first country to do so, in other words it capitulated in
this respect as well.

The only thing, apart from a few trifles, that Schwarzenberg allowed
Prussia by way of a face-saver was the joint summoning of conferences of
ministers of the states of the German Confederation. These were to discuss
the possibility of a reform of the Confederation, meeting not in Frankfurt
and not in Vienna, nor of course in Berlin either, but in Dresden. Prussia's
re-entry into the Confederation was thus to be formally effected by process
of negotiation. The Prussian Cabinet ratified this 'agreement' on 2 September.
The very next day Manteuffel presented it to the Lower House, clearly with
a view to giving angry minds an opportunity to let off steam.

With hindsight many historians have seen Olmütz, notwithstanding the
momentary humiliation, almost as a tactical victory for Prussia. The
settlement, they say, effectively prevented Schwarzenberg from parrying
Prussia's Union policy to put through his own idea for the solution of the
German question, an 'empire of seventy million' ruled by Vienna and
including the entire monarchy. A number of good reasons can undoubtedly
be put forward for this. But for immediate contemporaries what was
overwhelmingly predominant was the total humiliation of Prussia. Even
where it was seen, as it was by Prussia's arch-conservatives, as the outcome
of a policy that had been wrong all along the line, often the main emotions
were anger at Schwarzenberg's brutality and feelings of wounded patriotic
pride.

This was how Bismarck saw things too, and in this respect he was at first
very much closer to the reaction of the moderate conservatives and even of
the liberals than to that of the Gerlachs. 'As long as Prussia, our black and
white Prussia, is not assured by clear and conclusive treaties of rights in
Germany that are everywhere on a par with Austria's and take precedence
over everyone else's', he had written in the *Kreuzzeitung* on 13 November,

'we too want war.'[55] Subsequently, however, he agreed at the insistence of the Gerlachs to defend the policy of the government in a situation in which its own fate, given the mood of the country, was very much in the balance. This he did in a manner that doubly laid the foundations of his future diplomatic and political career: literally in that he thus placed the king and the advocates of the Olmütz agreement under an obligation to himself, and metaphorically in that he developed in this speech certain crucial features of his whole political outlook on life.

The fact that the Gerlachs and their associates even chose him, together with Kleist-Retzow, to be their spokesman in this perilous situation, which called for the most carefully considered approach on both the domestic and foreign policy fronts, shows how great a change Bismarck's standing had meanwhile undergone, particularly since his speech of 6 September 1849. He was now seen as the natural go-between for the different foreign policy positions within the conservative camp, as the man who knew how to bring out what those positions had in common and how to bring those positions together. To bring them together along their line, as the Gerlachs believed, the line of what was essentially a policy of supra-national conservative solidarity and principle. That there was in fact no question of this, that Bismarck secretly regarded even this policy as merely one position among many, a position that could be fallen back on when circumstances required but that could also be tactically deployed or if necessary even sacrificed – that only became clear later. Yet it was precisely this, one might say, that showed how completely right the Gerlachs were, at least in their estimate of his tactical and diplomatic skill: in the very moment when he seemed to be wholly their instrument he was already outmanoeuvring them – not so much through greater keenness of vision or intellectual superiority as because in his self-submission to the power at work in history he went as it were further than they did, believing as they did in the eternal truth of principles. The morality, the Christian basis of this ostensible submission to the power of God in history was something on which of course the Gerlachs themselves very soon cast doubt; they spoke of it as camouflaging an opportunism aimed solely at success and power. 'Revolutionary', 'godless' and 'wholly de-Christianized' were the terms that Ludwig von Gerlach eventually applied to Bismarck's politics, claiming that they were governed by the motto*suum cuique rapere* instead of by the conservative-Christian *suum cuique*, the device of Frederick the Great, to which admittedly even he had paid no more than lip-service.

The speech in which the provisional Minister-President outlined the terms of Olmütz to the Lower House on 3 December 1850 was by no means unskilful, given the circumstances.[56] Manteuffel's opportunity came with a debate, set for that day, in reply to the sections of the speech from the throne dealing with the German question. He used it to make a frank admission of the total failure of Prussia's Union policy – for which he personally, however, was in no way responsible. For the rest he concentrated in the main on explaining why the government had not wanted to go to war. The sacrifices involved would have been out of all proportion to what might have been achieved thereby. For the very foundation of the

Union, the principle of free agreements between the participant states and governments, had already been shattered before this. There had been nothing to justify a counter-action in Hesse purely from the standpoint of wounded honour since Prussian interests had in fact by and large been protected. Furthermore he stressed that 'there is always something distressing about the failure of a plan; the effect, however, is different upon the strong than upon the weak. The weak are thrown into a state of irritability; the strong may take a step backwards but they maintain their objective steadily in view and study by what other means it can be achieved.'

Such considerations could not of course obscure the fact that the government had experienced a complete fiasco as far as its German policy was concerned and that this had dealt a severe blow to Prussia's standing as a European power. The speech in which the leader of the liberal opposition, von Vincke, then took the government to task accordingly culminated with inner logic in a demand that the House pass a vote of no confidence in the ministry. Under the terms of the monarchical constitutional system then in force this took the form of an address to the monarch, asking that he should 'be pleased to put an end to the system by which the country has been placed in this disastrous situation and which is upheld by the present advisers to the Crown'. The second opposition speaker, the archivist Adolf Riegel, sided emphatically with Vincke: 'One feeling entirely consumes me: indignation, utter indignation at this latest act of our policy of which the ministry has just unexpectedly informed us. I can therefore only echo and thereby concur with the words contained in the address that is here proclaimed: "Away with this system of policy!"'

This emphasis gave Bismarck the cue he needed for the introduction to and indeed the whole tenor of his speech:[57] from the remarks of the – as to the delight of his party colleagues he ironically called him – 'martially-minded civil servant' who had spoken before him it could be seen how so grave and weighty a matter as the decision over war and peace between great powers threatened to become completely swamped by emotions – emotions, moreover, that sprang from very dubious sources. 'The draft address refers to this as a great age.' Here in Berlin, he said, he had 'seen nothing great except personal ambition, nothing great except mistrust, nothing great except party hatred. These are three great things that to my mind characterize this as an age of pettiness and give all who love the fatherland a gloomy view of our future.' In this sort of spirit matters were being discussed in a situation in which every comment by the Prussian parliament could decide between war and peace: 'And what kind of war, gentlemen? No expedition by individual regiments into Schleswig or Baden, no military parade through restless provinces, but a war on a grand scale against two of the three major continental powers, while the third, eager for booty, arms on our frontier and knows very well that Cologne Cathedral holds the treasure that would be just the thing to end the revolution in France and strengthen that country's ruler, namely the French imperial crown. A war, gentlemen, that will place us under the necessity of giving up some of the more remote Prussian provinces from the outset, in which large tracts of the country will be immediately overrun by hostile armies and in which our provinces will experience the horrors of war to the full.'

The trick was as transparent as it was effective: by invoking a war of European proportions and suggesting that the opponent at home was showing an irresponsible approach to the question, indeed casting moral suspicion on him, he went straight on to the offensive. Nor was that all. In so doing he raised the question at issue to a level where he could on two counts treat it as a matter of principle: first, to stormy applause from his political associates, with respect to the policy of the left as a whole; and secondly with respect to something akin to guiding principles of foreign policy generally.

That war was the continuation of *Politik* by other means, as Clausewitz had said, was something Bismarck took as unreservedly for granted as did most of the members of the parliamentary assembly he was addressing. But the crucial question was what in this extreme case, which so visibly increased the responsibility of those involved, was to count as 'policy'. Bismarck's answer to this question was unequivocal: the only kind of policy that was legitimate and at the same time morally justified was the one that had an eye to the interests of the community as a whole. The community as a whole, however, was for him not just in ideal circumstances represented by the state; it was – and here he was already deeply divorced from the traditional conservatives – in all circumstances identical with the state. The idea of a state being an illegitimate representative of the community struck him as purely and simply subversive, and he never understood that the concept of the unqualified identity of community and state was potentially no less revolutionary and could moreover lead to the eradication of all freedom.

On the basis of this ultimately absolutist concept of the state he was able to draw a very sharp distinction between party interest and the interest of the state, denouncing the former as illegitimate and indeed, if as here uninvolved third parties were affected, as immoral. 'It is easy for a statesman, whether' – as he stressed in a passing shot at the war party in the government itself – 'in the Cabinet or in parliament, to use the people's wind to give a blast on the war trumpet while warming his feet at his fireside or delivering rousing speeches from this platform, and to leave it up to the musketeer bleeding in the snow whether or not his system wins the day and reaps the glory. There is nothing easier, but woe betide the statesman who in this age fails to seek a reason for war that remains valid *after* the war is over.' And what could such a reason be that would in retrospect render endurable 'a long vista of battlefields and burning ruins, distress and destitution, a hundred thousand corpses and a hundred million in debts'? The salvaging of the Union constitution, the substitution in some tiny state of one minister for another, wounded honour understood as mere loss of face? All these the opposition had put forward as reasons. He who would act responsibly, however, had to examine how all these reasons related to a perfectly sober estimate of the interests of the state he represented: 'the only sound basis for a major state, and this distinguishes it essentially from a minor state, is national self-interest, not romanticism, and it is unworthy of a major state to fight for a cause that does not form part of its own interests'.

But what about the reasons put forward here, he asked, looked at in the light of such a maxim? There was much talk of wounded Prussian honour at the moment, particularly in the opposition camp. He, however, failed to see in what way that honour, starting with the honour of the army, actually was wounded. All military measures were bound by considerations of political expediency and had to be guided by the outcome of a sober assessment of the associated advantages and disadvantages. Every army or fleet in the world must accept even a retreat from time to time, when its government recognized that this or that objective was beyond reach for the moment. So anyone who pleaded wounded military honour was in reality undermining the authority of the political leadership and of the king as supreme commander. And in fact this was precisely what the opposition was aiming at. By invoking this alleged affront to Prussian honour they believed they had 'found the secret of leading the Prussian army into battle for the same principle as in March 1848 it had fought against in the streets of Berlin'. 'Try as you will', he challenged opposition members in what seemed a complete reversion to his earlier firebrand role, 'you will never succeed in turning the Prussian army, the army that on 19 March [1848], with the fury of the riled victor in its heart and loaded weapons in its hands but obedient only to the orders of its commander, accepted amisdst the insults of the adversary the role of the vanquished – you will never succeed in turning it into a parliamentary army; it will always remain the army of the *King* and seek its honour in obedience'. In fact these words were directed wholly at the military war party in his own camp, which was headed by the future William I, brother to the king. To point out to that party and to the conservative politicians who favoured it that a war would help no one but the opposition at home was in fact the burden of his whole speech.

Accordingly he also dismissed the second of the suggested reasons for war, the Hesse-Kassel question, with a disdain that inevitably aroused the liberals to extremes of indignation: 'The honour of Prussia does not in my view consist in Prussia playing Don Quixote to every offended parliamentary bigwig in Germany who feels his local constitution is in jeopardy.' In the *Kreuzzeitung* a fortnight before this he had spoken in even stronger terms of 'the romanticism of a roving knight in armour for "oppressed" peoples' to which Prussia ought to 'stop sacrificing its own interest'.[58] Now, in December, expressing himself in extreme terms and weaving into an apparently seamless robe conservative interests, the policy of the present government and the country's future foreign policy goals, he declared: 'I seek Prussia's honour in this: that Prussia should, first and foremost, hold itself aloof from every ignominious association with democracy, that in this present question, as in every question, Prussia should not permit anything to happen in Germany without Prussia's consent, that what Prussia and Austria, after joint independent consideration, regard as sensible and politically right should jointly be put into execution by the two equal protecting powers of Germany.'

Here he was indicating what in his eyes would constitute a real reason for war: the denial of Prussian parity with Austria in the control of the Confederation and indeed in all matters concerning central Europe. He called upon the government not to disarm until 'the free conferences have produced a positive result; then there will still be time to wage war if we are truly, in honour, unable or unwilling to avoid it'. This shows, incidentally, that Manteuffel had left even his closest party colleagues outside the Cabinet in the dark as to the extent of his capitulation at Olmütz.

Against this background of readiness for war on grounds of principle in the event of such a war really involving serious interests, Bismarck's fresh settling of accounts with the Union policy, to which he devoted the last part of his speech, gave a particularly fierce impression. It had been, he said, even if Radowitz had undoubtedly 'wanted the best for Prussia', a 'hermaphroditic product of timorous rule and tame revolution'. It could have produced stable results only if the government had plumped determinedly for one or the other. But with the one way, the way of unconditional Prussian supremacy, blocked by the whole internal construction and constitution of the Union, that ultimately left only the other way, a pact with the revolution. 'Let those people not deceive themselves who believe they could start such a war under the banner of the Union *and stop it too.*' If the Prussian government were after all obliged by circumstances 'to go to war for the idea of the Union', it would 'not be long before the Unionists had the last shreds of the Union mantle torn from their backs by powerful hands, and there would be nothing left but the red lining of that most flimsy garment.'

This was the quintessence of the entire speech: that Prussia's only real chance in a war against Austria at the present time lay in allying itself with the left, with democratic nationalism, in other words with the revolution, and playing the part 'played by Turin in Italy'. Because in view of the current distribution of power between the two power blocs led by Prussia and Austria, a decision along traditional lines could probably be arrived at only by involving third parties. The result of that, however, would be 'that the focus of all German questions is necessarily shifted to Warsaw and Paris'. Surely no one seriously wished for that kind of outcome. In other words, Prussia could win only if either in foreign policy or in domestic policy terms it sacrificed its traditional substance. Under these circumstances a Prussian war for the Union inevitably put him 'vividly in mind of the Englishman who fought a successful encounter with a sentry in order to be able to hang himself in the sentry-box, a right he claimed for himself and for every free Briton'.

At the end of his speech Bismarck once again emphatically warned his listeners against letting themselves be drawn into a 'propaganda war', a 'war of principle' on the side of the left, a war that would lead Prussia 'to ignominious ruin, even in victory'. Here he was expressing the heartfelt thoughts of the Gerlachs and their associates quite as much as when he said that he 'recognize[d] in Austria the representative of and heir to an ancient German power that has often and most gloriously wielded the German sword'. He must also have won their undivided approval when he declared that if the majority of the House demanded a 'war of principle', this was in his view 'no reason for war with Austria but for war with this House', for dissolution and fresh elections. But however much else there may have been between his assertion that 'the only sound basis for a major state . . . is national self-interest and not romanticism' and his warning against a 'propaganda war' or 'war of principle' – this was undoubtedly where, as far as he himself was concerned, the decisive arguments lay. In other words, under the heading 'romanticism' he lumped everything that did not directly serve to uphold and extend the power of the state.

In December 1850 it was only the left as yet, in the shape of liberal and democratic ideals, that he said the state must not be allowed to become subject to in terms of its foreign policy. But ultimately the same could be said of the right as well; the same point could be made with regard to its principles and with regard to the idea of conservative solidarity. 'One clings to principles', he had once, years before, written sarcastically to his wife, 'only for as long as they are not put to the test; when that happens one throws them away as the peasant does his slippers and walks after the fashion that nature intended.'[59] Putting them to the test, however, meant confronting them with interests, one's own and those of the state that one was backing and that one served. While still going into battle for his arch-conservative friends, Bismarck was already the spokesman of a 'reason of state', that, freed from all ties, aimed purely and simply at power.

Of course, this was no more an abstract development taking place on a theoretical level than was anything else in Bismarck's life. For a man of sober judgement such as himself it had been evident for some time that the successful counter-revolution in Prussia was not going to lead to a parliamentary constitutional system on the English pattern, the outcome he had once longed for as the basis for a successful political career. Instead what was in prospect was a neo-absolutism with mere constitutional embellishments. With a weak monarch, the people who would have the say would be bureaucrats such as Manteuffel and advisers who were not accountable in constitutional terms such as the members of the so-called 'Camarilla' headed by the Gerlach brothers. 'If you grasped firmly', Bismarck said of Frederick William IV in a confidential conversation held many years after this, 'all you were left with was a handful of slime',[60] and again in his memoirs he noted disdainfully that the king had been lacking 'not in political foresight but in resolve'.[61]

In such a situation it was inevitable that Bismarck found the role of a parliamentary spokesman for the conservatives comparatively uninteresting as being that of a man who would have to supply rational justifications for decisions already taken and as it were subsume those decisions under the principles of his own political group. The object of his Olmütz speech was therefore also to recommend himself for high office. It was to be expected, of course, that once the battle had been won such outstanding combatants as Kleist-Retzow and Bismarck would be rewarded. But Bismarck knew only too well that, particularly in the kind of semi-absolutist bureaucratic system that with the appointment of Otto von Manteuffel as Minister-President was now becoming definitively established in Prussia, politically successful outsiders who lacked the usual formal qualifications and career experience were treated with extraordinary mistrust. The best way of removing such mistrust was for the person concerned as it were to overcompensate in point of substance for his lack of formal qualifications, for him to lay particular emphasis on the dominant principles of public administration and diplomacy and extol them as his personal guidelines. In this case, however, the principles were those of the power, interest group and equilibrium politics of the eighteenth century with the proviso, of course, that in pursuit of them the status quo at home must always be preserved. And although in Bismarck's case no particular opportunist considerations were required for him to embrace them, since his own thoughts and beliefs had for a long time lain in the same direction, personal calculation did undoubtedly play a part in the way in which he apportioned the emphasis between respect for a conservative politics of principle and a politics of national interest.

Four months after his Olmütz speech, of which the conservatives had distributed 20,000 copies throughout the country, the desired result materialized. For some time now Bismarck had let it be known that, not least because of his 'very straitened', indeed 'sorry financial situation',[62] he aspired to public office: 'My estates came to me so burdened with debt', he told Ludwig von Gerlach, 'that once I quit the modest independence of my own four walls scarcely enough of my regular income remains for me to wear la cape et l'épée with decency.'[63] Early in 1851 he had entered into negotiations regarding the position of chief minister in the tiny north German state of Anhalt-Bernburg, which was wholly dependent on Prussia. 'The Duke is an imbecile and the Minister Duke', is how he described the advantages of the position in a letter to his wife.[64] Not long afterwards there was talk of a job as Landrat or district administrator. Probably in neither case was Bismarck seriously interested. After all, his friend Hans von Kleist-Retzow, whose services to the conservative cause were certainly no greater than his own, was being talked of as a Regierungspräsident or even an Oberpräsident, the top administrative positions in region and province respectively; he eventually became Oberpräsident in Koblenz. Why should not something comparable emerge for him too? And 'comparable' was not the word to describe either the office of minister of a tiny state or that of Landrat, or the mere title of Kammerherr – Chamberlain – which he was offered at the beginning of April. What was comparable, however, was the post of Prussian Bundestagsgesandte or envoy to the Federal Diet, for which as he learned at the end of April Leopold von Gerlach, the king's adjutant-general and now one of the most influential men in Prussia, had mentioned his name first to Frederick William IV and subsequently to Manteuffel, the Minister-President and Foreign Minister.

It had been clear since the end of March 1851 at the latest that the Dresden conferences agreed to at Olmütz with a view to reforming the German Confederation would end up simply re-establishing the *status quo ante*, in other words the 1815 constitution and the Frankfurt Diet in its old form. Neither side was prepared to meet the other's wishes. Austria, predictably, refused to grant Prussia an equal share in the control of the Confederation. Prussia for its part therefore saw no reason why it should agree to the whole of the Habsburg Empire entering the Confederation, especially since as well as the medium-sized German states Russia and France also stood beside it on this question. So the legation in Frankfurt, empty for almost three years, had to be manned again in a hurry. For this purpose a man must quickly be found who would be capable of holding an intermediate position between confrontation and excessive co-operation with Austria. In the wake of the developments of the last few months and years, which even in the diplomatic corps had produced entrenched positions and aroused powerfully partisan emotions, this was no easy task. After one of the direct negotiators, Count Alvensleben, had declined, the situation positively favoured an outsider. In view of the anti-Austrian mood permeating the conservative camp, however, even an outsider was hard to find.

Thus it was that from the narrow circle of possible candidates one man really stood out, the man who had so impressively stated in public that the preservation of Prussian interests and a settlement with Austria were reconcilable and who had left it up to the individual listener where he wished to place the special emphasis. Gerlach therefore had a comparatively easy passage with his proposal to the king and subsequently also to Manteuffel, although at first glance there was a great deal against it: Bismarck's total lack of experience in the diplomatic sphere; what was not only in the eyes of bureaucrats such as Manteuffel his extremely inadequate education; his youth; his notorious hot-headedness; and not least a wider misgiving to the effect that it might be counter-productive generally to push office patronage too far by such 'violent promotions', as Ludwig von Gerlach put it, and give the job of envoy to the Federal Diet to a man 'whose official position hitherto has been merely that of a failed candidate for the regional civil service'.[65] Prince William, the future king, was certainly not alone when he reacted to the news with the remark: 'And this *Landwehrleutnant* [a junior officer in the Home Guard] is to become our Envoy to the Federal Diet?'[66] 'The fellow would even take command of a frigate or perform an operation for gall-stones', the newspapers of the day suggested, paraphrasing something that was said of Lord John Russell.

Bismarck and Oberpräsident designate Kleist-Retzow were in a sense quite right when in the light of their new offices they invoked God's mercy upon themselves in special measure. As always in such cases, however, Bismarck was perfectly serious. In this he combined in characteristic fashion his feeling of superiority over the mere expert, the 'bureaucrat' who had risen 'through examinations, connections, study of the files, seniority', with a now certain faith in a divine order affecting every last detail of existence. The words in which he clothed that faith have since become largely ossified in mere formulae and therefore tend to strike the modern reader as empty and meaningless. On May 1851, for example, he wrote to his wife: 'I am God's soldier, and I must go where He sends me, and I *believe* that He is sending me and that He is cutting out my life as He needs it.'[67] Or again, two days later: 'God helps me along, and with Him I am more equal to the task than most of our politicians who, but for Him, might be in Frankfurt in my place. I shall perform my office; it is up to God whether he gives me the wit to do so.'[68] The profusion of such remarks and the straightforward way

85

in which he came out with them put it beyond doubt that here was indeed the source of a substantial portion of the courage and self-confidence that were on his own estimate required if, as a complete newcomer, he was to prove himself in what was 'currently the most difficult post in our diplomatic service'.[69]

On 8 May 1851 he had a protracted farewell audience with the king. It was finally settled on this occasion that he would take over the post after a two-month transitional period during which the St Petersburg envoy, General von Rochow, a brother of the Prussian Minister of the Interior in the 1840s, would formally head the legation and as it were show him the ropes. According to Bismarck's memoirs, Frederick William remarked during the course of their conversation that he, Bismarck, clearly possessed great courage if he was prepared, 'just like that', to enter upon what was for him an 'unfamiliar office'. He replied, he tells us, in the following words: 'The courage is entirely Your Majesty's in entrusting such a position to me, although of course Your Majesty is not obliged to uphold the appointment should it prove a failure.'[70]

This remark by the budding diplomat was highly characteristic of the man, not only then but also later. By laying the formal responsibility at the door of a higher authority, as it were, whether the king or indeed a supernatural power, he gave himself more room for manoeuvre and greater scope for taking risks and conducting experiments. At the same time he managed in this way to avoid committing himself too precisely with regard to content. Already in this situation, as in the dramatic autumn of 1862 before his appointment as Minister-President, he thrust the relationship of personal trust right into the foreground and subsequently derived from this tie an exceptional measure of freedom in matters of detail.

On the day of his interview with the king he was initially appointed Privy Legation Councillor – 'an irony', as he wrote to his wife, 'with which God is punishing me for all my abusive remarks about privy councillors'.[71] Two days later, immediately after the end of the parliamentary session, he left for Frankfurt. In the middle of July 1851 Rochow, who would have liked to have the job permanently, reluctantly returned to St Petersburg. As arranged, Bismarck was now formally appointed Prussia's envoy to the Federal Diet.

The Junker whom many even among his peers had been inclined to regard as a failure, the passionately committed party man of the revolutionary period, had with one bound become a top diplomat of a major European power, a man to be reckoned with beyond the comparatively very limited circle within which he had moved hitherto. It was indeed a 'violent promotion'. When in 1852 a flysheet by the liberal businessman Friedrich Harkort calculated what good business politics had become for one ex-candidate for the regional civil service, notwithstanding the polemical nature of the publication it was at the same time an indication of how dramatically Bismarck's rise was received by the general public.[72]

It was also, of course, received as a sign of how far the state and the traditional ruling class were now prepared to go, under the influence of the challenge from the process of economic and social change and the new forces it had released, in the direction of abandoning the traditional qualification requirements and giving absolute priority to the principle of adherence to the party line. The liberal *Nationalzeitung* saw the appointments of Bismarck and Kleist-Retzow as representing the final victory of the efforts of the 'Junker Parliament' of 1848 and hence not only of political but also of social reaction. And many contemporaries took the same view. The figure of the new Prussian envoy to the Federal Diet was seen almost as a symbol of the state of internal developments in Prussia and in Germany as a whole; he was the embodiment of state-imposed reaction.

Nor was that all. He could also stand as a symbol of the destruction of all national hopes and expectations, of Prussia's ignominious submission to the dominant position demanded by a reactionary and anti-nationalist Austria, of the abandonment of the whole tradition, going back to Frederick the Great, of an independent policy for Prussia as a great power. They were aware in Vienna and in the capitals of the medium-sized German states that even in the arch-conservative camp of which Bismarck continued to be regarded as a representative there were limits to what could reasonably be expected and that the conservative principle must not be placed under too great a strain at the expense of Prussian interests. But even here the dominant feeling was one of expectation that with the new man the spirit of conservative solidarity of the restoration years after 1820, a spirit so favourable to their own objectives, was about to return to the Frankfurt negotiating table.

The new envoy to the Federal Diet was thus at first almost universally regarded as a guarantee that the revolution had been successfully overcome, both within individual states and as affecting international relations, and was now a thing of the past. That Bismarck himself embodied a radical metamorphosis of that revolution seen as a principle of dramatic political, economic and social change, that through him it was ultimately, moving along quite new paths, to reach its goal – that was something no one suspected at the time, least of all the man himself. And that the means of which over the next twenty years he often thoughtlessly availed himself in order to make Prussia great and to maintain and strengthen the traditional power of the Prussian Crown and the Prussian state might in themselves be ends far greater and more momentous than those he used them to pursue – that was something he contrived to recognize only in so far as his faith taught him to distinguish between human calculation and divine control and to leave the actual course of history, the actual outcome of the historical process, entirely to the latter. Yet it was precisely in his releasing of means that contained their own end that lay not only the secret of his success but also his importance in terms of world history, in other words what we call historical greatness in a supra-personal sense.

PART TWO

'Let Us Rather Undertake Revolution than Undergo It'

[3]

Reasons of State and International Politics:

Envoy to the Federal Diet

If we look at the basic political and social ideas and at first only roughly outlined objectives with which Bismarck entered upon his first public office in 1851 and if we compare them with what at the end of his career, almost forty years later, was the actual political, social and economic situation obtaining in central Europe, one thing stands out immediately: he can hardly be regarded as one of history's great preservers. For they were forty years of stormy and often breathtakingly rapid change in almost every sphere. Considering the period in the light of one of Bismarck's favourite maxims, namely that a wave, while it will carry things along, cannot be steered, we have to say instead that he was a man of revolutionary change in both senses of the word and that he clearly owed his success in the main to an ability to sail before the storm. It was something that gave his political associates an uncomfortable feeling about him from very early on, at a time when his opponents still believed they could pigeon-hole him precisely. He nourished in them a strong suspicion that using him against the revolution, against liberalism, against nationalism and against the destruction of every traditional way of life would quite possibly be a case of 'out of the frying-pan into the fire'.

Not that they regarded him as in any way a revolutionary in disguise. But one thing they did see more and more clearly: that his unconditional pursuit of certain objectives, particularly in the field of power politics, often appeared to render him blind to the consequences that would flow from their achievement. 'He wishes à tout prix to remain possible, now and *in the future*', is how his closest comrade-in-arms in the first years of his minister-presidency, War Minister Albrecht von Roon, once put it. 'But – the means to that end! Will they be justified by it?'[1] The 'acheronta movebo', the readiness in emergencies to enter into coalitions of all kinds, the apparent indifference to the possible long-term political or social consequences of his own actions, which in others made for caution – all this gave rise to an impression of irresponsibility, of a gambler who inadvertently played into the hands of his political opponents.

91

Such verdicts bore in each case upon individual stages of his political career and applied to a greater extent to the years before 1870 than to the two decades that followed. Even in historical retrospect, though, there is no mistaking the fact that here was a key element of his political personality. He himself, when asked about this, repeatedly stressed in a wide variety of ways that all this applied only to the means and that there could never have been any question of the ends or objectives not mattering. 'The statesman', he said once towards the end of his life, 'is like a wayfarer in the forest who knows in which direction he is walking but not at what point he will emerge from the trees. Just like him, the statesman must take the negotiable paths if he is not to lose his way.'[2] But what he defended as the 'art of the possible' against a dogmatic approach to politics was for him undoubtedly also, on occasion, a plumbing of the feasible, regardless of what the wider consequences might be. There is no question but that the fascination of what bold action made possible more than once had him in its grip.

The crucial element, of course, lies not in the question of where, say, what was feasible dictated his objectives; on the whole his image of the wayfarer being aware of his general direction is fair comment here. Surely it lies instead in the fact that he believed he knew his 'general direction' very early on and in very clear terms, that he was sure of himself in an age that, marked by political upheavals and an ever-accelerating process of economic and social change, was increasingly unsure of itself.

When in the summer of 1851, at the age of 36, he took command of the Frankfurt legation, he was well aware that he first had to learn his new trade; he was still a 'diplomatic infant', as he stressed in a letter to his mentor Gerlach.[3] But it was his equally firm conviction that personally as well as in terms of the matter in hand he stood on solid ground. That ground was Prussia's national interest both abroad and at home conceived in terms of the unassailable legitimacy of monarchical rule and a simultaneous commitment to the traditional order. And that ground was at the same time his faith in a personal God who manifested himself in the reality of earthly being. For him the two were inextricably linked; they gave him his bearings and lent meaning to the obvious one-sidednesses of his own existence and his own actions. The charge of narrowness, of being blind to wider issues, therefore left him as cold as did the charge of extreme partisanship. As a Christian he felt released from an unbearable and existentially intolerable responsibility for an unascertainable whole, for the principles of the world order, as it were; consequently devotion to a concrete, calculable interest took on for him the character of a universal idea. He believed he was working towards the hidden objectives of a higher power, objectives that it was impossible for man to comprehend and of which he could the more effectively be the instrument the more completely he accepted his own individual existence.

This unqualified acceptance of his own existence and of a special angle of interest that he labelled 'the Prussian national interest' lay at the root of the strength and assurance of his performance as a politician and the uninhibited way in which he made use of whatever means lay to hand. In this respect, and within the narrow bounds of which he was himself thoroughly aware, he was an early maturer, as it were, in an age in which all relationships and the existing order found themselves in a state of radical upheaval. He no more represented what was to become of that age than did anyone else in those years. Quite the contrary. The world that proceeded to emerge was soon no longer the world that his feeling for and outlook on life, his values and his view of man might have led him to imagine as desirable. The industrial economy, the modern big city, the bureaucratization and regimentation of every aspect of life, mobility as a principle of existence – all that was totally alien to him. And yet he played a decisive part in bringing it about, admittedly without a hard and fast plan and often, as far as the wider consequences were concerned, adopting as a mere means what had as its goal an entirely new order.

No doubt this called for a 'mature' approach, an acceptance of narrowly restricted objectives, a renunciation of the idea of self-fulfilment in one's own life through planning for the future and through ideas, of self-realization through history. 'For the man who in an uncertain age is also of uncertain mind multiplies evil and increasingly spreads it abroad', Goethe had written in *Hermann and Dorothea*. And entirely in the spirit of German idealism he had gone on to say: 'But he who remains of firm mind forms the world within him.' This may have been true in personal terms but was hardly so in terms of the historical world, at least not in times of major, dramatic upheavals. No, the figure of Bismarck shows with especial clarity that the nature of the firmness that meets such an age is clearly in many respects a matter of complete indifference, indeed that the true tendencies of the age develop only out of the resistance offered to them. It has rightly been said of Hitler that his anachronistic programme was completely and utterly without effect but that against his will and as it were behind his back the period of his rule was one of violent and precipitate change in the social sphere as well. Much the same is true of Bismarck, though with the fundamental difference that he did not presume to know what a higher power allegedly wanted. He never once doubted that a superior will might run counter to his own intentions and place what the individual wanted in a quite different context.

From this standpoint he himself may have found it less surprising that in resisting his time he became wholly its man and helped to bring about a world that in many respects was not his own. For posterity, and especially for the biographer, the question presents itself in more difficult terms, even where the facts as such are plain to see. For we have a clear view from the start not only of the tension between what had been willed and what came about. We also see a process of becoming that often unfolded in almost complete detachment from what was specifically willed, although the latter created essential prerequisites for the former and was in turn crucially determined by it.

Recently many historians have resorted to attributing to Bismarck secret knowledge and a secret plan that – in terms of his own objectives, too – brings him back closer to the overall trends of contemporary development, particularly in the economic and social spheres. Apart from the fact that no one has explained why sources that otherwise flow so freely should have retained only a very flimsy and uncertain trace of this, the theory turns

Bismarck into a positive superman who for decades was playing a kind of double game with daredevil virtuosity – a life that could only seem possible in the intellectual puppet theatre of a scholar's study. The fact that a determined conservative, a man of tradition holding what was in many ways a wholly traditional view of political problems, should *de facto*, in terms of results and consequences, have become a man of not merely rapid but also revolutionary change hardly receives a satisfactory explanation from this quarter. Indeed, by placing too much emphasis on what Bismarck allegedly planned and desired, such constructions are more likely to push aside and cover up the problem as such.

If on the other hand we accept that Bismarck really was the man of relatively limited objectives that he presented himself as and in full awareness saw himself as, this central problem emerges clearly. Furthermore, an explanation begins to emerge that at least has the advantage of not needing to bring universal developments and the individual will violently into one context and at the same time of admitting of other interpretations of each individual case. It rests on the assumption that the self-assurance of his own position, which was based not only, indeed not even primarily on the concrete and objective – Bismarck chopped and changed often enough here – seemed to allow him a degree of nonchalance with regard to his choice of means and allies that he either underestimated or ignored as a factor with an importance of its own. The basis of this position was confidence and resignation at one and the same time. It raised national self-interest and a power-political interest that oscillated between that of the established authorities and his own to the status of a principle, while leaving everything else to a higher power. That this effectively freed politics from all obligations was no problem for Bismarck as a Christian and as a man who still took certain cultural and moral obligations entirely for granted. Here too, however – indeed here in particular – the consequences were enormous.

Bismarck first tried this position out as Prussia's envoy to the Federal Diet in Frankfurt, that is to say in an office that imposed objective restraints on the politician, albeit in a large and important setting. As a member of parliament his competence had hitherto extended to all departments, as it were, and he had spoken on almost every subject that came up on the agenda. In response to the challenge of the revolution he had as a matter of course seen all politics in an inner context and as a unity affecting and embracing human existence at least in all its communal forms. Nothing about this basic approach changed with his appointment to the new post. Yet it was inevitable that from now on he should concentrate more on foreign policy, particularly on Prussia's relations with Austria and on the constellation of the European powers – though in a manner, admittedly, that tended virtually from the outset to burst traditional bounds and upset traditional modes of behaviour.

His brief, at least as his backers saw it, was further to normalize relations with Austria in the direction of a joint alliance against the revolution and to prevent a fresh confrontation. This did not mean that he was to steer clear of any kind of conflict and yield on every point. But he was expected to pay strict heed to the limits and to keep the overriding interest of conservative solidarity permanently in view. Whether with his already fully developed ideas about power politics Bismarck would ever have been prepared to accept this kind of self-restraint need not concern us here. For the circumstances and attitudes that he found in Frankfurt stood in contradiction to that brief from the outset, as did his own personality. 'I was certainly no opponent of Austria's on principle when I came here four years ago', he wrote to his Foreign Minister, Manteuffel, at the end of February 1855, 'but I should have had to disown every drop of Prussian blood had I wished to retain even a moderate affection for Austria as its present rulers understand it.'[4]

Although Prussia had finally bowed to extreme Austrian pressure and renounced its 'German policy', it had become clear to all that, of the European great powers, Prussia was still the one that most vehemently strove to better the position hitherto assigned to it in the system of those powers. In the eyes of the representatives of classical diplomacy, Prussia was still the troublesome upstart that had first appeared on the scene a hundred years earlier, under Frederick II. And once again, as in 1815, the German Confederation appeared to offer the means of pinning down the military state on the Spree in a regional organization dominated by Austria and containing its expansionist ambitions as a European great power.

That Confederation now once again embraced through the representative form of a congress of envoys all the states and city-states that had come together in 1815 for the 'preservation of the external and internal security of Germany'. As a result of hereditary consolidations and renunciations of sovereignty there were now only thirty-six of them instead of the original forty-one: thirty-two territories and four free cities, including the seat of the Federal Diet, the former 'Freie Reichsstadt' or 'Free Imperial City' of Frankfurt.

The object of the Confederation was and continued to be the preservation of the status quo, the existing state of affairs in its legal, social and power-political aspects. As a result it immediately refocused on itself, as in the decades prior to the revolution, the hostility of all those forces that sought to alter that state of affairs. From this point of view, then, there was an almost unbroken tradition spanning the period before and after 1848–9. On the other hand the events of the preceding months and years had radically altered relations within the Confederation. In particular the power-political antagonism between Austria and Prussia had broken out in the most acute form, an antagonism that in the years before 1848 had been bridged by close co-operation on the basis of jointly held conservative principles amounting to a regular 'system of prenotification' between Vienna and Berlin. It was now no longer the revolution alone and the activities of national, liberal and democratic forces that the great majority of the members of the Confederation saw as the crucial threat. To a scarcely lesser extent their fears centred on Prussia, which had sought to break the Confederation up and in the persons even of many of its conservative representatives such as Radowitz had entertained somewhat ambiguous relations with the revolution.

This was the atmosphere that Bismarck found in Frankfurt. Gone was the spirit of conservative solidarity of which his political associates in Berlin dreamed. The mistrust that positively leapt out at him from that quarter would probably have greeted any newly installed Prussian representative. But there is no doubt that in him it found a particularly suitable object right from the beginning. With no adequate education and no diplomatic experience whatsoever, a man who owed his rise to the revolution, of all things, even if it was as its opponent, he appeared to his colleagues as the very archetype of the upstart. To this extent he seemed to embody a Prussia that, quite without regard to the principles of its domestic policy – another respect in which it resembled Bismarck – was out to upset the traditional order in the international sphere and alter this to its advantage.

To live and let live – that was once again the watchword in Frankfurt, both literally and metaphorically. In both respects, what this called for was a recognition of the existing state of affairs complete with its conventions and its traditional pecking-order. The ease of diplomatic intercourse, the close relations between the diplomatic community and the city's middle class, the liberality of its life-style and its all-round cosmopolitanism were all rooted in that. And that was what Bismarck, however much he enjoyed life in Frankfurt among his family and friends and however unwillingly he eventually parted from the city in 1859, questioned from the very outset in two capacities: as the representative of a power that had been more or less violently coerced into such a recognition, forced back into the old order, and as himself, an over-confident diplomatic outsider who from the day of his arrival refused to let anyone impress him and who denounced as mere pretence many things that embodied and represented basic political and social attitudes.

He did this not only in the countless letters with which from the moment of his taking office he literally bombarded both his Foreign Minister and, as head of the Camarilla and 'chef de cuisine politique', Leopold von Gerlach.[5] He not infrequently demonstrated it in public as well with an uninhibited directness that further underlined the arrogance and presumption of his demeanour and strengthened the impression that, like so many outsiders and upstarts, he had an eye only for power relationships, for hierarchies – for the skeleton of human relations, in other words, rather than for its flesh and blood. An example of this was the way in which he took such pains, even in respect of ridiculous formalities, to make sure that the Austrian envoy, the 'Präsidialgesandte', should appear as no more than a *primus inter pares*; the fact that he had immediately removed his uniform jacket when the Austrian appeared in an informal suit merited, to his mind, the same repeated mention as the fact that he had promptly breached the latter's 'privilege' of smoking cigars during sessions.

For the vast majority of his fellow envoys the official business of federal politics and the contacts and problems between states that passed through Frankfurt on the whole scarcely represented a full-time job, particularly since much of it was dealt with largely by subordinates. Most of them kept a large household, liked travelling and did a great deal of it, pursued various interests, including business interests, and in short enjoyed life in a wide variety of ways. The new Prussian envoy was different. After spending the

first few months in the 'Englisches Hof', at the beginning of October he
moved out of town to what in comparison with the palace of the Austrian
envoy was a rather modest house in the Bockenheimer Landstrasse, a
matter of yards from the legation chancellery. Moreover, he showed from
the very first day that he had no intention of leading the easy life of a great
lord but meant to work with all the means and energies at his disposal for
the interests of his country. Nor was that all. He also made little secret of
the fact that he for his part regarded the majority of his colleagues – the
Saxon Nostitz, for example, or Reinhard from Württemberg, Trott from
the electorate of Hesse, or Marschall from Baden – as diplomatic drones and
'caricatures of periwigged diplomats'.[6] According to Bismarck, most of
them basked in the brilliance of their social renown and exhibited a degree
of self-importance out of all proportion to the actual power of their states
and to the significance of the decisions they reached on behalf of those
states. It was the realities of power that were crucial. And on this level the
representative of Prussia as a European great power was entitled, together
with the representative of Austria, to precedence and to priority in all
decision-making – quite without regard to any kind of seniority, to the
standing and experience of the individual diplomat, or to the figure he cut in
society.

The comparatively modest life-style imposed on him by his own financial
situation – 'my own little bit'[7] – and by the traditional parsimony of the
Prussian state, which in the fifty years of the Confederation's existence
never purchased a legation building of its own, thus received a provocative
justification: Prussia's representative had no need to parade himself with
great pomp, least of all for the benefit of people whose word carried only
minor weight in the crucial political matters of the day. Even if he had to go
about on foot, Frederick the Great had urged his envoy in London (who
was kept similarly hard up), he must never forget that an army of a hundred
thousand marched unseen behind him.

Accordingly, apart from the social duties incumbent on his office,
Bismarck cultivated a highly bourgeois, family-oriented life-style in
Frankfurt, a life-style characterized by an almost casual liberality in terms of
the comings and goings of visitors, the eating and drinking that went on
and the way in which work was mixed with pleasure – initially in the
Bockenheimer Landstrasse, where following Herbert and Marie his second
son Wilhelm was born at the beginning of August 1852, and then, when the
house changed hands less than a year later and the new owner moved in
himself, in the city from October 1852 onwards. Here in the Grosse
Gallusstrasse between the Rossmarkt and the Taunustor, where the legation
chancellery itself moved two years later, he spent the greater part of his time
in Frankfurt, until in May 1858, eight months before his recall, he and the
chancellery moved once again, this time to the Hochstrasse, which was also
in the city centre.

Bismarck's life-style in Frankfurt at the same time suited the social
inexperience, not to say shyness, of his wife Johanna, who for one thing had
great difficulty with French, which was still very much the language of the
diplomatic world. The same style remained typical of his private life even

during his years as Minister-President of Prussia and as Chancellor of the Reich. His personal contacts and dealings continued, with relatively few exceptions such as the celebrated parliamentary soirées, to be confined to a very small circle of select friends and acquaintances, a circle that, centred as it was exclusively on Bismarck, remained appallingly provincial in terms of its intellectual and human calibre.

In the Berlin of the 1870s and 1880s people had long become accustomed to the fact that the Chancellery of the Reich was anything but a centre of the intellectual or artistic life of the capital and that music, painting, science and literature played a very small part within its walls, despite the fact that the master of the house had many of the requisite qualifications as far as aptitude and earlier inclination were concerned. In Frankfurt, however, his life-style further reinforced the impression of a proudly self-assured outsider who boasted of nothing but his country's power and his own special relationships with his monarch and with his head of government. The opinions of many of his Frankfurt colleagues chimed with this impression. As the Austrian envoy Count Thun put it with polite restraint soon after Bismarck's arrival, the new Prussian envoy appeared to him 'to belong exclusively to that party that has an eye only to the specific interests of Prussia and places no great faith in what can be achieved by the Federal Diet. Having never previously been in the diplomatic service or even held public office, he has no proper knowledge of affairs and argues all matters purely in accordance with his previous parliamentary experience.'[8] The emotions and antipathies that his behaviour was capable of arousing among his diplomatic colleagues are reflected in the vehemence – unusual even in secret diplomatic communications – with which Thun's successor, Baron Prokesch von Osten, characterized him: 'Behind his occasional gentlemanliness, an arrogant, mean disposition full of swollen-headed self-conceit; with no awareness of law, lazy, lacking in sound knowledge and in respect for the same; a skilful sophist and word-twister full of petty and underhand resources; full of envy and hatred of Austria, hence also his continuous campaign against the presidential powers; a non-believer, but one who carries his Protestantism like a banner.'[9] And even Count Rechberg, the future Austrian Foreign Minister, spoke in 1855 of how 'with his petty politics and with his choice of means, in which he allows no considerations to deter him, not even those that a gentleman owes to his government as he does to himself', Bismarck had 'seriously harmed his reputation with his colleagues'.[10]

Certainly none of these verdicts – and they were backed up by a host of others – does justice either to Bismarck himself or to the kind of calculation, political perspicacity and sheer political passion, overriding all other considerations, that governed his conduct in Frankfurt. But they do serve to characterize the atmosphere in which he moved, and which he himself spread about him, and with it the background that undoubtedly influenced his behaviour and his political ideas and attitudes to a greater degree than a purely abstract exposé of the positions and problems is often prepared to concede.

This is particularly true of his relationship to Austria, now reinstated as the leading power in the German Confederation. People have often spoken in this connection of a wavering between confrontation and co-operation, of what for all its antagonisms was in many ways an ambivalent relationship. However, the immediate impression of his life and work in Frankfurt clearly contradicts this. A great deal of evidence of such wavering can certainly be adduced, evidence that was provided by Bismarck himself over a period of many years and that moreover tallies completely with his basic tactical concept of always, if possible, keeping two paths open. And undoubtedly Rechberg showed great perception when in his verdict on Bismarck delivered in 1855 he went on: 'Ambitious above all things, he has already shown on several occasions that he knows how to adapt his opinions to the circumstances. However ardent his hatred of Austria may appear today, in altered circumstances he would surely not withhold his services from a policy based on reaching an understanding with Austria.' But during his Frankfurt period it was his 'hatred of Austria' that clearly predominated – and did so, moreover, with very much the sort of emotional groundswell that one senses through Rechberg's words.

Bismarck was convinced that from the point of view of Prussia's interest as a nation and as a great power the existing situation in central Europe was intolerable 'if only because of our geographical deformity', that Prussia and Austria were here 'breathing each other's breath' and that in the long run one of them must 'yield to or be forced to yield by the other',[11] and he reiterated that conviction too often in these years for there to be any possible doubt that it was sincerely held. In fact at times he became literally entangled in it in a way that threatened to cloud his sense of reality with illusions of possibilities for which all domestic, foreign policy and military requirements were lacking. An example was when in the spring of 1859 he remarked in a letter – afterwards quoted repeatedly and often quite uncritically – to General von Alvensleben about the war then looming between the Habsburg monarchy and Sardinia-Piedmont with its French ally, the war of Italian unification: 'The current situation yet again holds the jackpot for us if we just let Austria's war with France really bite and then move south with all our armies, carrying the border posts with us in our knapsacks and banging them in again either at the Lake of Constance or wherever the Protestant confession ceases to predominate.'[12] Or when he wrote to Moritz von Blanckenburg on 12 February 1860: 'This clinging to the half-Slav, half-Romance hybrid state on the Danube, this whoring with Pope and Emperor is at least as traitorous to Prussia and the evangelical confession, indeed to Germany, as the meanest, most barren Confederation of the Rhine. The most we can lose to France is provinces, and that only for a time, but to Austria we can lose all of Prussia, now and for ever. *Less* than that Vienna is not interested in as an ultimate objective.'[13] Ludwig von Gerlach was not entirely wrong when he observed on one occasion: 'He does have a tendency to forget the world and its governance for his own notion of it.'[14]

But Bismarck made these statements at a time when a change of course in Prussian domestic policy seemed to him to have cut off all hope of his ever acquiring a substantial say in the shaping of his country's foreign policy.

This meant that the counterpoise effect of direct responsibility in one form or another was removed in those years. In the years before, however, that counterpoise had been continuously and obviously present, particularly since from the outset Bismarck regarded his envoyship as the first rung on a ladder leading to the top job in the Prussian Foreign Office; he was always as it were anticipating higher responsibilities. This is clear from his exhaustive memoranda even on matters of only peripheral formal concern to the Prussian legation in Frankfurt. As a result, this concentration on Prussia's relations with Austria into which his whole environment, right down to the minor details of social life, continually prodded him did not in the end, despite his occasional obsessions, have a narrowing effect but on the contrary revealed to him for the first time the full dimensions of his own future policy.

For one thing the constant search for constellations within which Prussia could successfully hold its ground against Austria led him finally to reject the whole idea of prior commitments, the whole concept of permanent blocs of individual states, irrespective of whether these were formed on ideological, historical, or any other grounds. And for another – and this was perhaps even more important – he added in this connection, if at first often in the purely theoretical form of diplomatic sand-table exercises, to the traditional instruments of foreign policy, including as possibilities forces and tactics that had scarcely seemed usable as such hitherto. In these two things lay the true significance of the Frankfurt years, which in terms of tangible results yielded virtually nothing. Bismarck was not unjustified in complaining repeatedly of the pointlessness of his work at the 'Danaids' water butt in the Eschenheimer Gasse'.[15] The years between 1851 and early 1859, the period Bismarck spent in Frankfurt, saw as little change in the constitution of the Confederation, the formal distribution of political weight within it and the functions it performed as it saw – at least up until 1858 – in the overall political situation in central Europe.

This was the period of victorious reaction. Movement and change came either from outside or – with mounting dramatic impact – from the social transformation that, together with its economic preconditions, increasingly constituted a sort of self-generating and unstoppable process. Anyone who for his part was looking for changes of a power-political nature that would benefit his country but had no wish to interfere with the recently re-established internal balance of power needed to turn his attention to these two spheres. This is just what Bismarck did. And the two spheres, the social and the economic, shaped and determined his politics both as to form and as to content.

A natural consequence of his position was that he was particularly concerned with whatever affected central Europe from outside in a challenging and upsetting manner. But the insights of his student days, his basic understanding of the crucial impulses governing political and social life and the orientation of his public career as originally conceived led him entirely as a matter of course to see foreign relations and foreign policy developments not in isolation but in terms of their interaction with the march of economic and social change and with the shifts in the distribution of political weight and changing constellations of interests that resulted. So it is idle to argue about which sphere, domestic affairs or foreign affairs, enjoyed priority as far as he was concerned and essentially governed his behaviour. His experience was such that both came more and more to form a single unity. Although professionally and by his own inclination his interest centred over long periods on foreign policy, he always saw it as part of so dense a web that the problem of which came first as far as he was concerned simply disappears in practice. If he did occasionally talk about foreign affairs as being for him 'an end in themselves' and as counting for 'more than the rest',[16] it was only in defending himself against the charge that foreign policy served him as a mere means to an end, in other words that domestic policy took clear precedence over it in his eyes. He never, so far as we know, claimed that the opposite was the case. Indeed we can even say that his predilection for foreign affairs, leaving aside the circumstances of his path through life for the moment, rested not least on his realization that in this sphere the individual, for all his calculations and painstaking analyses, was to a very much greater extent than in other spheres of politics placed in the position of the gambler, whose winning or losing was in the last analysis decided by unpredictable forces.

When after 1871 the questions of the internal constitution and the structuring of relationships within the newly founded Reich came to dominate the scene, he was once again, as he had been as a young man, 'bored to death'. For him this was 'poor hare-hunting'; as he exclaimed to a group of parliamentary associates in 1874, 'Ah, if it was a question of bagging a big, powerful boar – an Erymanthian boar, why not? – then I'd be with you, then I'd stir my stumps again'.[17] His whole life long it was not the implementation of a plan or the application of an idea that attracted him but the challenge and the opportunities associated with a particular situation or a particular pattern of relationships that he came up against, the risk involved in taking up such a challenge. The foregone conclusion interested him as little as the apparent non-starter, even though the former might represent the historically potent and the latter the genuine challenge. The undecided aspects of reality constituted his field. Whether in the context of the historical process they represented problems of peripheral or central importance were in his eyes abstract, philosophical questions that did not concern him or inhibit him in the slightest.

But where were such undecided aspects of reality to be found in greater number than in the sphere of foreign policy, especially in a period when the always highly unstable balance of power in Europe was continually shifting not only for political but above all for economic reasons? If for him foreign affairs counted for 'more than the rest' it was for this reason: he ultimately had his roots in personality and not in the thing itself. He thus of course brought to this a 'subterranean' element, a deeply subjective and emotional content that, when it found adherents and was even backed up by an ideology, inevitably became destructive in its effects. That is another story, part of the long story of Bismarck's indirect responsibilities, a story that through the medium of blind imitation and success-worship brings out very clearly the darker side of his being.

101

So there were incentives from many sides for Bismarck to throw himself into his new job with unusual energy and passion and himself become an engine of disturbance and change from the very beginning. This he did by seizing every available opportunity to prod power relationships within the Confederation into movement and in particular to make repeated attacks, both covert and open, on the precedence and effective hegemony of the Habsburg monarchy, claiming that these were merely dictated by the situation and questioning their permanence.

His first really big opportunity was offered by Austrian policy itself. This also provided the first demonstration of his ability to bring every single means, every single force that offered itself as it were into a common focus. It was the question of the form to be taken in future by relations between the Habsburg monarchy and the Prussian-dominated Zollverein or Customs Union.

Not least under pressure from Russia, Austria had had to be content on a federal level with a simple restoration of the *status quo ante* in the shape of the 1815 Confederation. Austria's more ambitious plans for extending the Confederation to include all its subject nations and turning it into an 'empire of seventy millions' effectively ruled from Vienna were blocked for the time being. With their main objective temporarily out of reach, Schwarzenberg and his Minister of Commerce von Bruck sought at least to push ahead with another policy introduced at the same time, namely a tariff agreement for central Europe.

Here too, however, they immediately came up against Prussian resistance. The leaders of that country, partly because they were aware of the political importance of the whole question but also with a view to the interests of a substantial section of the Prussian economy, were not prepared to make any concessions. And in the subsequent struggle for those members of the Customs Union in southern and central Germany who were vacillating for political reasons it very soon emerged that the entwinement of economic interests within the Customs Union and its members' economic dependence upon Prussia as the dominant power even in territorial and transport policy terms were already so far advanced that it had become impossible to break up this bloc in the face of resistance from Berlin. In a counter-move the Prussian government even succeeded in persuading a number of Confederation members who had hitherto been holding back, namely Hanover and a series of smaller north German states associated with Hanover in the so-called 'Steuerverein' or Tax Union, to affiliate to the Customs Union, eventually to a great extent sealing this off against Austria.

In this Prussia's hand was not a little strengthened by what was now a clearly pro-Prussian attitude on Russia's part, which helped to break down the last remaining resistance of the south German states, notably Bavaria. On this basis Berlin eventually even felt strong enough, in February 1853, to conclude a trade agreement with Austria that made great concessions to the economic interests of the monarchy, for with the political problem as such out of the way the Berlin government had no further reason to refuse a compromise in the purely economic sphere, particularly since this took account of the interests of certain branches of the economy in Prussia itself.

The negotiations on all these questions, which crucially determined relations between Prussia and Austria in the years between 1851 and 1854, indeed virtually up until 1866, and remained an essential element in the two powers' dealings with each other, were conducted either directly at government level or through the Customs Union administration or special delegations. The Prussian legation in Frankfurt was only very marginally involved. 'Most things arrive from Berlin already complete', was Bismarck's repeated complaint.[18] Indeed the main task of the legation can be said to have been to pursue a policy of appeasement and co-operation at a level at which no fundamental political decisions were up for consideration for the moment.

Neither, however, was Bismarck for a moment prepared to play second fiddle like this, simply doing the honours and embracing the 'immoderate conviviality of the Confederation's Phaeatians'.[19] Nor was he inclined to let himself be ousted, even if it was only by circumstances and by the nature of the questions under consideration, from the central process of foreign policy decision-making in which his appointment to the Frankfurt post, to what he had supposed to be 'currently the most important post in our diplomatic service', had promised to involve him. While many of his Frankfurt colleagues in what he scathingly referred to as 'the stock-pile of notabilities that goes by the name of Federal Assembly'[20] were perfectly happy to be rather out of things, he forcibly insisted on being consulted or at any rate listened to.

For those immediately concerned this undoubtedly looked a great deal like importunity. Even we, looking back, would surely do well to be quite clear in our minds, as we read the many letters and memoranda from those years, about the situation in which they were written. For all the professional competence that Bismarck acquired in an astonishingly short space of time, his job and what he took to be his job still parted company in many areas. This meant that, over and over again, Bismarck was arguing from a position of knowing that even his own government regarded him as an intriguing and irritating outsider.

This was particularly true of the discussions regarding Austria's projected tariff agreement and the continued existence of the Customs Union, discussions in which he immediately attempted to intervene. He found his way straight to the heart of the matter, quickly isolating the crucial points, unfolded a whole series of extremely clear-sighted suggestions and bold tactical concepts, and repeatedly set everything in the wider contexts of German and European politics. Nevertheless, the impression was inescapable that the new man obviously saw himself not so much as an envoy in the usual sense, an official who was bound by strict instructions and obliged to refer even matters of detail back to the Foreign Office, but more as a kind of junior partner to the Foreign Minister who in accord with the latter or if necessary even over his head sought to pursue a broadly based plan of his own.

The tariff question was in fact the business of the Federal Diet to the extent that in July 1851 the majority had appointed a commercial policy committee that, after co-opting experts in the persons of officials from the ministries of the individual states, was to re-examine and if necessary revise the proposals worked out at the Dresden conferences. But it was clear from the outset that the Prussian government was in no way prepared to deal with the question at this level, even though it dispatched to Frankfurt its best man in this field, namely Rudolf Delbrück, who at the age of only 31 had been placed in charge of the relevant department at the Ministry of Commerce in 1848. Delbrück's chief task was presumably to keep the whole affair on a tight rein and to make sure it did not develop into a federal issue, as the Austrians wanted.

The intention of his Berlin masters, therefore, was that Bismarck should on this point, although formally the superior and enjoying 'consultative' status, take his lead entirely from Delbrück and for the rest remain right in the background. This he did only outwardly, however, in fact availing himself of every opportunity actively to intervene and to bring his own views and indeed his own person to bear. If in terms of substance little more than nuances were involved here, these were nevertheless highly indicative of Bismarck's position. But it was above all in his pursuit of them that he was soon showing a greater degree of independence than could possibly be welcome to his Minister-President and Foreign Minister, Otto von Manteuffel.

This was foreshadowed as early as the autumn of 1851, when the agreement with the Steuerverein necessitated the premature cancellation and re-negotiation of the Customs Union treaties, which were not actually due for renewal until 1853. Looked at objectively, this was the prelude to the great struggle for the control of economic policy in central Europe and hence for political hegemony in the region, a struggle that was to culminate in the war of 1866. But there is reason to doubt whether the Manteuffel government saw its own policy on that level and whether its individual measures were dictated by grand political calculations aimed accordingly. On the contrary, the principle behind it was much more one of retreat from the far-reaching plans and objectives of Radowitz's Union policy and a restoration of the *status quo ante* on the foreign affairs front too, not least in order to forestall Austrian plans that called it in question. So what looked like an offensive move on Prussia's part, namely the consolidation of the area covered by the Customs Union in the north, was in reality a defensive move, a preventive measure against the expansionist policy that Austria was continuing to pursue in this field. Indeed it was possibly an attempt to prepare for the not entirely unlikely event of a withdrawal by the south German states by creating a fresh basis for its economic policy, a smaller but more compact one.

But whatever elements of timid or at least over-cautious retreat may have been present in that policy initially, elements that subsequent developments obscured almost entirely, Bismarck at any rate sought from the outset to give it a quite different interpretation and push it in a quite different direction, urging that the possibilities contained within it should be exploited to the full. Accordingly he immediately hailed the treaty signed with Hanover on 7 September 1851 as a major coup, heralding a new phase of Prussia's policy as a great power. All measures and all political considerations must now be harnessed in the service of that policy.

This fell like a spotlight on a question that was being discussed rather in the sidelines, the question of what attitude Prussia should take to the counter-revolutionary revision of the Hanoverian constitution for which the Hanoverian knights had applied to the Federal Diet, there being reason to fear that such a revision would bring to power in Hanover a government leaning more strongly towards Austria. The inherent conflict between a politics of principle and a politics of national self-interest was imperiously swept aside by Bismarck: 'Hanoverian law is of less account to me than Prussian law, and in the last resort I shall drop the knights for the treaty of 7 September', he wrote to Manteuffel early in October 1851.[21] Six days later he made himself even clearer: 'However uncompromising my aversion to sacrificing the law to politics in my own country, I possess sufficient Prussian egoism not to observe the same degree of scruple with regard to Hanoverian law, and were Your Excellency to ask for my opinion I would humbly suggest that he should support in Hanover only such a ministry as would be prepared to fall in with our policy as embodied in the treaty of 7 September, whatever its political colour.'[22]

This was the basis on which at the end of November 1851 he conducted that justly celebrated conversation with the Austrian envoy to the Federal Diet, Count Thun, an elegant Epicurean from a prosperous family of 'imperial counts'; five years older than his Prussian colleague, as a successful career diplomat and as 'presidential envoy' he set the tone in Frankfurt in many respects. During the course of that conversation, in parrying Austrian objectives Bismarck very clearly elucidated his own attitude and basic approach. Whether the conversation went quite as he described in his report to Manteuffel is open to question; we lack the other side of the picture, Thun not having sent Vienna a report of his own. So we must allow for the fact that Bismarck may have put some things in rather milder but others in even sharper terms than he saw fit to pass on to Manteuffel.[23]

Bismarck's opinion of the nature and direction of Schwarzenberg's policy, of which he took Count Thun to be an advocate, had been clear from the beginning. It was 'never to be expected of Austrian statesmen of the Schwarzenberg school', he had written in his first unofficial report to Manteuffel only a fortnight after his arrival in Frankfurt, 'that they will adopt or observe the law as the basis of their policy for the sole reason that it is the law; their attitude appears to be more that of a brazen-faced gambler who seizes his opportunities, seeks in exploiting them at the same time to feed his personal vanity and to this end drapes himself in the jauntily disdainful negligence of a fashionable gentleman of the more frivolous school'.[24]

The moralizing undertone need not be taken too seriously. Its purpose was to draw a sharp distinction between Schwarzenberg's politics of power and self-interest and what was alleged to have been Austria's politics of law and of principle in the period up until 1848, which the Gerlachs and their circle saw as the basis for the future co-operation between Prussia and

Austria that he, Bismarck, was to promote. It was his way of trying to justify why he immediately adopted an anti-Austrian stance; significantly, in his conversation with Thun he took up the charge that Prussia rather than Austria was behaving like a gambler not at all in an indignant fashion but as constituting in some ways an apt comparison. What he objected to above all was Thun's attempt to disguise what to him, Bismarck, was the quite unambiguous character and direction of Austrian policy under Schwarzenberg and to brand Prussia as the troublesome intruder upon a harmonious development in central Europe grounded in nature and history.

Asked about 'Austria's aggressive policy towards the Customs Union', Thun replied, according to Bismarck, that Austria could not tolerate being 'excluded, even more brusquely than it had been previously from the Customs Union, from a fresh body embracing the whole of the rest of Germany'. For this reason the Austrian government aspired not only to closer links with the Customs Union but also to an extension of the powers of the Confederation in the field of tariff and trade legislation, in other words to a strengthening and consolidation of the Confederation. This of course meant a consolidation, indeed an enhancement of the hegemony of the Habsburg monarchy in central Europe. Since, however, this was in conformity with historical evolution and with the circumstances arising out of that evolution it was quite all right: 'A predominant Austrian influence in Germany was in the nature of things, he said, provided that Austria devoted itself to Germany without self-seeking; were it to violate this last condition, Prussia would take Austria's place, but if it respected that condition the task of Prussia lay in a similar dedication, jointly with Austria, to the interests of the whole.'

The words reflected the self-assurance of the representative of an ancient great power that had repeatedly dominated this part of the world and had just prevailed yet again over the newly emergent rival minor power. At the same time, however, there also rang through them a readiness to agree on a different level than appeared to be attainable on the basis of the selfish power interests of the individual state. In this there was an echo of the old imperial idea as there was of the idea of the unity of the nation in its specific historical form. And there was no mistaking, even in Bismarck's report, the appeal to the effect that states must serve higher ends than the mere consolidation and extension of their own power.

For Bismarck, however, these were just phrases, forms of words designed to obscure the true core of conflict on the power-political front: 'He spoke like Posa [the grandiloquent marquis in Schiller's play, *Don Carlos*]', Bismarck summed up, 'and exhibited Greater German zealotry.' He went on ironically: 'To complete his train of thought I pointed out that the existence of Prussia and further of the Reformation constituted a regrettable fact but one we were both powerless to alter; we must reckon with facts, not with ideals.' He also told him that 'a Prussia that, as he put it, "renounced the inheritance of Frederick the Great" in order to be able to dedicate itself to its true destiny as Lord High Chamberlain to the Emperor did not exist in Europe, and before I sent home a recommendation for such a policy the issue would have to be decided by the sword'.

Thun, of whom even in later years Bismarck often said sarcastically that 'deep down' he regarded 'the existence of Prussia as an irregularity',[25] then proceeded to liken Prussia to a man 'who, having *once* won the hundred-thousand-taler jackpot, now bases his budget on a yearly repetition of that event'. This was tantamount to saying that Prussia owed its present position of power largely to a fortunate concatenation of circumstances. Many people in Europe shared this opinion, particularly among the older-established great powers. It would soon lose its power again if it started to retrace Frederick the Great's steps with a policy of 'all or nothing'. Such a policy may have made Prussia great, but even on that occasion it had only narrowly escaped disaster.

Even in Prussia itself there were many who thought like this. Granted, Prussia's power was now much more firmly grounded than it had been in the eighteenth century under Frederick, partly as a result of territorial acquisitions, notably that of the Rhineland, and not least in consequence of economic developments; in the period between Frederick's death in 1786 and 1850 the national income had increased almost fivefold, whereas that of the Habsburg monarchy, for example, had risen by no more than about two and a half times – with a simultaneous sharp increase in the national debt. The revolution had shown, however, that in spite of this the power of the state rested on most uncertain foundations at home. For this reason Prussia's room for manoeuvre seemed very much more restricted than many were inclined to believe, considering the matter from a more mechanical, statistical point of view by counting heads and square kilometres and calculating economic power. The room for manoeuvre, at any rate, that was available to a policy of which the prime objective was the preservation of the established political and social order in Prussia itself.

This was the position adopted by those conservatives in the government and in the circle around the Prussian king who largely for this reason had opposed Radowitz's Union plans and taken the path that led to Olmütz, in other words the same conservatives as had sent Bismarck to Frankfurt in order to reach a settlement with Austria in spite of an apparent redistribution of political weight that needed to be taken into account. Bismarck, however, thought quite differently, and he took the opportunity to make this clear to Manteuffel as well, whom he saw as proceeding along the right lines with the September treaty and with the repulsion of Austrian advances in the field of tariff and trade policy. He reported having replied to Thun that 'if these views were as clear in Vienna as they were with him, I must say that I foresaw Prussia's having to rely on the aforesaid lottery once again; whether it won or not was in the hands of God'. He went on to say that the whole conversation had been 'conducted in a rather jocular tone' and had never lost the 'character of objective friendly consideration'. But it had 'fortified [him] in the conviction', Bismarck added, clearly revealing his own political line, 'that Austria must experience the importance of our alliance or our aversion before it will understand the value of it or act on that understanding'.

In other words, between Prussia and Austria as two European great powers there could be relations only at a European level. A commitment to what would nowadays be called a multi-polar regional alliance was in contradiction to the interests of both as great powers unless it implied the clear subordination of one to the other. That kind of subordination, however, was conceivable only if one of the two were voluntarily or involuntarily to withdraw from the circle of the great powers.

On sober consideration, therefore, the only policy open to Bismarck was one of strict demarcation in the sense of a separation and eventual mutual recognition of the two countries' spheres of influence. The problem of what form the relationship between the two powers should then take lay in the far distant future. There is a good deal of evidence, however, to suggest that Bismarck was already thinking in terms of a kind of condominium covering central Europe, a special alliance that if necessary would even be equal to the combined pressure of Russia and France on its flanks.

This kind of perspective had the effect then and later of confusing many people and causing them to speculate wildly about Bismarck's ultimate objectives. Initially, however, the struggle to demarcate the respective spheres of influence was absolutely central as far as he was concerned. That struggle was inevitably the more bitter and goaded a wider variety of enemies into action for the fact that the price of a favourable outcome for Prussia was the destruction of a wealth of traditional relationships and commitments. In pursuing that struggle Bismarck was determined to use every means, including trickery and violence, and to mobilize every force, even those that might one day make a sorcerer's apprentice of him.

This was the nucleus of his policy. For this he pleaded and fought for the next twenty years, sticking to it with the utmost tenacity. It is this alone that lends a deeper meaning to the bewildering diversity of his individual moves and places them in their proper context. His objective, from whichever angle we look at it, was first the division of eastern and eastern-central Europe between Prussia and Austria – as far as possible, of course, in Prussia's favour. This meant the destruction of what was left of the Old Empire, the destruction of the German Confederation, but also a decisive rejection of the idea of a German nation to be united politically, at least in so far as that idea implied anything more than a pattern for changing the map of central Europe, in other words a means to an end.

At the beginning of the 1880s, when the division of spheres of influence between Austria-Hungary and Prussia-Germany had long been a *fait accompli* and had provided the basis for a new and close alliance, Bismarck had the documents of his Frankfurt period published virtually in their entirety.[26] He wanted to prove to the many people who doubted it how straightforward his policy had been from the beginning and how directly, in spite of all the detours dictated by circumstances, he had pursued his objective. In essence he was certainly right, but even though he often gave quite unvarnished expression to his intentions in those years the inner core of those intentions undoubtedly remained hidden at the time from the overwhelming majority even of informed contemporaries.

For one thing this was because open statement of his objectives came across as a particularly skilful camouflaging of what he was really after: 'I played my cards straight', he said once, describing his tactics in retrospect. 'Against supposed cunning I set stark truth. It is not my fault that people often did not believe me and subsequently felt most offended and disappointed.'[27] But it was also due to the fact that the true context was revealed only to the very few simply because of the information that was available at any one time. Here the historian, like the reader of those documents published in the 1880s, finds himself in a situation that is often taken far too much for granted: that of knowing not only more than virtually every contemporary but even more than the principal actor himself. Because of course the latter could never be sure how long he would be able to stick to his goal with a calculable chance of success.

So however clearly the line appears in retrospect to have been drawn, the problem of keeping open a quite different course was still there for someone who, though prepared to take every risk to get his way, was not prepared to commit political suicide for what he ultimately realized was a lost cause. Here too what he really wanted depended upon the circumstances, upon the given and of course continually changing possibilities. The clear line of his policy was in this context the clear line of what from the standpoint of the Prussian national interest were the possibilities available at any one time. To that extent it neither possessed a binding principle nor did it rest on clearly defined, limited and consequently calculable objective goals. Instead, despite all its clarity in retrospect, for contemporaries it was in the true sense of the word incalculable. This explains why the man who, as the documents appear to show, steered so unequivocal a course during those years should at the same time have laid himself increasingly open to suspicion, not only with regard to his methods but also with regard to his ultimate policy objectives.

This was already manifest on the occasion of his first full-scale political mission when in the summer of 1852, at the climax of the dispute about tariff policy, he was sent to Vienna. In March of that year he had further consolidated his reputation of being one of the fiercest and most implacable opponents not only of the revolution but of any form of political liberalization or democratization in a speech – much heeded even outside Prussia – in the Lower House of the Prussian Diet, to which after resigning his seat in the autumn of 1851, as required by law, he had been re-elected in his old constituency with a large majority. His chance had come in a debate about a small increase in the defence budget, a debate of which the opposition took advantage to demand a further middle-class leavening of the officer corps and at the same time a strengthening of the middle-class reserve army, the Landwehr. In this debate Bismarck had once again taken up his old bone of contention with the liberals as to whether, unlike in the years after 1806 in which the main features of the Prussian army constitution had been laid down, there was now a gulf between government and people, between state and society. Again he had denied this emphatically, as he had in 1847, and warned against mistaking the 'population of the big cities', which in many instances allowed itself to be led by 'ambitious and deceitful demagogues', for the 'true Prussian people':

'the latter will know', he had said threateningly, 'how to bring the big cities to heel, should they rise up once again, even if it means obliterating them from the face of the earth'.[28]

The speech had made clear that although he was now a diplomat his basic political stance had lost none of its definition. He was still the man of the arch-conservative Gerlach brothers and their circle, the extreme right-wing group that was now largely in command of the king. The fact that after the debate, which had been marked by a certain amount of personal bitterness, Bismarck had been challenged to a duel by Baron von Vincke, one of the leaders of the liberal opposition since the time of the United Diet, served only to heighten this impression. So that when shortly after this Prince Schwarzenberg, the real advocate of a new kind of great power role for Austria, quite unexpectedly died on 5 April 1852 at the age of only 51 and both the Camarilla and the king himself felt that the time had come for a fresh Prussian initiative in favour of compromise and a policy of conservative solidarity, Bismarck very naturally seemed to them to be the right man to launch such a move.

Frederick William IV summoned him to Potsdam at the end of May 1852 and said he wished to send him on a special mission to Vienna as official stand-in for the ailing Prussian ambassador, Count Arnim, whom he had been nominated to succeed. He gave Bismarck a personal letter to Emperor Francis Joseph, written in his own hand and describing his special ambassador as a man 'who here in Prussia is hailed by many and hated by some for his knightly and unconstrained obedience and his implacable hostility even to the very roots of the revolution'. The Prussian king went on to say that Bismarck enjoyed his unreserved confidence extending to and indeed with particular regard to the treatment of the problems currently at issue between Prussia and Austria. Those problems ought, Frederick William added, to be treated in the light of his 'unchanging, urgent hope', which had received a boost from the recent visit of the tsar, 'that Your Majesty and I are wholly at one in the truth that our triple, steadfast, devout, and vigorous concord is the *one thing* capable of saving Europe and our mischievous and yet so beloved German fatherland from the present crisis'.[29]

This invocation of the spirit of the Holy Alliance of 1815 and hence of the tenor of Prussian-Austrian relations in the decades preceding the revolution undoubtedly corresponded to the king's innermost conviction. 'In Germany', he had written to the English prince consort a matter of months before the revolution of 1848, 'it is only the existence of the Confederation, Austria and Prussia that keeps the wild animal' – the 'tyranny of parties' and the revolution – 'grinning behind bars.'[30] Bismarck was quite clear about what was expected of him. 'I understood my mission', he wrote to Manteuffel shortly after its completion, 'as being more or less to organize relations between the two Cabinets in as friendly a manner as possible without giving any ground on the tariff question, without creating unnecessary tensions and without allowing the importance of the tariff question and the divergence of opinions on the same to grow any more than necessary and begin to influence other questions as well as relations in general between our two powers.'[31]

But can he really have wanted seriously to conduct such a mission with the firm intention of succeeding in it when for the last year he had been warning his Foreign Minister on every conceivable occasion against making any concessions to a power that was after much more than a restoration of pre-1848 conditions and was so obviously seeking to push Prussia to the wall on the international stage, in the German Confederation and over commercial policy?

What made Bismarck feel obliged once again to lay before Manteuffel his conception of the nature and purpose of his mission was some information he claimed to have received from Hermann Wagener, the editor-in-chief of the *Kreuzzeitung*, to the effect that 'the rumour is being very deliberately put about in Berlin that I did not properly understand my mission in Vienna or even that I exceeded my instructions'.[32] Such a view did in fact exist. Moreover Bismarck knew exactly where it was held: on the one hand in the circle around the king's brother, the Prince of Prussia, where the 'shame' of Olmütz was still keenly felt, and on the other hand at the Foreign Ministry itself, where Manteuffel had followed with steadily increasing mistrust the actions of an envoy who so obviously enjoyed the confidence of the king and the Camarilla and whose plans and activities manifested an independence that was difficult for one trained in the bureaucratic concept of a hierarchy of command to swallow. Both sides found themselves united, following the Vienna mission, in the suspicion that Bismarck had made more concessions to the Austrians in accordance with the policy of conservative principle and solidarity pursued by his political patrons than were compatible with the Prussian national interest. At the very least, they felt, he had sought to take certain steps in this direction and prepare the ground for others.

The suspicion that he had committed 'Haugwitzisms'[33] was one that Bismarck, despite intense efforts directed mainly at the Prince of Prussia, the potential successor to the throne, never really succeeded in eradicating. The episode shows how the two camps ultimately saw him, namely as an out-and-out careerist for whom the different positions on this question were merely means to an end and who backed now one and now another, depending on whom he was talking to and which he ascribed greater weight to at the time. Manteuffel in particular was convinced after the Viennese interlude that Bismarck was simply looking for a favourable opportunity of forcing him out of office and that he subordinated everything to this objective. He felt very much strengthened in this conviction by the extremely lively public discussion that ensued. This culminated in a series of articles by Wagener in the *Kreuzzeitung* – which was promptly seized as a result – in which the government, that is to say Manteuffel himself, was accused of excessive softness towards Austria, an accusation that Manteuffel inevitably saw as nothing but a relief attack for Bismarck's benefit and an attempt to put the latter into power by hook or by crook.

The true picture was very much more complicated. Even in his memoirs, written more than forty years later, Bismarck stressed in connection with his description of the Viennese mission and its consequences that he had never seriously aspired to ministerial office under Frederick William IV.[34] This had been because of his conviction that he 'would not, as minister, achieve what I would regard as a *tenable* ministerial position vis-à-vis the King'. In addition to a series of reasons bearing on the person of the king and on his special relationship with him, he also mentioned a material argument: it had been clear to him 'that the objectives of Prussian foreign policy as I envisaged them did not wholly coincide with those of the King'. However much Bismarck tended virtually throughout his memoirs to adjust the facts and his own and others' opinions to the way in which he wished to have developments viewed in retrospect, we can largely go along with him as far as this argument is concerned, particularly since it is corroborated by contemporary accounts.[35] He was alluding here to the situation that continued at least until 1871 to characterize the foreign policy contemplated by and, depending on the circumstances, also pursued by him: that foreign policy largely lacked a domestic base. This repeatedly forced him into dare-devil manoeuvres that not infrequently called his credibility very seriously in question. The Viennese interlude already made this very clear.

The positions occupied by the Prussian king, the Camarilla and Manteuffel on the one hand and by Prince William and his circle on the other were in fact by no means so far apart as outwardly appeared to be the case. They might very well have come to agree on a common policy, particularly following the death of Schwarzenberg. After all, under the effect of the revolution and of the failure of the Union policy both sides were in a defensive posture. A modified restoration of pre-1848 conditions inevitably appeared thoroughly acceptable to them.

Not, however, to Bismarck. He always saw the rejection of Schwarzenberg's plans and Prussia's whole policy towards Austria at the same time from the angle of a possible large-scale Prussian counter-offensive, a reversal of the Schwarzenberg approach in Prussian terms. But it seemed at first that there was no one in Prussia who could be won round to this, at least not in the conservative camp. So for the moment Bismarck had no alternative but to try at all events to keep the way open for such an offensive and in the mean time look around for allies.

Keeping the way open for a future offensive meant for a start, in terms of his narrower sphere of influence, that the Confederation must be kept as insignificant as possible – as a matter of principle, not simply until such time as, for example, the question of more adequate Prussian participation in its leadership was settled. There was 'nothing to be done' with the Confederation, he stated quite openly to Leopold von Gerlach as early as the beginning of December 1851: 'The only way of achieving anything in Germany is through associations within the Confederation, the Customs Union, the military convention, and so on.' And to Ludwig von Gerlach he wrote eighteen months later that the Confederation would never become 'anything other than an insurance (and a poor one) against war and revolution'.[36]

Accordingly he spent years waging a bitter campaign in the Federal Diet, not infrequently over quite ludicrous details and matters of form, guided only by one stubbornly held objective: never to let it provide a viable basis for an Austrian policy of hegemony in central Europe. As he put it himself in a letter to Manteuffel in March 1858, 'My period of office here, nearly seven years of it, has . . . been one continuous struggle against encroachments of all kinds, against the incessant attempts that have been made to exploit the Confederation as an instrument for the exaltation of Austria and the diminution of Prussia.'[37]

In the majority of cases he had been in complete agreement with his minister in point of substance. But the longer-term view was only poorly developed in Manteuffel, to say nothing of the far-reaching plans that it implied. This emerged less clearly in the field of federal policy, where thanks not least to Bismarck's constant obstructionism things were soon at a complete standstill, than in the questions of European policy then up for discussion and decision. The Frankfurt envoy put his oar in here to an ever-increasing extent, aware that after the failure of the Union policy and the immobilization of the Confederation this was the only area in which a way might be opened up for a fresh power-political offensive on Prussia's part.

His first opportunity of becoming personally and materially involved in this respect came with the final settlement of the Schleswig-Holstein question. This was one of those problems in relation to which the discussion about revolution and the right to self-determination clashed most obviously with the competing power interests of the different states; in other words, here the limits of a policy of principle and solidarity became very clear, both on the conservative and on the liberal side. It is no accident, therefore, that it later became not only a pivotal point but in a sense also a culmination of Bismarck's foreign policy.

At first sight the whole question seemed from the standpoint of current Prussian policy to be no more than an awkward legacy from the revolution, to be dealt with as quickly and unobtrusively as possible. The fact that the Prussian king and the Prussian army had in 1848, acting on behalf of the Frankfurt National Assembly, provided military assistance for the inhabitants of Schleswig-Holstein and their provincial government in their efforts to leave the Danish Federation was one that nobody in present-day Berlin was anxious to recall. Nor, of course, had the Prussians any wish to be reminded that in the summer of 1848, very much under pressure from the other European great powers, they had had to sign the Malmö armistice with Denmark, for it had been very like a capitulation; Britain and Russia in particular had been interested in ensuring that the 'Baltic Bosphorus' did not fall into the hands of another great power. Prussia had then gone to war with Denmark once again in the context of its Union policy. The end product, however, had been yet another diplomatic defeat, sealed in the Berlin peace treaty of July 1850; like Olmütz shortly afterwards, this was arrived at very much under pressure from an increasingly dominant tsardom.

Another chapter Berlin now wished to forget as quickly as possible was the one entitled 'Prussian national power politics in alliance with moderate liberalism'. This was not so easy, however, because in the mean time the

113

German Confederation had also intervened, at the request of the Danish king, and the European great powers had sought for their part to get a settlement accepted that bound all parties and looked like being capable of preventing a fresh outbreak of the conflict. The result had been the so-called 'London Protocol' of 1850. In this Russia, Britain and France had recognized the Danish king's sovereignty over the duchies and empowered the childless Frederick VII to regulate the succession in such a way as to guarantee the long-term integrity of the Danish state as a whole.

Simply to agree to this was more than Berlin – and especially Frederick William IV, who had only recently been so heavily committed – felt able to do. In order to save face at least to a degree Prussia demanded that a decision should first be made regarding the hereditary claims of Duke Christian August von Augustenburg, the man who stood closest to the Danish throne. Even Prussia conceded that Christian August's open support for the secessionist movement in the duchies in 1848 had rendered him as intolerable to the great powers as to Denmark itself. Nevertheless, the Berlin government inisisted that the duke be suitably compensated for his renunciation of the succession to the throne and of his possessions. Only then could it approve a final settlement. After a meeting between the Prussian king, the tsar and the Austrian emperor in May 1851 had in principle sorted out the succession in favour of the Russo-Danish candidate Prince Christian von Glücksburg, the care of Augustenburg's interests was entrusted to the Prussian envoy to the Federal Diet.

For Bismarck, therefore, it was a European policy question from the outset, and his efforts were immediately directed towards keeping the whole thing at this level and preventing the Confederation from becoming, on this issue, an independent factor in that policy. This could very easily have happened, given that legally, historically and materially the Schleswig-Holstein problem was in certain essential points a federal matter and Prussia and Austria were officially acting in Holstein as agents of the Confederation. There was also the fact that, with the Confederation now so clearly dominated by Austria, Vienna was inevitably interested in bringing it back into play at the European level and trying by this means as well to push Prussia even further into the background.

At first – and this shows how completely the policy not only of Manteuffel but also of the king and the Camarilla lacked an overall conception – this wider context was obviously not appreciated in Berlin. After Bismarck had in long and skilfully conducted negotiations persuaded Augustenburg to renounce his claims in return for a large financial indemnity and had thus removed the last obstacle to a final settlement of the question, he was instructed early in April 1852 to sound out what the chances of success might be for a Prussian initiative to involve the Confederation directly in the agreements that had now formally to be entered into. Berlin obviously thought that, with the actual decisions already made, such a move could only be interpreted as a gesture of goodwill on Prussia's part in being prepared to go back to the pre-1848 system of prior consultation between the two great powers in Germany on all matters of importance. Furthermore, it was felt in Berlin that the

114

responsibility for what to the German people were very unpopular decisions could in this way be shifted on to the Confederation.

But that was just what the members of the Confederation who had not up to now been directly involved in decisions on this question wanted at all costs to avoid, for reasons connected with their own domestic policies. This enabled Bismarck to support his flat rejection of such a move with the argument that it had no practical chance of succeeding, although in his private letters to Manteuffel he made no secret of the fact that the whole plan appeared to him to be based on an entirely false assessment of the situation and of Prussian interests. Such a move, he said, would play straight into the hands of Schwarzenberg's policy, the whole tendency of which was inevitably to see it 'as a goal that, if not attainable, was nevertheless to be aimed at . . . to absorb Prussia's external activity in that of the Confederation and to develop more and more the representation of the latter by the presidential power'. He went on, looking even farther ahead: 'The entry of the whole Austrian Empire into the Confederation would provide a basis and tariff unification at least a building-site for this system, and I have repeatedly had occasion, both in private conversation and in official proceedings, to convince myself that the presidency would welcome every opportunity of involving the Confederation in diplomatic negotiations as a single, integrated power.'[38]

Bismarck did concede in his letter, which was dated 6–7 April 1852, that following Schwarzenberg's death this 'system' might change. He even referred to such a change as being 'likely'. But he saw no reason for Prussia on that account to offer risky concessions in advance. Moreover, he sought to intercept the whole question by stating his conviction that it would take more than the 'united action of Prussia and Austria . . . to dispose the Federal Assembly to accede without reservation to the stipulations proposed and elect a delegate to implement them'.

Since the Austrian envoy Count Thun shared this opinion the question was effectively shelved for the time being, and in any case the attention of Vienna was wholly concentrated on forming a new government and no one was pressing for the opportunity to be exploited in the direction outlined by Bismarck. Together with the representatives of Russia, Britain, France, Austria, Sweden and Denmark, the Prussian envoy in London, Baron von Bunsen, put his signature to the 'Second London Protocol' on 8 May 1852. This once again recognized the unassailable integrity of the Danish state as a whole and awarded the succession to Christian von Glücksburg, whom the Germans scornfully referred to henceforth as the 'Protocol Prince'.

Even after the signing of the London Protocol the question of the Confederation's acceding to that agreement cropped up repeatedly, not least in connection with the problem of providing more effective protection for the people of Schleswig–Holstein, who were coming increasingly to feel treated by the Danes as second-class citizens. But although the Prussian king was prepared to consider such appeals for help and accordingly to make concessions on the question of federal involvement, his envoy in Frankfurt resolutely insisted on grounds of general policy that the Confederation must at all events be kept out of it. Moreover, he succeeded again and again in getting his way. Consequently Prussia, although the Schleswig-Holstein question provided a particularly vivid illustration of the collapse of its power, did in the end manage at least to uphold its claim to act independently of the Confederation and make decisions as a European great power.

It was not an enormous achievement, particularly since in substance it was associated with a total surrender. But it did very clearly show the drift of all Bismarck's political endeavours at this time, namely to win back for Prussian policy the greatest possible degree of autonomy and to shed all commitments that threatened to inhibit this or at least keep them at bay as far as possible. As he wrote to Leopold von Gerlach towards the end of 1852 in an attempt to make this palatable to his mentor, if the 'ultimately essential understanding between two great powers', Austria and Prussia, 'in *European* politics' was to be achieved, care must be taken that the 'threads' of such an understanding, which could not be spun from Frankfurt but 'only between Vienna and Berlin direct, from Cabinet to Cabinet . . . remain if possible untouched but at any rate unruptured by our domestic quarrel over *German* politics.' He went on ambiguously: 'Regarding the great and noble ideas of our most gracious Lord, Vienna will continue to be unreceptive as long as it does not once again find itself in deep water, and therefore our and Austria's German policies necessarily remain incommensurable. The advantage we achieve is that the consequences of our marital tiffs do not make themselves felt beyond the frontiers of Germany.'[39]

What he was saying was that in German politics there was no pursuing a joint course; the Confederation no longer provided a firm enough basis, and entirely new solutions must be found. In European politics, on the other hand, it *was* possible to make common cause, indeed it was still desirable to do so. And it might even be – the idea suggested itself and was without any doubt deliberately suggested by Bismarck – that this would lead to a solution of the problems facing central Europe. In other words, the policy of conservative solidarity to which the Gerlachs and their circle were so attached must as it were be pursued at the appropriate level, the level of the European great powers, far from the distractions and pettinesses of German politics. Only here, Bismarck suggested, was serious headway to be made, and his task was as it were to secure the rear for this kind of wider European policy by doing everything in his power to extricate it from all German entanglements.

There were few instances in which the ambiguity of Bismarck's foreign policy in these years and the way in which it was dictated by the situation found more vivid illustration than they did here. For in reality he was already looking only for an opportunity of playing the European card against Austria and outmanoeuvring the empire on that basis. It was not a shift in the level of the policy of conservative solidarity that constituted his true objective but the internationalization of the German conflict. It was at the international level, in the context of a change in the European balance of power, that he saw the best chance of that conflict being resolved in a way that would benefit Prussia.

Twice in the following years, in the Crimean War and in the Italian War, he thought he saw emerging just such a fundamental change in the European balance of power as favoured Prussia and its interests in central Europe. And on both occasions he did everything he could to move Prussian policy in the direction of exploiting that process of change – quite without regard to immediate political objectives and short-term interests but also without any misgivings about destroying at the same time a balance of power that favoured counter-revolutionary efforts in Europe. On neither occasion did he succeed. On the contrary, he enormously increased the number of his political enemies and was almost universally regarded as having largely wrecked any prospect of his ever being able to exert a decisive influence on Prussian foreign policy. His reputation of being not only a reactionary but at the same time an unprincipled gambler, a man with no sense of proportion and even perhaps with no tangible objective, received a powerful boost. At the same time the experience put him through the hard school of the outsider, forced by failure and frustration repeatedly to rethink and reassess his own plans but also to re-examine his own alliances on the domestic front.

What he proposed was again a Prussian power policy in which the element of risk was carefully calculated, in other words not at all the kind of gamble that Thun and with him many contemporaries accused him of perpetrating. Nevertheless, it is obvious that in view of the precariousness of his political existence, in view of the growing numbers of his political opponents and in view of his all-out determination to get his way he was even more inclined now than in later years to count as 'risk' only the danger of failure in the most immediate sense and to leave the question of the longer-term consequences of specific decisions and actions largely out of account. It was no accident, therefore, beyond the fact that his role during those years was essentially that of proposer and adviser rather than that of direct protagonist, that he got caught up at the time in the fiercest and most fundamental clashes regarding the nature and dangers of such a policy and was forced once again to define his precise standpoint.

That the wider European development he was counting on would not be long in showing itself was something of which Bismarck – unlike many of his conservative friends, who were hoping that things would progressively calm down on the foreign policy front as well – was convinced almost from the outset. Superficially the world of the 1815 treaties had in European terms too been largely restored after 1850. But with the possible exception of Britain there was scarcely a European great power that did not aspire to escape from its confines. In the case of France, on whose back the 1815 treaty structure had after all been erected, that aspiration was notorious. Louis Napoleon's coup of December 1851 was inevitably seen by the other powers as a beacon heralding an imminent fresh attempt by the French to shatter that structure. But Russia, too, the continent's other flanking power whose triumphant westward advance had been so unequivocally brought to a halt in 1815 but which had meanwhile achieved a position of steadily increasing dominance in central and eastern Europe as an embodiment of counter-revolution, could be expected to launch a fresh initiative if not to abolish at least to make important changes to the 1815 system in accordance with the new balance of power. Finally, as far as the two central European great powers were concerned they had both made it perfectly clear – Prussia with its Union plan, Austria with the Bruck-Schwarzenberg project for an 'empire of seventy millions' – that they too saw the *status quo ante* as a second-best solution.

So for every clear-sighted observer of the European scene there was really only one question: given that all the powers were in one way or another interested in a conflict, where was it going to break out? Once it had become clear that the new Napoleon was at first concentrating entirely on consolidating his position at home, most eyes turned towards Russia. Because in central Europe, in the aftermath of Schwarzenberg's death, a fresh Austrian venture was hardly to be expected for the time being; and Prussia seemed after its recent defeats to be urgently in need of recuperation.

Few could be in any doubt about the direction of Russian policy objectives. For more than 150 years now, ever since the late eighteenth century, the tsardom had been making repeated attempts to secure as large a share as possible of the European inheritance of the crumbling Ottoman Empire, including above all control of the Straits and hence of access to the Mediterranean. Each time it had come up against the stubborn resistance of the two western powers. They had eventually managed to secure the support of the two central European powers, who normally observed the strictest reticence on this issue, for the principle – backed chiefly by Britain – that the balance of power in Europe called for the preservation of the territorial integrity of the Ottoman Empire. As a result, the western powers had several times succeeded in asserting themselves against Russia, most recently in the Straits Agreement of 1841 barring Russian access to the Mediterranean.

However, now that Russia had placed the dominant power in central Europe, namely Austria, under so great an obligation to itself by helping to quell the Hungarian rebellion and by rebuffing Prussia's Union policy, the position looked radically different. It seemed more than likely that this was where Russia would launch any attempt to extend its power. Here St Petersburg could put to the test how solid was its standing as the leading conservative power in eastern and central Europe and whether it might venture the decisive thrust and set itself up as the dominant power on the European continent.

The first response from the power on which the attention of Europe's Cabinets was now naturally concentrated, since everything might depend on its decision, was as surprising as it was ambiguous: at the end of January 1853 Vienna appointed its specialist in eastern affairs, Baron Anton Prokesch-Osten, as its new envoy to the Federal Diet. Prokesch, by then nearly 60, had made a name for himself on several missions to the east. Study and travel, in both of which he indulged extensively, had familiarized him with the problems of the Ottoman Empire not only in the Balkans but also in the Near East; from 1834 to 1849 he had been his country's envoy in Athens, a scholar-diplomat of unique stature and importance. In 1849 he had been appointed Austrian ambassador in Berlin, which had had the unavoidable effect of turning him into a sort of symbol of Olmütz. With this in mind Bismarck reacted to him from the outset with deep scepticism, not to say aversion. As he remarked before Prokesch took up his post in Frankfurt, 'I think of him the way Old Fritz thought about the first Cossacks he saw: "That's the kind of — we're up against here."'[40]

The appointment of Prokesch to Frankfurt might mean that Austria was preparing to improve on the victory of Olmütz along the lines of its central European plans while Russia collected the prize for its support of the Habsburg monarchy in the Balkans – in other words, an extension of the power of both in an atmosphere of mutual connivance. But it might also mean that Vienna was attempting to mobilize the Confederation against a Russian expansionism that threatened its south-eastern flank and at the same time to achieve a reconciliation with the western powers – in other words, a reversal of all existing alliances. Finally, it was not completely out of the question that Austria might in a political high-wire act try to do both at the same time and in this way restore its post-1815 position as a continental power in a very much improved form.

But whatever the intentions of Austrian policy, Prussia, whose great power status many would have been inclined to dispute, might as a result of that policy find itself occupying a key position in the power struggle. By skilfully exploiting the situation it might conceivably obtain compensation for all the defeats of recent years. For this, however, it was necessary that Berlin should first of all retain a completely free hand and not commit itself prematurely on the basis of considerations that had nothing or at least nothing decisive to do with its own power-political interests. But there were few in the Prussian capital prepared to take this course. Instead a fierce conflict promptly broke out there, a conflict entirely of principle over whom Prussia should ally itself with in the event of war.

On one side there was the Camarilla. Disregarding all fears about Russian hegemony possibly extending too far, its members argued in favour of making common cause with Russia as the champion of a conservative order in Europe. Many may have hoped to see a reversal of the Olmütz alliance. But basically what they were looking for was a renewal of the link between the three conservative powers in the east as it had existed prior to 1848.

In opposition to the Camarilla, a tendency was increasingly emerging that favoured a link with Britain – partly for foreign policy reasons, the common denominator of which can be said to have been 'revenge for Olmütz', but also for domestic reasons. The watchword of this camp was that it was not autocratic reaction on the Russian model, not a 'tendential policy of Unholy-Holy Alliance'[41] that could bring rescue from a fresh revolution. What was needed was a policy of compromise between old and new elites, as in Britain, a policy of measured concessions to justified demands for reform coupled with a preservation of the basic monarchical and aristocratic structures of state and society.

This tendency, which found its mouthpiece in the *Preussisches Wochenblatt*, the 'Prussian Weekly' founded in 1851, and as a result became known simply as the '*Wochenblatt* party', saw itself as a kind of German Whig party, a successor to the liberal wing of the Prussian aristocracy that had already been in competition with the arch-conservatives back in 1848. Headed by the Prussian envoy in London, the scholarly Christian Josias von Bunsen, it comprised not only a substantial proportion of the younger generation of Prussian diplomats, chief among them Counts Albert von Pourtalès from Prussian Neuchâtel, Robert von der Goltz and Guido von Usedom, but also a number of members of the domestic civil service and of the landed nobility.

But above all it was the potential successor to the throne, Prince William, who in his increasingly blunt rejection of the policy of his brother and the Camarilla came to sympathize openly with the new political group; in particular he had long been a close associate of the official leader of the *Wochenblatt* party, Moritz August von Bethmann Hollweg, a son of the well-known Frankfurt banking family who had made a name for himself as a professor of law in Berlin and Bonn, as a Prussian councillor of state and as a member of both houses of parliament. The 'Case-Shot Prince' who had so vigorously quelled the revolution in southern Germany in 1848 was turning, it seemed, into a mentor of Prussian liberalism, a champion of the 'English way' to which it was now clear that from this quarter too the future in Prussia belonged – a development that Bismarck as one of the youngest members of what was still the dominant leadership in the country found highly alarming, not least as far as his own political career was concerned. In a major political memorandum addressed to the prince, who during the revolution of 1848–9 had several times assured him of his political sympathy, he sought to divert him from this course and swear him in to the old political line. 'Parliamentary Liberalism', he said among other things, might well 'serve as a temporary means to an end', but according to all the traditional principles of the Prussian state and the Prussian crown it could 'not itself constitute the end or purpose of our national life'.[42]

So the impending conflict over the direction of Prussian foreign policy was from the outset very much bound up with questions of domestic policy. The dispute about whether Prussia should look to the east or to the west turned increasingly into a battle of principle on the domestic policy front. In that dispute the Camarilla quite naturally expected its protégé in Frankfurt unreservedly to take its side – and that went for foreign policy as well. However much Bismarck agreed with his friends over domestic policy, this put him in an extremely difficult position. In the approaching European entanglement of which he had such high hopes for Prussia he found himself under pressure to bow completely to the will and opinions of others. He might even be obliged, if he did not want to jeopardize his political base, to look on impotently while Prussia hitched itself to Austria's wagon.

Whether Bismarck would eventually have submitted against his better judgement or whether he would have preferred to place his political career at risk must remain an open question, for it soon became clear that Frederick William IV was unable to decide unequivocally in favour of either position. 'My dear brother-in-law goes to bed a Russian every evening and gets up every morning an Englishman', the tsar mocked.[43] And Frederick William's wavering inadvertently favoured a policy that lay between the fronts, a policy of calculated temporization such as Bismarck supported.

Indeed for that very reason he was able to recommend it to either side as the policy of the lesser evil as compared to a decision in favour of the other. Since even the Minister-President himself was obliged to switch positions in the struggle for his own job and for the confidence of the king, Bismarck could even hope, in spite of Manteuffel's ever-wary mistrust, to find him ready in this case to listen to advice along such lines.

As early as 15 July 1853, shortly after Russia had, without declaring war, occupied the Turkish principalities of Moldavia and Wallachia on the Danube, he sought to win Manteuffel's support for this kind of policy of provisional neutrality. He really failed to see, he said, 'why without a cogent reason or strong inducement of any kind we should have to rush into taking sides' – and certainly not with Austria, at any rate not without a clearly stipulated *quid pro quo*. That would be tantamount to throwing away the trump card that this situation placed in Prussia's hand. 'The cases where in European politics Austria needs us or fears us' were 'the only ones where we can make progress in German politics'. He went on emphatically: 'If only I could hold this daily before His Majesty like a "My lord, remember the Athenians".' Armed neutrality, 'if possible in association with the other German states and Belgium, . . . would be a position in accordance with our interests and our dignity and one that would lend fresh vigour to our influence in non-Austrian Germany'. He hoped that Manteuffel's 'quiet cool-headedness' would 'not yield to the excitement of other advisers and we sustain no casualties; pour les beaux yeux de qui que ce soit, or purely for the glory of having been involved'. Of course, 'if we can get something out of it, that's different'.[44]

This was a formula that everyone could relate to the kind of policy he proposed. For Bismarck, however, it possessed a peculiar ambiguity, not to say baldness. 'Getting something out of it' meant for him an immediate power gain, an indisputable strengthening of the Prussian position, nothing less. This emerged very clearly from his attitude to the way things developed.

That was determined on the one hand by the sharpening confrontation between Russia and the western powers in alliance with the Porte, on the other hand by the vacillation of Austria. Like Prussia, Austria too had its influential supporters of all three conceivable positions: the arch-conservatives around Field Marshals Windischgraetz and Schlik, who like their counterparts in Prussia argued in favour of forming an ideological bloc with Russia and contemplated as a practical solution partitioning the Balkans into Russian and Austrian spheres of influence; the liberal conservatives around the Foreign Minister, Buol, the Minister of the Interior, Bach, and the envoy to the Federal Diet, Prokesch-Osten, who like the Prussian *Wochenblatt* party advocated an alliance with the western powers to contain Russian expansionism and ambitions of hegemony, their objective being at the same time a kind of Austrian protectorate covering the whole of the Balkans; and finally a very heterogeneous group of, on the one hand, adepts of Schwarzenberg's 'empire of seventy millions' policy led by the former Minister of Commerce and now Austrian ambassador in Constantinople, Baron von Bruck, and on the other hand supporters of the formation of a

121

central European bloc mediating between east and west along the lines of the Metternich system. They hoped by means of a policy of armed neutrality, a policy of 'waiting from a free standpoint', as the sympathetic old Metternich put it,[45] not only to get over the crisis but also to consolidate and extend the Confederation.

Of all positions it was inevitably the policy of armed neutrality, which in formal terms came closest to his own, that Bismarck found most disagreeable, threatening as it did, by way of the European crisis, to rob Prussia once and for all of its position as a great power. But that was exactly the direction in which Prussian policy was involuntarily moving under Frederick William IV and Manteuffel as a result of their shilly-shallying between a western and an eastern orientation. To prevent that from happening and yet nevertheless to keep Prussia on a neutral course, at any rate until such time as a more clear-cut outcome benefiting no one but Berlin appeared on the horizon – that was Bismarck's objective.

With it he stood almost completely alone, particularly since the naked power-political egoism reflected in it without any redeeming association with wider perspectives, not to mention ideals, was something that nearly everyone found repellent. Nor was that all: before long its advocate was scarcely able to escape the suspicion that with his exclusive emphasis on the basic reason behind every successful policy, namely its yield in terms of power and respect, he was ready when all was said and done to place himself at the disposal of any course, provided only that it was victorious. 'Bismarck is continually using and abusing his party colleagues. To him they are . . . post-horses on which to ride to the next stage', said Count Pourtalès in a letter written around this time. 'His knightly exterior hides nothing but a Judas, and I will not go one step of the way with him.'[46] The verdict 'opportunist loner', fatal for a politician, was very much in the air. That Bismarck did after all escape its consequences had less to do with his personal skill than with the very special circumstances that eventually formed a unique constellation in his favour.

The fact was that for years initially developments went against him. Granted, in the approach to and during the Crimean War Prussia did not commit itself unequivocally either to east or to west and also avoided any real rapprochement with Austria. But this was not the outcome of any deliberate calculation such as Bismarck had in mind but of the indecisive toing and froing of the domestic power struggle between the *Wochenblatt* party and the Camarilla. There could be no question of a 'policy of the free hand' followed up by decisive action. And if in the end Prussia did not find itself completely isolated, this was due purely to the fact that Austria had behaved even more imprudently and had in a manner of speaking fallen between every stool available. Its western orientation, referred to by Buol as a 'revolution in Austria's foreign relations', still existed on paper alone. All it had brought Austria was the enmity of Russia, without the commitment of the western powers. On the contrary, those sitting around the conference table in Paris when the peace terms between the western powers and Russia were negotiated in the spring of 1856 included Napoleon's protégé Count Camillo Cavour of Sardinia-Piedmont – the leading politician of the very power that in the name of Italian unification was the sworn enemy of Austria and of Austrian dominion south of the Alps. The Paris conference heralded the political constellation that was to lead by way of Austria's defeat in Italy to the rapid disintegration of the power of the empire, ending in the catastrophe of 1866.

No one had a sharper eye for this aspect of the situation than the Prussian envoy to the Federal Diet. In the ultimately futile struggle over the course of Prussian foreign policy, a struggle in which as a 'one-man party' he had increasingly run the risk of finding himself occupying a hopeless position in a no-man's-land between the fronts, he had repeatedly pointed out that the guiding principle of Prussian policy must be the undermining of Austria's foreign policy position; this constituted Prussia's sole interest in the so-called 'Eastern Question'. In the final analysis this had been the argument used by the foreign affairs representatives of the *Wochenblatt* party, namely Count Pourtalès, Bunsen, Prussia's representative in London, von der Goltz and Usedom. From it they had drawn what for reasons of domestic policy they saw as the obvious conclusion that to this end Prussia must ally itself with the western powers, particularly Britain, and bind these to it for the future. This was something Bismarck had rejected – necessarily so, since such a switch to the *Wochenblatt* party would have amounted to political suicide as far as he was concerned. But in substance, in calculation and in terms of foreign policy objectives he had always been much closer to this position than to the resolutely pro-Russian stance of his political friends. Secretly he had rejected the Austro-Prussian defensive and offensive alliance of April 1854 no less vehemently than the representatives of the *Wochenblatt* party, saying that with it Berlin was 'binding our spruce and seaworthy frigate to the wormy old warship of Austria'.[47] And he did everything in his power to prevent the Confederation from becoming a party to this alliance: 'Let's have no sentimental alliances', he warned as early as the end of February 1854, 'in which the wages of noble self-sacrifice must be the awareness of having done a good deed.'[48] On the day of the vote on this issue, 24 July 1854, the Austrian envoy Prokesch-Osten very fairly summed up Bismarck's attitude in his report as being based 'not so much on love of Russia as envy of Austria, not so much on any conservative principle as on a ravenous appetite for more power in Germany'.[49] In other words, he saw the problem of Prussia's eastern or western orientation purely and simply from the point of view of extending Prussian power at Austria's expense.

It had thus been in conformity with a deeper logic that in May 1854 Bismarck had been asked to mediate in the serious conflict between the Prussian king and his brother and heir, a conflict that brought the regime to the brink of crisis. The conflict had arisen out of the dismissal of certain leading representatives of the *Wochenblatt* party: Count Pourtalès, recently appointed under secretary of state at the Foreign Office, Bunsen, the London ambassador, and War Minister von Bonin. Their dismissal, brought about by the Camarilla, marked a decisive turning-away from the policy propagated by them and to some extent already being pursued on their own initiative.

Bismarck welcomed the fall of the Bethmann clique for domestic policy reasons; in fact he had been calling for it assiduously himself. He pointedly referred to Pourtalès, for example, with whom his relationship was one of mutual dislike, several times in letters to Leopold von Gerlach as one 'of the thickest numbskulls I have ever come across . . . with a faint touch of church, salon, scholarship and the brothel about him'.[50] But a return to a joint policy by the three conservative powers in the east, in which Prussia would inevitably find itself playing third violin, or even a passive association with Austria were alternatives he wanted his country to avoid at all costs. He must therefore have been very anxious to see that the opposite position did not collapse completely. It may even have occurred to him in this connection to wonder whether he might not himself be in a position one day to take the place of the Bethmann clique. Be that as it may, it was no accident that the rumour began to go the rounds in Berlin just at this time that the Prussian envoy to the Federal Diet occasionally spoke of the possibility not only of a Prussian–French alliance but also of an alliance with liberalism.

At the time, of course, all this was still extremely remote, even if it was already becoming apparent in substance. Bismarck's mission to Prince William evidently did little to bring him closer to him personally. At best it helped to pave the way for what remained a wholly superficial formal reconciliation between the king and the heir to the throne. In the eyes of the prince and his confidants, Bismarck was still a man of the Camarilla or, worse, a man of whichever battalions were stronger at the time – an impression that was further reinforced by his appointment as a 'royal peer' and member of the Upper House in November 1854. Being no more able than before to sanction a policy of unilateral alliance with Russia, even less one aimed at Austria, and seeing on the other hand only too clearly how short-sighted the policy of *de facto* neutrality remained, Bismarck found himself forced further and further into the position of an impotent outsider in whom even the Camarilla now placed only a qualified trust. 'Our foreign policy is rotten because it is timid', he wrote laconically to Kleist-Retzow towards the end of 1854; he himself seemed 'to have fallen into disfavour somewhat, or at least into dispensability'.[51] Even the memoirs still reflect the sense of helplessness that was his during those months: as 'the representative of Prussian policy' in Frankfurt it had given him 'an unavoidable feeling of humiliation and embitterment when I saw how in the face of what were not even courteously expressed demands on Austria's part we sacrificed any kind of policy and any kind of opinion of our own, retreating from position to position under pressure of feeling inferior and in fear of France and in trembling before Britain seeking shelter behind Austria's coat-tails'.[52] As he wrote to Leopold von Gerlach in August 1854, Prussia was 'to be reduced to the role of a source of money and recruits . . . without our being allowed any hand in the matter'.[53]

That was by and large how things remained until Russia's defeat in the Crimea in the autumn of 1855 and the institution of peace talks with Alexander II, who had succeeded to the throne in the spring of that year, following the death of Tsar Nicholas I. The upshot was that at first Prussia was not even invited to the conference table in Paris. As Bismarck noted at the time, there was not a great deal left 'from which my Prussian self-respect might take heart'.[54]

Granted, Prussia had eventually been asked to the conference at the instigation of France and Austria in order to avoid driving it into Russia's arms, though of course the Prussian representatives played no part in the negotiations, which reached their conclusion on 30 March 1856 with the signing of the Treaty of Paris. The important thing had been their simply being there. It was formal recognition of the fact that Prussia still belonged to the circle of the European great powers, over whose heads nothing could happen in Europe and who saw themselves as the guarantors of the new European order arrived at in Paris.

Outwardly that order was the same as in the years before the Crimean War, with a fresh acceptance by all the powers of the principle of the inviolability of Turkish national unity. In substance, however, it was radically changed, mainly as a result of the dissolution of the informal alliance of the three conservative powers in the east, which had been a crucial factor in European politics since 1815. Because that dissolution had not been coupled with any real reversal of alliances, in other words with a firm rapprochement between Austria and the western powers, and because on the other hand the plans laid by Bruck and others for forming a central European bloc in the shape of an expanded and strengthened Confederation had not come to fruition, the true victor of the Crimean War, as the choice of location for the peace conference showed, was France. Almost without any effort on his part Napoleon III suddenly held the strings of all Europe in his hand. To the traditional Anglo-Russian antagonism, which in the next few decades became more marked all over the world, there was now, only a few years after the Russian relief action in Hungary, added an antagonism between Austria and Russia that found permanent nourishment in the Balkans. As in the first half of the century it had been from Vienna, so in the second half it would have to be from Paris that the trimming of the European system, that on-going power-political transaction based on reciprocity, was effected. The international exhibition of 1855 and the peace conference of 1856 were brilliant outward signs of the fact that the centre of Europe had clearly shifted to the Seine. Politicians from all countries now began to make the pilgrimage to Paris, as the city increasingly recovered its former position as the intellectual and artistic capital of Europe as well.

In order to maintain and build on the leading role on the continent of Europe that had so to speak fallen into France's lap during the course of the Crimean War, one thing was needed above all, as Napoleon III saw clearly from the outset: it was imperative to prevent central Europe from coalescing into a more solid political entity and, for example, a reformed German Confederation presided over by Vienna from becoming an independent factor in European politics. To this end French policy needed to add to its anti-Austrian clientele in Italy an anti-Austrian clientele in Germany, in other words a German Sardinia-Piedmont. One possibility here was a sort of new Rhenish Confederation of the south German states. But it was a very uncertain one, especially in view of the attitude of German liberalism, which was particularly strong in the area and for protection against which the governments concerned still turned primarily to Austria. What inevitably looked like a much more promising, indeed almost ideal course was a corresponding rapprochement with the second great power in Germany, namely Prussia.

But who was there in Prussia to offer a hand in token of such a rapprochement? Certainly not the arch-conservatives, who were in power at the time. They saw Napoleon III as the embodiment of revolution and of the overthrow of all order. The same was true of the *Wochenblatt* party, which was in addition pursuing national ambitions with very obviously anti-French and anti-Napoleonic tendencies.

Unlike in Italy, therefore, there was as yet no obvious means by which French policy in central Europe might achieve its objective of checking Austrian power and neutralizing the German Confederation. In fact there was reason to fear that the kind of assault on Austrian hegemony in Italy that was being planned in Paris in the immediate aftermath of the Crimean War would lead to a nationalist reaction in favour of Austria as a 'German power'. Such a reaction might lead in turn to an unexpected strengthening of the German Confederation and usher in an expansion of the same. In other words, the Italian problem itself pointed to the need to secure a reliable partner in central Europe – reliable particularly in terms of its absolute opposition to Austria, even to an Austria that might be prepared to make concessions for the benefit of a common national cause.

This was the situation that had emerged at the end of the Crimean War. It was anything but stable, of course. Things had changed too much too suddenly, and the temptation for Austria as well as for Russia to change them again was too great for the Treaty of Paris to amount to anything more than a cease-fire. This was 1856, not 1815, France was not Metternich's Austria, a conformity of systems no longer existed, and competition on the power-political front was far more pronounced and had far deeper roots, both national and economic. From the French point of view, then, the only way to maintain the circumstances of 1856 was offensively: by strengthening France's power position at Austria's expense, with the risk of unleashing in the Italian theatre of operations envisaged for this purpose a kind of German war of unification the outcome of which in turn threatened to throw the whole European situation into turmoil once more.

For all the uncertainty and instability of the new situation, however, the old relationships had unmistakably been overthrown. Accordingly 1856 became a year of major policy reviews and analyses of the future, of large-scale memoranda and long-range political forecasts. And it was no accident that one of the first to make his views on the subject known was the Prussian envoy to the Frankfurt Diet. For despite the failure of his suggestions hitherto and the fact that they had made him an outsider, he was tremendously excited by the new situation and what he felt to be its implications. This, he believed he saw as in a flash of lighting, could be the jackpot for Prussia and possibly for himself as well.

His great memorandum of 26 April 1856, the so-called 'Prachtbericht' or 'Showpiece Report', began by saying that the new fundamental fact on which all further considerations must be based was the key position that France now occupied in Europe: 'Meanwhile all [Cabinets] great and small, in expectation of the way things may turn out, are seeking to obtain or to retain the friendship of France, and Emperor Napoleon, however new and apparently flimsy the foundations of his dynasty even in France itself, can take his pick from among the alliances currently available.'[55] Russia, Austria, Britain, the medium-sized German states – all of them aspired from various motives to a rapprochement with France. But where was Paris, after sober consideration, going to place its choice, and what attitude was it advisable for Prussia to adopt in the circumstances?

What was to be expected initially was some form of association and political co-operation between the two flanking powers of the European continent, namely France and Russia. Here he was expressing a lifelong conviction and one that was soon to fill him with increasing anxiety. 'Of all the great powers it is these two that because of their geographical situation and their political objectives contain within them the fewest elements of antagonism, having virtually no interests that necessarily [!] clash.' Hitherto the Holy Alliance and the personal attitude of Nicholas I had 'kept the two estranged from each other'. But the Crimean War had already been 'waged without hatred' and had served 'France's internal domestic requirements more than its external ones'. Now, with 'Emperor Nicholas dead and the Holy Alliance smashed by Austria', he saw nothing 'to inhibit the two countries' natural attraction for each other'.

Schwarzenberg, he said – and here something akin to admiration showed through for this man who in many respects so resembled him – had clearly foreseen this situation. On it he had based his expectation of being able, in alliance with both powers, to have his way in central Europe for a long time to come. But the bottom had now been knocked out of that plan for good. 'Given the Russians' present antipathy towards Austria and given France's increased pretensions to influence in Italy, it cannot be assumed', Bismarck wrote, positively savouring his words, 'that Austria will automatically be called to be the third member of the alliance, although it will surely not be lacking in the necessary goodwill.'

So it was Austria's move, and Austria must think of an idea. In theory this would be a counter-coalition of the three remaining great powers, Britain, Austria and Prussia, and hence at the same time the German Confederation. On paper, and given sufficient cohesion, such a counter-coalition ought to be in a position to survive even the emergency of a war against the two powers flanking the European continent. 'That, however, is not how things stand.' Because who in central Europe, which would necessarily take the main burden, would want to risk a war on two fronts? The small and medium-sized states of the German Confederation? As far as they were concerned he had 'most convincingly learned last year that they regard it as their honourable duty to abandon the Confederation should the interests, not to mention the security of their own prince or country be jeopardized by clinging to the Confederation'. Why should they do otherwise? Why, for example, should they oppose a new Rhenish Confederation under French patronage, especially since the experience of history had taught them that 'if it comes to the worst [a French defeat] Austria and Prussia begrudge each other everything' and the countries of the Rhenish Confederation did not 'come off badly' in 1813–14. 'The Rhenish Confederation had its burdens', he went on sarcastically, 'but at least the inconvenience of a constitution, particularly tiresome for a prince, was not among them and each pleased his subjects after his own fashion, provided only that he furnished France with the necessary troops. That servitude had its rateable fleshpots and was not so arduous for the princes that in order to escape from it they would have needed to risk country and people and like that emperor in Bürger's poem go "through heat and cold, through the tents of war, eating black bread and sausage, suffering hunger and thirst" for the sake of their own and Germany's freedom.'

Nor did an 'essentially different way of thinking' characterize the 'successors of the Rhenish-Confederation princes' today. Since the collapse of the Holy Alliance which by virtue of its strength had kept the 'Third Germany' up to the mark, the 'inner rottenness of the Confederation' stemming from that way of thinking had 'become visible and obvious both abroad and at home'; as he had sneered in a private letter written three years before this: 'That well-known song of Heine's, "oh Bund, du Hund, du bist nicht gesund", will soon be adopted by unanimous resolution as the national anthem of the German people.'[56]

In mercilessly straightforward terms this was tantamount to saying that, be it only in the most extreme emergency, namely in the event of the threat of war, Germany as a political entity capable of taking positive action did not exist even in the loosest form. Such an entity was nothing but more or less vague historical reminiscence, mere wishful thinking. The only political realities in central Europe were the two great powers, Austria and Prussia. The remaining states would align themselves like iron filings with whichever pole was the stronger at the time – the idea of the so-called 'Third Germany' Bismarck also dismissed contemptuously as a mere fiction.

Even with regard to Austria's military strength one must be sceptical, in Bismarck's view, whether 'with the enemy's first successful thrust into the interior the whole artificial edifice of its centralized regiment of scribes [would not] collapse like a house of cards'. But even a more positive view of the monarchy's powers of resistance could not overlook the fact that, as far as a permanent alliance between Austria and Prussia was concerned, the most elementary prerequisites were wanting – at any rate for the present. Even if under extreme pressure such an alliance did come about, the massive divergence of interests between the two central European powers would always lead to one party seeking to get the better of and outmanoeuvre the other. Germany was simply 'too small for the two of us', he stated baldly.

With one eye on the Camarilla, however, he made an immediate qualification. It was this: 'according to Viennese policy'. The present divergence of interests was not pre-ordained, as it were, not a fact of nature. It was the outcome of a policy that for centuries had sought to curtail Prussia's living-space and Prussia's opportunities for development. Prussia had repeatedly had to wage defensive wars against that policy. 'For a thousand years the German dualism has every so often – since Charles V, regularly every century – regulated its mutual relations by means of a thorough-going internal war, and in this century too no other means but this will be capable of putting right the clock of historical development.'

This was to adopt a very relaxed approach to historical truth, running together claimed and actual power and dressing up the policy of a rising great power such as Brandenburg-Prussia in the seventeenth and eighteenth centuries as a purely defensive one. According to Bismarck, Austria's 'perfidy' had repeatedly forced Prussia to take up arms afresh. It was a constant that all thoughts of an alliance must take as their starting-point. His attitude towards 'the old fox' was that he would 'no more trust him in a new coat than in his mangy old summer one'.

Austria would in all likelihood use an alliance with Prussia purely 'to procure at our expense better terms for an understanding with France and if possible with Russia'. He went on: 'It will play Don Juan to every Cabinet when it can produce so stout a Leporello as Prussia, and true to that role it will always be ready to extricate itself from a tight corner at our expense while leaving us in it.' And even in the event of war Vienna would in the long run, whether victorious or defeated, seek to twist things in such a way that Prussia at any rate gained nothing or even had to foot the bill alone.

After five years of not infrequently rancorous skirmishing in the Federal Diet, all this flowed easily from his pen. Undoubtedly the animosity exuded by his words here and on other occasions was the genuine expression of a political fervour that threatened time and time again to blur the distinction between opponent and enemy. On the other hand it suited his plans only too well to give that fervour free rein. His chief task, after all, was to convince the king and the Camarilla, whom he could be sure his memorandum would reach either directly or indirectly. They continued, despite all disappointments, to cling to the idea of the Holy Alliance and to the concept of fraternal collaboration between the two German great powers against the revolution and against the impending dissolution of all internal and international order in Europe. Bismarck must try to make them understand that Austria had always treated such objectives with reserve and indeed with hostility in so far as it had repeatedly destroyed the foundations for that kind of rapprochement by its own actions.

In this way he was able to suggest indirectly that war might be unavoidable from this standpoint too, as well as from that of the historical situation and historical evolution: with its anti-Prussian policy, a policy dictated by naked power-political self-interest, Vienna was threatening to smash one of the strongest pillars of the traditional order in Europe. He carefully qualified this by saying that he would never advocate a preventive strike or suggest, for example, that Prussian policy as a whole should be directed towards 'engineering a decision between ourselves and Austria in the most favourable circumstances possible'. But it was his 'conviction', and one he had no desire to hide, that 'before too long we are going to have to meet Austria in a fight for our *existence* and that it is not in our power to prevent this because the way things are going in Germany offers no alternative'.

This was the nub of his whole argument: war was inevitable, there was no alternative. Prussia must fight for its 'Existenz' – a word imbued with all the political ideas with respect to Prussian domestic and foreign affairs that the arch-conservatives and the columnists of the *Kreuzzeitung* had been using it to invoke ever since the revolution. As far as Austria was concerned it was simply 'a question of time and opportunity', he wrote to Leopold von Gerlach two days later, '*when* it chooses to make the decisive attempt to hamstring us; *that* it intends to do so is politically speaking an absolute necessity'. Even if Prussia – for which read the Camarilla with Gerlach at its head – wished 'piously to avoid' war: 'Austria will wage it at the first favourable opportunity.'[57]

This raised one final, crucial question: however much there was to be said for this kind of anti-Austrian policy, did it not ultimately favour the revolution by driving a wedge between the defensive forces ranged against it? For Leopold von Gerlach and his circle, however – unlike for Manteuffel, for example – the revolution meant not just the liberals and the democrats but also Napoleon III and with him the power that, as Bismarck himself pointed out, had meanwhile become the new centre of gravity in Europe.

Admittedly Bismarck did not yet go so far as to advocate a Prussian alliance with France, although he had already drawn attention to the possibility in a sharply graphic manner some years before this: 'Some highly estimable people, including medieval princes, have preferred to make their escape through a sewer rather than be thrashed or throttled.'[58] He did, however, expressly recommend a free-handed policy of cultivating good relations with everybody from the position of the 'sought-after ally'. Nor was that all. If it should come, he said, 'to the realization of a Franco-Russian alliance for the purposes of war', in other words a Franco-Russian war against Austria, 'we cannot, I am convinced, be among the opponents of the same, because we should probably be defeated and possibly, pour les beaux yeux de l'Autriche et de la Diète, bleed to death even in victory'.

What Bismarck was here quite soberly envisaging, with very little attempt at concealment, was attacking Austria, the number one power in the German Confederation, from the rear as soon as Vienna got into difficulties on the foreign affairs front. And Prussia's only chance of success with such a policy lay in her seeking at the same time to get on good terms both with Russia and with France.

In the long run, therefore, his proposals did after all amount to a rapprochement with France. But for Gerlach this meant, over and above the monstrosity of a fratricidal war in central Europe, actually promoting revolution, pulling down the traditional order with one's own hands in a purely egoistical pursuit of power interests. 'My political principle is and remains the struggle against revolution', he wrote to Bismarck a year later, on 6 May 1857. 'You will not persuade Bonaparte that he is not on the side of revolution. Nor does he wish to be anywhere else, for that is what gives him his decisive advantages . . . But if my principle, like that of opposition to revolution, is right . . . it must always be adhered to in practice as well.'[59]

[4]

In No-Man's-Land

By this time the argument about the objectives and the direction of Prussian foreign policy that was developing between Bismarck and his arch-conservative political friends had pushed far into the realms of principle. Provoked by Bismarck's abstract chess-player's logic, Leopold von Gerlach had asked him the crucial question: what, for all his agreement over domestic policy, was his attitude to the conservative principles of foreign policy? The question had not been without a certain inquisitorial undertone. Bismarck felt he must justify himself if after all the stresses and strains of the past he did not want finally to lose the confidence of this faction and with it his political base: the mental state of Frederick William IV was giving increasing cause for concern, and Bismarck could scarcely be said to be close to Prince William, the man expected to succeed him. In the circumstances his declarations of principle, the fundamental importance of which he expressly emphasized by reproducing them in his memoirs, were inevitably also diplomatic documents, attempts to substantiate his position in such a way as to prevent his being anathematized as an unprincipled opportunist.

Nothing would be more mistaken, therefore, than to interpret Bismarck's contribution to the famous correspondence between him and Leopold von Gerlach in the spring and summer of 1857 as a programmatic confession of faith, so to speak, and to represent it as a key document of *Realpolitik*, of a politics of realism in which lack of principle was almost a matter of principle.

One is always reading that this is where the difference between a politics of principle and a politics of interest finally and irremediably came to a head: on one side the arch-conservatives, represented by Gerlach, who demanded that the struggle against revolution and for the traditional political and social order remain the overriding principle of all domestic and foreign policy; and on the other side Bismarck, who refused to subject Prussia's power interests to what was in intention and in terms of its spiritual and historical justification an essentially supra-national principle.

If we take a closer look, without allowing ourselves to be guided by the preconception, subsequently fostered by Bismarck himself, that what were being developed here were the principles of a wholly undogmatic foreign policy, indeed one open to every combination to the point of having no

131

principles, it becomes very clear that this was not at all a quarrel about principles but about appraisals and methods. Whether there was in fact something else *underlying* it we shall have to examine carefully at a later stage, because we are dealing here with fundamental questions of the evaluation and classification of Bismarck, his policies and the tangible results of those policies. But first let us look at the actual points at issue and the background to the conflict.

When writing his memoirs, Bismarck gave the chapter in which he dealt with this conflict in detail in the light of the most important letters the laconic title 'A visit to Paris'. That 'visit', which took place in August 1855, in other words before a military decision had been reached in the Crimean War, did indeed constitute the decisive prelude. The initiative for what was to be the first of a series of visits to 'Babylon', as he put it ironically to Leopold von Gerlach,[1] undoubtedly came from Bismarck himself; the international exhibition merely provided the occasion. Bismarck was one of the first politicians to turn towards what was emerging as a new centre of power and to seek to make personal contact with Napoleon III.

We know relatively little about the conversations that Bismarck had with the French emperor on this and subsequent occasions. But this much we do know: the whole logic of foreign relations dictated that Napoleon III should himself be very interested in making contact with the Prussian envoy to the Federal Diet. Bismarck was introduced to him as a man who enjoyed the confidence of the Prussian king and the conservative court, the 'parti du *Kreizzeitung*',[2] and who was at the same time an independent spirit engaged in Frankfurt in a bitter struggle against Austrian hegemony in central Europe. What is equally certain is that as early as 1855 Bismarck saw Napoleon as a potential partner for Prussia against Austria. As to whether he was also, beyond that, personally attracted to and impressed by a man whose political ambitions, fanciful though these had seemed at first, had found their fulfilment within the space of a few years at the expense of an apparently omnipotent liberal propertied middle class and who was now becoming an increasingly dominant figure in Europe as well, there we can only speculate. The same is true of the question whether he perhaps even saw him as a living symbol of the potential of a particular type of policy and a particular political system.

Bismarck himself resolutely denied both suggestions. He always did so, however, in contexts where the suggestion was bound up with the charge that he was arguing on grounds of personal sympathy for a rapprochement with France – as, for example, in reply to Frederick William IV in September 1855 and above all now in reply to Leopold von Gerlach. 'How can a man of your intellect', wrote Gerlach towards the end of April 1857, opening the great debate after various preliminary skirmishes in the years leading up to this, 'sacrifice principle to one single man such as this L[ouis] N[apoleon]? He impresses me too, notably by his moderation, which in a *parvenu* merits double recognition, but he is and remains our natural enemy, and the fact that he is and will inevitably remain that will soon emerge.'[3] 'The man does not impress me at all', Bismarck retorted.[4] Surely Gerlach knew him better than that: 'The ability to admire people is but moderately developed in me, unlike a defect of vision that gives me a sharper eye for weaknesses than for strengths.' As for what 'principle' he was supposed to have 'sacrificed', he frankly did not know what Gerlach was talking about. The principle of legitimacy, formulated in 1814–15 essentially in France's interest, or perhaps the principle of a sworn enmity between Prussia and France?

Bismarck, of course, knew only too well what Gerlach was getting at. But by starting off at a lower level, as it were, with more external, formal aspects, he gave himself a chance of explaining his own position without overstepping Gerlach's stimulus threshold. Nor was that all. By mentioning the formal principle of legitimacy and not the material principle of revolution that Gerlach saw Napoleon as embodying he managed at the same time to draw attention, without placing himself in a dangerously exposed position, to the problems of a conservatism that related not to a particular country but to Europe as a whole, politically and socially.

Was it seriously permissible, he asked rhetorically, to sacrifice Prussian national interests to a principle such as that of legitimacy? What, then, was the difference between the anti-Prussian behaviour of so incontestably legitimate a monarch as Louis XIV and that of Napoleon I? Clearly what was decisive was how France 'reacts to the situation of my country'. But this was something that depended on the political constellation and on the balance of interests at the time, not on how legitimately the French head of state occupied his throne. The question of the legitimacy of a ruler was a domestic rather than a foreign policy matter. In terms of foreign policy he saw 'France, without regard to its current ruler, purely as a piece, an unavoidable piece in the chess game of politics, a game in which it is my duty to serve only *my* king and *my* country'. Then, boldly equating the charge that he favoured a rapprochement with France out of personal sympathy for Napoleon III with the antipathy that an arch-conservative Prussian felt towards an illegitimate ruler in France, he went on: 'Sympathies and antipathies with regard to foreign powers and personalities are something my sense of duty in the foreign service of my country will not allow me to justify, either in myself or in others; therein lie the seeds of disloyalty to the master or to the country that one serves.'

In plain terms this meant that it was not he, a man guided solely by the Prussian national interest rather than by personal sympathies, who was sacrificing a principle but the man whose dislike of the person occupying the French throne led him to risk harming the Prussian national interest and with it, as history had always shown, the stability of Prussia's domestic institutions and circumstances.

This was very cleverly argued. It was also entirely in line with what he believed. But he was perfectly well aware of what slippery ground he was treading here. The older conservatives of Gerlach's stamp saw the connection between domestic and foreign policy in a very different light. In the spirit of the treaties of 1815 they were imbued with the need for a conformity of systems. It was this rather than what they too regarded as the somewhat superficial principle of the pedigree of the incumbent monarch that was implicit in the doctrine of legitimacy.

Without waiting for Gerlach's reply, therefore, Bismarck sought in a kind of postscript written a week later[5] to allay the suspicion, which rather suggested itself in such circles and had probably even been voiced on occasion, that in reality he not only sympathized with Napoleon III as a person but was himself a 'Bonapartist'. This meant someone who favoured a system of government of which the formal basis was the plebiscitary consent of the masses rather than collaboration with bodies representing the estates of the realm. Its essence was seen in a joining of forces between the representatives of mobile capital, particularly of new industries, and the government bureaucracy, between the propertied middle class and the state, with the government securing its monopoly of power by meeting the material interests of the middle classes half way. The whole system thus amounted to one of 'revolution from above'.

In line with this interpretation Bismarck had written to Gerlach back in December 1851: 'I would venture to say that, here in Prussia, Bonapartism is older than Bonaparte, only in a milder German form; this it lost to some extent when it was introduced in a more French form in the shape of the Hardenberg legislation translated from the Royal Westphalian Bulletin; now I find it embodied among us chiefly by the liberalizing bureaucracy; you will scarcely expect me not to oppose it in this form.[6] If he was suspected of aiming at such a policy himself, there was no more in it than in past attempts to construe a connection between a foreign policy position and domestic policy inclinations: in 1850, he reminded Gerlach, he and his political friends had been dubbed 'the Viennese in Berlin';[7] 'later they thought we smelled of Russian leather and called us Spree Cossacks'. His answer then as now was: 'I am Prussian, and my ideal for those concerned with foreign policy is that they should be free from preconceptions and their decisions independent of the effects of any aversion to or predilection for foreign countries and their rulers.'

As far as the charge of being a secret 'Bonapartist' was concerned, Gerlach proceeded to reassure him. He thought he knew Bismarck's domestic policy principles too well for that. But 'for that very reason' – and here he came right back to the crucial point – he found 'inexplicable how you regard our external policy'.[8] What Bismarck had set out in his very full letters and in his last memorandum to Manteuffel on 18 May[9] was quite right in many details and well worth heeding – 'but, if you will forgive me, it lacks the head and tail of policy, namely principle and objective'. Napoleon was after all on the side of the revolution. He was subject to 'the consequences of his position as that of an absolutism grounded in the sovereignty of the people'. And since in a tripartite alliance between France, Russia and Prussia the weakest party would be Prussia, such an alliance would necessarily favour so-called French interests, in other words 'supremacy in Italy first and subsequently in Germany'. That, however, meant quite simply victory for the forces of revolution with Prussia lending a helping hand. Because it was beyond question as far as he was concerned that France would in fact pursue such an expansionist policy: 'Revolutionary absolutism is by its very nature out to conquer, since it can only sustain itself at home when the same conditions prevail all around it.'

At this point Bismarck could undoubtedly have evaded further debate by arguing that of course he was not in favour of such a development either. What he was proposing was no more than a possible tactical rapprochement in order to be able to contain France the more effectively in the long run. But that would have been to duck the problems. In Gerlach and among his circle it might well have provoked even greater mistrust. Furthermore – and this was probably the crucial factor – Bismarck saw no divergence of principle at all but only two different appraisals of Napoleon III and his regime.

The 'difference' in their views, he replied to Gerlach at the end of May, lay 'in the foliage and not in the root'.[10] And he went on: 'The principle of the struggle against revolution is one that I too acknowledge as my own, but I do not consider it right to make Louis Napoleon out to be the sole or even the prime representative of that revolution.' In his opinion Gerlach was here confusing not only form and content but also origin and present reality. There was much that was of revolutionary origin, and as far as the legitimacy of many ruling houses was concerned this was quite a problem. What mattered was whether a regime had *de facto* abandoned the paths of revolution and ceased to act as a missionary for the same. Even Napoleon I would have been 'very happy' to have the revolution 'eradicated from his past after he had plucked and pocketed the fruit of it'. How much more true this was of Napoleon III.

Both were heirs to revolution, not agents of it: 'Louis Napoleon did not create the revolutionary conditions in his country, nor did he obtain power in opposition to a *lawfully* existing authority; he fished it like an abandoned possession out of the maelstrom of anarchy. If he now wished to lay it aside he would embarrass all Europe, and he would be pretty unanimously requested to remain.' What people called Bonapartism was clearly, in a post-revolutionary country such as France, the only alternative to revolutionary rule by the masses or to anarchy. This made it 'probably the only method by which France [could] in the long run be governed'. To make common cause with Napoleon III would in reality be to contain the forces of revolution – that was the conclusion that must inevitably be drawn, even if Bismarck did not say so openly. The true foundations of that method had been laid by the absolutist policy of the Bourbons, a dynasty of unimpeachable legitimacy: 'Bonapartism is a consequence, not the creator of revolution', he stressed once again in a memorandum addressed to Manteuffel three days later.[11]

But agreement with Gerlach was not to be reached. Gerlach insisted that Bismarck's assessment of the phenomenon of Bonapartism was wholly false in that it overlooked the fact that Napoleon III, like his uncle before him, was not the master but the slave of the constellation of forces that had carried him to power. He was at the mercy of the masses, who had been declared sovereign. By them he was driven onward, and the obligation to fulfil their changing wishes was the only thing that determined the direction of his policy. Bonapartism, said Gerlach, restating his standpoint quite clearly, was 'not absolutism, not even Caesarism'.[12] Absolutism might 'stand on a *jus divinum*, as in Russia and in the east'; 'consequently it does not affect those who do not recognize that *jus divinum*, for whom it does not exist, unless it occurs to such autocrats to regard themselves, like Attila, Mohammed, or Tamerlane, as a scourge of God, which after all is the exception'. And Caesarism was 'the assumption of an *imperium* in what is legally a republic and is justified by a state of emergency'. For a Bonaparte, however, 'revolution, which means the sovereignty of the people, is whether he wishes it or not his inward and in every conflict or exigency also his outward title'.

Nevertheless, Gerlach did once again expressly concede to his protégé that 'at root' they were in agreement. The 'whole difference' between them lay 'purely in their different views of the essence of this phenomenon'; there could be no question of a difference of opinion at the level of political principle. As things stood this was extremely important to Bismarck. But did it correspond to the truth as far as he was concerned? Was not the whole thing a sham in so far as all the Frankfurt envoy was really interested in doing was freeing foreign policy calculations from the trammels of an unyielding adherence to principle and a sense of missionary zeal without jeopardizing his own position? Was he not solely concerned with marshalling every available argument in order to prove that none of the foreign policy decisions currently under consideration undermined or even contravened the principle of the 'struggle against the forces of revolution'?

Such is the interpretation that has prevailed hitherto. It was formulated initially from the standpoint of National Liberalism and subsequently by historians who for all their differences were united by one thing: they occupied the basic position of those who in the eyes of someone like Gerlach stood on the side of 'revolution'. Accordingly they tended to interpret every argument against an attitude such as Gerlach's, which they found wholly anachronistic, as expressing an opposition on principle that was at most disguised for tactical purposes. All the more so when it came from the pen of a man whose practical operations on the foreign policy front were hailed repeatedly in the further course of events as embodying a *Realpolitik* that reckoned in purely power-political terms.

However, this kind of interpretation has always had to avail itself of certain somewhat problematical auxiliary constructions and pseudo-psychological elucidations. It makes extensive use, for example, of the assumption of a break in or at least a radical reorientation of Bismarck's foreign policy after 1870–1. It also explains his permanently schizoid if not actually negative relationship with Britain essentially in terms of his distrust of shifting parliamentary majorities, and it reduces his relations with France after 1871 to the basic fact of an ultimately irreconcilable divergence of interests that was finally sealed at Versailles. But if we take seriously Bismarck's arguments and expressions of principle in the crucial years 1856–7 there is little need for such constructions. Indeed it becomes clear that the much discussed problem of the relationship between domestic and foreign policy in the context of his overall political approach is by no means as ambivalent or complicated as it is often made out to be.

At the end of the 'Prachtbericht', his great memorandum of April 1856, there occurs a passage that is crucial in this connection and that he repeated in many different variations on the most diverse occasions. On the question of the need for a conservative alliance of interests between Austria and Prussia he wrote: 'In 1851, particularly in the early part of that year, the dangers of a revolutionary overspill from France and Italy were more obvious, and there was a feeling of solidarity between the monarchies against *that* danger . . . ; a similar situation would recur only if the French Empire were to be overthrown. As long as it stands it is not a question of holding off the democrats but of Cabinet politics, in which the interests of Austria do *not* in fact coincide with our own.'[13]

He could not have made himself more clear: as long as the existing political and social order at home did not appear to be in jeopardy from events abroad, for example from the formation of blocs on ideological grounds or from large-scale penetration by internationalist revolutionary movements, it was possible to pursue a foreign policy that was governed purely by the concrete political and economic power interests of the state in question, seeking to advance these in changing constellations and coalitions as circumstances dictated at the time. If this basic situation changed, entirely new elements came into play of which account would have to be taken accordingly. In other words, it went without saying that the prime consideration – and one wonders when in history it was ever otherwise – was the preservation at home of the kind of order that most closely corresponded to one's own interests and one's own ideas and that at the same time seemed most likely to enhance one's own political power.

'At the same time' – there, of course, lay the central problem as far as Bismarck was concerned. In a period of transition, of rapid economic, social and – inevitably, sooner or later – also political change, his personal power interests, if he meant like the Gerlachs to remain consistent, were tied to a sinking ship. A legend as old as it is tenacious maintains that not only did he long preserve that ship, the political and social order of the old Prussia, from finally going under but he even in a sense made it seaworthy once more. That, says the legend, is the foundation of his historical success.

In reality it is precisely the other way around. Anyone who makes even the most superficial comparison of conditions in Prussia around 1840 with those that obtained around 1880, bearing in mind as he does so that without the aid of the guillotine or the firing-squad the social hierarchy in a society as a rule changes only slowly, will see very clearly that the process of change was possibly more rapid here than in any other country on earth, the possible exception being Japan. In relation to Bismarck this means that he did not in fact remain consistent and that from now on his own power interests drove him farther and farther away from the ideas and interests not only of those who had been his political friends hitherto but subsequently also of the social group to which he belonged.

He had started out as a representative of a particular class, a spokesman of the landed nobility against an allegedly levelling absolutism that sought to revolutionize society from above. His secret ambition had been to make a political career as the leader of a major conservative aristocratic party in a monarchical state that had been forced back into the traditional corporative mould. Now, only a few years after the complete defeat of the forces of

137

revolution and hence of the political competition in the shape not only of the middle-class liberals and democrats but also of the liberal aristocrats, that idea had little further basis in reality. What was left was a small, arch-conservative Camarilla of non-responsible political advisers around a monarch who was in a permanent state of indecision on almost every issue and lived, moreover, under the shadow of mental illness. Also left was a Conservative Party that was sinking deeper and deeper into lethargy, was more and more often outmanoeuvred by what was still a very absolutist-minded bureaucracy, and was in addition drifting farther and farther away from any kind of coherent leadership. On the other hand it was obvious that the liberal wing of the Prussian aristocracy, now organized in the *Wochenblatt* party, was beginning to find fresh impetus – not only because it appeared to have the probable successor to the throne on its side but above all because in the light of developments in general it seemed to offer the more realistic alternative to the forces of middle-class liberalism that, albeit still largely beneath the surface, were making their presence felt once more.

There is relatively little talk of all this in the mountains of letters, memoranda and other writings that Bismarck produced in those years; here the all-prevailing theme is German and European foreign policy. But precisely that reflects the crucial process. As it were under the cloak of the diplomat, of the man concerned solely with foreign policy who resolutely refused to see foreign policy too much from the special point of view of domestic policy and positions on the domestic front, he effected the transition from a conservative party politician to that peculiar type that the transition from monarchical and bureaucratic absolutism to the party-political, parliamentary system produced and promoted in other countries besides Prussia. This was the type of the relatively independent Cabinet minister who walked a tightrope between the two systems but who of course ran the risk, in performing this balancing-act, of soon losing in terms of objective independence more and more of what he gained in terms of personal independence.

Whether Bismarck himself ever became aware that the period favoured such a specific type of politician is open to question. What is more likely is that, once he had finally crossed the Rubicon from being a party politician in the corporative sense to being this new type of 'man between the fronts' [or, as we should say in English, 'in no-man's-land'; *Tr.*], he was fascinated by the striking analogy with the kind of calculating pursuit of foreign policy interests and opportunities that he practised and wished to see practised. Be that as it may, the disappointment of his political expectations with regard to the Conservative Party, the intermediate position into which his foreign policy thinking had led him, the uncertainty of monarchical and ministerial protection, and not least the parliamentary and rhetorical gifts that were at present lying fallow – all this led him with a certain logic during these years to look for his political advantage in a situation in which a clash of competing powers and interests admitted of no clear solution, given the equilibrium of the forces on either side, and a settlement had to be reached by other means.

This policy of a precarious balancing-act between different powers and

138

interests, to preserve the given conditions of which even under altered circumstances became the rule of his political life, has with reference to contemporary theories been dubbed 'Bonapartistic'. Such a label, however, together with the historical analogy that it invokes, while drawing attention to certain superficial similarities in fact obscures what is most important. This lies not only in the fact that Bismarck was not, like the two Napoleons, an autocrat but occupied a position of far more than merely formal dependence on a ruler in his own right. It lies above all in the consequence of this, namely that his power was based solely on the existence of a precarious equilibrium between the claims to sovereignty and political muscle of the representatives of historical authority and those of so-called 'revolutionary' authority, in other words between the forces backing the old and new orders.

In post-revolutionary France this was not at all the case. Both Napoleon and the advocates of parliamentary liberalism took their stand on the revolution and on the democratic principle of the sovereignty of the people. Both felt their authority to be legitimized by the latter's consent. Granted, Napoleon I and after him Napoleon III manipulated that consent directly and above all through a policy of measured complaisance and of concessions more demagogic than real in all directions. That, however, in no way alters the fact that plebiscitary consent was an essential component of their authority.

But that is precisely what with Bismarck was never at any time the case. The building of a completely independent position of authority, for example the founding of a party that was wholly committed to himself as leader, while altogether conceivable, would not only have meant a radical break in his policy. Such a course would in all probability have resulted in a revolutionary confrontation. For in that case Bismarck would have had to destroy the existing balance and help the principle of the sovereignty of the people in one form or another to victory over the monarchical principle, the 'historical' authority.

But that is something that Bismarck, convinced royalist that he was and remained, never at any point in his life thought of doing, for all his readiness to try different combinations. What he strove for in both home affairs and international relations and what he continued to strive for until his fall was a policy of equilibrium between the various powers and interests on hand. His prime concern in both fields had to be that, however much things might change, the distribution of political weight should remain approximately the same – with the result that shortly afterwards this 'Konfliktminister', this advocate of confrontation with parliament, was himself setting up counterweights to an excessive power on the part of the Crown and in the further course of events sought by the most problematical of means to neutralize the growing importance of social forces.

Whether it would be possible in the long term to maintain so precarious an equilibrium in both domestic and foreign affairs is something he doubted himself. In both spheres he was constantly afraid of being overwhelmed by revolutionary forces that he felt could no longer be tamed politically. Against them he sought to draw up defensive fronts that were themselves difficult to reconcile with the system of equilibrium he was aiming at. The argument that on the other hand his policy of equilibrium was itself erecting an ever stronger bulwark against the trends of the time the longer it was pursued and hence threatened literally to usher in revolution by force was one he always rejected as tendentious. That kind of thinking, he said, was based on a wholly unprovable theory of progess and evolution, on the idea that man could look at God's cards, as it were, and predict the future course of world events; it brought his whole conception of history back into play. And with the same argument he fended off the charge that giving absolute precedence to considerations of power politics made impossible any kind of consistent policy aimed at definite objectives and governed by clear-cut principles. This charge too was based on a colossal overestimation of the power of man and an almost blasphemous underestimation of the power of the Lord of History. Politics, he declared as an old man, was the ability to effect 'in every changing moment of the situation that which will be least damaging or most opportune'; anyone who expected more of it or even wished to give it the character of a 'logical' or 'exact' 'science' was deceiving himself and others.[14]

But however he chose to defend and justify his position, that position itself was wholly unequivocal. And we can assume that it developed in this form as early as the final stages of the Crimean War or in other words, seen from the point of view of domestic policy, on the threshold of a fundamental change of course in Prussian home affairs.

In both spheres, home and foreign affairs, everyone who was in any way connected with Prussian politics at that time found that some attempt at a fundamental review and reorientation was literally forced upon them. Bismarck undertook it in the awareness of a man now 40 years of age that he must also get clear in his mind what direction his personal future was to take: 'One goes on imagining that one is at the beginning of one's life and that life proper is still to come', but in reality one was already 'over the top and it is downhill all the way now to the Schönhausen crypt', he noted on the eve of his fortieth birthday.[15]

Should he prepare himself for a future as a diplomat serving a changing series of governments that might even change their basic direction? Should he start to press his candidacy for the Foreign Ministry, of which there had been talk for years, with greater urgency now? Should he return to the parliamentary arena or even – this also occurred to him – give up all thought of a further career in politics? All these considerations were present as Bismarck's thinking got more and more down to basics, even though that thinking was for the most part concentrated on foreign affairs and the decisions needing to be made in that sphere. And although further evidence was hardly necessary it became obvious from the results to which his thinking led and the resistance with which it met that the condition of all his political planning was extensive personal freedom of action and decision. The basic theme was still the same, though the purely emotional rendition of the 23-year-old had now acquired an objective substance: 'I, however, want to make the kind of music I know to be good, or make none at all.' It was clear to Bismarck by this time at the latest that, for him, any office below that of chief minister in Prussia could only be a step on the way to that goal.

To everyone else, of course, it seemed equally clear that such ambitions were no more than pipe dreams about the future in the mind of a man who in reality had little or no future left. He already had a draft plan for exercising the office he aspired to and another for keeping himself in that office for a long time, yet his prospects of ever reaching that point were never dimmer than during the months in which his debate with Gerlach regarding the relationship between principle and self-interest in politics reached its culmination. And dim they were to remain for years to come.

Towards the end of October 1857 Prince William began to deputize for his brother, whose sanity had been precarious for some time and who had now suffered a stroke as well. This finally heralded the end of the Camarilla and of the ascendancy of all those forces to which Bismarck had owed not only his whole political career hitherto but also the chance of influencing affairs beyond the circle defined for him by his office. Bismarck immediately tried to adapt to the new situation and by building on earlier encounters to enter into closer relations with the prince. All that this brought him, however, was the mistrust of his former political friends, which in one or two of the less well-meaning such as Edwin von Manteuffel, Frederick William IV's aide-de-camp and head of his Military Cabinet, was already mingled with contempt. It did not prevent him from being recalled from Frankfurt almost as soon as the circles now in authority had taken up the political reins, with the prince's assumption of the regency in the autumn of 1858, and being transferred to St Petersburg.

In terms of the traditional hierarchy of ambassadorial appointments this was promotion. In fact it was a clear case of being put on the shelf – an 'honourable exile', as Bismarck himself called it.[16] For in the new policy that was about to be introduced there was no role of any importance for St Petersburg. Instead it was confidently expected that, following the defeat in the Crimea, Russian ambitions would turn to other objectives, possibly in Asia, and furthermore that domestic policy would now occupy the attention of the tsarist government to a greater extent than hitherto.

Berlin's new policy was based essentially on the programme of the *Wochenblatt* party, which Bismarck and his political friends had so passionately opposed; even in his memoirs he referred to the party with disdain as a 'coterie' and spoke of the 'rickety edifice' of the pro–western policy of the crown prince's court.[17] The unity of this so–called party was, as Bismarck knew only too well, an extremely loose affair. The bond that linked its representatives with one another and above all with the man who was now prince regent consisted chiefly of shared convictions in the field of foreign policy; Moritz August von Bethmann Hollweg, who had for many years been a close confidant of Prince William and leader of the *Wochenblatt* party, significantly became not Minister of the Interior but merely *Kultusminister*, responsible for culture, education and church affairs.

The central objective of their programme was an autonomous German policy for Prussia. This was to wipe out the 'disgrace of Olmütz' and bring about a solution of the German question to Prussia's advantage. To this end they aimed at a closer rapprochement with the western powers, particularly with Britain. At the same time they set out to win the support of the right wing of German liberalism, whose nationalism favoured a 'Kleindeutschland' and who had been prepared to make extensive concessions at Gotha.

That was the nucleus. And even here the prince regent had misgivings as to whether this was not going too far in terms of co-operating with the forces of middle-class liberalism, even if it was in the interests of Prussian power and his own throne. His advisers sought to allay these misgivings with the argument that it was precisely Prussian power, which as an old soldier he saw primarily as military power, that would be enormously reinforced by such a policy. In this way the Prussian monarchy would get its hands more firmly on the reins than hitherto.

Depending on who was using it, however, such an argument concealed very different positions. For some it expressed a genuine inner conviction; for others it was merely a means of reassuring the prince regent and preventing him from becoming restive. The *Wochenblatt* party did after all contain a sizeable group that was looking for very much more than a new and improved edition of the old Union policy. Among those who sympathized with the group was the prince regent's wife, Princess Augusta, who her whole life long regarded things Prussian with deep scepticism from the standpoint of her country of origin, the cosmopolitan and liberal Saxe-Weimar.

What the group aimed at was the gradual liberalization of Prussia, a genuine and not merely tactical alliance with the leading forces of the liberal middle classes with a view to forming a new and broader-based elite, an application, as appropriate, of the British model to a 'Kleindeutschland', a united Germany without Austria. In this spirit they invoked the tradition of Baron vom Stein and the Prussian reformers who had taken their lead from Britain. At the same time, however, they pointed to the fact, now emerging with every-increasing clarity, that the rapid progress of industrialization, particularly in Silesia and in the Ruhr district, together with all the economic and social changes that it brought in its wake, was creating conditions such as had hitherto existed in this form only in Belgium and above all in Britain. The conclusion was that only by following the political example of Britain could revolution and the complete overthrow of all order be avoided.

The principal representatives of this group were Bethmann Hollweg himself, the new Foreign Minister Count Schleinitz and the man now appointed minister without portfolio, the former Oberpräsident of East Prussia, Rudolf von Auerswald, one of the leaders of the liberal aristocracy of 1848 and a son of one of Stein and Hardenberg's closest associates in the period after 1806. Bismarck looked on with very mixed feelings as other members of the group moved into further key positions: Pourtalès, Bethmann's son-in-law, was sent to Paris in January 1859, von der Goltz went to Constantinople, Usedom became Bismarck's successor as envoy to the Federal Diet and Justus von Gruner, who for many years had been editor-in-chief of the *Wochenblatt*, became under secretary of state at the Foreign Ministry.

This wing of the *Wochenblatt* party gave an enormous boost to the expectations associated with the prince regent's assumption of office in October 1858 and the appointment of a new Cabinet at the beginning of November in the German public mind and particularly in the middle-class liberal camp. The carefully prepared speech that the prince regent delivered to the new ministry on 8 November 1858, publicly announcing the government's programme,[18] was seen as heralding and indeed ushering in a 'New Era' in Prussian and German politics – with the result that the elections to the Prussian House of Deputies held shortly afterwards led to a complete reversal of the existing majority situation. The various conservative groups were reduced to something like a quarter of their former strength, from 181 seats to 47. By contrast the liberals, led by Georg von Vincke, managed to increase the number of their seats by more than three times, from 48 to 151; together with the liberal conservatives of the left wing of the *Wochenblatt* party, they now had nearly 200 seats, a clear absolute majority.

Particularly the concluding sentences of the November programme appeared to justify those who had held for so long and through so many disappointments to the view that the Prussia of enlightened absolutism, the Prussia of the reform period, would one day assume the leadership of German liberalism and achieve its constitutional, national, economic and social objectives. 'Prussia must make moral conquests in Germany', the prince regent had declared, 'by wise legislation at home, by accentuating every ethical element and by seizing upon unifying factors such as the Customs Union, though this will need to be reformed. – The world must know that Prussia is everywhere prepared to protect the law. A firm, consistent and if necessary resolute conduct of policy, coupled with wisdom and circumspection, must earn Prussia the political respect and give it the position of power that it is not able to achieve by its material might alone.'

In all this people largely overlooked those passages that reflected the actual views of William himself and that in particular gave the principle that Prussia must everywhere appear as the champion of law its thoroughly conservative character. 'Above all I would warn against the empty cliché', the prince regent said, 'that the government must let itself be pushed farther and farther in the direction of developing liberal ideas because otherwise these will force their own way through . . . If all its actions bespeak truth, lawfulness and consistency, then a government is strong because it has a clear conscience, and that gives one the right robustly to withstand all evil.'

Unlike an expectant and optimistic public, which greatly overestimated the extent of the change of course, Bismarck took very careful note of these qualifications. 'The new ministry appears to have the best intentions as regards withstanding the push to the left', he wrote on 16 November to his brother Bernhard,[19] who was still managing the family estates – 'Bismarck translated into the harmless terms of a country squire of the Brandenburg March', as the future Chancellor Hohenlohe once called him.[20] Even so, in view of the reaction of the public Bismarck immediately added: 'How far it will succeed in this in the circumstances, only events will show.'

This surprisingly restrained and considered verdict, given Bismarck's basic political attitude and natural disposition, may have been largely due to the fact that the very brief section of the statement devoted to foreign affairs might well have been written by himself. 'Prussia must adopt the friendliest relations with all great powers', it said, 'without abandoning itself to foreign influences and without prematurely tying its hands with treaties.' Taken together with what had been said – undoubtedly out of the prince regent's deepest conviction – about the need for Prussia to be militarily strong, this amounted to the kind of policy that Bismarck was quite prepared to serve. 'If the gentlemen maintain contact with the Conservative Party', he suggested as early as 12 November, 'and if they honestly work towards an understanding *at home*, they may in terms of our *foreign* relations have an undoubted advantage over Manteuffel, and this is worth a great deal to me; for we "had fallen on hard times and ourselves knew not how". I felt that here most acutely.'[21] He was assuming, he went on, that the change of course in home affairs would be kept within limits, and above all he saw the appointment of the Prince of Hohenzollern as giving additional expression to a desire 'to have a guarantee against pure party government and against a slide to the left'. 'If I am wrong . . . I shall retreat behind the guns of Schönhausen and watch them govern Prussia on the basis of left-wing majorities.'

But in fact he was not willing to let it go at mere watching. Instead this upheaval, in which he suspected the political future of Prussia would be decided one way or another, prompted him once again to wonder briefly – and not without a degree of temptation – whether he should not, if it came to a showdown, swap his government career for the parliamentary career of a party politician: 'The prospect of brisk, honest battle without being hampered by any official ties, so to speak in political swimming-trunks', held 'almost as much attraction' for him 'as the prospect of a continued diet of truffles, telegrams and Grand Crosses'. He would, he hoped, 'feel ten years younger to find myself back in the same combat position as in [18] 48–9'.

In the last analysis, however, as he himself probably recognized, this was a kind of escapism. Because after the experiences of the recent past it had become very clear to him that in a monarchical bureaucratic state such as Prussia, in which the Crown insisted on its claim to executive supremacy, a right-wing aristocratic parliamentary opposition stood not the ghost of a chance in ordinary circumstances. It would have had to oppose the monarch without affirming, as the left did, the alternative principle of the sovereignty of the people and hence of the parliamentary majority of the day.

The monarchical principle or the sovereignty of the people – that was in abstract constitutional terms the great choice behind which the various political and social forces and interests lined up. The neo-absolutists of Manteuffel's stamp readily identified this choice with that between state and society. Accordingly, in the name of the monarchical principle they stood for a state above parties and social forces. It was a position for which Bismarck's background, political convictions and experience hitherto gave him no sympathy. On the contrary, he had a realistic awareness that the modern bureaucratic state was an institution that could rest on a wide variety of foundations. The freedom of action of its rulers at any one time might even, he suspected, be in inverse proportion to the degree to which they committed themselves unilaterally to a particular principle and to the forces and interests behind it.

Yet for that very reason he also saw quite clearly that in a situation such as the present one, in which the Crown's claim to sovereignty was crucially threatened, only those people had any prospect of reaching key positions of power who were prepared to accept that claim to sovereignty in principle and to defend it unconditionally against both right and left, in other words virtually to identify it with the state as such. To put it another way, he knew that in both historical and practical terms the doctrine of neo-absolutism was no more than a construction or, as we should say nowadays, an ideology. But he knew equally well that the only way to the centre of power at that time lay through practical recognition of that doctrine, specifically through the monarchical civil service. He therefore determined, upset though he was by his recall from Frankfurt, to remain in that service and wait this 'patch of bad weather' out 'in my bear skin, eating caviar and hunting elk'.[22]

He had to wait another three-and-a-half years. It was at the beginning of March 1859 that he had had to hand over his Frankfurt job to Count Usedom, a man whom he and his wife, who had meanwhile begun to feel quite at home in Frankfurt, henceforth pursued with passionate loathing as an ambitious schemer. Bismarck 'hated his enemies unto the fourth generation', but his wife hated them 'unto the thousandth', Gerson Bleichröder once aptly remarked[23] – the Berlin banker who, on the recommendation of Meyer Carl von Rothschild, now began his long service as Bismarck's private financial adviser and manager. After an extremely arduous six-day journey by rail and mail coach he had arrived in St Petersburg at the end of March and in a return to hotel accommodation had put up initially at the Demidov Hotel on the Nevsky Prospect. Not until mid-July did he find a very lovely house on the English Quay, right by the bridge over the Greater Neva to Vassiliy Ostrov, so that he could send for his family.

The journey to St Petersburg had given spatial expression to the distance that now separated him from the centres of decision-making. 'Russia stretched itself out beneath our wheels', he wrote home, 'the versts dropping litters at every stop'.[24] He arrived as Russia and Britain were making their last, admittedly very superficial efforts to forestall the military conflict that looked like breaking out over the future of Italy between France and Sardinia-Piedmont on the one hand and Austria on the other. Bismarck had no means of knowing, of course, how far Russia had already committed itself through its secret treaty with France of 3 March 1859. But from his very first talks with the Russian Foreign Minister, Prince Gorchakov, and subsequently with the tsar himself, who soon openly favoured him, it became quite clear to him that the situation he had forecast in his 'Prachtbericht' of April 1856 had meanwhile assumed reality: Russia was unequivocally aligned with France.

It inevitably made Bismarck all the more bitter that he should have been banished to St Petersburg at this precise moment, when the decisions in the Russian capital had long been taken whereas in Frankfurt and Berlin virtually all courses were still open, including the one he had suggested in 1856. Although it was clear to him that Berlin was certainly not waiting for his advice, he simply could not help letting his voice be clearly heard in a situation that in his opinion 'yet again [held] the jackpot for us', as he wrote to Gustav von Alvensleben, the aide-de-camp and personal friend of the prince regent, on 5 May.[25] In the period between his arrival in St Petersburg and the surprisingly quick conclusion of a peace treaty in early July 1859 he swamped the new Foreign Minister, von Schleinitz, and the prince regent himself with a flood of 'reports' and private letters. Expressed in many different ways and from many different viewpoints, the burden of these was always the same: this was the moment if not to solve the German question at least to place the relationship between the two German great powers on a better, more solid footing.

He brought all his Frankfurt experience to bear here as well as the fundamental insights he had gained with regard to the individual powers and the state of their interests. Nor did he forget to appeal to what he took to be special prejudices and predilections of whichever man he was addressing at the time, as for instance when for the prince regent's benefit he put the emphasis on military questions and on the need to inspire confidence even in one's opponent by one's candour and clarity, or when he praised Schleinitz for his level-headedness in the face of 'party passions'[26] in the present situation and extolled his statesmanlike attitude.

Fascinating though it is to trace all this in detail and to observe how he derived each of his proposed moves from an overall concept, the basic features of which had been laid down long before, and how flexibly he adapted himself to a constantly changing situation, nevertheless it was the monologue of an outsider who at no point had any real influence on the decision-making process; he himself once spoke both soberly and graphically of the 'need to evacuate the mind as well as the bowels'.[27] Like the memorandum of almost a hundred pages on the subject of the German Confederation and Prussia's position within it that Bismarck, summing up the experiences and arguments of nearly seven years in Frankfurt, had presented to Prince William at the end of March 1858,[28] the reports he sent from St Petersburg in the spring and summer of 1859 can have received only a cursory royal reading at best. And as far as Schleinitz was concerned, Bismarck cannot seriously have believed that a man who enjoyed the confidence of Princess Augusta was going to adopt as his own the suggestions of someone to whom she objected strongly as a champion of reactionary Junker politics; Schleinitz had been a mere 'harem minister',[29] the 'princess's darling'[30] who 'owed his career to petticoats alone',[31] were some of Bismarck's scornful verdicts on the man who later became Minister of the Royal Household.

It did of course have one function, this flood of memoranda and letters with which the 'pasha', as one of the secretaries at the St Petersburg legation, Kurd von Schlözer, sarcastically dubbed the bustling and always irritable new man, overwhelmed his superiors in Berlin. Here was someone continually offering alternatives to the policy that Berlin was in fact pursuing. Should that policy not in the long run lead to the desired objectives, people would probably remember those alternatives and be inclined to look at them through fresh eyes, particularly since their author did not set out from a fundamentally different position, as was the case with the decidedly pro-Austrian arch-conservatives in Prussia, but on the contrary referred to the latter's attitude as 'utter lunacy' that was 'not even of interest to the doctor any more'.[32] 'In many Berlin minds' the hope was clearly 'indestructible', he mocked in a letter to Otto von Wentzel, a close colleague during his Frankfurt period, 'that Austria, arm in arm with a powerful Prussia, will drive the devil out of hell in order to install him as a convert in the state chancellery.'[33]

The significance of the tactical function of Bismarck's initiatives is something we must rate the more highly for the fact that his first reactions to the prince regent's November programme made it very clear that in his opinion progress could be made in this way in both foreign and domestic affairs as long as the government steered a resolute course and did not let parliament and public opinion force it towards the left. And if we can believe what the former leader of the democrats, Hans Viktor von Unruh, wrote in his memoirs about a conversation with Bismarck in mid-March 1859, even at this point he already had a clear idea as to how that course could be held and how the kind of foreign policy that was envisaged could be given additional momentum.[34]

Unruh tells us that, on the way to his new post in St Petersburg, Bismarck explained to him that Prussia's objective must be 'to remove Austria from Germany proper'. In pursuing this objective it could expect no support of any kind from the small and medium-sized German states. This was even 'quite natural, since the individual states knew quite well that Austria could not absorb them whereas Prussia made them fear for their lives'. With such a policy Prussia stood completely alone as far as central Europe was concerned. Here, according to Bismarck, there was only one conceivable ally for Prussia, 'if it knows how to acquire and how to treat that ally', namely 'the German people'. And upon Unruh's showing surprise: 'Well, what do you expect . . . I'm the same country squire [Junker] as ten years ago when we met in the [Prussian] House, but I'd have no eyes and no brain in my head if I couldn't see clearly how things really stand.'

'There is nothing more German than the development of Prussia's special interests as properly understood', he had said with a different slant and with a different kind of emphasis in the great memorandum addressed to the Prince of Prussia twelve months before.[35] And two-and-a-half years later he again said expressly in a letter to Rudolf von Auerswald, one of the leading figures of the 'New Era': 'In the long run we have only one reliable mainstay (if we do not deliberately reject it), and that is the national strength of the German people, as long as it sees the Prussian army as its champion and its hope for the future and as long as it does not see us waging wars to please and promote other dynasties than that of Hohenzollern.'[36]

With regard to 'how things really stand', as he had put it to Unruh, two years later Bismarck expressed himself much more candidly in a letter to his old friend Albrecht von Roon, who was now War Minister.[37] It was his opinion, he wrote to Roon on 2 July 1861, that 'the chief failing of our policy hitherto has been that we have presented ourselves as liberal in Prussia and conservative abroad, holding the rights of our own King cheap and those of foreign princes in too much respect'. The kind of policy he envisaged was the exact opposite: 'As I see it, only through a change in our "external" attitude can the position of the Crown at home be relieved of the pressure that otherwise it will not in fact withstand in the long run, though I have no doubt of the adequacy of the means thereto.' Back in 1857, in the great debate with Gerlach, he had put this more vividly: 'We are a vain nation; we grow irritable when we cannot show off, and we have a lot of time for a government that gives us importance abroad and we will put up with a great deal in return, even when it hits our pockets.'[38] There is an almost aphoristic echo of this sentence in the letter to Roon: 'We are nearly as vain as the French; if we can persuade ourselves that we are respected abroad we will put up with a great deal at home.'

On top of such considerations there was Bismarck's personal bid for power. He believed he had every reason to back this card. Had not Unruh, as one of the leading members of the 'National Union' founded in the summer of 1859 to promote a unified Lesser Germany, told him at the end of a long letter about the German question written in September of that year: 'Since for me and for my friends too the national question is of primary importance, ruling out any kind of ulterior motive, you can infer that we, including Mr von Bennigsen [the president of the National Union], would be sincerely happy to see you appointed Minister of Foreign Affairs. Now more than ever Prussia needs a clear, firm, bold policy. The bolder it is, the less risky it will be, relatively speaking.'[39]

The 'alliance with the German people', later so much invoked, was thus from the outset conceived as a means to an end, both in general and in personal terms – although it is also true, and the fact is often overlooked, that this was from the outset a twofold end. Important though the domestic calculation was, there is no doubt at all that the foreign policy arguments he cited for Unruh's benefit were of equal importance as far as he was concerned, especially since the two were so perfectly complementary. In his eight years in the thoroughly bourgeois environment of Frankfurt, a city in which vital skeins of trade and supra-regional high finance ran together, he had gained a clear idea of the importance of making general appraisals of a situation and of the way in which it was likely to develop. He had seen how important it was to associate oneself with particular expectations, and he had observed on the other hand the marked propensity of the middle-class business mind to come to terms in good time with those who were likely to carry the day. Another thing he had come to recognize in Frankfurt, particularly under the influence of Austrian activities in this sphere, was the growing importance of an effective press and public relations policy in the field of foreign affairs as well. 'Parliament and the press could become the most powerful aids for our foreign policy', he put it programmatically in a letter written around this time to a Conservative Party colleague.[40] The conversation with Unruh shows that he understood how important it was in politics to take account of the opinions and hopes of those not directly involved in the decision-making process – and above all how important it was to stimulate their imagination. Doing this without adopting any kind of disguise and without implausible adaptation – 'I'm the same country squire as ten years ago' – became in fact the secret of his success, here as in the world of diplomacy. For the bewildered listener this stood everything on its head, making the truth look like tactics and mere tactics look like the truth.

The truth was really very simple. The prince regent was quite right: Prussia, the Prussian state as presently constituted, must make 'moral conquests' in Germany. It must thereby 'earn . . . the political respect and . . . the position of power that it is not able to achieve by its material might alone'. But the word 'moral' must not be understood in any narrowly middle-class way, nor above all must it be limited to domestic policy, as the liberals wanted. 'Moral conquests' must mean winning over public opinion, first in Prussia but then also beyond its borders. In Bismarck's view, however, and here he was wholly at variance both with the conservatives and with the liberal idealists, the most effective way of achieving this was by convincingly holding out to the public a promise of increased power and respect for the community of interests it represented.

To the conservatives this was an opportunistic appeal to the sovereignty of the people, and they called it 'Bonapartism'. And to the liberals it was demagogic corruption of the people because it invoked expectations without regard to their original content. The simple truth, in other words, was not so simple after all. It was if politics was in essence reduced to the principle of self-assertion: at home on the part of the existing political and social order, abroad on the part of the country's place in the system of powers, and in overall terms, taking in both spheres, on the part of the protagonist, the particular politician concerned. It was not simple if one liked to see politics serving specific ideas and programmes and a rational value system and world order of whatever kind. That, however, still seemed to be the prevailing trend of the time, and so it was; testimonies to a fundamentally different view acquired weight only as a result of further developments.

This explains why the 'simple truth' of this particular policy at first met with little response and sympathy even from those in whose interests it was conceived. Ultimately, of course, the prince regent and the more conservative of his advisers wanted nothing more than to reconcile particularly the educated and propertied middle class with the existing political and social order by means of tactical concessions. But they shrank from so unequivocally calling a spade a spade. Above all they were not prepared, should the worst come to the worst and the representatives of the liberal middle class not prove sufficiently co-operative but try to make further ground, to risk a major conflict.

This applied to the prince regent as well – with one possible exception, of which everyone must have been aware: William's whole education and indeed his whole life up until now had taught him to see himself as belonging to a line of Prussian soldier-kings. It was something he took for granted, and anyone who questioned it must reckon with his impassioned opposition.

It had not yet come to that, of course, when in the spring of 1859 Bismarck argued from St Petersburg expressly but in vain for an offensive Prussian policy in the Italian conflict, although the military question did already loom large here, the prince regent having made the possibility of Austria's receiving help from the Confederation dependent on his being given supreme command of the Confederation army. The 'New Era' system was still working. Its practical successes, chiefly at home, appeared to confound even those who, like Bismarck, while not regarding it as fundamentally wrong, sharply criticized the way in which it was applied. The fact was that the overwhelming majority of the Prussian liberals under Bismarck's old adversary, Baron von Vincke, showed great understanding with regard to the delicate situation of a ruler who, entrusted only with the regency, was attempting to steer a new course against the declared wishes of the old governing circles. Accordingly they counselled restraint and patience. And as far as foreign policy was concerned, although Bismarck, while basically approving of the government's anti-Austrian objectives, condemned its pursuit of them as too hesitant and indecisive, yet he can hardly be said to have had a genuine alternative to offer.

Simply Prussia's demanding supreme military control in a war involving the Confederation and Berlin's impenetrable 'at-the-ready' attitude pushed the Austrian and French emperors headlong, at the beginning of July 1859, into concluding what was for both parties a somewhat problematical peace in order to avert the danger of a growth in Prussian power in central Europe. What, then, might the reactions have been to Prussia's giving notice of withdrawal from the Confederation or even a military offensive in the direction of southern Germany, as Bismarck suggested? In such an event Prussia would certainly not even have found its ally 'the German people'. For the majority of the German public was unequivocally of the opinion that it was the Rhine, meaning the integrity of the German states in the face of French aspirations, that Austria was defending at the Po. Accordingly it even frowned on the 'at-the-ready' policy of the new Prussian government. Exploiting the situation in favour of a new version of the Union policy or some other form of Lesser German unification policy was a course supported by only a section of the Prussian liberals together with one or two political outsiders such as the democrats Arnold Ruge and Ludwig Bamberger or the future socialist leader Ferdinand Lassalle. In other words, Prussian policy during the Italian conflict can be said to have gone as far as it could go and its lack of success to have shown the extent to which it had already overplayed its hand.

Bismarck probably admitted as much to himself. Given the circumstances and given the entire situation, there was in fact no 'jackpot' for Prussia here. If he nevertheless continued almost to the end to insist that there had been, the clear inference is that already at this point in his career the tactical viewpoint played a large if not a decisive part: only a failure on the part of the persons and forces currently setting the tone in Berlin, with whose basic direction he largely agreed, at least in foreign policy and particularly with regard to Austria, could bring him from the sidelines into a decisive position. The thing to do, then, was to predict that failure and to do so with arguments that suggested he knew another way of achieving the same objective.

With this very much in mind and with a clear eye on the prince regent, Bismarck the diplomat, whose many memoranda had for years been dominated by the principle that successful power politics was in essence successful alliance politics, began early in 1859 to play up the military question. Whether in the downright martial letter to General von Alvensleben or whether in his famous letter of 12 May 1859 to Schleinitz with the sentence: 'I see our federal relationship as a Prussian infirmity that we shall sooner or later have to heal ferro et igni if we do not undergo a cure for it in good time and at a favourable season'[41] – he talked continually now about how everything depended upon Prussia's military might.

He also saw immediately how he could exploit the official government policy of lending weight to a possible Prussian intervention by obtaining supreme command of the Confederation army. This, he said scornfully, bound Prussia even more closely to a body, namely the Confederation, that all experience showed to have a permanent bias towards Austria. It gave Berlin a purely superficial, borrowed power. In the name of a Germany that at this level harboured nothing but the selfish interests of Austria and the small and medium-sized states, Prussia was once again – and voluntarily, too – placing itself in leading-strings. It was probably 'time we remembered', he wrote with provocative exaggeration in the above-mentioned letter to Schleinitz, 'that the leaders who expect us to follow them serve other interests than Prussia's and that the cause of Germany, about which they talk incessantly, in something they understand in such a way that it cannot at the same time be Prussia's cause, unless we wish to give ourselves up'. In order to be able effectively to serve the cause of Prussia the Prussian government must have at its immediate disposal an army strong enough – this was the tacit implication – to dominate central Europe on its own if necessary.

This was nothing new. To all intents and purposes it already formed part of the 'New Era' programme – a point to which Bismarck very deliberately drew attention. But he was one of the first to place it, anticipating the outcome, in the context of the experience of the Italian War and at the same time give the demand for armament a concrete objective. He was touching here, as he well knew, on a favourite idea of the prince regent's: effacing the 'disgrace of Olmütz', the work of the 'November traitors' of 1850, with the aid of a powerful army – an idea of which seven years later he had to struggle long and hard to prevent the literal execution when William, now king, wanted to follow up the Battle of Königgrätz by marching his victorious army into Vienna.

Those Prussian liberals of the Lesser German persuasion who in 1859 had, like Bismarck himself, demanded an anti-Austrian policy on Prussia's part that if necessary went to the last extreme followed him only shortly afterwards in his demand for an increase in Prussia's armed strength. In so doing they temporarily frustrated the calculation, which had immediately suggested itself on the basis of the events of 1848, that the military question would bring about a rupture not only with the liberals in parliament but also with that section of the government that was genuinely prepared to co-operate with them. For the time being, therefore, Bismarck could do nothing but wait – in the hope that a conflict of principle would after all break out sooner or later. To this end he concentrated more and more in the period that followed on formulating at every conceivable opportunity and vis-à-vis the most diverse interlocutors the objective alternatives not so much to the system as to the practice of the 'New Era', thus building himself up as a personal alternative.

'Zwischenzustand' (literally, 'intermediate state') is how Bismarck referred in his memoirs to the period between the end of the Italian War and his appointment as chief minister in September 1862. The word conveys very precisely the situation in which he found himself during those three years. Mentally and emotionally it was a deeply trying time in which the shadow of futility once again fell over his whole existence. Serious disorders, which with the exception of a near-fatal attack of pneumonia in the autumn of 1859 his doctors never managed properly to diagnose, went hand in hand with constant physical and psychological ill-health, a veritable 'bankruptcy of his private nerves'.[42] A quite new tone enters his private correspondence during these months, a blend of resignation and detachment in which formulae of Christian devotion alternated with reflections on the senselessness of believing in the permanence of anything whatever in the swiftly changing pattern of all human relationships. 'I should be curiously overestimating the duration and worth of this life', he wrote in a letter to Leopold von Gerlach at the beginning of May 1860, 'did I not wish constantly to bear in mind that after thirty years, and possibly from a great deal earlier, it is of no significance at all to me what political successes I or my country have achieved in Europe.' And in the same letter: 'From my twenty-third to my thirty-second year I lived in the country, and I shall never get the longing to return there out of my veins; I am in politics only half-heartedly.'[43] In another letter he complained: 'The feeling of *dwelling*, of being *at home* anywhere is one I have become a complete stranger to since Frankfurt.'[44] Soon after this we find him again saying that he could easily imagine going to London or Naples as legation chief[45] – but 'moving is more than a little like dying'.[46]

Such remarks make it clear how useless he felt in his present post, how dissatisfied he was, cultivating relationships that had no function in the present and whose function in the future was for others to decide. When he returned to Berlin in the spring of 1860 to attend the sittings of the Upper House but above all to investigate the lie of the land it looked for a moment as if the prince regent, urged on by his Minister-President, Prince von Hohenzollern, and Hohenzollern's deputy Rudolf von Auerswald, might decide to strengthen the right wing of the Cabinet by giving Bismarck the Foreign Ministry. But in the end this went no further than contacts between him and the prince regent, contacts that were agonizingly long-drawn-out because the prince regent wanted to leave doors open in every direction. It went no further than 'the cheap situation of an envoy in his leave hotel engaged in backstairs intrigues against his boss', as Bismarck described it to Leopold von Gerlach.[47]

Bismarck himself would apparently have been prepared to accept such an offer. 'I am doing my level best to get back to St Petersburg unmolested and resignedly watch developments from there', he wrote to his brother on 12 May 1860. 'If, however, the ministerial hack is nevertheless paraded for my benefit, my concern about the condition of its legs is not such as to prevent me from mounting.' By way of justification he said that the situation was so confused that he could not play unduly coy, although the other side ought not to assume 'that I should make no conditions at all were I to join this Cabinet'. He added: 'If we go on driving before the wind like this it will be a miracle and a great mercy if we do not run so firmly aground that such questions as the Jews and the land tax soon seem very unimportant.'[48]

In fact he was probably more worried that this might be his last chance and that the future might see the final triumph of those whose objectives were a parliamentary monarchy on the British model and a permanent alliance with the liberals. And that was where his candidacy was to founder. He was too clearly not the kind of man with whose help anyone could hope to broaden the base of the Ministry towards the right. As his behaviour in Berlin, for all its caution, put beyond the shadow of a doubt, he would try continually to bring the Cabinet round to his overall political line and so sooner or later break it up. He would not let himself be tied down or 'tamed'. So it was necessary that he continue to be excluded if the great compromise between the forces of the old and the forces of the new was to have a chance.

But did such a compromise have a chance anyway? Was it not inevitable that the question should sooner or later be asked: who in fact governs Prussia? Was there some way of avoiding the power question until such time as the new order, the new relationship between Crown and parliament and between the men and parties on which it rested, had become firmly established? Everything else, the future of Prussia and of Germany as well as Bismarck's whole political destiny, depended on the answer to this question.

[5]

From Army Reform to Constitutional Conflict:

Bismarck's Hour

That it was of literally vital importance for the 'New Era' to avoid the power question was something of which those who had presided at its birth were only too well aware. In positive terms it was a question of condominium through compromise, a system of joint rule within a balance of interests and opinions. And since it was obvious to all clear-sighted people that every contemporary trend favoured the forces of newness and change, the need was in fact to locate that compromise more towards the right wing of the political spectrum and to treat the representatives of the right with the greatest possible indulgence. 'No pushing' was the watchword that Georg von Vincke issued to the liberals.

Despite this awareness and the way in which it dictated the political practice of the parliamentary majority during the 'New Era', large sections of those groups of the Prussian nobility who had hitherto set the tone, the landowners, top civil servants and army officers, rejected all idea of compromise. They persisted in their rigid opposition to all attempts to reach an understanding with liberalism and with the middle classes. Their numbers were now much reduced. In the mid-1850s the Conservative Party, though split into various parliamentary groups, had still enjoyed an absolute majority in the Lower House and had thus clearly dominated both houses of parliament. In the landslide election at the beginning of the 'New Era' they had held only forty-seven seats, and in the election of December 1861 they collapsed almost completely, retaining a mere fourteen seats in the House of Deputies. Yet conservatives continued to occupy crucial positions of power and influence in state and society. To push them out of those positions would have been impossible, as things stood, by any but revolutionary means – whether that revolution came from below or whether it came from above.

An appeal to the masses was ruled out, even as far as the most committed liberals were concerned, by the experiences of 1848. And against a revolution from above there was the objection, not to be dismissed lightly, that it would simply be playing into the hands of a new absolutism. As a result there were even now, despite all their negative experiences, powerful forces in the liberal camp who preached patience and restraint and advocated further attempts to win round the conservative groups that still resisted. At the same time, however, a more resolute tendency was emerging. This affirmed that progress must be made and if necessary the resistance of those who were not prepared to reach a genuine compromise must be broken down. The confrontation actually crystallized around a question that ultimately determined not only the fate of the 'New Era' but in a sense the development of Prussia and of Germany for the next two generations: the question of the reform of the Prussian army constitution.

In substance the question was at first hardly in dispute. Agreement about the need for reform was as widespread as about the fact that such a reform must increase the fighting power of the army and with it Prussia's importance in power-political terms. Whereas forty years before this, in 1820, the Prussian army had been weaker than the French by only about 40,000 men, the gap had since grown to some 200,000 men, in other words the French army was now nearly three times as big as the Prussian. Much the same was true with regard to Austria, Prussia being in a position of clear military inferiority at this time, to say nothing of Russia with its gigantic army of around a million men.

There was another consideration that was no less important. The now nearly 50-year-old Prussian Military Service Law, which the War Minister of the day, Hermann von Boyen, had drafted in 1814 in the immediate wake of and wholly in the spirit of the Wars of Liberation, had sought to forge as close a connection as possible between state and nation on the basis of universal compulsory military service and the idea of forming a reserve army comprising all trained soldiers. In the mean time, however, the law had led to enormous injustices. With a rapidly expanding population only a steadily falling proportion of those liable to military service could in fact be called up. On the other hand an increase in regular units was out of the question both financially and on grounds of principle, Frederick William IV having promised to make no changes here without summoning a Diet and enacting a constitution. The end result was that more than two-thirds of those liable to military service enjoyed the possibility of being released from that liability by lot – with all the consequences that such a procedure usually implies.

Moreover, even the principle of the reserve army operated at best only in a very limited way. The Landwehr or Home Guard of the first and second reserves, which comprised all trained soldiers up to the age of 40 and had been conceived as an army of the 'people in arms', was in principle repeatedly approved of and acclaimed by the middle classes and by public opinion. In practice, however, people found it increasingly burdensome as a commitment that interfered with both their professional and their private lives. As a result it was becoming more and more difficult, for example, to find even halfway suitable candidates for selection as Landwehr officers.

To anyone taking an unprejudiced view of the situation it was obvious that theory and practice had developed along very different lines. The idea of the 'people in arms', shaping its destiny by its own efforts in this sphere as well, had remained no more than an idea, not only with regard to the longer-term intention of embedding the army constitution in a democratic-liberal national constitution. It had also emerged that the much-invoked 'spirit of the Wars of Liberation' was a mere illusion and that the Prussian army differed in no way from the armies of other absolutist states: during the revolution the overwhelming majority of it proved a loyally devoted tool of the Crown. Even the Landwehr battalions mobilized on that occasion to quell the uprising in Baden in 1849 were no exception. Nevertheless, in conservative eyes the Landwehr did constitute a certain element of insecurity. Consequently the years after 1848 saw a continuation of the efforts of the preceding decades to bind it more closely to the regular army or even to amalgamate the two.

Seen as a whole, however, particularly against the background of the conflict situation of 1859, the army question as such scarcely contained the combustible material it was subsequently to acquire. What was crucial was that the manner in which it was treated made clear how unsure were the foundations on which the 'New Era' system in fact rested. Above all it became increasingly obvious that the man who had apparently set everything in train and on whom all hopes were therefore concentrated at first had clearly been guided in his opposition to the forces, tendencies and persons that had prevailed hitherto not so much by considerations of principle as by personal considerations and by opinions of his own regarding details of policy. This was when the prince regent particularly revealed himself to be a man who thought entirely in terms of the political battlefronts of the 1820s and 1830s, when his opinions had been formed once and for all. 'A parliament that commands the military is the end of monarchy', was how the historian Friedrich Christoph Dahlmann, once of the 'Göttingen Seven', had summed up the quintessence of all historical experience.[1] And that was where the prince regent now saw the hard core of the whole problem; that was what he regarded as the real impulse behind every parliamentary initiative in this field.

William started out from the assumption that compromise on this question was not possible, that the other side would always be trying crucially to weaken the Crown. Accordingly he treated the liberal majority in the Lower House, constantly though its members indicated their willingness to compromise, as constituting from the outset an enemy to be outsmarted as far as possible and outmanoeuvred with a policy of the *fait accompli*. In this he naturally received the immediate and most enthusiastic support of all those who were opposed to the 'New Era' system on grounds of principle as well as out of a concern to preserve their positions and influence. This led inevitably – almost, as it were, automatically – to the other side eventually behaving and arguing in the way the prince regent had always supposed they would, which in turn confirmed him in his own dogmatic viewpoint. The whole conflict in a sense unfolded along the lines of the self-fulfilling prophecy, although the premises of that prophecy had more to do with the views and battle-lines of the past than with those of the present. Among other things this brings out the not inconsiderable

156

importance of the fact that the change of sovereign in Prussia did not this time involve a change of generation.

The first step taken by the prince regent and his closest political advisers on military matters, chief among them Gustav von Alvensleben, the adjutant-general, and Edwin von Manteuffel, the head of the so-called 'Military Cabinet', still admitted of justification on essentially pragmatic grounds as well as by the fact that they were sure that parliament would be in fundamental agreement with them on this issue. On the occasion of the demobilization following the Peace of Villafranca they simply left a couple of cadres as a basis for the future expansion of the armed forces, although the requisite funds had not even been applied for. But when further proceedings were brought up in Cabinet and the reform plans discussed in detail it very soon appeared that the prince regent regarded it as the prerogative of the Crown to decide this whole question on its own authority alone. Any idea of an accommodating approach and a policy of compromise vis-à-vis parliament he rejected out of hand. The War Minister, Eduard von Bonin, by now a convinced supporter of the 'New Era' system, promptly resigned – an occurrence the fundamental importance of which Bismarck sought, when writing his memoirs, to cover up with the remark that Bonin could not even have 'kept a drawer in order, much less a ministry', implying that he was merely incompetent and had eventually faced the fact.[2] Bonin was replaced early in December 1859 by General Albrecht von Roon, an avowed representative of the political right. The move brought into the centre of the political stage the man who was to play so important a part in the eventual appointment of Bismarck, a personal friend of long standing.

Albrecht von Roon, then 56 years of age, had been born into an impoverished Pomeranian noble family of Dutch origin and brought up in Pietist circles. He had received a scientific education, was regarded as absolutely reliable politically and as a general staff officer had quickly made a name for himself as a teacher at the army's military academy. In his capacity as military tutor to Prince Frederick Charles he had come into close contact with the royal family in the early 1840s; he had known the present head of the family since the Prussian army had marched into Baden in 1849, an operation that the latter had commanded and in which Roon had participated as chief of staff of an army corps. In 1858, now a divisional commander in Düsseldorf, he had presented a memorandum about the problems and perils of the existing army constitution, and as a result he had been invited in 1859 to join a special advisory committee appointed to prepare the reorganization of the army.

As his memorandum had made clear, Roon whole-heartedly shared his sovereign's basic opinion that the army must be exclusively an instrument in the hands of the Crown and one that could be used for its purposes not only abroad but also at home. And he was determined from the outset, if possible with even fewer reservations than the prince regent, to couple the army question with the power question, should the need arise, in other words to ask Parliament to bow unconditionally to the will of the crown. In the 'New Era' Cabinet, which for all its differences of temperament and opinion was bent on co-operation and achieving a balance of differing views, Roon was therefore the odd man out right from the start, though this emerged clearly only with the passage of time; to begin with he was seen simply as a departmental minister.

The Army Bill that Roon presented to the Prussian House of Deputies on 10 February 1860, a mere two months after his appointment, contained in purely objective terms only one contentious point, and in different circumstances it is quite conceivable that agreement would have been reached even on that. Together with the almost universally welcomed increase in the peacetime strength of the Prussian army from 150,000 to around 210,000 men, the Bill proposed, with reference to the need at the same time to enhance the army's striking power, a change in the composition of the army in the field in time of war. Hitherto this had consisted of the current three active and two reserve years and the next seven years of the so-called 'first reserve' Landwehr. Now the first three years of the Landwehr were to be added to the reserve and placed under the command of the regular officer corps. The remaining four years were to join the former 'second-reserve' Landwehr and like it serve only in the rear in any future war.

There was certainly something to be said on practical grounds for what would amount to a rejuvenation of the army and the release of older Landwehr personnel from the front line. But this was promptly thrust into the background by the suspicion that what the government was really after was a restructuring of the army in the interests of monarchical autocracy and the destruction of the principle, embodied in the Landwehr, of the 'people in arms' – the specifically 'middle-class spirit' that constituted 'the sole corrective' against the ever-perilous 'army-officer spirit', as Max Duncker, the crown prince's political adviser, put it.[3] The suspicion was further fostered by the fact that the War Ministry insisted on the new three-year period of compulsory military service – the increase dated only from 1856 – although many military experts considered a two-year period quite adequate for practical training. On top of this there was a whole host of indications from the War Ministry and from the circle around the prince regent, some of them deliberately put about but others undoubtedly authentic, showing that behind the whole Army Bill there was a spirit that no longer had anything to do with the expectations that people had associated with the 'New Era'. The committee of the House of Deputies appointed to examine the Bill under the chairmanship of Baron von Vincke therefore decided by an overwhelming majority, after weeks of discussion, to recommend that the House enact the Bill only on condition that the government agreed to a two-year period of service for the infantry and to the retention of the Landwehr in its old form.

It should have been clear to everyone that the prince regent, whose personal commitment on this issue was of the deepest kind, could not have conceded these points without losing face completely. It is an open question, of course, whether matters might have taken a very different turn had the liberal majority adopted a radically different approach with the object of winning the prince regent round on questions of general policy by being exceptionally forthcoming on this issue and eliciting his co-operation in a spirit of genuine trust. But it is doubtful whether the mood of the public and of their own supporters would have allowed the liberals to adopt such an approach in the first place – quite apart from the fact that that kind of tactical calculation was totally alien to most liberal deputies.

Nevertheless, a section of the party was still quite prepared to talk in terms of extensive concessions, not least because they were aware that their own position was by no means as strong as it appeared to be in the parliamentary arena. However, their readiness to compromise no longer met with a response. Instead Roon, with the vigorous support of the prince regent and the muted approval of the Cabinet – which thereby progressively abandoned its original direction – immediately set about outmanoeuvring parliament and peremptorily rejecting its claim to have a say in this matter. Roon argued that the new Army Bill did not fundamentally modify the 1814 Military Service Law but was concerned only with its practical implementation. The whole thing had been placed before the House of Deputies, he said, simply 'as a matter of courtesy'. It was possible to proceed without parliament and not offend against the constitution in any way.

This was to argue in purely formal terms, because without additional finance, the approval of which was indubitably parliament's affair, Roon's army reform could not be put into effect. Moreover, the argument was also false in substance in that the relationship between Landwehr and 'army of the line' was laid down in the existing Military Service Law and was not for the monarch to determine.

In spite of this the army was reorganized during the course of 1860 in accordance with the plans of Roon's ministry, including the dissolution of the appropriate Landwehr regiments and the formation of the same number of line regiments. The financial basis for these measures, which at one blow improved the military career prospects of the sons of the Prussian nobility out of all recognition, was provided in May 1860 by a supplementary budget that was passed almost unanimously. This was expressly described by the government as an interim arrangement pending a final settlement of the military question, but in reality it was used to bring about a *fait accompli*.

However the matter may have been argued in detail, this constituted a substantial undermining of parliament's right of budgetary control. The conflict over the army had in fact already become a constitutional conflict, although a large section of the liberals and the wing of the ministry that sympathized with them did endeavour by means of a belated agreement to prevent a conflict of this kind from breaking out openly.

By this time at the very latest Bismarck must have seen that some skilful manoeuvring over the army question would be capable of upsetting the whole 'New Era' system. It was now clear to everyone in the know that Roon, the head of the Military Cabinet Edwin von Manteuffel and with them almost the entire *Kreuzzeitung* party were intent on exploiting the situation and the prince regent's dogmatic prejudice on this very issue to effect a fresh and radical change of course. Bismarck was also aware that Roon was thinking of him in this connection, seeing him as a particularly suitable fellow combatant against a liberalization and parliamentarization of Prussia. Equally, however, he was aware that Manteuffel and a number of leading members of the *Kreuzzeitung* party shared this view only to a limited extent. Like the prince regent himself, many of them regarded him as too unstable, too flexible both with regard to principles and with regard to practical politics and the means to be employed in its pursuit.

This does not suffice on its own, however, to explain why Bismarck, who did everything to keep himself in the public eye as both a personal and a policy alternative, took hardly any part, even within the limits imposed on him by physical distance and the duties of his office, in the attempts to exacerbate the conflict beyond the antagonisms that already existed. The decisive factor here was that Bismarck's tactical programme and political objectives and those of Roon and his friends, for all their apparent agreement at a superficial level, diverged widely on essential points.

Take foreign policy, for example, where Bismarck was inevitably afraid that a fresh change of course would lead to a revival of the circumstances of the Manteuffel era with the perpetual struggle for what he called his 'ideal' of 'freedom from bias', of the 'independence of decisions from the effects of aversion to or predilection for foreign countries and their rulers'.[4] It was no accident that a last letter discussing fundamental principles was written to Leopold von Gerlach during this period. In it Bismarck once again argued passionately in favour of not excluding Napoleonic France from all coalition considerations on grounds of anti-revolutionary principle 'because you cannot play chess when sixteen of the sixty-four squares are forbidden to you by your own side'.[5] But in domestic policy too, although here he understandably expressed himself only with great reserve and in very general terms, he saw that a new version of a policy of bureaucratic neo-absolutist repression in the style of Manteuffel and Westphalen stood as little chance of success as did romantic notions of a restoration of the old, pre-revolutionary order.

During his time in Frankfurt and in the light of the many and varied experiences that life in one of the great commercial and financial centres of mid-nineteenth century Europe had brought him, he had come a very long way from his original views on this point. In 1848, leaving aside all differences of opinion over the standpoint of concrete self-interest, he had agreed in principle with his arch-conservative friends that the economic and social reforms of the Prussian reform period had been politically and socially detrimental. Like them he had seen Stein and Hardenberg as symbols of absolutist arbitrariness, the bureaucratic mania for change. Now, however, he saw very much more clearly that those reforms were part of an unstoppable overall development and that the state and its traditional ruling class must adapt themselves to that development in the interests of their own self-preservation. This had the effect of mitigating his anti-bourgeois feeling to the extent to which he became aware that in a whole series of areas there was a natural convergence of interests between the land-owning nobility and the commercial middle class; particularly the way in which the fronts had formed in the conflicts over customs policy had undoubtedly taught him a great deal in this respect, both in matters of principle and in matters of detail. They had made clear to him the connection, which arose out of the situation, between the national ideal of a 'Kleindeutschland', the economic interests of the middle class and Prussia's interest as a great power, as he interpreted it – a connection that he had since taken increasingly into account in his foreign policy calculations.

It is difficult to say at what point Bismarck realized that all this could be exploited not only for foreign policy but also for domestic policy purposes and that it might perhaps be possible, particularly on the basis of Prussia's traditionally liberal economic policy founded on the principles of free trade and freedom of trade and industry, to build up quite new coalitions on the home front as well. There is reason to suppose that the man who had been saying for years that, to take a realistic view, it was not shared principles but common interests that formed the basis of foreign policy coalitions should for some time have been secretly working along the same lines when it came to appraising domestic affairs.

As a result he found the self-evident successes of the 'New Era' system, particularly with respect to the political integration of the middle classes, very much less surprising and perplexing than did many other conservatives. Even the rapid recovery after the economic crisis of 1857 and the ensuing period of sustained prosperity fitted easily into this context as far as he was concerned: they were proof of the fact that there was a kind of natural convergence of different economic and social forces and interests that could probably be successfully focused in political terms as well. Nor was that all. He was also convinced that that focusing by no means implied so unambiguous a political objective as many people thought. Instead he started from the assumption that at least a section of the forces that supported the 'New Era' system from the middle-class liberal side could also be incorporated in the kind of political system that he envisaged. This meant, however, that he must not move into a position from which a compromise might be ruled out in the future.

In foreign policy, as he knew, there was no danger of this. Here he stood closer to the Lesser German national movement, which in 1859, after the Italian war, had organized itself in the National Union, than any other conservative politician in Prussia. This was even registered occasionally by that side, as we saw from Unruh's letter, while the prince regent's distrust of Bismarck was concentrated in precisely this area. In the field of domestic affairs, on the other hand, given the reputation that was now his he had reason to fear that, however skilfully he conducted himself, any kind of agreement would be impossible in the long run if he was seen as a man who had all too obviously stirred up by his own efforts the conflict to which he owed his appointment. A confrontational 'Konfliktminister' was something he wanted to be only in the sense that he could be expected to overcome conflict, not in the sense that his political existence appeared to be bound up with the same.

This undoubtedly implied an enormous overestimate of his own possibilities in the office of chief minister. It reflects the kind of prevalence he ascribed to purely interest- and success-oriented thinking in the field of domestic policy too and how little he was prepared to recognize convictions and principles as independent forces. He was very soon cured of that kind of overrating by the practical experience of his first few months in office. But at first it led him, thinking as he did that in the interests of his future ability to act he must not commit himself unduly in advance, to behave with extraordinary restraint, given the circumstances in which he found himself, and even to pass up opportunities that seemed to him potentially too compromising.

This came out most clearly in connection with the so-called 'homage question'. When Frederick William IV, by now completely insane, died on 2 January 1861 and the prince regent acceded to the Prussian throne as William I, it was the first change of sovereign since the transition to a constitutional state. A quite new ceremonial was therefore called for. The traditional hereditary homage in which ruler and representatives of the estates exchanged reciprocal vows of loyalty and obligation in the spirit of the medieval feudal system must be replaced by a coronation ceremony essentially only for display purposes, the monarch having already sworn an oath on the constitution.

This kind of break with tradition went very much against the grain with the new king, a man already in his sixties. Here too he would have liked to stick to the forms with which he was familiar from his brother's accession in 1840. In fact it would have been easy to dissuade him from this course by drawing his attention to the objectively unconstitutional character of an act of hereditary homage. After all, it presupposed the existence of old-style corporate bodies with political rights of their own in addition to the modern representative bodies. Instead, however, Roon and his closest advisers, particularly on the army side, encouraged him in this way of thinking. They declared that this was a unique opportunity to demonstrate the continuing independence and autonomous authority of the Crown for all to see. It would be a way of visibly standing up to the claims of parliament so forcefully advanced in discussion of the military question. Presumably they were quite clear in their own minds that in taking this line they were not only encouraging a demonstration of the power of the king but also provoking a constitutional confrontation. The homage question was obviously intended to provide the excuse for a radical change of system that if necessary would not stop at overthrowing the constitution with a *coup d'état*.

The man whom Roon saw from the very outset as the natural leader of such an undertaking was Bismarck. So it was to Bismarck that he addressed himself quite openly towards the end of June 1861, by which time the question had, as he put it, 'reached breaking-point' in the Cabinet and the king seemed at last to be prepared to dismiss the section of his ministry that still clung to the 'New Era' system and to set a collision course.[6] Bismarck did not shrink from publishing this highly revealing letter in his memoirs many years later, obviously in order to make quite clear the kind of course that he himself had not been prepared to follow.

The king could not give in, so Roon maintained, 'without ruining himself and the Crown for good and all'. Nor could the majority of his ministers: 'They would be slitting open their immoral stomachs, destroying themselves politically. They cannot help being and remaining disobedient.'

162

This was the big chance. Everything now depended on 'convincing the King that without proclaiming a change of system he can find the kind of ministry he needs'. Because if he gave in now, as even his closest relatives advised him to do – Roon was referring to Queen Augusta and the crown prince – 'we should be heading under full sail into the mire of parliamentary government'.

Roon did everything to bring the formal central question, the answer to which would determine whether he could put Bismarck's name before the king as a minister, into the proper light. That question was whether he, Bismarck, regarded 'the traditional hereditary homage as an assault on the constitution', as the liberal ministers did, or whether he too was of the opinion that such a view was 'a piece of doctrinaire humbug, a product of political commitment and party-political posturing'.

Bismarck could not of course tell Roon outright that he did not share his position on this question. That could have cost him the support of a man who, even among those who stood closest to him politically, was almost alone in seriously prosecuting his candidacy for ministerial office. But in the belief that by adopting such a course he would probably be jeopardizing his entire political future and would at best became the mere tool of a new Camarilla, he nevertheless went a very long way in his reply.

He simply did not understand, he answered with feigned naïvety, how the dispute about the homage question 'has taken on such importance for both sides'.[7] Of course the king had the right 'to receive the homage of every one of his subjects and of every body corporate in the land when and where he pleases'. If that right were in dispute then he, Bismarck, would be found on the king's side – 'although I am not in fact pervaded by any sense of the practical importance of exercising it'.

His position, even if he had given a formally positive answer to Roon's question, was more than clear. Moreover, he immediately went a step further. As a means to an end the whole homage question was far too subtle: 'The loyally royalist mass of voters will not understand the dispute about homage, and the democrats will distort it.' It would have been much better 'to stand firm on the military question . . . break with the House, dissolve it, and then show the nation how the King stands with regard to the people'.

Stripped of its polite trimmings, what this meant was: exploiting the homage question is nothing but Camarilla politics; it denies the fact that the government of a constitutional state requires popular support. If they wanted to impose a change of direction against the will of the majority in the House of Deputies and against the members of the government who sympathized with that majority, they must have a demagogically exploitable, solidly grounded point at issue. And not only that. What was even more important was to unfold prospects for the future that were as attractive as those held out by the present liberal majority. Currently, however, prospects for the future capable of mobilizing the popular imagination and popular expectations lay mainly – and here he returned to his own programme – in the field of foreign policy. Anyone wishing to cut the ground from under the feet of the present liberal majority must begin here.

To succeed, in other words, the tactics employed hitherto must be exactly reversed. Rather than at home, the demands of the people must be met in terms of foreign policy. In this way a large number of liberal voters could be estranged from their allegiance, and circumstances at home consolidated in the manner desired.

If we look at the situation as it was in the middle of 1861 and do not allow our judgement to be dictated solely by subsequent developments, this was an exceptionally bold calculation. Beyond mere tactical questions Bismarck, in proposing it, was not only going against Roon and Roon's political friends; he was also opposing the king himself, whose basic foreign policy direction was indeed still what Bismarck described as 'legitimist'. Never again did Bismarck speak out with such vehemence against the concept of a supranational solidarity of crowned heads as a guiding principle of foreign policy as he did in this letter. 'My loyalty to my sovereign is of Vendéan completeness', he put it at its most extreme, 'but as regards all others, not in one drop of my blood do I feel a trace of an obligation to lift a finger on their behalf.' And in a clear estimate of the consequences: 'I fear that in this way of thinking I am so far removed from that of our most gracious majesty that he will scarcely find me a suitable adviser to the Crown.'

Only a matter of days later Bismarck was able to put this to the test. When he arrived in Berlin on 10 July, officially *en route* for his summer leave, the king had already given in over the homage question and consented to a solemn coronation in Königsberg that was purely for show. Following this decision he had left for Baden-Baden to take the waters at the residence of his son-in-law, Grand Duke Frederick I. Whether he left his envoy instructions to follow him or whether Bismarck decided to do so on his own initiative is not certain. At any rate he continued his journey immediately, and shortly after his arrival in Baden-Baden he was received for a lengthy audience. During this Bismarck directly countered the liberal princes' plans for reforming the Confederation along Lesser German lines, plans for which Grand Duke Frederick and his newly appointed Foreign Minister Franz von Roggenbach sought to win William over while he was in Baden-Baden, by placing before the king his own ideas for Prussia's future foreign policy, particularly with regard to the German question. At the king's request he wrote these down immediately after the audience, and in the months that followed he reworked the written version several times until it reached its final form in the so-called 'Reinfeld Memorial' of October 1861[8] – a clear indication of the fundamental, programmatic importance he attached to this whole exposé.

Programmatic and fundamental it was indeed, that plan he laid before the king – albeit in a way that Franz von Roggenbach, for example, who communicated Bismarck's memorandum to his grand duke, found confirmed his opinion: 'an unprincipled Junker who wishes to make a career of political villainy'.[9] Here too Bismarck followed exactly the line he had already laid down for Roon's benefit: the wishes of the national party must be met, then things will calm down at home. He suggested that Prussia should take the lead in the demand for a fundamental reform of the German

Confederation and proposed for this purpose a representative body for the whole of Germany composed of delegates from the individual national Diets. This kind of '*national representation of the German people on the central authority of the Confederation*' was 'the sole and necessary cement capable of adequately countering the divergent tendencies of dynastic politics'. But it would probably 'at the same time mean with some certainty that the regrettable tendency of most German Diets to devote themselves primarily to minor tiffs with their own governments was provided with a healthy diversion along broader lines of greater service to the community, and the petty squabbles of the assembly halls of the estates gave way to a more statesmanlike discussion of the interests of Germany as a whole'. However, as Bismarck quite candidly admitted, it could scarcely be expected that the majority of the national governments within the Confederation would accept such a proposal for the reform of the Confederation. It was a question, initially, of taking up a clear position and mobilizing public opinion in Prussia's favour.

In other words, the whole plan was conceived primarily as a device for breaking up the Confederation and winning over popular reinforcements. How one might proceed in concrete terms – one idea was to set up a kind of counter-confederation through a parliamentary development of the Prussian-dominated Customs Union – was an area that Bismarck left very sketchy. The same was true of the catalogue of indispensable Prussian demands, among which a satisfactory solution of the supreme command question had for the benefit of the addressee of the later memorandum been moved up into first place.

What Bismarck was concerned with above all else were the methods of advance and the tactical objective: a demonstration in favour of the national party was simultaneously to relieve the home front and force the Confederation, that is, Austria and its closest associates, into mounting a counter-action. In essence the suggestions of the St Petersburg envoy boiled down to creating a new situation both at home and in foreign affairs through a policy of confrontation over the German question and then, having thrown this stone into the water, as it were, waiting to see how things turned out.

Roggenbach's immediate suspicion was to the effect that the German question was to be used in order to reach solutions at home that would favour the arch-conservatives and to bring the author of these proposals to power. And like Jacob Burckhardt of Basle among his contemporaries, many historians in our own day have followed him in this and stressed the primacy of motives relating to domestic affairs. This should be seen not least as a reaction to the fact that for many years the national and foreign policy interpretation largely prevailed, the question of the domestic policy aims and repercussions of a particular foreign policy having very much receded into the background. Particularly here, however, this kind of reversed approach can easily be misleading or at any rate excessively restrict our field of vision. For what is crucial and characteristic is in fact the way in which foreign policy and domestic policy arguments and aims interpenetrated and fell into a specific basic pattern. That pattern itself emerges from the situation and from the tactical objectives that, over and above all considerations of content, led Bismarck into that situation.

With the resolution of the dispute about the homage question, not only had the crisis of the 'New Era' system been temporarily overcome. There was also, as Bismarck had discovered during his brief passage through Berlin, the prospect of an initiative in the German question along liberal lines with the plan, which was already definite, to transfer the Foreign Ministry from Schleinitz to the ambassador in London, Count Bernstorff. From Bismarck's point of view, then, his objective in Baden-Baden could not be a positive but only a negative one. He had to try above all, with his improvised remarks about Prussian foreign policy in the German question, to turn the king away from the proposals being put to him by his son-in-law the grand duke and by Roggenbach without forcing him back into the rut of his old legitimist policy. He had to endeavour to underline William's reservations with regard to the domestic policy implications of a foreign policy of Lesser German nationalism and unfold an alternative that promised a comparable yield in terms of additional power and prestige for Prussia and the Prussian Crown without the consequences of the liberal course as far as home affairs were concerned. 'It would be possible', he told a party colleague, stating his objective quite plainly, 'to create a solidly Conservative national representative body and yet even reap the gratitude of the Liberals for it.'[10]

His reasoning therefore stemmed from his awareness of appearing in the role of an antagonist whose first concern it was to preclude a decision in favour of the rival tendency. Consequently we must beware of making too much of it in every detail, even if programmatic elements were of course reflected in it. What it essentially revolved around was dissuading the king from believing that there was always a reciprocal and indissoluble connection between foreign and domestic policy, in other words that a decision in favour of a particular policy in one sphere largely determined the course things would take in the other.

This was Bismarck's old struggle against the theory, supported by both legitimists and liberals, of a necessary conformity of systems between foreign and domestic policy. With greater emphasis than ever before he here made perfectly clear how he saw the connection between the two spheres: everything depended, at least as far as the relationship of foreign to domestic policy was concerned, on success rather than on attitude and intention. A government whose foreign policy was successful, he maintained, would always be master of the situation at home. A successful foreign policy, however, was not the product of a particular state's desires, expectations and convictions; it was the product of a sober calculation that sought to combine that state's own power interests with broader tendencies and needs.

This was the red thread of his whole argument. Moreover, this was also where the crucial element of content came in: the Prussian state must not, as the liberals wished, let itself be drawn into the service of national forces and tendencies. Rather it must draw them into its service. For in the one case it would become their tool in terms of domestic policy as well; in the other it would remain their master here too.

The kind of instrumentalization of the national ideal that Bismarck was now quite openly proposing was in stark contradiction to the straightforward thinking of the king. Not that he would have seen himself as a partisan of the national movement. But he was reluctant to pursue a policy that used other people's sincere convictions as mere means and thus contained elements of deliberate deception. Bismarck tried to take this into account by emphasizing the desire for order, power and military security as being the really decisive impulse behind the national ideal. The 'need to see the developing strength of the German people more tightly and more uniformly integrated' was 'emerging with daily increasing decisiveness', as he put it in the first version of the memorandum, continuing in similarly general terms: 'The upsurge in national feeling, part of the whole trend of the time, is pushing us, as is the demand for protection against attacks from abroad, towards the objective of closer German unification, at least in the fields of defence and material interests.'

But for all his efforts to bring the aspirations of the conservative Prussian state and the national movement closer together in terms of content as well – in a period in which the liberal and reformist components of the national ideal, though slowly becoming less important, were still very much in evidence – the basically Machiavellian nature of his proposals was difficult to conceal. It would have struck even a mind less sophisticated than the king's as pretty far-fetched when Bismarck sought to establish a causal connection between the rising tide of nationalism and the dissolution of the alliance between the three conservative powers of eastern Europe. It was the destruction of 'the system of defence erected against France and the revolution in 1815', he argued, that had given the desire for an entirely new order its real impulse.

Bismarck may have increased the Prussian king's misgivings with regard to the liberals' Lesser German plans, but he failed to win him over for his own plans and above all for the way in which he envisaged proceeding. On the contrary, he probably even heightened the mistrust with which William regarded him as far as foreign affairs were concerned. William saw Bismarck as a man capable of the most wild-cat combinations. Once in office, he would seek to steer him along paths that conflicted sharply with his own attitudes and beliefs. 'That's all we need, for a man to take over the ministry who is going to turn everything upside-down', he had told the Duke of Coburg, one of the group of liberal princes, in 1859.[11] And the conversation in Baden-Baden was hardly such as to make him revise that verdict.

Bismarck obviously felt this very acutely. He drew a crucial conclusion from it, one might say for all time: that in his relations with his monarch he must as far as possible avoid discussions of principle but instead seek to win his trust without programmatic commitments. As indeed he succeeded in doing a year later, in the critical situation of September 1862. Thus was the basis laid on which Bismarck, throughout the twenty-six years of their working together, always remained completely in charge and managed always to keep his naturally often somewhat cautious and reserved monarch in the dark with regard to his ultimate objectives.

For the moment, however, Bismarck left Baden-Baden if not as the defeated party at least as one who, yet again, had failed to carry the day. Roon and possibly even at this stage the king himself had wanted to use him on the domestic front as the strong man of the extreme right who looked not for compromise but for a fight and for a decision wherever conflict offered. But Bismarck for his part had not only refused seriously to commit himself over the homage question that so exercised the king; he had also sought to push the king along entirely new paths that, at least superficially, involved compromises and co-operation with elements to which the king was deeply opposed. And all in a sphere in which, unlike that of domestic policy, William had long distrusted Bismarck, regarding him, for all his undoubted shrewdness, as dangerous and unpredictable.

The unconditional side of Bismarck's character came out quite clearly in that July of 1861, where ambition had in fact caused him to waver on one or two previous occasions. He had no desire to become either the tool of Roon and his group or the servant of a foreign policy conceived at court and vacillating between Prussian power interests and legitimist convictions. He wanted either to be in a position to make his own decisions or to play no part. From now on he stood there, so to speak, with arms folded, waiting. What he stood for could not but be clear to every informed person by now, at least so far as its general direction was concerned; so too was what anyone would be letting himself in for who appointed him to a crucial political post. Whether he himself was fully aware that for the king too, who was becoming more and more embittered over the army question, he represented the *ultima ratio*, we do not know. But on one thing he was by now firmly resolved: not to have imposed on him any conditions that threatened unduly to restrict his future freedom of action and decision and turn him into a mere executive organ in matters of central importance.

The outcome of such an attitude must have been obvious even to him. Without a parliamentary base of any consequence, without a body of friends at court and enjoying the vigorous support only of Roon, whom he had now seriously disappointed, he could have little hope of actually being appointed to ministerial office with the kind of power to which he aspired. Even if we allow for a certain coquetry, a tendency towards understatement of a kind that accentuated his own sovereign independence, his letters during those months contain an unmistakable note of resignation and scepticism with regard to his own political future. He discusses which diplomatic post he would prefer, given the choice: Paris, London, or St Petersburg. Even going to Berne seems to him not entirely unthinkable, although he himself aims an immediate shaft of irony at this 'fixed idea': 'Boring places with attractive surroundings rather suit the elderly.'[12] There are repeated references to a possible appointment as Foreign Minister, but they are invariably dismissive. He finds the idea 'almost frightening, like the prospect of a cold bath', adding: 'My mind has become so dull since my illness that I have lost all my resilience in hectic situations. Three years ago I would have made a serviceable minister, but now the thought of it makes me feel like a sick trick rider asked to perform his leaps.'[13] When early in March 1862 the rumour reached his ears that the new Foreign Minister, Count Bernstorff, wished to resign after only a few months in office and he was to be designated his successor, he even said: 'I do not believe it is true but would turn it down if it were. All political differences aside, I don't feel well enough for so much excitement and vexation.'[14]

We cannot take such statements at their face value, of course, particularly since they were based on largely fictitious premisses. But they do reflect how little chance he saw of his being appointed in the circumstances and on the conditions that he envisaged. His intention in saying such things was not least to prepare himself and those around him for the far more likely prospect of the final collapse of his candidacy for ministerial office – however difficult he found it to accept such a prospect. For the basic preconditions for the kind of policy he had in mind did indeed appear to be crumbling away during those months.

At the coronation in Königsberg on 18 October 1861, which Bismarck attended, the antagonism between the king and the liberal majority in the House of Deputies had received a further dramatic boost. Indignant at the attitude of the liberals, who in June had once again approved the funds for the reorganization of the army only on an interim basis, refusing to incorporate them in the budget proper, he had greeted the members of the Lower House simply as 'advisers' to the Crown. This was evidence of a very curious interpretation of the constitution. It was further underlined by the fact that the army delegation at the coronation celebrations included the commanding officers of the new regiments that had meanwhile been created on the government's own initiative with the aid of funds that had been only provisionally approved. These officers inevitably appeared as a virtual embodiment of the spirit that had dictated the speech with which William had closed the session of the Diet early in June 1861. Since the government 'will lose sight neither of the introduction of the appropriate legal rules nor of the establishment of regularly ordered budgetary provisions in the sphere of army administration', he had said on that occasion with regard to the interim approval of funds, 'I am able to overlook the form of the approval, which does not affect the central principle of this major measure'.[15]

For a large section of the Liberal Party, which was already split into several groups, this had proved to be the last straw. The next day its left wing, calling itself the 'German Progressive Party', finally parted company from what now became known as the 'Old Liberals' and the 'Left Centre' tendency, which continued, albeit with growing misgivings of their own, to adhere to the policy of 'No pushing' and of extensive readiness to compromise.

The new Progressive Party, on the other hand, demanded that the promises of the 'New Era' as understood by its members should now be put into effect. In addition to the systematic implementation of the liberal constitutional state at home, the party stood above all for a resolute policy of federal reform in the liberal direction of a Lesser Germany.[16] Bismarck had immediately taken note of the latter as being the point on which the new party might be drawn into his own strategy and indeed brought under control as far as domestic policy was concerned; in fact this was one of the possibilities to which his Baden-Baden proposals had very tangibly related. But it was precisely here that the king had been unwilling to go along with him. He saw the new party simply as a revival of the enemy of old, the embodiment of the fundamental conflict of systems of his youth in pre-1848 Europe, the revolution in a fresh guise.

For the old soldier the fronts were now clear once again. He resolved immediately to triumph or be defeated in open battle and not become involved in obscure manoeuvres and political tricks. A similar mood prevailed among a large number of the members of the new party, despite all the disappointments of the past and regardless of the experience that their own position had proved too weak for a frontal assault once already.

This mood received an extraordinary boost when with the fresh elections to the House of Deputies held on 6 December 1861, very much in the shadow of domestic confrontation, the Progressive Party abruptly became the strongest group with 106 seats. Together with the likewise swollen ranks of the 'Old Liberals' and the 'Left Centre', liberals now held some 260 of a total of 325 seats. A crucial trial of strength was now virtually inevitable, with both sides arming for a decisive encounter.

For the liberal majority this meant the full implementation of parliamentary rights with regard to the budget and on top of that a commitment on the part of the government to respect the will of the parliamentary majority. For the conservatives around Roon it meant the rejection of any kind of co-operation and if necessary a military coup to preserve the traditional distribution of power in state and society.

From the end of 1861 onwards, in other words after the Progressive Party's massive victory at the polls, quite specific plans were being drawn up in the Military Cabinet and at the War Ministry for dealing with the popular uprising that would allegedly follow the dissolution – regarded as inevitable sooner or later – of the recalcitrant Lower House. It was obvious that this side wished to persuade the king, who was prepared to sign the requisite secret operational orders, to go on to repeal important sections of the constitution and return to the kind of bureaucratic absolutism with purely formal constitutional trimmings that had prevailed in the days of Manteuffel.

Others, however, not least members of his own family including his wife and his eldest son, were urgently drawing the king's attention to the hopelessness of such a course – of which the public soon got wind from the rumours that were flying around. His son-in-law, the Grand Duke of Baden, who had affected a very much more decisive change of course in his own country two years previously by placing the government in the hands of the leader of the liberal parliamentary majority without reservation and without any ulterior motives of a purely tactical nature, implored him in mid-March 1862 not to pursue an anti-parliamentary policy and not to abandon the position above the government and above party that was allotted to the monarchy under the constitution. In doing so he would be going against the realities of life itself: 'Parliament is after all simply an image of human life in general, where the most diverse views meet and clash and each has its justification in so far as it rests on genuine conviction. Parliaments are the legitimate expression of that conviction – an arena in which victory and defeat are possible but above which the Crown stands as an impartial judge, respected by victors and vanquished alike.' The only feasible course was therefore to choose a ministry that 'can count with certainty on one or another of the parties pre-eminent in parliament'. If necessary the king must go to the country to find out whether that government and that party enjoyed the confidence of the electorate.[17]

William was indeed 'going to the country'; that was the occasion of the grand duke's letter. On 6 March 1862 a slender majority in the Prussian House of Deputies had adopted a motion put forward by one of its number, the Berlin municipal treasurer Adolf Hagen, calling upon the government to break down the budget in such a way that parliament could satisfy itself that it concealed no items for a secret continuation of the army reorganization. The king had reacted by dissolving the House of Deputies on 11 March and ordering fresh elections. At the same time, however, he had *not* done what his son-in-law had recommended, which was to appoint a government that could 'count with certainty on one or another of the parties pre-eminent in parliament', among which neither of them included the fourteen-strong *Kreuzzeitung* party. In place of the old ministry, which had sought to embrace the widest possible spectrum of political opinion from right to left, the Cabinet appointed in the middle of March 1862 was so constituted that it could not be seen as anything but a brusque refusal of any further co-operation with parliament. 'We are at the graveside of the New Era', wrote Max Duncker around this time.[18] The new head of the government was the former president of the determinedly anti-liberal and anti-reformist Prussian Upper House, Prince Hohenlohe-Ingelfingen. He was joined by a number of largely unknown conservative bureaucrats such as the former Breslau police chief, Gustav von Jagow, a friend of Bismarck's from university days, who became Minister of the Interior, a member of the High Consistory of the Protestant Church, Heinrich von Müller, as the new Minister of Culture, Education and Church Affairs, and the Berlin Director of Public Prosecutions, Count Leopold zur Lippe, as Minister of Justice.

The reaction of the liberal public was not long in coming. 'I think it's a good sign, in fact', sneered Karl Twesten of the Berlin Superior Court of Justice, one of the leaders of the Progressive Party: 'They want a ministry to slap the country and parliament in the face, and . . . have to resort to an obscure police chief and a public prosecutor, names that are unknown not only in parliamentary life and among the public but even within the bureaucracy. Next time they'll have to choose an NCO and a police sergeant.'[19] How the king can seriously have hoped to win the election with so undistinguished a government, which was seen merely as a veiled threat rather than as a recognizable political alternative, is almost incomprehensible.

Obviously, however, he really did think that with the aid of massive government influence in the run-up to the election it would be possible to achieve a complete reversal of the previous majority situation in favour of those political groups that were prepared to give their more or less unconditional support to the government, particularly over the question of army reform. 'There is absolutely no question of reaction, etc.', he replied to the Grand Duke of Baden early in April 1862, 'but the elections must be influenced by legal means in order to produce a House with which one can govern.' 'Not one word' of the 'New Era' programme of 8 November 1858 was he altering. But neither was he going to let himself be pushed in a direction 'in which', as he naïvely wrote, exposing his hopes for the elections as pure wishful thinking, 'men wish to go and I do not wish to go and may not go'.[20]

He was greatly encouraged in such wishful thinking by the man who was the real political brain of the new government, War Minister von Roon – not because he himself seriously believed in the prospect of electoral success but because he was counting on a passionate reaction on the king's part when an oppositional majority was once again voted into parliament. For it would take that kind of emotional reaction, as Roon knew only too well, to overcome the inhibitions and obstacles that stood in the way of what he was aiming at, namely a return to the Manteuffel system and a determined struggle against parliament and the social groups behind the majority in parliament. A policy that could be implemented only by means of a coup and a breach of the constitution inevitably appeared to the king as tantamount to the abandonment of beliefs that had guided him for years and of expectations placed in his reign not only by others but also by himself. Since the pursuit of such a policy would also involve deep and unavoidable conflict within the king's own family, Roon could foresee that only a quite exceptional situation would persuade him to set his misgivings and reservations aside.

Roon's adversaries in the king's immediate entourage – Queen Augusta, the crown prince and the Grand Duke of Baden – knew this too. The latter had drawn attention, as head of the group of liberal princes, to the consequences such a change of course in domestic affairs would have for Prussia's position in Germany and for the German policy it had just begun cautiously to introduce. Remarks along these lines had drawn a highly irritated reaction from William, who had made it clear that neither inside Prussia nor in the German sphere was he any longer prepared to get involved in deals of any kind with the liberal national movement.

William insisted that he still stood by the ideas, discussed with the grand duke, Roggenbach and Bernstorff in the summer and autumn of the previous year, for a reform of the Confederation along the lines of a modified resumption of the old Lesser German Union policy. But that kind of reform could only proceed from a free agreement between the German princes. He would not be forced into any other course: 'The compulsion of the now dissolved House that it must determinedly drive us in the aforesaid direction quite clearly means revolution and civil war in Germany.' If Austria and the majority of the small and medium-sized German states opposed Prussia's plans, then those plans must wait: 'What else is to be done? Time must do its work and gradually pave the way for good sense. Do you know of an alternative course?'[21]

This was perfectly logical in its way: if one was demanding at home that popular forces be subordinated to monarchical control, one could not hand them the initiative in the field of foreign policy by renouncing the ideal of solidarity and co-operation between crowned heads. Prussian ambition and Prussia's national expectations must be forgone if they could be satisfied only by means that included the possibility of violence, civil war and a revolution – even a veiled one – in the existing order of things both at home and abroad.

Less than six months before Bismarck's appointment William thus once again decisively rejected his whole foreign policy programme, indeed his whole basic approach to politics. He was moving closer and closer to the position that Metternich had once elevated to the status of a principle: that the struggle for the supremacy of the monarchical central power on primarily bureaucratic and military foundations allowed of no compromises with the national and liberal movement, however advantageous they might appear at the time. In view of this there could be as little serious question of Bismarck's being appointed Foreign Minister – though rumours to this effect naturally received a considerable boost with his sudden recall from St Petersburg in mid-March 1862, just when the new ministry was being formed – as there could be of a surrender in the conflict with the majority in the House of Deputies.

Already a much more likely prospect by this time was one very few people even suspected, namely that the king would abdicate and leave the way free for the alternative represented by the next generation in the persons of his son and his son-in-law. For the situation must have begun to look more and more hopeless, particularly after the announcement of the result of the fresh elections to the House of Deputies held on 6 May 1862, on the outcome of which the king had staked so much. An overwhelming majority of the electorate decided against the government and those political groups that more or less openly supported it and its position on the current issue. Despite wholesale attempts to influence voters not one of the candidates for the new ministry was elected. The Conservative Party lost a further three seats and was now reduced to eleven; in eight out of the ten Prussian provinces not a single conservative was returned, the party making a mark only in Silesia and Pomerania, where its candidates were drawn exclusively from the nobility. Even the so-called 'Catholic party' paid for its stance on the quesiton of army reform with the loss of twenty-one of its fifty-four seats in the old House. Finally the Old Liberals, the ones who had been prepared to compromise, dropped from some ninety seats to around fifty and promptly split into a wing that remained ready to co-operate and a left wing that henceforth always voted with the opposition majority.

That majority, whose members, drawn predominantly from the civil service and the propertied middle class, had clearly dominated the poll in every province except Posen and Pomerania while in East Prussia, Berlin, Brandenburg, the Rhine Province and Westphalia they had taken nearly all the seats, now numbered some 250 deputies if one included the sympathetic independents. In other words, it comprised almost two-thirds of the House, with the Progressive Party, now up a further twenty-nine to 135 seats, largely calling the tune.

That this huge parliamentary majority would suddenly agree to make substantial concessions was of course beyond all reasonable expectation. It was completely unthinkable that it would submit to the sort of monarchical control that William had in mind. His political plan now appeared to have lost for good any kind of basis within the existing constitutional system – especially since he had once sworn never to govern with the *Kreuzzeitung* party, as his brother had done, and a liberal-conservative parliamentary grouping such as might have been to his taste was not available. Egged on by Roon, Edwin Manteuffel, Alvensleben and a bevy of mere courtiers, William had become increasingly entangled in a concept of the monarchy and of the monarch that was by now almost without foundation not only in the constitution but also in political and social reality.

That concept was in a curious way politically anaemic, governed by supposed principles barely capable of concealing the fact that the Crown was in danger of losing its essential functions in a fresh separation from society. In the years after 1849 the section of the Prussian Conservative Party that aimed at a restoration of the old, pre-revolutionary order had endeavoured to harness the Crown in the service of its idea of the state and consequently its interests, the liberals having failed in their attempt to revive, in a modified form, the one-time alliance between monarchy and third estate, between the king and the middle class. Rivalling both concepts, a third doctrine had been formulated in a variety of versions to the effect that the Crown must leave the way clear for itself to co-operate with all groups in society. It must seek to assert its traditionally leading role both within various coalitions and at the same time as supreme conciliator and arbiter of interests.

One thing all tendencies were agreed on, however, was that some form of co-operation with powerful social forces was imperative, although this realization had been forced on the bureaucratic neo-absolutists of Manteuffel's stamp more by the situation, namely the need to co-operate politically with the old world conservatives as represented by the Camarilla. Even the present king had accepted this view as heir to the throne and as prince regent. Now, however, with the elections having shown that the policy he was pursuing obviously had no adequate social foundation any more, he found himself on the retreat into the old and now hopeless absolutist position of a purely bureaucratic supremacy backed by the army. To be sure, the fact that even advocates of that policy had meanwhile come to believe that such a position could no longer be sustained without a coup and a full-scale military dictatorship ultimately led him to shrink from this too, or at least to give more and more serious consideration to the alternatives of acquiescence and abdication.

Far beyond the actual points of issue, then, it was a quite exceptional situation in which Bismarck did eventually get his chance, a situation whose special uniqueness at the same time laid the foundation for the special uniqueness of his political position and his political opportunities in Prussia.

Literally bogged down in specific political objectives and in the view that a king could not yield on what seemed to him questions of central importance without losing face, William was inclined to give up one way or the other – by abandoning the basic political ideas that had guided him hitherto or by stepping down from the throne. He avoided both courses by summoning Bismarck, but only at the price of his claim to political leadership, of transferring the actual authority to lay down guidelines to his new chief minister.

He may already have glimpsed this himself at the time. Even clothed in the phraseology of royal service, it was too clear a case of a personal pretension to power and leadership that he was faced with here. He had not wanted to be a neo-absolutist dictator, but nor had he been prepared on the other hand to ascribe a dominant political role to the parliamentary majority of the day – so in the end he placed himself under the direction of a man who promised him an honourable way out of this dilemma and asked for nothing in return but his complete and utter confidence. In so doing he instituted that curious German form of constitutional monarchy, midway between the older, essentially absolutist type and the more recent type with parliament essentially in charge, though its relative durability in Prussia and subsequently in the German Empire was of course a product of a whole series of other factors.

Nevertheless, we must not underestimate the specific situation obtaining in 1862 and the personal factors involved in that situation. Both of these, in positive and in negative terms, created opportunities and restricted opportunities. At the same time they altered the realities at a crucial moment in time to the advantage of one party and the disadvantage of the other. To ignore this is to blind oneself to the alternatives of the historical process, to its openness to constantly fresh developments and thus to the very stuff of history itself.

Following the elections of 6 May 1862, everything was indeed open throughout that whole summer – not least because of the attitude of the king. If he abdicated, the victory of the left-wing liberal majority was assured, at least for the moment, since the crown prince more or less openly sympathized with it. If he decided to continue the struggle, then possibly the hour had come for the neo-absolutists of the Roon school, who were determined to go all the way. Nor, thirdly, was it yet certain that the king would not after all bow to the arguments of his non-military entourage and the majority in his present ministry and agree to a last-minute compromise.

In a sober appraisal of the foundations of their strong position in parliament, a position clearly favoured by the three-class electoral system, a large section of the liberal majority was quite prepared to make it easy for the Crown to come round if it would only give some indication that it would seek in future to co-operate with parliament honestly and without ulterior motives. 'The only possible form for a fruitful national life in Prussia at present is the parliamentary form under intelligent royal leadership', is how the historian Heinrich von Sybel, a member of the 'Left Centre' group in parliament, put it in a letter to Robert von Mohl, Baden's envoy to the Federal Diet. 'Parliament without such leadership is not yet up to the task, and not for a long time has the monarchy been up to it without parliament.'[22] Like Karl Twesten of the Progressive Party, Sybel too endeavoured during those weeks to reach a broad-based agreement that, looking beyond the present conflict, promised to usher in a genuinely new era in relations between Crown and parliament.

A major role in all this was played by these people's concern about the repercussions of any further aggravation of the conflict on the German question and on the prospects for their own programme in this sphere, for the champions of compromise were at the same time the principal advocates of a resumption of Prussia's Union policy along liberal lines. However, even if at this point in time they would angrily have rejected the idea, this made them potential allies of the man who had told the Prussian War Minister a year before that the 'chief defect' of the policy of the present Prussian government lay in the fact 'that we act like Liberals in Prussia and like Conservatives abroad'.[23] To be sure, such an alliance was still a long way off – very much farther off than Bismarck had originally imagined in his blend of contempt for people and for alleged principles and of thinking purely in terms of results. But as far as his own position and his behaviour during those months were concerned, this optimism was undoubtedly of crucial importance. It gave him that confidence of victory with the aid of which he eventually persuaded the king to continue the struggle and relinquish his abdication plans.

After his sudden recall from St Petersburg, which had been accompanied simply by the information that the king had not yet reached a final decision regarding his further utilization but that it would probably be a question of either London or Paris, Bismarck arrived in Berlin on 10 May, four days after the election. The first thing he heard there was that he was regarded as Hohenlohe's likely successor as Minister-President, in other words that the king had obviously resolved, in response to the election result, to appoint here and now a ministry that would proceed to set full sail on a collision course. 'We lack . . . a mere trifle at this stage', Roon wrote ironically in a private letter on 18 May, 'and that is the *brains* of the ministry.'[24]

The detailed talks with the king, which in Bismarck's own words covered 'everything but future diplomatic postings',[25] had clearly gone off to William's satisfaction. They had allayed many of his misgivings regarding the 'flightiness' of his potential chief minister, the quality that back in mid-March, on the occasion of the last change of government, had moved the queen to the impassioned outburst: 'But for God's sake not him for minister. It is a great mistake to believe that our country can be served by a man such as Bismarck, who will surely stop at nothing and is the terror of everyone because he has no principles.'[26] But in the end another consideration had proved stronger: to wait and see how the newly elected House of Deputies would react and not to slam all the doors straight away. In addition there was Bismarck's request that he should at the same time be given the Foreign Ministry as Bernstorff's successor. A fresh constitutional clash in the electorate of Hesse, which was once again becoming a problem within the Confederation, and a dispute with Austria over the question of the compatibility of Prussia's commercial treaty with France and the 1853 agreements between Prussia and Austria had made it seem inadvisable just now to swap horses in mid stream, as it were.

These were very pragmatic considerations. Ultimately, however, what lay behind them was the king's concern regarding Bismarck's foreign policy plans and the kinds of expectation and objective that Bismarck associated with these on the home front as well. That concern prompted him to seize almost with relief on the occasion when Bismarck, rather earlier than originally planned, 'exploded' on 21 May and issued a final demand for 'a post or my dismissal'. At this Bernstorff suggested sending him to Paris, a move that had been under consideration for some time. But at the same time the king told him that he was not to regard this decision as final. Indeed he openly gave him to understand that the Paris posting was to be seen purely as a sort of temporary retirement.

Which is exactly how Bismarck did see it from the start, even if the experiences of those two weeks in Berlin had had a further sobering effect on him with their constant shilly-shallying, the volatility and lack of resolution of almost everyone involved, the prevailing atmosphere of petty jealousy and a downright frightening lack of purpose on the part of those who had to make decisions on the government's behalf. He never even seriously considered moving into the Prussian legation building in the heart of Paris, on the Quai d'Orsay opposite the Tuileries. 'It is more an escape attempt I am making than a new residence I am taking up', he summarized both his appraisal of the situation and his mood in a letter written on 25 May to his wife, who since the middle of the month had been living with the children at her parents' house in Reinfeld, wholly uncertain as to what the future might hold.[27] He said that he thought the next few weeks of the session of the House of Deputies before the summer recess would very likely bring the decision. 'In eight to ten days I shall probably receive a telegram summoning me to Berlin, and then the whole performance will be over', he told Johanna on 1 June in a letter written immediately after his first audience with Napoleon III. He went on: 'If my opponents knew what a good deed they would be doing me by winning and how sincerely I wish them that victory!'[28]

This was surely not said without the secret vanity of the man who believes himself indispensable in a particular situation. But on the other hand he was sufficiently level-headed to know that the way out of the situation that he promised to furnish would for its part be no more than an attempt, an experiment, without any guarantee of success: 'If it is to be, then *s bogom* [in God's hands], as our coachmen used to say when they took the reins. Next summer we'll presumably be living at Schönhausen.' Furthermore, for all his ambition and will to power the price of the fulfilment of his hopes also appalled him: the total involvement in responsibility and in the business of politics, the virtual sacrifice of almost everything not directly related to this, in short the self-imposed one-sidedness of his whole future existence, which as he knew could be crippling in its effects.

It was no accident, then, that he spent the three-and-a-half months separating him from his appointment, which he now regarded as certain, once again living a kind of double life. On the one hand he used them to explore the terrain for his future policy as it were *in situ* – not only in Paris but also in London, which he visited in late June on the occasion of the international exhibition. On the other hand he once again broke out – though he knew it was for a mere escapade – of the world that from now on would no longer release its hold on him as one of its principal representatives and most important figures, try as he repeatedly might to get away from it in the knowledge that it threatened to stifle him and devour him inwardly with its routine. The beginning was thus at the same time a farewell, a painful awareness of things sacrificed – the more so because what they were being sacrificed to was still a mere hope, an expectation, a possibility.

In Paris Napoleon III was of course largely abreast of the state of affairs in Berlin and Bismarck's possible future role; both had been discussed often enough not only in diplomatic circles but also in the press. He therefore received him from the outset as a potential partner on the European stage. Following on from their talks in the 1850s, he tried in particular to find out what Bismarck thought of the chances of a more or less close co-operation between Prussia and France. 'He is an enthusiastic supporter of German unification plans, that is to say Lesser German ones, certainly not including Austria', Bismarck reported in a private letter to the Foreign Minister written towards the end of June 1862. During the conversation he, Bismarck, had been 'placed rather in the position of Joseph vis-à-vis Potiphar's wife'. Napoleon had had 'the most lascivious alliance proposals on the tip of his tongue', he told Bernstorff. 'Had I shown at all willing, he would have made himself clearer.'[29]

That was on 26 June. The next day Bismarck accepted Napoleon's invitation to Fontainbleau. Here the French emperor did make himself quite clear. Bismarck, deliberately emphasizing the dramatic character of the proceedings, reported the crucial exchange to his Foreign Minister word for word.[30] To Napoleon's question: 'Do you think the King would be inclined to conclude an alliance with me?' he replied that he was sure that Wiliam I had no personal objection to him and that earlier misgivings in Prussia with regard to a rapprochement with France had also largely disappeared. However, he saw no immediate 'motive or objective' for such an alliance.

For anyone in the know, of course, this ostensible statement in fact implied a question. Moreover, it was one that Napoleon immediately took up, though in a way, it is true, that made him appear almost as Bismarck's *alter ego*: 'I'm talking about an alliance not with a view to some hazardous undertaking; but I feel that Prussia and France have so many interests in common as to provide the foundations for a close and lasting association as long as prejudice and partisanship do not stand in its way.' He went on to make himself even clearer: 'It would be a great mistake to seek to *give rise* to events, but they occur even without our help and without our being able to calculate their strength and direction; one must therefore arm oneself in good time and be on the look-out for means of meeting them and being able to capitalize on them.'

In the further course of their conversation Napoleon had indicated,

Bismarck said, that his own appointment and the simultaneous arrival in Paris of the Russian envoy to Berlin, Baron Budberg, had evidently given rise to a kind of panic in Vienna. As a result the Austrian ambassador had been empowered to conduct alliance negotiations on a major scale. In order to avoid the charge of naïve wishful thinking, Bismarck added immediately that of course there was no need to take this hint at its face value. He also left it an 'open question', of course, 'how unconstrained these remarks were and what they were calculated to achieve; but', he went on, 'they cannot be a complete fabrication'. The Austrian envoy, Prince Richard Metternich, was indeed showing remarkable signs of activity – remarkable above all because he was a somewhat 'simple and unenterprising character'. London was obviously also of the opinion that Russia and Austria 'were trying to steal a march on each other in Paris in order to bring off secret treaties with France'.

Moreover, he continued, expressing his own attitude to Napoleon's offer, a sober appraisal of the situation as a whole, over and above all matters of detail, favoured such a course. The initial objective of Russian policy under Gorchakov was as far as he knew the 'dissolution of the alliance of the Western powers'. And as far as Austria under Rechberg was concerned, he regarded it as 'capable of *any* combination that gives it the upper hand over Prussia in Germany'. He went on: 'In Vienna they will sacrifice Venetia and the left bank of the Rhine if they gain in exchange, on the *right* bank, a federal constitution with Austrian supremacy assured. Sentimental Germanity [*Deutschtum*] has never in centuries been the guiding principle of Vienna's Hofburg, and talk of Germany is only tolerated there as long as it serves as a leading-rein for ourselves or the Würzburgers [an allusion to the Würzburg conference of the small and medium-sized German states; *Tr.*].'

That a Franco-Austrian alliance had not come about since 1852 was really not due to any lack of inclination on Vienna's part. It was due solely to Napoleon's 'lack of confidence', Bismarck wrote, 'in the future of Austria, which is not in a position to sail with the currently powerful wind of its [subject] nationalities'. The conclusion he drew from all this was admittedly not 'that we should endeavour to conclude an alliance with France on specific terms but that we must pursue no policy that would involve our depending upon the loyal federal partnership of Austria against France and that we must not let ourselves be guided by the hope that Austria will ever *voluntarily* agree to an improvement of our position in Germany'.

Particularly the latter point once again made it very clear that, although he was only too well aware of the king's attitude towards the kind of co-operation with France that, given this situation, literally thrust itself upon them, Bismarck was not prepared to modify or even so much as camouflage his foreign policy programme. That programme was the corner-stone of his whole political plan – as much, admittedly, as a means to an end as as an end in itself. Any change threatened to destroy what that plan essentially rested on – in terms of domestic policy, too, as well as with regard to his own future – namely the calculation that only success justifies the taker of action and with him the cause he espouses and represents. So there could be no question of either the situation itself or consideration for the king and his misgivings determining Bismarck's stance here – as Roon, for example, failed to understand at all, caught up as he was in that situation and concerned only to remove objections to Bismarck. The only consideration that counted as far as Bismarck was concerned was how, if he was appointed, he could get as quickly as possible into a starting-position that promised success on the foreign policy front.

This was also how he saw his six-day visit to London at the beginning of July. He was received both by Lord Palmerston, the Prime Minister and for many years the architect of British foreign policy, and also by Earl Russell, the Foreign Minister. He sent a detailed report of his talks with these two leading representatives of British liberalism in the pre-Gladstone period to William I himself,[31] undoubtedly with the intention, in part, of counteracting the inevitable impression made by the report of his conversation with Napoleon III. Moreover, this also gave him the opportunity, and this was no less important to him, of setting the king against a possible rapprochement with Britain such as the representatives of the former *Wochenblatt* party and the so-called liberal group of princes headed by the Grand Duke of Baden and by his own son had long been suggesting to him.

However much Bismarck had in other cases, particularly with regard to the France of Napoleon III, resisted making foreign policy coalitions dependent on domestic policy considerations, in this case he very deliberately played the domestic policy card in order to put it to the king that co-operation with Britain was quite impossible. He tried by roundabout means as well to persuade him that a Lesser German unification policy under Prussian leadership, as advocated by the liberal group of princes and the National Union, would in reality not begin to elicit British support. In the process he also worked in with extraordinary skill the domestic policy possibilities allegedly contained in his own programme.

He had been 'somewhat surprised', his report averred, by the 'lack of understanding' that he had encountered in both politicians regarding 'our domestic circumstances'. This applied particularly to the Prime Minister, Lord Palmerston: 'He regards it as an unavoidable necessity that Your Majesty should choose a ministry from among the oppositional majority in the House of Deputies. He did not know the Prussian constitution in detail but derived the necessity for always choosing the Crown's advisers from the parliamentary majority from the nature of representative constitutions in general.' He, Bismarck, had tried to explain to him that things were very much more complicated and that tied up with the army question was something that was presumably not entirely without importance as far as Britain, too, was concerned, namely the stability of internal and external relationships in central Europe. In this connection he had been somewhat disconcerted to find that Palmerston 'and, to an only slightly lesser extent, Lord Russell too were in a state of complete ignorance about the direction pursued in the field of foreign policy by the party in Prussia from which, in the opinion of the British ministers, a new Prussian Cabinet ought to be formed.'

Palmerston set great store by 'seeing Prussia remain on good terms with

Austria for the present and having any disturbance of the peace among members of the German Confederation prevented'. Yet he was wholly unaware 'that precisely in this direction our parliamentary majority, were Your Majesty to give them the helm, offers very little security in that the so-called Progressive Party demands as one of the first items of its programme an approach to the German question that would necessarily lead in fairly short order to a break with our partners in the German Confederation and in particular with Austria'. When he, Bismarck, had gone so far as to explain to him 'that the resistance of the majority over the military question would disappear and every contribution requested for the army be approved without any problems should Your Majesty deign to hold out the prospect of the army being used to support a policy such as that advocated by the National Union', Palmerston declared this to be simply a 'misrepresentation of the facts that I permitted myself, as he saw it, in the interests of a reactionary party-political stance'.

Whether the conversation – from which Bismarck also and again very deliberately reported that on the Schleswig-Holstein question both politicians sided entirely with the Danish national party – really took this form must remain an open question. After all, it suited Bismarck's plan rather too well that Britain should if possible be kept out of all combinations not only on foreign policy but also on domestic policy grounds.

It may indeed have come as a surprise to him that people in London had only the vaguest idea about domestic conditions in Prussia and particularly about the national objectives of the Progressive Party. Immediately on his return to Paris he wrote concurrently to his wife and to Roon that 'the British ministers know less about Prussia than about Japan and Mongolia'.[32] But if we believe no more than the gist of the note that the Saxon envoy, Count Vitzthum, made for his own benefit about a conversation held at the same time between his close friend Benjamin Disraeli, the leader of the conservative opposition, and Bismarck, the latter did in fact give far more open expression to the conclusions that he himself drew from the domestic and foreign policy situation as far as Prussia was concerned.

He may at least have hinted that a Prussian government headed by himself would react to London's taking sides – whether with the liberal opposition in Prussia itself, or with Austria and the preservation of the German Confederation, or even with the Danish nationalists – by adopting highly unorthodox counter-measures. If Britain did not stay out of things it would gain nothing and experience only unpleasant surprises, finding itself faced with coalitions that the reports of British diplomats had hitherto pronounced impossible. A little later Napoleon's verdict with regard to Bismarck's bold combinations was: 'Ce n'est pas un homme sérieux.'[33] Disraeli, however, apparently said: 'Take care of that man! He means what he says.'[34] Though whether this was also the opinion of the two leading foreign affairs representatives of the British government of the day is more than doubtful.

On the other hand there is no doubt that for Bismarck this brief visit to London confirmed what he thought: the real decisions would be arrived at on the continent. Britain was too remote from the conditions obtaining in central Europe. It was too preoccupied with other problems; provided the continental balance of power was more or less preserved, it would shrink from any risk of becoming involved in developments in which it could not see its way with absolute clarity.

This was something Bismarck banked on at least until 1870 – and as things turned out he was right. If Gorchakov sought a 'dissolution of the alliance of the Western powers', then let him devote his energies to that end. He, Bismarck, was convinced that in reality such an alliance, at least in a form that would take any strain, simply did not exist and that Napoleon not only desired but positively needed an understanding with Prussia. Even if they kept him waiting they would still be able to count on him. The king need have no worries at all on that score.

William, however, was very much more alarmed than Bismarck had thought possible. With explicit reference to the tête-à-tête with Napoleon III he once again refused to give Bismarck the Foreign Ministry. He made it clear that he would use him, if at all, only for domestic affairs, as a declared 'Konfliktminister'. Bismarck for his part was still determined not to consent to this. On the other hand he was by no means as sure as he liked to pretend in later years that he was not in danger of missing his moment, this so favourable moment when the king seemed to be dependent on him and looked as if he might be influenced by him in any direction. Stuck in Paris, Bismarck simply ran around in circles, growing more and more tense. 'I am not in good health, and this interim existence with its "if and how" suspense but with no actual business to attend to is doing nothing to steady my nerves', he wrote to Roon in mid-July.[35]

He wanted to get away, as far away as possible, to put actual distance between himself and all the toing and froing, the everlasting speculation and vacillation. For this his estate in Pomerania, despite the fact that he had not seen his wife and children for months, struck him as quite unsuitable. Besides, to reach it he would have had to travel via Berlin, where he dreaded being detained yet again for days on end without a decision. So when on 17 July he at last received the six weeks' leave for which he had applied, he resolved to spend them in France, travelling largely at random but with the vague object of seeing something of southern France and the Pyrenees.

After a detour to Trouville, where the delights of a family bathing resort very quickly palled, he boarded a train for the south on 25 July. He described this leisurely journey by way of Blois, Bordeaux, Bayonne, San Sebastian and Biarritz in almost daily letters to his wife, written with a colourfulness, a graphic immediacy and a feeling for landscape and for the mood of the moment that bring out that other Bismarck, a man of exceptional sensitivity who for all his ambition and for all his political passion at the same time felt oppressed and constrained by his future prospects, sensing that they barred quite different avenues to him and cut off quite different ways of life.

He was no longer, however, the man to let such feelings overwhelm him or knock him off course. Bismarck had learned only too well by now that freedom, openness and independence of perception were inextricably bound up with one's own anchoredness, one's being in many respects committed, and that such perspectives as offered themselves were unthinkable without a firm standpoint of one's own in life. That, apart from everything else, was what distinguished Biarritz from Wiesbaden, the 1862 escapade from that of 1837. In Wiesbaden he had been looking for a shape for his inner self; he had been in search of a way of life. In Biarritz he discovered that the shape he had meanwhile found and the outward existence that was now his had not sapped but in fact preserved his inner self.

Biarritz was of course Catherine Orlov, the 22-year-old wife of the Russian envoy in Brussels, Prince Nicholas Orlov, a man he had known casually in St Petersburg.[36] Before her arrival on 7 August, though he had felt very well and had read and bathed a great deal and written a great many letters, he had also been bored, his thoughts travelling to Berlin while he made plans for further travel in France. From then on it was only the day that counted for him, only the life he was living in that otherwise not particularly exciting southern French seaside resort.

That he very quickly fell in love with Catherine Orlov is beyond question; he himself quite unashamedly let it show in the letters that he continued even now to send to his wife at the rate of two or three a week. Yet, for all the intensity of his feeling, that was not what really mattered. Johanna, a stranger to jealousy in any superficial sense, possibly grasped this at once. 'Cathy', his 'niece', as he liked to call her, stressing and thereby contriving at the same time to diminish the age gap between them, did not plunge him into any kind of inner conflict. Nor did she alter or confuse his relationship with Johanna in any way. What happened was that her naturalness, her spontaneity and her carefree youthfulness swept Bismarck off his feet principally in the sense that he rediscovered his own youth in her, rediscovered it, moreover, in a form that was stripped of all the uncertainties, hesitancies and self-doubt that had inevitably been bound up with it. The knowledge that life was something pleasant and worth living in other terms than those of his hopes for the future, the projections of his own objectives and expectations, indeed that a feeling of being himself and a feeling for the beauties of existence could emerge only from a state of almost purposeless immobility – that was what those days brought him more than anything else. They were days of fulfilment rather than of yearning, days of a spontaneous, self-generated enjoyment of life – for which the feeling of being in love was both stimulant and outward expression. Neither here nor subsequently was there ever so much as the shadow of a suggestion of bounds overstepped or not overstepped. Quite obviously this was never a problem.

The chief element in the situation was the charm of the unspoken, of an erotic sympathy and of a certain playfulness, a mutual fascination, fostered by outward circumstances, that irradiated everything and embraced and enlivened everything without the tension of it ever becoming intolerable. Catherine Orlov spoke in retrospect of a 'time full of foolishness, gaiety and poetry in an enchanting natural setting', of a 'free and independent existence that was so full of dreams'. And almost ten years later, in June 1871, Bismarck for his part once again evoked the 'happy hours, the carefree life that we were able to live there and that is so far removed from this clamorous existence whose troubles oppress me today'.

That was the tone throughout – a 'Paradise Lost', as he called it [in English; *Tr.*] in a letter to Catherine written in September 1863, of which he was reminded daily by things he carried in his cigar-case: one of her pins, 'a little yellow flower . . . picked in Superbagnères, some moss from Port de Vénasque and an olive twig from the terrace in Avignon'. Early in October 1864, using a meeting with Napoleon as an excuse, he once again embarked on a journey into the past. And although he himself was somewhat sceptical and his official business left him only a limited freedom, the magic of that past was so powerful that at least intermittently the old atmosphere came back.

In 1864 there was of course no longer any question of an extension of leave being taken for granted, nor any further chance of the kind of journey into the unattainable on which he set out with the Orlovs in the Pyrenees on 1 September 1862. Mountaineering expeditions in the Pyrenees had been in fashion for some time. The party climbed the Pic du Midi and spent the night in a mountain hut in order to see the sun rise over the Pyrenees. They walked up the Col de Vénasque together and enjoyed a commanding view of Spain. In daily excursions in the bosom of nature they experienced a wealth of constantly changing external stimuli. For Bismarck it was above all confirmation of a return to strength and health, a *joie de vivre* that was not dependent on success and immediate self-affirmation. The wistful feeling that it would all be over in a few days, that it was no more than an interlude, lent it a special enhancement.

Because although he was unreachable for days on end and for quite a time was cut off from all news there were limits to his carefreeness, and not at any point did he sever a single mooring. He had meticulously indicated the places where letters would reach him by *poste restante*, and he had taken the precaution of informing the Foreign Minister in advance that he might want an extension of leave. He had also carefully worked out whether by his absence he perhaps ran the risk of missing a crucial moment. Biarritz and the Pyrenees amused him, they distracted him, they gave his thoughts a different direction from the one that tormented him, but that was all.

When he reached Toulouse on the evening of 10 September he did not need first to grope his way back to reality, to find his feet again, as it were. Quite the contrary. He had expected to find a letter there from the Foreign Minister with the decision about a possible Cabinet reshuffle. Receiving instead only a letter from Roon that bore the date 31 August and told him that everything was still in the balance,[37] he determined immediately to force such a decision one way or another without waiting for further information. Things could not go on like this, he replied to Roon from Toulouse on 12 September. His plan now was with Bernstorff's permission to come to Berlin in the very near future and discuss everything else orally: 'This time I must know where I stand.' He was very happy to remain in Paris, but he could not go on squatting on packed suitcases. 'Procure me certainty one way or the other and I shall paint angels' wings on your photograph!'[38]

What may at first sight appear to be impatient insistence on the part of a man who was not even properly up-to-date was in reality a precisely calculated thrust. Before his leave, back in the middle of July, Bismarck had outlined his own political plan of campaign, so to speak, in two letters carefully tailored to their respective addressees.

In the first of these, a private letter to Count Bernstorff, the Foreign Minister, he had expressly warned the latter against letting the House of Deputies force his hand in any way and rob him of the initiative. While it was certainly his opinion that the government must show 'calm resolution' in countering 'every undesirable cancellation of an item of military expenditure', it should 'never [make] a Cabinet or dissolution issue' out of it but let 'the House complete its work'. He went on: 'The longer the House sits and talks, the better things stand for the Crown in the eyes of public opinion.' Parliament, after all, plainly lacked 'individuals that keep it from being boring'. If the government eventually prorogued the House for a month and let 'the district court judges learn something of their representatives' expenses', Bismarck suggested, 'the gentlemen may come back in a more reasonable frame of mind'. He concluded: 'Patient and persistent attempts to reach agreement simply lead us into the passage between the Scylla of conditions at home resembling those in the Electorate of Hesse and the Charybdis of parliamentary rule.' As far as his own possible entry into the ministry was concerned, he declared that it would become meaningful and worthwhile only at such time as the budget proposals as a whole foundered on the antagonism between the House of Deputies on one side and the Upper House and the Crown on the other.[39]

Bismarck's letter to Roon, written on the same day, was no different in substance.[40] Here too the gist of his advice was to the effect that the House should be left to stew in its own juice for the time being. One must rely on the public sooner or later losing interest in these endless parliamentary battles of words and hope that this would take the wind out of the opposition's sails, especially if the civil servants in the House, above all the judges, who constituted something like a third of the 240 or so members of the left, were to be threatened with financial losses. It was just that in Roon's letter this was all put in very much more martial terms and Bismarck spoke only indirectly of the difficult passage between the Scylla of absolutism and the Charybdis of a victorious parliamentarism.

He compared his own entrance at the height of the conflict to the 'production of a fresh battalion in the ministerial battle-order'. This might make 'an impression', he suggested, 'that is not being achieved at the moment' – 'especially if preceded by a certain amount of verbal sabre-rattling with expressions such as octroyation and even a gentle *coup d'état*'. Then his 'old reputation for irresponsible violence' would come to his aid, and people would think: '"Now we're for it."' 'Then', said Bismarck, confident of victory, 'all the watchers and waverers will be inclined to parley.'

His anti-parliamentarism likewise received much greater emphasis in this letter, not least with an eye to that 'military expert', King William, who was furious at the opposition of such mere 'laymen' as the majority of the elected deputies were in his estimation. 'I am amazed at the political ineptitude of our parliament', Bismarck stated with deliberate condescension, posing as the superior statesman. In terms of education the members of parliaments elsewhere were undoubtedly 'no cleverer than the flower of our class franchise, but they do not have the childish self-assurance with which ours exhibit their ineffectual private parts stark naked in public as being something exemplary. However did we Germans get our reputation for shy modesty? There is not one among us that does not know more about everything from war-making to dog fleas than all the trained experts put together, whereas in other countries there are many who will admit to knowing less than other people about many things and are consequently content to keep quiet.'

But that was by the way, an attempt to get into the good books of a man who, since the homage question, had had his doubts as to whether Bismarck really was a wholly committed champion of the power of the Crown and was not in fact speculating on being able to pursue his own policy in a balancing-act between Crown and parliament as the real beneficiary of the conflict. Such was indeed quite clearly Bismarck's objective. And now, in the middle of September 1862, as he already knew from the parliamentary calendar, the crucial moment for the realization of that objective had come. Now he would be used as he had hoped to be used when he advised against embarking upon detailed negotiatioqs with the House: as a saviour in the hour of the king's greatest need, as his last way out. The circumstance that in July he had described as an obstacle to his joining the ministry, namely the intention at all events to appoint him only Minister-President without a portfolio of his own, was now without importance, not because he would seriously have been prepared to forgo the Foreign Ministry to which he aspired as well but because he was convinced that in the circumstances it would eventually drop into his lap.

The extent to which he had thought out his plan of campaign in every detail is shown by the fact that he informed Bernstorff as early as mid-July of his intention to come to Berlin after his leave and discuss everything else orally. His only worry was lest the government should after all embark on compromise negotiations before the actual final debate and final vote. And however much 'out of this world' the Biarritz days seem to have been, significantly that worry caused him to address himself once again to Bernstorff in the only political letter that he wrote during his whole leave and to warn him against changing the tactics adopted hitherto.

'The thing the ministry had to aim at in the interests of its own plan of operation, namely the dulling of public opinion', he wrote with reference to newspaper reports of the current committee proceedings in the House of Deputies, 'these clever politicians are offering it on a plate. It would be a great shame ever to send these blatherskites home; kept simmering over a moderate heat, they will provide a splendid ingredient for our constitutional cuisine, and the Crown will ultimately have them to thank for the preservation of the royal rights.'[41] The notepaper, incidentally, bears the initials 'C.O.'; it was 'borrowed from a Russian friend', as Bismarck wrote in explanation – a further indication of how closely attuned he remained even here to the probable course of events in Berlin, enjoying his own freedom and lightness of heart in the knowledge that he was leaving nothing undone, for Catherine Orlov liked to do her letter-writing in the open air, far away from the hotel. And on one such occasion, Bismarck, thinking over the whole situation, obviously decided it might be a good idea to give Bernstorff this further reminder of his duty.

So Bismarck's movements throughout formed part of a carefully worked-out plan of campaign. There was no element of what romantic exaggerations of his 'escapade' have been very ready to call spontaneous decision. Of course, as Bismarck was only too well aware, whether that plan would in fact lead to the desired objective scarcely depended on him. The calculations that lay behind it with regard to the circumstances and to the behaviour of the people concerned might be frustrated at any time. And, unlike in so many critical situations in later years, this time he had no real alternative at his disposal. If one side gave ground or the king even gave up altogether by abdicating, Bismarck had shot his bolt, probably for ever.

Initially the government in Berlin had behaved exactly as Bismarck envisaged. In its detailed discussions of the budget the House of Deputies was left largely to its own devices. A not inconsiderable number of opposition members continued to look hopefully for signs of a readiness to compromise on the part of the government, but no such signs were in evidence. On the contrary, on 14 and 18 August the semi-official *Sternzeitung* published an article that to all appearances put forward the view of budgetary law advocated by the arch-conservatives around Kleist-Retzow and Ludwig von Gerlach as representing the government's opinion. According to that view, if parliament and the government failed to agree on the new draft budget proposed by the latter, this would revive the right of the executive to dispose of the state's revenues and expenses on its own account – in accordance with the last budget to have been passed, but possibly also deviating from it if special circumstances required.[42]

Bismarck himself had taken this very line eleven years before, in one of his last speeches in parliament on 24 February 1851. On the subject of what was to happen if a budget duly proposed by the government was not adopted, he had declared on that occasion, 'the constitution says nothing at all'. He had added: 'Nowhere does it state that in such a case the former right of the government to make disbursements from state funds has been revoked.'[43]

The *Sternzeitung* article did not put it as clearly as that, namely that in the event of a clash between parliament and government the ministry could revert to pre-constitutional, absolutist methods. But it did point out, as Bismarck had done, that the constitution was clearly not complete here. It possessed a 'loophole', which the government must if necessary fill by taking action on its own initiative, since it was responsible for the continued existence of the polity and its institutions. This suggestion alone sufficed to provoke a storm of public protest, a storm that extended far beyond the circle of those who for their part rejected any compromise with the king.

What lay behind such a suggestion did indeed make a mockery of all modern constitutional thought. It implied no less than that the Crown was bound by the vote of parliament on financial matters only for as long as it managed to reach agreement with it. Failing this, it was for it and not parliament to decide how public funds were to be used. Anyone who was familiar, even in outline, with the evolution of the constitutional parliamentary state since the archetypal conflicts in seventeenth-century England was aware that, without the kind of full and unqualified right of budgetary control that the Prussian constitution, too, granted to parliament, that body was in practice powerless. Any attempt to deprive parliament of that right by trickery of one sort or another meant that a 'cold' *coup d'état* was at least in the planning stage.

The almost unanimous reaction on the part of the public obviously brought this home to ministers very clearly and caused them to shrink from so intransigent an attitude. In a so-called 'Immediatbericht' or 'direct report' to the king on 9 September a unanimous Cabinet – that is to say, including War Minister von Roon – accepted the view that in the event of the government's budget being rejected 'the constitutional foundation of the administration [was] removed'. A 'burning conflict' of this kind was not something that the government could 'allow to continue'. If it did 'it would be wholly abandoning the ground of the constitution because it would thereby be assuming the authority to defray public expenditure in defiance of the express decision of the existing national representative body and in the absence of a statutory budget'.[44]

The simple choice remaining was between immediately dissolving the House of Deputies once again and – even if ministers did not say as much openly – the government relenting. The Cabinet thus explicitly repudiated the theory that there was a 'loophole' in the constitution here and that that 'loophole' allowed it to carry on its business without an approved budget. On the eve of the crucial week of the parliamentary session from 11 to 18 September it was anxious to persuade the king that in view of the hopelessness of the prospect of fresh elections the government must urgently seek a compromise.

William, however, continued to turn a deaf ear to such arguments. He declared that he would not evade a conflict and would accordingly even support a government that was prepared to rule without a legally approved budget. Despite this the ministers, again including Roon, did after all attempt during the dramatic parliamentary discussions that now ensued to reach a compromise with the section of the opposition that was prepared to negotiate. In this they appeared to be successful. On 16 September it looked as if they were going to be able to agree on the basis of a motion, framed by Stavenhagen and Sybel of the 'Left Centre' and by Twesten of the Progressive Party, that made approval of the army reform programme dependent on a return to a two-year period of military service.

In effect this would have been an almost total victory for the government, the majority of the army leaders having pronounced a two-year period entirely adequate. In other words, the opposition's partial success would have been so in little more than appearance. Yet even that seems to have been too much for a by now completely obdurate monarch. At the decisive session of the Crown Council on 17 September he rejected the emergent compromise – only shortly after Roon had at least hinted to the House of Deputies that the government was thinking of accepting it. Despite the urgings of the majority of his ministers – the exceptions being von Jagow, the Minister of the Interior, Count zu Lippe, the Minister of Justice, von Mühler, the Minister of Culture, Education and Church Affairs, and Agriculture Minister Count Itzenplitz – the king was not prepared to make the slightest concession. Instead he categorically demanded of his ministers that they should bow to his will or draw the consequences. Notwithstanding which his ministers, after a break in the Crown Council meeting during which the Cabinet continued in session and subsumed the opposition minority under the obligation of voting as one vis-à-vis the monarch, held fast to their opinion. Whereupon the king, now very much the sovereign laying down the law, gave orders to revoke all readiness to compromise – though he promptly added that he would abdicate if he failed to find a suitable fellow combatant and that he intended, as a precaution, to have the crown prince summoned to Berlin immediately.[45]

The question must remain open whether this was at first simply an extreme means of swearing his recalcitrant ministers in behind his unconditional collision course. Nor is it possible, in retrospect, to determine unequivocally whether in fact it succeeded and the ministers really did spontaneously commit themselves to trying to stand beside him implicitly in the circumstances or whether, as is perhaps more likely, the bombshell of the king's announcement served at first only to create general confusion, ruling out the possibility of any genuine decisions. It was now quite clear, however, that the king was not under any circumstances prepared to give in. On the other hand it was to be expected that the House of Deputies would react in the strongest possible terms to the explicit withdrawal, insisted on by William, of all suggestions to the effect that the government might be prepared to make concessions. On 19 September the House did indeed throw out the Stavenhagen-Sybel-Twesten motion by a huge majority; Twesten's initiative cost him his seat on the executive committee of the Progressive Party.

The conflict now threatened to assume proportions that finally broke the bounds of a dispute, however critical, at the level of parliamentary politics. Siding with the king in this situation, against so powerful a majority in both parliament and public opinion, meant taking a big personal risk as well. This in turn meant that the king, if he found anyone, was likely to find only servile careerists or political desperadoes rather than men with the ability to survive such a conflict politically and eventually discover a way out of it. There was reason to fear that the Crown would thus be actively steering the ship of state to destruction.

So even if William had at first used the possibility of abdication essentially as a way of putting pressure on his ministers, the course of events showed him more clearly by the hour that he was going to have to give that possibility serious consideration if he did not wish to find himself in a situation incompatible with his conception of the royal office.

Probably no one saw the lie of the land more clearly than Roon, who shared William's views to a great extent and had done all he could to encourage him in them. Precisely because he saw it so clearly, however, the kind of coolly calculating Machiavellism that has been said to have characterized his behaviour during those crucial days appears unlikely. Roon, we are told, employed every means to engineer the crisis, including that of himself siding with the party of compromise in the hope that this would drive the king to decisions that he would probably not have been prepared to make had the circumstances been different. However, quite apart from the fact that in this final phase it was the king who was doing the driving, it seems more than doubtful that Roon would have let himself in for so hazardous a venture. Because that was what it was, given the fact that the king might at any moment realize how isolated he had become and given the risk of his drawing conclusions that in any case ran counter to Roon's actual political intentions.

It is much more likely, therefore, that Roon, fearing that if the position was stretched any further the ship of state might capsize, really did regard a course correction as unavoidable but failed to convince the king – any more than he had been able nine months earlier to bring him round to the idea of risking a military coup if necessary. In which case he is more likely to have been in a state of panic after the decisive Crown Council meeting of 17 September than in one of satisfaction at having finally put matters on the right course. And it was no doubt in such a state that he dictated the famous and much-quoted telegram that was dispatched to Bismarck under a previously agreed cover name on the afternoon of 18 September: 'Periculum in mora. Dépêchez-vous.'

It was with Roon's telegram that Bismarck, writing his memoirs thirty years later, opened his own account of the events immediately leading up to his appointment.[46] This is a masterpiece of political myth-mongering. It has demonstrated its effectiveness even in cases where their knowledge of facts that conflict with it has forced historians to adopt a more critical approach and correct many details. In fact there is scarcely a grain of truth in it. It deliberately obscures the actual circumstances in the interests of creating an impression that the Parisian envoy, appearing at this point like a *deus ex machina*, saved the House of Hohenzollern in a moment of dire distress almost against the will of the then occupant of the throne. He, Bismarck, who twenty-eight years later was to be so ignominiously dismissed by the latest and currently incumbent scion of that house, William II, had single-handedly saved the dynasty from declining into a mere shadow existence along the lines of the English monarch.

To place his account on what looked like a solid footing he had first to make Roon appear as the real driving force against a policy of half-measures or of acquiescence. As little was said about Roon's ever having been prepared to compromise as about the fact that a possible agreement had been thwarted solely by the stubbornness of the king. Furthermore – and this completed the distortion of the picture – Bismarck represented himself as having responded purely as a matter of duty to the desperate appeal of a loyally-principled champion of the rights of the Crown. What no one could have inferred from his account was that in reality the initiative had lain almost wholly with himself and the famous telegram had nothing whatsoever of the character of a pre-arranged signal between two men conspiring to save the mortally threatened Prussian monarchy. For Bismarck failed to mention that he had made plans months before to put in a personal appearance in Berlin during what looked like being the crucial stage of the argument between parliament and government about the army budget. He further suppressed the fact that the king acceded on 16 September, in other words before the situation became critical, to his request to be allowed to come to Berlin to discuss his future employment. 'The King consents to your coming here now', Bernstorff had telegraphed him on the evening of the 16th, adding: 'And I advise you to come immediately since His Majesty will soon be leaving again.'[47]

Roon's telegram was no signal, then, but was meant quite literally: Bismarck should get a move on, otherwise he could say goodbye to his hopes. Unquestionably Roon did indeed, after the failure of the compromise attempt, see Bismarck as the one remaining hope of salvation from a seizure of power by the liberals under the heir to the throne, who more or less openly favoured them. But it is quite as obvious that, although Roon undoubtedly knew from Bernstorff that Bismarck would be coming to Berlin in the very near future, he did not begin to abide by the tactical plan that Bismarck had sought to urge upon him.

Had he been following it, he would never have stretched out his own hand in compromise. The whole aim of Bismarck's calculation was by holding fast to the government's position to bring about a situation in which the appointment of an out-and-out 'Konfliktminister', which was what Roon was always presenting him as, would virtually force itself upon the king. But it inevitably appeared quite senseless, in terms of that calculation, to risk provoking unpredictable reactions on the king's part by offering compromises that he was likely to see as a betrayal. Roon, in short, had obviously wanted to keep two courses open for himself. And, in the light of William's recurrent aversion to appointing Bismarck, up until 18 September it was probably the course of limited compromise that struck him as the more feasible and likely to succeed.

In reality the king himself was the only person who consistently pursued the tactics that Bismarck had recommended in his two letters to Bernstorff and Roon back in mid-July, although tactics in the sense of the deliberate deployment of specific means in the interests of an overall strategic plan is more than we can really speak of in this connection. It was a case of a vague, unyielding adherence to a royal image much coloured by emotion making his conduct appear to him as his duty.

William made a further attempt to define and justify that image in the draft deed of abdication that he drew up on the evening of 17 September, after the serious clash with his ministry.[48] Using language that was downright archaic, he began by invoking, in a variety of ways, the idea of divine right and the special sanctity and dignity of kingship and went on to infer from this a special form not only of the duty but clearly also of the judgement of the sovereign.

He had always, he said, sought to obey that obligating judgement in conformity 'with the sworn laws', including the constitution. This was no longer possible. Instead, as a result of the behaviour of the majority in parliament 'a conflict has arisen that We are unable to reconcile with Our duties toward the state and with the provisions of the constitution. We are unable to break either with the principles of Our own life or with the glorious history and past of Our dear fatherland. Such a break would be necessary, however, to remove the present conflict.'

In plain terms this meant that he would never bow to the view that the monarch was not above the constitution but was himself an organ of the constitution and as such could act only in concurrence with the other organs of the constitution. Should he fail to find adequate backing here, there was 'no other course open than to renounce the exercise of Our royal rights and hand these over to the rightful and legal successor who as yet has no historical and binding past'.

The successor, however, was not prepared to accept the crown in such circumstances. Instead the crown prince sought to convince his father, in the crucial discussions they had at the royal summer residence of Babelsberg near Potsdam on 19 and 20 September, that a change of sovereign just now might be far more momentous than what he saw as an objectively quite justifiable giving-in: abdication, he said, would be tantamount to capitulation and would seriously hamper his own exercise of the royal office right from the outset.

Since then historians have repeatedly asked whether the crown prince, who later reigned briefly as Frederick III, did the right thing in that situation or whether he did not pass up a crucial opportunity of putting not only his own but also Prussia's and Germany's future on a quite different course. However, quite apart from the fact that no one could have foreseen that the present king, already 65 years of age, would go on to achieve a positively biblical span, we must bear in mind that what in retrospect appears almost as the turning-point of the century was noticed by hardly anybody at the time. If one ruled out a military coup – something that in spite of everything the king was not prepared to contemplate, as the crown prince knew – the position of the crown inevitably looked so weak that the alternative of abdication or surrender would remain even if for the time being the crown prince firmly rejected an early succession. On the other hand, swift acceptance by the crown prince of his father's plan would in many ways, quite apart from all personal considerations and feelings of loyalty, have placed him in a somewhat awkward position. As things stood, however, he could hope that even without any over-hasty intervention the situation would develop in what for him was the desired direction of a settlement between Crown and parliament – whether through a compromise being reached after all or through the Crown, without his appearing to have had any hand in the matter, eventually falling to him as the saviour of his country from what everyone saw as an onimous crisis. He was able to feel the more entitled to this hope for the fact that the appointment of Bismarck, on whom the hopes of all those who wished to fight on at any cost were now concentrated, had repeatedly been ruled out by the king – though whether or not the latter continued to rule it out in their talks of 19 and 20 September cannot be said with certainty.

At any rate the crown prince had already clearly committed himself when Bismarck, after a 25-hour train journey, arrived in Berlin on Saturday, 20 September. A brief discussion with Roon showed him immediately that the moment he had been banking on had now come. Bernstorff and the Minister of Finance, von der Heydt, who as deputy Minister-President was *de facto* head of the government, had both tendered their resignations. The fronts had hardened completely. The king was obviously determined to go to the bitter end, be it abdication or an all-out struggle. 'Government by parliament, arming of the people, the King behind parliament no more than a president – I'm not going to stoop to that role', he wrote to the queen at the time.[49] Bismarck, however, was well aware that as far as he himself was concerned William still hung back, indeed recoiled from using him. 'He thought me more fanatical than I was.'[50] And he may already then have suspected who was behind this, namely Queen Augusta, who had once again committed her reservations against him to writing in July 1862, reservations that culminated in the charge of treasonable intriguing back in March 1848.[51]

So everything now depended on winning the king over – and doing so not so much with concrete proposals and a clearly defined programme as by means of a kind of emotional surprise attack based entirely on the feelings and on the monarchical understanding of himself by which William was guided. The crown prince, who in parallel to his two very full discussions with his father was trying in a series of meetings and talks to lay the foundations for a compromise on the government side initially, sent for Bismarck on the evening of the 20th. He obviously wished to discover whether any surprise proposals altering the entire situation were to be expected from this quarter and what Bismarck in fact had in mind – 'whether he [was] willing', as his adviser Max Duncker framed the question for him in advance, 'to join the ministry and on what terms and with what intentions'.[52]

The idea of compromising Bismarck by the mere fact of this interview, in other words by giving the king the impression that his Parisian envoy was addressing himself immediately and primarily to the rising sun, will scarcely have constituted Frederick William's motive here. Bismarck, though, saw at once the possibility of such an impression being created. He was therefore at pains to keep the interview as brief and formal as possible and to avoid going into the questions that really mattered. This alone showed how carefully everything was directed at the king's present emotional state and how accurately Bismarck assessed this. For William was indeed following his son's activities with all the mistrust of a man who sees himself being pushed into a premature retirement, even if it is on the basis of his own decisions and resolutions, and detects evidence of the unprincipled opportunism of those around him at every turn. Bismarck with his son – for the king that was as good as confirmation that he too had joined the party of compromise and was expecting it to win. 'He's no good either; he's already been to see my son', he is supposed, according to

Bismarck's own account, to have said to Roon on 21 September when the War Minister requested an audience for the Parisian envoy in Babelsberg after the Sunday service.

That was exactly what Bismarck took as his starting-point in the crucial interview with the king in Babelsberg on the afternoon of 22 September 1862. We only have Bismarck's own version of how that interview went.[53] Yet there is a great deal of evidence, in the outcome of that interview and in the subsequent course of events, to suggest that the gist of his description is correct.

What Bismarck had to do was to give the king the impression immediately that he had in him, Bismarck, an utterly devoted follower who was prepared to stand up for him and for his rights without any ifs and buts. If he succeeded in this, all objective divergences of opinion were of no importance, given the king's present mood and way of thinking, and this kind of personal pledge of fidelity could take the place of a concrete and specific government programme.

How his calculation worked out was described by Bismarck very candidly and with an unmistakable feeling of triumph in retrospect. The king, he said, had first represented the situation to him as he saw it and informed him of his decision to abdicate – to his surprise, as Bismarck claimed in his memoirs, a claim that was obviously false and arose purely out of his attempt to draw a veil over the events leading up to his appointment. Without going into the king's abdication plan any further, he had then informed the king that he was prepared, even in the present circumstances, to join the ministry and would not be put off by eventual further resignations. To the king's twofold query as to whether in that case he would support the full programme of army reform and stick to it even in the teeth of majority decisions of the House of Deputies, he replied without further ado with a twofold 'Yes'. Whereupon the king declared: 'Then it is my duty to try to continue the fight with you, and I shall not abdicate.'

With that the real decision was already made. Overwhelmed by Bismarck's expression of unconditional loyalty and unreserved support for his position, William was really only going through the motions, whatever illusions he may himself have entertained in this regard, when he now called upon Bismarck to discuss and to define the future programme of the government on the basis of an exposé that he had drawn up himself. Significantly this second part of the audience took place on a walk through the park of the royal castle.

Bismarck did not shrink in retrospect from referring to the king's exposé as a 'concoction', saying he had not known whether it 'had already served as a basis for discussions with my predecessors or whether it was intended to provide a guarantee against what he took to be my runaway conservatism'. At any rate he clearly succeeded in very quickly convincing the king that this was not the moment to discuss details. It was a question 'not of Conservative or Liberal of this or that persuasion but of royal supremacy or parliamentary rule'. The latter 'must be averted, even by a spell of dictatorship'. The king thereupon tore up the draft programme on the spot and took his stand on the special relationship of trust and loyalty that he,

Bismarck, offered him with the words: 'I feel like a . . . vassal who sees his liege lord in danger. Whatever I am capable of is at Your Majesty's disposal.'[54]

That was the crucial basis of their collaboration over the next twenty-six years. It was a partnership that in its reciprocal trust and above all in the mutual self-subordination of the one to discernment and will-power and the other to rank and the monarchical ideal is almost without parallel in history. Bismarck repeatedly harked back to the audience of 22 September, for example in a letter he wrote to William on 1 December 1863 in which he recalled 'that I see my position not as a constitutional minister in the usual sense of the word but as Your Majesty's servant, and that in the final instance I am obedient to Your Majesty's orders even when they are not in conformity with my personal views'.[55] Again, in a letter occasioned by the twenty-fifth anniversary of his appointment as Prussian Minister-President we read: 'The high position that I owe to Your Majesty's favour has as its foundation and as its indestructible core the Brandenburg liegeman and Prussian officer in Your Majesty's service.'[56]

Behind such language there undoubtedly lay genuine monarchical sentiments rooted in unbroken traditions and bound up with an inner need for a firm and, in the last analysis, metaphysically anchored order. Nor is there any doubt that Bismarck's personal relationship with the upright and quite unpretentious monarch who was eighteen years his senior also played an important part. 'It was hard work bringing the old gentleman round, but once you had won him for something he held fast to what had been decided. He was loyal, upright, de relation sure. You could depend on him completely', was Bismarck's affectionate verdict, looking back as an old man.[57] But the essence of the matter was that in Babelsberg Bismarck managed to obtain a kind of *carte blanche*. This placed him in a quite different position and gave him a quite different kind of scope for action than chief ministers, whether in an absolutist or in a parliamentary system, were usually provided with by their office even in the most favourable of circumstances.

When towards evening he took his leave of the king, it was not only his appointment as Minister-President and Foreign Minister that was 'in the bag'. Politically speaking, he had an almost completely free hand – albeit on two conditions that appeared in practice to reduce the latitude theoretically available to him almost to nothing, indeed that almost everyone believed would condemn the newly appointed head of the government to certain failure: he had to get the army reform programme through uncut, and he had to be able to show, within a short space of time, some kind of visible success.

He had no doubt that he could do both; in fact he had specific plans for both. But he was very soon forced to admit that reality was different in many respects from what, for all his flexibility and all his thinking in alternatives, he had imagined it to be from a distance. And if he did eventually manage to stand his ground successfully – indeed extraordinarily so – in the real world, this was due only to a relatively minor extent to himself and to his own actions. It had much more to do with a situation and with developments that were substantially independent of him but that favoured him in a way that defied all reasonable expectation. 'It is a lesson one learns well in this business, that one can be as wise as the wise ones of this world and yet at any moment find oneself next moment going out into the dark like a child', he wrote to his wife not two years later, following his first major foreign policy success in the Schleswig-Holstein question.[58] The admission reflects, although as a personal experience this was something he had long been familiar with, how much the experience of those first two years reinforced his doubts as to what was feasible, as to the potentialities of the individual and the calculability of things.

To a greater extent than any of his contemporaries suspected, fixated as they were on the struggle in hand and on the thoroughly self-assured, even provocative manner of the new Prussian Minister-President, these were years of apprenticeship. In them it became very clear to him that his own ideas in many respects no longer matched the realities of a rapidly changing world. The fact that here, unlike later, he was still able genuinely to learn proved to be the decisive foundation of a more than monetary success, in fact for one of the most successful political careers of modern times, in the course of which the faces of Prussia, Germany and Europe all underwent a radical change.

The day when all this began, this far-reaching transformation of the national and international maps of central Europe, was 22 September 1862. To that extent it is indeed a historical date and one that very vividly brings out the historical importance of a particular constellation of persons and circumstances. But what ultimately occasioned the success of the man and his policies goes far beyond the situation of the moment and the people who played a part in it, far beyond the dramatic events of those days. It was this alone that gave the whole thing the character of a crucial new departure; to seek in retrospect to discover that character in the drama of the moment would indeed be no more than an exercise in dramatization. On that 22 September nothing or next to nothing was as yet decided – as the man who now stood at the head of the Prussian government himself very quickly realized.

[6]

'Konfliktminister'

When on the evening of 24 September 1862 Bismarck read in the official government organ, the *Sternzeitung*, of his appointment as Minister of State and interim President of the Cabinet it may abruptly have brought home to him, in an initial moment of relaxation after all the drama of the past few days, the fact that, for all his stock of experience and all his self-assurance, he now had in many respects to start all over again. Eleven-and-a-half years had gone by since he had left Berlin and the little flat in the Dorotheenstrasse. That was when, as a young man of the far right in the revolutionary period, who with the exception of his Olmütz speech had made a name for himself primarily in domestic affairs and possessed no practical diplomatic experience whatever, he had been appointed to one of the most important posts in the Prussian diplomatic service. Meanwhile the situation had in a sense been reversed. The new occupant of 74 and 76 Wilhelmstrasse, the Presidential Chancellery and the Foreign Ministry, was now acknowledged even by his opponents to be a gifted and imaginative expert in the field of foreign affairs. Indeed he brought with him a reputation for being prepared, as far as foreign policy was concerned, to look in any direction. On the home front, however, he was still regarded as a reactionary of the first water, the spokesman of wholly anachronistic 'feudal' principles and interests, an 'obsequious country squire', as the Hessian liberal Friedrich Oetker put it.[1] And since he was taking up office as an out-and-out 'Konfliktminister', a politician who, it was assumed, would not shrink even from making an open break with the constitution and quelling the opposition by violent means, it occurred to hardly anyone at first to wonder whether his basic views and appraisals of domestic affairs had not meanwhile also undergone a change. Expectations, fears and political propaganda all tended in the one direction: that with Bismarck a man had taken up office who would seek to halt and indeed to reverse the course of history not only in the political but above all also in the social sphere.

Was that not indeed his objective? Had it not been his political watchword from the beginning that it was universally necessary to defend the existing order against the forces of change, of movement and of 'revolution' that allegedly undermined everything? And was not therefore everything new that subsequently emerged under his aegis merely a means to an end, a fresh form for an old content, designed purely to preserve the latter? Can one not similarly interpret his whole, highly successful foreign policy as nothing but an enormous relief manoeuvre for the benefit of the home front, including the three wars in which that policy initially culminated? 'It will in any case become clear as time goes on', the great Basle historian Jacob Burckhardt prophesied as early as the autumn of 1871, 'to what extent the three wars were embarked upon for reasons of domestic policy. For the space of seven years great advantage was taken of the fact that the whole world believed that only Louis Napoleon waged war for domestic reasons. Purely from the point of view of self-preservation', he went on, 'it was high time those three wars were waged. However, as regards the further internal developments that all this will yet bring with it, we shall probably often have occasion to shed tears.'[2]

Those few sentences anticipated every one of the arguments since assembled for the primacy of domestic affairs in the context of Bismarckian policy as a whole and for the essentially instrumental nature of his foreign policy. Nor is that all! Already with Burckhardt the whole thing was based on the thesis that Bismarck's policy was directed exclusively towards defence, towards resistance to change. The indisputably creative, innovative aspect of that policy, which in many fields launched completely fresh developments, is seen here as a kind of by-product, the outcome of a highly mobile and imaginative forward–defence strategy.

From Bismarck's own point of view this undoubtedly touches on an extremely important point. It was one that his traditionally conservative friends were already aiming at when, starting from quite different presuppositions and drawing quite different conclusions, they concentrated their specific criticism of Bismarck's policy on the fact that it was too unscrupulous and far too flexible in the defence of their common principles. Yet it is precisely this criticism from the old conservatives that brings out that other point that criticism from the opposing side has often lost sight of since then: that the original intention and guiding ideal of the individual agent is only one and often not the most important aspect of the historical process, that it is just as much a matter of how he acts, the way in which he carries out his intentions and the means and methods employed. To put it another way, what is crucial is the particular concrete outcome in reality.

Bismarck himself resolved the connection between the two in a special way by leaving the particular outcome of his own conduct and the question of the place that outcome occupied in more general developments to a higher power; in other words, he deliberately evaded in this respect what he saw as an intolerable responsibility. This gave him a measure of inner freedom of action enjoyed by hardly any of his contemporaries. The retrospective observer, however, once again has his attention drawn with especial emphasis to the fact that the reality, the deed, the outcome, cannot be interpreted at all adequately in terms of the intention behind it but is on the contrary often obscured and distorted thereby.

In our context, on the threshold of two-and-a-half decades during which Bismarck increasingly became the central figure in German politics, this means that the question of his original intentions and motives must recede even further, giving even greater prominence to the question of the actual results and the nature of the historical process on which they impinged and which was at the same time constantly reshaping them. Because only from this angle can Bismarck the historical agent be rendered visible in his achievements and his limitations, those imposed on him from outside as well as those for which he was himself responsible; only from here can it be shown what place he actually occupied, both as an individual and as a representative of particular political and social tendencies and forces, in the stream of historical development.

This becomes clear the moment we examine the situation in Prussia in the autumn of 1862 and the way in which Bismarck initially reacted to it. That reaction was in every respect inappropriate – even, that is, from the standpoint of a man thinking purely in terms of success. It showed that his appraisal of the circumstances was well wide of reality, and not in any merely temporary sense.

In terms of experience his horizon had without question broadened considerably since his political début. This was true not only of the field in which he had meanwhile come to feel he had a special competence, namely foreign affairs. It was also true with regard to social relations and economic life and to the changes and trends of development inherent in both.

This was not the result of theoretical study, let alone of any attempt at systematic penetration; neither at this time nor subsequently was there ever any question of his reading suitable material or making use of appropriate sources of information. It was all based on first-hand experience and observation, on private conversations, on preparation – admittedly very intensive – for special tasks such as the question of the continuation and expansion of the Customs Union in the 1850s, and finally on occasional bouts of very extensive newspaper-reading. However, the keenness of perception that he frequently manifested even in areas remote from his own concerns must not be allowed to blind us to the fact that his insights in many fields remained extremely limited and superficial, owing to the type of information with the aid of which he acquired them.

This is particularly evident in the case of Russia. During the three years of his stay in St Petersburg he managed by such means to form only a very imprecise picture of that country's internal relations, social structure and pressing problems. But much the same is true – and this was of far greater significance as far as subsequent developments were concerned – of the situation in central Europe, for the very reason that the Frankfurt years had in many ways considerably broadened his field of view here.

The fact is that the special circumstances that he had found in Frankfurt and the immediately adjoining territories and of which he had taken such careful note were in many respects atypical. They were certainly not representative of the rapidly changing political and social situation in Prussia itself during those years. Yet it was those special circumstances that obviously confirmed him in his appraisal of the future economic, social and political role of the middle classes; as he stressed repeatedly in later life, Frankfurt had been an 'eye-opener' for him.[3]

The middle classes, he believed on the basis of his Frankfurt experiences, would as a result of pressure from below in the shape of an alliance or even the mere prospect of an alliance between the government and the peasantry and the lower classes allow themselves to be successfully coerced back into the traditional order and held in check politically. What he overlooked was that the really dynamic element in the economic and hence in the social development of the period, namely the vigorous expansion of industry since the early 1850s, was only very weakly represented in the Frankfurt region, indeed had run into decisive resistance there from forces and interests that felt threatened by it and that possessed considerable political influence in the city.

What the pre-industrial middle class of merchants and tradesmen in this former imperial city-republic aspired to in the governmental and in the social sphere was a kind of order that preserved tradition, promoted business interests and was moderately democratic in politics at the same time as being essentially conservative in social matters. This was in complete conformity with the image Bismarck had formed of the so-called middle-class movement and its representatives in Pomerania, in the Brandenburg March, in Aachen and even in Berlin. It was an image he found most vividly embodied in the person of the Prussian *Kreisrichter* or district court judge, the type he once ironically described as the 'bourgeois provincial court official, humanistically enlightened and with no resistance to the principle of revolution'.[4]

Such an image was not entirely false. It reflected a type and a politico-social tendency that had largely dominated the scene between 1815 and 1848 and in many places still determined the appearance and objectives of German liberalism. But it obscured the far-reaching change that was everywhere in the offing, that radical alteration in the social landscape that could not remain without political consequences in the long run. This was true of the content of politics and it was true of the outward forms, the institutional and personal premises.

For all his level-headedness, Bismarck at first apprehended both only very one-sidedly, and he often drew far too hasty conclusions from his observations. He certainly had an eye, from his own first-hand experiences in the years before 1848, for the consequences of the dissolution of the traditional estate-owners' association in conjunction with the so-called emancipation of the peasantry and the way in which the principles of rational capitalist management had penetrated the agricultural sector. And he also saw that, in the wake of rapid economic change and against the background of entirely new market and labour relations between the middle classes and what as a result of population increases and the move from the land were the steadily swelling urban lower classes, more and more pronounced antagonisms were emerging that were becoming difficult to bridge by means of shared political principles and demands; his speeches in the years 1848–50 show this very clearly. Both observations led him – and not only after 1862, for example under the influence of the way in which Napoleon III operated, but as early as 1848–9 – to the conviction that the actual 'people', the urban and above all the rural lower classes, could be mobilized against the propertied middle class, virtually neutralizing it.

What escaped him, however, was the fact that economic developments after 1850, the sudden enormous increase in industrialization in conjunction with a sustained boom in almost every sector, brought about a further marked changed in the overall situation as compared with that which had emerged so clearly in 1848–9, although there was no basic shift in the trend underlying the whole process and the preconditions for social antagonisms likewise remained unaltered – or rather were becoming even more marked.

The change consisted primarily in the fact that those economic developments proved extraordinarily favourable to large sections of the middle class and strengthened the position of that class considerably, not only in material but also in political terms. In the wake of the economic boom of the 1850s the antagonisms between the propertied and educated middle class in the narrower sense and the so-called petty bourgeois strata of the craft trades and small-scale commerce and industry, antagonisms that had asserted themselves so seriously in 1848 were very greatly diminished. At the same time the present general prosperity, compared with the lean years before 1848, made the economic and social principles of liberalism appear in a very much more positive light – even deep in the ranks of the now rapidly emerging industrial working class, many of whose represen-tatives were still in the early 1860s backing the possibility of collaboration with the liberals. All of which explains the upswing that German liberalism had been enjoying as a political and also as an economic and social movement since the late 1850s and the self-confidence with which, not ten years after the fiasco of the revolution, its spokesmen demanded a share of political power.

It is possible to argue, on the basis of subsequent developments, that this heyday was only apparent. The very success of Bismarck's policy, it is said, showed that his analysis based on the experiences of 1848 was correct and that the conflicts of social and economic interest within the newly emergent middle-class society had already become unbridgeable. Yet this kind of argument, misled by the quite different economic situation that obtained after the crisis of 1873, fails to take account of the fact that in reality Bismarck owed his success not at all to playing off the middle and lower classes against each other. He owed it instead to the insight, painfully acquired after a whole series of setbacks, that he must reach a *modus vivendi* and achieve some kind of co-operation at least with certain sections of the middle class.

It was this alone that made possible the achievement of internal and external nation-building associated with his name and shaped the character of the Lesser German Empire. Having taken office as the saviour of the power of the Prussian Crown and the traditional ruling classes, he was very soon forced to recognize that the only way in which that power could be preserved was not by dividing the opposition camp but by dividing the power and sharing it with a section of that camp. One must add immediately that this was a recognition he found comparatively easy to make in that, as soon became clear, it promised to place his own power on a very much firmer footing. The fact remains, however, that to start with he completely and utterly misjudged the situation – and not in any merely

201

superficial sense, either. A sober look at his first steps in office – in other words, one not dazzled by his subsequent success – makes this very plain.

Outside the *Kreuzzeitung* party, now an almost insignificant presence in parliament, and the likewise not very numerous group of open reactionaries in the army and the administration, Bismarck's appointment as chief minister was universally greeted with extreme scepticism and virtually unanimous disapproval, not only inside Prussia but also beyond its borders. An imminent 'rule of the sword at home' and 'war abroad' were prophesied by Max von Forckenbeck, the reporting member of the budget committee and a future Mayor of Berlin.[5] The widely read *Augsburger Allgemeine Zeitung* characterized the new man as the 'kind of Minister-President with a uniform hidden under his dress suit'.[6] The *Kölnische Zeitung* thought Bismarck was undoubtedly 'that rare bird among the country squires of our eastern provinces, a man of wit and culture' who lacked neither 'personal charm' nor 'eloquence and drive'.[7] All of which, the paper felt, only made him the more dangerous.

Blended with this scepticism and disapproval, of course, was a widely held conviction that the appointment merely represented the last, desperate step of a monarch who, blinkered by the ideas and principles of a bygone age, had increasingly lost touch with the political and social reality of his time. 'With the employment of this man', wrote the well-known and influential journalist August Ludwig von Rochau in the weekly magazine of the liberal National Union, 'the last and most powerful bolt of the "by the grace of God" reaction has been shot.' He went on: 'Even if there is much that he has learned and unlearned, he is in no way a fully fledged statesman but merely an adventurer of the commonest sort, concerned only with what the next day may bring.'[8] Bismarck's fall, for most people a foregone conclusion, was expected within a matter of weeks or at most of months.

This opinion was so widespread that the new head of government found it difficult, even within his own camp, to find half-way suitable colleagues who looked capable of replacing the ministers who had resigned. With very few exceptions Bismarck's first Cabinet, the definitive composition of which he finally announced at the beginning of December 1862, consisted of men who, politically as well as in their individual spheres, were wholly lacking in independent judgement and were in some cases clearly not up to the job. Even politicians of a similar shade of opinion hesitated to put their careers at stake by joining this ministry. To a letter from Kleist-Retzow, his comrade-in-arms during the revolutionary period, who had criticized some of his ministerial choices, Bismarck added the sober note: 'We're glad to find and keep eight men'.[9] It was not just his reluctance to let anyone shine except himself that turned the review of his first ministry that he gave in his memoirs, recalling people like Itzenplitz and Lippe, Jagow and Mühler, into a veritable waxwork museum; 'incapable of running their ministries', lacking in 'understanding' of the government's overall political line, 'work-shy and pleasure-seeking' – such were the verdicts he passed on most of them.[10]

It was not surprising in the circumstances that the newly appointed head of government, who ostentatiously moved his family into the official residence at Wilhelmstrasse 76, the seat of the Foreign Ministry, as early as the middle of October, failed to find any co-operation even among the 'watchers and waverers' on whose readiness to compromise he had counted so confidently in his letter to Roon back in mid-July: an opportunist appraisal of the situation made it seem particularly advisable to have nothing whatever to do with the new man. This was very drastically brought home to Bismarck when on 30 September he took the first opportunity that offered of playing what he thought was a trump card, one he had long been sure would win him the trick.

In response to the rigid attitude of the Crown, parliament had on 23 September, with the eleven conservative votes dissenting, passed the budget after formally deleting all costs for army reorganization, in other words in a form that the monarch had already said he was not prepared to accept. This had emphatically confirmed William in his decision of the previous day to call in Bismarck. The decision of the House of Deputies 'to countermand the army reorganization' was tantamount to an intention 'to decree the ruin of the army and of the country', the king wrote to his wife on the evening of 23 September, she having continued until the last moment to speak out passionately against the new man. 'Faced with such conduct I could not hesitate nor would my conscience and my sense of duty any longer allow me to hesitate to set against this unflinching resolve one equally unflinching.'[11]

In this situation the new government at first had little room for political manoeuvre. It was generally expected to start by withdrawing the budget proposals and so attempt to gain time – time to establish itself in office but also to prepare fresh initiatives. The upshot, of course, could only be in doubt if the government unexpectedly showed itself willing to compromise. Even if behind the scenes there was lively concern that the new ministry might resort to violent tactics, in other words possibly attempt a coup, the opposition, with the public behind it, adopted a very confident air: as the press repeatedly averred, governing the country in defiance of an overwhelming parliamentary majority would soon prove impossible.

On 29 September, in Bismarck's first public statement as Minister-President, the government did indeed withdraw its budget proposals with the comment, regarded as purely formal, 'that the results of an immediate decision regarding the budget for 1863 would not be conducive to the future settlement of the questions at issue but would considerably increase the difficulties these posed'.[12] At the same time, after giving an assurance that it had no intention of creating a precedent in budgetary law by so doing, it announced that it would be submitting a revised budget together with an Army Reorganization Bill at the beginning of the next parliamentary session.

All of which sounded perfectly correct in constitutional terms when one remembered that this was a new and so far not even complete Cabinet. For the time being, therefore, the House of Deputies left it to the budget committee to find out in direct negotiations with the government whether the latter was simply playing for time that it intended to spend in achieving further *faits accomplis* or whether it was in fact, contrary to all expectations, working towards a compromise that would even be acceptable to the majority.

How the now-famous meeting of the committee on 30 September went in detail cannot be said with certainty; no minutes were kept of the proceedings, and the various reports diverge on many points. Nevertheless, if we take an unbiased view the general drift of Bismarck's remarks appears quite unambiguous. He was clearly at pains, not least through the relaxed and courteous manner in which he spoke, to defuse the tension, to play down the antagonisms and minimize the substance of the conflict, and to direct the attention of members back to what he alleged was the main aim of army reform: the strengthening of Prussian power as a prerequisite for a successful Prussian policy with regard to the German question.

Critical re-examination of the 1848 revolution and the reasons for its failure had led large sections of German liberalism, reacting to the thesis that the revolution had foundered on the internal antagonisms of its supporters, to accept the view that the chief reason had in fact been neglect of the power question. It had failed to build any solid power positions; above all it had not attempted to harness for its own purposes such forces and interests as were in fact present. To the detriment of its own cause it had pursued mere 'Idealpolitik' and not, to use the catchword coined by August Ludwig von Rochau in the mid-1850s, 'Realpolitik'.

Bismarck was of course familiar with this line of argument. He also knew that a great many Prussian liberals were in principle very much in favour of strengthening the Prussian army. He therefore sought, albeit for obvious reasons more by means of hints and allusions, to convince at least some members that in his opinion the fronts were drawn up quite wrongly and that domestic antagonisms threatened to obscure the community of interests that existed in the much more urgent and important spheres of external and national policy. Moreover, those antagonisms, he added, had been dramatized out of all proportion by an irresponsible press and by a 'host of "Catilinish characters" who have a major interest in upheavals'. In the same context and with the same objective he then uttered the now famous sentences: 'It is not to Prussia's liberalism that Germany looks' – this being a swipe at the half-hearted and largely unsuccessful foreign policy of the 'New Era', which even in the liberal camp had not been without its opponents – 'but to its power; let Bavaria, Württemberg and Baden indulge in liberalism, no one will give them Prussia's part for that; Prussia must collect and keep its strength for the right moment, which has been missed several times already; Prussia's frontiers as laid down by the Vienna treaties are not conducive to a healthy national life; it is not by means of speeches and majority resolutions that the great issues of the day will be decided – that was the great mistake of 1848 and 1849 – but by iron and blood.'[13]

What Bismarck was sketchily outlining here was probably, on closer examination, the furthest-reaching offer of co-operation along the lines of a resolutely pursued Lesser German national policy that any Prussian head of government had yet proposed. It chimed with his having immediately declared himself ready to accept certain liberals such as the historian Heinrich von Sybel, men who were regarded as being prepared to compromise, as ministers in his Cabinet. Indeed he even hinted that he was open to suggestions on the question of the two-year period of service. In return he was asking for a kind of truce on the basis of the constitutional status quo, in other words that the House of Deputies should forgo its claim to priority in budgetary matters and hence indirectly, as the English example had taught everyone, in other political matters as well.

To underline this he showed his interlocutors at the time an olive branch that he had brought from Avignon: he was looking not for conflict but for agreement in order that he should have his hands free for the great tasks that faced them all. It was an appeal to the liberals to take stock, an appeal that at the same time reflected Bismarck's assessment of the distribution of weight between national and liberal elements within the liberal majority.

In the longer term he was proved right, but in the short term, in fact at that dramatic evening session of the budget committee, he met with a rebuff that almost knocked him off course and gave rise to consequences that largely dictated his policy over the next few months. It was Rudolf Virchow, the celebrated pathologist from Berlin University and one of the most popular and combative leaders of the Progressive Party, a man of impressive stature and great rhetorical gifts, who first showed him that he had ventured a great deal too far, both in terms of what he had said and in the way he had said it, without adequately covering his rear.

Completely ignoring the offer of a joint foreign policy and a playing-down of the domestic conflict in that common interest, Virchow went straight for the weakest point and the one that could be best exploited against Bismarck, both journalistically and politically: the Minister-President, he said, clearly wished to promote his domestic objectives by launching a violent power policy in the field of foreign affairs.

Bearing in mind the foreign policy objectives of a substantial section of the liberal group in parliament, one detects more than a whiff of hypocrisy here. Bismarck had clearly invoked objectives that were primarily those of the Lesser German liberals, objectives the implementation of which, as many of those liberals admitted in their heart of hearts, would be a power question – with all the consequences that might ensue. 'For the honour and power of our country, should those assets need to be preserved or achieved by means of war, no sacrifice will ever be too great for us', the Progressive Party had said in its launching programme back in June.[14] Yet the argument was extraordinarily effective, not only with the general public but also in the eyes of all those – and they included the Prussian king – who viewed the new Minister-President with considerable mistrust in this very sector of foreign affairs.

Bismarck's downright confused reply made clear that he had spotted the danger immediately, but it was too late. Indeed when he immediately followed up with a protestation born of his recognition of that danger, it had the effect of a confirmation. As the *Berliner Allgemeine Zeitung* reported this declaration in indirect speech: 'To seek conflicts abroad in order to get over difficulties at home, there he must protest; that would be frivolous; he was not looking for deals; he was talking about conflicts that we would not be able to avoid, without our having sought them.'[15]

Here in the form of a refutation was a precise formulation of the suspicion for which the words 'iron and blood' formed the very graphic catchphrase. The country was threatened with a tyranny at home based on a policy of irresponsible adventurism abroad, was the almost unanimous outcry in the liberal press. 'You know how passionately I love Prussia', the historian Heinrich von Treitschke wrote that day to his brother-in-law, the future Culture Minister and Minister-President of Baden, Wilhelm Nokk. 'But when I hear so shallow a country squire as this Bismarck bragging about the "iron and blood" with which he intends to subdue Germany, the meanness of it seems to me to be exceeded only by the absurdity.'[16]

In underestimating the opposition on the domestic front and the forces behind it, trusting in the manageability and corruptibility of the House of Deputies as well as of public opinion and probably also overestimating the power of the position to which he had just acceded, Bismarck had as it were put his own head in the noose; even his staunchest fellow combatant, War Minister von Roon, spoke on the way home from the committee meeting of 'witty sallies' that did their cause little good.[17]

The other side naturally did not lose a moment in exploiting the situation. 'The man and the system must be attacked without quarter', Bismarck's former adversary in Baden–Baden, the Baden Foreign Minister Franz von Roggenbach, wrote on 3 October to Robert von Mohl, his envoy to the Federal Diet and a member of the government of the Frankfurt National Assembly in 1848.[18] Such was the tenor of all liberal comments after the 'iron and blood speech'. In this instance, however, there was a particularly ominous background as far as Bismarck was concerned.

The king was once again staying in Baden–Baden at this time. And it was not difficult to predict that his son-in-law, the grand duke of Baden, and the latter's advisers would attempt, with reference to this speech and to the storm of protest it had provoked both inside and outside Prussia, to revive William's old mistrust of the foreign-policy plans and objectives of his new Minister-President. William, however, was still much too much under the influence of Babelsberg, of the idea that this one man had stood unreservedly by him while all the rest betrayed him, to have been at all amenable to such an attempt. In fact he forbade any further interference in unmistakable terms and 'with brusque vehemence'. 'The whole manner of thinking is changed, the premises are false, consequently there is no discussing even the most logically formulated conclusions', the king's son-in-law complained.[19]

But Bismarck could not know this. He therefore thought it advisable in the circumstances to go as far as Jüterbog on 4 October to meet the returning king in order to reassure him and talk him out of any eventual doubts and misgivings with regard to the person of his new Minister-President as well as his political plans.

In his memoirs Bismarck described in the most graphic terms this scene in which he spoke darkly to the king of the scaffold and of the fate of English kings and ministers and managed to put heart in him once more only by means of a fresh pledge of unconditional loyalty.[20] It is another carefully staged contribution to the legend that he, Bismarck, saved the

House of Hohenzollern politically and preserved its position and power virtually against the will of its principal representative. Yet the episode as such, the very fact that he decided to make the journey, shows how badly Bismarck felt the ground shaking under his feet at this time and how clear was his sense of having made a crucial mistake.

His arrogant assertion that he knew better than anyone how to deal with parliament and with the public, better at any rate than conservative bureaucrats of the stamp of Manteuffel and his adepts, seemed to have been unequivocally disproved. On the contrary, his miscalculation had actually consolidated the enemy front, and he now found himself facing what was to all appearances an invincible phalanx. Moreover, his plan for radically altering the domestic alliances, for splitting the opposition by hiving off the group of those whose first concern was with the national question and with the achievement of economic unity between the states of the Customs Union, seemed to have failed completely, at least as far as his taking the lead in implementing such a plan was concerned.

This raises a question that is of central importance as regards our verdict on all that followed: did Bismarck nevertheless continue to hold fast to that plan or was he from this moment on pursuing quite different solutions? The former hypothesis is at first glance supported by the eventual outcome in the shape of the political constellation achieved after the war of 1866 and the foundation of the North German Confederation, the latter by the developments that now immediately ensued, up until the first external conflict situation that Bismarck survived with unambiguous success and clear gains in terms of power and prestige, namely the great Schleswig-Holstein crisis. What gives the question particular importance is above all the fact that it is indirectly bound up with the very much more momentous question of the fundamental nature of the political creation associated with the name of Bismarck: the German Reich of 1871. For depending on whether one regards Bismarck's alliance with a substantial section of the German middle class as having shaped his policy or at least a whole series of its constituent elements or not, one's view of the nature of that creation will vary very greatly.

In the former case one must ask oneself whether the widely held view of the 1871 Reich as a foundation in defiance of the spirit of the age or more precisely in defiance of the spirit of the middle class of that age is not too much influenced by wishful thinking with regard to the supposed ideals and actual objectives of that middle class, at least as far as central Europe was concerned. One must ask oneself, in other words, whether the constitutional, legal, economic, social and also intellectual and cultural organization of that empire, in so far as these things were institutionalized, did not very precisely reflect the hopes and wishes of the great majority of the German middle class. This means, however, that if the ultimately open support for Bismarck and his policy among the majority of even the liberal bourgeoisie was not simply a by-product of the success of that policy but in fact its objective, pursued from the start and never seriously abandoned, the very content as well as the tangible results of that policy appear in an entirely different light.

Whether this was so cannot of course be unambiguously determined. Indeed it must even be said that such a question, however essential to a comprehensive verdict, in a way does violence to historical reality, imputing as it does to that reality and to those acting within it a logical consistency and singlenesss of sense and purpose that to begin with were neither subjectively nor objectively present in them.

Bismarck's conclusion from the evident failure of this first step towards the implementation of his tactical plan was in fact to all appearances very much more pragmatic and indeed straightforward. He saw that he must be guided to an even greater extent by the concrete possibilities of success available to him at the moment and moreover that he must always keep open a variety of courses, which henceforth became his tactical byword and one he employed with ever-increasing skill. From now on he became very much more cautious and at the same time, while remaining unimpeachably conservative in his basic attitude to all questions of domestic policy, more ambivalent as regarded his concrete objective at any one time. As a result, however, the power constellations currently obtaining in reality and the actual distribution of political weight in state and society came more and more to influence his policy and its direction. He became, if you like, increasingly 'opportunist'. And herein lies an answer to the question that goes far beyond the individual and his specific desires and intentions.

Precisely because he allowed himself to be guided primarily by what was feasible and by what promised success at the time his policy, following this failed attempt at a rapprochement with a section of the liberal majority in parliament, had of necessity to make far greater concessions to middle-class interests than outwardly appeared to be the case at first. In other words, the heightened political antagonism literally wrested material concessions from him, particularly since he lacked a party-political power base of his own. This eventually led to an apparently total incongruity between the concrete results of the policy of the Prussian state under Bismarck's leadership and the steadily intensifying and increasingly polarized conflict that dominated the period of its planning and execution.

This is clearest in the case of the economic and commercial policy that as far as guiding principles and concrete measures were concerned the Bismarck government continued without a break. We must beware, however, of jumping to conclusions here. That policy, which was increasingly directed towards liberalization and free trade, had long been in accordance with the interests of the majority of the landed nobility in Prussia. Moreover, part of that nobility, particularly in Silesia, had begun at a comparatively early stage to commit itself in the industrial sector as well; one need think only of names like Schaffgotsch and Pless, Ballestrem and Henckel-Donnersmarck, all of whom acquired industrial interests on a major scale and began building up companies of their own as early as the 1840s and 1850s. So it would be quite wrong to see the uninterrupted continuation of the economic and commercial policy of the 'New Era' governments as proving simply that it was primarily a question of bribing the economic middle-class, as it were, that it was dictated mainly by a plan to bind that middle class to the conservative state and dissuade it from attempting to implement liberal political objectives: in fact there were very much more immediate economic interests on the part of the conservatives and the nobility at stake here.

On the other hand the existence of a convergence of interests between large sections of agriculture and commerce as well as between quite substantial sectors of new industry and the manufacturing trades obviously provided exceptional support for a policy aimed at splitting what looked like an over-powerful opposition. It was only natural, therefore, that Bismarck, the moment he came to power, should have sought both to reinforce this factor by taking appropriate action and at the same time to exploit it in order to make headway on his own terms over the German question.

Bismarck was quite familiar, from the intensive experiences of his Frankfurt years, with the importance attributed to commercial and particularly to Customs Union policy on the one hand in foreign affairs and on the other hand in relation to the different interest groups both in his own country and in others. And we can assume that even in the years after 1859, when his new job made this complex of questions seem more remote and it found a correspondingly minimal echo in his official papers and reports, he followed developments closely and made a note of the opportunities inherent in them. The principal event in this field, that is to say the one with the most far-reaching consequences, was Prussia's joining the Anglo-French free trade zone established by the Cobden Treaty in 1860. This took the form of a commercial treaty with France concluded at the end of March 1862.

The immediate economic significance of that treaty was not very great. Trade between Prussia and France was on a fairly small scale at that time, and expectations with regard to its expansion were not exactly effusive. What gave the agreement its importance were its indirect consequences for economic development in central Europe itself and above all its political repercussions. For both sides these had been at the centre of all considerations from the outset: Napoleon saw such a commercial treaty as an initial point of contact for the acquisition of a fresh political clientele, this time in central Europe, to go with his Italian one; and the Prussian 'New Era' government hoped that mere negotiations with France would give it a fresh lever against Austria that would force the latter to make concessions on the German question along the lines of Prussian plans for a Lesser German reform of the Confederation.

This latter calculation had misfired completely. In a counter-move Austria had mobilized almost the whole of the so-called 'Third Germany' against Prussia with the argument that this was an attempt by the Prussian government once and for all to mediatize the remaining German states economically and hence also politically; in the treaty negotiations, which were of course of direct material concern to the Customs Union, Prussia did indeed behave in a downright provocative fashion as the dominant power in that organization. Without making any progress either in the matter in hand or in the German question, Prussia had virtually had its hand forced by the Austrian counter-initiative: if it did not wish to suffer a severe diplomatic defeat with substantial consequences for its entire policy, it must close with France.

The French government had done much to make this an easy step for Berlin to take. The new Prussian envoy in Paris appointed shortly after this was able to report immediately with what emphasis Napoleon III had spoken of further improving Franco-Prussian relations. This had suited the then Prussian envoy, now Minister-President, very well but not the Prussian government and certainly not the Prussian king. Instead of the hoped-for entente with Austria they faced the threat of an ever-sharpening confrontation between the two German great powers. And it looked very much as if Napoleon III was banking on just that in the interests of his own continued hegemony in Europe; significantly, in the middle of October 1862 he dropped his old Foreign Minister Thouvenel in favour of Drouyn de l'Huys, who was reputed to lean more towards Austria.

Conservatives and liberals were in broad agreement in their assessment of the French emperor's real objectives. At the same time, however, both sides welcomed, as benefiting their respective economic interests, a commercial treaty with France that in practice meant the final economic separation of Austria from the rest of Germany – provided that the smaller Customs Union states signed it too. Since the continued existence of the Customs Unions had long been something that Prussia could forgo only verbally, for the purposes of putting its partners under pressure, conflict with Austria, which in the most extreme form only very few people wanted, looked almost inevitable.

This was the situation that Bismarck inherited when he took office. Irrespective of his own wishes and intentions in this connection, it left him very little room for manoeuvre. On the contrary it explains why from this point of view too, again relatively independently of any possible long-term tactical plan, it must have seemed to him urgently desirable to achieve a rapprochement with that wing of the liberals whose main objective was the solution of the national question along Lesser German lines. And even after the complete fiasco of that attempted rapprochement his foreign and economic policy course was largely laid down for him. It was a question of stopping the Austrian counter-offensive that had just reached a climax with the rejection of Prussia's commercial treaty by the two largest south German states, Bavaria and Württemberg, and with the simultaneous initiative launched by Austria and the medium-sized states in connection with the German question.[21]

In the middle of August 1862 Vienna had put before the governments of the Confederation a proposal to the effect that the Confederation be placed on an entirely new basis by the creation of a representative body made up of delegates from the parliaments of the individual states. This of course fell far short of the liberal demand for a directly elected German parliament. But the representatives of the Lesser German wing of German liberalism had great difficulty, against a background of constitutional conflict in Prussia, in portraying the whole thing as mere eyewash, particularly since Austria had itself joined the ranks of constitutional states meanwhile and was at the moment operating the constitutional system more genuinely than Prussia.

Many people were therefore inclined to see this as an initial, trend-setting step in the direction of a solution of the German question from the national as well as from the constitutional point of view. There was also the fact that, even after the Lesser German compromise of 1849, the majority opinion outside Prussia was in favour of a solution that included Austria – in formal terms, on the basis of the German Confederation being the successor to the Reich that had collapsed in 1806. At the end of October 1862, in competition with the Lesser German National Union, the Greater German Reform Union was set up and began to attract a substantial membership, particularly in the south; in Munich, for example, well over a thousand had joined within a few months.

So the Austrian initiative could certainly count on popular support. There were obvious discrepancies between its objectives and those of the small and medium-sized German states who went along with Austria but whose prime concern was for the preservation of their independence and sovereignty. Nevertheless, from Prussia's point of view there was an increasing danger of Austria stealing a march. That, however, meant that one of the traditional alternatives of Prussian policy was already blocked when Bismarck took office, namely the brandishing of a settlement between Prussia and Austria on the basis of the status quo and of joint national and power interests.

It was an alternative that the 'New Era' government had still made use of, even during the negotiations for the commercial treaty with France, almost always finding suitable partners for it in Vienna. Now and for the foreseeable future all that seemed to be over. Few registered this with greater misgiving than the Prussian king. But Bismarck too must have regretted that this alternative had clearly broken down, even though he had long been pursuing a determinedly anti-Austrian policy in federal affairs and with regard to the German question. For this considerably reduced his freedom of manoeuvre both at home and abroad. He could hardly couple his offer of co-operation over the German question and over commercial and Customs Union policy convincingly with a threat to the effect that the government was also in a position to ride roughshod over people's wishes in this connection and seek quite different solutions.

The dilemma became apparent only three days after Bismarck's appearance before the budget committee when the new Minister-President found himself obliged to defend a foreign policy resolution of the House of Deputies before an initially recalcitrant Upper House.[22] The resolution called upon the government to go further in the direction indicated by the commercial treaty with France and not let itself be put off by the opposition of one or two Customs Union states but on the contrary go to any lengths to overcome such opposition. In the circumstances this was a decisive challenge to Austria, which openly sympathized with those states, and in general to the coalition between Austria and the medium-sized German states. But it was also, and this was why the Upper House at first opposed it although the majority approved of the content of the resolution, an expression of parliament's claim to a role in laying down the general guidelines of foreign policy.

Bismarck himself, of course, decisively repudiated such a claim. But since there was no practical alternative available at the moment, it was quite impossible for him to oppose it with any force if he wished to avoid becoming deeply involved with the opposition members of the Upper House in matters of form and the problems of such a claim in the abstract. He had impotently to look on while the liberal majority set itself up as the spokesman of a policy of power and self-interest for Prussia and on the basis of his remarks to the budget committee virtually branded him, who had planned to do political deals on a major scale along these lines, as a security risk for Prussian foreign policy as well.

In such a situation, nothing came more naturally to a man such as Bismarck than to try with all his might to escape from this position of evidently having no foreign policy alternatives and if necessary to build up counter-positions artificially. This is not to say that he attempted arbitrarily to bring such alternative situations into existence; that would have been in deep contradiction to his view of the basic conditions underlying any kind of potentially successful foreign policy. It simply means that he was tempted to inflate their importance and supposed potential by means of propaganda that actually ran counter to his true opinion.

This is true above all of the alleged alternatives to his policy on the German question and consequently of his policy towards Austria in the years before 1866. In reaction to the long-prevalent and in many respects undoubtedly one-track view that was guided purely by the outcome, following the dissolution of Austria-Hungary and the military collapse of the German Reich in 1918 a whole series of historians inclined towards the theory that here too, as so often, Bismarck made sure almost up until the last minute, namely the outbreak of the 1866 war, that he always had two courses open to him. He had, it was said, constantly kept his eye both on the possibility of a settlement with Austria and on a kind of division of power in central Europe on the basis of the traditional collaboration of the three conservative eastern powers.

There is indeed a quantity of evidence apparently pointing in this direction. And there is no disputing the fact that in individual cases it is often very difficult to decide what was mere pressurizing and what Bismarck's actual objective. But that is not what matters. The crucial point is that the historical process itself made clear that the traditional course could no longer be pursued with any hope of success, indeed that even the threat to pursue it eventually appeared scarcely credible any more. Of enormous and hitherto often underrated importance in this were domestic developments, particularly in Prussia.

Following the failure of his attempted rapprochement with a section of the liberal majority, Bismarck's sole concern at first had been to gain time and get rid of the recalcitrant House of Deputies for a few months by adjourning it. However, the majority in the Upper House had rather put a spoke in that wheel by further escalating the conflict with an open breach of the constitution that placed even greater difficulties in the way of any possibility of agreement in the future. It had not only rejected the budget in the altered version passed by the House of Deputies, as it had a perfect right to do; it had at the same time approved the government's original proposals, thus laying claim to parliamentary rights that were in open defiance of the constitution. The House of Deputies had reacted with understandable vehemence. Even very moderate members now joined Max Duncker in speaking of a 'Ständekampf', a 'clash between middle class and squirearchy' in which surely no compromise was possible any more.[23]

This radical polarization, in which the liberals counted the new head of government on the side of the Upper House as a matter of course, had by no means suited Bismarck's original plan. He had had the king emphasize once again, in the speech from the throne on the occasion of the provisional closure of the Diet on 13 October, that the government was still concerned to reach agreement. It would in due course seek retrospective approval of or 'indemnity' for the payments that would have to be made, necessarily without prior parliamentary agreement, in the interests of an ordered continuance of state affairs. He had a report to the same effect placed in the *Norddeutscher Allgemeine Zeitung*; this paper had been founded in 1861, originally as a mouthpiece for Austrian interests, though from now on it became increasingly the central organ of the new Prussian government and its head, the 'switchboard' being provided by the 'Literary Bureau' at the Ministry of the Interior, which was headed by two senior civil servants, Ludwig Hahn and Karl Ludwig Zitelmann, a colleague of Bismarck's from Frankfurt.

On the other hand this polarization between the two houses of the Prussian parliament and the political and social forces behind them might contain a great opportunity. With skilful tactics the government could get out of the immediate firing-line and in the end perhaps even emerge as *tertius gaudens*. This was already the object of Bismarck's initiative, clearly directed at the liberal public, in the constitutional conflict that had been going on for years in the electorate of Hesse: in November 1862, openly threatening violence and acting in flagrant contradiction to his own position on domestic affairs, he forced the Elector, who was insisting on his monarchical rights, to come to an understanding with his parliament. And it was likewise the object of his policy towards Austria and of the first fundamental step that he took with regard to the German question.

In terms of content that policy was in many respects laid down for him already. From the beginning Bismarck left it in no doubt that he would oppose the federal reform programme put forward by Austria and the medium-sized states, in other words initially the so-called 'Delegates Plan', and that he would seek by every means to break down the Austrian-backed resistance particularly of Bavaria and Württemberg to Prussia's commercial and economic policy. This inevitably raised the question, however, whether the new Prussian Minister-President, supposedly so arch-conservative and concerned for the preservation of the existing order in domestic affairs, was actually thinking of putting the whole weight of Prussian power behind the foreign policy objectives of the left-wing liberal Prussian Progressive Party.

The question was asked not only in Vienna but also in St Petersburg and, from a different standpoint, in Paris. In foreign policy terms a great deal depended, for Bismarck and for Prussia, on the answer that he gave or that foreign envoys believed they could deduce from his remarks. Moreover, given the links that existed between the envoys and their governments as well as between them and the different political groups inside and outside Prussia, the question also possessed a domestic policy dimension that must not be underrated. Bismarck was undoubtedly fully aware of both when in December 1862, in several conversations with the Austrian envoy Count Károlyi, he portrayed with apparently total candour his own position and the conclusions that were in his view to be drawn from the present situation.[24]

Károlyi, who had been the Hofburg's envoy in Berlin since 1860 and came from a wealthy and respectable Hungarian family that had been rising to the highest offices in the imperial service since the eighteenth century, appeared manifestly fascinated by those conversations, however much their content must have disturbed him officially. The historical dimensions in which his interlocutor argued, the lofty circumspection with which he sketched his view of things and outlined the problems, 'proof' against 'the "brothers' war" claptrap' and recognizing 'only the uncomfortable politics of self-interest', doing 'one deal at a time, and for cash'[25] – all this possessed a strange attraction, opened up all kinds of perspectives and combinations, and made even the undisguised claim to power and the brutal challenge appear in an iridescent light.

Bismarck took as his starting-point the arrangement made in 1815 and the political practice of the decades before 1848, that system of co-operation and peaceful give-and-take between the two German great powers that the conservatives of both countries saw as the prerequisite for the preservation of existing internal relationships in central Europe. The reason why the system had worked, he claimed, was that Austria had rewarded Prussian loyalty over the major questions of European policy by leaving Prussia a largely free hand in 'German policy', that is to say primarily in its commercial and economic policy and in particular by not interfering in Prussia's 'natural sphere, north Germany'.

Historically speaking, the argument was scarcely tenable. But it did, with its reference to a period of extensive harmony and fruitful collaboration between the two powers, indicate precisely what all this was aiming at: the co-operation that had existed then could be restored if Austria would renounce its pursuit of the Schwarzenberg policy, in other words give up the attempt to achieve absolute hegemony in central Europe at Prussia's expense. Persistence in that attempt, Károlyi reported Bismarck as saying, would on the other hand 'lead sooner or later to a formal breach and ultimately to war': '"Nous croiserons les bajonettes"', as he stressed once again during their last talk on 26 December.

Anyone who did not want that must work towards a moving apart of the two powers, a clear division of spheres of influence and a co-ordination of their reciprocal interests. For Bismarck this meant in practice that Austria, 'instead of looking for its centre of gravity in Germany' and governing its non-German territories, principally Hungary, 'as an appendage', ought in future to look more to the east and south-east, in other words to 'shift [its] centre of gravity to Ofen [the Hungarian Buda; Tr.]', as the Austrian

Foreign Minister ironically put it. In return for Austria's voluntarily renouncing a claim to hegemony in non-Austrian Germany that could never be implemented without war, Berlin was prepared to make Austria's 'vital interests in Italy and the east' its own and give the empire 'unconditional support' in defence of them. In other words, Austria would once again be able to depend on Prussia in Europe. Austria's statesmen should seriously ask themselves whether such a policy did not serve the well-understood national interests of the empire better than a Schwarzenberg-style policy of conflict and confrontation, the success of which was more than doubtful and in any case to be achieved only by way of the destruction of Prussia.

This was undubitably a bold and, with its naked threat of violence, brutal look into the future, an anticipation of the historical reality of the years 1866–7. Indeed in a sense Bismarck was here already outlining developments up until the Dual Alliance between the German Reich and Austria-Hungary in 1879. That must not, of course, be allowed to blind us to the fact that from the Prussian point of view this was a maximum programme that Bismarck himself can hardly seriously have believed at this point in time would be realizable by peaceful means. According to a close colleague of the Prussian Minister-President, when as a result of deliberate Austrian indiscretions this sally became known in diplomatic circles in Berlin, people questioned whether Bismarck was still entirely sane, 'because how can an entirely sane person tell the representative of Austria: "You would do well to shift your centre of gravity to Ofen."'[26] The whole thing had as its primary object to persuade Vienna to enter into negotiations regarding what the Hofburg too might find an acceptable alternative to the present policy of confrontation.

Accordingly, in addition to his maximum programme Bismarck on this same occasion gave a clear indication of a kind of Prussian minimum programme. Implementation of this, he hinted, might possibly have the same effect. The minimum programme concentrated almost entirely on the demand for unqualified Prussian hegemony in north Germany. This was the 'air so vitally necessary to our political existence', as Bismarck put it. In a memorandum to the Prussian king dated Christmas Day 1862 he even went so far as to contemplate expelling from the Customs Union all states that did not unconditionally bow to Berlin.[27] As things stood, this was aimed primarily at Bavaria and Württemberg; in other words, it once again suggested a readiness on Prussia's part to confine itself, if necessary, entirely to the north German region, with the Main as its southern limit. South Germany appeared in this context as a kind of buffer zone between the two co-operating German great powers. The question of the fate and future shape of the German Confederation was left wide open, although Bismarck already ruled out continuance in its present form as being incompatible with Prussian interests.

In plain terms, what he was offering Austria was this: instead of a probably bloody battle for hegemony in central Europe, a sharing of real power in the region on the basis of the shared conservative conceptions of order held by the traditional elites of both countries. There was no mention in this connection of any compliance with the expectations and demands of the nationalists and liberals. On the contrary, the dominant element was this appeal to the solidarity of the forces of conservatism across all national boundaries, as for example when, according to Károlyi's report, Bismarck expressly regretted that with their conduct towards Prussia the other German governments and above all Austria were 'making it so very much more difficult to consolidate Prussia's conservative policy at home'.

Here too it was the pre-1848 situation as well as the basic political and social attitude of most of the then leading statesmen in central Europe that were being invoked – and hence once again the factor that had prevented a clash between the two German great powers at that time: their mutual renunciation of any initiative on the German question and any attempt to mobilize national forces in support of their own cause. At the same time Bismarck was hinting that he would give up his flirtation with the foreign policy programme of the Progressive Party, a flirtation that not only Vienna was following with deep distrust, as soon as Austria for its part dissociated itself from all plans for a 'Grossdeutschland' – plans that above all Julius Fröbel, a leader of the Greater German democrats of 1848, was propagating to not inconsiderable effect with the vigorous support of the Austrian Foreign Ministry.

For all the exaggerations and threats the whole thing was carefully thought out. It was aimed at those elements in the Austrian civil service and in the Hofburg in Vienna who, like a section of the arch-conservatives in Prussia, continued to see their political objective in a policy of agreement and co-operation between the two central European great powers.

Among these was Bismarck's former Austrian colleague in Frankfurt, the present Foreign Minister Count Rechberg. He too had a deep mistrust of Bismarck, referring to him shortly before his appointment as chief minister in Prussia as 'a person who is capable of pulling off his coat and mounting the barricades himself'.[28] But unlike the majority of his senior civil servants Rechberg, whom Bismarck in return once sneeringly referred to as 'an unusually stupid statesman',[29] was only too ready to look for possible alternatives such as he was being offered here, albeit in a form bristling with provisos, by the new Prussian Minister-President.

Following the failure at the end of January 1863 of the federal reform plan put forward by Austria and the medium-sized states – in which the balance had been tipped by, of all people, the Elector of Hesse, who had been deeply humiliated by Prussia – a period of probing accompanied the preparation of a fresh major initiative in the matter of federal reform. In it Rechberg, acting in agreement with Emperor Francis Joseph, who likewise favoured an Austro-Prussian rapprochement under conservative auspices, tried to find out what kind of plans and intentions underlay what Bismarck was saying.

Even a measure of doubt as to the future direction of Prussian foreign policy was a success as far as Bismarck was concerned. It gave him considerably greater scope, not only in foreign but also in domestic affairs. Theoretically at least it opened up changing possibilities of combinations in both spheres and consequently the opportunity to tempt or even to threaten his partner at any given time with a shift in the current pattern of coalitions and alliances. This was a method that Bismarck henceforth used with growing mastery.

It was not his method, however, that ultimately accounted for the success of his policy but a particular constellation to the tendencies within which Bismarck, for all his tactical manoeuvring, surrendered almost without reserve and at the sacrifice of convictions and objectives of his own that ran in a different direction. That constellation led him, in foreign policy and later also in many areas of domestic policy, *de facto* to implement the programme of Lesser German liberalism. He came to see with growing clarity that present and future belonged to that programme in many ways and that ever more powerful forces were pushing in that direction. He therefore, power-politician that he was, made it his own, as it were taking the political wind out of his opponents' sails. *Ipse faciam* – that was the watchword and the extent of the secret. The direction he took was consequently far more clear-cut than contemporaries and later generations have often thought. His much-invoked juggling encountered precisely defined limits in the realities of the given balance of power and interests.

This is true first and foremost as regards foreign policy. The memorandum of Christmas Day 1862 outlines the long-term objectives up until 1866 quite unequivocally:[30] 'liberation from the web of federal treaties'; exertion of the 'full force' of the 'weight inherent in the Prussian state' through internal development and reform of the Customs Union, that is to say through introducing the majority principle and a directly elected Customs Union parliament to represent not the individual states but the collective populations of the Customs Union countries and so consolidate those countries into a unity;[31] until then, in other words until the end of 1865 when the current Customs Union treaties expired, an essentially dilatory policy with the object of 'if possible ensuring the realization of our intentions for the period from 1 January 1866 without allowing ourselves to be distracted by a concern for bogus successes in the intervening interim period. That intervening period will in any case be filled with diplomatic battles over the shape of the future after the year 1865.'

This was the essence of what Bismarck was aiming at. From the outset he countenanced both possible solutions: the 'Greater Prussian' north German solution that he had described to Károlyi and the Lesser German solution in which he converged with the programme of the Progressive Party. But whatever efforts he made over the next few years in terms of propaganda and tactics to push the former solution into the foreground for reasons of both domestic and foreign policy, it was clear to him from the beginning that the forces pushing in the direction of the second would sooner or later prove overwhelming, once the traditional structure of central Europe and the German Confederation had been broken up. The forces concerned included not only those of Lesser German liberalism and with it a large section of the educated middle class in the German-speaking world; they also, indeed above all, included the economic interests of the Customs Union states and of their individual economic sectors, which in terms of their orientation and market calculations were crucially influenced by the

Customs Union. And they included not least the national idea that was now spreading to ever broader sections of the population, an idea that it was becoming more and more unthinkable should be left wholly unsatisfied in the long run.

For all of these a north German solution along 'Greater Prussian' lines was unacceptable and at best conceivable only as a transitional stage. And since on the other hand such a solution provoked considerable misgivings even in the conservative camp, misgivings that were nourished by the concept of legitimacy and the idea of the solidarity of crowned heads, its base in Prussia itself was exceptionally weak. The fact that Bismarck nevertheless managed, at least now and again, to put it forward with a measure of credibility as an alternative both at home and at the European level and to make use of it to entice or threaten counts among the political achievements that essentially laid the foundations of his success.

Although Vienna had been taking careful soundings in this direction since the end of January 1863, it was more than a year before he truly succeeded in so far concealing his ultimate objectives that people began to think he was himself wavering between different possible solutions and was in essence concerned only to correct the distribution of weight between the European great powers in favour of the one that was acknowledged to be the weakest. A platform for this was eventually provided by the European crisis over the Schleswig-Holstein question, the treatment and solution of which found him at the height of his political and diplomatic skills. Initially, however, he had as it were to fight his own reputation, which he had further reinforced with his speech to the budget committee, the reputation of being a foreign policy gambler who for domestic policy reasons would pay any price for successes on the power-political front. That reputation exactly fitted the image of the new Minister-President of Prussia that had already been pieced together from other sources in the capitals of Europe. And his next steps in foreign policy likewise accorded perfectly with that image.

It began with the Polish uprising of January 1863. As the product of a national liberation movement this promptly won the sympathies of almost all European liberals and of the powers who for various reasons co-operated with them. Particularly Napoleon III immediately scented an opportunity here of extending his influence as self-appointed protector of the national movement to eastern-central Europe as well. He hoped in this way to start doing business with those circles in Russia which supported a reformist policy oriented towards western Europe and were accordingly in favour of adopting a friendly attitude towards the Poles. Since even the chief minister in St Petersburg, Prince Gorchakov, was supposed to be at least intermittently this way inclined, Bismarck suddenly found himself confronted with a double danger: on the one hand that Russia might reach an understanding with the Polish national movement, thus encouraging it sooner or later to mobilize the non-Russian areas of former Poland as well; and on the other hand that the Polish question might lead to a Franco-Russian alliance. Such an alliance between the two flanking powers of the European continent spelled in Bismarck's eyes a probable end to all Prussian hopes with regard to extending its power and to the kind of solution of the German question that he envisaged.

He therefore made every effort, against the resistance of the majority of his likewise anti-Russian colleagues in the ministry, to nip such a development in the bud as quickly as possible. His objective was to lead Russia back to its traditional course of an anti-revolutionary and hence, at least as far as the peoples of eastern-central Europe were concerned, anti-national alliance between Berlin and St Petersburg.

This objective was served by a variety of ventures, chief among them the dispatch of the Prussian king's adjutant-general, General Gustav von Alvensleben, to the court of the tsar at the beginning of February. His mission was very clear: to explore the situation generally and beyond that 'to prepare the ground for the measures that can be taken jointly by both governments to quell the current uprising or further similar occurrences'. 'In our view', Bismarck went on in the directive to Alvensleben, '. . . the position of both courts with regard to the Polish revolution is essentially that of two allies threatened by a common enemy.'[32]

In a personal letter to Gorchakov, which he gave to Alvensleben to take with him, he even went a step further: 'We should like, with regard to any Polish *insurrection* as with regard to any danger from abroad, for that fine remark to be proved true that your Emperor made to Goltz in Moscow, namely that Russia and Prussia act against joint dangers in solidarity as if they were *one* country.'[33]

This was an offer, in other words, of full co-operation, not confined to the present case, between Prussia and Russia, a coalition along the lines of the Holy Alliance. If the convention that Alvensleben signed in St Petersburg on 8 February 1863 confined itself in formal terms to joint operations by the troops of both countries in pursuit of rebel forces, including permission for both sides to cross each other's borders, its actual significance went far beyond that. In his memoirs, in which he devoted a whole chapter to this episode, Bismarck called the agreement a 'successful move that decided the game being played inside the Russian Cabinet between the anti-Polish, monarchical faction and the pro-Polish, pan-Slav faction'.[34] He claimed that it had determined Prussian-Russian relations for the next few years and created important preconditions for the successes of Prussian foreign policy during that time.

Historians have largely accepted this assessment, although its expression in this form was undoubtedly coloured by the post-1890 estrangement between Germany and Russia that Bismarck so deeply deplored and by the tsar's rapprochement with France. At times it has even been claimed, surely also under the influence of contemporary hopes or fears, that it was here that the true foundations of the German national state were laid.

This is certainly an exaggeration, particularly since Russian policy towards Prussia and Prussian ambitions in central Europe continued during the following period to be characterized very much more by restraint and mistrust than by feelings of obligation and by any idea of the kind of far-reaching solidarity that Bismarck sought to invoke in his letter to

Gorchakov. Clearly, though, Prussia's attitude over the Polish question and the Alvensleben Convention did at least prevent a further rapprochement between Russia and France, which would have produced a highly problematical situation as far as Bismarck's future plans were concerned. To that extent the agreement must still be credited with great importance, even if it was more negative than constructive in terms of what it led to and further substantial efforts on the part of Prussian policy were required to keep Russia on a course of semi-benevolent neutrality with regard to Prussian ambitions in central Europe.

The price Bismarck had to pay for the momentary prevention of a possible alliance between the two flanking powers of the European continent and the victory of the conservative forces within the Russian state was exceptionally high. Not only did he now lose almost all credit in foreign policy terms too in the eyes of the liberal public both inside and outside Prussia; he also found himself faced with an *ad hoc* coalition of the two western powers and Austria, in reaction to the pact between Russia and Prussia. Led by France, this coalition explicitly opposed a policy of intervention against the Poles on the part of the two eastern powers. On the other hand Bismarck was probably right in placing a relatively low value on the internal coherence of the new alliance and its readiness, should the need arise, to make its actions suit its words. When the English ambassador, Sir Andrew Buchanan, on being told that if necessary Prussia would put down the rebellion itself, solemnly informed him, *'Europe* will never stand for this', Bismarck answered simply and soberly, so he told the king, 'Who is Europe?' And when the ambassador, of whom Bismarck had a low opinion on account of his liberal tendencies, replied, 'Several great nations', he embarrassed him with the further question 'whether those nations were at one amongst themselves in this respect'. Whereupon Buchanan, instead of giving a straight answer, had merely said 'that in his opinion the French government could not possibly tolerate a fresh suppression of Poland'.[35]

It did indeed very quickly transpire that France was the only really driving force here, while the other two behaved with cautious restraint. And when in the further course of events Bismarck signed a secret agreement with St Petersburg releasing him from the now virtually meaningless convention, the diplomatic counter-thrust that France had organized in the mean time hit Russia alone. This had the effect of giving the tsardom an additional push in the direction of closer co-operation with Prussia.

In spite of this tactical success the overall balance-sheet of the Polish crisis was anything but positive as far as Bismarck was concerned. Relations with France, to which he attached such great importance, came out heavily on the debit side. Despite unsolved problems in Italy, it seemed not entirely out of the question that Napoleon III might in the longer term contemplate a realignment in favour of Austria. Above all, Austria had acted in a way that further considerably enhanced its prestige in central Europe, particularly among liberals. Encouraged by this and by the potential support of the western powers and disregarding the failure of its 'Delegates Plan', Vienna felt able to press ahead on the German question and prepare a fresh major initiative without lengthy prior consultation with Prussia.

A further factor encouraging Austria's plans was that the behaviour of the Prussian government during the Polish uprising had now completely hardened the domestic fronts inside Prussia. Not even the most limited collaboration between Bismarck and any liberal group whatever now seemed at all conceivable. On this very question of German policy Prussia was regarded, for the present, as being for all practical purposes out of action. Many hitherto determined advocates of the Lesser German solution even began to wonder whether in the circumstances their position was still at all tenable or whether they must now contemplate a radical reorientation.

Here the Polish question and the government's handling of it were only one point among many, even if Bismarck's conduct had shocked precisely those on whose national aspirations he had based his own calculations. Of far greater significance was the dramatic way in which the internal conflict in Prussia was coming to a head.

What Bismarck had confidently announced to Roon in July 1862 as his tactics vis-à-vis parliament and the public had turned out to be wholly impracticable. None of his threats and enticements had even begun to have the desired effect. The liberal press saw to it that every piece of chicanery directed at a representative of the opposition and every alleged or actual instance of discrimination against or demotion of civil servants who sided with it received wide publicity. On the other hand it poured scorn on every government hint of a possible readiness to compromise and on every suggestion of co-operation, however conceived, representing these as simply an attempt at political bribery.

When the House of Deputies reassembled in mid-January 1863 it soon became clear that most members were determined not to accept any deals. Their manifest objective was to bring down the government as quickly as possible and secure the appointment of a ministry that at least came close to the views of the majority. 'The present ministry', Bismarck's private banker, Gerson Bleichröder, observed at the time in a letter to James Rothschild in Paris, 'is unpopular to a degree scarcely seen before in Prussia'.[36]

Bismarck therefore found himself with his back to the wall from the start. Not until 1890 was he ever again so sorely tempted to stage a coup than in the months that followed. He took no more than the first steps towards it in the end. But it is quite obvious that in home affairs he was drifting increasingly out of his depth during those months and was almost desperately looking for opportunities to get his feet on some sort of solid ground once more.

In the light of his subsequent success, this too has often been seen in a false perspective. What was mere groping around and a purely theoretical juggling with alternatives that in the last analysis were not even feasible, people have grandly represented as bold anticipations of the future or at least sought to see as the immediate expression of the forms and methods of power that he envisaged. Again it is the figure of Napoleon III that is invoked in this connection without it being made clear that the social background to his rule in a post-revolutionary society was radically different from that obtaining in Prussia.

No one saw this more clearly than Bismarck himself. In his desperate attempts to find ways out of the impasse in domestic affairs it undoubtedly occurred to him to wonder sometimes whether at least individual elements of Napoleon III's style of rule were not translatable into Prussian terms. This kind of consideration was reflected above all in the much-discussed talks that he held in the spring and summer of 1863 with Ferdinand Lassalle, the co-founder, first president and principal theorist of the *Allgemeiner Duetscher Arbeiterverein* or 'General German Workers' Association', the first working-man's party in Germany. In the thrill of speculation about the content of these talks, of which no authentic record survives and which already violently excited the imaginations of contemporaries, it is of course easily overlooked that they were quite without any outcome. Bismarck very quickly recognized that Lassalle's movement would be producing no really appreciable or, for his purposes, exploitable potential in the foreseeable future, although he found the talks stimulating in many respects and said in retrospect that he would have 'been happy to have a man of his [Lassalle's] gifts and intellectual sophistication as a neighbour on the next estate'.[37]

Lassalle was a mere 'dreamer' and his 'world-view' purely 'Utopian', as Bismarck told friends at the time. His 'opposition to the Progressive Party', however, was 'politically welcome'. The government 'could therefore allow his agitation to continue for a while provided that it intervened when the time came'.[38] He did in fact continue in the years that followed, particularly in connection with the question of workers' freedom of combination, to toy occasionally with the idea of promoting working-class interests for political ends.[39] But he can scarcely be said to have entertained with any real seriousness the thought of a possible alliance with the working-class movement, even if for no other reason than a tactical mobilization against the middle class.

What preoccupied him more forcibly was the possibility of bringing the mass of the rural population into the political arena against the urban middle class more effectively than hitherto by appealing to the anti-bourgeois and to some extent anti-capitalist resentment present in rural areas and to the more markedly conservative and monarchical feeling that prevailed there. Not that this had much to do with Napoleon III and his style of rule; it was a tactical plan common to the younger generation of Prussian conservatives since 1848 and the experiences of the revolution, a plan Bismarck himself had helped to shape and implement at the time. Yet here too, apart from some intensive promotion of the *Preussischer Volksverein* or 'Prussian People's Union' founded by Hermann Wagener in 1861, Bismarck was confined to purely theoretical speculations: the introduction of universal suffrage or even a limited alteration of the electoral law in that direction would, in the circumstances, never have been agreed to by the king and by the orthodox conservatives who were now dominant once again, especially in the Upper House.

What they were looking for was a rolling back of parliament's demands to the level of the Manteuffel era. They wanted to see the opposition tamed with the methods of absolutism and the authoritarian state. Bismarck could not help thinking that there was no future in this. Moreover, in many ways it ran counter to his own convictions, the convictions that had originally led him into the arch-conservative camp with its corporative view of society and its resistance to absolutism. Yet if he did not wish to resign he had no choice, for the moment, but to comply with these expectations.

He can scarcely be held to have demonstrated any great skill in the process. On the contrary, right at the start of this fresh round of the dispute with the House of Deputies, a mere three months after his much-quoted appearance before the budget committee, he once again very clumsily betrayed a weak point – and his political adversaries pounced on it immediately.

In the address – it was presented by Virchow – in reply to the speech from the throne at the opening of the Diet, which before the introduction of the parliamentary system of government constituted the counterpart to the government statement contained in the speech from the throne, the majority in the House of Deputies once again emphatically endorsed its view that the present conflict arose out of a clear breach of the constitution on the part of the government. A resolution of the conflict was possible only, it said, if the government returned to a constitutional position, in other words virtually capitulated to parliament. This conclusion, Bismarck claimed in the plenary debate on the address on 27 January 1863, showed the true nature of the dispute.[40] In reality it was not at all an abstract question of constitutional law and the practical application of individual paragraphs; it was a question of an attempt by parliament to use this opportunity to exceed its bounds and invade areas of power and decision-making reserved to the king and his appointed government. 'This address demands of the royal House of Hohenzollern its constitutional rights of government in order to transfer them to the majority in this House.' He went on: 'This would lead, however, to the House of Deputies being invested with sole supremacy; yet that kind of sole supremacy is not admissible in Prussian constitutional law.'

The Prussian constitution was based on the idea of a balance between the three legislative authorities, the government and the two houses of parliament, and 'none of those authorities can *coerce* the others into submission'. In other words – and this was the deeper significance of such a constitutional structure – they must co-operate with one another: 'The constitution therefore points in the direction of compromises for the purposes of agreement.' Instead of contenting himself with this and developing further an argument that few liberal constitutional lawyers would have questioned at the time, indeed that was very much in line with the ideal state put forward by contemporary bourgeois-liberal political thought, Bismarck promptly overdid it. He tried to persuade the deputies that, as things stood, it was they who had most to gain by this kind of compromise. 'If compromise is hindered by one of the authorities concerned seeking to enforce its own view with doctrinaire absolutism', he declared, 'the series of compromises is interrupted and conflicts arise in their place, and, since the life of the state cannot stand still, conflicts become power questions; whoever has the power then proceeds in his own direction, because the life of the state can never stand still, not even for a moment.'

From the mouth of a constitutional historian or a philosopher of law this might have been a realistic appraisal, but from the mouth of the Prussian Minister-President it sounded, in this situation, like sheer defiance. The House reacted accordingly, the climax of that reaction coming with the much-applauded and subsequently much-quoted speech made by Count Schwerin.[41] Schwerin, a member of the East Elbian nobility like Bismarck himself, was a man of unimpeachably monarchical views and a basic approach that inclined towards the conservative. But like many of his fellow aristocrats he was at the same time imbued with the necessity for a genuine compromise with the liberal middle class and consequently a convinced supporter of the 'New Era' system, which he had served as Minister of the Interior for almost three years.

What was at issue, according to the count, was not at all the constitutional status and power of the Prussian Crown. The House of Deputies supported these as strongly as did the government. And because this was so, because no one in that House was seriously thinking of altering the distribution of weight in the state as laid down in the constitution, he must state emphatically 'that the proposition in which the Minister-President's speech culminated, "*Might before right*, say what you will, we have the power and will therefore implement our theory", is not in my view one that is capable of sustaining the dynasty in Prussia in the long run . . . that on the contrary the proposition on which the greatness of our country rests as well as the esteem that the Prussian ruling house has enjoyed hitherto both at home and abroad and will ever continue to enjoy . . . is precisely the reverse: "*Right before might*: justitia fundamentum regnorum!" *That* is the device of the Prussian kings and will ever remain so.'

Bismarck surely had some justification, from his point of view, in regarding as political hypocrites those on the liberal left wing who were loudest in applauding these words spoken by a man who at the same time opposed the majority's address, counselling restraint and accommodation in this instance as well. Of course they too were fighting for power and for the position of dominant influence in the state. Of course their constitutional interpretations likewise served their own objectives. And of course they wished to reduce the influence of a monarch who was becoming increasingly hostile to those objectives. Here a certain school of history has fostered many a distorted idea with a view of the nature of politics and the relationship between constitutional law and politics that is somewhat problematic in its consequences. All too often this school has taken politicians with clearly definable convictions but also with interests, with overall objectives but also with personal expectations, and presented them as pure idealists who were defeated in a struggle with brute power.

The categories for this derived of course from the period itself; they were part of its style and also constituted one of the combat and propaganda weapons of the liberals. The victory of the liberal cause was intended to be seen not simply as historically necessary, so to speak, but as following from a proper implementation of the idea of law and the principles of a judicious constitutional order. This was something that Bismarck undoubtedly underrated, as he did the determination that he had himself aroused in his parliamentary opponents to accept no compromise and to force a decision in their favour.

Here again, as in the budget committee, no one acknowledged his guarded offer of possible collaboration and compromise. Nor did it make any difference that he repeated the offer several times, stressing in his brief reply to Schwerin's speech, for example, that he had 'described it not as an advantage' but merely as a necessity in the interests of the national life that, in the event of conflict, 'the one who is in possession of power . . . is obliged to use it'.

As the *Kölnische Zeitung* said as early as 16 January, Bismarck was a 'smooth talker' and the greatest caution was therefore called for.[42] Deliberately, all that the liberal camp was willing to hear in his remarks were the threats and the promises of further breaches of the constitution. Because as the opposition calculated, surely with some justification, could Prussia really afford, could the Crown and the numerically small ultra-reactionary wing of the traditional ruling class, notwithstanding the tangible instruments of power that they undoubtedly had at their disposal, really afford to brush parliament and constitution aside in a *coup d'état* and return to a purely autocratic regime? Would that not completely isolate them both at home and abroad in a period in which nearly everyone took it for granted that not only the objective interests but also the subjective desires, hopes and expectations of ever broader strata of the population must be taken into account? In other words, to put it briefly, was the present regime in Prussia not inevitably doomed to failure, and would not any compromise with it therefore be merely compromising?

The supporters of that regime could hardly invoke Russia as an example demonstrating the opposite. Russia was a backward country in every respect. European public opinion was largely unanimous in feeling that special conditions obtained there. Prussia, on the other hand, the country of enlightened despotism and of the great reforms of the early years of the century, could not in the public mind, as indeed emerged from foreign reactions to the constitutional conflict, lay claim to that kind of special status. In fact that was something people were more inclined to concede to Austria as a multi-nation state burdened with enormous problems of integration. If Prussia were to pursue a determinedly anti-popular and, in the language and perception of the period, anti-national policy, it would not only cut itself off completely from the rest of Europe; it would also so weaken itself that its government would virtually be inviting revolutionary upheaval and thereby digging its own grave.

For all his pragmatism and for all his passionate partiality in this situation, a man such as Bismarck, who so soberly took into account the growing importance of the popular factor in what had become his own special province, namely foreign policy, can hardly have been under any illusion as to the fact that the opposition's overall assessment of the situation was not entirely false. He would scarcely have agreed with the subsequently much-quoted view of Ferdinand Lassalle, who thought that the opposition was digging itself in behind a lot of big words and an abstract legal standpoint because it felt it lacked any real power and because it no longer dared appeal to the masses.[43] On the contrary, he saw that behind the opposition there was an economically and socially rising class whose self-assurance, in a period of exceptional prosperity, was growing steadily everywhere in Europe and whose demands could not in the long run be met with pure negation. In a speech to the House of Deputies in which he rebuked the opposition by saying that its unity was one of criticism alone and that it saw the balance of interests in far too simple a light, he gave as it were an involuntary indication of this. 'The pathway a Prussian ministry is able to take', he declared, 'is never very wide; the man from the far Left, when he becomes a minister, will have to move to his right, and the man from the far Right, when be becomes a minister, will have to move to his left, and there is no room on this narrow trail that the government of any large country is able to tread for the kind of sweeping divagations of doctrine that a man may unfold as an orator or as a member of parliament.'[44]

It made him all the more bitter, therefore, that his attempts to fragment the opposition's unity met with no success whatever. On the contrary, almost every one of his policy statements and concrete measures was exploited by the left wing for the purposes of locking that unity more tightly each time into a common defensive posture. He thought he knew the potential points of penetration, particularly in the field of foreign policy. And he found them blocked by vigilant adversaries who at the same time kept on provoking him into saying things that to the public ear were more revealing than persuasive. An example was when, defending himself against an old charge at the end of January 1863, he felt he must once again 'reassure' the House of Deputies, 'as if this internal conflict could induce us "to find in the prospect of external involvements a means of settling our internal differences": the means would be worse than the evil itself, and I have already on previous occasions, when I was likewise accused of pursuing it, described such a policy as frivolous'.[45]

All this threw him into a state of growing agitation, increasingly bringing into play emotions that exploded in uncontrolled outbursts, fanciful speculations about the future and attacks on the opposition that even from the standpoint of his own objectives could only be regarded as rash and ill-advised. Such an occasion was when, in the course of what was already a very heated debate about the Polish question and the Alvensleben Convention in the House of Deputies towards the end of February 1863, he further raised the temperature by not only repudiating any claim by parliament to even a consultative role in policy-making but also launching a vehement personal attack on, of all people, one of the leaders of the markedly nationalist wing of the liberals, Viktor von Unruh, making him and his political associates out to be notorious professional revolutionaries.[46]

Later, after 1866, he tried to put a fresh interpretation on this. He claimed to have been obliged, with the king starting to waver, to act the strong man, show how the House of Deputies could be dealt with and demonstrate that no danger threatened from that quarter. In reality the situation was probably the exact reverse: he was the one who felt driven into a corner and had reason to fear that the king would sooner or later see how weak and increasingly lacking in support his Minister-President's position really was. So he actually went looking for new bones of contention, which diverted attention from the material questions at issue and released a great deal of emotion and undirected aggression on both sides.

Only to a very limited extent could this be described as tactically inspired; a clear objective was scarcely discernible any more. No, this was a desperate struggle for political survival. It came to a head, following a series of massive affronts to parliament, with Roon and after him the whole government contesting the Speaker's right, in the context of clashes in the House over the Military Service Bill, to use his authority against members of the government – in other words to interrupt them, if the occasion arose, and call them to order. Even if certain legal arguments could be advanced in support of this, politically it was an unparalleled insult. What the government was demanding in the circumstances was that parliament should listen in silence to every attack launched upon it by the government, even down to personal smears directed at individual members, and that at no point did the Speaker have the right to intervene.

All the House of Deputies could do in response to this virtual declaration of war by the government was to issue a counter-declaration to the effect that all bridges were now finally burnt. By the overwhelming majority of 239 to 61 votes it passed an address to the king on 22 May 1863 that culminated in the words: 'The House of Deputies has no further means of communicating with this ministry; it refuses to co-operate with the present policy of the government. All further discussion only strengthens our conviction that between the Crown's advisers and the country there exists a gulf that cannot otherwise be filled than by a change of personnel and furthermore a change in the system'.[47]

Events now followed one another in swift succession. The king refused to receive the deputation that was to have handed him parliament's address. He replied to the House of Deputies in writing four days later with a vehemence that had never been heard from this quarter before, at least in public; even a section of the ministry, headed by the Minister of the Interior, Count Eulenburg, felt that the monarch had gone too far. What William said in his statement, which was not countersigned by the government, was that he must 'in all seriousness . . . oppose the efforts of the House of Deputies to use its constitutional right to participate in the legislative process as a means of restricting the constitutional freedom of royal resolutions'. They were trying in this way 'to prepare the ground for an unconstitutional dictatorship of the House of Deputies'. He went on: 'I repudiate this demand. My ministers enjoy my confidence, their official acts are performed with my approval and I am grateful to them for making it their business to oppose the unconstitutional aspirations of the House of Deputies for an extension of its power.'[48]

Next day, on 27 May 1863, he 'closed' the Diet, in other words he declared the session at an end without for the time being making use of his right to dissolve parliament; in that case there would have had to be fresh elections within a certain period, which the government was anxious to avoid. And five days later, on 1 June 1863, formally invoking the government's right to issue emergency decrees when parliament was not sitting, he signed a press decree that Bismarck had already been planning for some time.[49] This placed the press to a large extent under government control, even as far as content was concerned, giving the government the 'right' to confiscate and ban purely on the grounds of a paper's 'general attitude'. In practice this meant the abolition of the freedom of the press and the suppression of public opinion, which had hitherto spoken out almost unanimously against the government and its policy; of some 300,000 newspapers sold in Prussia every day, at least five out of six backed the opposition. Accordingly this blow against the press was almost universally regarded as the prelude to a dictatorship by decree – by *Ordonnanzen*, as such measures were called in Germany after the notorious 'Ordinances of St-Cloud' promulgated by Charles X of France in July 1830.

The reaction to this, both at home and abroad, overshadowed everything that had happened hitherto. To the delight of the liberals, even the Prussian crown prince joined in. Having first written to Bismarck and his father protesting vigorously against the government's measure, at a reception given in his honour by the city of Danzig on 5 June he publicly expressed his regret at this escalation of the conflict and made it clear that he personally had nothing to do with it.

This development at the same time revealed that there was no need in practice for the question of royal or parliamentary supremacy to be posed so acutely. It merely disguised the fact that here was a monarch seeking despotically to set aside the opinions and desires of the majority of the people of the country over which he ruled.

For a moment it may have looked as if this had lent the conflict an entirely new quality. If even the heir to the throne sided openly with the opposition, the position of the government and the reigning monarch threatened to become untenable, not least because precisely the most determined 'forces of order' must now ask themselves whether a continuation of the conflict did not place that order in greater jeopardy than everything else. It very quickly transpired, however, that a policy deliberately aiming in this direction was very far from the crown prince's mind. He did stand by his convictions, informing Bismarck that he was 'opposed in principle' to the political course he was pursuing and that he considered 'those who . . . are leading His Majesty the King along such paths' to be the 'most dangerous advisers for Crown and country'.[50] But at the same time he promised his father, who was furious with him, that he would refrain from making public statements in future. The dominant impression in the end was one of weakness and indecision, which led to disappointment among all those who had attached high hopes to the crown prince's speech; the whole thing turned out to have been no more than an 'Incident in Danzig', as Bismarck sarcastically entitled the relevant chapter of his memoirs.

This outcome had not been a foregone conclusion, of course, nor could anyone have predicted that the king would allow himself to be inveigled into so open a breach of the constitution as the press decree undoubtedly represented. Once he had taken that step, however, he was more than ever bound to his Minister-President and dependent on him and on his political skill. In view of this there is a strong temptation to place the emphasis on Bismarck's more and more solid establishment of himself in power and to look at and judge developments up until the summer of 1863 primarily from that angle. But there was another aspect, namely that the price of such an entrenchment in power was extraordinarily high, particularly since that power rested almost entirely on the life and health of a man already 66 years of age. Too high, one might think, for someone who, whatever he was, was not a politician of the status quo, a man content to hang on to what had once been achieved.

The fact was that, if it did not wish to proceed to abolish the constitution altogether and formally establish a neo-absolutist dictatorship – and there is little evidence that Bismarck seriously considered such a course and even less that the king would have gone along with it – the government was now almost completely paralysed. The opportunity of taking up a position between the contending parties and the social groups behind them, an opportunity that had seemed briefly to present itself in the autumn of 1862, had been passed up. Instead of the 'Ständekampf' of which Max Duncker had spoken there was now an ever-sharpening confrontation between the government on the one hand and the 'people' on the other. Bismarck may have had some justification for doubting the existence of an absolute identity of opinions and interests between 'people' and House of Deputies majority, but the legal basis for the opposite view and to an even greater extent its basis in public opinion were unassailable. No press decree from above and no amount of public relations work, however skilful, could shake that fact.

Entrenchment in office and in power did not mean a great deal in that situation. Without the instrument of legislation and with no public backing and no support to speak of for his other plans and objectives, that power lacked any real substance and was incapable of asserting itself constructively, at least at home. With regard to foreign relations, on the other hand, the government's freedom of action, as some noted with triumph and others with great concern, appeared very much less restricted. So the likelihood from the outset was that it would attempt to compensate in this sphere for its impotence in the other and to score successes abroad that would divert attention from the stagnation and conflict besetting it at home. Here too, though, the government's opponents hoped that such successes would become increasingly less feasible without the backing of the national public or that of the individual countries concerned, in other words without at least the approval and psychological assistance of popular forces and democratically legitimated interests.

The reaction of the powers to the highly unpopular behaviour of the Prussian government during the Polish uprising appeared to provide strong confirmation of this. It appeared to prove those people in Prussia right who warned against overestimating the danger from this quarter. What worried them, they said, was that other governments, in this case primarily the Austrian government, would attempt to exploit the situation to their own advantage and outmanoeuvre Prussia.

This was indeed Vienna's plan, as became clear to everybody early in August 1863, and the Prussian liberals found themselves thrown into serious disarray by it. The question was this: faced with the Greater German federal reform plans of an Austrian government that was clearly bent on liberalization at home, should they, despite the situation in Prussia, stick to their Lesser German plans and so support Bismarck's foreign policy in what might be a highly confusing fashion – or should they execute a decisive change of course? In fact close examination of the Austrian proposals, which fell far short of liberal expectations, made the decision a relatively easy one for them to take. Moreover, their representatives did not even need to take up a position officially but were able to confine themselves by and large to commenting on the decision that was now reached very swiftly.

Incomparably more difficult and indeed extremely menacing was the position in which Bismarck was himself placed by the Austrian proposals. Like everyone else, he had been expecting a fresh thrust from Vienna in the matter of the reform of the German Confederation and hence towards a solution of the German question. In the event he was clearly surprised by the skill with which Vienna went about it under the strategic direction of the man in charge of German affairs at the Foreign Ministry, Baron von Biegeleben.

At a specially arranged meeting on 3 August in Bad Gastein, where William I was taking a cure, Emperor Francis Joseph invited the Prussian king to a kind of summit conference of German rulers to be held in Frankfurt am Main on 16 August – in less than two weeks' time. The purpose of this gathering was to discuss and adopt a wide-ranging Austrian plan for the reform of the Confederation, although as far as the actual content of that plan was concerned the emperor confined himself to the very vaguest generalizations. Austria, in other words, deliberately bypassing William's Minister-President, tried to woo the Prussian king with the very point for which he was campaigning so passionately in Prussia, namely by invoking the monarchical idea and with it the concept of monarchical solidarity. The crowned heads of the states of the German Confederation, led by the Austrian emperor and the Prussian king, were to take it upon themselves, as in Vienna in 1814–15, to rearrange the pattern of relations in central Europe. They were to make use of their supremacy to put in their places all who sought in one way or another to misuse them as figureheads.

This forced Bismarck to start fighting on two fronts, as it were. Resolving immediately to wreck the Austrian intitiative not just in detail but in its entirety, he was obliged, a mere two months after the constitutional conflict had reached its climax with the closure of parliament and the promulgation of the press decree, to persuade his king to fall right back on the position of the strictly constitutional monarch who can make no far-reaching decisions without his responsible ministers. For this was the only way of countering at all convincingly the Austrian emperor's argument that there was no need for lengthy preliminary conferences and consultations: the reigning monarchs could proceed to the requisite discussions and pass the requisite resolutions at the conference, so to speak in a single operation, demonstrating to all and sundry that they had the reins firmly in their grasp. Under pressure of circumstances Bismarck himself now violated the fiction of monarchical self-government. He prevailed upon the king to cite that classical principle of constitutional law: 'Le roi règne, mais il ne gouverne pas' ('The king rules, but he does not govern').

The first time, namely in his letter to the Austrian emperor on 4 August in which he neither accepted the invitation nor definitely declined it, William, hard pressed by Bismarck, did this in a somewhat guarded form. He suggested that conferences of ministers of the principal powers of the Confederation should take place first, 'regarding the outcome of which a decision would eventually be made by the sovereigns'.[51] The Austrian government, however, disregarded this evasive manoeuvre. It insisted on its 'summit', which was opened on 17 August, amid much solemn ceremony invoking the imperial past, in the city where German emperors had once been elected and crowned. At Vienna's bidding the Council of Princes promptly adopted a resolution expressly requesting the Prussian king once again to join in its proceedings. King John of Saxony, who was said to be on particularly close terms with William, was charged with delivering this request to him in person at Baden-Baden.

The Prussian king now had to put his cards on the table. At first he was ready to give in; with 'twenty-five crowned heads and a king as courier', he said, he could do nothing else. Bismarck, however, who had accompanied him in the expectation of 'Frankfurt blusterings',[52] mobilized all his resources, including the threat of resignation, to dissaude him from this course; he would be 'quite happy to accompany him as his secretary but not as his Minister-President'.[53] Eyewitnesses of the dramatic encounter say the king was so upset he repeatedly burst into tears. Bismarck himself, on leaving the royal presence after hours of arguing, first had to demolish a huge wash-basin in the antechamber before he could recover his breath.

In the back of both men's minds was an awareness that what was at issue here was in many ways a decision of far-reaching and quite fundamental importance. A course had to be set. In the end the king yielded to his Minister-President's wishes. He decided to decline the invitation once again and to accept the grounds for doing so that Bismarck dictated to him. In the crucial passage of his letter William wrote that he could arrive at his 'resolutions only when the alterations to the federal constitution under discussion have been examined in detail, in a full and proper treatment of the matter by my advisers, as to how they affect the legitimate power positions of Prussia and the legitimate interests of the nation. I owe it to my country and to the cause of Germany not to make any binding declarations to my confederates prior to such an examination of the questions at issue; yet without such declarations my participation in the discussions would not be feasible.'[54]

Already implicit in this, in addition to the highly significant formal aspect and very closely bound up with it, was the actual substance of the Prussian refusal. Austria's federal reform plan, of which the representatives of the individual states of the Confederation had been informed officially and in full detail only on 16 August 1863, the day before the opening of the Frankfurt Council of Princes, suggested setting up a series of central institutions in addition to the present congress of envoys. Through these and above all through a major extension of its powers, the 'objects of the German Confederation', the Confederation was to be recast in the form of a federal state. It was to be headed by a new five-man directorate comprising the Austrian emperor and the kings of Prussia and Bavaria as permanent members and two other members sitting in rotation. In addition to the Federal Diet, which was to continue in existence, the plan also provided for an assembly of German princes meeting periodically and a further assembly of 'federal deputies', likewise meeting on a regular basis. These, however, were not to be directly elected but appointed by the parliaments of the individual states. Finally, to standarize jurisprudence a federal court was to be set up – as a logical extension of efforts to establish joint legislation in many areas, notably that of 'Wohlfahrt' or 'Welfare', which at that time covered economic, commercial and tariff policy.[55]

Against all this, against the 'Schwarzenberg policy in the posthumous form of the Congress of Princes', as he called it in his memoirs,[56] Bismarck made a firm stand, both through the mouth of the Prussian king and subsequently, in very much plainer terms, also in the *Norddeutsche Allgemeine Zeitung*. He did so with the twofold argument that the whole thing conflicted with the 'legitimate power position of Prussia' and the 'legitimate interests of the nation', the suggestion being that there was an inherent connection between the two.

Officially there was no word in all this of the Customs Union and of Austria's obvious attempt to use its federal reform plans to unsettle the political aspects of that institution, although in his Christmas memorandum of 1862 Bismarck had singled out this sphere as the real object of all future diplomatic arrangements. Nor did the idea of a Lesser German solution of the national question and possible coalition-building towards that end receive the least mention in formal terms. Yet the whole complex, under the headings 'legitimate power position of Prussia' and 'legitimate interests of the nation', constituted the substance of the three formal conditions under which, according to Bismarck, Prussia would agree to add its acceptance to the Federal Reform Act passed by a large majority on 1 September 1863. Those conditions were: a right of veto for both German great powers in the event of declarations of war by the confederation when it was not a question of repelling an attack on actual federal territory; parity between them in the control of the Confederation; and finally, in place of the assembly of delegates, a 'true national representative body founded on the direct participation of the entire nation'.

Whereas the first two conditions were traditional Prussian demands that had been brought out against every federal reform plan launched by Austria or the medium-sized states since 1850, the third one, particularly so far as its justification was concerned, went very much further in that it played off the nation against the princes, as it were. Even if Prussia's demands for a right of veto for both great powers in the matter of war and peace and for parity with Austria in the control of the Confederation were granted, the Prussian Cabinet declared in its summary statement about the Frankfurt Reform Act on 15 September 1863, 'the task of reconciling the divergent dynastic interests for the purposes of facilitating uniformity of action by the Confederation [was] not solved'. The statement went on: 'Summarily to decide disputes between them by majority votes of the governments represented on the directorate seems to us neither just nor politically acceptable. The element competent to mediate the particular interests of the individual states into a unity in the interests of Germany as a whole can basically be found only in the representation of the German nation.'[57]

With this Prussia's 'conflict ministry', whose head had already made the Prussian king execute a formal retreat to a position of scrupulous constitutionality in the clash over the Austrian invitation, itself took a stand on the crucial issue that was in line with the demands of the liberal national party. It identified itself with the latter's view that the German question could not be solved by monarchs and governments alone but only in collaboration with the German nation and through the appointment of a German parliament to represent it.

This was an extraordinary turn of events. The Prussian demands having been made in public, it opened up entirely new and far-reaching perspectives for everyone concerned. The overwhelming majority of liberal contemporaries, however, saw it as a purely tactical move. They doubted whether the Prussian counter-proposals 'could be meant at all seriously by such a government', as the National Union, the umbrella organization of Lesser German nationalism, put it in a mid-October resolution opposing the Frankfurt Reform Act.[58]

The objective, they argued, was on two counts a purely negative one. Bismarck was concerned only to parry the Austrian proposals and to confuse and if possible split the opposition at home, and to achieve these ends he would employ any means. 'This bare-faced attempt by the Bismarck ministry', the weekly newspaper of the National Union announced at the beginning of October 1863, 'to turn the jealousy that the Prussian national spirit feels towards Austria into a fresh prop for its shaky existence will come wretchedly to grief.'[59]

This accusation of a purely tactical calculation can certainly not be brushed aside completely, even in retrospect. On the other hand the call for a German parliament was entirely in line with the course that Bismarck had said years before was the only one likely to lead to a solution of the German question in Prussia's favour and that he had been trying to follow ever since, namely a rapprochement with the Lesser German national party and the forces behind it – even if he did talk in only vague terms of 'the German people' or 'the German nation'. Of course – and this is where the apparent contradiction is resolved – it had only ever been an essentially tactical rapprochement that he had had in mind, a backing-up of Prussia's and his own claims to power by those forces. The whole thing rested 'not on a political theory but on material Prussian interests', he noted in a directive to

Bernstorff. 'It is not the German governments but the German people that overwhelmingly shares the same interests as ourselves. Prussia needs a counter-weight to the dynastic policy of the governments and will be able to find it only in a national representative body'.[60]

The question of Bismarck's tactical motives must not, however, be allowed to obscure the really crucial element in this situation, which was that the co-operation to which it gave rise in many areas had practical consequences and begot actual results that went far beyond what had been intended. To put it another way, the indubitable skill with which Bismarck contrived, albeit only after several attempts, to harness the forces of national liberalism to his purpose ought not to blind us to the fact that the direction in which they pulled never rested with him and that the means he employed at the same time rendered him dependent.

In the autumn of 1863 this dimension of Prussia's response to the Frankfurt Reform Act was largely unapparent as yet. The function of that response was to block the whole initiative by making demands that Austria could not accept, and that function it fulfilled, aided by the fact that an impending European entanglement over the Schleswig-Holstein question seemed in Vienna's view to call for urgent co-operation with the other German great power. The national party, on the other hand, and the opposition within Prussia remained unimpressed. 'Only the German people itself, in a freely elected parliament, can determine its constitutional rights', the weekly newspaper of the National Union stressed once again in programmatic terms.[61]

The election campaign launched in the wake of the dissolution of the House of Deputies early in September was fought by the Left Centre and the Progressive Party on a platform of uncompromising hostility to the Bismarck government. At the end of October 1863 that platform brought them an overwhelming victory, despite muzzling of the press and massive government attempts to influence voters but also notwithstanding the ministry's stance on the question of federal reform and its declarations of intent on that subject. Particularly the liberally inclined civil servants from whose ranks many more than half the opposition deputies were drawn had found themselves exposed to ever-increasing pressure. Nevertheless, with more than 70 per cent of the seats in its control the liberal opposition now enjoyed an even more crushing majority than hitherto. And since they had won it under the banner of all-out war on the government, a compromise was now virtually out of the question; under the present constitution the Prussian monarchy stood no chance, Bismarck threatened darkly a few days after the election.

Following the immediate repeal of the Press Decree, which was publicly celebrated as a smashing defeat for the government, the parliamentary majority did everything during the next few weeks to demonstrate that it was still not prepared to have serious dealings with the Cabinet currently in office. Essentially it repeated the proceedings of the previous year: it rejected the government's Army Bill with its insistence on a three-year period of military service, it curtailed the budget accordingly, it protested vehemently against the adoption of that budget by the Upper House in the form proposed by the government, and it denounced the government's whole policy as unconstitutional since it lacked any basis in budgetary law.

Since a further dissolution appeared senseless in the light of recent experience, the only alternative from the government's point of view was once again to prorogue parliament – this time with no chance of arguing in constitutional law that it must be the king's constant concern to see that the majority will of the people and the majority will of parliament concur, *ergo* that he must if necessary use his influence to restore such a concurrence by proroguing or dissolving parliament. There seemed to be no denying now that the government was getting rid of parliament in order to implement its objectives without it and to that extent in defiance of the declared will of the majority of the Prussian people.

As to what those objectives were, the public was becoming increasingly unclear. 'Even the history of Byzantium scarcely provides such a picture of decrepitude and confusion as is offered by the present regime in Prussia', was the verdict of a leading article in the National Union's weekly towards the end of August 1863.[62] What in positive terms did he actually want, this man who after all had held the offices of Minister-President and Foreign Minister of Prussia for almost a year now? Was he really only interested in resistance, preservation, the defence of the status quo – a latter-day Metternich desperately on the look-out for ways in which to evade the pressures of political and social change? Did his political objectives really go no further than the acquisition and possession of power? Or was he in fact just waiting patiently for an oportunity to turn the whole situation upside-down and seize the initiative himself, for some external event that would change everything?

Ever since his accession to office people had suspected that he would try to use foreign policy successes and surprising moves in that sphere to divert attention from the situation at home and win support for himself. So when the Schleswig-Holstein question once again became acute in the autumn of 1863, friend and foe alike immediately saw it as a sort of test case for his real intentions and longer-term plans as well as for his ability to implement them. Would he now succeed, in a situation that stirred up deep political passions, in imparting a decisive turn to events or had people, whether in fear or in hope, hugely overrated him? If anywhere, it was over this question that success or failure stood to determine his entire political future.

[7]

The End or a New Beginning?

The Schleswig-Holstein question came to be of absolutely crucial importance for Bismarck, for the liberal national movement and for the configuration and evolution of the whole international situation. This is beyond dispute. Equally beyond dispute is the fact that in its origins and development this was one of the most intricate problems in nineteenth-century international relations. As Palmerston, the English Foreign Minister, commented wryly on one occasion, only three men had grasped it in all its ramifications: one was dead, the second had been driven mad by it and the third, he himself, had forgotten all about it. Yet the only way to understand the dramatic consequences to which it eventually gave rise is to examine at least in broad outline something of the complicated background to the problem.

Even after the succession question had been settled by the great powers in 1852, the duchies of Schleswig, Holstein and Lauenburg, which were attached to the Danish Crown by personal union, had remained a sore spot on the international political scene. This was true with regard to relations between the states involved and with an interest in the matter, and it was especially true with regard to the two national movements, the German and the Danish, that were competing for support in those parts. The aim of Danish nationalism was quite patently to extend the personal union into a real union, in other words to make the duchies an integral part of the Danish state, in defiance of international agreements, or at least to make Schleswig a province of Denmark. During the 1850s this aim had managed to win increasing acceptance inside Denmark itself. As early as 1855 a constitution had been adopted for a 'Greater Denmark' that gave the central parliament in Copenhagen wide-ranging legislative and financial rights in the duchies.

Protests had been lodged against this not only by the German Confederation as guarantor of the rights of the duchy of Holstein, which was a member of the Confederation, but also by the two German great powers as signatories of the Treaty of London. Prussia, however, in line with the policy of the then Prussian envoy to the Federal Diet, had at the same time been anxious to block any intervention by the Confederation and consequent enhancement of the standing of that organization by favouring direct negotiations between the two German great powers and Denmark. The move had not succeeded. But it had robbed the counter-measures of much of their weight and persuasiveness, particularly since at first neither Vienna nor Berlin had any interest in playing up the whole affair.

The Federal Diet had nevertheless decided in August 1858 to threaten the Danish king with *Bundesexekution*, a kind of federal enforcement order, in Holstein and Lauenburg unless he abolished the new constitution as far as these two territories were concerned. King Frederick VII had eventually bowed to this threat. But the highly unwelcome outcome of this had been that Schleswig, in a further violation of the Treaty of London, was in effect separated from Holstein. Without the support of Holstein and through it indirectly of the German Confederation, it had become even more firmly incorporated in the Danish state. The Danish government had continued along this road after 1858. At the end of March 1863 it had formally contested the section of the Treaty of London that dealt with Schleswig, recognizing special rights only for Holstein and Lauenburg.

This had pushed the antagonism between Germans and Danes to fresh heights. On the German side the chief vehicle of that antagonism was the German National Union, the liberal, Lesser German pressure group founded in 1859 and already numbering some 20,000 members. One of the key points of its programme from the outset was the solution of the Schleswig-Holstein question in German terms. It was a matter, as its weekly newspaper stated towards the end of April 1863, 'not merely of the mortgaged honour of the nation; it is also a matter of winning and securing a position that is of incalculable importance for the protection of our coasts, for the development of our sea power and for the whole political future of Germany'.[1]

Not least in view of the direct connection between the Schleswig-Holstein question and national and liberal aspirations, the Confederation had reacted only hesitantly – unlike the two German great powers, who protested immediately against the Danish violation in identical notes. To Bismarck's secret satisfaction it had thus further discredited itself in the eyes of the national movement. Not until the beginning of July 1863 had it decided to reinstitute the *Bundesexekution* proceedings against the Danish king in his capacity as Duke of Holstein and Lauenburg that had been in abeyance since 1858, at the same time calling upon the king to fulfil the terms of the Treaty of London with a constitution that upheld not only Holstein's rights but those of Schleswig too.

In making this demand the Confederation had formally exceeded its powers. On the one hand it was not a signatory to the Treaty of London, and on the other hand the sovereignty of Holstein and Lauenburg was being challenged by the Danish government only in matters of detail; as a whole it was not infringed. Copenhagen therefore took the opportunity not only to stick rigidly to its position but to give formal notice that it would withdraw from the Confederation should *Bundesexekution* actually be attempted. The Danish government coupled this with the statement that any further step would be interpreted as a declaration of war on Denmark by the Confederation. The Federal Diet thereupon approved an order against Holstein on 1 October 1863 and charged not only the two German great powers but also Saxony and Hanover with the task of enforcing it.

Since then events had followed one another in swift succession. Anxious lest the conflict should spread, both London and Paris had offered their services in mediation. Denmark had in fact taken up their offer; that is to say, it had declared itself ready to participate in fresh talks at a European level. At the same time, however, it had pushed ahead with the incorporation of Schleswig in the Danish state by hurrying through a new national constitution. And precisely at this point, two days after the Danish parliament's adoption of the new constitution on 13 November 1863, King Frederick VII had died. In other words, in the very moment in which the succession settlement for which the Treaty of London of 1852 had guaranteed the approval of the great powers should have come into effect its fundamental terms and conditions had been violated in the most flagrant fashion. Since in addition the legal requirements for a succession by the so-called 'Protocol Prince', Christian IX of Schleswig-Holstein-Sonderburg-Glücksburg, were not fulfilled with respect to Holstein and hence indirectly with respect to Schleswig, the Holstein parliament having not yet given the requisite assent to the succession settlement, the legal situation appeared to be wholly favourable to the recalcitrant Schleswig-Holsteiners.

It was the almost unanimous opinion of the German public that the powers, particularly the two German great powers, now had the choice between right and might. On the side of right in this situation there was not only positive law but also natural law in the form of the right of peoples to self-determination. Accordingly the Duke of Augustenburg, who had previously relinquished his rights, met with the almost unanimous support of the German public when in view of the new situation he claimed the succession in Schleswig and Holstein, not for himself but for his son. As early as 16 November the latter announced to the Confederation that he had ascended the throne as Duke Frederick VIII.

The wave of national enthusiasm under the influence of which a 'constituent assembly' of Schleswig-Holsteiners gathered spontaneously to swear allegiance to Frederick VIII seemed for a moment to sweep aside all possible objections to such a procedure on the grounds that it contravened international agreements: the majority of the small and medium-sized German states declared for Augustenburg and for the recognition of an independent principality of Schleswig-Holstein.

That was the situation in the second half of November 1863. Many of the leaders of the liberal opposition in Prussia registered with concern and with mixed feelings what an extraordinary opportunity appeared to present itself to the Prussian government here. All the greater was people's surprise, even in the immediate circle around the Prussian Minister-President, when Bismarck seemed to be wholly unaware of this opportunity and to lay himself open to the distinctly dangerous charge of neglecting German and consequently also Prussian interests.

His flirtation with the national movement, his advocacy of a German parliament, his alleged determination to press for a solution of the national question along Lesser German lines, indeed his much-invoked diplomatic skill now appeared in a somewhat diffuse light. Was his true objective here too, people asked themselves, the preservation of the status quo at any price? Was he now turning out, in foreign affairs as well, to be what people had long believed he was in respect of domestic policy: a reactionary of the first water, who hated any kind of change and who clung to everything, however fragile, that stood in its way?

Instead of leading Prussia to the head of the national movement, instead of mobilizing Prussia's military might for the German cause, the might that after all was supposed to have been strengthened and was to be strengthened further to this end, the Prussian head of government appealed to the sanctity of international treaties. And instead of supporting the actions of the Confederation and upholding Prussia's claim to a leading role within that organization, he was obviously concerned only to put relations between Prussia and Austria back on their old, pre-1848 footing, relinquishing all reform plans and proposed solutions of the German question.

Whatever bitterness this stance gave rise to not only among the national movement and the liberal opposition but also in the ranks of the former *Wochenblatt* party around Schleinitz, von der Goltz and Bernstorff, it came as a pleasant surprise to Vienna and the capitals of the other great powers. In Vienna a national pronunciamento would necessarily have been greeted with mistrust. An unleashing of national passions could have only fateful consequences for a multi-nation state; the most recent federal reform proposal with its rejection of a directly elected parliament had shown once again that even progressive elements were aware that they were walking a tightrope here. The danger that Prussia might turn this weakness to account had been an ever present one since 1848; now, with the Schleswig-Holstein crisis, it looked like becoming acute.

But it was not just the national implications of the whole question, namely its potential repercussions in Venetia, Bohemia and Hungary, that worried Vienna; in other respects too the emerging conflict threatened to put the empire at a disadvantage almost all along the line. Geographically, Schleswig-Holstein lay well beyond its real sphere of power and interest but well within that of Prussia. Any kind of direct intervention carried with it the danger of a straight confrontation on unfavourable terrain. There was also the fact that to repudiate international agreements seemed a particularly dangerous course for Austria to take since, as the Crimean War and the war in Italy had shown, few states were more dependent on the existence and effective functioning of a European legal system guaranteed by the great powers.

In view of all this, Vienna was exceptionally relieved when the Prussian Minister-President and Foreign Minister promptly indicated his readiness to collaborate very closely over the whole question. This was particularly true of the Austrian Foreign Minister, Count Rechberg, Bismarck's Frankfurt colleague in the 1850s. He had always taken a somewhat sceptical view of the essentially anti-Prussian activities of his senior civil servants, led by Ludwig von Biegeleben, and been more convinced than they were of the vital necessity for a peaceful settlement with Prussia. Nevertheless, he had gone along with their initiative on the question of federal reform, and in resisting Prussia's demands he had implicated himself in what Bismarck sarcastically called a policy of 'enterprising recklessness'.[2] Now, however,

Rechberg suddenly saw Prussia's minimum programme, which the Prussian Minister-President had unfolded alongside his maximum programme in talks with the Austrian envoy Count Károlyi less than a year before, in an entirely new light. Indeed he wondered whether Bismarck, schooled by his experiences on the domestic policy front, was not now a very much more conservative politician in foreign affairs as well than had hitherto seemed to be the case, a politician who, for all his continued ambitions with regard to power, did after all think very much more firmly in terms of the European legal and power system.

The same question was being asked in the Cabinets of the other great powers. Eventually they inclined more and more to the view that under these circumstances the Schleswig-Holstein question would not after all turn out to be so explosive as they had inevitably thought at first. A latent mistrust lurked everywhere, of course. Napoleon III in particular found it hard to imagine that Bismarck would entirely forgo playing the national card. Yet it was obvious that the image people had formed of the Prussian head of government changed appreciably once the Schleswig-Holstein crisis had broken out openly.

Considering this change in people's estimate of him on the internationl stage, this growing tendency to see him not as a troublemaker but as a co-guarantor of the European system, and contrasting it with the final outcome in the shape of Prussia's annexation of the disputed territories and the diplomatic isolation of Austria, which eventually went into the decisive battle for hegemony in central Europe without a single ally of any consequence to its name, the historian is already tempted to see that outcome as the product of a policy that was in the highest degree Machiavellian. As so often, this verdict – which is not infrequently associated with a secret admiration for a Machiavellism so perfect – rests on the assumption of an inner consistency of conduct, the systematic implementation of a long-term plan, an assumption that deduces an intention from a result, inferring the agent from the act, as it were.

Bismarck himself provided support for this view with his retrospective self-justifications, which he used quite deliberately to enhance his political prestige and with which he sometimes completely convinced himself. In reality we have to take as our starting-point, particularly in relation to the Schleswig-Holstein question, the fact that, apart from the very general objective that something must come out of it for Prussia in the end, it was predominantly negative factors at first that governed the stance Bismarck adopted and the actions he took. The end-result can be represented as the diagonal of a parallelogram of evils to be avoided, and what the Prussian Minister-President was mainly aware of at first was what he did not want.

The first factor was his determination to prevent any enhancement of the prestige of the German Confederation; this must continue to be seen as incapable of effectively representing the interests of Germany and the German states. There was also his concern that Austria might be tempted to use the majority it had obtained in August in the matter of federal reform to launch a major offensive against Prussia for the purposes of finally establishing its own dominance in central Europe. An initiative in this direction, problematic though it might be in essence from the point of view of the Austrian national interest, appeared not entirely out of the question in so far as the chief powers of the so-called 'Third Germany', namely Bavaria, Württemberg and Saxony, were backing the creation of a new medium-sized state. Their hope was that, in a reformed Confederation under Austrian leadership, this would tip the balance even more in their favour and further reduce the power of Prussia.

Another negative determinant as far as Bismarck was concerned was the development of a rapprochement between Austria and France. He was not at all sure whether this was a purely tactical move on the part of Napoleon III or whether it marked the beginning of bigger things, with Austria possibly making concessions in Italy in the interests of consolidating its power in central Europe. Perhaps the French emperor had seriously come round to the view that Austria, with its internal structural problems and the state of its public finances, presented a lesser long-term danger to France than Prussia did.

Bismarck was also oppressed by his habitual fear of a rapprochement between Paris and St Petersburg. This was now heighteneed by the fact that in the subsequent course of events Russia supported the bid for the throne made by the Grand Duke of Oldenburg, a relative of the tsar, and thus in practice came very close to the French position of a solution of the question in accordance with the principle of national self-determination. Finally a certain role, though hardly a central one, was played by the fact that Augustenburg had clear leanings towards the liberal group of princes and like them favoured the Lesser German unification programme. A triumph for him threatened in the circumstances to redound to the benefit of other forces. Even in Lesser German circles it threatened to strengthen the front of Bismarck's political opponents, particularly if it were to be achieved with the backing of Britain, for example, on whose support in solving the national question the Lesser German liberals and the German princes close to them had always banked. To forestall such an eventuality from the outset and if possible persuade Britain to hold its course of rigidly preserving the international status quo in Europe was therefore, for this as well as for other reasons, a further element determining his policy in relation to the Schleswig-Holstein question.

Moreover, this assumption that his conduct was largely dictated by negatives, as it were, that is to say by calculating how specific dangers could best be avoided, is supported not only by an analysis of the actual situation and of individual things he said and steps he took. It is supported to a perhaps even greater extent by his whole approach to politics, his basic understanding of the nature of political reality and of the political role of the individual. It was no accident that he gave the most striking expression to this at the climax of his success in the Schleswig-Holstein question. That success, as he knew only too well, was in certain essential respects the product not of his own planning and brilliant exploitation of the situation accordingly but of circumstances having favoured him – although of course he had not marched into the affair 'like a cadet sergeant' without being 'clear in my mind about the course for which I can answer to God', as he put it to a close associate in the very early days of the crisis.[3] Another thing he knew was that circumstances particularly favour the person who allows himself to be guided by them, wresting solutions from them rather than seeking to impose solutions on them.

In this sense Bismarck's policy with respect to the Schleswig-Holstein question presents itself as an outstanding example of an approach that was thoroughly unorthodox, dictated largely by circumstances and by changing conditions – in a word, pragmatic. It perfectly illustrates not only the possibilities but also the limitations of that approach. The limitations lay mainly in the early stages, in the preliminary decisions that determined the basic direction of the policy and, often almost unbeknown to the agent himself, narrowed the circle of possible alternatives from the outset.

First there was his conviction that the whole question could be solved only by war, as a Gordian knot can only be cut with a sword. He had stated this as early as the end of December 1862 in a letter to the Prussian envoy in Karlsruhe, Count Flemming,[4] and at the beginning of February 1863 he had reiterated it to the Prussian king in commenting on a proposal by the Grand Duke of Oldenburg that the Confederation, although not a signatory, should declare the Treaty of London null and void on the grounds of Denmark's infringements of it.[5] That conviction was his guideline. It formed the basis on which he solved the individual problems that subsequently arose, and above all it determined the steps he took in order to hasten the solution of other problems to his advantage.

Central to his policy were relations with Austria and the virtual exclusion of the German Confederation – in demonstrative fashion and in a way that should determine the future. The tool he chiefly used here was the argument of the sanctity of international treaties, the very treaties that he secretly regarded as untenable. In other words, seeing only one solution from the outset, namely the military one, he had both the time and the detachment to make a thorough calculation of the possibilities of each stage of a swiftly changing situation and to ascertain the prerequisites for an eventual end result – which after all a military decision, whichever way it went, would still by no means provide. This explains how a policy that was highly pragmatic in terms of detail, always leaving serious scope for a number of possibilities, can give the impression in retrospect of having been informed by a determination that knew perfectly well where it was going from the beginning.

At the beginning of that policy was a radical realignment of the fronts in central Europe. The full significance of this went almost unnoticed at first among Bismarck's passionately involved contemporaries. Prussia and Austria, who in late November and early December 1863 had at his instigation agreed, informally at first, on a joint policy of rigid adherence to the 1852 treaties, suddenly constituted a compact active unit over against the group of small and medium-sized German states, which were likewise collaborating ever more closely. They denied to the majority formed by that group in the Federal Diet – to 'the policy of minor states trapped in the web of club democracy [*Vereinsdemokratie*]', as Bismarck scornfully put it[6] –

the right to bring the Confederation into play as an autonomous element in the field of international affairs.

This arose *ad hoc* out of the fact that, from a wide variety of motives as far as individual members were concerned, a pro-Augustenburg majority had formed in the Diet that agreed with the German national movement in wishing to see Schleswig-Holstein, under Augustenburg, become a member-state of the German Confederation. What it implied, however, was that the Confederation was now being called radically into question no longer by just one but by both of the German great powers. At the very moment when, for the first time in its history, its policy enjoyed the support and approval of broad sections of the population, the Confederation was dealt a lethal blow. It soon became clear that neither Prussia nor Austria was prepared to have its foreign policy dictated to it by the Federal Diet. Indeed neither of them shrank from stating openly, in view of the situation that had now arisen, that in the final instance it was for the two German great powers to decide regarding the validity and binding character of Confederation resolutions.

This found expression principally in a bilateral agreement that Károlyi and Bismarck signed in Berlin on 16 January 1864. The agreement was of extraordinarily far-reaching importance. If both powers claimed the 'right' to disregard resolutions of the Confederation, there was no reason why this should not be done in future by one power alone.

In repudiating a series of Confederation resolutions that in practice aimed at establishing Augustenburg's rule in Schleswig and Holstein, Prussia and Austria announced that they would regard all further measures by the Confederation in this direction 'as incompatible with the constitution of the Confederation and exceeding its authority' and consequently as invalid.[7] What was actually at issue was the question of the occupation of Schleswig by Confederation troops and the problem of what purpose such an occupation, which Prussia and Austria also advocated, should serve. The majority in the Federal Diet was thinking more and more openly in terms of creating *faits accomplis* that would benefit Augustenburg. Prussia and Austria, on the other hand, had in mind a token occupation as a coercive measure against Denmark and the Danish king. Its purpose was to make Copenhagen comply in full with the terms of the Treaty of London, in other words to retract the November constitution.

That at least was the official justification that both powers stressed once again, also on 16 January, in a short-term ultimatum to Denmark. Even Austria, however, could no longer be in any serious doubt that, in the circumstances, the Treaty of London and its provisions were simply the legal title for a joint intervention by Prussia and Austria. A return in practice to the ground of that treaty seemed highly unlikely. The agreement between Prussia and Austria even touched on this quite openly: 'In the event of hostilities breaking out in Schleswig', this stated, 'and the existing treaty relations between the German powers and Denmark becoming invalid the courts of Prussia and Austria reserve the right to determine the future circumstances of the duchies purely by joint consent.'

With this a second crucial step had irrevocably been taken: Vienna had finally bound itself to Prussia. It had stated explicitly that it would approve a solution only if Berlin approved too. This meant, however, that in this respect too any resolutions of the Confederation aiming in a different direction were pronounced irrelevent in advance and the Confederation consequently put out of the running for good and all. And it also meant that from now on Berlin could at any time compel Vienna either to bow to Prussian demands or become involved in a conflict over a territory that lay far beyond its own sphere of influence and interest.

Moreover, Austria would have had to contemplate any such conflict from an extremely unfavourable starting position. In the peculiar situation in which it found itself, Vienna could count neither on the support of the Confederation nor on that of the German public – unless, of course, the Austrian government performed a complete about-face, radically disowning its own policy. This explains why, with the allied Prussian and Austrian troops under the supreme command of Field Marshal Friedrich von Wrangel occupying Schleswig from early February 1864, Bismarck felt that the moment had come to name, at least within the confidential confines of the Prussian Council of Ministers, the military objective he now envisaged. What he was after, he said on 3 February, was not the integrity of the Danish monarchy under the provisions of the Treaty of London but the amalgamation of the Elbe duchies with Prussia.

Once again he took it for granted that the conflict would escalate into a formal war with Denmark. The hopes of a negotiated settlement cherished in Vienna he treated as playing-counters with which to forestall a premature discussion of joint war aims. In other words, from a very early stage he scarcely saw them as constituting a serious problem. 'There has never been a time when Viennese policy was so largely dictated by Berlin both in outline and in detail', he had written triumphantly to the Prussian ambassador in Paris, Count Robert von der Goltz, back on 24 December 1863.[8]

What agitated him much more was the attitude of his own king. Under the influence of Schleinitz, von der Goltz and his son-in-law in Baden, William too was increasingly inclined to favour Augustenburg. He hoped thereby to make his peace with the majority in the Federal Diet and with the German national movement and perhaps even find the opportunity to launch a fresh version of the old Union policy. While at the European level Bismarck felt that he was beginning to hold more and more of the reins in his hands, at home they threatened to slip from his grasp altogether.

As early as the beginning of December 1863 he had felt compelled to resort to his most powerful weapon, the threat of resignation, in order to bring the king into line[9] – 'since Schleswig-Holstein', he was to say sixteen years later, he had 'had to wrest everything piecemeal' from his monarch 'with the desk revolver always within reach'.[10] Nor did the threat of resignation seem to him to suffice on its own. At a time when he might for the opposition's benefit have begun to lay cautious emphasis on certain potentially interesting consequences of Prussia's policy of intervention, he felt obliged once again to raise the pitch considerably in order to remind the king afresh of the priority of the domestic conflict.

Bismarck's chance to show the king how indispensable he was in the context of the domestic situation came in the debate about a government request for a loan in connection with the Schleswig-Holstein crisis on 21 and 22 January 1864. With the rejectionist attitude of the majority a foregone conclusion, it would have been easy for him, particularly in so delicate a foreign policy situation, to confine himself to a brief, cautious statement of the government's position. Instead he immediately took the offensive and, reversing the argument that had so often been used against him, accused the majority of harnessing a foreign policy problem in the service of the dispute over domestic policy and once again allowing this to dictate its whole attitude. 'The chief motive' behind the expected rejection was 'the lack of confidence in the present ministry; that is what it all comes down to, that is the focal point of your entire argument'. Once again the intention was 'to establish in Prussia the dictatorship of this House'. If opposition members were honest with themselves they would admit 'that this is a battle for the control of Prussia between the House of Hohenzollern and the House of Deputies'. Were the government to comply with the wishes of the majority in this situation, he went on, its members would no longer be 'ministers of the King' but 'ministers of parliament'. 'We should be *your* ministers, and that is something I hope to God we never come to!'[11]

The real target of this inflammatory language was clearly the now vacillating king, of whom Bismarck had written to Roon the day before this speech, likewise with the object of mobilizing suitable counter-forces: 'I have the presentiment that the Crown's game against the revolution is up because the King's heart is in the other camp and his trust bestowed more on his opponents than on his servants.'[12] But no one in the public sphere could know this. It was something of a double-edged success when, in agreeing to a further closure of parliament two days later, the king once again demonstratively backed his Minister-President and the latter's policy. In his speech during the final session Bismarck did make a further attempt to dispel all possible doubts to the effect that this agreement did not necessarily extend to the field of foreign affairs. He spoke of the 'desire' of the House of Deputies 'to place the foreign policy of the government under an unconstitutional constraint', indeed the tendency, in the event of war breaking out in Germany itself, to 'take sides against the Prussian fatherland in advance'.[13] Yet precisely this attempt to represent every other foreign policy but his own as capitulating to the opposition at home shows how much Bismarck was fighting with his back to the wall and what a threat his very foreign policy posed for him at this time.

A handful of opposition deputies saw this very clearly and attempted to exploit it politically. Once again they were led by Rudolf Virchow. He stated in the same debate, likewise for the obvious benefit of the king, that Bismarck was turning increasingly into an unadulterated *Kreuzzeitung* man, as witness his collaborating with Austria for the purpose of rigidly preserving the status quo: 'He is no longer the man who joined us with the feeling that he was going to accomplish something with an energetic foreign policy.'[14]

In rebutting what in the present situation was a somewhat dangerous argument, Bismarck for a moment lifted his mask, as it were. He replied to Virchow that he had 'acted on the principle: "Flectere si nequeo superos, Acheronta movebo!" I did incidentally, when I came here, cherish the hope that I should find in others besides myself a willingness, should the need arise, to sacrifice the standpoint of party to the overall interest of the country. I shall not, lest I offend anyone, go any further into how far and in whom I have been disappointed in this hope; but disappointed I have been, and of course that affects my political position and relations.'[15]

Here was a very brief glimpse of what was still, even at the height of the conflict, his real objective: to make common cause with the national movement and with the section of the middle class that was prepared to co-operate with him. But that objective was barred to him for the moment by the very short cut that seemed to many people, including to an increasing extent the Prussian king, to present itself on the way there. In his great argument with Robert von der Goltz, the ambassador in Paris who increasingly threatened to win the ear of the king, he made clear why in his opinion support for Augustenburg and the popular movement backing him would have the opposite effect to that which people hoped to achieve thereby.

Goltz, who for years had tended to pursue similar political objectives to Bismarck himself, particularly as far as combining a conservative domestic policy with a Lesser German foreign policy was concerned, had called upon the Prussian Minister-President to seize a unique opportunity by placing himself at the head of the Schleswig-Holstein movement and the small and medium-sized German states that supported it. If he did otherwise he would be jeopardizing not only his future 'but that of the dynasty, Prussia's position as a great power and the existence of the Conservative Party', for 'the effective severance of a German state from Germany, in the middle of the nineteenth century, without a fight, would indeed be a departure from Prussia's vocation'.[16]

Bismarck's reply to this letter from a man who presented himself to the king in scarcely veiled terms as a personal and practical alternative to Prussia's current foreign policy, the man who in a subsequent letter had spoken quite openly of a 'dictatorship of the Minister for Foreign Affairs' that was incompatible with the monarchical principle,[17] was as tough as it was fundamental. Who would be the victor, he asked in his crucial letter of 24 December 1863, if Prussia decided to make common cause with the governments of the small and medium-sized states in support of Augustenburg?[18] Even if contrary to all expectations they were to overcome 'at the side of Pfordten, Coburg and Augustenburg, backed by all the cheats and chatterboxes of the movement party,' the resistance that could certainly be expected from the other European great powers, the prize would be 'one grand duke the more in Germany who, fearful for his new sovereignty, votes against Prussia in the Confederation'. And what if one did not want this but sought to use the opportunity to settle the German question in

Prussian and Lesser German terms? For that there was one way only – and here Bismarck quite deliberately employed the past tense to indicate his opinion that such an opportunity had in any case gone by: 'We should have had . . . to pull the ground from beneath our allies' feet *by means of* an imperial constitution and still count on their loyalty. Had this failed, as is to be believed, we should have been made to look foolish; had it succeeded, we should have had our Union *with* the imperial constitution', in other words with the constitution of 1849. Prussia would thus have made itself – and with highly uncertain prospects of success into the bargain – a mere tool of Lesser German liberalism.

Goltz did not want this either. On the contrary, he had more time for a 'unification from above', for a Lesser German federal reform policy along conservative lines, than for the ideas of the liberal group of princes as formulated in detail by Roggenbach, and he was trying to persuade the king that this opportunity could be exploited 'to implement . . . Gagern's programme without an imperial constitution'. Bismarck evaded the obvious question as to how he himself saw things developing; he could hardly make Goltz privy to his 'innermost thoughts', he said 'after you have declared war on me politically'. But he did give sufficient indication for his direction to be quite clear at least in retrospect.

The whole of Europe was in a ferment, he declared in oracular fashion. France was literally spoiling for a fight, as Goltz himself had reported. The Polish question was still smouldering; in Galicia, too, revolution threatened. 'Russia has an army of 200,000 men in excess of its Polish requirements and no money for military fantasizing, so it must presumably be prepared for war.' He went on: 'I am prepared for war and revolution combined.' And to remove all doubt as to the fact that this diagnosis suited him perfectly he added: 'Nor am I the slightest bit afraid of war; on the contrary, I am also indifferent to revolutionary or conservative, as I am to all mere words. You will perhaps very soon be persuaded that war forms part of my programme too.'

This was said not only with a view to Schleswig-Holstein and the impending clash with Denmark. It was dictated by the fundamental conviction that he had once, in connection with the Crimean War and the policy he had proposed in that situation, expressed in the words: 'Major crises constitute the weather that promotes Prussia's growth in that they have been fearlessly and perhaps also very ruthlessly exploited by us.'[19] When all was said and done, a solution of the German question was to be found only on the battlefield. Everything else must be subordinated to this view: 'Our strengthening cannot come from parliamentary and press politics but only from great power politics backed by arms, and we have not sufficient force and vigour to squander it on a bogus front and on empty words and Augustenburg.'

Bismarck in no way denied that a rapprochement with the Lesser German national movement was desirable. 'Possibly', he stated with deliberate vagueness, 'other stages will yet ensue that are not so far removed from your programme.' He simply wanted the order of priorities to be quite clear. For him it arose out of what he believed to be the incontestable fact that a policy that allowed its specific direction and practical steps to be dictated not by the international situation and the opportunities it presented but by something else was doomed to failure.

This clash with the advocate of a rival model of a conservative Lesser German unification policy made it quite clear that Bismarck's policy was in essence – and this was what always disturbed his king about it – one of conflict. A genuine alteration of the status quo at the international level he regarded as obtainable only by war. The concept of peaceful change seemed to him a mere fantasy. And he likewise dismissed as a political illusionist anyone who supposed that drastic changes in this sphere could in the long run be achieved and maintained without changes in internal conditions and circumstances.

It was no accident that in the letter to Goltz he mentioned war and revolution almost in the same breath. Just as war not infrequently represented a direct or indirect answer to revolutions, it was at the same time, as Bismarck well knew, itself a revolution not merely in international relations but also, in its repercussions and impetus, with regard to internal fronts and dispositions. The conclusion he drew from this insight was as pragmatic as it was revolutionary. It was that in a decisive conflict situation everything may serve as a means for the agent involved. That very fact gives him an extraordinary advantage.

It is hard to say at what point Bismarck first saw the Schleswig-Holstein question as the possible point of departure for the really major conflict to decide the German question and from what point he accordingly envisaged that kind of mobilization of all available forces. Unquestionably the argument with Goltz and with his proposals gave him an early push in that direction. On the other hand the exceptionally unfavourable political situation at home at the end of 1863 and the beginning of 1864 made him hesitate at first and leave everything to the dictate of events.

As it happened , of course, this very quickly removed all uncertainty, paving the way for what many contemporaries, in the light of the outcome, called the 'German revolution'. Like all revolutions, this too unfolded in accordance with its own laws or rather with the general conditions that entered into and influenced it. In making use of it as a means, Bismarck at the same time cleared the way for it; he became its involuntary proxy, so to speak. At the climax of his political career the results he occasioned exceeded to a greater extent than ever previously or subsequently the objectives he had had in mind – perhaps the very mark of individual historical greatness as well as being its greatest paradox.

Following the virtual exclusion of the Confederation and the concerted independent action taken by the two German great powers, the conflict over Schleswig-Holstein and the political future of the duchies had predictably escalated into a full-scale war involving Austria, Prussia and Denmark. In this the two German powers initially figured as, so to speak, self-appointed enforcers of international law in the shape of the 1852 Treaty of London. The crucial change of policy came at the beginning of March 1864 when Prussia and Austria, after a campaign that had so far met with only limited success, themselves repudiated the London agreements, pleading Danish intransigence, and decided to carry the war beyond Schleswig into Jutland, thus attacking Denmark itself. With this change of policy Vienna finally cut off its own line of retreat. For even at this stage Austria dispensed with a firm arrangement regarding the allies' military objective, namely the political future of the duchies, and let Prussia fob it off with vague phrases and the prospect of an agreement before an eventual peace conference. Henceforth Austrian policy on this question really was 'dictated by Berlin both in outline and in detail'. Bismarck could now use this lever to intervene in Austrian policy overall.

This thoroughly favourable position – seen from Prussia's point of view – was further reinforced by the progress of the campaign. Shortly before the conference to which Britain had invited the great powers towards the end of February got under way in London on 25 April 1864, Prussian troops stormed the Düppel entrenchments on 18 April to register a major military victory, albeit one that was paid for with heavy losses. This enabled Bismarck to negotiate in London from a position of strength.

However, in the light of the not inconsiderable danger – about which his own king had repeatedly and urgently warned him – of even a heterogeneous coalition lining up against Prussia, the Minister-President proceeded with extreme tactical caution. As with Austria, he did not commit himself at the London conference regarding his military objective. He appeared to be leaving it to the other powers to work out a viable solution. The fact was, he was confident from the outset that such a solution was most unlikely to emerge, given the divergent interests of the powers. An additional and in this case very welcome factor as far as Bismarck was concerned was that, as well as the signatories of the 1852 treaty, London had also invited the German Confederation. Its delegate to the conference, the Saxon Foreign Minister Count Beust, brought with him what even after the failure of Bavaria's attempt to get him to commit himself and the Confederation to Augustenburg was yet another scarcely reconcilable position. The conference dragged on for week after unproductive week without Bismarck once having to show his hand. Only after the failure of all attempts at compromise did it reach a point at which the Prussian Minister-President for a moment saw his position as seriously threatened.

The party most responsible for the London conference taking so favourable a course for him and for Prussia was without doubt the actual enemy. Although Denmark agreed to a temporary armistice on 9 May, over the issue itself it remained utterly inflexible, trusting to the eventual assistance of Britain and to its own military might. The compromise proposal of a purely personal union between Denmark and the duchies, with both territories retaining full political independence, was categorically rejected by Copenhagen. Since at the same time exploratory suggestions regarding a possible partition of Schleswig to round out the Danish state – which would then relinquish the remaining territories – likewise met with absolutely no response from the Danish side, the conference increasingly found itself in an impasse.

As a result, the only potential solutions left on the agenda were ones that unilaterally favoured one side or the other. Meanwhile the situation was clearly such that the British support for which Copenhagen hoped would have led to the immediate collapse of the conference and to a military conflict of scarcely calculable proportions between the various great powers – a step to which the British government, notwithstanding the pro-Danish mood of a large section of the British public, could not bring itself to proceed.

As Bismarck pointed out when towards the end of May he soberly took stock of Prussia's position vis-à-vis the Austrian government, in practice this left only three solutions – two if one disregarded the French compromise proposal for a partition of the region according to the principle of national self-determination, in other words on the basis of a plebiscite; that was hardly likely to find favour with such multi-nation states as Austria and Russia, for whom the principle represented a threat. Those two solutions were: either political independence for Schleswig-Holstein within the context of the German Confederation, whether under Augustenburg or under the Oldenburg line of the House of Gottorp, or alternatively annexation by Prussia.[20]

This was the point at which the 'thin thread' by which in Bismarck's words[21] Prussia had up to now 'pulled' Austria along threatened to break. Although in his negotiating brief for von Werther in Vienna the Prussian Minister-President apparently established a perfectly clear order of priorities, mentioning the possibility of union with Prussia only in third place in the event of the failure of both the Augustenburg and the Oldenburg solutions, the cat was now finally out of the bag. It was clear that the Prussian government was giving very serious consideration to the possibility of annexation; in fact for some weeks the idea had been receiving a public airing in Prussia – with massive encouragement from above. It was a man who had been a close friend of Bismarck's for many years, Count Arnim-Boitzenburg, a prominent member of the Conservative Party, who in May 1864 launched a petition in favour of annexation that collected more than 70,000 signatures in the space of a few weeks.

Moreover, Bismarck at the same time had his envoy address a catalogue of stiff Prussian demands to Augustenburg: he must 'guarantee a truly conservative form of government', to which end he must rid himself 'of his previous contacts and associations' and instead of the 1848 constitution introduce a version of the traditional corporative constitution.[22] By now even Rechberg could scarcely escape the impression that Prussia, given anything less than total compliance on Augustenburg's part, would seek to torpedo this and subsequently the Oldenburg solution too.

What it all boiled down to once again was the programme of joint supremacy in central Europe that Bismarck had worked out in December 1862. As the price for continued close collaboration between the two German great powers in future he demanded Prussian control over the duchies they had jointly taken from Denmark – whether indirectly, through a monarchical vassal who was wholly subservient in every respect, or directly through formal annexation.

This brought Austrian policy to a crossroads. Vienna now had to decide whether it wished to continue along the path it had taken up to now or whether it wished to turn back at the last minute. Those who, like the majority of Rechberg's ministers and like the powerful Greater German party in the Austrian government and among the Austrian public, continued to regard as possible and practicable a settlement of the German question along Austrian lines, that is to say along the lines of the Frankfurt federal reform plan, were obliged to support the latter course. But anyone who, like Rechberg himself, was beginning to despair of such a possibility and was continually on the look-out for alternatives as to how the Austrian state, now threatened from within as well as from without, could be strengthened and secured in the longer term must inevitably, despite all the counter-arguments, be as fascinated as ever by this idea that Bismarck kept on presenting of a conservative alliance between the two German great powers.

The upshot was that Austrian policy remained undecided. In the face of Prussia's annexation plan Vienna did now take up the Augustenburg solution, which it had firmly rejected hitherto, and the Foreign Ministry instructed its delegate to the conference to press for that solution in London. But as Berlin quickly recognized there was no real determination to draw any decisive conclusions and implement such a policy even at the price of a possible break with Prussia.

Bismarck therefore saw only a small risk in taking up a position at the London conference in support of the Austrian proposal, which to Denmark's huge disappointment provoked not a curt rejection by the British government but merely a counter-proposal for a partition of Schleswig along the frontier dividing German from Dane.

Prior to the actual negotiations, however, the Prussian Minister-President felt it advisable, not least in view of the attitude of his king, to confront the claimant to the throne, Prince Frederick of Augustenburg, with the very extensive demands that he had already outlined for the benefit of the Austrian government. This he did during an interview at the Foreign Ministry on the night of 1 June 1864, an interview that gave rise to a great deal of comment both at the time and subsequently.[23]

Augustenburg, who had earlier been received in the most kindly fashion by King William, was of course quite clear in his mind that he must go a long way to meet Prussia, on whose attitude and future military successes everything depended – very much farther, in fact, than the popular movement backing him, at least outside Prussia, would consider justified. Nevertheless, there were bounds that, as he put it himself later, it would not only be 'contrary to his honour' but also politically suicidal for him to overstep: a mere puppet of Prussia and of the hated Bismarck regime was something he could not and would not be allowed to become.

Given this starting position, it was a simple matter for Bismarck to outmanoeuvre Augustenburg. The prince could either say amen to everything: to the points already mentioned as well as to the establishment of a Prussian naval port and the consequent radical restriction of his military sovereignty as well. That would probably have cost him his base not only in the duchies but also in the national movement and among the governments of the medium-sized states, because it can be assumed without hesitation that Bismarck would have arranged for dissemination and interpretation of the prince's concessions to that effect. Or he could raise certain objections, as indeed he did. In which case he supplied Bismarck, Bismarck's king, the Austrian government, the remaining powers and, in a suitably administered form, the Prussian public too with the proof they were all looking for that he did not offer adequate guarantees of constructive neighbourly relations, that he was ungrateful and that his policy was simply a fresh instance of small-state egoism.

In other words, it was virtually immaterial how Augustenburg acted, which in turn renders superfluous all questions as to whether he might have been cleverer in this, that, or the other respect. What Bismarck 'summed up' as – allegedly – his 'overall impression of the three-hour discussion' was in practice established from the very first moment, in fact was the object of the whole interview: 'That the prince regards us not with feelings of gratitude but as an unwelcome creditor to satisfy whom as incompletely as possible he is prepared to mobilize the support of the estates and even of Austria.'[24] Bismarck wanted a Schleswig that was independent in name alone, and all Augustenburg had to decide was whether or not he wished to be a sort of princely Minister-President.

Unreserved acceptance of the Prussian demands by the prince would probably have facilitated Prussia's relations with Austria for a time. But in the long run it would have put fresh curbs on the freedom of manoeuvre that Prussia had now acquired. So there are grounds for assuming that even in that event Bismarck would have sought to wreck Augustenburg's candidacy. Now, however, with the prince having expressed predictable misgivings and objections, he already had all the arguments he needed in order to put it to his king and subsequently to the Austrian government as well that the Augustenburg solution was intolerable – both from the point of view of Prussian interests and from that of conservative interests in general.

External circumstances made it possible for Bismarck to refrain completely from making official statements and so avoid a fresh anti-Prussian reaction among the German public. For just as he was secretly preparing to hedge his bet by holding out, chiefly for Russia's benefit, the prospect of Prussian support for the candidacy of Oldenburg, the London conference finally ran aground on the question of how exactly any partition of Schleswig was to be undertaken.

After weeks of toing and froing, during which the Prussian side quite deliberately placed a further obstacle in the way of agreement by deciding to take up the plebiscite proposal favoured by France but firmly rejected by Austria and Russia, the delegates of the powers eventually parted without a resolution on 25 June 1864. They left matters to be decided by further hostilities between Denmark and the two German powers. In fact they did more: the principle of the joint responsibility of the great powers in international disputes of this order of magnitude was in practice abandoned by them in this case, although London in particular still clung to it verbally and for a while a British intervention seemed not entirely out of the question.

After that the final military defeat of Denmark was merely a question of time. Only three days later, on 28 June, Prussian troops crossed to the island of Alsen in a move that once again made a powerful impression on the German public. Copenhagen having finally despaired of receiving any help from Britain, Denmark signed a provisional peace treaty on 1 August that was then simply confirmed by the definitive Treaty of Vienna of 30 October 1864. In this the King of Denmark relinquished all rights in the duchies of Schleswig, Holstein and Lauenburg in favour of the Austrian emperor and the Prussian king.

With this an important objective of the German national movement was achieved. The policy of the two German great powers, hitherto so decried, now appeared in an entirely new light. However, their joint stand in favour of Augustenburg at the London conference had also given rise to the expectation that the two powers would now simply hand over their prize – an expectation that for many people was no longer entirely unclouded, particularly since more and more voices were now being raised, mainly inside Prussia itself, in favour of Prussian annexation. This meant that Austria was once again faced with the question whether, with the war now over, it ought not to execute a decisive change of course and attempt, jointly with its traditional partners in the Confederation and in collaboration with the Schleswig-Holstein movement, to push the Augustenburg solution through, if necessary in defiance of Prussia.

Such a development had not been hard to foresee. From the Prussian point of view it was by no means without its dangers. And it is difficult to judge how things might have turned out had Austria determinedly adopted such a course at this stage of the proceedings. There was a whole series of reasons why it did not do so. Vienna's reluctance to take this step cannot be attributed simply and solely to the alleged incompetence and irresolution of Austrian policy.

One of the chief reasons was the extremely difficult financial situation that Austria had been in for some time and that the burdens of war had aggravated further; the national debt was now in excess of five times the country's total annual income, whereas in Prussia's case it amounted to hardly more than one year's income. This enormous burden of debt, coupled as it was with stagnating revenues, created extraordinary problems, particularly in home affairs, and constituted a strong incentive to the country's leaders to avoid any conflict on the foreign policy front at present – unless they wished to plunge into such a conflict like bankrupts, seeing no other way out. There was also the fact that, in the wake of the events of recent months, the traditional coalition within the Confederation looked like providing an extremely fragile base both in itself and in relation to the once-dominant power – if indeed they managed to get it together again at all, given that even a pro-Oldenburg party had formed in its bosom meanwhile. And finally a partnership with the Schleswig-Holstein movement, of however loose a kind, was something at which Vienna continued to shy, particularly since there was no predicting how Russia, which wanted

Oldenburg on the throne, would react to such a partnership and what attitude would be taken by France, which was all too obviously seeking to get back into the game by one means or another.

Bismarck nourished these reflections and anxieties on the Austrian side quite deliberately and from an early stage in a realistic appraisal of the dangers of a pro-Augustenburg initiative on the part of the empire. At the same time he stressed for the benefit of Rechberg and his associates but also for the benefit of Francis Joseph himself the advantages that continued collaboration would have for both powers and for the preservation of the traditional order in central Europe. In a directive sent to the Prussian envoy in Vienna on 14 July this was set out in programmatic terms: 'We regard the Danish conflict as being in essence an episode in the struggle of the monarchical principle against the European revolution, and we allow our handling of the duchies question to be guided by our views concerning its repercussions on that greater question of our time.' The most important result of the way in which the two German great powers had handled the Schleswig-Holstein affair hitherto was the 'furtherance of conservative attitudes' that could already be observed. To develop and underpin this must be their true objective. They must therefore, Bismarck stated in this document dating from the critical stage of the war, not jeopardize 'the great conservative interests that we are defending' even 'for the sake of temporary good relations with Britain'.[25] The same applied to Prussia's relations with France, as Bismarck added in another directive written on the same day.[26] Should Paris wish to start an unprovoked war it would be easy in the circumstances to keep France in check by means of 'harmonious collaboration' between the 'three continental great powers together with the rest of Germany', even if the power of France was 'reinforced by that of Italy'. For that kind of 'harmonious collaboration' would not merely be 'indicated in the nature of things'; it would also be 'guaranteed by the attitude of the monarchs and leading statesmen' concerned. Because presumably it was quite clear to everyone that in this context 'France's victory would be the victory of revolution'.

It is precisely this denunciation of France as the torch-bearer of revolution, coupled with the vision of a restoration of the alliance of the three conservative eastern powers and the veiled offer of an unconditional defence of Austria's interests in Italy, that exposes the markedly tactical character of Bismarck's whole line of argument. These were set-pieces from the political programme and credo of the arch-conservatives in Berlin and Vienna, which Bismarck had discussed often enough in critical and somewhat aloof terms. When in a letter to his wife from Karlsbad he speaks of 'a heavy day of Emperor and Rechberg work',[27] one senses how he had a mental picture of a stubborn old horse that had to be harnessed to the wagon by all available means.

Historians have nevertheless again sought to see this as the prelude to a policy that, not least in the conservative interest, was seriously on the look-out for alternatives to a military solution to the German dualism with all the domestic and foreign policy consequences that that would probably involve. The arguments and supporting evidence adduced here are not inconsiderable, particularly since they have been put forward with great brilliance and with an eye for the wider context. In the final analysis, of course, the theories and interpretations based thereon are confined to the realm of speculation. In an understandable endeavour not to see the course of events in too narrowly single-track a fashion, they underestimate from the very beginning the element of constraint that characterized Bismarck's policy. They ascribe to it a freedom it never in fact possessed. This becomes very clear when we soberly analyse the result to which that policy initially led.

That result was the draft of a Prussian-Austrian convention that Bismarck and Rechberg, after four days of talks, placed before their monarchs at Schönbrunn on 24 August. Into this went everything that Bismarck had put to the Austrians in repeated diplomatic thrusts over the past few weeks in terms of arguments in favour of continuing and possibly even extending the Schleswig-Holstein alliance between the two German great powers. Beyond that it also reflected the Prussian minimum programme that Bismarck had outlined to the Austrian envoy in December 1862 as a basis for possible collaboration between the powers. Only the main geographical orientation, the focus of Austria's future political interests, was slightly shifted in this definition of them, though without there being any change in intention, the principle of agreement on the basis of a clear demarcation of spheres of influence remaining the same. Vienna's proper direction of thrust was now stated to be Italy, the revision of the 1859 treaties and in particular the reincorporation of Lombardy in the empire. In return Vienna promised Berlin, should its revision policy be successful, to accept Prussian annexation of the duchies and so recognize Prussia's absolute hegemony in northern Germany. The empire demanded only that the consequent shift in the balance of power be compensated for in the Confederation as well by the admission of certain Austrian territories that had not previously been members.

Behind the whole thing, then, was a readiness on Austria's part to consent in future, at least in practice, to parity in the control of federal affairs, in other words to a policy for the Confederation that, as in the period before 1848, should be the instrument of an agreed policy on the part of the two German great powers. This was the significance of both sides' once again stressing their determination, come what might, to dictate to the Confederation how the Schleswig-Holstein question was to be settled and not to get involved in any deals with the other members of that body.

What lay behind such considerations seems even in retrospect to open up quite extraordinary perspectives. It appears to indicate an alternative to the formation of a Lesser German national state that could have led Europe in a quite different direction and might possibly have spared it a great deal. In practice, notwithstanding Napoleon, the sympathetic attitude of the British public and the successes of 1859, the principle of national self-determination and the national ideal had hardly spread beyond western Europe as yet. The whole of central and eastern Europe was still dominated by states that had evolved historically, states that in their peculiar cultural and religious traditions, in their shared history and language, in their economic constitution and administrative organization, and not least in the feeling of oneness among their subjects were after all something more than mere dynastic agglomerations. Burdened though it was with problems that others did not face in so acute a form, Austria still in principle represented the prevailing type of state and society in that part of the world and not, as it did a few decades later, a political and social breed that seemed almost archaic, a monument to a rapidly disappearing historical past. And it still seemed conceivable that the frontier lines that the western European revolutions of the eighteenth century had crossed only locally and temporarily and within which the social structure in particular was still essentially determined by tradition might continue to be held and possibly even be reinforced; with respect to Italy the draft convention even contemplated a kind of 'roll back'.

The conservative thinking of the time clung to all this. And it is not surprising that in the subsequent course of events such arguments, seen in the light of the devastating triumphs of ultra-nationalism and of dramatic social upheavals, should have appeared in a fresh perspective.

However, this ought not to blind us to the fact that even at the time such a way of looking at things was a product of mere wishful thinking. Its spokesmen sought desperately to conceal from themselves the fact that in reality form had long outlived content here and the real revolution was bound up not with ideas and external power but with an inexorable process of change affecting all economic and social relationships. What this kind of thinking, anchored as it was more firmly than ever in the past, represented to itself as possible was largely without any foothold in reality or any chance of effective implementation, and significantly this was true even at the more superficial level of day-to-day politics. Because it was obvious, when all was said and done – and, sober pragmatist that he was and remained, Bismarck is unlikely not to have seen it too – that all the requisite preconditions were lacking for a revival of a policy of containment and anti-revolutionary bloc-forming along pre-1848 lines, even in the field of current inter-power relations.

The question we have to ask ourselves is who, apart from Vienna itself – and even there a different course was conceivable – who in Europe had any interest in joining an anti-French front under the banner of the struggle against revolution? Britain, as of course even the Hofburg knew, was ruled out from the start. What about Russia? There too the pro-western, pro-French party was going from strength to strength. It was increasingly directing attention towards domestic policy matters, including the obligatory social reform – particularly in the sphere of agrarian structure, where an initial important step had been taken with the abolition of serfdom in 1861 – but also urgent problems of judicial and administrative reform as well as the whole sphere of education and training. This meant that for the kind of crusading mentality that would have been required here, given that there was now little serious conflict between French and Russian interests, the proper conditions did not currently obtain in Russia either. Added to which, the shift in Russian interests from Europe to Asia in the aftermath of the Crimean War still very largely dictated the country's foreign policy orientation.

That left the states of the German Confederation. But here too the situation – as compared to 1859, for instance – had changed considerably. As the two German great powers had appeared to be co-operating ever more closely, so the small and medium-sized states had for their part drawn closer and closer together. The objectives pursued by individual governments were anything but uniform. Yet in no case was there any suggestion of a determinedly anti-French policy. On the contrary, these states saw Napoleon III as a kind of natural protector who might support their own endeavours.

Realistically, then, Prussia was the only partner that presented itself for a revisionary policy conceived as anti-French and anti-revolutionary. Yet that was unquestionably too weak a basis for a political course set on offensive operations and conflict. It was therefore in keeping with an entirely sober assessment of the situation that both the Austrian emperor and the Prussian king should have refused to ratify the draft submitted to them by their respective Foreign Ministers.

But an approach unclouded by wishful thinking has to go a step further. It has to ask whether the proposed partnership, the terms of which may have been largely formulated by Rechberg for the Austrian side but which in substance went back to Bismarckian proposals, was not in fact, as far as Prussia was concerned, aimed at diversion and deception from the outset. Was it not simply intended as the tow-rope by means of which Prussian policy might continue to pull Austria along in its wake until such time as Berlin, given a situation unfavourable to Vienna, saw fit to sever it? Are those historians right after all who see developments from the Danish peace until 1866 primarily in terms of a deliberate, planned preparation for armed conflict on Prussia's part, a run-up to the decisive struggle for hegemony in central Europe?

Posed in that exaggerated form, the question is undoubtedly wide of the mark. It suggests once again, this time from the other direction, a freedom of decision and alternative possibilities that simply were not present in that kind of way. And once again it was not the intention of the individual historical agent that was crucial but the pressure of circumstances, to which with a greater or lesser degree of flexibility the agent adapted himself. To put it another way, the question of whether or not Bismarck's policy towards Austria was dishonest from the start and intended solely to deceive and trick is ultimately of secondary importance. What matters is that it had to acquire an appearance of deceitfulness and trickery in retrospect if it did not wish to run aground itself – on the impossibility of its alleged or actual objectives ever being achieved in practice.

For this much is certain, whatever the intentions of those directly involved: the substance of and basis for a Prusso-Austrian partnership at this time were so feeble from the very beginning that such a partnership could not possibly have lasted. Not only did it run counter to the spirit of the age, to the liberal as well as to the national ideal, and to the prevailing trends within the international system and among those who chiefly upheld it; it was also incompatible with quite concrete and ultimately invincible interests and *de facto* decisions of long standing.

This emerged in the immediate aftermath of Schönbrunn when Austria tried to take this special relationship between the two states that Bismarck had so vigorously invoked and put it to the test, as it were. At issue was the question of the economic and commercial relations of the two countries, specifically Austria's relations with the Prussian-dominated German Customs Union.

Since 1862, the year of the Franco-Prussian commercial treaty and of Austria's counter-offensive, culminating in the July 1862 proposal to set up a central European free trade area, Vienna had gradually been giving ground. In direct continuation of the policy that Prussia had pursued for years and that enjoyed the vigorous support of the country's principal economic interest groups, Bismarck had shown himself utterly unyielding in the face of all Austrian advances. He had concentrated entirely, as he had said he would in the December memorandum of 1862, on using the treaty renewal due in 1865 at the latest to bind the Customs Union even more tightly together and seal it off against Austria. In order to achieve this objective he had even gone so far, at the end of 1863 – in other words, at the first climax of the Schleswig-Holstein crisis – as to cancel the Customs Union treaty by way of a precaution. The intention was to bring the governments involved under increased pressure from interested parties and from their own budgetary interests.

The Customs Union question in particular, of course, belies all attempts to portray Bismarck as a wholly free agent by showing the extent to which he was himself a prisoner of circumstances. The organization now constituted so solid a network of interests that breaking out of it or dissolving it in favour of other combinations scarcely seemed a serious possibility any more. The negotiations for its renewal were therefore, however tough and long-drawn-out, no more than a bluffing contest over details.

At least, they were for the northern and central German states, which duly submitted with varying degrees of alacrity to the terms imposed by Prussia as the dominant power. What was not quite so certain was how the two southern German kingdoms of Bavaria and Württemberg and in their wake Hesse-Darmstadt and Nassau would react. This had been Bismarck's starting-point in the December memorandum of 1862. Not the least of the eventualities reflected in his Prussian minimum programme as outlined to Károlyi was that Bavaria and Württemberg might indeed decide to withdraw from the Customs Union.

Of course, such a step would have made political sense only if it had formed the prelude to a rival initiative on a grand scale. The actual organizer of the resistance, the Bavarian Foreign Minister Ludwig von der Pfordten, an exceptionally flexible and imaginative thinker who in different circumstances might have had the makings of a major opponent of Bismarck, was fully aware of this. His attempt to torpedo the Customs Union negotiations therefore took as its aim an idea that Bavaria had been pursuing for decades, namely the creation of a third centre of power in central Europe. This, it was believed in essence, would constitute a 'Kerndeutschland', a German nucleus with a corresponding power of attraction over all German territories.

However – and it was this that sealed its fate – such an idea was unacceptable, despite the more pro-Austrian than pro-Prussian attitude of its advocates, to Austria's conservatives as well as to those who spoke for the interests of the Austrian Empire as a whole. It carried the risk of a dissolution of that multi-nation state following from the creation of a national centre of gravity that lay outside Austria and beyond Austrian control. So for the role of protector of a group of states working towards this end, greatly though Vienna was inclined to support their concrete actions as a counter-weight to Prussia, Austria was hardly a serious candidate. On the other hand it became clear once again that states that were keen to leave the Customs Union for essentially political reasons had no intention whatever of bowing to any plans for a Greater Austrian tariff union in the Schwarzenberg tradition; so radical a reorientation seemed more than their domestic economies could reasonably be expected to undergo.

In this state of affairs, which really could not be said to have been brought about by Bismarck's personal skill but was a product of circumstances, existing interests and decisions previously arrived at, all Vienna could hope for in the economic and commercial sphere too was a partnership-type solution along the lines of the 'spirit of Schönbrunn'. The plan for a central European tariff union together with all the political objectives that lay behind it no longer had any chance of becoming reality, as Rechberg was forced to admit. The only possibility was a special relationship with regard to commercial and economic policy similar to the general political understanding with Berlin and the Customs Union that Austria appeared in the mean time to have achieved.

Even this kind of special relationship, however, was fiercely opposed by economic policy experts inside Prussia, with Rudolf von Delbrück at their head. In view of the interests involved on both sides, they argued, the scope for viable compromises was virtually non-existent, and the whole thing would only lead to fresh tensions. For the same reasons they objected to Rechberg's request that the new Customs Union treaty about to be concluded should once again incorporate a provision to the effect that before the expiry of that treaty negotiations should be put in hand regarding a possible tariff union with Austria. This too, they claimed, was simply sowing the seeds of fresh conflicts and evading a straightforward clarification of the whole situation.

Objectively speaking, both points were difficult to refute. And it has yet to be shown satisfactorily that the position taken up by Delbrück and his senior civil servants was dictated not by economic policy considerations alone but by preferences with regard to national policy and reservations about Austria – to say nothing of a hostile bias against their own government, of which Bismarck spoke at the climax of the dispute.[28] But, greatly though the whole episode irritated him at first, the Prussian

Minister-President did not close his eyes to the logic of the counter-arguments. Indeed, once he had calmed down they provided him with further evidence that the restoration of an anti-revolutionary alliance between Prussia and Austria favoured by the conservatives of both sides was a mere illusion.

Nevertheless, he energetically set about the task of making it look as if he was co-operating with Rechberg as fully as possible. As he had stressed in a letter to his ministers von Bodelschwingh and von Itzenplitz towards the end of August 1864, it was 'of the greatest importance for us to secure the goodwill of the Viennese Cabinet and to strengthen the position within that Cabinet of the ministers who support the Prussian alliance'.[29] Rechberg, he repeated several times, must be placed in a position, even after the decision had in practice already been taken, where he could give the impression in public and also for his emperor's benefit that nothing whatever had been decided as yet and that positive progress would soon be made on the fresh basis of a special relationship between the two states.

In the end, however, such a policy was decisively rejected by the Prussian king, who on the basis of the forecasts of experts in economic and commercial policy argued precisely that the good relations with Vienna that had now been achieved could be preserved only if the Austrian public and Austria's political leaders were told the plain truth and were left in no doubt as to what was possible and what was not. While Bismarck was briefly absent from Berlin the decision was taken, following a threat of resignation by Delbrück, to accede to none of Austria's requests and to rule out a tariff union altogether, in other words to provide for no reopening of negotiations in the new Customs Union treaty. The decision was not in fact finalized and communicated to Austria until after Bismarck's return at the end of October. Nevertheless the deed, if not so much in substance as in how it was handled formally, was a decision against Bismarck. It very clearly showed the limits to a policy of compromise with Austria inside Prussia itself, even if and in fact precisely when it was interpreted, as it was by Bismarck, purely from the point of view of Prussia's power interest.

Those limits became visible in Austria too around the same time. The Greater German party under the leadership of Minister of State von Schmerling urged the emperor not to let himself be pushed any farther by Bismarck and by his own Foreign Minister, who was obviously conforming entirely to Bismarck's line. Austria would gain nothing by pursuing such a course, as Berlin's treatment of its requests with regard to commercial and customs policy showed very clearly, and in the future it stood to lose everything. The idea of an Austro-Prussian condominium in central Europe was obscuring the fact that the manner of its present collaboration with Prussia increasingly undermined the foundations of the hegemony Austria had enjoyed hitherto. Those foundations lay in its alliance with the small and medium-sized German states and in its support for all those forces and interests that opposed Prussia and Prussian hegemony.

In fact Francis Joseph was not prepared, after the obvious failure of the Frankfurt plan and the visible successes of Austro-Prussian collaboration over the Schleswig-Holstein question, wholly to accept this argument and undertake a fresh change of course in favour of the Greater German party. But nor was he unimpressed by the fact that his Foreign Minister, who was coming under such heavy fire from this quarter, was obviously himself a prey to ever-increasing doubts as to whether his policy of co-operating with Prussia really did rest on premisses conducive to the furtherance of Austrian interests.

Those premisses, as Bismarck had constantly stressed to Rechberg, were the conservative ideal, the principle of the anti-revolutionary solidarity of crowned heads and the regulatory function of the two German great powers in the central European region. Even after Schönbrunn he had several times repeated this in lengthy private letters. 'Unity of Germany against internal and external enemies', 'restoration of the foundations of monarchical government' and 'neutralization of revolution' – such, according to his letter of 8 September 1864, were the objectives jointly to be pursued and the foundation of 'an active common policy'.[30]

What increasingly disconcerted the Austrian Foreign Minister, however, was not only the fact that emphasis on such common interests went hand in hand, more and more obviously, with a complete absence of any concrete progress over the tariff question. A great deal more disturbing was the radical manner in which Bismarck dismissed everything that did not seem likely to further the very narrowly defined power-political interests of both sides. This tendency reached its climax in a letter of 29 September 1864 in which Bismarck sought once again to play down the importance of the tariff question in the context of the wider concept of future collaboration between the two powers and to persuade Rechberg that Prussia's wholly intransigent behaviour in this respect did not affect the real issue.

The foundation of that collaboration lay, the Prussian Minister-President stressed, in the convergent power-political interests of the two states and nowhere else. That was why he was backing it with all his might, in other words 'not because I am aware of our common membership of the German Empire but purely on the grounds of my assessment of the interests of Prussia and its Crown'. That, he went on, ought to be Rechberg's attitude too: 'I believe . . . we should be surer of the progress of our common course if we were both to take our stand on the practical ground of Cabinet politics without allowing the situation to be obscured for us by the fogs that emanate from the doctrines of German political sentimentalists.'[31]

This was supposed to render Rechberg immune to the arguments of the Greater German party and of his colleague Schmerling. But at the same time it was just the sort of thing to scare someone like Rechberg stiff, for the Austrian Foreign Minister was after all very much a politician of conservative principle, and to revive the old misgivings that the outspoken statements of his Frankfurt colleague had aroused in him back in the 1850s. 'It increases to a more than ordinary degree the difficulties of conducting business', he told Francis Joseph when he showed him Bismarck's letter, 'when one is dealing with a man who so openly professes political cynicism as to reply to the passage in my letter where I say that we must make the maintenance of the Confederation and of the legitimately acquired rights of the German princes the foundation of our policy . . . with the outrageous piece of claptrap that we both take our stand on the practical ground of Cabinet politics without allowing the situation to be obscured for us by fogs emanating from the doctrines of German political sentimentalism. This is language worthy of a Cavour. Holding fast to what is lawful is foggy sentimentalism! The task of keeping this gentleman in check and talking him out of his megalomanic utilitarian politics . . . is one that exceeds human powers.'[32]

This may not have been meant quite as pessimistically as it sounded. But since Francis Joseph currently saw no other course than that of continued collaboration with Prussia he inevitably gained the impression that Rechberg, severely disappointed in his more far-reaching expectations, was no longer the right man to pursue such a policy successfully. 'Very true, alas', he noted in the margin of the letter, 'except that the alliance with Prussia is still the only right one in the circumstances, and we must therefore continue our thankless efforts to keep Prussia on the right lines and within the fold of the law.'[33]

So Rechberg's dismissal at the end of October 1864 did not indicate any change of course. On the contrary his successor, Count Mensdorff-Pouilly, a politically undistinguished cavalry general who had been used for occasional diplomatic jobs and whose most recent post had been as governor-general of Galicia, was to pursue the policy of Austro-Prussian co-operation, if at a slightly more disabused level, so to speak. Not even inside Austria itself, however, was this entirely clear. The Greater German party therefore reacted to Mensdorff's appointment with increased activity and did everything in its power to introduce a new policy. As expressed principally by Ludwig von Biegeleben, its objective was to use an alliance with the small and medium-sized German states and an understanding with Napoleon III to create the preconditions for a fresh initiative aimed at reforming the Confederation to Austria's advantage. In this it did not shy even at the prospect of a confrontation with Prussia.

This was the complete opposite of what, written in Biegeleben's own hand, had been agreed at Schönbrunn. It shows that Vienna too had fundamental alternatives to hand, that the Austrians were likewise always playing to deceive and outwit their opponent of the time. The big difference was simply that in Vienna no agreement was reached, no real decision was made as to the course to be pursued and people oscillated perpetually between the possible alternatives, whereas in Berlin a decision was now arrived at very swiftly.

Rechberg's dismissal meant the removal from the scene of the one man who in Bismarck's estimation might possibly have been prepared, on the basis of a sober and at the same time traditionally conservative view of things, to alter the organization of central European affairs in the direction of joint supremacy for Prussia and Austria. Now, however, the anti-Prussian tendency would sooner or later regain the ascendancy; a situation would arise in which Prussia might possibly be able to assert its interests only by violent means. 'Should the Schmerling policy gain the upper hand in Vienna', Bismarck had prophesied to the king from Biarritz on 10 October, 'we must be prepared not only for a striving for the support of the western powers but also the establishment of closer relations between Austria and the medium-sized states; presumably', he had added, 'Austria would then immediately take steps over the Holstein question by bringing motions before the Confederation in the interests of the medium-sized states.'[34]

Certainly Bismarck had never lost sight of such a possibility; characteristically he had already taken the French ambassador to Vienna, the Duke of Gramont, on one side at Schönbrunn and made very extensive advances to him regarding a rapprochement between Prussia and France. But that was nothing unusual with Bismarck. It formed part of his normal procedure always to air all the possibilities and as far as possible keep things in a state of flux – a procedure that confused his contemporaries and has continued to confuse historians, misleading them into often untenable constructions.

After Rechberg's fall, however, Bismarck obviously saw very little chance, if we examine all his statements in the light of the secondary intentions that underlay them, of reaching even so much as a temporary agreement with Austria under the conditions obtaining at the time. Rechberg's fall as it were provided him with practical proof that the idea of forming an anti-revolutionary bloc made up of Prussia and Austria lacked the power and was too feebly anchored in the reality of existing forces and interests to be of any use as far as extending and consolidating Prussian power was concerned – the sole objective he was using it to pursue. In other words, the conservative ideal could obviously not be harnessed in the service of Prussian power; the 1815 situation was not reversible in favour of Berlin and of a Prussian hegemony in central Europe. So all that was in fact left now was something he had always kept in mind as a possibility and circled round without ever working it up into a precise programme: the harnessing not of the conservative ideal and all that went with it but of the liberal and national ideal, the reality of the newly emerging forces and interests.

Hitherto it had been only individual factors that he had envisaged using as tools: commercial policy interests, the Lesser German ideal, the principle of representation. They could be incorporated as self-contained elements in an essentially conservative overall picture. Now, however, he found himself with no choice but to yoke them together in a way that gave him reason to fear that he might be putting himself in the position of the sorcerer's apprentice, who summons up forces that, applied to a particular objective, eventually elude control to an ever-increasing extent.

Bismarck was indubitably aware of this, despite the pressure on him to decide and to act. His 'Acheronta movebo' was not simply one of his favourite expressions; he also knew the context from which it was taken. And he was always quite clear about how much risk attached to a political appeal to the 'underworld'. It was one thing to recruit auxiliary troops by unorthodox means; it was another to mobilize a whole army of forces that could perhaps for a short while be focused on a common objective but that over a more extended period would hardly consent to remain in step without far-reaching concessions.

This also explains why, despite the fact that he was now finally convinced that a confrontation was unavoidable, he spent the whole of 1865, with the international situation very much in his favour, in a state of some vacillation: there was no getting away from the fact that developments, once set in motion, might overshoot the desired objective and the sceptical 'fert unda nec regitur' he so often quoted turn out even in its first part to have been an exaggerated hope. The complaints about the burdens of official business and the constraints of his existence began to increase in frequency again around this time, indicating very clearly that Bismarck found himself at a crossroads. He had a presentiment that the next step would finally cut him off from the past and carry him into a highly uncertain future.

His Schleswig-Holstein policy and developments at home since his taking office had in a sense, even if such had been far from his original intention, led him back into the past. In both spheres, that of domestic as well as that of foreign policy, he had allayed the initial misgivings of the conservatives. He now appeared more than ever before to be inwardly their man as well, an unqualified opponent of all the tendencies of the age that radically challenged the traditional order. With him, they were able to believe, the old Prussia, the monarchical authoritarian state on its traditional corporative foundation, had come back to life. The temptation may have suggested itself very strongly to Bismarck to continue to comply with such estimates of himself and the expectations associated with them and to see his true objective in the revival and reinvigoration of Prussian power within the traditional framework.

However, he was not only ambitious enough but also level-headed enough to see clearly that this, precisely when considered from the standpoint of Prussian tradition, was only a pseudo-alternative. Prussia could hold its own in its internal and external form only if it aspired beyond that form, if in order to preserve its own essence it made itself the spearhead of change. The choice, as he expressed it in parallel to his statement regarding a possible revolution, was between being the hammer and being the anvil; in a time of such upheaval there was no third alternative. Yet he personally was a far cry from the textbook image of the smith: the forces and interests concerned here were supra-individual ones. The only thing the agent could do was to try, in a specific situation and at an opportune moment, so to combine and contrast those forces and interests that, as it were, their parallelogram favoured an attempt at a solution that was in line with his own intentions.

So when he hesitated in the months following Rechberg's fall he was at the same time waiting – waiting for a constellation of circumstances that would admit of not just a minor but a major solution. Such a solution must not simply free the Prussian state from the shackles of the German Confederation and the German dualism. It must also lead it out of its domestic stalemate, which in the present circumstances, all the harsh words on both sides notwithstanding, appeared to be insurmountable.

That Bismarck was now finally ready, against all the expectations of his current political friends, to contemplate a reversal of the domestic fronts as well seems on sober examination to be as clear as the fact that such a constellation of circumstances was not at the moment in sight. Only one of the requisite preconditions was so far fulfilled and even that one, formally speaking, only in part: the assured continuance of the Customs Union in its present form and in conjunction with acceptance of the free trade agreement with France.

In October 1864 the two southern German kingdoms of Bavaria and Württemberg, with Hesse-Darmstadt and Nassau following in their wake, had decided to accept Prussia's terms and approve an extension of the treaty for a further twelve years. An agreement along these lines came into final effect in May 1865. This meant, of course – and it was undoubtedly a most significant fact – that the basic premiss of the Prussian minimum programme of 1862, namely the possibility of southern Germany with-drawing from the common customs, commercial and economic zone, now no longer obtained. However, before Prussia could embark with any prospect of success on the maximum programme outlined on the same occasion, at least three crucial conditions must be fulfilled. First there must be a readiness for conflict amounting to a mood of military determination on the part of Prussia's leaders, some of whom had only recently been nursing the ideal of an arch-conservative condominium of the two German great powers in central Europe. The second requirement was for an international situation that, as in the Danish War but this time in a very much broader context, made it appear possible and practicable to isolate the conflict and confine it to the chief protagonists and their immediate supporters. Finally it was necessary to establish in the mind of the political public both inside and outside Prussia a Prussian war aim that, even if perhaps only in the light of the prospects it opened up, looked attractive enough to set in train a reorientation of opinion, at least in certain circles, and pave the way for a realignment of the political fronts. The fact that the money needed for a war was difficult to obtain, given the conflict with the House of Deputies, did of course play an important part. But it was hardly of such decisive importance as to have governed Bismarck's timing, as has recently been alleged: even with the requisite finance largely assured, Bismarck continued to temporize until the above-mentioned cardinal conditions seemed to him to be in some measure fulfilled.

With regard to the first of those conditions, this was relatively quickly the case, despite persistent misgivings about the consequences to which a large-scale conflict with the traditional conservative overlord of central Europe might give rise. The problems – which the other side could aggravate whenever it chose – of a condominium on one's own doorstep, so to speak, were too enormous not to have fostered an eagerness to bring such a situation to an end at all costs, including that of an armed conflict. At the crucial meeting of the Prussian Crown Council on 29 May 1865 it was not only agreed that the objective must be the annexation of the duchies by Prussia. In accepting Moltke's remark 'that to accomplish this objective Prussia must not shrink even from the prospect of war with Austria', a remark that was at first more technical in its implications, dictated by the chief of staff's calculation of the chances of military success, the council at the same time accepted the possibility of a military confrontation – except, that is, for the crown prince, who protested vehemently against their entertaining the idea of waging a 'civil war in Germany'.[35]

The second condition was not so easily fulfilled. Bismarck may, as Moltke noted, have assured the Crown Council meeting of 29 May that in the event of a war between Prussia and Austria 'France and Russia would presumably abide by a benevolent neutrality' – Britain clearly not even rating a mention any more after its conduct in the final phase of the Schleswig-Holstein crisis. In reality France's attitude was still uncertain. Whatever happened, Paris could be expected to demand a decisive say in the matter and to attempt to get its position respected by one side or the other. And how Russia might then react was likewise impossible to predict. More precise soundings and more detailed agreements were needed here if Prussia did not wish to risk a major European war.

Caution was all the more recommended since it was widely expected that, with France's attempt to gain a foothold in Mexico already beginning to look like a failure, Napoleon III would soon be turning his main attention back to central Europe. So although the international situation following the conclusion of the Treaty of Vienna was not unfavourable as far as Prussia was concerned – or was at any rate more favourable than it had been for many years – Bismarck had good reason to argue for a postponement of the final decision and, despite mounting friction with Austria, to advise against pushing forward too fast.

There was also the fact – and this is probably the true explanation of his much-discussed hesitation and indecisiveness throughout 1865 – that annexation of the duchies as a war aim appeared to be neither popular enough nor comprehensive enough to be of much help in making any real breach in the front of public opinion and the various political groups inside and outside Prussia. Yet just this seemed for two reasons to be urgently desirable, indeed almost indispensable: to strengthen Prussia's position before and during a war, and to provide opportunities for exploiting an eventual Prussian victory.

If, when it came to war, it was a question of no more than a territorial extension of Prussian power, on the one hand this was a positive challenge to the other powers to demand compensation, just as in almost all the so-called 'Cabinet wars' that had been fought before. On the other hand there was a danger, given this kind of starting situation, that a possibly heterogeneous but none the less powerful anti-Prussian coalition might form behind the 'war of brothers' watchword and under the banner of hostility to the brutal power state, a coalition with strongpoints even inside Prussia itself. And even should Prussia succeed in overcoming both obstacles there was reason to fear that any new initiative would once again produce and perpetuate the old fronts. In short, war was in many respects an unpromising prospect, even capped by military success, if it opened up no other perspectives and invoked no other aims than the acquisition of an additional Prussian province.

In fact the prospect of a territorial victory prize and Prussia's military successes in the Danish War had already caused a series of influential representatives of the opposition to waver somewhat in their former estimate of Bismarck and his policy; they were headed by the historian Heinrich von Treitschke and the 'Prussian Almanachs' he had so much to do with. On the whole, however, the opposition persisted in its unqualified rejection of the government and of all idea of compromise. As things stood it was scarcely to be expected that anything would change in this respect if Prussia were to implement its annexation plans in one form or another. On the contrary, the greater part of the opposition was still committed to the Augustenburg solution. This was regarded as the truly national as opposed to the narrowly Prussian one. The idea that the latter would in the end turn out to be of greater benefit to the national cause found little echo at first, although it had already been voiced on several occasions.

The different standpoints had emerged very clearly when, at Bismarck's instigation and in the teeth of resistance from the group around the adjutant general, Edwin von Manteuffel, that persisted in flirting with the idea of a coup, the Prussian parliament had been reconvened in the middle of January 1865. All the main government proposals – the Military Service Bill, presented for the fifth time, a Bill providing for the expansion of the Prussian navy, not at all an unpopular measure in principle and one that after the experiences of the Danish War was urgently necessary, and of course the budget – were eventually thrown out by an overwhelming House of Deputies majority. And in the debates about them as well as about the government's many attempts to intimidate opposition representatives it became clearer and clearer each time how much the fronts had hardened, heightening the impression of a hopeless trench warfare situation.

Yet amid this growing rigidity a development was beginning to emerge that attentive observers in the opposition camp must have found most disquieting. Their footing in constitutional law with regard to the central issue, the dispute over the budget and the government's claim to be able, in the event of conflict, to govern without an approved budget, was still virtually unchallenged as far as the general public was concerned. That apart, however, the relationship between might and right no longer looked as clear-cut as it had at the beginning of the conflict. The chief reason for this was that in its feeling of practical impotence, which over the years had assumed extraordinary proportions, the opposition had repeatedly claimed a right of intervention and decision even in cases where, though it seemed justified in the event, there was no constitutional or statutory provision for it. For example, the opposition tried to countermand direct administrative measures or to quash verdicts that courts had handed down with complete formal correctness. The upshot of such efforts was to provide unwitting support for the government's thesis that in the state, that is to say in the field of public law, all questions were ultimately power questions. For it was possible to argue that the behaviour of the majority in the House of Deputies showed that it was not in the least concerned with upholding the established law but only with asserting its claim to power under the guise of a variety of legal arguments.

Even if in individual cases it was not difficult to refute, on the whole this was a somewhat dangerous argument. It was apt to reinforce another trend that was likewise highly problematical as far as the opposition was concerned, namely that the public was slowly growing accustomed to the incumbent regime, particularly in the light of its recent successes in foreign policy and on the battlefield, and that it really was beginning to reduce this detailed and highly complicated dispute over the discrepant legal positions to the question of claimed and actual power.

All this was still in the very early stages; it was more in evidence in connection with the Schleswig-Holstein question at first than in the sphere of domestic policy. But the implicit trend towards a legal relativism and towards a one-sided emphasis on the idea of power was one the dangers of which far outreached the present conflict, as precisely the more level-headed opposition members had increasingly to admit to themselves as time went on. Despite all the differences, therefore, behind the scenes there were attempts to reach a compromise over the original point at issue, namely the problem of army reform and in particular the three-year period of military service, and so perhaps pave the way for an agreement over the budget question, the constitutional problem at the heart of the whole dispute.

Significantly it had been the government that had taken the first step here, making it very clear right from the start of the session that it might well be prepared to reach an understanding along these lines. 'Give up the idea of testing your budgetary right on the army question', Count Eulenburg, the Minister of the Interior, had told the House of Deputies on 24 January 1865, while Bismarck was delivering a speech in the Upper House that likewise made a strong bid for compromise. 'Look for some other subject, some other field in which you believe you must assert your rights . . . You will find the government prepared, so far as practical circumstances do not render this impossible, to entertain the reading of the relevant sections of the law on which you insist. Let the army question disappear from the scene', Eulenburg went on almost imploringly, 'and it will then be a useful lesson to us for the future; then the whole struggle that has preoccupied us for the last three years and that, if you do not yield on this point, will continue to preoccupy us indefinitely will after all be of some use to our country and will contribute more than you think to the development of our constitutional life.'[36]

However, when a group of deputies led by the 'New Era' War Minister von Bonin took up this offer and presented what from the opposition standpoint was a very generous compromise proposal with regard to the army question, insisting only on a top limit for the army's peacetime presence, that proposal did not meet with the approval of the government after all. Those who had been ready to compromise felt tricked, their opponents within the opposition camp felt vindicated and, instead of there being a relaxation of the fronts, from April onwards they hardened even further.

But what only very few insiders knew at the time was that Bismarck himself had suffered a severe defeat here. He had received a forceful reminder of the extent to which he was shackled by the conditions under which he had taken office. Against the vote of the entire Cabinet, that is to say including the War Minister, the king had refused to take so much as a step in the direction of compromise, having already been sharply critical of

Eulenburg's speech.[37] 'Any kind of restriction imposed on the strength of the army', he had declared, was a curtailment 'of the power of the king'.[38]

The men behind this were the head of the Military Cabinet, General Edwin von Manteuffel, and with him the group that wished to push the monarch into a *coup d'état* and the establishment of an absolutist military dictatorship – into a 'Düppel at home'. And however much Bismarck might secretly fume he had no choice at this point in time but to bow to the verdict of his king, a verdict whose foundations in a wholly absolutist view of the royal office he had himself spent years in reinforcing. The threat of resignation that he later used repeatedly and with success in such cases was out of the question here. The chances of an attempted compromise over domestic policy were too difficult to assess, as Bismarck well knew, and the foreign policy situation was too complicated. There was also the fact that the matter under discussion was dearer to the king's heart than any other. The Minister-President did, however, draw one conclusion from the whole affair that crucially affected the further course of events: he must first smash the influence of the group around Manteuffel before looking for a decision on the question of the duchies and on relations with Austria and with the German Confederation. Otherwise there was a danger that such a decision might benefit that group rather than himself and the policy that he was pursuing.

This was one reason why he argued at the Crown Council meeting on 29 May 1865 – to which the king, without previously consulting him, had invited the leaders of the armed forces, Manteuffel included – for a postponement of any definite decision regarding the whole question. He did so all the more energetically for the fact that Manteuffel, who had earlier tended to favour the idea of forming a conservative bloc with Austria, had in his constant concern to keep in the closest possible touch with the monarch recently switched his allegiance to the war party and was therefore not to be separated from the king by such a decision.

But for Bismarck this was not the only reason for postponement. Foreign policy motives were also important, prompted by the still entirely open question of how the other great powers, France in particular, would react. And of equal importance was the fact that, to his mind, certain crucial prerequisites seemed to be wanting in the areas of public opinion and the mood of the population for a successful action on Prussia's part and above all for the successful exploitation of a Prussian victory.

It was this aspect of the situation that, notwithstanding the failure of the latest attempt to reach a compromise, governed his behaviour towards the House of Deputies during the months that followed. There were still repeated clashes, of course, particularly since Bismarck knew only too well that the Manteuffel faction was very much on the look-out for further evidence of alleged softness and weakness with which to make the king suspicious of him. But at the same time he let it appear on a number of occasions that a fresh beginning was an ever present possibility as far as he was concerned.

On 1 June 1865, for example, in what became a very heated debate about a government request for a loan intended for the military development of

Kiel Bay and the enlargement of the Prussian fleet, he stated that he could 'only regret that, given the existence of so many points of agreement, an understanding over foreign policy should nevertheless continually elude us'. He went on: 'Were it possible for us to hold full and frank discussions with you in good time, well in advance, regarding all our plans for the future, I believe you would give your approval to more of them than you have felt able to up to now.'

In all this there was no shortage of ironic reflections on the competence of many deputies in the field of foreign affairs or of fresh attacks on alleged attempts by the opposition to widen to its own advantage the scope allotted to parliament under the constitution. But the keynote throughout remained this scarcely veiled offer of collaboration over foreign policy. Bismarck went so far as to explain why, unlike opposition spokesmen, he was not of the opinion that on the occasion of the negotiations for the renewal of the Customs Union treaty, given a certain amount of pressure, 'political advantages' could have been pushed through 'in favour of a federal arrangement' – from which anyone could infer that he was wholly in agreement with the objective as such. In this sense the closing passage of his speech too, for all the ambivalence and severity of its wording, contained a very clear programme. He could not deny, he summed up as it were from the negative standpoint, 'that it makes a painful impression on me when I see that, in the face of a major national question that has preoccupied public opinion for twenty years, the assembly that all Europe regards as representing the cream of Prussian intelligence and patriotism can rise to no other attitude than one of impotent negativism. Gentlemen, this is not the weapon with which you will wrest the sceptre from the hand of kingship, nor is it the means', he added on a warning note, 'by which you will succeed in imparting to our constitutional arrangements the kind of stability and further development that they require.'[39]

These tactics were construed at the time, as they have been subsequently, as representing a combination of the stick and the carrot. The fact that the session ended shortly afterwards with Bismarck attacking the majority in the bluntest terms seems to confirm this interpretation as much as did his statement at the subsequent meeting of the Council of Ministers to the effect that it would be 'impossible to govern' in the long run 'with the existing constitution'. 'A fundamental modification of the same' was 'unavoidable'.[40] The question must be asked, however, whether both were not merely evidence of the dilemma he was in with regard to home affairs.

His attempt to open a dialogue with the majority had once again come to nothing. On the other hand there was a group standing by that advocated giving up this eternal shilly-shallying and resorting to the remedy of a *coup d'état*. If one believed deeply that this policy was wrong but was not at the moment able to offer a feasible alternative, the obvious thing to do in the circumstances was to out-bluster the competition in one's own camp in order to gain time. The abruptness of Bismarck's tone towards the members of the House of Deputies, his threats of fresh hostilities and the significantly vague suggestion of a possible decisive campaign against the opposition can equally well be interpreted as so many ways of defending himself against reproaches from within his own ranks. Those reproaches culminated in the assertion that he was insufficiently decisive and was failing to take advantage of an opportune moment to effect a cure that would do away with the whole conflict, roots and all.

If in this case too we forget about professed plans and intentions and concentrate on what actually happened, there does seem to be a great deal to be said for such an interpretation. On the one hand Bismarck clearly did play for time over the next few months, and on the other hand he made no preparations for a coup. Instead he stuck steadfastly to his programme of bringing at least a section of the opposition round to himself and his policy. At the same time he concentrated his efforts on getting Edwin von Manteuffel, who was always trying to meddle with his foreign policy as well, particularly with regard to a possible rapprochement with France, removed from the immediate environment of the king and sent away from Berlin – efforts that eventually met with success when Manteuffel was 'promoted' to the governorship of Schleswig in August 1865.

A prime example of gaining time was the new understanding with Austria represented by the so-called Gastein Convention of August 1865, an understanding that hardly anyone had still believed possible. This is another thing that historians have sought to place in the context of a policy of fundamental alternatives with regard to the German question. Yet the events leading up to it and those springing immediately from it are, soberly considered, quite unequivocal in their implications: the whole thing, from Prussia's point of view, was another temporary halt, the last stage on the road to the great confrontation.

Despite Francis Joseph's openly avowed intention of sticking to the policy of collaboration with Prussia, relations between the two countries had been steadily worsening since the resignation of Rechberg. Even after allowance has been made for all the difficulties and problems that inevitably arose out of the joint administration of the duchies, it has to be admitted that the party to blame for this was quite clearly Prussia. Berlin had taken every imaginable opportunity to point out to the Austrians that here in northern Europe, far from their natural sphere of influence, they ultimately had nothing to lose and would do better, in the interests of future good relations, to quit the field as soon as possible. That Austria should have reacted by moving gradually back towards the pro-Augustenburg position of the majority in the Confederation was only logical: if it handed the duchies over to Prussia, either now or later, it would be exposing itself as a dupe in the eyes of the whole world and risked suffering what might be a fatal loss of prestige in Germany.

The two powers were thus in a position of open confrontation as early as the summer of 1865. In a fundamental statement communicated to the Viennese Cabinet back in late February,[41] Prussia had made clear that it would consent to an independent Schleswig-Holstein only on condition that that state acknowledged complete Prussian supremacy in the military and economic spheres. Moreover, Berlin continued to reject emphatically any involvement on the part of the Confederation. The Prussian government repeatedly and insistently called upon Austria to abide by the traditional principle of the sole responsibility of the great powers. Vienna on the other hand was more and more clearly seeking to rejoin its old coalition within the Confederation and the pro-Augustenburg majority among the German public. As early as the beginning of April its representative in the Federal Diet had declared that Austria was prepared to surrender its rights to Augustenburg if Prussia would do the same.

At the same time, however, the Austrian government let it be known through confidential channels that, given suitable co-operation on Prussia's part, it was prepared to modify this stance: mention was made of territorial compensation in southern Germany or Silesia, of the Hohenzollern principalities or of Glatz, a territory ruled by a count. Berlin would hear nothing of this, answering instead with the repeated demand, which on 31 July became an ultimatum, for joint action against the Augustenburg movement in the duchies since this represented a threat to public order and to the authority of the new powers in the land. If Austria failed to co-operate, the Prussian government said, it would proceed on its own. Since this was something Vienna could scarcely tolerate, the immediate result would have been to make open conflict unavoidable.

In this situation the party in Vienna that favoured a conservative partnership with Prussia asserted itself once again. Its chief spokesman, Foreign Minister Count Mensdorff and the emperor's personal confidant, Count Moritz Esterhazy, used as their principal argument that the domestic situation in Austria, the growing danger from liberal and revolutionary-nationalist currents in a time of steadily worsening economic and financial conditions, made such a conflict unthinkable.

The domestic situation in Austria was indeed highly precarious. It was made even more so by the leader of the Greater German party, Minister of the Interior and Minister of State von Schmerling, failing to place relations with the Hungarian part of the country on a satisfactory fresh footing. When as a result of this Schmerling gave up and tendered his resignation at the end of June, the bluffing match was as good as over.

The fact that Bismarck chose this moment to step up his campaign by bringing every weapon to bear, not least that of financial pressure, once again demonstrates with the utmost clarity that he was not prepared to make even the smallest Prussian sacrifice for the ideal of a conservative partnership. On the contrary, he made it perfectly plain, as soon as Vienna showed itself willing to negotiate, that the concessions must all be on the Austrian side. And while he was in Bad Gastein, the Prussian king's favourite spa, conducting the relevant negotiations with a man who enjoyed the full confidence of the emperor and the group around Esterhazy, namely the Viennese envoy to Munich, Count Blome, he was having inquiries made in Paris and also at the seat of the Italian government in Florence as to how those capitals would react in the event of war breaking out between the two German great powers. In other words, he was quite patently operating on the brink of a war, the financing of which had seemed assured since the middle of July 1865 even without parliamentary assistance, largely as a result of the activities of his banker, Gerson Bleichröder.

Hence the pressure that he brought to bear on Austria and on the Austrian negotiators. Only such pressure can explain why Vienna eventually agreed, under the terms of the Gastein Convention ratified by Francis Joseph and William on 20 August 1865, to concessions that finally undermined its position with regard to the Schleswig-Holstein question as well as thoroughly unsettling its relations with its supporters in non-Austrian Germany. The empire gave its consent to a *de facto* division of sovereignty in the duchies: Vienna was to administer Holstein, Prussia was to administer Schleswig, while the Austrian emperor sold his rights in Lauenburg to the Prussian king for two-and-a-half million Danish taler. At the same time the Austrians agreed to the inclusion of both territories in the German Customs Union and to the establishment of permanent transport and communications links between Prussia and Schleswig across Holstein territory.

The whole thing, although the fact was sketchily disguised by high-sounding phrases and Prussian bows in the direction of its Austrian partner, was an unqualified triumph for Berlin and for the man in charge there. Bismarck's elevation to the status of a hereditary count on 15 September 1865, the day on which Prussia formally took possession of the duchy of Lauenburg, showed the world how highly the Prussian Crown valued the achievement of its first minister. 'In the four [!] years since I appointed you to the head of its government', William's letter recorded, 'Prussia has assumed a position that is worthy of its past and that moreover promises a felicitous and glorious future.'[42]

In the Gastein negotiations there had been talk at first of the *de facto* division of sovereignty and administration being made definitive and Prussia and Austria each annexing one duchy. This would undoubtedly have whipped up an even greater storm in the forum of German public opinion and among Vienna's traditional allies. For it would have meant relinquishing a further demand that the German side had been putting to Denmark repeatedly for decades, namely the principle of the indivisibility of the duchies. Consequently the Austrian Cabinet had suggested describing the whole thing as an interim measure and abiding by the principle of the joint responsibility of both monarchs for the future of the duchies.

Bismarck had promptly and readily agreed to this. However, what looked like friendly complaisance and might be seen as a prelude to the policy of closer Austro-Prussian co-operation aspired to by Vienna and its new chief minister, Count von Belcredi, was in reality a piece of cool calculation. Because keeping it an interim measure put Prussia in a position where it could set a match to the fuse at any time, in other words force Austria into a fresh conflict over the question of finalization whenever it wished. It was the fundamental and eventually fatal mistake of Viennese policy to believe that the conservative partnership with Prussia could be achieved in any other terms than those outlined by Bismarck in December 1862, namely the moving apart of the powers and the precise delimitation of their respective spheres of interest and influence.

The much-debated question of the importance of the Gastein Convention can therefore be answered quite clearly as regarded the Austrian side as well. It demonstrated the inability of the ruling party in Vienna consistently to carry out a decision already arrived at in practice and actually make the requisite sacrifices. That decision was: to give up its Greater German and moderately liberal federal reform policy, to apply itself to reorganizing the Austrian Empire in a way that should take due account of the importance of Hungary and to achieve a settlement with Prussia in order to have its hands free to set about solving this problem.

With the government reshuffle of July 1865 and the repeal of the liberal umbrella constitution of 1861, with the increasingly preferential treatment accorded to the Hungarian element in Austria's political make-up and with the final abandonment of the objectives of the Schleswig-Holstein movement and the break with the pro-Augustenburg governments of the small and medium-sized German states, that decision had already been implemented in several essentials. Yet Austrian policy still shrank from drawing the ultimate conclusion, namely voluntary surrender of the victory prize in the Danish War as well as of its old attachments within the German Confederation in favour of a long-term settlement with Prussia. Without that, however, Gastein was meaningless, indicating only weakness and indecision rather than a readiness to embark on a genuinely new policy.

The question has to be asked, of course, whether this kind of bold anticipation of the eventual outcome of 1866 without any need for a war and under conditions more favourable to Austria was in fact a practicable possibility. On the other hand, seen from this point of view it is once again quite clear that in the run-up to 1866 Bismarck was not interested in an alternative objective but only in alternative means. If the objective – Prussian supremacy at least as far as the River Main and the removal of the conditions that had prevailed within the Confederation until the outbreak of the Schleswig-Holstein crisis – could be achieved through a general agreement between Austria and Prussia, so much the better. If not: 'Flectere si nequeo superos, Acheronta movebo.'

But that was easier said than done. However deeply Bismarck may have been convinced, following the establishment of a fresh interim solution at Bad Gastein, that an armed conflict was inevitable sooner or later, it must have seemed as doubtful as ever whether it really would be possible to recruit auxiliary troops from the 'underworld', in other words from what conservatives called the 'revolutionary camp'.

Certainly the general feeling of outrage among the German public at the 'disgraceful horse-trading' of the Gastein Convention was directed primarily at Austria: it inevitably appeared that Vienna, without any immediately comprehensive interest such as Prussia possessed and in betrayal of its recently professed faith in the law, had sacrificed the interests of the nation and of the Schleswig-Holsteiners. Furthermore, as became clear in the discussion about the continuation and future objectives of the all-German Schleswig-Holstein movement and its organizations, people were increasingly beginning to ask themselves, particularly in sections of Prussian liberalism, whether a solution of the German question along the lines pursued by Bismarck, namely those of successful power politics, ought not at the moment to take precedence over the solution of the constitutional question in their own terms. As the former Foreign Minister and present Minister of the Royal Household, von Schleinitz, the confidant of the queen, put it bitterly towards the end of October 1865, they began to 'bow to a successful act of violence'.[43] And finally Florence and Paris, the two foci of the revolution in Europe as the conservatives saw them, were beginning to associate a conflict between Prussia and Austria with the expectation, quietly yet persistently fostered by Bismarck, that there would be something in it for them too in territorial and power-political terms.

But all these things were and remained so many unknown quantities in Bismarck's balance-sheet of the chances of success, a balance-sheet that, as we know today, could not even put on the credit side a firm faith in the benevolent neutrality of Russia. Here too there were endless vacillations, and the temptation for St Petersburg to try to have its say in the matter was as great as its inclination to pay Austria back once more for its stance during the Crimean War.

Probably nothing illustrates better how shaky Bismarck felt his own base to be than the consideration he gave to appealing, if the worst came to the worst, to the revolutionary-nationalist movements inside Austria's multi-nation empire. This would indeed have meant mobilizing forces the furtherance of which could have turned out sooner or later to constitute a threat to Prussia itself; one need think only of the Polish minority in that country.

However favourable Prussia's starting position may meanwhile have become in many respects, a war with Austria and its probable allies among the states of the Confederation continued to represent an extraordinary risk. This was true even in the purely military sphere. Despite its defeat in Italy and despite the economy measures that were cutting deeper and deeper into its army budget, as a military power Austria still seemed to be at least Prussia's equal. And whether the Prussian forces would be adequate in purely numerical terms to fight on several fronts simultaneously against the smaller states of the Confederation appeared doubtful to many people. Even if they did prove adequate, the war threatened to be a long one, and that would increase the risk of the other great powers intervening as well as the likelihood of the whole thing ending in compromise. And one of the first victims of such a compromise would undoubtedly, sooner or later, have been Bismarck himself – for having contrived the entire episode and failed to bring it to a properly satisfactory conclusion.

So it is quite wrong, looking at the situation as a whole, to speak of Bismarck as having pursued a policy of calculated or calculable risk in the period leading up to 1866. He nourished this legend himself, in interpretations of his own success, and many historians have repeated it after him – even and indeed especially those who have stressed the seriousness of the alternatives allegedly contemplated and, depending on the circumstances, furthered by him. The impression given is altogether that of a man who was in complete and virtually risk-free control of every stage of the game, since he always made sure that he had a way out.

In reality what he did in 1866 particularly, for all his shrewd calculation of details and for all his indubitable skill and his ability to bide his time, was to stake absolutely everything on a single card in a game in which, besides skill and mastery of the rules, chance and luck tipped the scales at the crucial moment; it was no accident that even on the Berlin stock exchange most people reckoned right up until the war that Vienna would emerge as the victor. Man's very natural tendency to indulge in wholesale retrospective rationalization of the historical process is in danger here, under the influence of the success of the outcome, of obscuring important preconditions of that success. An exaggerated image of the great man in terms of his rationality and his ability to dominate and control all circumstances and situations can easily have the effect of pushing into the background what contemporaries who were involved in the same events saw as his 'unpredictability'. 'It will be seen when there is a storm that we can swim better in heavy seas than others can', he had prophesied on one occasion in 1865.[44] That was precisely what remained to be seen.

[8]

1866

Bismarck had been stressing over and over again since the 1850s that the existing federal relationship must eventually be 'healed *ferro et igni*', because as things were at present Prussia and Austria were 'smothering each other' – literally 'breathing each other's breath away'. And for all his openness to new developments he had repeatedly set forth very precise plans for achieving that objective: to eliminate the Confederation to a great extent in the event of such a conflict, to keep Russia and Britain out of it, to secure at least the benevolent neutrality of France, and above all to mobilize the Lesser German national movement for his own ends. So far he had definitely achieved none of these objectives. Indeed it was already possible to foresee that such a constellation of circumstances, which would of course have constituted the ideal, was not going to present itself. Yet even when it eventually became clear that, given conditions at the outset, no certainty of success was going to be forthcoming, he did not hesitate to have 'another go at the aforesaid lottery' of a power politics in the style of Frederick the Great that put the punter's own existence at stake, as he had announced to the Austrian envoy to the Federal Diet, Count Thun, at the end of November 1851.[1]

This was at the same time the individual element, which here in particular we must not underestimate, in the decision of 1866. Much undoubtedly pointed in this direction, and a good deal had already been decided in advance in the shape of the Customs Union, the resolutions of 1848-9 and the formation of political groups in central Europe. But whatever factors went into the decision-making process, its concrete outcome depended on the process itself and hence on those who, whether pursuing a plan or responding to a situation, were active within it. Bismarck, however much he ultimately wove everything together, undoubtedly belonged to the latter group: the reality that emerged in the autumn of 1866 and that decisively influenced developments was not at all something he had consciously planned in that form in advance. This gave him an advantage and a certain superiority over the more rigid planners and those who took a less flexible line. But it also heralded, even at this stage, what the price of success might be in terms of dependence upon his own *ad hoc* creation.

After Gastein, when it had finally become clear that Austria, even under an arch-conservative government averse to the liberal concept of a

277

centralized Greater Germany, was not going to agree to a settlement with Prussia on the terms once stipulated by Bismarck, the Prussian Minister-President resolutely set a collision course. In practice this meant mobilizing and exploiting all factors that appeared likely to damage the Austrian position and improve the Prussian, without regard to the consequences that might arise from harnessing them together and from such developments and self-generating processes as this might set in motion. 'If revolution there is to be, let us rather undertake it than undergo it' – that was the watchword now.[2] And Bismarck complied with it to an extent that eventually made his old conservative friends turn their backs on him in horror.

His first step was to create as much confusion as possible not so much with regard to the objective he was aiming at as with regard to the paths he was likely to take. He hoped this would enable him to keep everything in a state of flux and use the reactions he obtained to make his own decisions. It was to this end that he let Napoleon III know early in September 1865, in reply to an inquiry from the French emperor disguised as a suggestion, that he now had no intention whatever of making common cause with the Lesser German national movement. On the contrary, he noted with satisfaction that the governments of the small and medium-sized states of the Confederation, whose attitude to that movement, he said, was anything but benevolent, were siding more and more closely with Prussia.[3] At the same time he issued a directive to the press to the effect that the support the national movement and a section of the German public was receiving from the British and French governments for its estimate of the Gastein Convention showed what should be thought of forces that were prepared to make themselves dependent on foreign powers: it was therefore Austria's duty as president of the German Confederation to proceed against those forces in conjunction with Prussia. And whereas in this case he portrayed Prussia as a bulwark of the status quo and the forces of conservatism, shortly afterwards he was instructing the newly appointed governor of Schleswig, Edwin von Manteuffel, to favour the representatives of the 'so-called national party' in his staffing policy – 'without entertaining too many misgivings with regard to the position of those men on other matters'.[4] 'If Mensdorff relapses into Würzburg policies', he hinted ten days later, he would not hesitate 'to rub a bit of black, red and gold under [Vienna's] nose' in turn. The same applied to Austria's German clientele: 'A German parliament would put the special interests of the small and medium-sized states in their place.'[5] That would soon teach them that it was better not to irritate Prussia. 'What are the little princes after?' he sneered.[6] 'The governments are more reactionary than I – who would even make use of the party of change if it were to Prussia's advantage; they want most of all to stay on their thrones, and while they may be afraid of us they are even more afraid of revolution.' In other words, he for his part ruled out completely any possibility of a counter-move on the part of those small and medium-sized states, for example along the lines of von der Pfordten's 'Third Germany' policy: 'Were there an Ephialtes among the ministers of the medium-sized states, the great German national movement would crush him and his master.' At the same time, however, in his dealings with Austria he used such an eventuality as something for which they must be quite prepared.

Behind this smoke-screen of deliberately contradictory statements – though of course they reveal which elements he hoped to use for his purposes – he pressed on purposefully in the direction of a confrontation with Austria. In addition to the permanent skirmishing in the duchies over staffing and administrative questions, the attitude to be adopted towards the persistently pro-Augustenberg popular movement and the treatment of the claimant to the throne himself, he was continually building up new positions and fronts at the German as well as at the European level: at the German level by seeking to widen what since Gastein had become an enormous gulf, on the one hand between Austria and the small and medium-sized states and on the other between the empire and the forces of liberalism and nationalism; and at the European level by wooing Austria's natural enemy to the south, the new kingdom of Italy, with economic concessions and the scarcely veiled hint that in a war between Prussia and Austria it might gain Venetia. He further endeavoured, though without committing himself with regard to a possible material *quid pro quo*, to draw Napoleon III as close to Prussia as possible. The impression he strove to convey in Paris was that France stood to gain at all events from lending its support to Prussia, if only in terms of a permanent strengthening of its continental hegemony.

Although the government in Vienna was rather inclined to delude itself after Gastein, preoccupied as it was with pressing domestic problems, it became less and less possible as time went on to ignore what all this was leading up to – even though only a fraction of Prussia's activities came to light and was known about at the time. Yet even so Vienna was unable to make up its mind to take the final step and by voluntarily sacrificing Holstein give up Austria's traditional position in central Europe for the sake of a shared dominion and a policy of co-operation with Prussia extending over a wide area.

It was thus left with no alternative but to take up the challenge and try to win back its old allies in central Europe. An initial step in this direction appeared to be the fact that on 23 January 1866 a public meeting was held in Altona, clearly with the consent of the Austrian government, at which thousands of people demonstrated in favour of the convocation of a Schleswig-Holstein Diet. Afterwards Vienna expressly denied having approved the content of this campaign in any way, let alone having had any part in bringing it about. But when the Prussian government issued a sharply worded protest against what it saw as support for the attempt to go back on the Gastein resolutions, the Austrian government reacted – and this was the crucial point – by finally deciding to make a stand against Prussia. As Count Esterhazy put it, they must now at least 'show their teeth'.[7]

The tone and content of the Prussian protest left the Viennese Cabinet with little choice.[8] It suggested, for example, that Vienna was obviously prepared to give up the fight they had jointly agreed to wage against 'the common enemy of both powers, revolution'. Austria, it said, far from standing by the contents of agreed treaties, was even seeking to come to terms with revolutionary forces. If the empire did not immediately dissociate itself from this policy, the conclusion was unavoidable that what Prussia had 'honestly striven for' in terms of an 'intimate mutuality with regard to overall policy between the two powers [could] not be realized'. In which case the Prussian government must 'gain complete freedom for its *entire* policy and make of the same such use as we regard as being consistent with Prussia's interests'. This threat, framed by Bismarck himself, concluded the note dispatched to the Prussian envoy in Vienna for direct communication. Nothing could have been plainer: either Austria renounced any kind of independent policy in Holstein, knuckling under completely to the interests of the dominant power in northern Europe if it could not agree to cession – or a clash was inevitable.

When the Austrian Council of Ministers, presided over by Francis Joseph, decided in Ofen/Buda on 21 February 1866 not to give way yet again, it as good as decided to go to war.[9] Its own envoy was asked to communicate the information that Austria was not a power to allow 'its honour, influence and reputation to be disparaged or itself to be ousted from rightfully acquired positions without a fight'.[10]

Admittedly the Austrian ministers were unanimous in looking for 'the preservation of the country's honour and dignity as well as of its interests' once again 'through diplomatic channels'; for the present, concrete preparations for war were to be made only 'on paper'. But there could no longer be any doubt that they were now disposed to bar Prussia's way come what might. And that disposition, given the attitude of government circles in Berlin, meant that war could no longer be avoided .

At a meeting of the Prussian Crown Council held on 28 February 1866, a week after that of the Austrian Council of Ministers, it was assumed by those present, with the sole exception of the crown prince, that war was virtually inescapable. The almost unanimous opinion of the council was that, without deliberately provoking it, they must now put the emphasis on diplomatic and political preparations for an armed conflict.[11]

This was simply giving official confirmation to something that had already been established for some time – despite the fact that the king was repeatedly assailed, right up until the very eve of war, by doubts and misgivings that necessitated his Minister-President 'playing the part of clockmaker every morning, winding the run-down mechanism up again', as those in the know expressed it.[12] The most important thing about this Crown Council meeting was that at it Bismarck formulated Prussia's actual military objective and outlined the means by which this was to be achieved.

In a major historical survey of the development of relations between Prussia and Austria and the situation in central Europe since the end of the old Reich he swept aside everything that had been discussed over the previous few years in terms of a possible permanent understanding and division of hegemony as well as all the expectations and objectives that had long been associated with these in the conservative camp. Prussia, Bismarck maintained, was 'the only viable political creation to have emerged from the ruins of the old German Reich'. This was the foundation of its legitimate claim 'to take the lead in Germany'. Austria, on the other hand, had 'always jealously opposed Prussia's natural and legitimate strivings in this direction by not allowing Prussia to assume control of Germany, although incapable of doing so itself'.

That campaign had known 'only one or two interruptions for specific, temporary purposes'. Thus the foundation of the German Confederation in particular was not to be seen as a serious attempt to end the conflict. On the contrary the Confederation had 'from the outset been conceived simply as a means of effectively defending German lands against France'. It had 'never acquired a proper national existence'. All efforts by Prussia to reshape it along these lines had been 'frustrated by Austrian resistance'.

In this connection Bismarck did not hesitate to describe the year 1848 as having represented a great opportunity for Prussian policy: 'Had Prussia then sought to lead and control the movement not from the platform but with the sword, it would probably have succeeded in bringing about a more favourable outcome.' At the same time this put into words his own tactical plan. This was that Prussia must now finally make common cause with the German national movement, whose natural leader it was, though it must also resolutely lead it to Prussia's advantage.

What Bismarck unfolded at that crucial meeting of the Prussian Crown Council, in the presence of his two chief rivals from his own camp, General von Manteuffel and the Prussian ambassador in Paris, Count von der Goltz, was the Lesser German programme complete with the historical justification that mainly non-Prussian historians such as the Saxon Heinrich von Treitschke or Ludwig Häusser from the Palatinate had provided for it. Prussia, it had been stressed repeatedly in these quarters, must be the spearhead of the national movement. Nor had there been any shortage of sabre-rattling, particularly after the experiences of 1848. But what if not only Austria but also a number of the small and medium-sized states of the Confederation should oppose such a policy of unification, in other words if, besides the Austrian emperor, other legitimate monarchs should put their veto on it? Could Prussia seriously consider riding roughshod over the much-invoked foundation of any kind of conservative order, the monarchical principle?

The answer given by most representatives of Lesser German liberalism was quite clear. Theodor Mommsen, the celebrated classical historian who was himself a prominent member of the Prussian Progressive Party, had put it in the plainest of terms six months before this in an open letter to the president of the German Diet of Deputies (*Abgeordnetentag*; a free assembly of representatives of the individual national Diets) dissociating himself from the Schleswig-Holstein movement in the interests of the future of Germany: there must be an end, he had said, to the 'sovereignty swindle' that was 'sapping the marrow of Germany'. It was now 'written in letters of fire that the choice for us is between subordination to a German state [*Grossstaat*] and the ruin of the nation'.[13] But this was also the answer given by the supposedly so arch-conservative Minister-President of Prussia. 'We are coming close', he had warned a party colleague in a letter written around the middle of September 1861, 'to making the whole unhistorical, ungodly

281

and unlawful sovereignty swindle of the German princes, who are using our federal relationship as a pedestal from which to play the European power, into the pet child of the Prussian Conservative Party.'[14] And to Roon he had written in July of that year: 'My loyalty to my sovereign is of Vendéean completeness, but as regards all others, not in one drop of my blood do I feel a trace of an obligation to lift a finger on their behalf.'[15]

Whether the principle of legitimacy could in any case provide the foundation for an international order had been the major point at issue between himself and Leopold von Gerlach back in the 1850s. Gerlach had suspected at the time that their ways would part sooner or later. One could not, in Gerlach's view, employ principles in accordance with considerations of mere advantage, keeping them for use at home and otherwise not bothering about them.

Such had also, at the time, been the opinion of the man who was now king. As Bismarck had added in the same letter to Roon: 'I fear that in this way of thinking I am so far removed from that of our Most Gracious Majesty that he will scarcely find me a suitable adviser to the Crown'. Now, however, even William no longer took exception to his Minister-President setting Prussia's power interests, which for the first time were wholly identified with the interests of the German nation, above the ideal of the solidarity of crowned heads; his only stipulation was that no crowns must be toppled, but even that was forgotten a few months later. What the crown prince had referred to at the end of November 1865 as 'Otto Annexandrovich's piratical policy' had finally won general acceptance.[16] Indeed, with regard to principles in politics, as Bismarck once scoffed in his old age, the same question applied as the Frankfurt Rothschild had been in the habit of addressing to his chief accountant: 'Mr. Meier, if you please, what are my principles today with regard to American hides?'[17]

In terms of this kind of basic *Realpolitik* the Crown Council further agreed with Bismarck that increased efforts must now be made to talk to and reach agreements with the two chief opponents of the 1815 settlement and the principles underlying it, namely the kingdom of Italy and Napoleonic France. In the case of Italy this meant seeking to further Prussia's own success by assisting a power that had risen by the revolutionary route to implement the principle of national self-determination in the teeth of what was historically lawful. And if the line adopted towards France continued to be one of refusing to enter into any firm commitments, Bismarck had already stressed to the French government back in the autumn that the natural field for French expansionist ambitions was 'wherever French is spoken in the world'.

He had further indicated to Paris that for Prussia too the principle of national self-determination now counted for more than what was historically lawful, more than the traditional order, by holding out the prospect of a partition of Schleswig in accordance with that principle. But what had hitherto gone no further than mere probing and could have been regarded as a Machiavellian chess move that might be rescinded at any time, as Gastein had shown, was now given out as official Russian policy. With this Prussia crossed its Rubicon and finally declared war on the traditional order in central Europe. The land of successful counter-revolution had itself turned revolutionary.

This was true also, although it was even less discussed either in principle or in detail, of the question of future domestic policy and the forming of coalitions on the domestic front. Although Bismarck drew a firm distinction between the national movement, on which Prussia must lean and which it must at the same time lead, and the liberal opposition, no one could seriously doubt that the two were at least in part identical and that the government had decided to launch a policy of rapprochement with regard to the opposition. Reference was made, the minutes of the Crown Council meeting tell us soberly, to the 'beneficial effect' that the whole thing would have 'on the solution of the domestic conflict'. There was also the fact that abandoning the principles of a traditional, legitimist foreign policy would inevitably throw at least the arch-conservatives into opposition to the government. This would therefore sooner or later be forced, if it did not wish to find itself without any kind of base, to look around for fresh allies.

Of course, an understanding of objective necessities and appropriate programmatic statements and resolutions was one thing; practical implementation of them was quite another. The list of things that appeared necessary to the preparation of a successful campaign against Austria was now clearly drawn up: an alliance with the Lesser German national movement and, as an inescapable consequence of this, a rapprochement with at least part of the liberal opposition; an attempt to reach an understanding with the remaining states of the German Confederation; securing the support of Italy and the benevolent neutrality of France; and keeping Russia and Britain out of the whole affair. Under the influence of Bismarck's subsequent success, however, it is easily overlooked that, for all the bold and imaginative initiatives of Bismarckian policy, only a fraction of these prerequisites actually obtained when in the summer of 1866 the clash came. In fact the attempt decisively to reduce the risk and prepare a reserve position in case of unexpected developments and a result that would impose a compromise had succeeded to only a very limited extent. The thing remained a lottery, to be decided by the luck of the battlefield.

The military leadership, confident of the strength of the Prussian army, had made only one stipulation: Moltke, the chief of staff, insisted that a second front be set up to the south of the empire by means of an offensive alliance with Italy. And here Prussia did indeed achieve its one truly decisive success. Although the preconditions for this appeared very favourable in the light of Italy's burning ambition to get its hands on Venetia, it was by no means a foregone conclusion. For Bismarck had already played this card prematurely, in the run-up to Gastein. He therefore had first to break down the very understandable mistrust of the Italian government, which felt that it was being used as a pawn in the chess game between Berlin and Vienna.

This he managed to do after lengthy and difficult negotiations with General Govone, a relatively young officer who had distinguished himself in the Crimea and at Magenta. The original plan had been to send Moltke on a special mission to Florence, but then in March 1866 the Italian chief minister La Marmora had dispatched this personal confidant of his to Berlin, where Govone had once served briefly as military attaché. A secret treaty limited to three months' duration was signed on 8 April. In it Italy undertook to declare war on Austria the moment an armed conflict broke out between Prussia and the empire. Furthermore both powers promised each other to conclude no 'peace or armistice except by mutual consent'. Prussia, the treaty said expressly, was obliged to give such consent only if Austria was prepared, as well as ceding the kingdom of Lombardy and Venetia to Italy, to hand over to Prussia 'Austrian districts with the same size of population as that kingdom'.[18]

The Italian government finally made up its mind to sign such an agreement only after Napoleon III, appealed to by Florence for advice, had encouraged it to do so. Napoleon had immediately added, however, that he was not committing France to anything thereby. It was quite obvious what he was thinking of: in the approaching conflict he wished to play the part of *tertius gaudens*, the successful mediator who is afterwards rewarded accordingly. Hence his concern not to commit himself prematurely.

Bismarck, who knew Napoleon personally very well from their many discussions, soon saw through this. He concluded from it that a benevolent neutrality in the sense of permanent support for Prussian policy and its objectives was out of the question, not to mention a treaty of neutrality in corresponding terms. The course he continued to steer resolutely even now, one of confining himself to vague intimations and a reference to the French-speaking world in dealing with the question of possible future compensation, was therefore governed more by negative considerations than, as a certain nationally oriented school of history has been fond of maintaining, by positive considerations with regard to resisting French claims to German-speaking world in dealing with the question of possible future compensation, threatened only to sharpen appetites and increase the propensity for each side to get the other to promise it even more and then add both together to the final account.

That the Prussian Minister-President was quite correct in his assessment of the general trend of French policy was shown very clearly by the way in which Paris subsequently received Vienna's overtures aimed at preventing an eventual rapprochement between Prussia and France, which Vienna feared might at any moment find concrete expression in a treaty. In return for a neutrality that it had decided on in secret long before, France secured a guarantee in the secret convention it signed with Austria on 12 June 1866 of the cession of Venetia even in the event of an Austrian victory. This rendered the war between Austria and Italy completely meaningless. Paris further obtained a series of extremely wide-ranging if purely oral assurances with regard to the future pattern of relations in central Europe.[19]

France, said Paris, would in the event of an Austrian victory raise no objections to a territorial expansion of the empire in the region, at least not as long as it did not, in conjunction with a reorganized German Confederation, threaten the balance of power in Europe. This French assurance, set out in a separate note, was reciprocated on the Austrian side by an oral declaration, in other words one that was not signed by both parties, to the effect that Vienna 'would have no objection to a territorial rearrangement enlarging Saxony, Württemberg and even Bavaria at the expense of mediatized princes and even turning the Rhine provinces into a new, independent German state'.[20]

The whole thing amounted to a Rhenish Confederation with even greater power than before, and this Austria accepted. And the price that Paris would demand of Prussia when the time came promised to be just as high. The conflict between the two German great powers was to secure French hegemony on the continent of Europe once and for all – that was Napoleon's great objective.

It is scarcely possible, in view of this, to speak of Bismarck as having scored a major diplomatic success with his stalling policy towards France. His scope for manoeuvre was in fact virtually non-existent and France's temporizing neutrality decided on in advance. Only an unexpected swift military victory that upset everybody's calculations was able to prevent the French plan from succeeding whatever the outcome.

On the other hand it was precisely that plan that caused Britain and particularly Russia to temporize at first. Both countries were worried lest they place themselves at a disadvantage by committing themselves prematurely and have the French emperor outmanoeuvre them yet again. For it was still Napoleon's France rather than Bismarck's Prussia that was regarded as the truly central power in European politics. The general opinion was that the big event would begin only once the minor event, the one between Austria and Prussia, was over or had at least entered its critical phase.

It is only by bearing this in mind that we can understand the general consternation that followed Königgrätz/Sadowa and Nikolsburg and the deeper reason for the French desire for 'vengeance for Sadowa'. Suddenly and surprisingly the distribution of power in Europe was, if not turned upside-down, nevertheless very decisively altered. And this without the 'Areopagus' of the European powers having at least tacitly given its prior consent.

In the field of international politics, then, the situation as it existed was in fact ultimately to Bismarck's advantage, though there is no justification for overrating his own part in bringing that situation about, as has so often been done. In national politics, however, and in the closely associated sphere of domestic affairs Bismarck at first had almost no success at all. As always since his first major approach in the speech to the budget committee in September 1862, his efforts to open a dialogue with and reach an agreement with the Lesser German national party fell victim to the almost universal verdict that they lacked all credibility. Who, after all, was going to regard the advances of a man who even now never missed an opportunity of violently opposing the representatives of that national party on the Prussian domestic front as anything more than mere tactical manoeuvres?

The latest brief session of parliament in January and February 1866 had once again not only brought the two sides no closer but had further aggravated their differences. As soon as the House had assembled the opposition had passed a resolution, again moved by Virchow, declaring the personal union of the duchy of Lauenburg with the Prussian Crown agreed to at Gastein to be invalid without the consent of parliament. Apart from the legal questions involved, this was clearly intended to demonstrate yet again that the opposition was not prepared to co-operate in any way, even in the field of foreign policy.

Whether or not this was politically wise in view of the government's undeniable foreign policy successes in the Schleswig-Holstein affair and the growing impression that these were making on public opinion inside Prussia, it was the expression of a very clear-cut plan. This was to wreck in advance any attempt to loosen cohesion and unanimity of the opposition through the medium of foreign policy – even at the cost of creating fresh points of conflict.

Bismarck had made a further vain attempt to dismiss the suspicion 'that in my political conduct I was using external policy merely as a means to internal policy and to furthering the government's struggle against the demands of parliament . . . Foreign affairs are for me an end in themselves', he had stated almost aphoristically, 'and rank higher with me than the rest'.[21] The question that not only Virchow but above all the lawyers Rudolf Gneist and Karl Twesten asked was: how in this context could one have any faith in a man who even on recent form used any and every opportunity to harass the liberal opposition as well as individual representatives of it, drive them into a corner and outmanoeuvre them politically?

In this and other connections the members of the House of Deputies had with tremendous passion recited to Bismarck the catalogue of the government's sins. Particularly bad blood, for example, had been created by the illegal banning of a banquet that the citizens of Cologne had offered the Rhineland deputies in the previous year and subsequent use of police and army physically to prevent the banquet from taking place. And the exasperation of the House had been no less over the attempt to restrict parliamentary privilege and make deputies answerable in the criminal courts for making and propagating allegedly false statements of fact.

Incidents of this kind had kept on cropping up, and in the end any possibility of agreement was more remote than ever. On 22 February 1866, to the accompaniment of grave reproaches directed at the opposition by the Minister-President, the king once again ordered the closure of parliament.

In spite of all this, Bismarck stuck unswervingly to the necessity for a rapprochement with the national movement. In fact he now came out with concrete proposals that, if they were to succeed, required such a rapprochement. These constituted a revival of his old plan to summon a German parliament, which would then decide on the reform and reorganization of relations among the states of central Europe.

This plan, which in March 1866 took the form of an official Prussian motion in the Federal Diet and as such was presented there on 9 April, the day after the signing of the offensive treaty with Italy, pursued a twofold objective from the start.[22] On the one hand the mobilization of the Lesser German section of the national public was intended to lift the imminent conflict with Austria, particularly vis-à-vis France and the principle of national self-determination so vigorously propagated by France, out of the sphere of a purely power-political clash between two European great powers and at the same time to strengthen the Prussian position; 'a German parliament is of more use to us than an army corps', Bismarck noted laconically around this time.[23] And on the other hand the plan was designed to put pressure on the small and medium-sized states of the German Confederation.

The crucial change, as compared with the original formulation of the plan in the Baden-Baden/Rheinfeld Memorial of 1861, was that the proposed parliament was now no longer made up of the delegates from the individual German Diets but was to be the product of direct general elections. This, it inevitably appeared, was a thoroughly revolutionary act, an appeal to the people as the supreme authority, so to speak. It was the appeal, however, of a man who was using it to pursue not only revolutionary but also arch-conservative objectives: revolutionary in so far as the nation was being enlisted against the existing territorial and power-political order in central Europe and against those forces in the individual governments of the states of the Confederation that opposed Prussian objectives; and arch-conservative because, at least at first glance, the nation was at the same time being led into the field against the liberal opposition – against an opposition that claimed to represent the people but that actually, according to Bismarck, did not do so at all.

The people, as he had been saying over and over again in recent years, were in reality conservative and loyal to the king; that was the direction their nationalism took. 'Direct elections . . . and universal suffrage', he told the Bavarian Minister-President, von der Pfordten, at the end of March, 'I regard as greater guarantees of a conservative stance than any artificial electoral system designed to produce contrived [!] majorities.'[24] And as he told Count Bernstorff, the Prussian ambassador in London, on 19 April: 'In a country with monarchical traditions and a loyalist mentality universal suffrage will, by doing away with the influence of the liberal bourgeois classes, also lead to monarchical elections.'[25]

Accordingly he had even given occasional thought to introducing universal, direct suffrage in Prussia, where 'nine-tenths of the people [were] loyal to the King' and were 'prevented from expressing their opinion only by the artificial mechanics of the electoral system'. 'The advocates of the three-taler census have obviously not yet learnt that the bourgeoisie has always been the curatrix of revolution while below the three-taler mark nine-tenths of the "people" are good royalists', he had written to a party colleague back in 1854.[26] And in his rebuttal of Austria's federal reform scheme, too, the proposal he had put forward in the autumn of 1863 for a directly elected German parliament had at least hinted in this direction.

It is only too understandable that all this should since have excited people's imaginations in the highest degree. The arch-conservative in domestic affairs in league with democracy, in other words with the lower strata of society, against the traditional as well as against the new, middle-class elites – so wholly Machiavellian a plan held and continues to hold an extraordinary fascination. In the process, of course, Bismarck's actual objectives and success, in particular his expectation of success, have all too easily been overlooked. To put it more bluntly: expectations and political plans have been attributed to Bismarck in this connection that he never entertained at all.

The Prussian motion was not in fact, even in part, intended in any constructive spirit but in a purely destructive one. That it would prove unacceptable to the majority in the Federal Diet could have been predicted with relative certainty; there is little argument about that. But what could also have been predicted – and in concentrating on the remoter perspectives of the whole thing as well as on its supposedly revealing character people have usually overlooked this – was that even among those directly concerned, namely the future voters, the motion would meet with only a very limited response. Bismarck was not in fact counting on any spontaneous, enthusiastic agreement from this quarter. His calculations were aimed in a quite different direction; their true target was the middle-class liberal movement, on which he hoped to put pressure by this means. He did not really wish to mobilize the powers of the 'underworld' and govern with their support but simply to parade them before the liberal middle class, using them as a threat.

Universal suffrage, as he knew full well, had since 1848, since the sharpening of social antagonisms in the course of the revolution, been associated in the minds of the majority of liberals with the very gravest misgivings. It was by no means far-fetched to suppose that the prospect of the Bonapartist regime so frequently invoked even at that time might induce them to give in and agree to a compromise. Particularly since Bismarck did not stint the siren-songs to the effect that such a compromise would be to the liberals' advantage not only with regard to their national objectives but also in party-political terms. An example was when, having told the House of Deputies at the beginning of February 1866 that he maintained a very careful distinction between foreign and domestic policy, with 'foreign affairs' ranking 'higher than the rest', he went on to say: 'And you, gentlemen, ought to be thinking along the same lines, because after all any ground you lost at home you could very quickly make up under, say, a liberal ministry, such as might possibly ensue.'[27]

Such intimations of the party-political advantages of collaboration on the foreign policy front and the influx of support that could be expected from the powerful liberal parties outside Prussia, intimations that were tailored to a discussion already going on within the party, were not without their effect in the long run. At first, however, they did not pay off at all. The Lesser German, liberal-minded national public simply did not take the threat implicit in the Prussian proposal seriously. Which meant that the enticement that lay behind it also lost its point.

Liberal publicists had themselves conjured up the spectre of Bonapartism often enough. It now emerged very clearly, however, that this was primarily an instrument of propaganda and that they did not believe in such dangers themselves. That Bismarck might actually succeed in using the democratic franchise to create a parliamentary majority loyal to himself was something that only a few dreamers supposed, men like Lassalle's successor as president of the General German Workers' Association, Johann Baptist von Schweitzer, who were themselves always fantasizing about getting a democratic majority together. And even then such an estimate probably needed a certain amount of stiffening with government funds. The great majority saw the proposal as not only an all too transparent piece of calculation but also an unrealistic one, and they reacted accordingly. If Bismarck went on like this, *Kladderadatch* maintained, the magazine would have to cease publication; it could not keep up with him.

In view of the trend of public opinion it was already virtually certain that the governments of the small and medium-sized states of the Confederation were not going to let the Prussian motion put them under any kind of pressure either. The response to the initial Prussian approach of 24 March as to how people would react in the event of a conflict and what attitude they took towards the question of federal reform had already shown that the overwhelming majority were not prepared to change course and support Prussia's plans. Subsequently, when the motion was presented, it inevitably looked like a concession when the majority in the Federal Diet did not throw it out immediately but referred it to a committee for consideration. It was not by chance that it reached this decision at the instigation of the Bavarian government and its Minister-President, von der Pfordten.

From the outset Bavaria had occupied a key position in Bismarck's attempt to lift the approaching clash between the two German great powers above the level of a purely power-political conflict of interests and tie it in as closely as he could to the German question, thus strengthening Prussia's position as far as possible. As early as 14 February he had instructed the Prussian envoy in Munich, Prince Reuss, carefully to sound out the Bavarian Minister-President as to 'how far, when and in what direction action might be expected on his part' in the 'German national question'.[28]

In response to this approach von der Pfordten had outlined a possible peaceful solution of the conflict between Prussia and Austria: consideration should be given to declaring the north German region, including the duchies, to be Prussia's exclusive sphere of power and influence and altering the constitution of the Confederation accordingly. Whereupon he had become the first and only German head of government to whom Bismarck had the Prussian motion submitted – in initial outline on 8 March and *in extenso* on 24 March – for his approval.

This indicates with complete clarity what the whole business was all about: the remaining states of the Confederation were to be threatened with defeat at the hands of a majority not only from below, by a German parliament, but at the same time by the largest and most populous member-states apart from Austria, namely Bavaria in the south and Prussia in the north, and thus pressed into talking about a reorganization of relations in central Europe and already at this stage preparing themselves for fresh coalitions. Here too the motion in the Federal Diet was a means to an end, intended to pave the way for quite different solutions.

Unlike the liberals, von der Pfordten at first went along with this. There can be no question, however, of any real assent to Bismarck's professed plans and certainly not of a prelude to a confidential partnership over the German question in future. What von der Pfordten was thinking was that he could use the motion and beyond it the policy of the man who was proposing it in the interests of Bavaria and a possible Bavarian hegemony in southern Germany. He thus placed himself – and this is what really matters – on exactly the level at which Bismarck himself was operating with all his calculations and suggestions: namely that in politics everyone will try to use everyone else as a means to an end and will always take up a proffered gamble in the hope of successfully outplaying the other party.

The majority of liberals did not react in this way and in fact refused to get involved at all – and that was where Bismarck went wrong. His miscalculation points once again to the great gulf that existed between the two sides in terms of their basic understanding of the nature of politics. The thing that had been alienating Bismarck from his arch-conservative friends for a long time and to an ever-increasing extent now separated him from the liberal majority too.

The main claim of both camps, at least in their own view, was that they practised a politics not so much of self-interest as of conviction. They were pervaded by the idea that the objectives they were pursuing were more than just the objectives of a particular political and social group. Both factors introduced a certain relative dimension into the question of momentary success or failure and offered some protection, if only within limits, against the temptations of opportunism. But they also rendered the respective parties inflexible, dogmatic and incapable of proceeding in small stages, and they implied a pretension to an overall political and social absolutism that tended to be a stranger to compromise. There was thus as it were a deeper historical significance in the fact that in the concrete decision of 1866 both positions in practice came to grief. Only then did a politics of compromise become possible, a politics employing other categories than purely those of victory or defeat.

Bismarck, however, was involved in this only indirectly, as the principal exponent of what was eventually an extremely successful brand of power politics, the results of which destroyed the very basis of many traditional positions and necessitated a general reappraisal. To begin with, his attempt to bring the Lesser German liberal national movement into play met with complete failure – precisely because of its leaders' refusal to entertain anything that ran counter to their own convictions, even when it might have been utilized and exploited in a tactical fashion to suit their own purposes.

This completely undermined all Bavaria's ideas that it might serve its own interests in southern Germany by advocating an effective federal reform policy and a peaceful settlement between the two German great powers. In the end Munich was prepared to do no more than help Prussian policy to save face by preventing the majority in the Federal Diet from throwing the Prussian motion out straight away.

Even if the Federal Diet did then embark on formal discussion of the Prussian proposals, this could not hide from anyone the fact that Bismarck's plan – to effect a realignment of the fronts in central Europe on the eve of an armed conflict with Austria – was a complete non-starter at this level too. It was now clear that the overwhelming majority of the states of the German

Confederation would side with Austria and in the event of war would draw the appropriate military consequences.

This fact, together with its fear of a surprise attack by Prussia and Italy, finally prompted the Austrian government, towards the end of April, to prepare for war. In the light of the outcome the phrase coined by Tsar Alexander at the time that Vienna was 'resigned to war'[29] is apt to create a false impression here. If the Austrians finally decided on war only with grave misgivings, these had little to do with the way they thought that war would turn out. They were determined much more, financial considerations apart, by anxiety that in fighting a conservative power Austria might be destroying certain essential foundations of its own supremacy.

At any rate, convinced that a clash was inevitable, Vienna now set about trying to seize the initiative. In a note of 26 April that in practice marked the abandonment of the Gastein Convention the Prussian government was informed that Austria would allow the fate of the duchies to be decided by the Confederation, in other words that it would appeal to the Confederation as arbitrator. This was in itself a kind of declaration of war. For it was clear that the majority in the Confederation would decide in favour of a new medium-sized state. And it was equally clear that Prussia had no intention of accepting such a decision.

Nevertheless, throughout the whole of May there were attempts to prevent the war at the last minute. These were made by Bavaria and subsequently by a quasi-private party, namely the brother of the Austrian *Statthalter* or governor in Holstein, Anton von Gablenz, who, a Prussian subject himself, began at the end of April to travel back and forth between Berlin and Vienna with a plan of his own. The nucleus of all these attempts was a division of power in central Europe that left northern Germany largely to Prussia. According to the proposal made by Gablenz, which Bismarck received very positively at first, the duchies – with the exception of Kiel, which was to belong directly to Prussia as a naval port – were to constitute a separate state under a Prussian prince. In the last analysis, however, the time for such compromises was past. Both sides were pressing for a decision on the battlefield, Austria more openly in this final phase than Prussia, which outwardly appeared to be more ready to compromise. All they were really concerned with at this stage was occupying the better starting position.

In the end this looked more favourable to Austria than to Prussia almost all along the line. The secret treaty of 12 June between the empire and France came as the culmination of what had been a very positive development for Vienna. In fact at the time it was possible to see this more as a safeguard against the consequences of a Prussian defeat than as an initiative designed to weaken the enemy. On the other hand Bismarck's attempts to recruit new allies in central Europe for the coming clash or at least widen the circle of neutral powers had all ended in failure; he had not even managed to persuade the immediately threatened medium-sized states of Saxony and Hanover to alter their traditional political course. The only allies Prussia had left were the small states lying directly on its borders in northern and central Germany. Moreover, all his efforts to open a dialogue with the Lesser German national movement had come to nothing. The same was true of his advances to the opposition inside Prussia. The dissolution of the Prussian parliament on 9 May 1866 more or less marked the end of both, despite its being associated with the hope that fresh elections, held in different circumstances, would lead to a more favourable outcome as far as the government was concerned.

Bismarck, in other words, had not succeeded in breaking out of the circle of hostility and isolation that continued to surround both himself and his ministry. In this context there was an almost symbolic quality about the attempt made on his life by a Tübingen student named Ferdinand Cohen-Blind, a stepson of Karl Blind, a veteran of the Baden revolution of 1848–9 now living in exile in London, in the Berlin avenue of Unter den Linden on the afternoon of 7 May 1866 – at almost exactly the moment when copies of the *Kreuzzeitung* appeared on the Berlin news-stands with an article entitled 'War and Federal Reform' in which one of Bismarck's political mentors, Ludwig von Gerlach, dramatically dissociated himself from the Prussian Minister-President and his 'revolutionary policy'. The would-be assassin had been waiting for Bismarck on the tree-lined footpath along which the Minister-President was returning – unaccompanied, as he often was – from the royal palace to the Wilhelmstrasse. He missed him at first, and Bismarck managed to disarm his assailant single-handed, with two further shots that Cohen-Blind let off during the scuffle merely grazing the skin.

Not even this attempted political assassination, however, produced any discernible change of mood. In fact there were numerous expressions of regret that the enterprise had failed. 'The attempted murder of this murderer condemned unanimously by an entire people is not in the least surprising', was the opinion of the Stuttgart *Beobachter*, the organ of the Württemberg democrats. 'No one will venture to call this young man a bad German who has given his life to free the fatherland from such a monster.'[30] And as the Bonn historian Heinrich von Sybel wrote a week after the attempt, 'Everything is dominated by the bitter, tenacious, all-pervading hatred that the mismanagement of domestic affairs has provoked over the past four years and that, as it unfortunately happens, Bismarck has by virtue of his importance and his way of going about things focused upon his own person.'[31]

Attributing to the failure of the assassination attempt symbolic significance of a positive sort was something that, apart from the king and the circle of his immediate colleagues, only Bismarck himself was prepared to do. 'I several times had the impression', said a friend of the family who was present when Bismarck returned and who heard his first account of the incident, 'that he now felt himself to be God's "chosen instrument" to bring blessings upon his country.'[32] The underlinings in the two devotional books that Bismarck had for many years carried with him everywhere he went provide additional evidence of how powerfully the whole episode confirmed his deep conviction that success and failure in the lives of individuals as of communities are subject to the will of a higher power. They also show how great was his need of such confirmation at this point in his career.

For apart from the situation in Prussia and within the German Confederation, now appealed to for a decision, foreign policy developments at the European level too were not, in this final phase, exactly encouraging for the Prussian Minister-President. Bismarck did not know that Napoleon III was even now launching an attempt to break up Prussia's alliance with Italy by making Florence an offer to the effect that it would take Venetia from Austria and give it to Italy without a struggle. But it was quite clear to him that the French emperor was anxious to get Prussia somehow under closer control and tie it down to certain specific conditions.

In particular there hung over him like a sword of Damocles the fear that Napoleon might propose a European congress for the peaceful settlement of the questions at issue and that he might persuade Russia to take part. For in St Petersburg the argument was steadily gaining ground that Prussia, as its motion before the Federal Diet showed, was in reality doing more and more to place itself at the head of the revolutionary national movement. Berlin was thus, all protestations to the contrary notwithstanding, becoming a danger to the traditional order in Europe.

How seriously Bismarck regarded this development can be gauged by the fact that he spared no effort to rebut such assertions. In this connection – and here the whole passionate unconditionality of his nature stands revealed – he saw the assassination attempt as nothing less than a gift from heaven. That same evening he instructed the Prussian envoy in St Petersburg, Count von Redern, to point out to Gorchakov 'and if possible to His Majesty the Emperor [tsar] himself . . . that the attempt upon my life was made by a Württemberg *republican* and that accordingly the revolutionaries of southern Germany at least regard me not as a promoter of their plans but as the representative of the monarchical principle and are trying to get rid of me, seeing particularly my German reforms as I see them myself, namely as an obstacle to their plans, that in other words my position is not after all what it has been represented to the Emperor as being'.[33]

Almost simultaneously, however, he embarked on a venture that, had St Petersburg known about it, would have satisfied the Russians beyond all doubt that Bismarck was anything but a conservative in the sense associated with the monarchical principle and the Holy Alliance. It would have been taken as conclusive proof that the Prussian Minister-President was prepared to do a deal with any and every power and political movement, provided only that such a deal served the interests of Prussia. With the declared aim of setting up a third, internal front against Austria Bismarck got in touch with certain Hungarian revolutionaries who had emigrated after the suppression of the Hungarian revolution in August 1849.

The original initiative came from the Prussian envoy in Florence, Count Usedom. He had excellent contacts with Hungarian emigrant circles in Italy, some members of which had taken an active part in the Italian revolt against the Habsburg monarchy and saw the Risorgimento as the model for the successful prosecution of their own cause. Usedom was aware at the same time that King Victor Emanuel was already thinking about mobilizing a Hungarian auxiliary unit in the event of war with Austria; in the king's immediate entourage there was a man serving as adjutant, General Stefan Türr, who had fought in Garibaldi's army and was a literal embodiment of the comradeship in arms that existed between Hungarians and Italians.

It was with a notable lack of enthusiasm at first that Bismarck accepted Usedom's suggestion in the middle of May that Prussia might consider something similar and make common cause with Florence in this respect as well. Indeed he warned against taking any ill-considered steps that were not very carefully covered. In fact, however, reviving old ideas and associations, he had just taken up a very similar thread himself.

That thread led to a colonel of the Hungarian revolutionary army of 1848-9 by the name of Kiss de Nemeskér. Brother-in-law to the former French Foreign Minister, Thouvenel, Kiss had meanwhile become adviser to Prince Napoleon, a cousin of the emperor who had been elevated to the Senate and made a general. As spokesman for the Hungarian emigrant community he obviously played an important part behind the scenes. Whether it was in this capacity or as an emissary of certain circles in French politics that Kiss was in Berlin for the first week of May onwards is not clear. Once there, at any rate, he became the middleman in certain crucial exchanges of information and contacts, the eventual upshot of which was that Bismarck, through Usedom, invited General Türr to Berlin and together with him and another leading Hungarian revolutionary of the years 1848-9, General Klapka, who was called in shortly afterwards, discussed in detail the formation of a Hungarian legion.

Things quickly progressed to a point where on 11 June, only a day after Türr's arrival in Berlin, Bismarck was instructing Usedom to make a binding commitment to the Italian government to reimburse half the costs of such an undertaking and to ask them for an advance in order that matters might be put in hand from the Italian end immediately. 'I am pursuing my objective with the clearest of consciences as it seems to me to be right for my country and for Germany', he told a French journalist around this time. 'As far as means are concerned, I use those that, in the absence of others, present themselves to me.'[34]

As a result of an indiscretion, the purpose of which was to counteract the alleged belittlement by Prussia and the German public of the role of the Italian army in the war of 1866, the whole process became known not first to posterity but, at least in outline, as early as the middle of 1868, at a most unfavourable time for Bismarck. On 21 July 1868 La Marmora, who two years before had been not only chief minister but also supreme commander of the Italian army, used a speech in the Italian parliament to inform the world that at the time he had let himself be guided to a great extent by the wishes and recommendations of Prussia.[35] It was not Italy, he said, but Prussia that had abandoned their common course in 1866. In proof of which La Marmora read out a telegram that Usedom had sent him on 17 June 1866, calling upon him in what for a diplomatic communication were most unusual terms to march on Vienna directly and at once, thus striking 'at the heart of Austria's power', and to link up with the Prussian troops 'in the centre of the imperial monarchy itself'. And not only with the Prussian troops; on the contrary Prussia hoped and expected, Usedom had said further, that a 'corps made up of national elements', marching south from Silesia, would link up inside the monarchy with the 'national armed forces soon to be formed' and likewise march on Vienna.[36]

The disclosure of this information from top secret files created an enormous sensation. Bismarck promptly denied having had any part in the affair and attempted to represent the whole thing as an unauthorized initiative on the part of the envoy, who he said had based his action on quite untenable premisses and mere suppositions. But of course nobody believed him. Everyone was convinced that Usedom had been acting on behalf of and with the full backing of the Prussian government. What people had often suspected now seemed proven beyond doubt: this man would stop at nothing to achieve his ends. The professed defender of the traditional order and the monarchical principle had been prepared for the sake of success to ally himself with declared enemies of that order and that principle. People in many places wondered: where would the man ever draw the line?

Then as subsequently, however, the significance of the whole episode was often wrongly appraised. This is true above all with regard to what it can tell us about the character of Bismarck's policy as a whole. Whereas it was once said of Heinrich von Sybel's glorifying and apologetic history of the founding of the Reich that in it the tiger Bismarck was falsely portrayed as a pussy-cat, since then the opposite tendency has often prevailed. The tiger now has to be made to appear as brutal and as dangerous as possible and above all utterly unscrupulous in his choice of means.

Even if the Prussian Minister-President was prepared to use everything possible as a means to his end, forgetting for the time being about possible consequences, nevertheless he deliberately did not go beyond a certain point: the means must not be allowed to become an end, nor must the opponent of the day and what he stood for be destroyed. In practice this meant that even the alliance with the forces of revolution was intended only to coerce the opponent into taking stock of his position. The aim was to induce him, in the light of the dangers that threatened from those forces, to give up his opposition.

His constant assumption in all this, essentially dictated by his experiences in 1848–9, was that those forces could be controlled. The danger in any given case, discounting extreme situations, was confined in his view to the imaginations of the fearful. Whether he was not mistaken here, failing above all to see that the true threats sprang from quite other factors than he supposed, is another question. At any rate it cannot be said, even with respect to what was an extremely dangerous set of circumstances for Prussia in May and June 1866, that he pursued a policy of 'all or nothing'.

It was not only his own shrewdness that advised him against this but the whole situation. Granted, he enjoyed being sarcastic at the expense of those who were always talking about Europe and the European public and about what that public was allegedly not prepared to accept. But he knew perfectly well that there were limits here, to overstep which would lead to incalculable risks. And he also knew that the maxim 'Let him who desires peace prepare for war' enshrined a general truth in its converse form as well. In other words, he who regarded a war as inevitable to implement certain specific objectives must see to it that war did not unleash additional objectives. Otherwise there was a risk of its bursting all bounds and eluding political control.

To keep war subject to politics in this way was to prove as difficult as the balancing act that Bismarck performed in the run-up to the war in order to block any intervention if not by Europe at least by the two chief continental powers, France and Russia. Predictably Napoleon had once again floated the idea of a congress of the European great powers and the parties directly involved. This was to attempt to settle the points at issue by process of negotiation. After much toing and froing the French emperor managed to win both Britain and Russia round to the idea. On 24 May 1866 these powers issued a joint invitation to Austria, Prussia, Italy and the German Confederation, thus once again expressly underlining the separate existence of the latter under international law. The specific points of discussion proposed by the inviting powers without prior consultation with the parties involved were the question of what was to happen to Schleswig-Holstein, the Italian question and the problem of reforming the German Confederation, at least as far as this affected the interests of the other powers and the balance of power in Europe.

Bismarck saw with perfect clarity that such a congress could succeed only at the expense of the very objectives that Prussia was out to achieve. For the congress would naturally start from the status quo and seek to negotiate modifications of it by a process of mutual compensation. On the other hand he knew that Prussia of all parties could not possibly refuse the invitation. That would have branded Berlin as the power that intended to change the existing order unilaterally and without regard to the opinions and interests of the other powers.

Austria for its part was in a very different situation. It stood for the preservation of the existing order and of a legal system that had hitherto enjoyed internationl acceptance. It could argue, particularly with regard to the 'Italian disagreement' referred to in the text of the invitation, that the projected congress called all this into question from the outset, simply by the way in which the agenda was drawn up.

This was in fact the position that Vienna adopted, confident of its own strength and of the success of the talks it had initiated with France. It made its acceptance of the invitation dependent upon all participants in the congress pledging in advance that they would agree to no territorial expansions or increases in power on either side.

In view of the way things turned out, this decision on Vienna's part may seem somewhat questionable, not least from the tactical standpoint. In a kind of negative collaboration between the two parties headed for a military confrontation it freed Prussia from all anxiety regarding a joint intervention by the remaining European powers. And it left Austria looking, if not like the aggressor, at least like a power that was opposed to any kind of international co-operation for the joint removal of tensions and settlement of crises. However, if we bear in mind the situation as it was in late May and early June 1866 and the attitudes that the powers concerned could be expected to adopt, Austria's reaction appears in a substantially different light.

From virtually none of those powers could Vienna expect unconditional, active support for its position. On the other hand it had good reason to fear that at the congress too its cause would be forced on to the defensive – a situation the empire had been in for a long time now, not so much against Prussia as against the voices of liberalism, the national ideal, economic developments and the resultant opportunism of most of those who had been its partners hitherto. In such a situation it was not after all so unthinkable that a determined attack might constitute the best defence. If on account of a variety of illusions many chances had already been missed, that need not mean that what at least the Hofburg saw as a promising opportunity must once again be renounced in favour of what would surely now be a somewhat dubious compromise. It is not hard to imagine the tones in which the boldness of such a decision would have been praised in many quarters had the outcome been the reverse of what it was.

On 1 June 1866, the day when the Austrian government in practice declined the invitation to the projected congress, it took the decisive step in the direction of war. In an official statement issued on that day by its Frankfurt envoy, von Kübeck, it placed the decision regarding the future of the duchies in the hands of the Federal Diet. In so doing Vienna dissociated itself not only from Gastein but also from any conceivable continuation of a policy of compromise with Prussia. The expected reaction was not slow in coming. In an order to the Prussian envoys to the major powers in Paris, London, Florence and St Petersburg as well as to those in Munich and Frankfurt, Bismarck took up the gauntlet on 4 June with the statement, to be communicated officially, 'that we can see nothing in this action by the Austrian government except a deliberate, direct provocation and a desire to force a rupture of relations and war'.[37] Five days later, on 9 June, following the final collapse of the congress project, Prussian troops invaded Holstein, though without the intended engagement materializing. And the day after that Prussia submitted a federal reform plan in Frankfurt aimed at excluding Austria from the Confederation and introducing a fresh division of supremacy within that organization, this time between Bavaria and Prussia.

Berlin did not of course believe the proposal had any chance of succeeding. Rather it contained the official expression of Prussia's war aim, beyond the definitive acquisition of Schleswig-Holstein, and as such constituted an informal declaration of war on Austria. The latter's response was clear and expected: the Viennese government moved on 11 June that the non-Prussian army of the Confederation be mobilized to protect the 'internal security of Germany and the threatened rights of its confederate members.'[38] When a vote was rushed through three days later the motion duly received the expected majority. Apart from Prussia itself only the Hanseatic towns, the two Mecklenburgs, Holland for Luxembourg and a series of small central German states voted against it, while the grand duchy of Baden was the only state outside Prussia's immediate sphere of influence to abstain. The Prussian envoy to the Federal Diet, von Savigny, thereupon declared in a statement prepared well in advance that the federal treaty, having been 'breached', had now 'lapsed' and that his own job was 'at an end'.[39] Even the extremely short-term Prussian ultimatum to Hanover, Saxony and the electorate of Hesse to declare their neutrality and furthermore to adopt the Prussian federal reform plan was intended solely to achieve a final clarification of the fronts. Its rejection immediately triggered off the first act of war in the shape of the invasion of those states by Prussian troops and as a direct reaction a resolution on the part of the Confederation to give military assistance to its threatend members as swiftly as possible and force Prussia back into due compliance with federal law.

The parties to the conflict thus found themselves, by what in terms of federal law were very complicated ways that were to keep the lawyers busy for a long time, and without a formal declaration of war, embarked upon hostilities that many people had long rgarded as inevitable – indeed, despite all misgivings, even necessary – and that others had seen as a disastrous eventuality of unforeseeable dimensions and consequences. But what kind of war was it, looked at from a distance of more than a century? A German 'war of brothers'? The first war of unification? An eighteenth-century Cabinet war fought with nineteenth-century weapons? A readily chosen way out of internal conflicts? Or a historical fatality, the outcome of a malefic constellation of circumstances that could no longer be properly controlled by peaceful means?

Contemporaries assembled a mass of arguments for each and every interpretation at the time, and only a few new ones have been added since. Their relative value and importance have of course changed continuously, depending on the historical situation and experience dictating the verdict at any given moment. It is not only our estimate of war in general, our readiness to see it, if not as a legitimate instrument, at least as a kind of *ultima ratio* of politics, that has changed fundamentally under the impact of two world wars. Its supposed justification by the objectives implemented with its aid has also come to look more and more suspect, both morally and in regard to content.

What, then – as had to be asked in the light of future developments – of its creative power, something contemporaries scarcely disputed as yet though they only partially approved of its practical consequences? Did not the results to which it gave rise turn out to be highly unstable, creations of very slight historical substance and duration? And did it not on the other hand destroy much that was positive and that might have been capable of evolving in a quite different direction? Was it not, in the last analysis, merely symptomatic of an inability to cope with conflicts in a truly creative way and arrive at fresh syntheses that would last?

Such questions are not only necessary and legitimate; in the light of subsequent events they literally force themselves upon us. They are still, however, for their part too heavily influenced by a view that the war of 1866 and that of 1870–1 fostered and two world wars seemed subsequently to confirm: that war in general has been the great catalyst and indeed modifier of historical evolution, as it were independently determining the substance of that evolution.

Yet precisely this is not true at all or is true to only a limited extent of the Bismarckian wars of 1866 and 1870–1, unlike the two world wars, if we consider those wars as such, their course and immediate consequences. They were 'Bismarckian' wars not in the sense of any rather superficial question of who was to blame for them but in the sense that each of them helped to bring to fruition the kinds of interest and objective that Bismarck in principle regarded as enforceable and achievable by peaceful means as well, in other words through the medium of agreement and compromise, taking into account the interests and objectives of the other party concerned.

Military success undoubtedly lessened the victor's willingness to make concessions and increased his inclination to impose the compromise he had thus anticipated, so to speak. Yet with a single, admittedly fateful exception, namely the annexation of Alsace and Lorraine, in neither case did he go beyond just such a previously projected compromise. This called simply for the removal of the contradictions that had arisen between form and content, between existing legal and treaty relations in Europe, particularly central Europe, and the actual distribution of power in the broadest sense, in other words not merely at governmental and inter-governmental level.

War was seen as an instrument of violent redressment. It was seen as a means of preserving in a modified form the internal and external order in Europe as Bismarck saw it by preventing those contradictions between form and content from eventually becoming too powerful and venting themselves independently. Already visible here, behind the image of the unscrupulous Prussian power politican who was always ready for war, is that of the European peacemaker of the post–1871 period, however much the two images appear to contradict each other at first glance. What draws them together is precisely the thing that at the same time characterizes the wars of 1866 and 1870–1, namely that neither the one nor the other aimed at anything really new but sought to preserve as much as possible of the status quo while simply giving fresh form to a content that was already present and was in any case pressing for recognition and acceptance.

The wars of 1866 and 1870–1 and their consequences appear in this light as representing the minimum amount of change that could not be avoided. Indeed, the man who essentially determined their course and outcome can even be said to have taken to such lengths his attempt to channel the new economic, social, national and more narrowly political forces that were pressing for such change that the old tensions between form and content very quickly reappeared and came once more to dominate the scene.

In other words, however revolutionary many of their internal and external consequences were, particularly in the effects and impulses to which they gave rise, these were in many respects – to coin a deliberately paradoxical phrase – conservative wars. In terms of the distribution of power both internally and internationally and the definition of political and social scales of value they did not, in their course and in their outcome, rise above the lower limit of the kind of change that seemed to be imperative if crucial elements of the status quo were to be preserved. 'The unification of Germany', the ageing Bismarck said tersely on one occasion, 'was a conservative achievement.'[40] The so-called wars of unification were in this sense fitting tools for a man who in the pursuit of his essentially conservative aims, directed at preserving the basic structure of the existing order, was bold or even unscrupulous enough to make use of everything that promised effectively to further that pursuit.

Bismarck was aware, of course, that he was operating in a highly dangerous area here and that in this instance in particular he might easily find himself in the role of the sorcerer's apprentice. He was not so much concerned about the long-term effects of the changes thus implemented by military means, which are what have principally concerned posterity; it was his conviction that these largely eluded the calculations and potential influence of the agent directly involved. He did, however, concentrate with an intensity that took him to the verge of total mental and physical exhaustion on keeping the instrument of war very firmly under his control at every stage.

This was the tacit condition, as it were, on which he had taken up that instrument without any great inner scruples. Even in the event of failure, this must remain a controlled war. Because otherwise, instead of controlled changes in the internal and international spheres there was a risk of uncontrolled developments erupting. Instead of the controlled effects of a 'revolution from above' there was a risk of revolution from below. 'If with the Confederation in its present form we were to face a major crisis', he put it once on the eve of the conflict with reference to the cold war within the Confederation, 'a wholesale revolutionary upheaval in Germany is the most likely outcome, given the instability of circumstances as they are at present. That kind of catastrophe can be precluded only by timely reform from above.' [41]

The danger, as Bismarck knew, was considerably increased by the type of war that the Prussian military leadership, under the decisive influence of the chief of staff, Helmuth von Moltke, envisaged waging. From the start it was no limited engagement in the style of eighteenth-century warfare that they planned, one answering to possibly wide-ranging but at the same time precisely defined and hence limited political objectives; what they had in mind was an unlimited, 'total' war that aimed to destroy the opponent's military might as completely as possible.

Clausewitz, the man who had analysed this type of warfare in detail with reference to Napoleonic practice and described its methods and consequences, may have wished to see it harnessed unreservedly in the service of politics. It was perfectly obvious, however, that making the military objective unlimited as a matter of principle could very easily lead to a removal of all limits as far as political objectives were concerned. At any rate the military leadership could be expected during the course of the war to press for all political decisions and actions to be subordinated to the military objective – to say nothing of the destructive and irrational passions, the desires for revenge on the one side and the wholly exaggerated expectations on the other, that this type of warfare threatened to release.

In the war of 1866 it was Bismarck's additional good fortune, as it were, over and above Prussia's military success as such, that because of the surprising brevity of the campaign all this had only a very limited effect. The first encounter went rather badly as far as the Prussian troops were concerned: on 27 June the Hanoverian army under General von Arentschildt fought a successful defensive engagement against them near Langensalza, a victory so prestigious that, little though it did to prevent the eventual military defeat of the Guelf monarchy, the supporters of that monarchy drew on it for a long time to come. After that, however, Moltke's plans paid off to an extent that surprised even the Prussian leadership. His strategy – to confuse the Austrian army as it marched into the Bohemian Basin by having the three Prussian attacking armies make separate approaches and then defeat it in an encircling action – led to an overwhelming success between Königgrätz and Sadowa on 3 July 1866. Although the military perfectionists saw it as not quite complete since a large proportion of the Austrian army managed to escape at the last moment, militarily it meant that the war was already as good as decided. For even though Vienna did manage to beat the Italians in the Battle of Custozza on 24 June and finally to crush them in a naval engagement off the island of Lissa (Vis) on 20 July, the real power of the empire was smashed at Königgrätz and a complete conquest of the country only to be staved off by political means with the conclusion of a swift peace.

This was what Bismarck now worked towards. His principal war aims had already been achieved: a free hand for Prussia in northern Germany, the dissolution of the German Confederation and the removal of Austrian hegemony and Austria's claim to hegemony in central Europe. The main thing to be done now was to make what had been achieved permanently secure. Here the Prussian Minister-President had to contend with two quite different counter-forces linked in a kind of negative collaboration: with Napoleon III, who saw all his calculations upset and who sought to use the time between the actual military decision and the conclusion of the peace to implement at least some of his original objectives and the concessions already made to him by Austria; and with those sections of the Prussian leadership that now began to tailor their objectives to Prussia's overwhelming military success.

The latter included the King of Prussia himself. Undoubtedly one of the heaviest burdens of Bismarck's political career was having to combine the diplomatic defensive battle against Napoleon III with combating all attempts to overstep the limits of the objectives originally set. It was more than just his enjoyment of a neat turn of phrase that prompted him to remark as an old man: 'My two greatest difficulties were first to get King William into Bohemia and then to get him out again.'[42]

The whole thing was further complicated by the fact that within those limits Bismarck was pressing for a far more radical course of action than the king at first felt to be compatible with the conservative ideal and with his own feeling for justice. That some of the princely colleagues who had fought against him should forfeit crown and country while others escaped largely unscathed struck him not only as deeply unjust but also as potentially dangerous. Was this not tantamount to abandoning the principle of the divine right of kings to the arbitrary dictates of power, thus countenancing the allegation that might was right? Who was going to believe in the monarchical principle any more if one of its chief champions, the King of Prussia, did not hesitate to topple from their thrones such old-established rulers as the King of Hanover, the Elector of Hesse and the Duke of Nassau? And if one was going in for power politics in the style of Frederick the Great, why spare Austria, of all countries, and Saxony too, the actual enemies, instead of recouping land and money from them?

Bismarck's most urgent argument in this connection was that this was the only way of concluding a peace with Austria without the intervention of third parties, the only way in which an extension of the war, with a highly uncertain outcome, could be avoided. 'Provided we are not excessive in our demands and do not think that we have conquered the *world*', he had written to Johanna as early as 9 July, 'we shall also achieve a worthwhile peace. But we are as quickly carried away as we are cast down, and I have the thankless task of pouring water into the bubbling wine and pointing out that we are not the only inhabitants of Europe but live in it with three other powers that detest and envy us!'[43]

The weight and realism of this argument were difficult to refute. As early as 5 July Napoleon III had taken an approach by Austria as an excuse for intervening with an offer to mediate between the warring parties. Naturally, the offer at the same time contained a tacit threat. Bismarck was therefore in a hurry to agree to it, though his intimates heard him mutter through his teeth: 'In a few years' time Louis will probably be sorry he took sides against us like this; it may cost him dearly.'[44]

The French intervention may indeed have appeared somewhat partisan when Napoleon III based it on Austria's offer to give up Venetia and sought in this way to prise apart the military alliance between Prussia and Italy. But of course anything else would have been quite futile from the standpoint of French interests. Prussia was now the military victor, and compensations were going to be obtained only by putting pressure on the victor, not by aiding and abetting him.

It was with such compensation that the negotiations between Berlin and Paris were primarily concerned. These were conducted over the following weeks partly between the Prussian legation in the French capital and the government there and partly between Bismarck and the French envoy Benedetti at Prussian headquarters in Nikolsburg.

Bismarck's tactics on this occasion, over and above all questions of detail, was one of delay. It was not unlike a rather dangerous tightrope-walking act. For although the French army and French public opinion were neither psychologically nor materially prepared for an effective intervention – an undubitable achievement of Prussian policy – France as a power constituted a threat even unprepared. Prussia must therefore on no account take the risk of provoking uncontrolled reactions on the part of the French emperor, who was nothing like as firmly in control at home as he had been in the 1850s and early 1860s. Above all he must not be given the impression that he was on the way to becoming a mere piece on the chessboard of his Prussian opponent, who continued to cherish a certain secret sympathy for him.

The skill and intuition that Bismarck exhibited over the next few weeks were undoubtedly of a very high order indeed. They show him at the height of his diplomatic powers, powers acquired through long years of dealing with many different types of resistance at home. The nationalist school of history, particularly prone to swaggering in this connection, has in its overemphasis on Bismarck's success and on his skilful outmanoeuvring of his opponent only imperfectly grasped the really crucial element here. Bismarck's real and quite extraordinary achievement in this respect lay in the fact that he managed within the limits of what was humanly possible to protect Prussia's relationship with France and in particular with Napoleon III and to keep it in being. He managed it by not merely refraining from any kind of outward expression of triumph but actually seeking to represent everything as the product of circumstances and to keep the prospects for the future wide open from the French point of view as well.

The much-discussed question of what sacrifices the Prussian Minister-President would have been prepared to make had things turned out less favourably for Prussia and the pressure from France been stepped up thereby loses much of its importance. Bismarck's actions in 1866 were primarily those of a Prussian statesman who knew perfectly well that the open hostility of France, even if a favourable international situation did momentarily put Prussia in a position to avoid its consequences, would be highly dangerous for Prussia and for the preservation of the territorial and power gains it was on the point of making and that it might even constitute a threat to the country's very existence. A coalition between France, Austria and Russia for the preservation or restoration of the status quo on the European continent was not just an unrealistic nightmare. Dams had to be thrown up against such an eventuality in at least two directions. The question still seemed wide open whether in the case of Austria this could be done successfully in future, and since the Russian position was by no means as secure as had long been thought, France began to look less like potentially the next opponent on the battlefield and more like a possible partner. To keep it as such, if necessary at the cost of certain minor territories that in the national sense belonged to Germany, was something Bismarck could not and indeed must not rule out in principle in the interests of what was so far the only state he represented.

He was aware, of course, that he had to set his threshold very high here not only in deference to his king but also with regard to his future relations with the German national movement. But he cannot be said to have ruled out such a deal under any circumstances from the word 'go'. It formed the basis of his inner flexibility and of his credibility as a partner in the negotiations with the French.

Bismarck went into those negotiations with the trump card of Prussian self-restraint even in the wake of its triumphant success on the battlefield. If Napoleon III had been secretly afraid that Prussia would now invoke the national principle and immediately lay hands on southern Germany, he was pleasantly surprised. It emerged from the negotiations that von der Goltz conducted with Napoleon III and the French government on Bismarck's behalf that even Prussia took the view that, following the dissolution of the German Confederation, southern Germany should remain wholly independent. Possibly it should constitute a separate South German Confederation. All Prussia demanded – but this it demanded unreservedly – was hegemony in northern Germany. For the rest, it said, Berlin had no objection to an eventual plebiscite in the nationally mixed areas of northern Schleswig to determine the future of that part of the duchy.

Von der Goltz did not bring all this out as Prussia's programme straight away. By arrangement with and in consultation with Bismarck he allowed it to look like the outcome of the negotiations. In this way the ambassador gave Napoleon III the impression that he was himself playing the part of the broker who, in coming up with the compromise, as it were covers his own expenses in the process. The ambassador further said that Prussia might well be prepared, in the event of a happy outcome to the whole affair, to discuss a minor surrender of territory in the south, amounting for example to a restoration of the so-called 1814 frontiers. Whether or not this statement was quite as unauthorized as most historians, taking their cue from things Bismarck said on the subject, would have us believe, it certainly suited the overall situation very well. In that situation it was Prussia's overriding concern to show the French emperor present and future in what should appear a promising light for France.

In view of the probable reaction of the German national movement and its possible exploitation by Prussia, Napoleon III acted very cautiously and hesitantly at first. When he did venture to take up the suggestions of the Prussian ambassador and demanded first the 1814 frontiers and finally, in a formal draft treaty of 5 August 1866, the entire Bavarian Palatinate and the districts of Hesse on the left bank of the Rhine, including Mainz, he met with an unambiguous refusal from Bismarck. It was combined with an open threat to unleash the forces of German nationalism against France, should this be necessary.

The fact was that the situation had meanwhile undergone a decisive change. It had become obvious that a French intervention on behalf of Austria was scarcely to be expected any more, with Paris instead clearly engaged in coming to terms with the victor. Consequently the political leadership of the empire had made its own decision to work towards a swift peace. One reason for this was that the Prussian terms, presented in the guise of a French proposal for mediation, seemed extraordinarily moderate. There was no mention of straight surrenders of territory. Even the customary war indemnity demanded of Vienna was within reasonable bounds, which given the state of Austria's public finances was particularly important; after subtraction of Prussian debts, it was eventually set at 20 million taler. The bill – as Bismarck, with the agreement of the French emperor, had stated quite openly early on – was to be footed by others: Hanover, the electorate of Hesse, Nassau and what had hitherto been the free city of Frankfurt, which was not only the seat of the Federal Diet, now to be dissolved, but above all the most important financial and commercial emporium in central Europe. All of them were to lose their independent status and become provinces of Prussia, just like the long and hotly disputed Elbe duchies of Schleswig and Holstein, which everyone now regarded as Prussia's natural victory prize.

In the circumstances, all that had stood in the way of a rapid conclusion of peace between Prussia and Austria was resistance within the Prussian camp,

Vienna having evinced only verbal misgivings at thus leaving its northern and central European allies in the lurch. In his memoirs, Bismarck heightened the drama of that resistance. Again, current considerations played a crucial role here, specifically his irritation at what he said was an attempt by the youngest scion of the house of Hohenzollern to play down his, Bismarck's, part in the successes of Prussian policy and in laying the foundations of future relations between Germany and Austria. Nevertheless, the evidence of immediate contemporaries, men who were influenced by such considerations and by the experience of future developments, likewise reveals that there was in fact a very deep-rooted and fundamental conflict involved here.

Apart from all the superficial expectations it was a question of the object of the war and the fruits of victory. In voicing his misgivings with regard to the Prussian peace terms as formulated by Bismarck, William I was expressing on behalf of many like-minded people in the higher echelons of the country's military and political leadership a déeper unease about the way the whole affair was turning out. What was he after, they asked themselves, this man who had promised to rescue the Prussian monarchy from revolution at home and from further humiliation and loss of power abroad and who had now so obviously attained his goal? Were the prophets right, perhaps, who had predicted that those who had believed they could make use of him were in for a big surprise? Did he mean to go so far as to curtail the victors' victory in order that he should eventually appear as the only really triumphant party?

Such questions understandably suggested themselves. The answer, though, lies at a deeper level. It lies in the insight that distinguished Bismarck from the overwhelming majority of those victors and accounted for his paramountcy in the years to come. That insight told him that the victory so far achieved was a highly superficial one and that the watchword was still, indeed now more than ever: 'If revolution there is to be, let us rather undertake it than undergo it.' And Bismarck was more than ever determined to undertake it.

[9]

'Revolution from Above'

'If in spite of this due representation there is no obtaining from the *vanquished* what the army and the country are entitled to expect, that is to say a heavy war-expenses indemnity from Austria as the principal enemy or quite strikingly extensive territorial acquisitions . . . the *victor* will have to swallow this bitter pill at the very gates of Vienna and let posterity be the judge.' Such was the decision, as noted in the margin of Bismarck's vote on the question of the peace terms, that William I had agreed to accept after prolonged and agonizing discussions during which the supposedly so imperturbable Prussian Minister-President, on the verge of a nervous breakdown, had several times burst into fits of tears.[1]

The posterity appealed to by the Prussian king has been almost unanimous in celebrating the sparing of Austria as one of Bismarck's very greatest achievements, an act of wise moderation that in fact made possible all that followed, principally the successful establishment of the Lesser German national state. It had implications that went far beyond the immediate power-political and foreign policy context. This was something more, as the Prussian king sensed very clearly in his level-headed way, than a piece of *Realpolitik* based on a calculation of interests. It was also more than just a foreign policy arrangement offering as broad a perspective as possible, though this was the aspect on which Bismarck repeatedly laid special emphasis in his negotiations with the representatives of other powers as well as within his own camp. It had to do at the same time with the future foundations of the Prussian state, both with regard to domestic policy and with regard to territorial and power-political considerations.

In the moment of its greatest triumph, seen in traditional absolutist and military terms, the Prussian monarchy was to impose a twofold restraint on itself. On the one hand it was to forgo taking any tangible 'revenge for Olmütz', for example by marching into Vienna. On the other hand it was to allow fundamental principles of the traditional political order to be pronounced, in its name, a mere fiction, whereby it was openly conceded that a modern state of any size rested on essentially different foundations and that it had long owed its power and internal cohesion to quite other factors.

This meant that the new Prussia and what was emerging as the new area of direct hegemony around its sovereign territory – the future North

German Confederation – would in this respect too be essentially new political creations with a crucially altered basic structure. Future developments were to follow not the traditional pattern of the expanding sovereign state of the time of Frederick the Great, which the Prussian king and his generals were particularly given to recalling in the summer of 1866, but an entirely different plan: the conversion of external, military, power-political successes into internal structural changes. Although in the long term these might be of more use to the cause and position of the monarchy than anything else, at first they had the look of a retreat in the very moment of victory.

On the domestic front too, then, it was a question, for Bismarck, of choosing between an imposed, victor's peace and a peace by negotiation. This was something the Prussian king only dimly suspected at first in the discussions of the peace terms held among the Prussian leadership in the little Moravian town of Nikolsburg. His son the crown prince, on the other hand, who had been thoroughly at odds with Bismarck at least since the events surrounding his Danzig speech in the summer of 1863, very quickly saw that on the basis of the new situation Bismarck was prepared to show moderation and seek an understanding and had decided to turn over a new leaf not only vis-à-vis Austria but also at home. Not least for this reason he gave Bismarck his strong support, and under his influence the king eventually abandoned his opposition. So it was that on 26 July 1866, in the castle of the Dietrichstein princes in Nikolsburg, the family seat of the wife of the incumbent Austrian Foreign Minister, where the king and his immediate staff had been in residence for the past week, the preliminary peace was concluded with Austria on the terms drafted by Bismarck. The final peace treaty was signed in Prague just four weeks later, on 23 August.

That peace included two additional concessions to French policy that at the same time served to parry for good and all any further French aspirations for compensation. It formally laid down that a plebiscite would be held in the northern districts of Schleswig to determine which country those districts should belong to in future – as never in fact occurred. And it stipulated that in future the south German states, whether singly or in a confederation, should 'have an international, independent existence'; the possibility of a link between an eventual confederation in southern Germany and the projected North German Confederation must not be allowed to jeopardize this international independence of the southern states.[2]

Neither concession seemed to Bismarck to be of much importance. He had offered the plebiscite in Schleswig himself in the knowledge that its practical implementation would be largely left to the discretion of Prussia. And as for consolidation of the Main 'frontier', the stipulation to this effect offered him not inconsiderable advantages in terms of both foreign and domestic policy. Abroad it not only demonstrated Prussia's self-restraint, thus calming the fears of the European great powers; it also offered the possibility of playing south German fears of a new Rhenish Confederation and French mistrust of Prussia and the German national movement off against each other. And at home it provided additional justification for a course he already intended to pursue, namely concentrating on northern Germany and on the political stabilization of that region, as well as making such a course seem unavoidable for the time being in the eyes of the liberal national movement. It thus threw up an additional dam against an overflow of national forces and the formation of a self-generating and possibly almost uncontrollable revolutionary national movement of the kind that Italy had seen six years earlier.

By combining both elements Bismarck managed, as a direct and immediate consequence of the Treaty of Prague and its fixing of the River Main line, to draw the south German states closer to Prussia and keep the national and liberal forces in the south at a distance. By pointing explicitly to French ambitions in southern Germany he induced the governments of Bavaria, Württemberg and Baden to conclude alongside their peace treaties secret defensive and offensive pacts with Prussia in the event of a French attack; Hesse-Darmstadt was left out of this because of the allegedly pro-French sympathies of its Minister-President, Reinhard von Dalwigk. At the same time he suggested to the liberal movement in southern Germany, the majority among which was now swiftly falling into line with Prussia, that precisely in the interests of the national cause it must contain itself in patience, await consolidation in the north and in the south work for the idea, not as yet very popular there, of a Lesser German national state. Bismarck's argument right up until immediately before the war with France in 1870–1 was that they could not simply go at unification like a bull at a gate. They must allow things to mature and await a favourable constellation of circumstances.

This line of argument was not going to convince anyone unless Bismarck came in principle to be regarded as a champion of the national cause. That, however, presupposed a fundamental change of attitude on his part towards at least certain sections of the liberal movement. For it was liberalism that continued to provide the chief vehicle of the national ideal; an anti-liberal nationalism was not yet a force with mass appeal.

Just such a rapprochement between Bismarck and a section of the liberals did in fact emerge a relatively short time after Königgrätz and Nikolsburg, the Prussian Minister-President having already declared before the war: 'You'll have constitution enough when we've won.'[3] But opinions are still divided, as they were then, on the question of whether, in taking this step, the liberal camp was succumbing to mere self-deception as a result of a blend of opportunism and gullibility or whether it had adequate reason to revise its traditional stance as well as its assessment of the political situation and of the opportunities that situation held for it. To put it in more pointed terms, was that section of the German liberal middle class that now increasingly resolved to co-operate with Bismarck – though in fact such co-operation was rarely full and unreserved – breaking faith with its own past and with its political convictions and objectives and setting up in their place mere success-worship and the yardstick of furthering its own material interests; or was it acting in pursuit of a calculation that possessed an undeniable inner rationality, practical chances of success – even in terms of the liberals' own beliefs and ideals – and to that extent historical plausibility?

The answer to this question is of central importance as regards our verdict on what followed. For that very reason we must beware of falling in with the widespread tendency to see the process purely from the standpoint of the eventual outcome – without regard to the fact that quite other factors, factors scarcely foreseeable at the time, also played a part. It is a view in which an ultimately unpolitical dogmatism easily takes on the appearance of the highest political wisdom and morality, whereas the attempt actively to influence and if possible take advantage of certain developments already in progress and constellations of forces actually to hand appears, in the light of its eventual failure, as having been problematic from the start and prompted by dubious motives.

If we take a sober look at the situation with which Prussian and German liberalism and the German liberal middle class found themselves confronted in the summer of 1866, we have to admit that it was as confusing as it was seductive. Königgrätz was without question a victory for the political opponent, for all that that overwhelming military success left even many liberals, especially in Prussia, not unimpressed and prompted them to reflect on the extraordinary perspectives that it opened up; it was certainly 'a marvellous feeling to be there when history turns a corner', as even Theodor Mommsen noted at the time.[4] The monarchy, the military leadership, most of whom were violently anti-liberal, the hated conflict ministry under Bismarck and the whole arch-conservative Prussian ruling class were not only placed in a stronger position as a result of that victory; they now had broad sections of the population behind them and were on the verge of becoming the new nucleus of crystallization for people's hopes of national unification.

The new elections for the Prussian House of Deputies, held on the very day of the Battle of Königgrätz, 3 July 1866, in other words before the victory became known, had already shown that a massive shift of mood was under way. The conservatives had gained more than 100 seats, shooting from 35 to a new total of 136. The Left Centre and Progressive parties, on the other hand, had lost almost as many, dropping from 247 in the old House to 148 in the new. This had cost them their parliamentary majority, for the Old Liberals with twenty-four instead of nine seats as hitherto were expected to come down on the other side.

Given the successes of government and army, the liberal camp was well aware in the following days and weeks that this was only the beginning of a most adverse development as far as the liberal cause was concerned. Bismarck's much-derided plan to summon a German parliament on a universal suffrage basis, a plan that kept on cropping up under various guises in the semi-official press, now appeared in a quite different and for the liberal opposition distinctly ominous light. It looked as if the only question now was whether Bismarck would translate his military and foreign policy triumph into domestic terms in a more Bonapartist or, as the military party and probably the monarchy too envisaged, a more traditional, neo-absolutist fashion.

All the greater were people's astonishment and bewilderment – and in arch-conservative circles their indignation – when at the beginning of

August 1866, after a whole series of somewhat dubiously received hints and veiled announcements in the preceding weeks, it finally emerged as certain that Crown and government were looking for an understanding with the liberal opposition and were anxious to bring the years of conflict to an end with a compromise. The king's government, it was proclaimed in the speech from the throne with which the newly elected Diet was opened on 5 August 1866, stood by its view 'that the maintenance of a well-ordered administration, the fulfilment of its legal obligations towards its creditors and civil servants and the upkeep of the army and of state institutions were matters of life and death for the state'.[5] The executive had therefore been acting in a kind of state of emergency, and that had constituted its justification for effecting payments and conducting affairs even without a duly approved budget. However, the government conceded and had indeed never denied that its actions had lacked the 'legal foundation' clearly prescribed for them under the constitution and that it was not in the general interest that this state of affairs should be allowed to continue. It would therefore be approaching parliament for retrospective approval of the expenses decreed without such a legal foundation. It would be asking for 'indemnity' – a concept that comprised a renunciation of sanctions on parliament's part and, in a form that was psychologically very shrewd, tacit recognition in principle of parliament's right to impose such sanctions. 'I am confident', ran the climactic passage of the king's speech, every nuance of which Bismarck had carefully weighed in advance, 'that recent events will so far contribute towards effecting this indispensable understanding that my government will readily be granted the indemnity in respect of the period of administration without a legal budget for which parliament is to be approached and that with this the conflict that has prevailed hitherto will be brought to a close for all time.'

The question that everyone both inside and outside Prussia was driven to ask was: what are we to make of this? The government's step threw into disarray virtually all the ideas that right as well as left had formed hitherto about the Prussian Minister-President. Both sides had seen him as a man who was trying if possible to set aside parliament as the body representing the people, his model being the authoritarian state built on monarchical and military foundations, and who did everything, even down to conducting foreign affairs, principally with that in mind. External, power-political successes, as opposition spokesmen headed by Virchow and Twesten had been saying for years, served no other purpose. They were indeed elements in a thoroughgoing 'politics with a purpose', one 'in which foreign relations are reduced to something transacted purely for the sake of the conflict at home'.[6] Now here was the same man saying that the whole constitutional conflict together with much of what had been built up in connection with it in terms of fundamental positions of principle was, if not a mishap, at any rate a kind of misunderstanding that must be wiped from the slate as speedily as possible. Indeed he was openly courting a parliamentary majority and had the king say in the speech from the throne: 'Government and parliament, working together in harmony, will have the task of bringing to ripeness the fruits that must grow from this bloody seed, if it is not to have been scattered in vain.'

This was the high-point of Machiavellism, this attempt to make the opponent at home an apparent partner in his success and to corrupt him from the safe position of the real victor, said some: Virchow and Hoverbeck, Schulze-Delitzsch and Harkort, Jacoby and Waldeck. They argued for decisive rejection of the Indemnity Bill. Approval of it, Waldeck declared in an impassioned appeal, would be tantamount to a 'renunciation of everything that the opposition has been fighting for through the period of conflict'.[7]

Perhaps they had been wrong in many respects; perhaps they had been too quick to dismiss Bismarck's many concealed or even quite open offers of co-operation since his speech before the budget committee in the autumn of 1862, said others: Twesten and Forckenbeck, Unruh and Lasker, Duncker and Siemens. At any rate they must now, after history itself had, as Twesten put it, 'granted indemnity' to Bismarck's ministry,[8] look at this fresh offer very carefully – precisely in the interests of their own cause.

Both sides saw, of course, that just such a sundering of the opposition might be one of the main aims of the whole initiative. But it was argued that to base one's decision on such a consideration would be to abandon any kind of independent policy and condemn oneself to mere positive or negative reactions to a presumed tactical calculation by the other party, and on both sides of the debate the argument seemed irrefutable. And since neither group was able to convince the other, the dissolution of the old opposition into two autonomous parliamentary groupings was ultimately unavoidable. The split took place during the winter of 1866–7. Alongside the Progressive Party there now emerged a National Liberal Party. Under the leadership of the Hanoverian Rudolf von Bennigsen, the former chairman of the German National Union, this announced that it was ready to co-operate with Bismarck unconditionally in national and foreign policy matters and conditionally with regard to domestic affairs.

The day on which this new party – on which Bismarck was to rely for parliamentary support over many questions for the next twelve years – actually came into being was 3 September 1866, the day when after a three-day parliamentary battle the Prussian House of Deputies voted on the government's Indemnity Bill and half the old liberal opposition, despite what for some members were severe misgivings, came down in favour of it. But it was also the day – and we cannot judge the one thing without the other – when the conservatives too found themselves at a crossroads. It had been clear from the outset, of course, that they would approve the government's Bill; to reject it would have made no sense. But there was no mistaking the fact that the majority of conservatives regarded most of what the government and Bismarck had done since Königgrätz and the great conservative election triumph of the same day with increasing unease and deep hostility.

The arch-conservative wing under Ludwig von Gerlach had already dissociated itself from Bismarck and what it foresaw as the revolutionary

311

consequences of his policy before the war. As Gerlach had said in the crucial *Kreuzzeitung* article of 8 May 1866, it delivered Germany up to political and social upheaval and arbitration by the dictator on the Seine. 'Oesterreich Preussen Hand in Hand, sonst Deutschland ausser Rand und Band' ('Austria [and] Prussia hand in hand, otherwise Germany [will be] out of all control'), was how he had sought in clumsy verse once again to adjure his political friends.[9]

The great majority of conservatives had not followed him, even though many of them privately conceded that the one-sided emphasis on Prussian power interests, the expulsion of legitimate princes and the complete disregard of tradition in the field of foreign affairs struck at the root of essential conservative beliefs and principles and threatened in the long run to undermine the credibility of their own position. But when it became clear that a great deal of what for years they had been led into political battle to defend was now being set aside and that they were to share the fruits of victory with the old opponent, who had played no part in it, their restiveness began to assume alarming proportions. 'One's enemies one can deal with, but one's friends!' Bismarck complained to his wife as early as the beginning of August 1866.[10]

All of a sudden loyally principled conservatives and such members of that party as had seen Bismarck chiefly as the appropriate tool to implement their own beliefs and promote their interests found themselves shoulder to shoulder with those liberals who remained in opposition. Both sides observed, albeit from diametrically opposite viewpoints, how groups of self-styled realists within their respective camps more or less swept aside everything that had hitherto constituted the basis, aim and substance of their political activities. On the conservative side this was the so-called Free Conservative Alliance under the chairmanship of Count Bethusy-Huc, a Silesian estate-owner who had sat in the House of Deputies since 1862. This separate group within the Conservative Party eventually became a separate party, the Free Conservative Party. Its collaboration with Bismarck was very much less reserved and went very much further than that of the National Liberals; drawing its members mainly from among top diplomats and civil servants, representatives of the higher nobility of Silesia and the Rhineland and a number of businessmen, the party even became known later on as 'the Bismarck party *sans phrases*' – as we might say, 'the Bismarck party, period'. However, this did not alter the fact that what was beginning to emerge here was a kind of double party of the centre, which at least as far as legislation was concerned increasingly assumed the functions of a government party or rather a government coalition.

Like the war and the peace just concluded, all this occurred with quite breathtaking rapidity. And since it was connected in substance with and happened at the same time as the integration of the annexed states within the new Prussia and the establishment of the North German Confederation during the autumn and winter of 1866–7, the impression inevitably imposed itself upon contemporaries and posterity alike that this was part of an all-embracing revolutionary historical process, launched and controlled from above by the executive power, that was bursting all the shackles of tradition and the traditional order and everywhere setting in motion something entirely new.

'Revolution from above' – that was the watchword with which people tried at the time and subsequently to master their own bewilderment and make sense of a fundamentally altered situation. This was 'the German revolution in the form of war, led from above rather than from below, as it is in the nature of monarchy to do', said Johann Caspar Bluntschli, a Swiss constitutional lawyer teaching in Heidelberg and a man of the liberal centre, as early as June 1866.[11] And as the historian Heinrich von Treitschke summed up at the end of the year: 'Our revolution is being completed, as it was begun, from above, and with the limited understanding of subjects we are groping in the dark.'[12]

Ludwig von Gerlach had warned from the other end of the political spectrum against 'foundering in revolution' back at the beginning of May 1866, and those both inside and outside Prussia who shared his views now saw that warning as borne out in full. 'Now, however, through you, revolution from above has become the fashion', the Austrian Field Marshal Baron von Hess wrote to the aged Wrangel, his comrade-in-arms in the Danish War, in October 1866. 'Beware, and doubly so, lest in the fullness of time, you having flushed away all sense of justice, it should seize upon you! Then you will be done for!'[13] Bismarck met such warnings at the time with the confident assertion that 'only kings make revolution in Prussia';[14] in other words he did not dispute the fact as such, particularly with regard to his own policy. Later on he was no longer quite so sure, and Marx's dictum about the 'royal Prussian revolutionary'[15] who unintentionally did the work of quite other political forces would perhaps after all have given him pause for thought.

But in 1866 that lay far in the future. At the time people from right and left believed that with the concept of a 'revolution from above' they had found at least the beginnings of an explanation of the extremely confusing fact that, without a revolution in the traditional sense, indeed under apparently conservative auspices, fundamental changes were taking place in the most diverse spheres of existence within a very short space of time.

The year 1866 does in fact represent a crucial turning-point in the history of central Europe, much more so than the actual founding of the Reich in 1870–1, which in many respects merely translated into reality what had been laid out four years before. The external and above all the internal order of the old Germany, its party spectrum and constitutional system, its prevailing legal principles in the economic, social and administrative spheres, and many of its traditional political and social norms were fundamentally changed by the events of that year. Abrupt though the caesura was, however, in reality it represented simply the breaking through of very much deeper, longer-term trends of development, the opening of the curtain, as it were, on a set that had been in place for a long time. Consequently any interpretation that portrays and dramatizes the whole thing essentially in terms of political manipulation on the part of one great individual does no more than touch the surface.

It is true that that individual played an exceptionally large part. The year

1866 undoubtedly shows Bismarck at a high-point of his political creativity and effectiveness. But for that very reason the premisses and basic structure of his political achievement appear here with perfect clarity: his absolute determination and readiness to move with the times with as his one guiding objective the affirmation of his own power and that of his state. The times, however – and this has often got in the way of people's understanding of these matters – were moving in a different way, at a different speed and under the influence of different currents than contemporary and subsequent wishful thinkers were and have been prepared to admit. To put it another way: to say that in 1866 and 1870–1 Bismarck was erecting a bulwark against the spirit of the age is a piece of well-meaning self-deception that refuses to take account of the realities of historical development in Germany and uses a single figure to create for itself, usually with the aid of the idealized example of Britain, the illusion that things might have turned out quite differently.

In fact it is precisely Bismarck's policy, with its primarily power-oriented opportunism often amounting to a complete lack of principle, that reflects those realities with sober clarity. He saw that in his day, of all the conceivable possibilities, a parliamentary majority offered the best foundation for a powerful, effective executive as well as one that was relatively independent of the throne and the person currently occupying it. So he secured such a majority where an analysis of the overall political, economic and social situation and its emergent trends of development showed it to be most solidly grounded – irrespective of ideological objections and traditional front formations. He saw that in the long run the power of Prussia could be effectively and permanently enhanced only in collaboration with the Lesser German national movement and in particular with the economic interests inside Prussia itself and in the neighbouring countries that the Customs Union had increasingly focused on Lesser Germany as a national objective. Without ever completely ruling out alternatives, he pursued a foreign policy line that in its consequences gradually cut off all other possibilities. Finally and most importantly, he saw very early on that a particular political and social constellation, a state of equilibrium between the forces and powers of the past and those now emerging in the wake of a process of fundamental economic and social change, was exceptionally favourable to the power of the state, the political executive and the man at its head. Consequently he made every effort to fix that state of equilibrium in institutional terms by boosting the trend that was moving almost in the manner of a natural growth in that direction – wholly indifferent to the accusation that in so doing he was furthering the affairs of his political opponents. What mattered was the securing and preserving of power, his own and that of the institutions on which it was founded and by which it was enhanced.

It was to this end that in the months and years after Königgrätz Bismarck set about establishing and organizing the North German Confederation, which was in turn to have a decisive influence on the shape of the Reich of 1871. That Confederation was the expression in political terms of a highly realistic understanding of the way things were going economically, socially and politically; it was much more a consummation of something for which the time was ripe than the manipulative creation of an individual. It was formally called into being even before the conclusion of the final peace treaty with Austria by means of an agreement that Prussia signed with fifteen small north German states on 18 August 1866.[16] Over the following weeks the agreement was acceded to by all the former states of the German Confederation lying north of the River Main, Hesse-Darmstadt respecting this boundary-line – drawn chiefly for France's benefit – quite literally by joining only in respect of its province of Upper Hesse. The parties to the agreement committed themselves to setting up a new Confederation on the basis of the Prussian reform proposals of 10 June 1866. In conformity with those proposals it was to have a constitution that was to be initially 'determined' by the delegates of the governments concerned and then submitted to a federal parliament 'for discussion and agreement' – that parliament to be elected according to the 'imperial' electoral law of 1849, in other words by universal, equal, direct suffrage.

If we except the annexations on the one hand and the restriction to the area north of the Main on the other, Prussia was abiding by all the principal points that it had declared on the eve of hostilities to be the political objective of the war. Now, however, the whole thing appeared in a completely new light. Before Königgrätz the overwhelming majority among the German public and the governments approached had seen the Prussian proposals as a tactical, propaganda move, a means of breaking up the old Confederation and uniting behind Prussia all who for whatever reason were dissatisfied with things as they were. Now it became apparent that Berlin had been in earnest after all. Behind what had seemed to be mere tactics there was obviously a clearly defined concept for reshaping the internal organization of central Europe.

Again, as in so many other spheres, the image that people had hitherto formed of the Prussian Minister-President began to waver. In this respect too people felt compelled to reconsider, though in the process it was their own wishes that very quickly pointed the way. The fact that Bismarck obviously intended to give the new Confederation a more pronouncedly federal form with an overall representative body as a unifying element led many in the liberal and national camps to overlook at first the qualifications with which the whole thing was hedged around.

The point of departure was still the *Staatenbund* principle: a group of monarchs and governments who came together in a Confederation while in principle preserving the sovereignty of their individual states. It was Bismarck's avowed intention that none of this should change. The joint parliament, the integration of armed forces, the federal presidency and the powers of joint organs were to counteract the centrifugal tendencies within such an organization, with which people were all too familiar after years of experience with the German Confederation. They were not to dominate, however, and certainly not to pave the way for a centralized state that was federal only in terms of its formal structure, which was what the historian Heinrich von Treitschke was calling for, for example. That emerges very clearly from the draft constitution for the new Confederation that was eventually placed before the delegates of the allied north German

315

goverments in mid-December 1866. In its most important points this was Bismarck's own work, reflecting very precisely how he wished to see the political weight distributed.

This was where the main emphasis lay. The liberals' basic view that a constitution must first and foremost serve to put a check on power and to distribute it accordingly was one that Bismarck had always dismissed as being unpolitical or as camouflaging claims to power of its own. Apart from the general one of regulating the use and distribution of political power and so making it accountable, there were no universal constitutional principles, he said. As he had repeatedly pointed out in a variety of ways between 1849 and 1851, if a constitution was to be more then simply a piece of paper its basic structure must be a product of the historical development of the polity concerned. Only if the actual distribution of power in state and society was taken into account would a constitution have validity.

During the constitutional conflict he had honed this view to a fine point. If the organs of the constitution failed to reach agreement, he said, then the one in possession of real power went ahead on its own. Even over the indemnity question he had not in principle retreated from this position. On the contrary, both he and the king had stated that in any future emergency they would be able to act no differently. At the same time, however, this kind of calculation of future power relations threw a particularly clear light on his basic approach to constitutional questions, namely that what mattered was to reach an understanding with the new social forces in order to compensate in good time for a prospective crumbling away of the traditional foundations of the power of the state.

That calculation did not take only the middle classes into account, though they were undoubtedly in the forefront of all his thinking at this time. It was also, if in a very much vaguer form, directed at broader sections of the population, whom it sought to involve either as a counter-weight to an augmented middle-class bid for power or as a factor in their own right. The means by which this was to be achieved was direct universal suffrage. Hence Bismarck's insistence on this system. Indeed he wanted to have it established from the outset as an indispensable component of the new constitution. Only when, following the confederate governments, the Prussian Diet had likewise accepted the 'suffrage of revolution' for the future parliament of the North German Confederation – against considerable resistance from both conservatives and liberals – did it seem to him that conditions were finally right for constitutional legislation along the lines he envisaged.

As if to underline this, shortly after the decisive vote of mid-September 1866 he left Berlin for an extended holiday, returning only at the beginning of December. He spent it, following what was probably the most exhausting summer of his career, as a guest of Prince Putbus on the Baltic island of Rügen. During this cure, shielded from the distractions of day-to-day business, he drafted two documents that became famous as the 'Putbus Dictates'.[17] Dated 30 October and 19 November respectively, they laid down the principal features of the new constitution, which was in essence to become the constitution of the German Reich and as such to remain in force until 1918.

The Putbus Dictates took the form of loosely worded suggestions for those who had been charged with preparing a draft constitution. However, in view of the influence and authority that Bismarck now possessed in areas extending far beyond his actual official position, they acquired the status of wholly binding guidelines.

They took as their starting-point preliminary drafts that had been made by Lothar Bucher and Robert Hepke, two high-ranking officials in the Foreign Ministry, and Max Duncker, the crown prince's adviser for many years, who was employed in the same capacity as Bucher and Hepke in the Staatsministerium. Bismarck's chief initial criticism was to the effect that the drafts were 'too centralistically federal for the future accession of the south Germans'. He went on: 'In form we shall have to stick more to the confederation of states [Staatenbund] while in practice giving it the character of a federal state [Bundesstaat] with elastic, inconspicuous but far-reaching forms of words.' It was therefore advisable to designate as 'central authority . . . not a Ministry but a Federal Diet [Bundestag]', in other words a body consisting of delegates from the individual governments, as in the old German Confederation. 'The more we continue the previous forms', he remarked in this context, 'the more easily the thing can be done, whereas an attempt to have a fully grown Minerva spring forth from the head of the Presidium will run it aground in professorial disputations.' That, expressed in almost flippant terms, was precisely what it was all about: no generalized constitutional discussion, the greatest possible continuity from the external point of view – then 'the thing can be done'.

The 'thing' in question was the solid, permanent establishment of the hegemony of the Prussian state and the Prussian government. That was the supreme reference point; all the rest, the extent of possible modifications and compromises as well as the question of the form and substance of the individual institutions, could be derived from and determined by that. This explains the ease and rapidity with which Bismarck made his decisions in this field and with which he declared himself agreeable even to apparently very far-reaching alterations, and it accounts for his flexibility and indifference where formal considerations were concerned: everything that ran counter to this claim to hegemony or appeared even remotely to jeopardize it was rejected; regarding everything else, Bismarck was prepared to listen to reason.

Accordingly in both the first and second 'Dictates' he tackled apparently quite crucial problems with a relatively light touch, for example the question of the shape the federal executive should take in future or whether the Bundestag, that is to say the body that was initially to be designated as the actual 'central authority', should one day become a sort of Upper House on the British model. He even wanted to leave open at first the question of whether the King of Prussia should be accorded 'a position as head of the empire [Reich] or that of a primus inter pares with regard to the other members of the Confederation'. 'Establishing a monarchical federal state or

317

German empire will run into more formal problems', he remarked in this connection, 'than implementing the second system, which ties in with traditional federal concepts and will therefore more easily find favour with the parties concerned, even though', he went on, quite candidly stressing the crucial point, 'it guarantees Prussia the same position of dominance.' Looking back two years later, he put it like this: "The form in which the King exercises sovereignty in Germany has never particularly mattered to me; to the fact of his exercising it I have devoted all the strength of endeavour that God has given me.'[18] And the King of Prussia meant first and foremost the Prussian government with himself at its head.

Not for one moment was there any question of his effectively sharing power with the 'Bundestag' or, as it later became, 'Bundesrat' or 'Federal Council'. He intended from the outset to use the Prussian representatives to steer it along his own course on all important questions. The thing he had constantly in mind here was 'the accession of the south Germans': it was a question of ensuring that even then that body remained under the tight rein of Prussian government policy.

In the debates of the 'constituent' Diet of the North German Confederation, the three hundred or so members of which gathered for their first session in the White Hall of the royal palace in Berlin on 24 February 1867, twelve days after their election, he defended this plan with the utmost firmness and the repeated threat that if necessary he would allow the whole constitutional and unification structure to founder over this issue. In particular he rigorously rejected the liberals' demand that independent, accountable federal ministries be set up. What eventually emerged as a formal compromise here was in fact, when looked at more closely, no compromise at all but an unequivocal victory for Bismarck and a clear defeat even for Bennigsen's National Liberals.

On a motion by the independent knight's-estate-owner Carl von Saenger, a liberal of the old school who supported the government and had very close links with Max Duncker, the majority decided to impose a special political accountability on the office of the Prussian presidential envoy to the Federal Council. It was to become a separate organ of the constitution – as it were, a unique federal ministry. The draft constitution 'adopted' by the Prussian government at Bismarck's direction on 9 December 1866 had already hit upon the title 'Federal Chancellor' – 'Bundeskanzler'; a title that appealed to ancient traditions – for this office.[19] At the time there had still been talk of its being filled by Karl Friedrich von Savigny, the former Prussian envoy to the Federal Diet and a friend of Bismarck's youth. Before long, however, Bismarck had come to appreciate the possibilities implicit in such a function. And from then on there had been only one candidate as far as he was concerned. The majority decision of the Diet of the North German Confederation represented the crowning of his efforts, so to speak; there is every indication that Saenger's motion was drawn up under his direct influence.

It is thoroughly ironical, therefore, that the whole thing should have gone down in history as the 'Bennigsen Amendment'. Bennigsen had for procedural reasons coupled Saenger's motion with one of his own that looked beyond accountability for the Federal Chancellor and set its sights on accountable federal ministries, in other words on a federal government bearing collective responsibility. Under massive pressure from the Prussian government and its Minister-President, however, the Diet voted on 27 March 1867 to adopt only the first part of the motion and reject the second. In token of what was supposed to be a compromise, it thus threw out the very thing that even markedly co-operative liberals such as Bennigsen regarded as absolutely essential if the power of the executive and above all of the man at its head were to be kept within bounds.

Apart from that the politically very heterogeneous majority in the Diet reacted to the concrete situation and the circumstances obtaining in exactly the way Bismarck had envisaged when drawing up the constitution. He had expressed his intentions very clearly in the relatively concise observations in the Putbus Dictates regarding the role and function of the future central parliament or Diet of the North German Confederation. 'We stand by the programme announced before the war', he emphasized in the first Dictate, 'to the effect that federal legislation shall come into being through agreement between the majority in the Federal Diet [Bundestag] and parliament.' That legislative activity must get under way as soon as possible. This was justified on pragmatic grounds in terms of the need to provide the new polity with a common basis in law as well. But the thinking behind it was to keep the people's representatives busy from the very first day by giving them practical work to do. On the one hand he wished to see a high value placed on the new parliament both in the interests of domestic equilibrium and with a view to mobilizing the nation as a whole; it had been conceived as 'an anchor of salvation and cementer of our unity', as he put it in a speech in the Imperial Diet fifteen years later.[20] On the other hand he was concerned to keep the political vigour and dynamism of the new representative body under control and as far as possible eliminate all risks to his own position and power. His remarks in connection with the framework directive regarding the position of the future central parliament make this very clear.

Obviously a prey to misgivings as to whether universal suffrage alone would be capable of putting the liberal middle class under sufficient political pressure from below, he invited consideration of whether it might not even be advisable to have the Diet 'result from a variety of electoral procedures'. One possibility, for example, would be to have half the members elected by universal suffrage and the other half by means of an extensive property qualification. His plan amounted to institutionalizing social differences, as it were, by giving separate representation to a kind of monied aristocracy; the sort of figure contemplated was the hundred highest taxpayers in each constituency, the constituencies numbering some hundred thousand inhabitants.

He did say immediately that for him these questions did 'not occupy first place in order of importance'. Nevertheless, the plan clearly reveals the basic line he was pursuing with regard to the German parliament. It is this alone that explains the sentence at the end of the first Putbus Dictate: 'The main thing as far as I am concerned is: no attendance fees, no delegates, no census, unless the latter goes to the lengths indicated above.' Decoded, this meant that on no account was a kind of professional politician supported by attendance fees to be created, a 'parliamentarian by trade'[21] whose political existence rested on a party-political base that received additional organizational backing from an indirect electoral procedure.

'Attendance fees mean paying the educated proletariat for the professional practice of demagogy', the Prussian Minister-President declared during talks with representatives of the confederate governments, putting his view at its most extreme.[22] What Bismarck wanted to see was the kind of politician who was a notability in his constituency, with which he was very closely associated and to which he was committed in terms of his middle-class status as well, and on whom the government could exert direct influence, whether by concessions or through the medium of threats and appeals to the primary electorate. Accordingly, and remembering the more stubborn resistance shown by the civil servant members of the House of Deputies during the conflict period, he even went so far as to suggest a measure making civil servants ineligible for election. The aim must be 'a living representative body enjoying a relationship of unbroken reciprocity with the people', as he later explained in public, concealing his true motives: in his opinion this could come about only if 'large numbers of the employed classes' were 'directly represented'.[23]

Bismarck was enough of a politician, however, not to be dogmatic about this plan. Particularly over the question of the eligibility of civil servants, on which the Diet, almost two-thirds of whose members were civil servants, clung vehemently to the opposite position, he did in fact subsequently give in. But this then rendered his victory over the question of attendance fees meaningless in practice, as soon emerged. Contrary to Bismarck's intentions, it even led to civil servants continuing to dominate the parliamentary arena while the element of direct representation of economic and social interests remained rather less pronounced for the present.

With a view to co-operating with the new liberal moderates in future, Bismarck went some way towards meeting the eighty-strong National Liberal parliamentary party even over the very hotly disputed budget question. Departing from the original Bill, he declared himself agreeable to annual presentation of a detailed budget. The sole exception was the military budget, which for the time being was fixed. The level at which it was fixed, however, itself had a time limit on it. After much toing and froing it was agreed that the Diet's right of budgetary control should be extended to this sphere too from the end of 1871.

But all Bismarck's real or apparent concessions during the constitutional deliberations of the Diet of the North German Confederation cannot obscure one basic fact: the constitution of the new polity that was adopted by an overwhelming majority on 16 April 1867 – there were only fifty-three dissenting votes – and that came into force in the summer was in its principal points not a compromise but an unambiguous triumph for the man who shortly afterwards took the helm of the new state as Federal Chancellor, invested with quite extraordinary powers.

This, along with the implementation of the principle of a scarcely veiled Prussian hegemony, was the second crucial point. Only to a very limited extent can one speak of the realization of a particular national concept or the further development of certain traditions, even though much of a more or less ingenious nature was said and written at the time and has been subsequently by jurists and historians alike. On the contrary, if we start from the various constitutional formulations of a conservative national concept in the years before 1866 and from Bismarck's own positions during the revolutionary period and the period of reaction that followed it, not to mention those he occupied in the years of conflict, it becomes clear that both the strengths and the weaknesses of that constitution consisted precisely in its large measure of detachment from principle, system and dogmatism. Every attempt to lessen that detachment and retrospectively invest the constitution with the character of a system is not only misleading; it actually obscures the essential point. This lay in the perception and conviction that both the successful use of power and the preservation of power were bound up with contingencies that largely eluded abstraction and generalization. As Bismarck put the point eleven years later: 'Theoretically there is much that can be said about it [the constitution]; in practice it was the impress of what was actually present at the time and possible in consequence, given the limited amount of stretching and adjusting that could be done at that moment.'[24]

Only the institutionalization and engagement of forces and trends of development actually present, as Montesquieu had already pointed out, make possible an orderly and organically progressing polity. Yet Bismarck went far beyond this general principle of conservative political thought, a principle that was set against the normative thinking of the Enlightenment and of liberalism, just as in many respects he lagged behind it. What he wanted was to make use, through the medium of a constitution, of a certain power-political constellation but also certain prevailing ideas and expectations in order on the one hand to stabilize power positions and on the other hand to facilitate the use of power: to keep at a minimum the 'grave hindrance inherent in the friction of the artificial machinery of a constitutional state', as he once significantly put it in the rough draft of a letter to William I.[25]

The two things, as the Prussian Minister-President knew, were often difficult to combine, the one calling for solidity and the other for mobility. But precisely in this situation of an increasingly pronounced plurality of positions and interests, particularly the agrarian, aristocratic and traditional on the one hand and the commercial, mobile, dynamic and forward-looking on the other, a constitution seemed to him to be a better way than almost any other of linking the two requirements. For him it was thus tool and platform at one and the same time. And as he fully appreciated, not least from his experiences during the conflict period and because of the crises in which Napoleon III's system was becoming more and more deeply entangled, the only way in which it could serve him successfully as a tool was if he himself firmly abode by it and accepted its rules even in the event of momentary defeat.

On the basis of this interpretation Bismarck emphatically defended himself against a charge that was levelled against him several times, particularly in the context of the discussion about universal suffrage, to the

321

effect that Napoleon III and his regime were the real model behind his draft constitution. As he stated in the Diet of the North German Confederation on 28 March 1867, for example, anyone who thought this was 'a deeply laid plot against the freedom of the bourgeoisie in association with the masses to set up a Caesarean type of government' had misjudged his real intention.[26] They certainly had, for his fundamental political calculation, as embodied in the constitution, was precisely *not* aimed, like Napoleon III's, at excluding the middle class from the political arena. 'Forming worker battalions and stirring up the poorer classes against the propertied middle class', as Karl Twesten had put if from the National Liberal benches,[27] were in Bismarck's eyes at most things he could use as a threat, not a recipe for success. He was much more interested in finding an additional prop for his own power in the section of the middle class that was prepared to co-operate with him. In this way he sought to arrive at a middle position, supported by both sides, in the as yet undecided struggle between the forces of past and future, between the static and dynamic elements in society. The whole plan was based on the urgent need for compromise that arose out of the situation then obtaining and that favoured the government as the natural mediator – though only for a while, namely for as long as the period remained so markedly transitional in character and the opposing forces that put their stamp on it continued in something like equilibrium.

At this point in time, however, at least at the political level, that was only to a limited extent the case. The military and foreign policy triumph of the arch-conservative leaders of army and state and the forces associated with them, the general shift of mood following Königgrätz and the new readiness to bow to success had all led to an extraordinary strengthening of the forces of intertia, which only a few years before had been forced on to the defensive along a broad front. Bismarck's persistent concern after Königgrätz and Nikolsburg was therefore to re-trim the ship of state, as it were, by redistributing the weight, not just superficially but in terms of its very substance. That was what the Indemnity Bill was for. That was what the constitution was for with its 'parliamentary high-pressure engine', Bismarck's expression for the Diet of the North German Confederation, elected by universal suffrage, with which he wished to 'exert . . . leverage'[28] on and practice 'intimidation by parliamentary movements'[29] against all opposing forces – already, of course, with the prospect of future rivalry between the Diet and the Prussian House of Deputies, contemplating one day 'bringing down parliamentarism with the help of parliamentarism'.[30] And that was the purpose particularly of the fundamental reforms that were introduced as soon as the new federal state had been constituted.

Anyone considering those reforms purely from the point of view of the political distraction of the liberal middle class is undoubtedly falling short of the whole truth, although this was a by no means undesirable side-effect as far as Bismarck was concerned. As early as 1848–9 he had been forever pointing out to his party colleagues the fundamental importance of 'material interests' in political life and of all practical measures in this field. And he knew only too well that every intervention in the existing economic and social order, particularly in a time of such upheaval, was in the highest degree a political matter and that indeed decisions crucial to the future were being made here. So there can be no question of his not having been fully aware of the importance and potential repercussions of the reforms that were put in hand from 1867 onwards on his political responsibility. On the contrary, the immediate and longer-term consequences of those reforms, which created vitally important legal prerequisites for the continued growth and development of modern industrial society in central Europe, were very deliberately taken into account in his political calculations.

Here, however, we must immediately introduce a qualification of quite crucial significance as far as evaluating his policy is concerned. He saw and accepted the importance and repercussions of the reforms he introduced. Yet in the final analysis he did this only because he regarded the process itself, the process that they helped along and in which they were one factor among others, as inevitable. Here too, as in his approach to politics as a whole, he bowed to the ineluctable 'unda fert nec regitur'. The idea that the ever-accelerating dissolution of the traditional economic and social order could be permanently halted and that order preserved was one he rejected with relentless clarity of vision. Slowing the process down, channelling it, keeping it within bounds – these he thought possible in principle; all his positive and negative measures in this field rested on that conviction. But to set oneself up in opposition to it was in his estimation to be overwhelmed or simply swept aside by it.

So it was as a reluctant reformer that he presented himself, someone who found himself faced with a choice he frequently invoked – that of being hammer or anvil. As he saw it, it was a question of either placing himself at the head of a development that he deplored but regarded as unstoppable, even of accelerating matters in order to drive that development in his direction and exploit it to his own advantage – or of seeing it sooner or later force him on to the sidelines. The fundamental conviction of most liberals, and particularly of those who were prepared to co-operate, was that this would happen anyway. Bismarck, on the other hand, was confident that by making limited concessions and by continually trimming and re-trimming the balance he would be able to hold his own.

However, we must not let this blind us to something else, namely the plain fact – which had an effect far beyond all political calculations and crucially influenced the future – that in the years following 1866 it was a government still regarded as conservative that created certain basic preconditions for the acceleration of the process of economic and social change, the process known as 'modernization', in central Europe. This raised fundamental doubts about whether political progress and social change did in fact go hand in hand. The ambivalence of progress, particularly when speeded up like this, suddenly came to light. Many people began to ask themselves in alarm, echoing the historian Jacob Burckhardt of Basle, a liberal of the old school, whether freedom and a life truly fit for human beings had not been very much better provided for under the old systems. 'A certain supervised amount of wretchedness, with promotion and in uniform, begun and ended each day with a roll on the drums – that would be the logical next step.' Thus Burckhardt saw the prospects for the future in 1872, speaking of a Europe of mindless 'non-stop night trains' that would replace the Europe of old.[31]

It is one of the ironies of history that this acceleration of progress brought forth an increasing scepticism with regard to progress, which then redounded to the benefit of the conservatives. In both cases Bismarck turned out to be the beneficiary of and driving force behind that development: when the factors that he had furthered after 1866 threatened to become too powerful he made use of the growing pessimism about progress felt by large sections of the middle class to apply the opposite lock, as it were, and once again give greater weight to the other side.

But for the time being contemporaries were presented with a somewhat astonishing spectacle that exerted a powerful grip on their imaginations. The Prussian Minister-President, after four years of being denounced as the high priest of political and social reaction, now sought to tread the path of peace and understanding both at home and abroad. He further set about giving this polity essentially of his own creation, the North German Confederation, the most modern economic and social constitution, legal system and administrative structure in the whole of Europe.

And Bismarck's entirely personal contribution to this great and momentously important work of reform must not be underestimated. This is true not only with regard to its basic political direction and the political calculation that lay behind it but also with regard to many individual aspects. However, the practical implementation, the technical and political co-ordination of the whole thing were in the hands of someone else, a man who for the next ten years virtually personified the collaboration between the Prussian government and the liberals in all its possibilities and limitations, namely Rudolf von Delbrück. This is rightly referred to, therefore, as the 'Delbrück Era'. It began with the appointment of this top civil servant in the Prussian Ministry of Commerce as president of the newly founded Federal Chancellery in August 1867 and ended with his resignation in April 1876 on the threshold of a general change of course.

Delbrück's line on economic policy and, inseparably bound up with this, on general policy as well had been familiar to Bismarck for many years. The two men, almost the same age, had already worked very closely together back in the 1850s, when Bismarck was Prussia's envoy in Frankfurt. Then it had been a question of the Customs Union and of combating Austrian attempts to join and alter that organization. Granted, Delbrück had sided more or less openly with Lesser German liberalism from an early stage, and it had been in this spirit that in the spring of 1862 he turned down the offer of the Ministry of Commerce in a Cabinet that was increasingly set on a collision course in domestic affairs. In practical matters of economic and commercial policy, however, there had often been a broad measure of agreement between him and Bismarck. This had been true not only of the Customs Union question in the 1850s but also of almost all the decisions of principle with regard to economic and commercial policy that had been taken up until 1866 – not least of the commercial treaty with France that Bismarck had so welcomed in 1862. In each of those decisions Delbrück had played a leading role. That the Prussian national interest was best served in fiscal as in overall power-political terms by a liberal economic policy and by co-operation with the middle classes in this field was a view in which Bismarck was confirmed primarily by Delbrück's arguments and by the undeniable success of Delbrück's practical measures. Indeed it was thanks to Delbrück, who was very much his superior in terms of economic expertise, that Bismarck arrived at that view in the first place.

For this reason it is not possible to speak of Bismarck's having been guided, either directly or indirectly, by Delbrück and by the forces behind him. If Bismarck now, after 1866, cleared the way on the home front as well for the kind of economic policy advocated by Delbrück, he did so only after careful consideration of the problems and possible alternatives. There can be no question of his not having been aware of the real motives of those who were pushing in this direction.

Most of the economic reforms that Delbrück introduced in his new position had to do with standardizing the law, that is to say with bringing the Confederation into line with the norms prevailing in Prussia; in his graphic way Bismarck spoke of a 'diarrhoea' of statutory regulations that befell old and new subjects alike.[32] It began with the statutory establishment of the principle of freedom of movement and settlement throughout the Confederation and the standardization of weights and measures. There followed the adoption of a 'German Commercial Code', limited at first to northern Germany, and the establishment of a supreme commercial court based in Leipzig. The climax was reached in June 1869 with the passage of a trading and industrial code based on the principle of general freedom of trade. That completed the internal standardization of the new market or economic area, which with the introduction of a north German criminal code towards the end of May 1870 finally became one region under the law as well.

But standardization and adaptation were merely the rubric under which practical changes on an enormous scale were put into effect. Particularly drastic for the non-Prussian parts of the Confederation was the fact that within a very short space of time all their bases of calculation and all their protective institutions were abolished. They found themselves plunged abruptly into the cold bath of a largely liberalized economy in which those soon came to dominate who had long been acclimatized to it.

But this second conquest of northern Germany by the Prussian economy was only one aspect, albeit one that was particularly dramatic in its effects. Of far greater consequence was the fact that the concept of the self-regulation of the economic and hence also of the social order was now finally elevated to the status of a principle, with the state, in other words, largely relinquishing control in this field. This was and has been seen by many people as a triumph of liberalism, making up for much of what liberalism was denied in the more narrowly political sphere, even if at the same time it turned it increasingly into the party of a particular class, a particular interest, further diminishing its power to integrate and its ability to represent society as a whole. However, if we look at things less in terms of the history of dogma and more in terms of straight history, it very quickly becomes apparent that the truth was rather different.

Particularly in Prussia economic liberalism and political liberalism had parted company at an early stage, in the wake of the reform period and its concrete effects. The same was true of the classes of society that respectively supported them. While the land-owning aristocracy had steadily been coming round to economic liberalism and the *laissez-faire* principle even with regard to social affairs, the middle class had been growing increasingly sceptical. It saw the dissolution of the traditional economic and social constitution more and more in terms of an instrumentalization of that process by the state and by the traditional elites with their knack of adapting themselves to developments. Representatives of the middle class accordingly even devised a sort of model of a 'middle-class society' that was not only pre-industrial but also in many respects pre-capitalist. Setting their model up as a political ideal in opposition to the modern economic society that was beginning to emerge, they sought under its aegis to prevent an all too rapid transition to such an economic society, the social consequences of which they increasingly felt to be disastrous.

This explains why in southern Germany, the real home of German liberalism, the process of economic liberalization made poor headway in comparison with Prussia. In none of the south German states, for example, was the principle of freedom of trade accepted before the 1860s, and even then it was in the teeth of considerable opposition. On the other hand the fact that a town such as Mannheim, which in the first half of the nineteenth century constituted a kind of precursor of economic and social development in the south, very soon also became a centre of Lesser German unification efforts under Prussian leadership shows that it was quite specific middle-class groups that, not least because of their own economic interests, argued with particular vigour for that course. They even continued to do so when the 'Prussian' course began to appear in a somewhat dubious light, politically speaking. One must have faith in progress, their argument ran, regardless of who brings it about and with what motives.

It was a course, however, in which the overwhelming majority of south German liberals did not follow them in the years before 1866, the years of Prussia's constitutional conflict. Even after Königgrätz and the understanding between the Prussian government and the majority in the House of Deputies, warning voices were repeatedly raised against the obvious ambivalence of progress on the Prussian model. The very fact that a conservative government so energetically embraced economic liberalism was in their eyes additional proof that the inner connection between a liberal economic constitution and a liberal political constitution was not after all as direct and unproblematical as the ideologues of economic liberalism liked to maintain. Admittedly they too felt for the most part that a free state without a free economy was inconceivable in the long run. But they had their doubts as to whether conversely a liberal economic constitution necessarily brought a liberal political constitution in its train.

In southern Germany such doubts fell on fertile ground. When Bismarck tried by developing the Customs Union internally to draw the south German states closer to the North German Confederation and to harness economic liberalism as an effective instrument of unification in this sphere too, he experienced a nasty surprise: the elections to the so-called 'Customs Parliament' held in the spring of 1868 produced a quite unexpected result. Moreover, even the liberal members who then arrived in Berlin to represent the south conducted themselves with a great deal more scepticism and reserve than the Prussian Minister-President had initially allowed for.

So there are certain problems about talking in blanket terms about the economic reforms introduced during the period of the North German Confederation as representing a triumph of liberalism. We cannot even speak without major reservations of a straight political deal whereby liberalism was compensated for its co-operation and self-restraint in other areas. Very much more immediate reasons of state were paramount here, namely the direct and not least fiscal interest that the Prussian state had in a liberal economic system. That system had already proved itself in the past as being of outstanding value to the state in strengthening its power both at home and abroad. So was not the obvious course to remove the last remaining barriers and start enjoying all the advantages of an uninhibitedly developing economy?

It was obvious, however, only to someone who in concentrating on the immediate power interest of the state had rid himself of all the misgivings that had been so frequently expressed in conservative circles in particular with regard to the social consequences of such a system. In other words, to someone who, like Bismarck, defined the limits of the feasible far more narrowly than did many conservative partisans of state control and who at the cost of forgoing any kind of state intervention in what he regarded as an inexorable process of economic and social change sought within those limits to develop the power and authority of the state to the full. In this way the concept of power finally took precedence over any kind of social policy objective.

Such a development was of course based on a quite specific assumption, namely that the country's traditional elite, the land-owning aristocracy of the regions east of the Elbe, far from finding its former economic and social position threatened by complete economic liberalization, had on the contrary found that this operated to its advantage. Irrespective of that, however, the process as such was of quite crucial importance. It permitted a stabilization, at least in the medium term, of the traditional political system and the power positions existing within it. For it freed it, at least temporarily, from the suspicion of being a mere bulwark of the traditional and progressively less workable economic and social order. The fact that the traces were being cut here, so to speak, even enabled the state increasingly to appear and be represented as the organ of a 'judicious collective will' over and above the individual groups in society and their conflicting interests – just as the political philosophy of German Idealism and early liberal political theory had once postulated.

To Bismarck himself this kind of ideological approach to the concept of the state was quite foreign. In fact, having seen himself as a conservative all his life, although precisely in this field he was not acting at all like one, he inevitably found it deeply repugnant. There are plenty of examples of the way in which he continued even in old age to react whenever the state

327

sought as a demanding, 'authorized' abstraction, the 'ideal' embodiment of the community, to enter his private sphere and affect him in his capacity as landowner, taxpayer, or businessman.

What was true of the economic policy and the economic policy reforms of the North German Confederation period ultimately applies to all the reforms introduced during that time. All of them, even though most contemporaries were scarcely aware of the fact, resulted in a strengthening of the state by way of a final break with old ties, old systems and old forms coupled with a decisive modernization of its institutions and instruments.

This is most apparent in the sphere of administrative reform. Even in the old absolutist days this had already been an indication of the continuing process whereby the state was becoming independent of traditional society and its patterns of organization. In Prussia this process, which significantly reached its climax in the French Revolution, had in the years after 1806 been partly advanced by the Stein-Hardenberg reforms and partly held back by them. Those reforms had after all, in imitation of the British model, aimed to give the new middle-class society that they sought to create a role in administration from the start. The resultant set-up, with centralized state administration and local autonomy existing side by side, contained the elements of a great deal of friction. Moreover, it had led, in the further course of events, to the lower and middle levels of government, namely local and regional administration, falling more than ever into the hands of the traditional ruling class.

In his youth, prior to 1848, Bismarck had been one of those who resolutely defended the new system that so greatly benefited their own class against all attempts by government to change it. Even after 1848 and during the 1850s he had on several occasions opposed the very minor concessions that the state had made to the revolution, for example in the field of manorial jurisdiction. After 1866, however, in the administrative incorporation of the annexed territories, in the development of a federal bureaucracy and in the efforts of the ministerial bureaucracy to tighten the administrative structure and bind it more closely to central government, he came down strongly on the side of those who advocated a powerful, centralized state administration. Indeed he spoke up more and more frequently in the years to come for an extension of the bureaucratic machine, which had hitherto been tailored solely to an 'agricultural state'.[33] Before the 1860s were out, for example, he was proposing a separate government 'control authority' for the stock exchange. He also argued at an early stage for institutions that would actively look into the 'situation of the working classes'.

It is in only apparent contradiction to this that in the early 1870s Bismarck was more on the side of the opponents of the long-overdue administrative reforms at local and regional level that Count Eulenburg, the Minister of the Interior, finally felt obliged to introduce under pressure from the Free Conservatives and the National Liberals. These administrative reforms aimed at giving renewed authority to the local government bodies that had had their powers severely curtailed since the neo-absolutist Manteuffel era. Even though the reforms benefited new social strata, the whole thing amounted once again to a weakening of the bureaucratic centralized state.

In other words, Bismarck's apparently conservative arguments in this connection merely disguised the fact that any diminution of the administrative powers of the state, however loathsome these might individually be to him as a private person, ran counter to the political line he pursued in principle and in practice. Significantly, though, when in the early 1870s a conflict arose over this question between the House of Deputies, with its majority of National Liberals and Free Conservatives, and the Upper House, which clung fiercely to the traditional rights of its members in the local sphere, he came down firmly on the side of the House of Deputies. Granted, he had little liking for the idea of setting up new local government institutions at district and regional level, thus providing a potential opposition with an additional base. But he was even less anxious to give the state under his management the reputation once again of being ultra-conservative socially and a fundamental obstacle to any kind of progress. That, as he knew, was more dangerous than anything else, not only with regard to current party alliances but with regard to his political position overall. If they continued to make difficulties for him and sought to force him on to an extreme right-wing course, he had flung at his conservative critics at the beginning of 1868, 'you shall have government at district level that looks like the work of a lot of district court judges'.[34] Then they would see where their 'republican muddle-headedness' had landed them.[35]

That the conservatives could no longer depend on their former standard-bearer to any but a very limited extent was further demonstrated during the long struggle over the legal unity first of the North German Confederation and subsequently of the Reich. Although Bismarck scarcely intervened himself, the whole process of legal and procedural standardization, regulation of the stages of appeal and final and complete nationalization of the judiciary, including the last remnants of manorial jurisdiction, did after all take place on his direct political responsibility. And it was he who eventually overcame the joint opposition of particularist and conservative forces.

So the final establishment of the modern, bureaucratically centralized, institutional state in central Europe with all its legal forms and institutions that were so important in the development of industrialized society was essentially Bismarck's work. There is a gulf here in biographical terms as well between the arch-conservative's protest against the political unreliability and ubiquitous and arbitrary interference of the bureaucratic institutional state prior to and during the 1848 revolution and the measures and decisions that brought that kind of state to a new peak of power and influence after 1866. It is not surprising that associates and opponents alike – and most of his contemporaries were first one and then the other – could no longer make head nor tail of the man who had moved so far in a relatively short space of time.

Where was the link, the element of continuity and dependability in all the man's manifest lack of principle? Could one seriously, without deluding oneself, come to any other conclusion than that here was an opportunist power politician through and through, a man who subordinated everything to success and to the acquisition and consolidation of personal power?

Ludwig Bamberger, a left-wing liberal politician and journalist who, fascinated by Bismarck's personality and achievements, was one of the first to write about him during these years and to attempt to interpret his policy, answered this question with a definite 'no'. But at the same time he stressed that it was precisely this so-called lack of principle in a sort of historical stalemate between the forces of old and new that constituted the foundation of Bismarck's success. To put it another way, he was the man of the hour because the hour called for an opportunist balancing-act if everything was not to stagnate.

This corresponded to the view of many contemporaries, particularly on the political left. It cushioned people's uneasy perplexity at finding themselves for practical reasons, in the interests of their own programme and their own political objectives, forced again and again to support Bismarck's policy in substance although most of them were as sure as ever that in terms of its motives and secret goals it scarcely chimed with their own beliefs and interests. But was Bamberger's interpretation correct? Does it still get to the heart of the matter when viewed from a distance of more than a century?

To begin with we must note that it exercised its own very powerful influence on the historical process; in other words, it was itself a historical datum of the first order. Because the fact that Bismarck, at the height of his success in the years following 1866 in respect of both domestic and foreign policy, was regarded by substantial groups in both political camps, the conservative as well as the liberal, as a purely success-seeking, opportunist power politician created a credibility gap that could have been filled only by his abandoning what had hitherto been fundamental policy positions. His very successes, together with the means by which they were achieved, destroyed old loyalties and ties in the given situation without generating new ones. They led to a kind of isolation in which only continued success, his own obvious indispensability and the concentration and keying together of effective power positions provided stability and security.

In other words, Bismarck actually came under pressure from the estimates and interpretations of his policy that his actions and methods provoked; he was in danger, one might say, of being overwhelmed by people's image of him. That is one point. Another is that the categories of the feasible, of what promised success, of what would advance things politically, can be said to have dominated his thinking in these years to a greater extent than ever before. He was rightly seen more and more as a man for whom the prospects of success constituted if not the sole at least the essential determinant of any course of action. This basic approach made him in a much broader sense a man of his time, a man who helped the currents and prevailing tendencies of that time to break through and assert themselves. That same approach, however, meant that the very first false step would place his entire political existence in jeopardy. For hardly anyone had occasion to identify with him personally or see him as symbolizing a specific political direction and set of convictions.

There is a series of indications that after 1866 Bismarck became more and more clearly aware of the danger this represented both to him personally and to the political system that he embodied. That danger could prove fatal if he failed to build into the newly emerging political and social order some element that exercised an integrating effect beyond even the most skilful distribution of power-political weight and beyond any purely success-seeking manipulation, sowing the seeds of fresh loyalties.

Just such an element already lay to hand, of course, and Bismarck had already mobilized it for his purposes in a variety of ways. This was the national idea. In this respect too, however, the year 1866 represents a turning point. Prior to that date it was the purely tactical aspect that was paramount, the attempt to harness the national party for his concrete power-political objectives. That aspect retained its importance after 1866 and was indeed a key element in his policy right up until his dismissal. But from now on he came increasingly to see that the national idea had long since ceased to be the banner of a particular party and a particular politico-social group and its special interests, capable of being exploited in that sense. Its cachet and its power had come to consist much more in the fact that it had a unifying effect that spanned all political divisions and all divisions of class and interest and that even spanned denominational barriers. 'We could no longer count on German nationalism as on a united force', Bismarck pointed out on one occasion, impressed by this development, 'if we failed to maintain the religious peace that has existed in Germany hitherto.'[36] The national idea, together with all the hopes and expectations that depended on it, changed after 1866 from being a distinctly oppositional ideology, as it had been up until 1848–9, to being an integrative ideology. It overlaid existing loyalties from right to left of the political spectrum, whether those loyalties were of a political, social, dynastic, or denominational nature. This meant, however, that mobilization of the national idea virtually imposed itself upon a government that was trying for its part to free itself from such traditional loyalties and ties and transcend the bounds they set.

So there was very much more to it than a heightened willingness to make tactical concessions to the national party, particularly the National Liberals, when the Bismarck government associated itself more and more closely with the national idea in the years after 1866. The move reflected the very urgent need to place what for all its deliberate points of contact with the past was in certain essential points a new political and social order on a new foundation. It was a question of giving it a different sort of inner cohesion and for this purpose drawing, in political terms, 'the diagonal of forces actually to hand', as Bismarck explained in the Diet of the North German Confederation towards the end of May 1870.[37]

The appeal was directed primarily at the conservatives, for whose benefit he had said in the Upper House early in 1867: 'A great state is not governed in accordance with party opinions; the sum total of the parties existing in the country has to be carefully weighed and out of that a line drawn that a government as such can pursue.'[38] The statement reveals Bismarck's understanding of the fact that the dynastic idea of the state anchored in traditional conceptions no longer possessed sufficient integrative power to bind the new creation firmly together and give it internal stability.

That insight represented a complete break with his former political friends and their views. It led Bismarck to the recognition that the monarchical principle and the system of government that was based on it could survive politically only on condition that its advocates associated themselves with the national idea and indeed became its standard-bearers. This explains why Bismarck wanted the Lesser German national state to be founded strictly as a confederation of German princes and why on this occasion he directed all his energies towards ensuring that the popular, parliamentary element, on which he had meanwhile come to rely very heavily, was kept and was seen to be kept in second place: the object was to offset the manifest loss of importance suffered by the dynastic factor and to underline the new, national legitimation of the dynasties.

Already implicit in this is an answer to the much-debated question of whether it would have been possible in principle for Bismarck to abide for any length of time by what had been achieved. That answer too is a very clear 'no'. And the reason for it is not so much that Bismarck was dependent on the support of the National Liberals and would not have been able to make too many demands on their patience. The deciding factors arose instead out of the structure of the whole order that he called into being in the years after 1866. That order lacked any truly stabilizing and integrating element as long as the state was not at the same time a national state, focusing on itself all the various expectations that a steadily growing public associated with such a state. In other words, there was quite clearly an inner necessity after 1866 to make progress in the matter of national unification and to revise the results of 1866 to this end.

In apparent contradiction to this is the fact that Bismarck himself repeatedly denied during those years that any such necessity existed. He was not prepared, he said, to let himself be driven into taking risks that could not be assessed in advance. He delivered a serious warning in this context against the 'wordy restlessness with which people not involved in the business of government search for the philosopher's stone that will immediately establish German unity'. It concealed, 'as a rule, a shallow and in any case impotent lack of familiarity with realities and their effects'. One could put the clock forward, 'but time will go no faster for that, and the ability to wait while circumstances unfold is a prerequisite of practical politics'.[39]

However, such statements can also be interpreted as an attempt to use every available means to counter the impression that one was dependent on swift successes. And probably they were in fact directed primarily to that end. For Bismarck was only too well aware that in both domestic and foreign policy he now had to traverse an area of considerable danger and that he risked coming under pressure on the way and becoming dependent on other forces. He must therefore pretend to have neither a firm plan of action nor any more precise ideas about timing. No, he said, as far as future developments were concerned he was thinking in terms of relatively long periods of time and was prepared, moreover, to settle for what had already been achieved, namely a federal state uniting northern Germany under Prussian leadership.

How much of this was mere tactics emerges very clearly from a sober examination of developments in the period immediately preceding the war of 1870–1 and the founding of the Reich. On condition, that is, that we do not get involved in the sort of discussion of war guilt that seeks to nail a culprit and tends to see everything primarily or even exclusively from that point of view. Only then does it become clear that Bismarck's policy after 1866, even and indeed especially as far as foreign affairs were concerned, was dominated by his awareness of the incompleteness of the overall situation. It contained within it dangers for Prussia and for Bismarck's own person and position that positively demanded that things be done and decisions be made. Contrary to Bismarck's own statements, therefore, his watchword had to be not patience but action.

It is not inconsistent with this that for long periods he preferred to act reactively, that is to say to build his own actions on those of others. Knowing as he did that he had to move, the obvious course was to make the crucial moves apparently from the defensive in order not to let his opponent have the advantage of marking time in a rest position. That the attacker in fact must formally be the defender had been one of Bismarck's political axioms from the very beginning. And that a Prussia now extended to include all northern Germany down to the Main and reaching out for southern Germany as well must inevitably appear as a power that aspired not merely to a minor supplementary adjustment but to a further major change in its favour – that was beyond question in Bismarck's eyes, though not in those of a national movement that claimed as it were a natural right to unification nor in those of its historiographical issue. He would scarcely have entertained seriously the sophistries with which contemporaries and historians on the German side sought and have sought to conceal the fact that, if we take the status quo as our criterion, German policy after 1866 was clearly on the offensive while that of the other powers, principally France, was on the defensive.

French policy itself, however, made a substantial contribution towards obscuring that fact. In a move that was as poorly prepared as it was poorly executed France attempted in the spring of 1867 to correct both abroad and at home the disastrous impression to which its various manoeuvres during 1866 had given rise.

At issue was the grand duchy of Luxembourg. This had belonged to the German Confederation since its foundation in 1815 as being a former territory of the Reich, once attached to the Austrian Netherlands. From 1815 it had been attached by personal union to the kingdom of the United Netherlands until in 1839 it was partitioned, with the agreement of the European powers, betwen Holland and the new kingdom of Belgium. The smaller part, which included the city of Luxembourg, a *Bundesfestung* or federal fortress, had remained under the supreme authority of the Dutch king, had joined the German Customs Union in 1842 and had for decades accommodated a federal garrison of Prussian troops. Following the Treaty of Prague, which turned the grand duchy into an independent European state, that garrison had not at first been withdrawn, Prussia citing its existing bilateral agreements with Holland. This did not necessarily mean that Prussia was determined to protect the country against any kind of outside intervention or even build the fortress up into a western advance post. Paris was more inclined to see it as the practical securing by Prussia of potential compensation material, there having after all been repeated mention of this kind of compensation in the negotiations that had been going on between Prussia and France since July 1866.

However, when in the winter of 1866–7 Paris asked Prussia, in return for France's having refrained from interfering hitherto and in the interests of further good relations, to make the Dutch king cede the territory to France, Bismarck took refuge in the argument that, in view of the negative reaction that could certainly be expected from the German public as well as from the Prussian king and his generals, he could not possibly take any initiative in this respect. Admittedly he allowed the impression to subsist that he had no objection in principle to this kind of territorial adjustment in France's favour. But at the same time he pointed France in the direction of direct negotiation with the Dutch king. He further made it a condition that in the event of an agreement between Paris and The Hague Prussia's public image must be that of the party taken by surprise and not that of secret accessory. In this way he eventually achieved the very position he had wanted to achieve: although he was the one who was looking for the really radical modifications of the status quo as confirmed by the Treaty of Prague, he now appeared to be acting on the defensive, and this gave him an ever greater degree of control over the situation.

The business basis of this thrust by the French was their offer to Prussia, made in August 1866, of the closest possible co-operation in future to the mutual advantage of both nations. During the second half of August agreement had been reached between Bismarck and the French ambassador in Berlin, Count Benedetti, to the effect that, given such co-operation and on the basis of such a relationship, France would have no objection to the inclusion of the south German states in Prussia's sphere of control. In return France counted on Prussian support in the acquisition not only of Luxembourg but also of Belgium.

That had been the draft of a bilateral agreement,[40] and Bismarck had undoubtedly taken a very active part in framing it. However, in the further course of events it became possible to present it as a unilateral offer on France's part. The fact was that, in his confidence in his future partner and in the successful outcome of the negotiations, Benedetti had committed what for a diplomat was the almost unforgivable blunder of writing out the draft, as it had been discussed by both sides, in his own hand and giving it to Bismarck to place before the Prussian king. All his efforts to regain possession of this embarrassing and damaging document had met with failure.

In the talks held through the autumn and winter of 1866–7 both sides had largely been marking time. Bismarck had not let it appear that he intended to steer a different course. But he had, as far as Luxembourg was concerned, expressed himself with ever-increasing reservations. Consequently France's move in opening negotiations with the Dutch king in March 1867 was prompted by more than simply the wish to score a tangible success that could be turned to account at home as well. It was at the same time an attempt to overcome the stagnation afflicting their reciprocal relations and to draw Prussian policy out of hiding, as it were. In this it succeeded, though in a way that gave rise to the suspicion that Bismarck had nicely calculated the course and outcome of the whole affair in advance and deliberately led French policy up the garden path.

There is still no reliable, positive proof of this. The fact is, however, that Paris felt it had been duped and drew the appropriate consequences. And that was what mattered. Because from this point on it was clear that unification along Lesser German lines, in other words the incorporation of the south German states in the North German Confederation, was going to be achieved only in the teeth of more or less open resistance from France.

So regardless of whether one starts from a piece of deliberate stage-management on Bismarck's part or an accidental chain of circumstances, at the end of the so-called Luxembourg crisis Prussia and France found themselves head-on to each other. And to Bismarck this certainly came as no surprise. His basic understanding of politics had convinced him from the outset that France would stake everything on preventing a further shift in the European balance of power to its disadvantage. All Bismarck's dealings with France after Königgrätz and Nikolsburg were based on the assumption that French policy could not have the slightest interest in becoming the patron of a Lesser German unification process. Instead Paris would continually seek to harness Prussia to French interests and eventually to outmanoeuvre it, offering nothing in return. The possibility of a peaceful, long-term balance of interests was in this case never seriously on the agenda as far as Bismarck was concerned. On the contrary, from the beginning of 1867 onwards he increasingly regarded a military clash as unavoidable. When he discovered from French documents seized in 1870 that a group of people in French politics really had thought an agreement possible and had believed in Prussian co-operation, he was genuinely astonished.

So it was with France's Luxembourg initiative, too: he took it for granted from the start that France had something else in mind as well – in the first place the precautionary containment of Prussia. It was 'difficult', he wrote to his ambassador in Paris early in 1867, 'not to detect a desire to compromise us in the eyes of Germany and Europe and possibly isolate us'.[41]

It was indeed highly likely that France would use the successful acquisition of Luxembourg, which could after all, in accordance with a mainly historically oriented German national idea, be claimed for the future German national state, to undermine Prussia's claim to be the protecting power of all non-Austrian Germans. From that point of view it was entirely logical that during the Franco-Dutch talks, taking as his pretext the permanent consultations about military co-operation between north and south in future, Bismarck should have made public Prussia's hitherto secret defensive and offensive alliances with three of the four south German states. This enabled him to intercept such negative consequences in advance, as it were, and to demonstrate for France's benefit that he did business only for cash. That the Dutch king happened to take the publicizing of the alliances as his reason for making a possible sale of Luxembourg to France dependent upon the express agreement of Prussia could be seen as an unfortunate concatenation of circumstances and a highly personal decision on the part of William III. And what of the fact that in reaction to this Bismarck positively ordered a parliamentary interpellation from the National Liberals, thus provoking a storm of anti-French protest? Here again it was and is possible to argue quite straightforwardly that this was the only way out of an obvious dilemma: either to give such agreement and so bring discredit on Prussia's position as the protector of and supreme power in Germany or to withhold it in the absence of any external pressure and so forfeit all credibility in Paris in future as being a setter of diplomatic traps.

As things stood, however, the doubt subsisted that Bismarck might in fact have been prepared to make concessions, as he was always asserting, and that the whole thing had come to grief purely as a result of French bungling and the over-anxious attitude of the Dutch king. This interpretation even gained momentum in the weeks and months that followed. The Prussian government now concentrated entirely on providing France with an honourable retreat. At the ensuing conference of the great powers in London, Prussia voted for Luxembourg to be made neutral. Moreover, Prussia's diplomats as well as the government press made every effort, in spite of the still-echoing agitation at home, to present this solution as a clear success for French policy.

Nevertheless, the prevailing conviction in Paris from now on was that co-operation with Prussia on the basis of securing and developing the semi-hegemonial position France had occupied in Europe hitherto, in other words with Berlin joining it as a kind of junior partner, was no longer a possibility. Granted, it had become obvious at the height of the Luxembourg crisis and the national agitation in Germany that Bismarck, rejecting the advice of many hotheads and even that of the Prussian chief of staff, von Moltke, did not want to have a war develop over this issue. But that could equally have been because, on sober consideration, the situation was not yet ripe for such a war and the risk was therefore in every respect too great. In the north the constitution had not even been adopted as yet, so that the entire internal organization of the new state was still theoretically open to radical re-examination. And it seemed at least doubtful whether the south would solidly follow suit and afterwards, in the event of a joint success, take its place in the North German Confederation without further ado. In short, at this point in time there was much more to be said on the Prussian side against a war with France than simply Bismarck's much-quoted reflection: 'If it comes to war, we shall immediately be faced with a whole series of wars: whoever is beaten the first time around will simply wait till he has got his breath back and then start all over again.'[42] On the other hand the Chancellor noted coolly in private as early as the beginning of July 1867: 'Luxembourg was the limit of our peaceableness; if that does not secure peace, then there is no keeping it.'[43]

A similar assessment of the situation from the opposite point of view lay at the basis of French policy. As a result Paris was now determined to abandon its old course of controlling developments in central Europe by trying to tie Prussia up in a joint alliance and to embark instead on one of straight containment of Berlin through the construction of an appropriate system of alliances. The most obvious partner in such an enterprise was Austria, and French policy had already extended feelers in that direction during the Luxembourg crisis. Following a series of diplomatic soundings, two meetings between the two emperors were staged with great ostentation, one in Salzburg at the end of August 1867 and the other in Paris in October of that year, on the occasion of the World Exhibition.

A change in Vienna had meanwhile placed one of the most determined opponents of Prussian policy in the past, the former Foreign Minister of Saxony, Baron Friedrich von Beust, in charge of the external affairs of the empire. After the decision of 1866 Berlin had positively forced his dismissal in Dresden. Nothing was more natural than that Beust, whom no less a person than Schwarzenberg had once called 'my best lieutenant', should in his new office make every effort to revise that decision. In late June 1867, following the settlement with Hungary, he was also appointed head of government with the title 'Imperial Chancellor' and so finally became one of the key figures in Austrian politics. Since he had long been spoken of as enjoying particularly good personal relations with Paris, he must have seemed the ideal partner for a French policy that was in the process of realigning itself and as such the very incarnation of the dangers now threatening Prussia.

Beust, however, was a sober realist, or rather, as his opponents put it at the time and later, an out-and-out opportunist. He allowed himself to be guided primarily by what in the particular state with which he was concerned at the time was most feasible politically and most likely to bring success. 'One can expect nothing from bullocks but beef and nothing from Beust but ambitious, scheming Saxon domestic politics – as long, that is, as the Kingdom of Saxony provides the frame for the picture to be glorified, namely that of Friedrich Ferdinand von Beust', Bismarck had sneered in his days as envoy to the Federal Diet.[44] Although Beust's real political objective was without question the revision of the decision of 1866, he was soon forced to admit to himself that neither of the two politically pre-eminent nations of the empire, the German nor the Hungarian, seriously aspired to such a revision with the means available. The Austrian Germans did not because scarcely anyone was prepared to wage a fresh 'war of brothers' side by side with France. And the Hungarian nation did not because such a revision would have called into question again its newly acquired parity within the monarchy.

There was also the fact that an alliance with France directed towards a revision in central Europe could have been seen as a positive invitation to St Petersburg to intervene on Prussia's behalf and subsequently recoup itself in the Balkans at Austria's expense. Russian policy was indeed no stranger to considerations of this kind. Bismarck very soon found himself confronted with an offer of closer co-operation between Russia and Prussia, an offer about which he was far from enthusiastic, however important Russian backing inevitably appeared to him. The fact was, he was afraid that this might be the prelude to an attempt on the part of St Petersburg to regain the position of dominance on the continent of Europe that it had enjoyed in the years after 1848–9.

Beust thus had a good many reasons for receiving the advances of the French with a degree of reserve and for dragging his feet over the question of a possible alliance. In particular Vienna called for greater regard to be paid to its Balkan and eastern interests, which in concrete terms meant French support even in the event of a clash with Russia. 'France must either make a determined stand against Russian policy with regard to Turkey and Austria or offer us cast-iron guarantees against Russian encroachments through the medium of a joint agreement with Russia', Beust said in the negotiating programme that he submitted to Francis Joseph before the latter's meeting with the French emperor in Salzburg.[45] But Paris was reluctant to get involved in this direction for fear of becoming wholly dependent on the decisions and policies of Vienna and making a definite enemy of St Petersburg.

The government in Berlin could only speculate about all this at first. Thus the danger of a possible rapprochement between France and Austria inevitably, not least because of Beust himself, appeared to be very much greater than it actually was, looked at in retrospect – notwithstanding Bismarck's opinion of Beust that if one subtracted 'his vanity from his abilities' there was 'little or nothing left'.[46] The Austrian envoy in Berlin, Count Wimpffen, spoke of 'serious worries' on the part of Bismarck and the Prussian government in connection with the Salzburg meeting,[47] while French diplomacy put it as high as 'feverish anxiety'.[48] Even the British ambassador, Lord Loftus, carefully weighing his words, reported 'some mistrust, not without elements of concern'.[49]

Every step in the direction of a closer rapprochement with the south therefore seemed, in the wake of the Luxembourg crisis, to be burdened with substantial additional risks. On the other hand progress on the national question appeared to be not only desirable but absolutely vital to the continued existence of the political system Bismarck had erected as well as to his own position within it. The Chancellor of the North German Confederation therefore began to walk a tightrope in the full knowledge that every false step, every failure, whether in home or foreign affairs, could plunge him into the abyss.

Even in this situation his tactics remained unchanged. While doing his best to remain in the background and on the defensive, he sought to encourage and even to accelerate developments that then obliged his opposite number at the time to take action, which in turn enabled him to exploit the new situation in what appeared to be a purely reactive manner. This was true of his German policy in the narrower sense, in other words of his policy towards the south German states. But it was also true of the European policy that embraced and ultimately imparted movement to his German policy.

In his German policy Bismarck aimed by way of developing existing institutions and relationships, in other words in formal terms adhering strictly to the status quo, to reach a point at which he hoped the unification process would to a certain extent become self-generating. On the one hand this was a question of endeavouring to draw the south German states ever closer to the North German Confederation through the medium of adapting their military systems to the Prussian or north German system and through the practical co-ordination of co-operation – though such endeavours met with no really striking success until 1870. On the other hand Bismarck relied on the existing close economic tie of the Customs Union, in other words on a card that he had already been playing with great success for many years.

In the 1866 talks between Prussia, France and Austria regarding the future organization of relations in central Europe this economic tie between north and south, which had been in existence for more than thirty years, had not been questioned by anybody nor even seriously touched upon. Not by Vienna because it was quite clear that the decision of 1866 at the same time represented the final decision in the struggle that had been going on for years regarding the relationship between the empire and the Customs Union. And not by Paris because that organization guaranteed a connection between the western and central European economic regions that was extremely important to France on account of its own economic interests. Bismarck was therefore able to assume with reasonable certainty that in taking steps here he need fear no objections from outside. Consequently, not only was it the obvious course to proceed to develop the Customs Union internally in order to bind the south German states and those of the North German Confederation more tightly together, as it were pre-empting a decision at government level; the idea also suggested itself of using that development to bring the forces of the national movement into play institutionally at a new, inter-governmental level.

That objective was served by the implementation of a plan that had first cropped up on the eve of the 1848 revolution. Originally put forward by supporters of Lesser German liberalism, it had been thrown into the debate on several occasions since from various quarters and in a variety of forms. Its essential aims were two in number: first, the periodic conferences of representatives of the governments of the member-states of the Customs Union were to be turned into a permanent body, a 'Customs Diet' on the analogy of and in competition with the Federal Diet of the German Confederation; secondly, an elected 'Customs Parliament', representing the citizens of the Customs Union, was to be set up alongside the 'Diet'. Behind those aims was a two-pronged political programme of transforming a quasi-confederate organization into one run on the lines of a federal state and of restructuring the whole thing internally in the direction of parliamentary democracy. Both were to provide a model and a vehicle for the modification of relations generally within the region covered by the Customs Union.

That objective was so clear that no one could be in any doubt as to what it meant when the Prussian government, as announced by Bismarck before the Diet of the North German Confederation as early as the middle of March,[50] took up that plan at the conference of representatives of the Customs Union states that it convened in Berlin at the beginning of July

339

1867 and put the whole political as well as economic weight of Prussia behind its implementation. Having not made a great deal of progress so far – this was how Paris and Vienna and Munich and Stuttgart inevitably saw it – Berlin was now trying to mobilize popular forces. These were to move things along from below or at least exert pressure from that direction – as Bismarck had already tried to do once with his federal reform proposals of the spring and summer of 1866.

Following the failure of his attempt in the spring of 1867 to unleash, in immediate connection with the Luxembourg crisis, an accession movement at the level of states and governments, Bismarck was now going one level deeper, as it were. This was not without its dangers, not only from the standpoint of the more inflexible conservative and monarchical traditionalists but also from his own. It threatened further to increase the already much-enhanced importance of the forces of parliamentary democracy and in the longer term to increase his own dependence on them. Yet it seemed to Bismarck, faced as he was with a foreign policy situation in which only a concatenation of particularly favourable circumstances could bring about any radical change, to be the only way of making progress.

Only in this way, as he saw it, could the south German states be pressurized into making a move. It was a question of creating a situation in which a violation of the terms of the Treaty of Prague and the agreement between Prussia and France would appear to be justified on the grounds that otherwise there was a risk not only of the internal status quo in central Europe being destroyed but also of a dangerous overflow of national forces beyond the confines of Lesser Germany. Once he had successfully mobilized them, Bismarck meant to present himself as the tamer of the forces of nationalism as they affected both domestic and foregin policy. Lesser German unification was to be made to seem the minimum concession that must be made in return.

A prerequisite of the plan, however, was that the appeal, indeed the irresistibility of the national movement must be clearly in evidence in north and south. The national party must therefore achieve a more or less triumphant victory in the elections for the Customs Parliament set at relatively short notice for February–March 1868.

Those elections, which took place only in the south German states, the north being represented by the already elected members of the Diet of the North German Confederation, were held under the new electoral law of northern Germany and not the property qualification suffrage, conditional upon a certain minimum of income or assets, under which the Diets of all the south German states had been elected hitherto. The north German system directly suggested itself in the interests of the internal homogeneity of the new body. But it was also intended to increase the weight of the expected popular vote. In the event, however, and to the enormous disappointment and dismay not only of the representatives of the Lesser German national party but also of Bismarck, it served only to expose glaring political and social antagonisms in the south.

Even in Baden, which wanted to join the Confederation and was dominated by an overwhelming liberal majority in parliament, the elections brought the national party to the brink of defeat. Bavaria and Württemberg saw the triumph – in the shape of the future Patriots' Party, the Württemberg People's Party and various particularist groups – of political forces that, while differing widely in terms of their own objectives and basic political attitudes, were united in one respect: namely, in their objection to a 'Prussianization' of the south in military and educational matters and in the economic and administrative spheres as well as in their concern that their own domestic circumstances were to be 'synchronized' with the political system obtaining in Prussia. Nor should the denominational aspect be underestimated – the fear of being placed in a helpless minority by Protestant Prussia. As a result the Lesser German national party, which was in fact seen less as a national than as a 'Prussian' party, won just twelve of a total of sixty-five seats in the two south German kingdoms. Even taking the other two south German states into account as well – only Hesse-Darmstadt voted overwhelmingly for the Lesser German liberals – the result was more than disappointing: of the ninety-one members returned by the south, including Luxembourg, which of course still belonged to the Customs Union, twenty-six fell to the national party as constituted by the National Liberal and Free Conservative groups in the Diet of the North German Confederation. And even they included some who secretly shared many of the misgivings voiced during the election campaign.

Even allowing for the protest-vote factor and the exaggerated fears of the electorate, particularly on the economic score, the Customs Parliament elections of the spring of 1868 made it quite clear that Bismarck's policy was still very largely without a popular base in southern Germany. His change of course after 1866, while it had been noted here by the liberal parties, had not impressed broader sections of the population. On the contrary, the rapprochement between a section of the liberal middle class and the expanding power and authority of the Prussian state had intensified fears of a specific form of class domination by the propertied bourgeoisie, an unholy alliance between a still semi-absolutist state and the traditional elites on the one hand and the new middle-class forces on the other.

Fears of this kind had already been entertained by a section of the democratic left during the revolution of 1848–9. Now they were also seized upon by the Catholic movement in the south, which in its clashes with liberalism over cultural, educational and religious policy was increasingly directing its appeal towards broad sections of the population, thereby bringing existing economic and social conflicts of interest into play as well. Although party-political and tactical considerations were clearly dominant here, this had a whole series of positive aspects and side-effects: above all it meant that the Catholic Church and the Catholic movement began to look at the social question and the consequences of economic and social change in less conservative terms than hitherto, with the Bishop of Mainz, Wilhelm von Ketteler, emerging around this time as the chief representative of this tendency. On the whole, however, it introduced a strongly demagogic element into the discussion. It contributed substantially towards sharpening political and social antagonisms to a degree that ultimately played into the hands of the opponents of all change and all progress. It was this tendency that Ludwig Bamberger had in mind when, shortly before returning from exile in Paris, he spoke in the immediate aftermath of the decisions of 1866 of the 'spectre' of a 'Caesarism' allegedly fostered by the propertied middle class 'with which infants on the Swabian Alp are now sung to sleep in fear'.[51]

For the time being at any rate, the 'spectre' had done a thorough job. With regard to the unification question as Bismarck saw it, there was no progress to be made at the moment along the path of parliamentary democracy and the mobilization of popular forces. And the Chancellor of the North German Confederation took good care from then on to venture no further in this direction. When not two years later it was officially proposed by the National Liberal Party through the mouth of one of its most distinguished parliamentary spokesmen, Eduard Lasker, that Baden should be admitted to the North German Confederation, thereby unleashing a popular movement in favour of accession, Bismarck brusquely rejected the proposal.[52] That was not the way to go about it. Any progress in this field would depend solely on the international constellation and the unanimous decisions of the south German governments.

The Prussian Minister-President could not afford to jeopardize yet again the opinion prevailing in most European capitals to the effect that the overwhelming majority of non-Austrian Germans aspired to belong to a Lesser German national state under Prussian leadership. It was too important, not to say indispensable an element in the field of international politics. For only with the aid of this positive preconception could the argument now repeatedly advanced, chiefly by France, that Prussia was out to destroy the balance of power in Europe be, if not invalidated, at least set against far more ominous prospects for the future. Whoever opposed Lesser German unification under Prussian leadership and within the suggested bounds of reasonable self-restraint, ran the tacit counter-argument, would be courting an explosion of nationalism – initially in central Europe but with predictable consequences in other parts of the continent as well, particularly in the east and south-east. And then, instead of the kind of balanced order to which Prussia continued to aspire, chaos would very soon prevail.

It was a striking thought. It tied in with what many politicians and publicists in Europe feared – particularly in Britain and Russia, on whose attitude so much depended as far as Prussian policy was concerned. However, Bismarck was unable to parade this purportedly so threatening nationalism in practice except under quite specific circumstances, namely some external menace or affront to German national self-awareness. That meant that in this respect too Prussian policy must remain apparently on the defensive and await an opportunity of making some progress on the back of a mobilization of national feeling triggered off from outside.

It was clear from this that more depended on the course of international politics than whether external circumstances were favourable or unfavourable. Only from this quarter – as must have seemed obvious in the light of developments in the south – could a change in the overall constellation be expected such as looked like creating a fundamentally new situation in

German internal relations too, relations between north and south. For the forces opposed to a Lesser German national state under Prussian leadership, to the incorporation of the south in the North German Confederation, continued to make headway even after the Customs Parliament elections. And this process, which culminated in the electoral triumph of the Patriots' Party in Bavaria in 1869 and the subsequent resignation of Prince Hohenlohe, the Bavarian Minister-President who had co-operated with Bismarck, in turn had repercussions on the Lesser German national parties in the south. Here too people became more critical, in the light of their electoral defeats and trends of development in public opinion, with regard to the positions taken up after 1866. They stressed that they were not under any circumstances prepared to be forced into line by the north. Indeed there was evidence here and there of a revived tendency to favour a Greater German solution, one that included Austria. The sweeping press campaign that Bismarck organized from the late autumn of 1868 against Beust and his revisionist German policy needs to be seen in this context as well.

Bearing all these things in mind gives us a direct insight into not only the main lines but also the tactics of Bismarckian policy after 1868. It becomes clear why he once again concentrated almost exclusively on the international scene and rejected with growing nervousness all moves on the home front that threatened to affect that scene in undesirable ways. The same is true of the line he was pursuing in all this. There can have been nothing he looked for more eagerly than the appearance of international problems that would force France – as his chief foreign policy adversary – into action of a possibly risky kind and allow Prussia to exploit the resultant situation to its own advantage.

Bismarck did not, however, fall into the temptation of creating suitable constellations himself. It was his conviction that this was almost bound to lead to whoever tried such a thing eventually being hoist by his own petard. 'That German unity would be furthered by violent events I too regard as probable', he wrote in this connection in a directive to the Prussian envoy in Munich, von Werthern, towards the end of February 1869. 'But the vocation to induce a violent catastrophe is quite another matter . . . Arbitrary intervention in the evolution of history on purely subjective grounds has always resulted in merely knocking down unripe fruit; and that German unity is not at this moment a ripe fruit is in my opinion obvious.'[53]

Bismarck's own attitude is characterized much more accurately, even in this specific case, by his variously worded analogy of the person walking in a wood who is aware of his general direction – he knew that very precisely – but not of the point at which he will come out of the wood. 'At least I am not so arrogant as to assume that the likes of us are able to *make* history', he wrote around this time to Gottfried Kinkel, a democrat from the 1848–9 period who was now living in Zurich as a professor of art history and who, disregarding all former political barriers between them, had got in touch with him over the national question. 'My task is to keep an eye on the currents of the latter and steer my ship in them as best I can. The currents themselves I cannot direct; even less am I able to create them.'[54]

In relation to the concrete situation this meant that setting a trap for

343

French policy in accordance with a carefully prepared and precalculated plan executed with military precision was inconsistent with the basic structure of his policy, tactically as well as in principle. This had nothing to do with any kind of moral consideration; he did not in any way reject the idea of exploiting an 'unlooked-for opportunity' such as, 'an upheaval in France, for example, or a war between other great powers'.[55] No, what was crucial was his conviction that any kind of planning, any kind of precalculation in politics had to work with so many unknowns that it made sense only if the person doing the planning and precalculating at the same time held himself constantly in readiness for as many possible courses and quite distinct outcomes. 'It would be to misunderstand the nature of politics to suppose that a statesman could draw up a far-reaching plan and rigidly dictate to himself what he wished to do in one, two, or three years' time', he said once in later life.[56]

Implicit in this is something that is entirely logical but that we often disregard when forming historical judgements, particularly since the historical agent himself connives at it in retrospect: what at first dimly presented itself as one possibility among many and was then, still together with others, exploited with varying degrees of concentration and varying expectations of success, eventually being brought to what remained to the last an uncertain outcome, assumes in the light of a successful outcome the appearance of a skilfully contrived plan, a bold stroke of genius, or, depending on one's point of view, a piece of out-and-out devilry. Only if we get this clear in our minds will we be able to reach a historically balanced and in some degree fair judgement regarding the much-discussed immediate background to the war of 1870–1.

Contrary to popular opinion, however, the question of responsibility and hence of 'war guilt' will be touched on only peripherally in the process. Neither side stumbled into that war with any deep reluctance, and certainly neither side was dragged into it. It was taken for granted at the time by those who made the decisions on both sides that the instrument of war was the *ultima ratio* of politics and a means – albeit an extreme one – of settling conflicts that could be resorted to as and when it was appropriate. Consequently the question of responsibility must be a question of the estimated chance of success that either side associated with it, in other words of the motives that made exacerbation of a conflict to the point of war appear not at all unwelcome in the final analysis. And the answer to that question can emerge only from an examination and appraisal of the situation as a whole, not from the analysis of somewhat diffuse individual initiatives and individual actions arising out of a wide variety of contexts, even if in retrospect those initiatives and actions appear to form a direct and highly revealing chain of cause and effect. As the Austrian historian Heinrich von Srbik once very rightly remarked, 'The argument about "war guilt" never gets to the bottom of things'.[57]

The starting-point of the crisis of 1870 that triggered off the Franco-Prussian War was the plan to place a Hohenzollern prince on the vacant Spanish throne. The vacancy was due to a left-wing coup by officers of the Spanish army, who in September 1868 had brought to an end the still wholly absolutist reign of Isabella II of the House of Bourbon and who now aspired, under the leadership of General Prim, to make Spain a parliamentary monarchy on the British model.

In their search for a suitable monarch the new rulers of Spain, if they did not wish to expose the country to the risk of never-ending rivalries and civil war by elevating some grandee, were faced with the usual problem: they must find a king whom the rest of Europe's princes would accept as an equal in accordance with the prevailing dynastic laws. This presupposed his being a member of a currently or formerly ruling house. It pointed the Spanish military government, as it had pointed Belgium in 1830 and Greece in 1832, in the direction of central Europe, the region that two generations before had seen the passing of the Holy Roman Empire, the home of hundreds of once independent and consequently equal-ranking royal families. An occurrence that lay less than two-and-a-half years in the past further directed their attention to a quite specific family, the south German collateral line of the Hohenzollerns, which had given up its independence in favour of the principal, Prussian line after the revolution of 1848: in April 1866, likewise following a coup, the second son of Charles Anthony, former ruling prince of Hohenzollern-Sigmaringen, had been placed on the throne of Romania as King Carol I.

So it came as no great surprise when, after a parliament had been summoned and a liberal constitution adopted, the newly appointed Spanish government under General Prim, having made various other soundings and considered other possibilities, chose the hereditary prince of that family, Prince Leopold. To what extent there were promptings from Prussia to this effect at an early stage of the proceedings can no longer be unequivocally established. What is certain is that the Prussian Minister-President followed Spanish developments in general and the succession question in particular with great attention from the outset. 'It is in our interests', ran a telegraphed instruction to the Foreign Ministry early in October 1868, 'that the Spanish question should remain open as a fontanel of peace, and a solution agreeable to Napoleon is unlikely to be the one beneficial to us.'[58] It was obvious that the idea of a closer, dynastically based tie between Berlin and Madrid must immediately appear as a solution 'beneficial' to Prussia.

On the other hand the sources make it perfectly clear that the whole affair was at first of only minor importance as far as Bismarck and Prussian policy were concerned. This was chiefly because for a long time it was not possible to predict what direction the deliberations and decisions of the Spanish army leaders and the individual political parties would finally take and what prospects of success an eventual candidature might in fact have. Following a prelude in the spring of 1869, serious exploration of the whole question and of the Spanish terrain did not begin on Prussia's part until the winter of 1869–70, when it began to look as if something might actually come of the affair.

Before that the paramount factor was quite obviously fear of losing face, even indirectly, in the event of an unsuccessful commitment. When Benedetti, the French ambassador in Berlin, tackled Bismarck in May 1869 about the rumours of a Hohenzollern prince possibly being a candidate for the Spanish throne, he received a very clear-cut reply: neither the candidate envisaged by certain circles in Spain nor his father had reacted positively; furthermore the Prussian king, as head of the Hohenzollern family, was more than sceptical with regard to such considerations.

This was not to be taken at face value, of course. But it did show that from the outset the Prussian Minister-President was aware of the risk of French policy exploiting such a candidature against Prussia and representing it as evidence of unbridled Prussian expansionism – however much the French approach may have confirmed him in his opinion that the whole thing also offered not inconsiderable political opportunities.

Inevitably, such an approach did indeed almost force itself on the framers of French policy. After all, the French government had a manifest interest, not least for domestic policy reasons, in successfully standing up to Prussian policy wherever this appeared to exceed the terms of the German national interest. In this way France would be able once again to present itself as the upholder of the European order and possibly even make quite concrete compensatory gains without coming into conflict with the principle of national self-determination.

Since 1866 the foreign policy of Napoleon III had been in a quandary that affected the French emperor's political system as a whole, dependent as this very largely was on its successes. From the beginning it had backed a revision of the 1815 settlement along national lines and had allied itself with the forces and powers that were working in the same direction. It had followed the same broad line, all fluctuations and attempts to secure its rear notwithstanding, with regard to developments in central Europe as well. Accordingly it had for long periods directed its political sympathies towards Berlin rather than Vienna. Favouring what appeared to be the weaker of the two German great powers and what both territorially and in power-political terms was the more restrained nationalism of the Lesser German persuasion would, it hoped, best serve French power interests. It would provide fresh proof for the basic Napoleonic contention that that interest was best taken care of in a European system of national states, indeed that such a system would lend permanence to French hegemony.

That calculation had been very seriously upset by events at Königgrätz and Nikolsburg. A review of French policy therefore positively imposed itself – a fact that Bismarck immediately and very soberly took into account. On the other hand, and this was the real dilemma that French policy was in, such a review threatened to undermine the foundations of the Napoleonic system.

In essence that system was based on the fact that broad sections of the French public believed that, despite many disadvantages, it guaranteed the nation's interests: economic and social progress, peace at home, prosperity and national honour. The French Empire appeared – and it was on this that its indubitable political successes rested – as the chief agent of progress and of a future peace among nations; Napoleon, seen in this light, was the antithesis of the traditional type of monarch associated with stagnation and reaction. Were Napoleon to abandon a position on which his press and propaganda laid repeated and explicit stress by allying himself, no longer for what he alleged to be merely tactical reasons but in this case clearly in terms of essentials as well, with those who sought to defend the existing order by every means against popular forces and interests, not only would his prestige be placed in jeopardy; his entire system would be at risk.

How far this was already the case was shown by the fact that the political parties that had been successfully thrust aside in the early 1850s were once more beginning to gain ground and to demand a restoration of the parliamentary, constitutional system in place of the plebiscitary, pseudo-democratic system. On top of the final collapse of the Mexican venture, the attempt to use the Austrian emperor's younger brother, Maximilian I, to set up a kind of satellite empire in the New World, came the rebuff over Luxembourg. Furthermore – and this was far more serious – in the aftermath of 1866 French economic and financial circles suffered a severe setback in European markets. Adapting the government's propaganda slogan, 'L'empire, c'est la paix', Paris in those days adopted the motto, 'L'empire, c'est la baisse'. In the face of all this Napoleon III found himself obliged in 1869 to make far-reaching constitutional concessions to the parties and the opposition, concessions that virtually turned the empire into a parliamentary monarchy. In the so-called 'empire libéral', parliament and the parties had at least an equal say from now on.

The Napoleonic right had done its utmost, right up until the end, to halt this development. Its advocates continued to rely on successes on the foreign policy front. Led by the French ambassador in Vienna, Duke Antoine de Gramont, they too of course saw the in-built dilemma, as it were, for French foreign policy, namely that it could not dissociate itself from the national principle and from the idea that it was the spokesman of the nations and of their true interests. They now tried to tread a new path that would avoid the dilemma.

That path was fundamentally different from the one that French policy had pursued before 1866 and to which a section of Napoleon's diplomatic corps, headed by a Minister of State, Eugène Rouher, endeavoured to cling even after that date. They disputed the existence of a true alliance between Prussia as an expanding great power and the German national movement. Prussia, they began to argue in the immediate aftermath of the decision of 1866, was not in fact pursuing a German policy at all but a 'Greater Prussian' policy. Furthermore, this served no other interests than those of political and social reaction. It was therefore, they said, not only in its own interests but also in the true interests of the German people that Napoleonic France should continue to think in terms of taking 'revenge for Sadowa' and revising the decision of 1866.

The whole thing, in other words, amounted to questioning the alleged identity of Prussian and German national interests and seizing every available opportunity of demonstrating the opposite. But what could possibly lend itself more fittingly to this than a dynastic question that they felt would hardly affect the German public and that was on the other hand of considerable importance to France? If Prussia were to back a Hohenzollern candidate for the Spanish throne, must it not become clear to everyone that Berlin's reckless pursuit of power and confrontation had nothing to do with the interests of the German people but on the contrary had the effect of earning that people the hostility of other nations? Consequently, as far as the French government and in particular the Napoleonic right were concerned, the rumours for Spain signalled not only a danger but at the same time a substantial opportunity: that of inflicting a serious defeat on Prussia at no great risk and possibly obtaining after all that compensation for 1866 that was so desirable from the standpoint of domestic affairs. Moreover, French policy did, in the further course of events, make very successful use of that opportunity – until at the very last moment it committed a crucial error.

So both sides, the Prussian and the French, saw the Spanish succession question at a relatively early stage as offering a chance to impart some movement to international affairs in the direction of their own interests and objectives. That this applied to the French side as well can be deduced not least from the fact that Paris avoided putting a stop to the whole business from the beginning by making its intentions clear in Madrid. For it was obvious and must have been so to Paris too that the Spanish government would not have acted in defiance of the stated wishes of so powerful a neighbour. Only one conclusion can be drawn from this, namely that the French government, anxious to keep open at least the possibility of a poker game, did not want, before the game had even started, to prevent its potential opponent from accepting the invitation and venturing a stake.

At any rate, Berlin was left to decide for itself whether to become involved in the question in an active way. Bismarck thus found himself in the kind of situation he had been determined to avoid. He must leave his cover, as it were; he must, if not actually go on the offensive, at least take steps on ground where the other side might be lying in wait. There can be little doubt that he toyed with the idea of calling the whole thing off and was frequently assailed by fears that he might be stumbling into a trap. When in the early months of 1870 he nevertheless seized the initiative and made a serious attempt to persuade both sides, the Spaniards and the Hohenzollern family, to put Prince Leopold on the throne, it was because of his own increasingly pessimistic appraisal of the overall situation.

At the international level, not only did the rapprochement between Paris and Vienna appear to be making some progress. The attitude of the British government and of the British public towards France and the Napoleonic regime had also begun to take a more favourable turn as far as France was concerned since the constitutional reforms of 1869 and the appointment of the constitutionally and liberally minded Émile Ollivier as chief minister on 2 January 1870. And in St Petersburg Prussia's refusal to commit itself positively to Russian interests in the Balkan and Black Sea regions tended to benefit those who warned against indirectly supporting constant extensions of Prussian power for no visible return.

But above all it was developments in central Europe that, from Bismarck's standpoint, provided every justification for taking a negative view of the future. The anti-Prussian current in the south was swelling all the time. And in the north, too, more and more voices could be heard, principally from Catholic and formerly non-Prussian quarters, drawing attention to the other side of the decisions of 1866. Much that had hitherto seemed to be simply a transitional stage on the way towards a German national state – a prelude and as such provisional – assumed a different character when seen in terms of a very much longer road to that objective. Even within the National Liberal camp people were once again beginning to ask whether the national idea was not still, for Bismarck, a mere means to an end. Was the Chancellor perhaps, even now, not in the least concerned with bringing about German unity but purely with securing power interests – those, to be precise, of the Prussian state, of his class and above all of himself?

In this situation the fundamental lack of trust that always potentially surrounded him once again came to a head. It now placed him and the political system he personified very much under pressure to produce results. He felt very clearly that he could not go on marking time any longer without putting a great many things at risk once more. As the crisis of the autumn of 1869 concerning Finance Minister von der Heydt and the government's budgetary policy showed, notwithstanding all his triumphs he was no longer fully master of the situation on the domestic policy front. And it was not by any means fanciful on his part to fear that a development he had himself done so much to urge on and accelerate might one day in the not too distant future roll right over him.

Only by bearing in mind this whole constellation of circumstances, which Bismarck himself registered acutely and without any illusions, can one understand why with the Spanish succession question, in defiance of his tactics hitherto, he finally let himself in for something in which dangers and opportunities were, from the Prussian standpoint, precisely balanced and in which the risk of failure and defeat was exceptionally great: no more promising target presented itself, and Bismarck absolutely had to make some headway.

The whole affair entered its crucial phase towards the end of February 1870 when after reciprocal exploratory talks the Spanish privy councillor Don Salazar y Mazarredo, acting on behalf of the Spanish government, presented the official proposal for a candidature for the throne – first in Düsseldorf, to the Sigmaringen line, and afterwards to the head of the family in Berlin. Both Charles Anthony and the Prussian king still had great misgivings. However, Bismarck now brought all his powers of persuasion, backed up by every single available argument, to bear on laying those misgivings to rest. The letter he wrote to the Prussian king on 9 March 1870, summarizing and elucidating his point of view once again,is a classic example of a Bismarckian *argumentum ad hominem*.[59] He brought into it all the avowed or secret guiding principles, all the ideas and illusions and all the desires and hopes that occupied the mind of the man he sought to convince.

A Hohenzollern on the throne of Charles V – that, he bade his king imagine, would, quite apart from all practical advantages in the military and diplomatic spheres as well as in terms of commercial policy, have enormous consequences for the standing of the dynasty as a whole and for Prussia's position in Germany. 'The House of Hohenzollern' would in consequence very soon 'be accorded such respect and occupy so high a position in the world as have their analogy only in the Habsburg antecedents since Charles V'. The Prussian people's 'pride in a glorious dynasty' had already in the past been 'a powerful moral stimulus behind the development of Prussian power in Germany. That driving force will increase mightily if the German nation's need for recognition abroad, a need that has received so little satisfaction hitherto, is met by the dynasty's occupying an unrivalled position in the world.' Were the House of Hohenzollern to refuse, on the other hand, it would not only be repulsing a 'nation of sixteen million people that is asking to be saved from anarchy'. It would give rise, if the already mooted candidature of a Wittelsbach were given a chance, either to an 'ultramontane reaction at home' in sympathy with the 'anti-national elements in Germany' or to a republic. This might in turn result in a corresponding change of system in France, releasing a violently anti-German nationalism. Public opinion in Germany would ultimately lay the blame for such a negative development at the door of those 'with whom the rejection of the Spanish crown originated'. In such a case the Hohenzollern dynasty and with it the Prussian government would emerge from the whole episode weakened rather than strengthened. Besides their reputation, their power position too would be substantially diminished.

The idea that the Hohenzollern family would, with the acquisition of the Spanish throne, finally 'catch up' with the Habsburgs, the family of Charles V, the emphasis on the implicitly leading role of the monarchy in political life, the evocation of an enormous increase in both the national and the international prestige of his dynasty – all that inevitably made a most powerful impression on the Prussian king. Bismarck hoped that it would push his misgivings into the background, especially since his Minister-President did not say a word about possible entanglements with France; on the contrary, he predicted that kind of danger more in the event of a refusal and the resultant complication of the whole situation.

The king, however, remained sceptical and could bring himself only to tolerate the decision of the Sigmaringen family. On the other hand Bismarck's line of argument has continued down to our own day to impress a whole series of historians who have thought they saw more in it than simply an attempt to overcome the king's resistance by means of arguments tailored wholly to his personal preoccupations. They saw and have seen behind it the concept of a supra-national power position for the Hohenzollern dynasty, and they argue that this was part of a large-scale plan. The ultimate objective of that plan is supposed to have been the establishment of a national emperorship as the final political authority in and at the same time integrator of a German national state.

For proof they point mainly to the plan, first aired by Bismarck early in 1870, to bestow on the Prussian king in his capacity as 'Holder of the Presidency of the North German Confederation' – as the not exactly memorable official constitutional formula had it – the title of emperor. This, they say, was the counterpart to and true reason for the attempt to increase the national and international prestige of the Hohenzollern dynasty by placing a Hohenzollern prince on another throne. Through the medium of the head of the dynasty, as future emperor, that increase in prestige was to be made to redound directly to the benefit of the North German Confederation. It was supposed to make the Confederation irresistibly attractive to the peoples of the south German states. A further consideration is said to have been that having a prince from the Catholic branch of the family mount the throne of Spain would allay denominational misgivings about a Lesser German national state ruled by the Protestant royal family of Prussia.

All of which seems highly plausible at first glance. On closer examination, however, it soon becomes clear that the whole thing is simply an artificial construction that to a great extent stands the actual situation on its head. It is unlikely that Bismarck, faced with the outcome of the Customs Parliament elections and subsequent political developments in the south, seriously believed that setting up an emperorship in northern Germany would trigger off a sudden rush to join the Confederation. Moreover, it was obvious that such an upgrading of the holder of the presidency of that organization would tend on the contrary to heighten the misgivings of the south German governments and monarchs, particularly those of Bavaria.

The function of this altogether not very felicitous plan, which was in fact soon shelved, was probably quite different – as so often, Bismarck spoke of his motives here only in contradictory terms always tailored to the particular situation. For one thing the increasingly restless and unruly national party within the North German Confederation was to be offered something capable of firing its imagination once again in a politically fairly harmless way by giving it something to look forward to. But above all – and probably this was the really crucial point – it was to be demonstrated for the benefit of the other great powers that Prussia was now wholly taken up with the internal development of its own sovereign territory and in that respect also aspired to formal equality of status with the continent's other three empires. This supposition is supported by the fact that the plan disappeared from the scene the moment France and, in the wake of France, Britain too began to construe it as an expression not of self-restraint but of expansive national aspirations. So if there was any connection between the emperorship plan and the Spanish succession – the one was shelved as the other really came to the fore – it was at most that the plan was to provide additional cover for Prussian activities with regard to the Spanish question and further emphasize the defensive character of Prussian policy in general.

Whether the Spanish succession question would eventually impart the kind of movement of which Bismarck hoped to take reactive advantage remained open almost up until the last minute. So, accordingly, did the potential outcome of the whole affair. An armed conflict, a peaceful settlement, a clear diplomatic defeat for one side or the other, or even a surprising resolution of the whole problem as a result of developments inside Spain – any one of them seemed possible almost to the end.

The idea of this kind of openness characterizing the whole constellation of circumstances was downright intolerable to many contemporaries as they looked back on the affair, and it has remained so for many historians right up to the present day. Consequently, for more than a hundred years people have been trying with considerable acumen to ferret out Bismarck's true plan, the precise political objective he had in mind. Was it deliberately to provoke a war of unification? Or merely to pave the way for unification by inflicting a diplomatic defeat on the French? Or was it simple crisis management in the face of irresponsible or aggressive behaviour on France's part? To adopt this approach, however, is fundamentally to misunderstand the nature of what we are dealing with here. The fact is, precisely that kind of advance objective formed no part of Bismarckian policy – or did so only to a very limited degree. Bismarckian policy was multi-track even to the extent that it made allowance for every possibility not only as an outcome but also, and in the same breath, as a starting-point for further, wholly new actions and especially designs.

Consequently not only Bismarck's own statements, which in any case were almost always tactical in intention, but also those of the individual contemporaries acting alongside him contain examples of every plan and every objective that were at all conceivable in the given situation. When Bismarck, looking back, repeatedly stated in different contexts and in relation to quite distinct historical situations that history made its own way here, in essence this was neither mystification nor was it to identify successful action with history itself. On the contrary, it represented his understanding not only of the limitations of his own plans and actions but above all – and it was this that was most characteristic – of the need repeatedly and quite deliberately to make the reservation that those plans and actions were provisional and dependent on circumstances.

Particularly in his handling of the Spanish succession question Bismarck was continually making that kind of reservation. As he had learned only too well, this was a question in which everything depended on the circumstances of the moment. In the middle of March 1870, all his Minister-President's efforts and arguments notwithstanding, the king himself had cast the only vote in the Prussian Crown Council against the candidature of Prince Leopold. Since the potential candidate declined to accept the candidature unless William voted accordingly, it looked as if that was the end of the matter. On 20 April Leopold and his father even sent the Spanish government formal notification of their refusal. 'The Spanish affair has taken a wretched turn', Bismarck wrote to Delbrück around the middle of May 1870, summing up the situation. 'Indubitable reasons of state have been subordinated to the private inclinations of princes and to ultramontane female influences. Irritation over this has for weeks been placing a heavy burden on my nerves.'[60]

It was surely no accident that it was a liver complaint that kept Bismarck away from Berlin from mid-April onwards. Not only was the attitude of his king giving him trouble; there was another, no less important factor on top of that. While diplomatic soundings and discussions with Madrid had been going on the whole time, regardless of the king's resistance, the overall political situation in Paris, the situation on which Bismarck's calculations had been based since the introduction of the 'empire libéral' and the appointment of Ollivier's ministry, had undergone a further decisive change.

The Napoleonic right, which had agreed only with great reluctance and under pressure of circumstances to the concessions granted to the political opposition, used the enhanced prestige those concessions had bestowed on the emperorship in order partially to retract them. On 8 May 1870 the French nation was asked in a referendum to approve the alterations to the constitution that had been made over the past few years. At the instigation of the right a clause was introduced into the wording to the effect that the French people at the same time 'approved' the decree passed by the Senate on 20 April 1870. To the less well informed it inevitably appeared that this decree of Napoleon's senate, a body dominated by the group that had been in control of the regime hitherto, was entirely in line with the constitutional reforms to be voted on. In fact, however, the text of that decree laid emphasis on principles that were scarcely compatible with those reforms and that amounted to a restoration of the Napoleonic system. Above all it stressed that the head of state was still the true bearer of political responsibility vis-à-vis the 'nation', in other words not the government as backed by a majority in parliament. Accordingly it was open to the head of state to appeal to the sovereign people at any time through the medium of a plebiscite.

This meant that the right was determined, in the event of a conflict, to play parliament and people off against each other by employing every means of influence and demagogic simplification – this was widely used – available to the state. Those who had pushed the liberal reforms through and were now of course compelled to stand up for them had to look on impotently while this process proved successful in the very plebiscite concerning the reforms. Admittedly the larger towns produced many more votes against than in other Napoleonic plebiscites, but an overwhelming majority of more than 80 per cent formally approved not only the constitutional reforms but also, and at the same time, their modification and curtailment in practice.

The immediate outcome of this success on the part of the opponents of reform, the price of which was of course a further forfeiture of trust among large sections of the country's intellectual leadership, was a fresh government reshuffle on 15 May 1870. Although Ollivier remained in charge as a figurehead for the compromise with the parliamentary left, the basic direction of the government was altered substantially as the principal spokesman and 'strong man' of the Napoleonic right joined the Cabinet in the person of Duke Antoine de Gramont. He took over the Foreign Ministry from Count Daru, who favoured compromise and a policy of cautious restraint. A group thus came to the fore in foreign affairs that propagated a decidedly anti-Prussian policy directed towards a revision of the decisions of 1866 and that sought to use that policy to strengthen the foundations of the regime at home.

This development can scarcely be said to have caught Bismarck entirely unawares. It was too much in line with what he had allowed for from the start in his sober appraisal of the objective interests of the other side. Yet the changes in the political constellation in Paris marked a major turning-point for him too: they represented a very considerable shift in the spectrum of potential French reactions on the international scene. This was particularly true with regard to an absolute determination not only on no account to tolerate any further extensions of Prussian influence but to seize every opportunity of actively and demonstratively putting Prussian policy in its place and so making good such changes in the balance of power as had taken place since 1866. Probably the most tangible object towards which the eyes of Napoleon III and his government were directed in this context was Belgium. The implication, however, was that the Spanish succession question and a possible Hohenzollern candidature for the Spanish throne would be seized on by the French, if the slightest opportunity arose, in order to bar Prussia's way. A man such as Bismarck, to whom the French scene was particularly familiar – for the last twenty years he had followed it more closely than almost anyone – could be in no doubt about this.

In other words, whatever different courses and outcomes Bismarck may have regarded as conceivable and possible before 15 May, it must have been clear to him now that there was no getting round a confrontation if Prussia continued to press the Hohenzollern candidature. His decision to become actively involved once again and urgently to recommend to the Sigmaringen family in a letter of 28 May that they accept the candidature on the grounds that this would constitute a 'service' to 'both countries', Germany and Spain, unmistakably reflects the fact that he no longer wished to avoid that confrontation because he now regarded it as inevitable, given the interests at stake on both sides.[61] And since neither side could really afford a serious diplomatic defeat, not least for domestic reasons, armed hostilities were now an immediate prospect.

At the very least it was a possibility with which both sides now had to reckon. Of course, the firebrands in both camps excepted, both Paris and Berlin would have preferred to achieve their respective political objectives without a war, by subjecting the other to a severe diplomatic defeat. This is so tritely self-evident that one wonders why such dogged disputes have been waged over the point on both sides. The theory that Bismarck was aiming solely at this kind of diplomatic victory over France right up until the last minute, and that the war was ultimately triggered off by the immoderate and uncontrolled behaviour of the other side, fails like its French counterpart to take account of the fact that the chances of inflicting so severe and politically momentous a defeat on the other side in the given situation were extremely slim from the outset. In other words, that kind of attempt to clear one or the other side of blame is based on wholly fictitious premisses. It relies on the idea that the power that was momentarily driven into a corner could have admitted defeat without first having played all its cards, as it were, which both sides unquestioningly took to include having recourse to war. Since this was hardly a realistic expectation, escalation of the conflict to the point of war was the probable outcome, while a lasting success without war would be such a stroke of luck as was scarcely to be taken into serious account. Because in the final analysis one of its prerequisites would have been, if not the immediate collapse of the opposing government, at least a loss of authority on a scale that it could scarcely have coped with in the long run.

It has been argued that Bismarck sought to avoid precisely this kind of pressure to seize the bull by the horns by building up a pretence to the effect that the Prussian government was in no way involved in the whole affair. He did indeed do everything to maintain such a pretence and to prevent the other side from getting its hands on any proof to the contrary. When at the beginning of June, without the knowledge of the still reluctant Prussian king, he dispatched Lothar Bucher, a senior Foreign Ministry official, on a second secret mission to Madrid it was with instructions to the effect that, while dealing very vigorously with the whole affair, he should treat it as a purely dynastic, quasi-private matter and not as something that concerned the state. Accordingly he was to urge Madrid to deal only with the Sigmaringen family direct.

The Prussian Minister-President kept strictly to this course during the weeks that followed. The acceptance of the candidature by Prince Leopold on 19 June and the consent of the Prussian king given two days later were treated as occurrences to which, in the words of a letter of 11 June to the crown prince, he did 'not attach *official* importance'.[62] Bismarck wrote that letter from his Varzin estate in eastern Pomerania, to which he had retreated on 8 June for a holiday and a cure. There, 300 kilometres from Berlin, he was virtually unreachable as far as all official contacts were concerned. That too was part of his plan to appear as uninvolved as possible.

But can he seriously have hoped to deceive the other side with this pretence? Did he really think that it would enable him to evade a counter-thrust if necessary, to give in without losing face in public? Hardly. On the contrary, he probably envisaged a situation from the outset in which the French government would try to knock a hole in that pretence. When it did so, it could be expected to expose in one form or another the true motive behind its counter-initiative, namely containment of Prussia and Prussian national ambitions. And then, the thought suggested itself, German national feeling would all of a sudden come into play: the nation would feel humiliated through its protecting power, Prussia, and would demand appropriate counter-measures. But that would result in all misgivings and reservations with regard to Prussia and Prussian control being thrust into the background, at least temporarily. One could then expect to see a kind of national united front comprising the vast majority of existing parties and political forces with corresponding repercussions on the future shape of central Europe.

So it all came down to manoeuvring Paris, whose reactions could be predicted with some certainty, into an unfavourable starting position. It was a question of presenting France internationally but in particular to the German public as the power that seized on every pretext to confirm and reinforce its hegemony at Prussia's expense. According to the original plan French policy was to be confronted as far as possible with *faits accomplis*; every effort was to be made to ensure that the delay between the official announcement of the candidature and the actual election of the king in accordance with the law passed by the Spanish parliament on 7 June 1870 was kept to a minimum. This part of the plan miscarried, with a mistake in the decoding of a telegram from the chief Spanish negotiator in Germany playing a key role. As a result the election was set by the Spanish government for 1 August and not, as intended, for a date very much sooner after publication of Prince Leopold's official declaration of acceptance.

However, this was not of such crucial importance as has often been supposed. When the 'Spanish bomb', as William I put it,[63] 'went off' on 2 July 1870, the day the Spanish chief minister officially informed the French ambassador of the Hohenzollern candidature, French reactions immediately focused almost exclusively on Prussia. That was where Paris was looking for a decision. On 4 July, less than forty-eight hours after the Spanish announcement, the French chargé d'affaires Le Sourd appeared at the Foreign Ministry in Berlin in place of the absent Benedetti and demanded to know the extent of Prussian government involvement. On the same day the Prussian ambassador in Paris, Baron von Werther, found himself listening to some sharply worded reproaches and threats not only from the French Foreign Minister but also from chief minister Ollivier. Hermann von Thile, the secretary of state at the Foreign Ministry, stated as he had been instructed to 'that as far as the Prussian government is concerned the affair does not exist'.[64] Werther, on the other hand, much to Bismarck's displeasure, allowed himself to be drawn into discussion of the issue to the extent that he agreed to report directly to the Prussian king on the occasion of a long-projected visit to Bad Ems, where William was taking a cure at the time.

A further two days later Duke Antoine de Gramont delivered in the French Chamber of Deputies the speech that he had announced immediately and that had been looked forward to with great excitement. With it he departed from the sphere of more or less secret diplomatic negotiations and proceeded publicly to commit the government. 'We do not believe', he declared to tumultuous applause from the overwhelming majority in the Chamber, 'that respect for the rights of a neighbour people obliges us to suffer a foreign power to disturb the present balance of power in Europe to our disadvantage by placing one of its princes on the throne of Charles V, so jeopardizing the interests and honour of France.' The French government still had hopes 'of the wisdom of the German and the friendship of the Spanish people'. But, he went on, 'should things turn out otherwise we shall know, strengthened by your support and by that of the nation, how to do our duty without hesitation and without weakness'.[65]

The threat was as unequivocal as it was massive: if the candidature of Prince Leopold was maintained, France would intervene with every means at its disposal. Since Spain could confidently be expected to capitulate sooner or later under such heavy pressure, particularly with both Britain and Russia letting it be known that they were in sympathy with the French threat, maintenance of the candidature inevitably appeared suicidal – unless the other side, namely Prussia, was bent on war at all events, regardless of how favourable or unfavourable conditions might be for it at the moment.

To let himself be pushed along like this and simply take his chance was not of course Bismarck's way. He therefore affected, behind the smoke-screen of his pretence that this was purely a Hohenzollern matter – and one concerning only the south German, Catholic branch of the family at that – to beat a retreat. Afterwards he sought to persuade contemporaries and posterity alike that his objective had been to evade the French counter-thrust in this way. However, the king, in his utter straightforwardness and love of peace – read: in his political maladroitness – had almost thwarted his plans. By trying on his own account to persuade the prince to withdraw his candidature and on top of that getting involved in negotiations with the French ambassador, Benedetti, who had meanwhile hurried to Bad Ems, William had placed Prussia in an extremely difficult position. Only the immoderate nature of the French demands, which culminated in the request that the king rule out his ever consenting to such a candidature at any time in the future, had saved the day. This had made it possible for him, Bismarck, to proceed to counter-measures.[66]

This is without a doubt the most meticulously stylized and the most vividly and colourfully embellished historical legend that Bismarck launched upon the world. Entire generations accepted it at face value, and even the majority of historians have swallowed it more or less whole. And yet on sober examination Bismarck's calculations and tactics in this final phase are downright obvious. This prompt retreat in an affair that the Prussians had been preparing and pursuing for a long time was inevitably seen in Paris as indicating a weakness in the Prussian position. This in turn was virtually guaranteed to thrust upon the French idea of exploiting that weakness as much as possible for their own domestic and foreign policy objectives – unless, of course, it dawned on them that this was exactly what the other side intended. However, in view of the national agitation that had gripped France and the temptation to turn it to account politically, this was hardly likely.

Now, given the fact that the Prussian government could not officially be addressed on the matter and Bismarck could not even be reached, where else was such an attempt to begin but with the Prussian king, at whom the version according to which this was a purely family affair, concerning only the House of Hohenzollern, pointed an additional finger. But there was scarcely anyone whose reactions Bismarck could predict more precisely than those of William I, the man with whom he had lived in the closest proximity for many years and on whose actions and decisions his political life entirely depended. Having been averse from the outset to a member of his family standing for the Spanish throne and being at the same time decisively opposed to another war, he could be expected, with a degree of probability verging on certainty, to do everything to placate and pacify the French – thereby literally provoking them into making a further precipitate thrust.

For Paris must attempt eventually to go beyond the king and somehow bring the Prussian government into play as well, luring it out of its reserve. Only in that way could it counter the irritating claim, which stood in the way of complete success, that Prussia as a state had no concern with the whole affair: whatever might happen, it left the Prussian government cold and did not affect it. Only if France achieved a breakthrough here would it be truly victorious. It was possible to predict, in other words, that the French government would go on and on giving the screw another turn. And it was equally possible to predict that this process would reach a point where it would be a simple matter for the Prussian side to represent the French demands in the eyes of the German and international public as intolerable exactions out of all proportion to the given occasion.

Bismarck had been waiting for this moment with some serenity ever since the 'Spanish bomb' had 'gone off'. Not until 12 July did he leave Varzin to travel to Bad Ems via Berlin. His serenity arose out of his conviction that he had after all now achieved the apparently defensive position for which he had worked so hard. When on the evening of 13 July, after detailed discussions of the situation in Berlin, the now famous report reached him from Bad Ems concerning the latest developments and the king's discussions with the French ambassador, he did not in the least, as he subsequently tried to have people believe, act on a sudden inspiration or out of a feeling of having been saved at the last moment from impending defeat. He acted in the knowledge that the moment had now arrived for the decisive counter-attack on which all his thinking and planning had been focused for days.

Benedetti had lodged his government's first complaint with the Prussian king in Bad Ems on 9 July. He had asked him about his attitude to the whole question and requested information as to how, in view of the French attitude, he saw things developing. As arranged, William had put forward the Bismarckian version on that occasion: he had been asked for his advice and approval on this question not as King of Prussia but as head of the Hohenzollern family. He could hardly have withheld his consent. For the decision at issue had been one for the Sigmaringen branch alone to make and answer for. Accordingly, neither could he attempt to reverse that decision.

In fact, however, he had written to Prince Charles Anthony the very next day, on 10 July, at least suggesting that his son withdraw his candidature. The reaction was swift: on 12 July Prince Leopold announced that he was no longer standing. With that William considered the matter taken care of and the conflict settled. He was therefore genuinely taken aback when the French government said it was still not satisfied. Through the Prussian ambassador in Paris it demanded not only formal approval of the withdrawal but also a declaration on the part of the king that in consenting to Leopold's candidature he had had no desire to offend the interests and honour of the French nation. It further demanded through its own ambassador that the Prussian monarch enter a binding commitment never to give his consent to a revived candidature.

William was prepared to go a very long way in the interests of avoiding a conflict. Consequently he strove even now to keep the negotiating option open. Even to his way of thinking, however, a formal letter of apology and an assurance of the kind demanded were hardly compatible with the dignity of a great power and its royal family. But in any case he could do nothing further on his own; he had to bring in his government, at last taking the step that Paris wanted him to take. However, by waiting until now to address himself to Bismarck in the now famous telegram authorizing his Minister-President to make public the information it contained as he saw fit, the king had unwittingly – because his guiding intention had been to avoid a clash if at all possible – brought about just the sort of escalation of demands that Bismarck had been counting on.

It was now a simple matter for Bismarck to push the original question at issue into the background and to hold France up to the world and particularly to the German public as the power that was seeking to use the Prussian king's obvious love of peace and preparedness to compromise for the purposes of humiliating him and with him Prussia and the German nation that relied on Prussia as its protecting power. According to the 'Ems Dispatch' that Bismarck cut to two sentences and distributed to all Prussian diplomatic missions late in the evening of 13 July for immediate publication, after Paris had been informed by Madrid through official channels of the withdrawal of Prince Leopold's candidature the French government had sought through its ambassador to make the Prussian king promise 'never again to give his consent, should the Hohenzollerns revert to their candidature'. The revised message went on: 'His Majesty the King has refused to receive the French ambassador again and has informed the latter through the duty adjutant that His Majesty has nothing further to say to the ambassador.'[67] The original had spoken only of 'an adjutant', and the bit about having 'nothing further to say' had referred quite explicitly to the present state of information.

The reaction to this laconic yet provocative disclosure, which ruled out any further negotiations, could be predicted with complete certainty. The only possible answer to such a slap in the face, if Napoleon III and his government wished to survive politically, was a declaration of war. It came, following the mobilization order passed by the French Cabinet on 14 July, on 19 July 1870. With this the alliance requirements laid down in the offensive and defensive treaties with the south German states were formally fulfilled. In fact the decision of the south German governments had been made days before: since publication of the Ems Dispatch the overwhelming majority of the German people had been behind the Prussian government and the allegedly deeply offended Prussian king.

In the light of this the capitals of the remaining great powers lost the last vestiges of an inclination actively to intervene in the conflict, let alone become directly involved in it, as had been a distinct possibility for a long time in the case of Austria-Hungary, for example. Subsequently Bismarck's much-cited coup with Benedetti's handwritten treaty draft of 1866 merely reinforced a general tendency on the part of the powers to stay out of things. By the time Benedetti's document, which spoke of France acquiring Belgium, appeared without its date of origin and consequently with every appearance of immediate topicality in *The Times* of 25 July, London too had long since decided not to intervene at this stage.

For the second time in four years Bismarck had succeeded in politically and diplomatically isolating an armed conflict between Prussia and another European great power to such effect that no other state had any immediate reason for or direct interest in becoming involved. Once again, as in 1866, the controlling groups and forces in the remaining states were convinced that this war was going to adjust tensions that had become intolerable – tensions that arose, they said, not least from the contradiction between formal pretensions and political and social reality. Furthermore, the feeling was again prevalent that in its probable consequences the war would remain at the lower limit of what was clearly inescapable in terms of change. To put it another way: the state of suspense surrounding Prusso-French relations, particularly the question of the future of the south German states and hence the central European situation in general, now appeared to hold more danger than a clarification of those problems by force of arms. On top of which there was the fact that the conflict in question was between two states whose leaders experience showed to be aware of the limits that the interests of the other powers set upon the outcome of such clarification.

The capitals of Europe expected a politically limited war for objectives that had been fixed in advance. This was true first and foremost with regard to the Prussian or German side. Prussia's war aim seemed quite clear: to unify non-Austrian Germany by incorporating the south German states in the north German federal state set up after 1866. Most neutral politicians and a large part of the European public assumed that when that was accomplished a major European storm centre would have been removed. On the other hand people were less certain about whether France's efforts to halt the Prussian advance in central Europe might not, if successful, become metamorphosed into a fresh striving for hegemony. For that reason neutral observers, particularly in Britain – here the revelation in *The Times* was of course very effective – were initially more mistrustful of France and tended to sympathize with the Prussian side.

This changed abruptly when after a series of surprisingly swift Prusso-German victories the main body of the French army was defeated near Sedan on 2 September, Napoleon III was taken prisoner and the French Empire collapsed. With this 'second Königgrätz', it was widely believed, Prussia had achieved its objective. Now it was up to Berlin to terminate hostilities as soon as possible and avoid further bloodshed – particularly since the newly formed provisional government in Paris immediately indicated its willingness to negotiate and make peace, dissociating itself from this 'Napoleonic' war.

Instead of taking it up on this, however, the Prussian government confronted Paris with a demand that pushed peace into the remote distance and changed the situation completely, indeed aroused fundamental doubts regarding the nature and objectives of Prusso-German policy: it called for the cession of Alsace and part of Lorraine. All over Europe people now began to wonder whether perhaps this was not at all, on Prussia's part, a war with a clear-cut political objective in the shape of Lesser German national unification, the kind of war that Prussia had demonstrated in 1866 by sparing Austria and respecting its territorial integrity, but a war of conquest that burst all such bounds, a war in which desires and objectives at any one time were determined by what had already been achieved.

This was without doubt the crucial question, and it arises in retrospect as well. Was the policy of making careful allowance for the interests of the other great powers, of preserving the foundations of the European power system despite all alterations of it in Prussia's favour – was that policy mere camouflage to see the Hohenzollern state through to the point at which it seemed strong enough to throw off all fetters? In the wake of further developments there were many people outside France who answered that question in the affirmative. On the other hand the majority of German contemporaries spoke at first of this having been simply a case of seizing a favourable opportunity to remedy a past injustice. Territories had been returned to Germany that had for centuries belonged to the Reich and possessed solid links with German culture. It had had nothing to do with any policy of conquest, and there could certainly be no question of a prelude to a policy of European hegemony.

The further course of events did, however, reveal more and more clearly what a liability the annexation of Alsace and Lorraine represented and just how much politically disastrous mistrust it brought upon the resurrected Reich and its policy. Accordingly there was an increasing tendency on the German side to hold it up as a unique political blunder on Bismarck's part, made under pressure from the military and above all from the German public. But that opinion survived only for as long as Bismarck's foreign policy after 1871 was seen as a model of a circumspect and successful peace policy in contrast to the imperialist adventures and prestige-seeking of his successors – in fact the whole thing is a classic example of the way in which historical judgements depend on the course of historical developments. When under the effect of National Socialist foreign policy people began to see the question of continuity in a new and rather sharper light, a major shift of emphasis literally imposed itself. The tendency now was to represent Bismarck as the man really responsible for leading the nation down the fateful road of a policy of conquest. Not the least important factor behind this reassessment was a desire to play down the historical handicaps impeding German–French relations, now that these had taken so positive a turn.

Yet neither did this interpretation stand up to sober examination for long. Today it is beyond question that in the immediate aftermath of the first victories of the allied German armies there arose a spontaneous demand among the most varied sections of the German people for a territorial victory prize in the shape of the recovery of the 'old German imperial lands in the West'. Equally beyond dispute, however, is that Bismarck's decision to ask France for Alsace and part of Lorraine and to brook no compromise was arrived at quite independently and under no sort of external pressure. He did not, in other words, abide by the much-invoked 1866 model of extensively sparing the opposing great power. In fact his action here may even put 1866 in an entirely different light: was his prudent restraint towards Austria at that time, for which of course Bismarck's Prussia more than compensated itself in other areas, perhaps already in essence a preparation for what was considered the inevitable clash between Prussia and France?

That is undoubtedly an oversimplification. But the question nevertheless emphatically arises: what were Bismarck's reasons for ruling out from the start a genuine peace with France based on compromise and agreement – and doing so, as afterwards emerged, quite regardless of the regime in power there and even of the opinions of the military party in his own camp?

Over the last hundred years this question has received a whole kaleidoscope of answers. Most of them, no matter how contradictory, find some support in one or another of Bismarck's pronouncements, either at the time or subsequently. Because he did in constantly changing circumstances, each time with a different objective, mention, pretext, suggest, deny and with lame-seeming arguments rule out or confirm virtually every conceivable motive for his action – completely confusing contemporaries and posterity alike, as he did so often. This was part of the very essence of his politics, which in order to keep things in a constant state of flux and not unnecessarily deprive himself of a single possibility sought by every available means to eschew any kind of clarity at a certain level, occasionally to the point of self-deception. An answer to the question of the motives behind the annexation decision can therefore be derived only from a general interpretation of Bismarckian foreign policy and its ultimate objectives and determinants.

If anything was permanent in Bismarck's political thinking and in his basic ideas it was his conception of the behaviour of the great powers as being, unlike the smaller states, the truly autonomous subjects of the political sphere. That behaviour was in his opinion guided in every case by quite specific basic interests and directions of interest, some of them natural, some historical. They arose out of the geographical position, social structure, economic situation, traditions and, embracing all these, historical self-awareness of the power concerned. It was his firm belief that no political group and tendency in any state could in the long run ignore basic interests of that kind. They were the continuum with which every representative of another power must reckon for as long as the state concerned continued to rank as a great power and had not, like Spain, Portugal, Sweden, or the Netherlands, for example, dropped back to being a second-class power.

In the case of France such basic interests included, to Bismarck's mind, the existence of a weak central Europe with two great powers in a state of maximum rivalry. Paris had for centuries seen this as the crucial prerequisite for the dominant role it sought to play on the European continent, indeed for any permanent guarantee of its great power status. It would therefore, all statements and assurances to the contrary notwithstanding, always attempt to restore such a constellation whenever a favourable opportunity presented itself. 'They have not forgiven us for Sadowa and will not forgive us our victories now, no matter how generous our peace terms', he remarked to a colleague shortly after Sedan.[68]

What seemed to Bismarck to be the self-evident conclusion was that the great power Prussia, as it expanded to become the great power 'Kleindeutschland' – an increase in power that the other European states as it were tacitly accepted by their non-intervention – must therefore stake everything on weakening France, above all in geo-strategic terms, to such an extent that reasonable profit-and-loss calculations would in future deter French policy from any solo attempt to revise what Bismarck was hoping would be the results of the war in central Europe. 'The only correct policy in such circumstances', he noted as early as 21 August 1870 in a directive to the

Prussian ambassador in London, Count Bernstorff, 'given an enemy who *cannot* be won over as a sincere friend, is at least to render him a little more innocuous and make ourselves more secure against him, for which it is not enough to raze those of his fortresses that threaten us; only the surrender of some of them will do.'[69]

In other words, unlike when he was dealing with Austria in 1866, Bismarck assumed from the outset that the antagonism between France and its eastern neighbour was going to be insurmountable. Many of his remarks between 1866 and 1870 indicate that he even saw this as the price of German unification. He dismissed as political illusionism any attempt wilfully to ignore the fact in any way.

There was undoubtedly, on top of this, a whole series of motives for the annexation demand that arose out of the situation. It is obvious, for example, that the initial refusal by the French to agree to any cession of French territory – a refusal with which the Prussian Minister-President had reckoned – and the resultant continuation of the war beyond Sedan were very welcome to Bismarck in the light of the still unresolved domestic situation within Germany. But that was simply a consequence that could be turned to account, not a true reason for the decision to annex. This was based quite unequivocally on his assessment of the present and future power-political situation in Europe, which led him to the belief that a permanent antagonism between Paris and Berlin was inevitable whatever happened.

Whether that assessment was wrong is something we can only speculate on in retrospect. But what can be said with some certainty is that Bismarck took as his starting-point the kind of distribution of political weight in Europe with which he had become familiar in the twenty years of his political career. In the early 1850s Prussia had ranked as the weakest of the five great powers. Since then Berlin had gradually caught up, as it were; indeed it had proved itself the military superior first of Austria and now of France as well. But unlike many of his contemporaries the Prussian Minister-President, with his precise knowledge of the situation and of all the circumstances, rated the luck factor in all this very highly. He was very far, again unlike some others, from projecting this present success into the future and assuming a permanent condition of power-political superiority on the part of Prusso-Germany.

In this kind of cautious mood the 'genius of the actual', as he has fittingly been called,[70] was inclined to underestimate what others, particularly outside central Europe, could already see very clearly and had begun at an early stage to experience as a threat: the rapid expansion of the population and extraordinary growth of commerce and industry brought factors into play in central Europe that gave the political unification of the region a quite different dimension and perspective. Mentally still very much bound up with Prussia and its limited power resources, Bismarck did not at first fully appreciate the extent of the shift in political power that those factors implied. Accordingly he was wrong in his assessments of others' reactions to the new situation.

In other words, Bismarck's annexation decision was based on power-political premisses and on considerations of balance as attributed to the other powers that were no longer abreast of reality, so to speak. It took a major international crisis, the so-called 'Is War in Sight?' crisis of 1875, to bring home to him the fact that the other powers had meanwhile come to regard the enormous growth in power of Prusso-Germany as a very serious threat. Only then did he realize how ready they were to band together in a kind of containment coalition if necessary in order to prevent any further expansion of the new power.

That such a coalition could under certain circumstances provide the foundation for a French policy of revision was in 1875 the insight that governed Bismarck's further activities on the foreign policy front. In 1870 he was still a long way from that. On the contrary, for all Bismarck's dynamism in other respects, particularly in the field of foreign policy, his annexation decision reveals a markedly static element in his political thinking and his political imagination. It resulted in one of the very great handicaps for the future policy of the Reich and a highly problematical restriction of his freedom of action in a rapidly changing foreign policy situation.

A different question altogether is whether Bismarck could in fact seriously have evaded the annexation demand that after the great victories of August and particularly after Sedan arose ever more forcefully from the German public. He had had to wrest a lenient approach to Austria in 1866 only from his king and the majority of the army leadership. A policy of leniency towards France could have been pushed through only against the opposition of a substantial section of German public opinion. And that would in turn, particularly in southern Germany, have diminished people's readiness to become reconciled, in the interests of German unification, to the internal form of the new state, initially at any rate. It would have given additional impetus to the critics of simple accession to the Prussian-dominated North German Confederation.

So Bismarck might well have thought in terms of going along with the German national movement over the annexation question in order to induce it to give in and make tacit concessions in the field of domestic and constitutional policy. But from the point of view of historical reality that kind of calculation remains strictly in the subjunctive. In fact Bismarck did not at any time weigh the advantages of annexation on the domestic policy front against its potential foreign policy disadvantages. His decision to annex was firmly esablished at a very early stage – by mid-August at the latest. From then on he did in many respects apply it to domestic policy ends, not least in the direction suggested. But, the decision once made, he never seriously questioned it in principle.

As in 1864 and 1866, so too in the war of 1870–1 he did not allow himself to be pushed either one way or the other. Although appearances, with the widely unexpected annexation demand, seem at first to contradict this, the war of 1870–1 was likewise a limited war, one whose objectives were clearly defined from the outset. In it, politics were once again clearly paramount. It remained a means to an end that had been established in advance. Bismarck passionately opposed every attempt to have him alter, as a result of circumstances or on allegedly humanitarian grounds, the course that seemed to him to spring imperatively from this relationship of means to end.

Accordingly he followed the activities of the army leadership with the gravest mistrust from the very first day of the war. After the experiences of 1866 he was convinced that army leaders, in particular the spectacularly successful chief of staff, von Moltke, were inclined to subordinate politics to their military calculations or rather to steer what they regarded as an appropriate political course on their own initiative. It was therefore important to keep a close watch on the 'demigods' all the time and hold them very firmly in check politically. The resultant implicit conflict, which at times overshadowed everything else, reached an initial climax in the winter of 1870–1 over the question of bringing the war to an end as swiftly as possible by military means.

Although his diplomatic efforts had so far been thoroughly successful, it was Bismarck's constant preoccupation that the other great powers, who had remained neutral hitherto, might after all decide to intervene. In that preoccupation both he and Roon, the War Minister, advocated smashing the resistance of the French by first softening up and then seizing their capital, Paris. Moltke was emphatically against this, citing primarily technical reasons but also considerations of a humanitarian nature. At the same time he pointed to the disastrous impression that such a proceeding would inevitably make on the international public – which Bismarck dismissed as merely 'censing with empty talk', attributing it to a 'plot hatched by women, archbishops and men of letters'.[71]

Actually, the chief of staff's counter-proposal was hardly more humane in its implications. He wanted the complete military annihilation of the enemy, in other words a 'war of extermination' along Napoleonic lines that would allow the German side a 'dictated peace'. The problem of the particularly bitter resistance offered by the capital under the leadership of the political left Moltke reckoned to solve in practice by starving the city out: its inhabitants, as the crown prince's chief of staff, Count Blumenthal coarsely opined, were welcome to 'die like mad dogs'. He went on: 'We could not . . . care less what happens to the Parisians; after all, they have brought it upon themselves.'[72]

This conflict of principle, which went far beyond considerations of military expediency or differences of opinion between individuals, culminated in mid-January 1871 in a bitter quarrel over the terms of surrender for Paris. Bismarck eventually decided it in his favour, admittedly not so much by his own efforts as because he was backed by the king. Although this has been characterized as a conflict between political and military leaderships and as a struggle over who should have the last word in decisions during the war and on questions immediately concerning the war, that only touches the surface of the picture. In essence it was not in fact a question of the demarcation of powers of decision-making, of 'the military's antiquated departmental jealousy', as Bismarck once put it.[73] It was a question of two diametrically incompatible basic approaches to politics, each of which inevitably resulted in practice in a radically different kind of policy.

Granted, Moltke professed that the only thing that he and his colleagues were concerned about was carrying out a political mission with military means and being given a free hand in the selection and deployment of those means as experts as against mere laymen – 'civilians in cuirassiers' tunics', as the Chancellor was sarcastically referred to among the general staff.[74] But it must have been clear even to Moltke that the relationship between means and end was in reality more complex than that and could not be reduced to so simple a formula. That formula gave the appearance of being valid only when the political and military leaderships were united in one person, as in the case of Napoleon I; it was from the Corsican that Clausewitz himself, the great idol of the Prussian army leadership, had taken his cue. Only then did 'the continuation of politics by other means' signify that the leading statesman selected from the means and opportunities available those that suited his political objectives and seemed most likely to further them. Where this was not the case, the possibility existed that the choice of military means might jeopardize the political objective. No one could be blind to that unless he was incapable of seeing not only war but also politics from any other point of view than that of total victory or crushing defeat – the 'all-or-nothing' approach; unless, in other words, he ultimately believed the life of the individual and that of states to be subject to the supposed 'law of the jungle'.

In the wake of the triumphant military successes of the past six years that kind of thinking was undoubtedly beginning to make headway in Prussia and in the section of the German public that was sympathetic to Prussia, and doing so among civilians to a much greater extent than among the military: Moltke and the victorious generals were at that time far less controversial and far more popular figures than Prussia's leading statesman. This in turn, by a sort of feedback effect, increased the tendency to reduce politics to the simple categories of success-oriented military thinking, indeed to regard any kind of manoeuvring, any kind of looking for compromise, as being beneath the dignity of the strong.

Undoubtedly there were also entirely personal reasons for Bismarck's observing the growing prestige and popularity of the army leadership with suspicion. But it was principally concern for his basic approach to politics and for his concrete policy that caused him to react to the doings of the military with increasing touchiness and irritation. On his taking office his enemies had described him as 'the kind of Minister-President with a uniform hidden under his dress suit'.[75] Actually it was more the other way around. Outwardly he liked, chiefly for reasons of political calculation, as a manifestation of his position and his stance, to cultivate a martial appearance. He dressed more and more often in uniform, particularly after his appointment as commander-in-chief of the 7th Heavy Cavalry Regiment of the Landwehr and his promotion to the rank of major general in September 1866. During the French War he was scarcely ever seen in civilian clothes. Moreover, his whole nature undoubtedly lent itself to a certain brisk directness – in contrast to the highly reserved and rather sensitive-seeming Moltke. In substance, however, as indeed the dispute with the army leadership in 1870–1 revealed, he was very far removed from the thinking and the underlying political ideas of many leading officers. He saw forces at work here that threatened to destroy what was accepted without discussion in European diplomacy and European politics in terms of shared positions and habits, a kind of minimum consensus that sustained all conclusions, decisions and actions.

Granted, Bismarck took many opportunities to pour scorn on those who talked in emphatic terms about Europe, about a European public and about what, seen in this light, seemed in their opinion to be possible and what not. He called it a mere camouflaging of selfish interests, and particularly when such opinions were voiced by the British he professed to see them as no more than a stubborn, unimaginative clinging to existing forms and conditions. But even he was convinced deep down that a great deal did in fact depend on the way in which his own actions and the objectives that were presumed to lie behind them were appraised in the mind of something like a European public. The game, he knew, was played in accordance with certain basic rules, which it was advisable to infringe only in the direst emergency.

Back in Frankfurt in the 1850s he had extolled the power politics of Frederick the Great in provocatively strident terms for the benefit of the Austrian envoy to the Federal Diet. Then as now, however, he had been quite clear in his mind that the true key to success even in Frederick's day, contrary to popular opinion, had been not a policy of isolated military strength but the exploitation of a particular international constellation, which included taking constantly into account the forces and interests at work in it. It was this and not an isolated military triumph that was the thing that mattered here, too. It was a question of securing for the actual aim and outcome of this war, namely the foundation of a Lesser German national state, a kind of consensus of European opinion and of giving the new political creation something of a permanent footing therein.

The way to that objective had been difficult enough even within his own camp right up until the end. After the outbreak of the war, after the emotional fusion of the nation against France and after the victories jointly won it had been generally taken for granted that a return to the *status quo ante* was out of the question. But although Bismarck repeatedly brought that general expectation into play, together with the now enormously increased strength of the national movement in the south as well, he was nevertheless firmly determined not to let it pressurize him, especially as far as the internal structure and constitution of the new state were concerned. And this in turn lent albeit unintentional support and encouragement to all those who, particularly in the two south German kingdoms, in Württemberg and to an even greater extent in Bavaria, feared two things: mediatization of their states by Prussia or a process of increasing centralization within the national state that would eventually destroy every shred of their independence. To reassure them, win them round and in doing so build into the internal organization of the new state additional counter-weights to the parliamentary and democratic forces that were so obviously fostered by the whole development – that was his chief task in the aftermath of the August victories and the triumph of Sedan.

It shows him at the height of his political and diplomatic skills but at the same time in a very obvious dilemma that called for those skills in the very highest degree: between particularism and centralism, between the monarchical principle and the sovereignty of the people, between Prussia's interests and those of the larger state and between the different power factions within the Prussian leadership itself he had to negotiate compromises that inevitably had the character of improvizations – and artificial and thoroughly temporary ones at that. In almost no case could they be based on clear principles or on the recognized demands of powerful groups and forces. On the contrary, in the majority of cases they boiled down to balancing or more precisely cancelling out such demands and principles against one another. As a result, in the end they left both sides dissatisfied.

The more so since in most cases it was not a question of compromises reached between two partners in the interests of the division and joint exercise of power but of arrangements imposed in greater or lesser degree from outside, arrangements of which the actual beneficiary appeared to be a third party. What this meant, however, was that the sovereign command and the quite extraordinary skill that Bismarck displayed at this crucial time in handling the various forces, interests and demands and his way of drawing them together in the direction in which he wanted to go at the same time inhibited and postponed a genuine and politically fruitful settlement between them. Such a settlement could have proceeded only from the pressure towards compromise inherent in a situation of concrete political responsibility. As it was, *Idealpolitik* and a *Realpolitik* uninhibitedly extolled by some and damned by others once again abruptly parted company.

On the one hand this fell in with Bismarck's objectives, particularly in so far as these were of a purely power-political nature. On the other hand, however, it threatened what very soon became known in characteristic fashion as his achievement. For all the exultation that had attended its birth, the new political creation lacked that basic consensus of what has been jointly fought for, even in the context of the bitterest political debate, that character of truly achieved inner unification.

Bismarck was well aware of the dangers implicit here. But he could not, from his point of view, see in the given constellation any possibility of effectively countering them. 'Let's put Germany in the saddle, so to speak: it will know how to ride', he had said in 1867.[76] What he had been suggesting was that people should not attach excessive importance, as predetermining all future developments, to the nature of and initial form assumed by a German national state. He hinted at something similar now, whether directly through his dealings with the National Liberal Party leaders or indirectly through the government press and his various principal negotiators, chief among whom was Rudolf von Delbrück. But ultimately these were mere formulae of appeasement. In reality he was very much concerned to use this opportunity to build into the constitution of the new state permanent buttresses against the possibility of parliamentary democracy overwhelming the forces of the past as well as to reinforce the buttresses already present in the constitution of the North German Confederation.

The watchword issued in the aftermath of 1866 regarding consideration for the south German monarchies once again served as a kind of political shield here. Behind it he was able to conceal his endeavour to distribute the weight in such a way as to obviate, at least for the immediate future, a preponderance not only of parliamentary but also of centralist forces. For this was where he saw the really threatening tendency for his own position as well. He was aware, after all, that in the context of a radically changing society the national idea and a national parliament embodying it increasingly operated as the real instrument of integration and as the supreme point of reference for individual and collective loyalties. He may have stressed repeatedly: 'It is not yet proven in practice that parliamentary government as it has evolved in Britain over a long and highly distinctive history could settle and become established in another major state.'[77] But secretly he was well aware that such proof would not be long in coming. Indeed, he went further: he suspected that the parliamentarism of British provenance – highly aristocratic and elitist even in its middle-class manifestation – that constituted the pattern by which most continental liberals were guided would very soon be replaced by a national, democratic type of parliamentary system. And this, without the appropriate counter-weights, would prove very much more irresistible, would tolerate only a parliamentary type of government organized along strictly party-political lines and would very quickly sweep away all power positions that rested on any other foundation.

This kind of critical forecast was his point of departure, the motivating basis, as it were, of his practical policy and of his individual moves in the matter of the type and form of the definitive fusion into one state of all of non-Austrian Germany. Above all it determined the limits of the concessions he made to new forces and tendencies, concessions that he had always regarded as in principle inescapable and that formed so essential an element of his policy.

It was clear from the outset, as he saw it, that the final unification must come about strictly in terms of a freely negotiated alliance between monarchical governments that appeared to be largely sovereign even with regard to internal affairs. The parliamentary and democratic element, which in 1866 had played a not inconsiderable role, was to be very much less important this time. In the given situation this meant the accession of the south German states to the North German Confederation through the medium of individually negotiated treaties and the simultaneous accentuation of the character of that confederation as being an association of 'prince and free cities'. This way of going about things suggested itself for other reasons as well. It seemed not least to offer the best way of overcoming the substantial resistance of Bavaria in particular. But what was crucial was Bismarck's firm determination on no account to let himself be forced into any greater degree of dependence on the national movement and the liberal middle-class forces by which it was organized. That he sought to keep those forces for ever at the ready, as it were, and was constantly parading them – that was in line with the nature of his policy always to make sure of having suitable means of exerting pressure and issuing threats. But he never, in this situation, seriously considered a fundamentally different course of action, let alone actual mobilization of the national movement against monarchs and governments that resisted him – especially since, unlike in 1866, he was very soon master of the situation. Only the unexpectedly long duration of the war subsequently gave rise to somewhat altered circumstances.

On the Prussian side the negotiating line and objective in the unification question had been more or less officially established only a matter of days after Sedan: a memorandum of 13 September 1870, composed on Bismarck's behalf by the head of the Federal Chancellery, Rudolf von Delbrück, laid down the route to be followed and the result to be worked towards in the negotiations about to be opened with the south German states.[78] Shortly afterwards Delbrück was putting that result before representatives of the Bavarian and Württemberg governments at the first talks in Munich.

Here there was little inclination at first, particularly on the Bavarian side but also on the part of Württemberg, to engage in the proposed accession negotiations. They were thinking much more in terms of reopening the whole question of unification and the Confederation including, as the first question to be answered, how the south German states could share in the territorial war gains or, in the event of the annexation of Alsace and part of Lorraine, be suitably indemnified by Prussia. For all their formal courtesy, however, and for all their oft-repeated assurances that of course all the details were open to discussion, Bismarck and his negotiating team were immovable in their insistence that as far as Prussia was concerned the only course open to the south German states was that of accession.

However, in contrast to what was being demanded by the crown prince, for example, the Prussian Minister-President avoided any kind of direct pressure right up until the end. He relied on the power of the facts, facts that the still recalcitrant forces would be less capable of escaping, the less they appeared to be arbitrarily engendered or susceptible of alteration. He believed he could have all the more confidence in this for the fact that both Hesse-Darmstadt and Baden had already predictably announced their readiness to join the Confederation without further ado soon after Sedan – the government of Baden as a spokesman of the Lesser German nationalist forces in the south out of deep conviction for many years past, the Hessian government under pressure from its own National Liberals and the fact that one province of the country already belonged to the North German Confederation. How, in the circumstances, and in view of the existing close network of economic ties within the Customs Union, were the two south German kingdoms, let alone Bavaria on its own, to sustain an independent existence? The question must be positively forcing itself, Bismarck believed, on Munich and Stuttgart. So why compel them to join, thus provoking permanent internal resistance, when an apparently voluntary accession could form the basis of a solid partnership – not least against the forces that were betting politically on a very much more rigid national union and on a national parliament that was to take precedence over all other political factors?

This did not of course smooth the path of the accession negotiations held in Versailles in October and November 1870 at which delegations from the governments of the individual south German states came together in separate rounds with representatives of Prussia and representatives of the North German Confederation. Bismarck's watchword to the effect that everything must be based on the free decision of the future partner led on the contrary to some tough as well as tedious haggling over points of detail. And even after the negotiations had been concluded it took a dip into the coffers of the Prussian state before the King of Bavaria was finally persuaded to give his consent. On top of a large initial payment on account, Ludwig II was promised an annuity from the fortune of the Hanoverian royal family, the so-called 'Guelf Fund', which Prussia had sequestered in 1866, with his trusted adviser, Count von Holnstein, who had organized the whole thing, receiving 10 per cent of each payment.

Affected by this generous understanding shown to his craze for building, the Bavarian monarch hesitated no longer before offering the Prussian king the imperial crown on behalf of the princes of Germany. His letter to this effect had been drafted by Bismarck himself, who wished thereby to lay special emphasis once again on the character of the new state as a confederation of sovereign monarchs.

The means employed may not exactly have been the most graceful, but in essence Bismarck got his way all along the line – and in a manner that allowed the other side to sign with the feeling of having driven a hard and successful bargain. This was possible only because the Chancellor of the North German Confederation consistently avoided giving any evidence in public of what he thought of the concessions made by the Prussian north German side. In this connection the criticisms levelled at the results of the negotiations by the Prussians and by the national movement even suited him very well.

With the so-called 'Reservatrechten', special prerogatives granted to Bavaria and to a lesser extent to Württemberg, Bismarck had, according to his critics, taken his readiness to compromise to the limits of what was acceptable. That Bavaria should retain its own railway, postal and telegraphic administration and so be able to demonstrate its sovereignty daily for all to see, and that the same should apply to Württemberg in respect of its postal service – that might pass. Similarly the principle of the independent taxation of beer and spirits could be tolerated as a curiosity, albeit an expensive one. But that the Bavarian army should in practice retain complete autonomy and the commander of the federal army, the future emperor, be granted only a 'right of inspection' in peacetime to enable him to assure himself of the 'combat-readiness' of the Bavarian forces – that seemed more than questionable. The same applied to the right accorded to the King of Württemberg to continue to maintain his own army administration and appoint his own officers.

It was widely felt that the uniform and unifying bond that was to embrace the nation had here been loosened unjustifiably from the very outset in favour of particularist forces and interests. The view that decentralizing elements had been introduced in a problematic manner into what was in any case a not very strongly centralized federal constitution received further reinforcement when it became known that a separate Federal Council

371

committee for foreign affairs was to be set up with Bavaria in the chair and permanent seats for the representatives of Saxony and Württemberg. It looked as if even the principle of central direction of foreign policy, a key principle in any federal state, was not to be adhered to. A further sacrifice was being made to the aspirations of the kingdoms towards independence, one that would further weaken the cohesion of the Confederation as a whole.

Actually, as Bismarck had foreseen, most of the concessions turned out to be more or less meaningless in practice. The much-discussed committee of the Federal Council met only once in the next thirty years. Nor was there ever any doubt that Bavaria and Württemberg, with their more or less independent armies, were unconditionally 'loyal to the Reich'. As Bismarck had anticipated, the new state very quickly developed stronger and stronger internal bonds, and all its principle elements began to look for unified leadership and representation. This very quickly neutralized the centrifugal forces and tendencies, despite the fact that these had appeared at first to receive support from the concessions made to the two south German kingdoms.

What was left was a special relationship of trust between Munich and Stuttgart on the one hand and the current political leadership of Prussia and the new confederation on the other. This enabled Bismarck repeatedly to play the federalist card against the centralist and centralizing forces virtually without risk and indeed ultimately at least to suggest that he saw the idea of a dissolution and re-foundation of the Reich as a potential political remedy.

In this respect too, then, the conclusion of the treaties with the south German states between 15 and 25 November 1870 was a personal triumph for Bismarck. Those treaties represented the practical inauguration of the Lesser German federal state. 'German unity is a fact, and so is the emperor', he announced triumphantly to his colleagues after signing the treaty with Bavaria.[79] The formation of the new state, which received the historically resonant name of 'Deutsches Reich', had not only followed the pattern that he had envisaged for it from the outset, with the last parliament, that of Bavaria, giving its assent to the treaties on 21 January 1871, albeit by a very small majority. The founding of the state had also created a political constellation, a distribution of power, such as seemed likely to secure his own position in the long term. It remained to dramatize the founding of the Reich in as symbolic a manner as possible in order to lend permanence to the solution achieved and to its specific character in particular. The whole thing must also be made finally secure on the foreign policy front.

The act of proclamation in the Hall of Mirrors at Versailles on 18 January 1871, which was how the foundation of the new empire was presented theatrically, provoked unease and some secret criticism even among contemporaries, despite all the widespread and unifying joy at what had been achieved. 'I cannot begin to describe to you', one of the royal participants, Prince Otto of Bavaria, wrote to his brother, Ludwig II, 'how infinitely and agonizingly painful I found the scene . . . It was all so cold, so proud, so glossy, so strutting and boastful and heartless and empty.'[80] Today's spectator, looking back on it, is even more inclined to see the whole thing as a disastrous demonstration of the superiority of the victor, the military monarchy that was triumphant all along the line, in foreign affairs, in the field, but also in domestic affairs.

At the heart of the land they had conquered, surrounded by their generals, courtiers and diplomats, the German princes celebrated the unification of Lesser Germany as an act of confirmation and reinforcement of their sovereignty and of their claim to complete political paramountcy. The public, parliaments, the actual driving forces behind unification in the economy and in society – these receded into the background, eclipsed by this self-portrayal of the 'Fürstenstaat', the 'state of princes', which was later made the occasion for a national holiday and which now very substantially influenced the external image of the new national state. And there may have been some unintentional additional symbolism for the more distant future in the fact that the man who had brought the whole thing about, he who now stood at the foot of the imperial throne as a loyal paladin, should on this day of all days have come to feel the displeasure of his royal master over the question of the latter's title. The only title possible in constitutional law, that of 'German emperor', the Prussian king had been unwilling to accept right up until the last minute. It was, he said, the title of a 'brevet major', a retired captain without a captain's pay or a captain's authority to command, a mere name with no special rights and no proper office. If he was going to be anything, then 'Emperor William' – the appellation with which his son-in-law, the Grand Duke of Baden, cleverly got round the whole question when asking for the three cheers – wanted to be 'Emperor of Germany', monarch of the Reich, in order to make clear to the whole world the increased power of the House of Hohenzollern.

The ingratitude and lack of understanding shown by his monarch on this occasion scarcely upset Bismarck any more, although they brought home to him once again how shaky were the foundations of his own position. He was used to them by now and was inclined to pay the king back in kind, occasionally displaying similar whims and moods. 'Were it not for the wonderful footing I have in religion', he once vividly expressed it around this time, 'I should have launched myself at the whole court bottom-first long ago.'[81] Only three days after the proclamation he had nothing but irony left for the whole procedure. 'This imperial birth was a difficult one', he reported to his wife on 21 January. 'Kings have their strange cravings at such times just like women before they deliver to the world what they cannot after all keep from it. As *accoucheur* I several times experienced a fierce desire to be a bomb and blow up, bringing the whole building down in ruins.'[82]

The thought that really troubled him was that the national feeling of triumph and superiority, which was affecting ever wider circles and had received a further stimulus from the scene in the Hall of Mirrors, might now, by way of the army leaders and the princes with the Prussian king at their head, take full effect in the field of foreign policy too and sweep aside all caution and restraint. It was around this time that the dispute between him and Moltke as to how to proceed came to a head. At the same time it was touch and go whether the peace-seeking elements around Adolphe

Thiers and Jules Favre would manage to assert themselves in the provisional French government or whether Léon Gambetta, the War Minister and actual organizer of the second *levée en masse* in French history, the people's war that followed Sedan, would retain the upper hand. Moreover, the risk of an intervention by the other great powers seemed to be still very much on the cards.

That risk had recently become acute when Russia tried to seize this opportunity to get the 1856 Treaty of Paris revised in its favour. St Petersburg particularly wanted to see the neutralization of the Black Sea revoked. So far Bismarck had succeeded in preventing a chain reaction. On the one hand he had suggested a conference on the whole question. And on the other hand he had managed to stall the two parties principally interested, namely Russia and Britain, by making both sides veiled offers of Prussian support. But his tactical manoeuvring had resembled a tightrope act. It was uncertain right up until the end whether the two powers might not abruptly come to terms with one another and use that agreement as the starting-point for a joint peace initiative. And while engaged in that tightrope act, which called for all his diplomatic skills, Bismarck found himself facing an increasing tendency within his own camp to fail to take at all seriously the dangers and risks he was thus seeking to avoid. Instead people were inclined to rely entirely on their own so impressively proven strength and military superiority and lose sight of the conditions and prerequisites on which their success up to now had been based. 'I often worry that we shall yet be punished for this arrogant overrating of ourselves', he wrote to his wife towards the end of November 1870.[83] And in conversation at a Versailles dinner table on 2 December he said with reference to the domestic situation in Germany: 'I am extremely worried. People have no idea of the situation. We are poised on the tip of a lightning conductor; if we lose the balance I have been at pains to create, we shall find ourselves on the ground.'[84]

The experience of those weeks not only placed an enormous burden on his nerves. It also hugely enhanced his mistrust of the abilities and discernment of those around him and indeed gave him, at the climax of his political career, a kind of pessimistic detachment from the beneficiaries of his achievement and consequently from that achievement itself. This was not continuous; it was punctuated by moods of exultation and by acute disappointments. But it did reinforce his already very pronounced inclination to rely politically on no one but himself. From now on he showed an even more marked tendency to attribute either ignorance or ill will to political partners whose views failed to coincide completely with his own. In fact it was not so much his extraordinary success that, for all his power, isolated him inwardly from his environment to an ever-increasing extent. It was his keen perception of the growing blindness of those around him to the ever present possibility of failure, his awareness of the *hubris* that came increasingly to characterize the entire ruling class of the young German state.

In the concrete situation of January 1871 the dangers – of which most people had very little idea, given the prevailing mood of national exuberance and their feeling of superiority – in fact melted away to a great extent in the space of a few days. Many people saw Bismarck, who had undoubtedly played the largest part in causing them to do so, as simply an opinionated dramatizer. On 25 January the Prussian king finally settled the conflict between the army leaders and Bismarck regarding the future course of action, both military and political, in favour of his Chancellor and Foreign Minister. On 28 January the armistice agreement with the provisional French government was signed after negotiations had continued almost up until the last minute with both sides, that is to say with representatives of the Napoleonic regime and with emissaries of the new government; it formed the basis of the provisional Treaty of Versailles of 26 February, which was ratified immediately afterwards by the national constituent assembly meeting in Bordeaux. Lastly, the Straits Conference met in London on 1 February and after lengthy negotiations, which further engrossed the attention of Europe, settled the Black Sea question very much in accordance with the wishes of Russia.

With that the danger zone was finally traversed. The political newcomer in central Europe was now tacitly accepted by all sides and peace with France virtually assured. The definitive peace treaty, which under the influence of the army leadership compelled the French to cede the fortress of Metz but left them Belfort and which fixed the war indemnity at 5,000 million gold francs, followed after detailed and protracted negotiations just under three months later.

'We finally signed yesterday', Bismarck had written to his wife on 27 February, referring to the conclusion of the provisional treaty, 'getting more than I consider useful for my political calculations. But I have to pay heed to feelings from above and below that, you see, do *not* calculate.'[85] This was certainly not true as stated. But it does show how, as soon as the tension of recent weeks let up a little, he was assailed by doubts and misgivings as to whether he had not perhaps after all gone a step too far, so placing himself and the newly founded Reich in conditions of dependence that might have been avoided. In the weeks that followed, when after all the clashes and conflicts of the past few months the sense of success and of what had been achieved first began to make itself really felt, such sceptical considerations naturally receded into the background once again, particularly since the immediate fear that the French National Assembly might withhold its consent very quickly proved to have been groundless. The triumphal procession back to Berlin through a united Germany, his elevation to the rank of prince on the day of the ceremonial opening of the new Imperial Diet, 21 March 1871, the award to the freedom of the capital, which was followed by many others – all this was not without effect. All the negative experiences that over the past few months had cut him off from those around him, filling him with ever-increasing scepticism with regard to other people's abilities and political judgement, now received positive corroboration, as it were: he was, so he was assured from all quarters, the greatest statesman of his time, the determined yet circumspect man of action among so many mere planners, debaters, even waverers. And all the pinches of salt with which he took this verdict and all his meditations on how closely Palm Sunday was followed by the Crucifixion could not prevent his not exactly underdeveloped sense of his own value from receiving a further substantial boost. It brought him increasingly up against the temptation to believe that he was in tune with the intentions of the Lord of History, to whom from now on he more and more frequently referred.

In the realm of day-to-day politics, however, disenchantment set in very swiftly. The concrete tasks requiring attention in a society that was changing at an ever more dramatic rate were not such as could sustain continued self-glorification for any length of time. Bismarck responded to this on the one hand by tending increasingly to retire to his estates for months on end on the pretext of ill health and complain about the boring nature of the daily political round. On the other hand it gave him an exceptionally clear eye for the forces of change, to which what had been achieved was if anything only a beginning and which therefore rendered it increasingly relative.

When Bismarck and Jules Favre, the French Foreign Minister, put their signatures to the peace treaty with France's bourgeois republic in Frankfurt am Main on 10 May 1871, that republic found itself facing a crucial trial of strength with an organized coalition of parties and groups of the extreme left, the so-called Commune, in its own capital. This questioned the existing order, whether in France or elsewhere, with drastic pretension. At the same time it appeared that the new order of things in central Europe was under attack with regard to both its internal and its external validity from the professedly arch-conservative quarter of the Catholic Church and the political and social forces that supported it. And to cap it all even the parties and forces of the centre showed no inclination to stop at what had been achieved. On the contrary they were pressing with increased activity, using as their base the unified platform of the Reich as already secured, for the internal development and indeed reorganization of the Reich along their lines.

The worries that had assailed Bismarck after the conclusion of the provisional peace treaty and that he had at first brushed aside now seized him in even greater measure. Was he no more than a sorcerer's apprentice? Had the forces that he had apparently directed with such skill and made to cancel each other out in reality been using him? Had they merely gone along with him in order to be able the more surely to destroy what he had sought to effect and maintain with their aid? Had Ludwig von Gerlach been right when he called him blind, power-mad and incapable of predicting and calculating the consequences of his actions? And was the feeling of superiority perhaps no more than the arrogance of the man who fails to recognize the symptoms of decline?

It did not take a great deal of psychology to temper and set aside such questions and gloomy forebodings. But they returned again and again in the light of further developments and gradually crystallized into veritable nightmares. It has rightly been pointed out that in addition to the much-invoked 'cauchemar des coalitions', the fear of an overwhelming alliance against him, Bismarck suffered from a 'cauchemar des révolutions', a fear of the internal dissolution and destruction of what he had just created. And were they just nightmares? Did not the German Reich of 1871 stand on wobbly foundations both at home and abroad right from the start? Had it not been initiated and pushed through by forces, interests and expectations that could not begin to maintain it in that form but simply had to destroy it? Had Bismarck not melted together, with as much skill as violence, ingredients that were by nature incapable of forming an alloy? Was the creative element, the combination of old and now, the enforced compromise, actually the destructive one?

All this has been under discussion now for more than a hundred years. The discussion has become very much more intense and critical since the internal destruction and eventual dissolution of the Reich, since what is often referred to even today simply as Bismarck's creation turned out to have been one of the shortest-lived political creations of all time. Occasionally, of course, it is only answers that are discussed, and historians are too busy proving things to ask the questions that really need to be asked. And, as tends to happen, old answers determine seemingly quite new ones that appear to turn everything upside-down, and the positive hero-image is replaced merely by a negative one using the same kinds of argument and the same cosy simplifications. But if there is one approach that is definitely wrong it is this one. Because this much seems in retrospect to be scarcely open to question, namely that Bismarck achieved only a very limited measure of control over his creation and over the problems and trends of development inherent in it or lent additional impetus by it. He ultimately found himself in many respects faced with a situation that was insoluble for him on his terms. In the end, perhaps like every major actor on the stage of history, he was really no more than a sorcerer's apprentice.

Notes

With a few exceptions, these notes are confined to direct references to sources. It goes without saying that a work of this kind, besides having recourse to original sources, both printed and in manuscript, is based on an enormous number of specialist studies, monographs and synoptic accounts. Historians will find reflected in discussions throughout the book the various interpretations, contentions and controversies of past and current research. To refer to these individually, however, would not only have made the book very much longer; it would also have been somewhat pointless. The specialist requires such references only in exceptional cases, and experience shows that the general reader has little interest in a complicated scholarly apparatus.

L.G.

Alphabetical list of the abbreviations used in the notes

Die auswärtige Politik Preussens: Historische Reichskommission (ed.), *Die auswärtige Politik Preussens 1858–1871, diplomatische Aktenstücke*, 10 vols (Munich/Berlin, 1933 ff).

H. von Bismarck, *Privatkorrespondenz*: Walter Bussmann and Klaus Peter Hoepke (eds), *Graf Herbert Bismarck. Aus seiner politischen Privatkorrespondez* (Göttingen, 1964).

Bismarck-Jahrbuch: Horst Kohl (ed.), *Bismarck-Jahrbuch*, 6 vols (Berlin, 1894–9).

Busch, *Tagebuchblätter*: Moritz Busch, *Tagebuchblätter*, 3 vols (Leipzig, 1899).

Duncker, *Politischer Briefwechsel*: Johannes Schultze (ed.), *Max Duncker, Politischer Briefwechsel aus seinem Nachlasse* (Stuttgart, 1923).

Eyck, *Bismarck*: Erich Eyck, *Bismarck, Leben und Werk*, 3 vols (Erlenbach/Zurich, 1941–4).

Grosse Politik: Johannes Lepsius, Albrecht Mendelssohn-Bartholdy and Friedrich Thimme (eds), *Die grosse Politik der europäischen Kabinette von 1871–1914, Sammlung der diplomatischen Akten des Auswärtigen Amtes* (Berlin, 1922–7).

Grossherzog Friedrich I. von Baden und die Reichspolitik: Walter Peter Fuchs (ed.), *Grossherzog Friedrich I. von Baden und die Reichspolitik 1871–1907*, Vol. 1: 1871–9 (Stuttgart, 1968); Vol. 2: 1879–90 (Stuttgart, 1975).

GW: Otto von Bismarck, *Die gesammelte Werke* (the 'Friedrichsruh Edition'), 15 in 19 vols (Berlin, 1924–35).

Hank, *Kanzler ohne Amt*: Manfred Hank, *Kanzler ohne Amt, Fürst Bismarck nach seiner Entlassung 1890–1898* (Munich, 1977).

Hatzfeld-Papiere: Gerhard Ebel (ed.), *Botschafter Paul Graf von Hatzfeld. Nachgelassene Papiere 1838–1901* 2 vols (Boppard, 1976).

Heyderhoff, *Liberalismus*: Julius Heyderhoff and Paul Wentzcke (eds), *Deutscher Liberalismus im Zeitalter Bismarcks. Eine politische Briefsammlung*, 2 vols (Bonn/ Leipzig, 1925–6).

Huber, *Dokumente*: Ernst Rudolf Huber (ed.), *Dokumente zur deutschen Verfassungsgeschichte*, 3 vols (Stuttgart, 1961 ff).

HZ: *Historische Zeitschrift*.

Keudell, *Fürst und Fürstin Bismarck*: Robert von Keudell, *Fürst und Fürstin Bismarck, Erinnerungen von 1846 bis 1872* (Berlin/Stuttgart, 1901).

Kohl, *Reden*: Horst Kohl (ed.), *Die politischen Reden des Fürsten Bismarck*, 13 vols (Stuttgart/Berlin, 1892–1905).

Lucius, *Bismarck-Erinnerungen*: Robert Lucius von Ballhausen, *Bismarck-Erinnerungen* (Stuttgart/Berlin, 1920).

Marcks, *Bismarcks Jugend*: Erich Marcks, *Bismarck. Eine Biographie*, Vol. 1: *Bismarcks Jugend 1815–1851* (Stuttgart/Berlin, 1909).

Nachlass Bismarck: Archives of the Bismarck family at Friedrichsruh.

Oncken, *Rheinpolitik*: Hermann Oncken (ed.), *Die Rheinpolitik Kaiser Napoleons III. und der Ursprung des Krieges von 1870/71. Nach den Staatsakten von Österreich, Preussen und den süddeutschen Mittelstaaten*, 3 vols (Stuttgart/Berlin/Leipzig, 1926).

Poschinger, *Wirtschaftspolitik*: Heinrich von Poschinger (ed.), *Aktenstücke zur Wirtschaftspolitik des Fürsten Bismarck*, 2 vols (Berlin, 1890–1).

Quellen zur deutschen Politik Österreichs: Heinrich von Srbik (ed.), *Quellen zur deutschen Politik Österreichs 1859–1866*, 5 vols (Munich/Berlin, 1934–8).

Roon, *Denkwürdigkeiten*: Albrecht von Roon, *Denkwürdigkeiten aus dem Leben des Generalfeldmarschalls Kriegsministers Grafen von Roon. Sammlung von Briefen, Schriftstücken und Erinnerungen*, 3 vols, 4th edn (Breslau, 1897).

Rothfels, *Bismarck und der Staat*: Hans Rothfels (ed.), *Bismarck und der Staat, Ausgewählte Dokumente*, 3rd edn (Darmstadt, 1958).

Rothfels, *Briefe*: Hans Rothfels (ed.), *Otto von Bismarck, Briefe* (Göttingen, 1955).

Schoeps, *Bismarck über Zeitgenossen*: Hans-Joachim Schoeps, *Bismarck über Zeitgenossen, Zeitgenossen über Bismarck* (Frankfurt/Berlin/Vienna, 1972).

Sempell, 'Unbekannte Briefstellen': Charlotte Sempell, 'Unbekannte Briefstellen Bismarcks', in *Historische Zeitschrift*, vol. 207 (1968), pp. 609–16.

Tagebuch der Baronin Spitzemberg: Rudolf Vierhaus (ed.), *Das Tagebuch der Baronin Spitzemberg geb. Freiin von Vernbüler, Aufzeichnungen aus der Hofgesellschaft des Hohenzollernreiches*, 4th edn (Göttingen, 1976).

Tiedemann, *Aus sieben Jahrzehnten*: Christoph von Tiedemann, *Aus sieben Jahrzehnten, Erinnerungen von Christoph von Tiedemann*, 2 vols (Leipzig, 1905/9).

Werke in Auswahl: Gustav Adolf Rein, Wilhelm Schüssler, Albert Milatz and Rudolf Buchner (eds), *Otto von Bismarck, Werke in Auswahl, Jahrhundert-Ausgabe zum 23 September 1862*, 8 vols (Darmstadt, 1962–80).

Introduction

1 G. F. W. Hegel, *Vorlesungen über die Philosophie der Weltgeschichte*, in J. Hoffmeister (ed.), *G. F. W. Hegel. Sämtliche Werke*, Vol. XVIII A, p. 90.

2 Speech of 17 May 1847: Kohl, *Reden*, Vol. 1, pp. 8 ff.

3 Letter to Johanna, 18 May 1847: GW, Vol. 14, p. 89.

4 Said in conversation with the journalist Friedrich Meyer on 11 August 1867: see GW, Vol. 7, p. 222.

5   One person to whom Bismarck spoke of politics as an 'art' was the editor of the *Hamburger Nachrichten*, Hermann Hofmann, in the 1890s: see GW, Vol. 9, p. 399.

Chapter 1: Between Two Worlds

1   GW, Vol. 14, p. 46.
2   On 22 September 1870: see Busch, *Tagebuchblätter*, Vol. 1, p. 229.
3   In conversation at table on 28 September 1870: see Busch, *Tagebuchblätter*, Vol. 1, p. 249.
4   Busch, *Tagebuchblätter*, Vol. 2, p. 23.
5   ibid., p. 426.
6   Letter to Wilhelm Harnisch, 16 February 1849: Rothfels, *Briefe*, p. 121.
7   Said in conversation with Robert von Keudell on 18 June 1864: Keudell, *Fürst und Fürstin Bismarck*, pp. 160 ff.
8   Nachlass Bismarck, A 1. In the *Collected Works* (GW, Vol. 14, pp. 65 ff.) the text of this letter was, like so much else, arbitrarily mutilated in the interests of 'cleaning up' Bismarck's image. As well as the sentence beginning 'As a little child . . .', quoted here, the following sentence is also missing: 'There is perhaps nowhere I have sinned more grievously than against my parents, but especially against my mother.' See Sempell, 'Unbekannte Briefstellen', pp. 609 ff.
9   GW, Vol. 15, p. 5.
10 For Goethe on Heeren, see *Tag- und Jahreshefte 1811*, in *Gesammelte Werke* (Sophienausgabe), Vol. 36, p. 71. The German titles of Heeren's books mentioned here are *Ideen über Politik, den Vekehr und den Handel der vornehmsten Völker der Alten Welt* (1793, 1796) and *Die Geschichte des europäischen Staatensystems und seiner Kolonien* (1809).
11 GW, Vol. 15, p. 6.
12 *Graf Alexander Keyserling, Ein Lebensbild aus seinen Briefen und Tagebüchern* (1902), pp. 542 f.
13 GW, Vol. 15, p. 6.
14 Letter to Gustav Scharlach, 18 June 1835: GW, Vol. 14, p. 6. 'Schulenburg' was a mutual acquaintance.
15 Bismarck's essays were published in *Bismarck-Jahrbuch*, Vol. 2, pp. 3 ff.
16 Letter of 21 October 1837: *Bismarck-Jahrbuch*, Vol. 3, p. 28.
17 Marcks, *Bismarcks Jugend*, p. 141.
18 Letter of 30 August 1837: GW, Vol. 14, pp. 8 f.
19 Letter of 7 September 1837: GW, Vol. 14, p. 9.
20 Letter to Gustav Scharlach, 13 September 1837: GW, Vol. 14, p. 11.
21 Letter of c. 6 December 1837: GW, Vol. 14, p. 11.
22 Letter to Scharlach, 9 January 1845: GW, Vol. 14, p. 30; 'rl' = *Reichstaler*.
23 Letter of 25 January 1835: GW, Vol. 14, p. 12.
24 Marcks, *Bismarcks Jugend*, pp. 153 f.
25 Letter of 7 April 1834: GW, Vol. 14, p. 4.
26 Letter to Gustav Scharlach, 14 November 1833: GW, Vol. 14, p. 3.
27 The copy for his father was enclosed with his letter of 29 September 1838: GW, Vol. 14, pp. 14 ff.
28 See Sempell, 'Unbekannte Briefstellen', p. 610. Charlotte Sempel gives only a selection of the excisions – mainly references to debts and love affairs – that the

editors of the *Collected Works* made throughout in a way that is quite indefensible in a work of scholarship; cf. note 8 above.

29 See the letter to Johanna of 13 December 1847; GW, Vol. 14, pp. 57 f.

30 Letter of 25 February 1855; see Appendix to *Gedanken und Erinnerungen*, Vol. 2 (1901 edition), p. 246.

31 Letter to his brother-in-law, Oskar von Arnim, 16 August 1861: GW, Vol. 14, p. 577.

32 GW, Vol. 14, p. 47.

33 Letter to Johanna, 13 February 1847: GW, Vol. 14, p. 58.

34 Letter to Johanna, 13 February 1847: Sempell, 'Unbekannte Briefstellen', p. 613. This passage too was suppressed by the editors of the *Collected Works*.

35 Letter to Gustav Scharlach, 9 January 1845: GW, Vol. 14, p. 31.

36 Letter to Johanna, 13 February 1847: Sempell, 'Unbekannte Briefstellen', p. 613 (another passage suppressed in the *Collected Works*).

37 Letter to Oskar von Arnim, 31 October 1843: GW, Vol. 14, p. 23.

38 Letter to Louis von Klitzing, 10 September 1843: GW, Vol. 14, p. 21.

39 Letter to Oskar von Arnim, 31 October 1843: GW, Vol. 14, p. 23.

40 Letter of 15 April 1844: Nachlass Bismarck, A 32.

41 Letter to Oskar von Arnim, 31 October 1843: GW, Vol. 14, p. 23.

42 Letter to Gustav Scharlach, 4 August 1844: GW, Vol. 14, p. 26.

43 Letter to Gustav Scharlach, 9 January 1845: GW, Vol. 14, p. 31.

44 Julius von Eckardt, *Lebenserinnerungen*, Vol. 2 (1910), p. 123.

45 Letter to Heinrich von Puttkamer, c. 21 December 1846: GW, Vol. 14, p. 47.

46 Letter from Marie von Thadden to Moritz von Blanckenburg, 7 February 1843: Marcks, *Bismarcks Jugend*, p. 244.

47 Letter to Heinrich von Puttkamer, c. 21 December 1846: GW, Vol. 14, p. 47.

48 Marcks, *Bismarcks Jugend*, pp. 244 f.

49 Letter to Heinrich von Puttkamer, c. 21 December 1846: GW, Vol. 14, p. 48.

50 Letter of 3 July 1851: GW, Vol. 14, p. 230.

51 Telegram of 28 July 1887: GW, Vol. 14, p. 975.

52 Telegram to his sister, 12 January 1847: GW, Vol. 14, p. 49; letter to his brother, 31 January 1847: GW, Vol. 14, p. 50.

53 Letter to Johanna, 4 January 1851: GW, Vol. 14, p. 187.

54 Letter of 17 February 1847: GW, Vol. 14, p. 60.

55 Said in conversation with Keudell and Abeken on 18 August 1865: Keudell, *Fürst und Fürstin Bismarck*, p. 221.

56 Quoted in A. O. Meyer, *Bismarcks Glaube. Nach neuen Quellen aus dem Familienarchiv*, 2nd edn (1933), p. 64.

57 Letter to Andrae, 26 December 1865: GW, Vol. 14, p. 709; written in answer to his letter of 24 December 1865: *Bismarck-Jahrbuch*, Vol. 3, pp. 213 ff.

58 GW, Vol. 14, p. 533.

59 Letter to Johanna, 20 July 1864: GW, Vol. 14, p. 672.

60 See A. O. Meyer, *Bismarcks Glaube. Nach neuen Quellen aus dem Familienarchiv*, 2nd edn (1933), p. 64.

61 On 28 September 1870: Busch, *Tagebuchblätter*, p. 247.

62 In conversation with Keudell on 31 May 1857: Keudell, *Fürst und Fürstin Bismarck*, p. 57.

63 Kohl, *Reden*, Vol. 1 pp. 21 ff.

64 Stenographic Reports (ed. Bleich), 1756.

65 Said to Christoff von Tiedemann on 7 May 1875: Tiedemann, *Aus sieben Jahrzehnten*, Vol. 2, p. 33.

Notes

Chapter 2: The Way into Politics

1 GW, Vol. 15, p. 15.
2 Drafts of the speeches can be found in Kohl, *Reden*, Vol. 14, pp. 4 ff. (hunting rights), and Marcks, *Bismarcks Jugend*, p. 475 (patrimonial jurisdiction).
3 *Denkwürdigkeiten aus dem Leben Leopold von Gerlachs*, Vol. 1 (Berlin, 1891), p. 150.
4 For a facsimile of Augusta's hand-written note, see E. Zechlin, *Bismarck und die Grundlegung der deutschen Grossmacht*, 2nd edn (Stuttgart, 1960), after p. 254.
5 In *Erinnerung und Gedanke*: GW, Vol. 15, pp. 29 f. He had already advanced this version in conversations with Hohenlohe on 24 October 1874: *Denkwürdigkeiten des Fürsten Chlodwig zu Hohenlohe-Schillingsfürst*, Vol. 2 (Stuttgart/Leipzig, 1907), pp. 135 f.; and with Tiedemann early in November 1877: Tiedemann, *Aus sieben Jahrzehnten*, Vol. 2, pp. 208 ff.
6 Quoted in H. Hofmann, *Fürst Bismarck 1890–1898* (Stuttgart, 1913), p. 184.
7 G. Küntzel, *Die politischen Testamente der Hohenzollern*, 2nd edn, Vol. 1 (1919), p. 104.
8 Kohn, *Reden*, Vol. 1, pp. 77 f.
9 Eyck, *Bismarck*, Vol. 1, p. 90.
10 Letter from Roon to his wife, 20 March 1848: Roon, *Denkwürdigkeiten*, Vol. 1, p. 142.
11 Speech on 2 April 1848: Kohl, *Reden*, Vol. 1, pp. 45 f.
12 Letter to Johanna, 26 May 1847: GW, Vol. 14, p. 91.
13 Letter to Ludwig von Gerlach, 7 July 1848: Rothfels, *Briefe*, p. 114.
14 Kohl, *Reden*, Vol. 1, pp. 53 ff.
15 Letter to Albert von Below, 12 April 1848: GW, Vol. 14, p. 105.
16 Kohl, *Reden*, Vol. 1, pp. 130 ff.
17 Schoeps, *Bismarck über Zeitgenossen*, p. 158.
18 GW, Vol. 1, pp. 1 f.
19 Letter to Hermann Wagener, 25 August 1848: GW, Vol. 14, pp. 111 f.
20 'Den Rücken gegen den Mist, die Front gegen den Feind – das ist adelig.' Ludwig von Gerlach, in a speech to the 'Junker Parliament' on 19 August 1848: Jakob von Gerlach (ed.), *Ernst Ludwig von Gerlach, Aufzeichnungen aus seinem Leben und Wirken 1795–1877* (Schwerin, 1903), Vol. 1, p. 541. What Gerlach meant was that they should concentrate less on their interests and more on their common ideals (he assumed their community of interests).
21 On 12 November 1848: ibid., Vol. 2, p. 27.
22 Letter to Johanna, 20 July 1849: GW, Vol. 14, p. 130.
23 R. Hübner (ed.), *J. G. Droysen, Historik*, 6th edn (1971), p. 291.
24 *Briefe zur Beförderung der Humanität*, 5. Sammlung (1795), Letter 57, Supplement, pp. 147 f.
25 Benjamin Constant, *De la liberté des anciens* . . .
26 In the *Mainzer Zeitung*, 9 June 1848.
27 GW, Vol. 14, pp. 105 f.
28 Probably in May 1863: GW, Vol. 4, p. 118.
29 Letter of 26 March 1861: GW, Vol. 14, p. 568.
30 Dictate of 9 November 1876: *Grosse Politik*, Vol. 2, p. 88.
31 Quoted in F. Meinecke, *Weltbürgertum und Nationalstaat* (1908), p. 361.
32 In conversation, 9 June 1848: GW, Vol. 7, p. 13.
33 Letter to Johanna, 2 March 1849: GW, Vol. 14, p. 125.
34 Letter to his brother Bernhard, 18 April 1849: GW, Vol. 14, p. 127. St Paul's

Church (the Paulskirche) in Frankfurt was the meeting-place of the short-lived Frankfurt National Assembly of 1848–9.

35 Kohl, *Reden*, Vol. 1, pp. 81 ff.

36 Speech of 21 April 1849: Kohl, *Reden*, Vol. 1, p. 92.

37 Letter from Frederick William IV to Baron von Bunsen: Huber, *Dokumente*, Vol. 1, p. 327.

38 Reply to the deputation from the German National Assembly, 3 April 1849: Huber, *Dokumente*, Vol. 1, p. 329.

39 GW, Vol. 15, p. 50.

40 Memorandum of 20 November 1847: J. M. von Radowitz, *Deutschland und Friedrich Wilhelm IV* (1848), pp. 39 ff.

41 Letter of 6 November 1851: H. Böhme (ed.), *Die Reichsgründung* (1967), p. 75.

42 Huber, *Dokumente*, Vol. 1, p. 291.

43 Letter to Gustav Scharlach, 4 July 1850: GW, Vol. 14, p. 161.

44 For Radowitz's 'Union plan', see P. Roth and H. Merck, *Quellensammlung zum deutschen öffentlichen Recht seit 1848* (1850–2), Vol. 2, pp. 573 ff.

45 Three Kings Alliance of 26 May 1849: Huber, *Dokumente*, Vol. 1, pp. 426 ff.

46 The articles, which appeared on 26 and 31 August 1849, were reprinted in *Bismarck-Jahrbuch*, Vol. 1, pp. 472 ff.

47 *Denkwürdigkeiten aus dem Leben Leopold von Gerlachs*, Vol. 1 (Berlin, 1891), p. 620.

48 Kohl, *Reden*, Vol. 1, pp. 103 ff.

49 Article in the *Kreuzzeitung*, 20 May 1849: Schoeps, *Bismarck über Zeitgenossen*, p. 171. Bismarck was punning on the word *Schwindel* as meaning both 'fraud' and 'vertigo'.

50 Lucius, *Bismarck-Erinnerungen*, p. 20.

51 K. F. Vitzthum von Eckstädt, *Berlin und Wien in den Jahren 1845–1852* (1886), p. 247.

52 Kohl, *Reden*, Vol. 1, pp. 235 ff.

53 Letter to Johanna, 29 September 1850: GW, Vol. 14, p. 164.

54 Letter to Hermann Wagener, 7 November 1850: GW, Vol. 14, p. 179.

55 Reprinted in *Bismarck-Jahrbuch*, Vol. 3, p. 414.

56 Manteuffel's speech is included in Kohl, *Reden*, Vol. 1, pp. 258 ff.

57 Speech of 3 December 1850: Kohl, *Reden*, Vol. 1, pp. 261 ff.

58 Article in the *Kreuzzeitung*, 19 November 1850: *Bismarck-Jahrbuch*, Vol. 3, p. 415.

59 Letter to Johanna, 14 March 1847: GW, Vol. 14, p. 79.

60 Said to Lucius on 14 April 1872: Lucius, *Bismarck-Erinnerungen*, p. 20.

61 GW, Vol. 15, p. 49.

62 Letter to Ludwig von Gerlach, 8 July 1850: *Werke in Auswahl*, Vol. 1, p. 308.

63 Letter to Ludwig von Gerlach, 6 September 1850: ibid., p. 309.

64 Letter to Johanna, 20 January 1851: GW, Vol. 14, p. 190.

65 Jakob von Gerlach (ed.), *Ernst Ludwig von Gerlach, Aufzeichnungen aus seinem Leben und Wirken 1795–1877*, Vol. 2 (Schwerin, 1903), p. 124.

66 Quoted in A. O. Meyer, *Bismarcks Kampf mit Österreich am Bundestag zu Frankfurt 1851–1859* (Berlin, 1927), p. 33.

67 GW, Vol. 14, p. 207.

68 GW, Vol. 14, p. 209.

69 Letter to Johanna, 28 April 1851: GW, Vol. 14, p. 206.

70 GW, Vol. 15, p. 58.

71 Letter to Johanna, 7 May 1851: GW, Vol. 14, p. 209.

72 See F. Salomon, *Die deutschen Parteiprogramme*, Vol. 1 (1912), p. 59.

Chapter 3: Reasons of State and International Politics: Envoy to the Federal Diet

1 Letter from Roon to Moritz von Blanckenburg, 16 January 1870: Roon, *Denkwürdigkeiten*, Vol. 3, p. 159.
2 In conversation with the Austrian historian, Heinrich Friedjung, on 13 June 1890: H. Friedjung, *Der Kampf um die Vorherrschaft in Deutschland 1859–1866*, Vol. 2 (1898), p. 521.
3 Letter to Leopold von Gerlach, 28 December 1851: GW, Vol. 14, p. 245.
4 Letter of 28 February 1855: GW, Vol. 2, p. 23.
5 Letter to Gerlach, 13 April 1854: GW, Vol. 14, p. 353.
6 Letter to Hermann Wagener, 5 June 1851: GW, Vol. 14, p. 237.
7 Letter to Johanna, 14 May 1851: GW, Vol. 14, p. 211. With that and with his salary they could 'live here, but in straitened circumstances'.
8 Thun's report of 21 September 1851: A. O. Meyer, *Bismarks Kampf mit Österreich am Bundestag zu Frankfurt 1851–1859* (Berlin, 1927), p. 44.
9 Quoted in E. von Wertheimer, *Bismarck im politischen Kampf* (Berlin, 1929), p. 34.
10 Letter from Rechberg to Count von Buol, 9 May 1955: ibid., p. 49.
11 Letter to Leopold von Gerlach, 19/20 December 1853: GW, Vol. 14, p. 334.
12 Letter of 5 May/23 April 1859: Rothfels, *Briefe*, p. 247.
13 ibid., pp. 266 f.
14 Jakob von Gerlach (ed.), *Ernst Ludwig von Gerlach, Aufzeichnungen aus seinem Leben und Wirken 1795–1877* (Schwerin, 1903), p. 148.
15 Letter to Leopold von Gerlach, 19 December 1857: GW, Vol. 14, p. 482.
16 Speech on 3 February 1866: Kohl, *Reden*, Vol. 3, p. 27.
17 Quoted in H. von Poschinger, *Fürst Bismarck und die Parlamentarier*, 2nd edn, Vol. 1 (1894), p. 87.
18 Letter to Leopold von Gerlach, 22 June 1851: GW, Vol. 14, p. 221.
19 Letter to Manteuffel, 12 March 1856: GW, Vol. 2, p. 133.
20 Letter to Leopold von Gerlach, 6 February 1852: GW, Vol. 14, p. 249.
21 Letter of 3 October 1851: GW, Vol. 1, p. 66.
22 Letter to Manteuffel, 9 October 1851: GW, Vol. 1, pp. 70 f.
23 Bismarck's conversation with Thun: GW, Vol. 1, pp. 104 f.
24 Report of 26 May 1851: GW, Vol. 1, p. 4.
25 Letter to Manteuffel, 16 February 1852: GW, Vol. 1, p. 250.
26 See H. von Poschinger (ed.), *Preussen im Bundestag 1851–1859, Dokumente der K. Preuss. Bundestags-Gesandtschaft*, 4 parts (1881–4).
27 In conversation with the editor Anton Memminger, 16 August 1890: GW, Vol. 9, pp. 93 f.
28 Speech on 20 March 1852: Kohl, *Reden*, Vol. 1, pp. 410 ff.
29 Letter from Frederick William IV to Francis Joseph, 5 June 1852: *Bismarck-Jahrbuch*, Vol. 6, pp. 51 f.
30 Letter to Albert, November 1847: J. Hansen, 'König Friedrich Wilhelm IV. und das liberale Märzministerium Camphausen-Hansemann 1848', in *Westdeutsche Zeitschrift für Geschichte und Kunst*, Vol. 32 (1913), p. 64.
31 Letter of 21 July 1852: GW, Vol. 1, p. 207.
32 loc. cit.
33 Letter to Leopold von Gerlach, 2 August 1852: GW, Vol. 14, p. 275. Christian von Haugwitz was Prussia's envoy in Vienna and subsequently Prussian Foreign Minister in the early years of the nineteenth century. His contradictory

policies led to Prussia's complete political isolation and eventually to the defeat of 1806.

34 *Erinnerung und Gedanke*, GW, Vol. 15, pp. 64 f.
35 By his conversation with Keudell, for example, on 31 May 1857: Keudell, *Fürst und Fürstin Bismarck*, p. 57.
36 Letter of 1 May 1853: GW, Vol. 14, p. 304.
37 Letter of 14 March 1858: GW, Vol. 2, pp. 297 f.
38 Letter of 6–7 April 1852: GW, Vol. 1, p. 155.
39 Letter of 4 December 1852: GW, Vol. 14, p. 283.
40 Letter to Leopold von Gerlach, 21 January 1853: GW, Vol. 14, p. 289. 'Old Fritz' was of course Frederick the Great.
41 O. Graf zu Stolberg-Wernigerode, *Robert Heinrich Graf von der Goltz* (1941), pp. 58 f.
42 GW, Vol. 1, p. 375.
43 Eyck, *Bismarck*, Vol. 1, p. 237.
44 GW, Vol. 1, p. 355.
45 Quoted in H. von Srbik, *Deutsche Einheit*, 3rd edn, Vol. 2 (1940), p. 230.
46 Letter from Pourtalès to Bethmann Hollweg, 16 October 1853: A. von Mutius, *Graf Albert Pourtalès* (1933), pp. 75 f.
47 Letter to Manteuffel, 15 February 1854: GW, Vol. 1, p. 427.
48 Letter to Leopold von Gerlach, 20 February 1854: GW, Vol. 14, p. 345.
49 *Aus den Briefen des Grafen Prokesch von Osten 1849–1855* (1896), p. 380.
50 Letter of 13 April 1854: GW, Vol. 14, p. 353.
51 Letter of 12 December 1854: GW, Vol. 14, p. 374.
52 GW, Vol. 15, p. 71.
53 Letter of 15 August 1854: GW, Vol. 14, p. 365.
54 Letter to Leopold von Gerlach, 11 February 1856: GW, Vol. 14, p. 432.
55 Memorandum of 26 April 1856, the 'Prachtbericht': GW, Vol. 2, pp. 138 ff.
56 Letter to his sister Malwine, 22 December 1853: GW, Vol. 14, p. 336.
57 Letter of 28 April 1856: GW, Vol. 14, p. 441.
58 Letter to Leopold von Gerlach, 19–20 December 1853: GW, Vol. 14, p. 334.
59 H. Kohl (ed.), *Briefe des Generals Leopold von Gerlach an Otto von Bismarck* (1912), pp. 211 f.

Chapter 4: In No-Man's-Land

1 Letter of 15 September 1855: GW, Vol. 14, p. 415.
2 Letter from Bismarck to Manteuffel, 29 April 1857: GW, Vol. 2, p. 208.
3 Letter of 29 April 1857: H. Kohl (ed.), *Briefe des Generals Leopold von Gerlach an Otto von Bismarck* (1912), p. 206.
4 Letter to Leopold von Gerlach, 2 May 1857: GW, Vol. 14, pp. 464 ff.
5 Letter to Leopold von Gerlach, 11 May 1857: GW, Vol. 14, p. 469.
6 Letter of 28 December 1851: GW, Vol. 14, p. 244.
7 Letter of 11 May 1857: GW, Vol. 14, p. 469.
8 Letter from Gerlach to Bismarck, 21 May 1857: H. Kohl (ed.), *Briefe des Generals Leopold von Gerlach an Otto von Bismarck* (1912), pp. 213 ff.
9 GW, Vol. 2, pp. 217 ff.
10 Letter of 30 May 1857: GW, Vol. 14, pp. 470 ff. Cf. the very similar memorandum of 2 June 1857: GW, Vol. 2, pp. 227 ff.
11 GW, Vol. 2, p. 229.

12 Letter of 5 May 1857: H. Kohl (ed.), *Briefe des Generals Leopold von Gerlach an Otto von Bismarck* (1912), pp. 216 ff.

13 GW, Vol. 2, p. 144.

14 Address to a deputation from Jena University, 30 July 1892: GW, Vol. 13, p. 468.

15 Letter to his brother Bernhard, 26 March 1855: GW, Vol. 14, p. 396.

16 Under secretary of state von Grüner to Bismarck, 28 February 1859: Supplement to *Gedanken und Erinnerungen*, Vol. 2 (1901), p. 286.

17 GW, Vol. 15, pp. 68, 80.

18 For the prince regent's speech on 8 November 1858, see E. Berner (ed.), *Kaiser Wilhelm des Grossen Briefe, Reden und Schriften*, Vol. 1 (1906), pp. 445 ff.

19 GW, Vol. 14, pp. 494 f.

20 *Denkwürdigkeiten des Fürsten Chlodwig zu Hohenlohe-Schillingsfürst*, Vol. 2 (Stuttgart/Leipzig, 1907), p. 119.

21 Letter to his sister Malwine, 12 November 1858: GW, Vol. 14, pp. 493 f.

22 Letter to his sister Malwine, 10 December 1858: GW, Vol. 14, p. 495.

23 F. Stern, *Gold and Iron: Bismarck, Bleichröder, and the Building of the German Empire* (London, 1977), p. 455.

24 Letter to Johanna, 28 March 1859: GW, Vol. 14, p. 507.

25 Rothfels, *Briefe*, p. 247.

26 Report of 12 May 1859: GW, Vol. 3, p. 36.

27 Letter to Gustav von Alvensleben, 17 June 1859: GW, Vol. 14, p. 527.

28 Foreign Office staff sarcastically dubbed it 'Mr. Bismarck's little book': GW, Vol. 2, pp. 302 ff.

29 E. Feder (ed.), *Bismarcks grosses Spiel, Die Geheimen Tagebücher Ludwig Bambergers* (Frankfurt, 1932), p. 323.

30 'Mignon der Prinzessin': GW, Vol. 15, p. 88.

31 Said to Poschinger, January 1893: GW, Vol. 9, p. 306.

32 Letter to his sister Malwine, 1 May 1859: GW, Vol. 14, p. 516.

33 Letter of 3 February 1860: GW, Vol. 14, p. 544.

34 For Unruh's conversation with Bismarck, see H. von Poschinger (ed.), *Erinnerungen aus dem Leben von Hans Victor von Unruh* (1895), pp. 207 ff.

35 Memorandum of March 1858: GW, Vol. 2, p. 317.

36 Letter of 30 November 1860: GW, Vol. 14, p. 565. He wrote in similar terms to a leading member of the Conservative Party, probably Alexander von Below-Hohendorf, on 22 August 1860: GW, Vol. 14, pp. 561 f.

37 GW, Vol. 14, p. 571.

38 Letter of 2 May 1857: GW, Vol. 14, p. 467.

39 Letter from Unruh to Bismarck, 12 September 1859: *Bismarck-Jahrbuch*, Vol. 4, p. 156.

40 Letter to Alexander von Below-Hohendorf, 3 April 1858: GW, Vol. 14, p. 487.

41 GW, Vol. 3, p. 38.

42 Letter to Schleinitz, 19 December 1859: GW, Vol. 3, p. 67.

43 Letter of 2–4 May 1860: GW, Vol. 14, p. 549.

44 Letter to Otto von Wentzel, 10 April 1860: GW, Vol. 14, p. 545.

45 Letter to Johanna, 17 May 1860: GW, Vol. 14, p. 551.

46 Letter to his sister Malwine, 26 March 1861: GW, Vol. 14, p. 567.

47 Letter of 2–4 May 1860: GW, Vol. 14, p. 550.

48 GW, Vol. 14, p. 553.

Chapter 5: *From Army Reform to Constitutional Conflict: Bismarck's Hour*

1 F. C. Dahlmann, *Die Politik, Auf den Grund und das Mass der gegebenen Zustände zurückgeführt* (1835; new edition 1924), p. 111.
2 GW, Vol. 15, p. 141.
3 In a speech in the House of Deputies on 15 September 1862: see Michael Gugel, *Industrieller Aufstieg und bürgerliche Herrschaft* (Cologne, 1975), p. 101.
4 Letter to Leopold von Gerlach, 11 May 1857: GW, Vol. 14, p. 469.
5 Letter of 2–4 May 1860: GW, Vol. 14, p. 549.
6 Letter from Roon to Bismarck, 27 June 1861: *Bismarck-Jahrbuch*, Vol. 6, pp. 194 ff.
7 Letter to Roon, 2 July 1861: GW, Vol. 14, pp. 570 ff.
8 GW, Vol. 3, pp. 266 ff. On the Baden-Baden Memorial, see H. Oncken, 'Die Baden-Badener Denkschrift Bismarcks über die deutsche Bundesreform (Juli 1861)', in HZ, Vol. 145 (1932), pp. 106 ff.
9 Letter from Roggenbach to Max Duncker, 25 August 1860: Duncker, *Politischer Briefwechsel*, p. 220.
10 Letter to Alexander von Below-Hohendorf, 18 September 1861: GW, Vol. 14, p. 578.
11 Ernst II, Duke of Sachsen-Coburg-Gotha, *Aus meinem Leben und aus meiner Zeit*, Vol. 2 (Berlin, 1888), p. 497.
12 Letter to his sister Malwine, 7 March 1862: GW, Vol. 14, p. 582.
13 Letter to his sister Malwine, 17 January 1862: GW, Vol. 14, p. 581.
14 Letter to his sister Malwine, 7 March 1862: GW, Vol. 14, p. 582.
15 Speech on 5 June 1861: Proceedings of the Prussian House of Deputies 1860–61, 3, 1865.
16 For the founding programme of the Progressive Party, 6 June 1861, see L. Parisius, *Leopold Freiherr von Hoverbeck*, Vol. 1 (1897), pp. 210 ff.
17 Letter from Frederick I of Baden to William I, 14 March 1862: H. Oncken (ed.), *Grossherzog Friedrich I. von Baden und die deutsche Politik*, Vol. 1 (1927), pp. 326 f.
18 Letter to K. Francke, 13 March 1862: Duncker, *Politischer Briefwechsel*, p. 324.
19 Letter to Gustav Lipke, 19 March 1862: Heyderhoff, *Liberalismus*, Vol. 1, p. 82.
20 Letter of 2 April 1862: H. Oncken (ed.), *Grossherzog Friedrich I. von Baden und die deutsche Politik*, Vol. 1 (1927), pp. 329 f.
21 loc. cit.
22 Letter of 13 July 1862: Heyderhoff, *Liberalismus*, Vol. 1, p. 105.
23 Letter to Albrecht von Roon, 2 July 1861: GW, Vol. 14, p. 571.
24 Letter to Perthes, 18 May 1862: Roon, *Denkwürdigkeiten*, Vol. 2, p. 84.
25 Letter to Johanna, 17 May 1862: GW, Vol. 14, p. 586.
26 E. C. Conte Corti, *Wenn . . . Sendung und Schicksal einer Kaiserin* (1954), p. 137.
27 GW, Vol. 14, p. 588.
28 GW, Vol. 14, pp. 589 f.
29 Letter of 26 June 1862: GW, Vol. 3, p. 381.
30 Letter to Bernstorff, 28 June 1862: GW, Vol. 3, pp. 382 f.
31 Report from London, 8 July 1862: GW, Vol. 3, pp. 384 ff.
32 Letter to Johanna, 5 July 1862: GW, Vol. 14, p. 599.
33 Said after Bismarck's farewell audience: Schoeps, *Bismarck über Zeitgenossen*, p. 67.
34 F. Graf Vitzthum von Eckstädt, *St. Petersburg und London*, Vol. 2 (1886), p. 158.

35 Letter of 15 July 1862: GW, Vol. 14, p. 600.
36 On Catherine Orlov, see Fürst Nikolai Orloff, *Bismarck und die Fürstin Orloff, Ein Idyll in der hohen Politik* (Berlin, 1936), which is also the source of the letters quoted here.
37 Letter from Roon to Bismarck, 31 August 1862: *Bismarck-Jahrbuch*, Vol. 3, pp. 273 f.
38 GW, Vol. 14, p. 619.
39 Letter to Bernstorff, 15 July 1862: GW, Vol. 3, pp. 388 ff.
40 Letter to Roon, 15 July 1862: GW, Vol. 14, pp. 600 ff.
41 Letter to Bernstorff, 24 August 1862: GW, Vol. 3, p. 397.
42 The *Sternzeitung* article was reprinted in *Die innere Politik der preussischen Regierung von 1862 bis 1866* (1866: official collection of documents), pp. 26 ff.
43 Kohl, *Reden*, Vol. 1, p. 313.
44 K. Ringhoffer, *Im Kampf um Preussens Ehre, Aus dem Nachlass des Grafen Albrecht von Bernstorff* (1906), pp. 533 ff.
45 On the Crown Council meeting of 17 September 1862, see E. Zechlin, *Bismarck und die Grundlegung der deutschen Grossmacht*, 2nd edn (Stuttgart, 1960), pp. 295 ff.
46 GW, Vol. 15, pp. 177 ff.
47 GW, Vol. 3, p. 399, n. 3.
48 H. O. Meisner (ed.), *Kaiser Friedrich III., Tagebücher von 1848–1866* (Leipzig, 1929), pp. 498 ff.
49 Letter to Queen Augusta, 23 September 1862: A. O. Meyer, *Bismarck*, 2nd edn (Stuttgart, 1949), p. 176.
50 GW, Vol. 15, p. 169.
51 Facsimile of Queen Augusta's verdict, in her own hand, in E. Zechlin, *Bismarck und die Grundlegung der deutschen Grossmacht*, 2nd edn (Stuttgart, 1960), after p. 254.
52 Duncker, *Politischer Briefwechsel*, pp. 334 f.
53 GW, Vol. 15, pp. 178 ff.
54 Keudell, *Fürst und Fürstin Bismarck*, p. 110.
55 GW, Vol. 14, p. 658.
56 Letter to William I, 26 September 1887: GW, Vol. 14. p. 977.
57 In conversation with the historian Erich Marcks on 17 March 1893: E. Marcks, *Männer und Zeiten*, 2nd edn, Vol. 2 (1916), p. 71.
58 Letter to Johanna, 20 July 1864: GW, Vol. 14, p. 672.

Chapter 6: 'Konfliktminister'

1 F. Oetker, *Lebenserinnerungen*, Vol. 3 (1885), p. 334.
2 Letter to Friedrich von Preen, 12 October 1871: F. Kaphahn (ed.), *Jacob Burckhardt, Briefe* (undated), p. 358.
3 F. Oetker, *Lebenserinnerungen*, Vol. 3 (1885), p. 336.
4 Letter to Manteuffel, 18–19 June 1852: GW, Vol. 1, p. 191.
5 On 24 September 1862: see Philippson, *Max von Forckenbeck, Ein Lebensbild* (1898), pp. 101 f.
6 On 29 September 1862: see O. Nirrnheim, *Das erste Jahr des Ministeriums Bismarck und die öffentliche Meinung* (1908), p. 65.
7 Issue of 26 September 1862: ibid., p. 61.
8 Issue of 3 October 1862.
9 Marginal note on a letter from Kleist-Retzow, 18 December 1862: H. von

Petersdorff (ed.), *Bismarcks Briefwechsel mit Hans Hugo von Kleist-Retzow* (Stuttgart, 1919), p. 56.

10 GW, Vol. 15, pp. 204 ff.

11 A. O. Meyer, *Bismarck*, 2nd edn (Stuttgart, 1949), p. 176.

12 Kohl, *Reden*, Vol. 2, p. 15.

13 *Berliner Allgemeine Zeitung*, 2 October 1862: Kohl, *Reden*, Vol. 2, p. 30.

14 See L. Parisius, *Leopold Freiherr von Hoverbeck* (1897), p. 211.

15 Kohl, *Reden*, Vol. 2, p. 31.

16 Letter of 29–30 September 1862: M. Cornicelius (ed.), *Heinrich von Treitschke, Briefe*, Vol. 2 (1918), p. 238.

17 Quoted by Bismarck himself: GW, Vol. 15, p. 194.

18 Heyderhoff, *Liberalismus*, Vol. 1, p. 118.

19 Letter from Frederick I of Baden to Charles Alexander of Sachsen-Weimar, 2 October 1862: H. Oncken (ed.), *Grossherzog Friedrich I. von Baden und die deutsche Politik*, Vol. 1 (1927), pp. 333 f.

20 GW, Vol. 15, pp. 193 ff.

21 See the letter from Rechberg to Károlyi, 10 July 1862: *Das Staatsarchiv*, Vol. 3 (1862), pp. 228 f.

22 On 2 October 1862: Kohl, *Reden*, Vol. 2, pp. 40 f.

23 *Aus dem Leben Theodor von Bernhardis*, Vol. 5 (Leipzig, 1898–1906), p. 7.

24 Talks with Károlyi on 4, 12, 18 and 26 December 1862: *Quellen zur deutschen Politik Österreichs*, Vol. 2, pp. 614 ff., for Károlyi's account; Bismarck gave his own account in a circular to the missions, 24 January 1863: GW, Vol. 4, pp. 40 ff.

25 Letter from Bismarck to Bernstorff/London, 21 November 1862 (concerning a conversation with the Austrian ambassador to Paris, Count Metternich): GW, Vol. 14, p. 628.

26 Keudell, *Fürst und Fürstin Bismarck*, p. 124.

27 The so-called 'Weihnachtsdenkschrift': GW, Vol. 4, pp. 29 ff.

28 H. von Poschinger, *Bismarck und die Diplomaten 1852–1890* (1900), p. 24.

29 Letter to Schleinitz, 13 March 1861: GW, Vol. 3, p. 190.

30 GW, Vol. 4, pp. 30 ff. Using the cancellation of the Customs Union as a policy instrument was mentioned by Bismarck as early as 3 March 1858, in a letter to Alexander von Below-Hohendorf: GW, Vol. 14, pp. 468 f.

31 Bismarck had mentioned his plan for a Customs Parliament in conversation with the Hessian liberal Friedrich Oetker on 15 October 1862: F. Oetker, *Lebenserinnerungen*, Vol. 3 (1885), pp. 334 ff.

32 Directive for Alvensleben, 1 February 1863: GW, Vol. 4, pp. 48 f.

33 Letter of 2 February 1863: *Werke in Auswahl*, Vol. 3, pp. 68 f.

34 GW, Vol. 15, p. 216.

35 Bismarck's account in the *Promemoria* of 11 February 1863: GW, Vol. 4, pp. 57 f.

36 Letter of 25 January 1863: F. Stern, *Gold and Iron* (London, 1977), p. 29.

37 In a speech on 17 September 1878: Kohl, *Reden*, Vol. 7, p. 258.

38 Keudell, *Fürst und Fürstin Bismarck*, pp. 175 ff.

39 See his speech to the House of Deputies on 15 February 1865: Kohl, *Reden*, Vol. 2, pp. 328 ff. See also the letters to Minister of Commerce von Itzenplitz, 26 January and 24 August 1865: Rothfels, *Bismarck und der Staat*, pp. 317 ff.

40 Kohl, *Reden*, Vol. 2, pp. 78 ff.

41 *Stenographische Berichte des preussischen Abgeordnetenhauses*, 1863, pp. 60 ff.

42 O. Nirrnheim, *Das erste Jahr des Ministeriums Bismarck und die öffentliche Meinung* (Heidelberg, 1908), p. 152.

43 Ferdinand Lassalle, *Über Verfassungswesen, Ein Vortrag* (1862).
44 Speech on 29 January 1863: Kohl, *Reden*, Vol. 2, p. 93.
45 Kohl, *Reden*, Vol. 2, p. 98.
46 Speech in the debate on the Polish question, 26 February 1863: Kohl, *Reden*, Vol. 2, pp. 125 ff.
47 Huber, *Dokumente*, Vol. 2, pp. 61 ff.
48 ibid., pp. 63 ff.
49 It is mentioned in Bismarck's letter to Senfft-Pilsach, written on 23 March 1863: GW, Vol. 14, p. 638.
50 Letter of 30 June 1863: Appendix to *Gedanken und Erinnerungen*, Vol. 2 (1901), pp. 350 f.
51 Huber, *Dokumente*, Vol. 2, p. 121.
52 Letter to Johanna, 12 August 1863: GW, Vol. 14, p. 650.
53 Quoted in Prince Kraft zu Hohenlohe-Ingelfingen, *Aus meinem Leben*, Vol. 2 (1905), p. 354.
54 Letter of 20 August 1863: Huber, *Dokumente*, Vol. 2, p. 122.
55 Austria's federal reform plan: H. Schultess, *Europäischer Geschichtskalender*, Vol. 4 (1863), pp. 47 ff.
56 GW, Vol. 15, p. 228.
57 GW, Vol. 4, pp. 166 ff.
58 Resolution of 16 October 1863: Huber, *Dokumente*, Vol. 2, p. 138.
59 *Wochenzeitschrift des Nationalvereins*, 3 October 1863.
60 Directive to Bernstorff, 8 October 1863: GW, Vol. 4, p. 178.
61 Issue of 22 October 1863.
62 Issue of 23 August 1863.

Chapter 7: The End or a New Beginning?

1 Issue of 24 April 1863.
2 Directive to von der Goltz/Paris, 17 February 1863: GW, Vol. 4, p. 62.
3 Said to Keudell on 30 November 1863: Keudell, *Fürst und Fürstin Bismarck*, p. 136.
4 Letter of 22 December 1862: GW, Vol. 4, pp. 27 f.
5 *Promemoria* of 3 February 1863: GW, Vol. 4, pp. 50 ff.
6 Letter to von der Goltz, 24 December 1863: GW, Vol. 14, p. 659.
7 Austrian-Prussian punctation of 16 January 1864: Huber, *Dokumente*, Vol. 2, pp. 165 ff.
8 GW, Vol. 14, p. 659.
9 Letter to William I, 1 December 1863: GW, Vol. 14, p. 658.
10 Said to Dr Cohen, 2 November 1880: GW, Vol. 8, p. 385.
11 Speech on 22 January 1864: Kohl, *Reden*, Vol. 2, pp. 285 ff.
12 Letter to Roon, 21 January 1864: GW, Vol. 14, p. 661.
13 Kohl, *Reden*, Vol. 2, p. 305.
14 *Stenographische Berichte des Preussischen Abgeordnetenhauses*, 1864, p. 821.
15 Kohl, *Reden*, Vol. 2, p. 278.
16 Letter from von der Goltz to Bismarck, 22 December 1863: *Bismarck-Jahrbuch*, Vol. 5, pp. 231 f. Only a fragment of the letter survives.
17 Letter from von der Goltz to Bismarck, 31 December 1863: Nachlass Bismarck, B 47, 26. An incomplete and undated version of the letter was printed in *Bismarck-Jahrbuch*, Vol. 5, pp. 238 ff.
18 GW, Vol. 14, pp. 658 ff.

19 Letter to Manteuffel, 15 February 1854: GW, Vol. 1, p. 427.
20 Directive to von Werther/Vienna, 21 May 1864: GW, Vol. 4, pp. 436 f.
21 In conversation with Keudell, 22 April 1864: Keudell, *Fürst und Fürstin Bismarck*, p. 154.
22 GW, Vol. 4, p. 436.
23 For Bismarck's note about the interview, written on 3 June 1864, see GW, Vol. 4, pp. 448 ff.; for Augustenburg's report of 2 June 1864, see K. Jansen and K. Samwer, *Schleswig-Holsteins Befreiung* (1897), pp. 731 ff.
24 GW, Vol. 4, p. 450.
25 GW, Vol. 4, pp. 461 ff.
26 GW, Vol. 4, pp. 464 ff.
27 Letter to Johanna, 23 June 1864: GW, Vol. 14, p. 669.
28 Letters to Roon and Thile, 16 October 1864: GW, Vol. 14, pp. 683 f.
29 Letter of 27 August 1864: GW, Vol. 4, p. 545.
30 GW, Vol. 4, p. 554.
31 GW, Vol. 4, p. 562.
32 *Quellen zur deutschen Politik Österreichs*, Vol. 4, p. 348.
33 ibid., p. 349.
34 GW, Vol. 4, p. 570.
35 *Die auswärtige Politik Preussens*, Vol. 6, pp. 174 ff.
36 *Stenographische Berichte des preussischen Abgeordnetenhauses*, 1865, p. 62.
37 In a letter to Bismarck, 25 January 1865: Nachlass Bismarck, B 125. The king was critical of the attitude of the whole ministry in a further letter to Bismarck, 18 March 1865: loc. cit.
38 Letter to Roon, 3 June 1865: *Kaiser Wilhelms des Grossen Briefe, Reden und Schriften*, Vol. 2 (1906), p. 106.
39 Kohl, *Reden*, Vol. 2, pp. 371 ff.
40 On the Cabinet meeting of 19 June 1865, see A. Stern, *Geschichte Europas seit den Verträgen von 1815 bis zum Frankfurter Frieden von 1871*, Vol. 9 (Stuttgart, 1923), p. 587.
41 Directive to Werther/Vienna, 22 February 1865: GW, Vol. 5, pp. 96 ff.
42 Letter of 15 September 1865: appended to *Gedanken und Erinnerungen*, Vol. 1 (1901), p. 121.
43 Letter to Queen Augusta, 31 October 1865: Graf zu Stolberg-Wernigerode, *Robert Heinrich Graf von der Goltz* (1941), p. 418.
44 On 20 February 1865: Keudell, *Fürst und Fürstin Bismarck*, p. 187.

Chapter 8: 1866

1 As reported in his letter to Manteuffel, late November 1851: GW, Vol. 1, p. 105.
2 Telegram to Edwin von Manteuffel, 11 August 1866: GW, Vol. 6, p. 120.
3 Reply to Napoleon, 1 September 1865: GW, Vol. 5, pp. 286 ff.
4 Letter of 11 September 1865: GW, Vol. 5, p. 293.
5 Said to Keudell on 21 September 1865: Keudell, *Fürst und Fürstin Bismarck*, pp. 227 ff. Würzburg had been the seat of the conference of the small and medium-sized German states – the so-called 'Third Germany'. Black, red and gold were the colours of the German 'tricolore' of 1848.
6 O. Graf zu Stolberg-Wernigerode, 'Ein unbekanntes Bismarck-Gespräch aus dem Jahre 1865', in HZ, Vol. 195 (1962), p. 361.
7 *Quellen zur deutschen Politik Österreichs*, Vol. 5, p. 203.
8 Directive to Werther/Vienna, 26 January 1866: GW, Vol. 5, pp. 365 ff.

9   *Quellen zur deutschen Politik Österreichs*, Vol. 5, pp. 202 ff.

10 Directive to Károlyi/Berlin, 1 March 1866: *Quellen zur deutschen Politik Österreichs*, Vol. 5, p. 233.

11 *Die auswärtige Politik Preussens*, Vol. 6, pp. 611 ff.

12 GW, Vol. 7, p. 123.

13 Letter of 28 September 1865: Heyderhoff, *Liberalismus*, Vol. 1, p. 254.

14 Letter to Alexander von Below-Hohendorf, 18 September 1861: GW, Vol. 14, p. 578.

15 Letter of 2 July 1861: GW, Vol. 14, p. 571.

16 Letter from the crown prince to Schweinitz, 30 November 1865: W. von Schweinitz (ed.), *Briefwechsel des Botschafters General von Schweinitz 1859–1891* (Berlin, 1928), pp. 20 f.

17 Said in conversation with the English writer Sidney Whitman on 3 April 1895: GW, Vol. 9, p. 420.

18 Huber, *Dokumente*, Vol. 2, pp. 190 f.

19 Oncken, *Rheinpolitik*, Vol. 1, pp. 265 f.; supplementary note, p. 267.

20 Duke of Gramont to Drouyn de Lhuys, 12 June 1866: Oncken, *Rheinpolitik*, Vol. 1, p. 268.

21 Speech in the House of Deputies on 3 February 1866: Kohl, *Reden*, Vol. 3, p. 27.

22 Huber, *Dokumente*, Vol. 2, pp. 191 ff.

23 Said to Ernst von Coburg-Gotha on 26 March 1866: H. O. Meisner (ed.), *Kaiser Friedrich III., Tagebücher von 1848 bis 1866* (Leipzig, 1929), pp. 545 f.

24 Directive to Reuss/Munich, 24 March 1866: GW, Vol. 5, p. 421.

25 *Werke in Auswahl*, Vol. 3, p. 692.

26 Letter to Alexander von Below-Hohendorf, 22 February 1854: *Werke in Auswahl*, Vol. 2, p. 7.

27 Kohl, *Reden*, Vol. 3, p. 27.

28 GW, Vol. 5, p. 381.

29 Wilhelm von Schweinitz (ed.), *Denkwürdigkeiten des Botschafters General von Schweinitz*, Vol. 1 (Berlin, 1927), p. 195.

30 Issue of 10 May 1866: O. Bandmann, *Die deutsche Presse und die Entwicklung der Deutschen Frage 1864–1866* (1910), p. 176.

31 Letter to Hermann Baumgarten, 14 May 1866: Heyderhoff, *Liberalismus*, Vol. 1, p. 284.

32 Keudell, *Fürst und Fürstin Bismarck*, p. 261.

33 Telegram to Redern/St Petersburg, 7 May 1866: GW, Vol. 5, pp. 490 f.

34 J. Vilbort, *L'Oeuvre de M. de Bismarck 1863–1869, Sadowa et la campagne de sept jours* (1869): GW, Vol. 7, p. 120.

35 Schultess, *Europäischer Geschichtskalender* (1868), p. 427, and La Marmora, *Un po' più di luce* (1873).

36 Usedom's telegram is reprinted in Huber, *Dokumente*, Vol. 2, pp. 208 ff.

37 GW, Vol. 5, pp. 524 ff.

38 Huber, *Dokumente*, Vol. 2, p. 204.

39 ibid., pp. 206 f.

40 Address to the committee of the Kiel Conservative Union, 14 April 1891: GW, Vol. 13, p. 421.

41 Circular to the missions, 27 May 1866: GW, Vol. 5, p. 514.

42 In conversation with the English writer Sidney Whitman, mid-October 1891: GW, Vol. 9, p. 157.

43 GW, Vol. 14, p. 717.

44 In conversation with Abeken and Keudell on 5 July 1866: Keudell, *Fürst und Fürstin Bismarck*, p. 295.

Chapter 9: 'Revolution from Above'

1   Direct report of 24 July 1866: GW, Vol. 6, p. 81.
2   The concessions were in article V (Schleswig) and article IV ('international independence'): Huber, *Dokumente*, Vol. 2, p. 218.
3   Said to Johannes Miquel, late May 1866: GW, Vol. 7, p. 119.
4   Letter to his brother Tycho, 18 July 1866: A. Wucher, *Theodor Mommsen, Geschichtsschreibung und Politik* (1956), p. 68.
5   Kohl, *Reden*, Vol. 3, pp. 48 ff.
6   Said by Twesten in a speech to the Prussian House of Deputies on 3 February 1866: *Stenographische Berichte* p. 79.
7   Said on 1 September 1866: ibid., p. 152.
8   Said on 2 September 1866: ibid., pp. 194 f.
9   *Krieg und Bundes-Reform* (volume publication 1870), p. 12.
10 Letter to Johanna, 3 August 1866: GW, Vol. 14, p. 720.
11 Letter to the Swiss politician Dubs, 23 June 1866: J. C. Bluntschli, *Denkwürdigkeiten aus meinem Leben*, Vol. 3 (1884), p. 160.
12 In a letter to G. Reimer, 1 December 1866: M. Cornicelius (ed.), *Heinrich von Treitschkes Briefe*, Vol. 3 (1920), p. 103, n. 1.
13 O. Regele, *Feldzugmeister Benedek, Der Weg nach Königgrätz* (1960), pp. 479 f.
14 Busch, *Tagebuchblätter*, Vol. 1, p. 568.
15 Quoted in E. Engelberg, 'Über die Revolution von oben', in *Zeitschrift für Geschichtswissenschaft*, Vol. 22 (1974), p. 1193.
16 Huber, *Dokumente*, Vol. 2, pp. 224 f.
17 GW, Vol. 6, pp. 167 ff. They appear in a more complete form in Keudell, *Fürst und Fürstin Bismarck*, pp. 311 ff.
18 Letter to Roon, 27 August 1869: GW, Vol. 6b, p. 134.
19 GW, Vol. 6, pp. 188 ff.
20 On 12 June 1882: Kohl, *Reden*, Vol. 9, p. 368.
21 Bismarck used the expression 'gewerbsmässige Parlamentarier' in conversation with the Saxon minister von Friesen early in January 1867: R. Freiherr von Friesen, *Erinnerungen*, Vol. 3 (1910), p. 10.
22 Quoted in O. Becker, *Bismarcks Ringen um Deutschlands Gestaltung* (Heidelberg, 1958), pp. 141 f.
23 Speech to the Prussian House of Deputies, 18 January 1869: Kohl, *Reden*, Vol. 4, p. 98.
24 Speech of 5 March 1878: ibid., Vol. 7, p. 156.
25 February 1869: *Bismarck-Jahrbuch*, Vol. 1, p. 80.
26 Kohl, *Reden*, Vol. 3, p. 247.
27 Quoted in K. Pollmann, 'Der Parlamentarismus im Norddeutschen Bund', lectureship thesis (Brunswick, 1978), p. 447.
28 Quoted in O. Becker, *Bismarcks Ringen um Deutschlands Gestaltung* (Heidelberg, 1958), p. 166.
29 Letter to Eulenburg, 17 January 1867: GW, Vol. 6, p. 238.
30 Said to the Saxon minister von Friesen early in January 1867: R. Freiherr von Friesen, *Erinnerungen*, Vol. 3 (1910), p. 11.
31 These two quotations from letters to Friedrich von Preen, 26 April 1872 and 20 July 1870: F. Kaphahn (ed.), *Jacob Burckhardt, Briefe* (undated), pp. 364, 345.

32 In a letter to Thile, 29 July 1867: GW, Vol. 14, p. 735.
33 Letter to Minister of Commerce von Itzenplitz, 2 February 1868: GW, Vol. 6a, pp. 229 f.
34 Quoted in Julius von Eckardt, *Lebenserinnerungen*, Vol. 1 (1901), p. 141.
35 Letter to Alexander von Below-Hohendorf, 25 February 1869: GW, Vol. 14, p. 749.
36 Directive to Usedom/Florence, 21 October 1867: GW, Vol. 6a, p. 86.
37 Speech on 24 May 1870: Kohl, *Reden*, Vol. 4, p. 375.
38 Speech on 15 January 1867: Kohl, *Reden*, Vol. 3, p. 118.
39 Directive to Werthern/Munich, 25 February 1869: GW, Vol. 6b, p. 2.
40 See Oncken, *Rheinpolitik*, Vol. 2, pp. 94 f.
41 Directive to von der Goltz/Paris, 8 January 1867: GW, Vol. 6, p. 223.
42 Letter to Catherine Orlov, 6 June 1867: Fürst Nikolai Orloff, *Bismarck und die Fürstin Orloff, Ein Idyll in der hohen Politik* (Berlin, 1936), p. 119.
43 Letter to Keudell, c. 6 or 7 July 1867: GW, Vol. 14, p. 729.
44 In a letter to Leopold von Gerlach, 18 December 1853: GW, Vol. 14, p. 332.
45 Quoted in H. Lutz, *Österreich-Ungarn und die Gründung des Deutschen Reiches* (1979), p. 75.
46 Said in December 1866: H. von Poschinger, *Fürst Bismarck und die Parlamentarier*, Vol. 2 (1896), p. 51.
47 *Die auswärtige Politik Preussens*, Vol. 9, p. 180.
48 *Les Origines diplomatiques de la guerre de 1870–1871, Recueil de documents publié par le Ministère des Affaires étrangères*, Vol. 18 (Paris, 1910–12), p. 195.
49 A. Loftus, *Diplomatic Reminiscences 1862–1879*, Vol. 1 (1894), p. 193.
50 In a speech on 11 March 1867: Kohl, *Reden*, Vol. 3, pp. 168 ff. (specifically pp. 180 f.).
51 L. Bamberger, *Politische Schriften von 1848 bis 1868* (Berlin, 1895), p. 331.
52 In a speech on 24 February 1870: Kohl, *Reden*, Vol. 4, pp. 305 ff.
53 Directive of 26 February 1869: GW, Vol. 6b, p. 2.
54 Letter of 21 July 1869: GW, Vol. 14, p. 752.
55 Dictate for William I, 20 November 1869: GW, Vol. 6b, p. 166.
56 In conversation with the historian Heinrich Friedjung on 13 June 1890: H. Friedjung, *Der Kampf um die Vorherrschaft in Deutschland 1859–1866*, Vol. 2 (1898), p. 522.
57 H. von Srbik, *Deutsche Einheit: Idee und Wirklichkeit vom Heiligen Reich bis Königgrätz*, Vol. 4 (Munich, 1942), p. 462.
58 Dated 3 October 1868: GW, Vol. 6a, p. 412.
59 GW, Vol. 6b, pp. 271 ff.
60 Letter of 13 May 1870: GW, Vol. 14, p. 776.
61 Letter to Charles Anthony, 28 May 1870: GW, Vol. 6b, pp. 324 f.
62 GW, Vol. 6b, p. 332.
63 Letter to Charles Anthony, 6 June 1870: J. Dittrich, *Bismarck, Frankreich und die spanische Thronkandidatur der Hohenzollern, Die 'Kriegsschuldfrage' von 1870* (Munich, 1962), p. 406.
64 R. H. Lord, *The Origins of the War of 1870* (Cambridge, Mass., 1924), p. 121.
65 Oncken, *Rheinpolitik*, Vol. 3, pp. 396 f.
66 GW, Vol. 15, pp. 301 ff.
67 GW, Vol. 6b, pp. 368 ff.
68 To Keudell on 6 September 1870: Keudell, *Fürst und Fürstin Bismarck*, p. 457.
69 GW, Vol. 6b, p. 455.
70 'Genie des Gegenwärtigen': K. Scheffler, *Bismarck* (1919), p. 25.
71 Letter to Johanna, 28–9 October 1870: GW, Vol. 14, p. 797.

72   *Tagebücher des Generalfeldmarschalls Graf von Blumenthal aus den Jahren 1866 und 1870–1871* (1902), p. 161.
73   Letter to Johanna, 12 September 1870: GW, Vol. 14, p. 792.
74   P. Rassow (ed.), *Paul Bronsart von Schellendorf, Geheimes Kriegstagebuch 1870–1871* (1954), p. 311.
75   Quoted in O. Nirrnheim, *Das erste Jahr des Ministeriums Bismarck und die öffentliche Meinung* (1908), p. 65.
76   In a speech to the constituent Imperial Diet of the North German Confederation on 11 March 1867: Kohl, *Reden*, Vol. 3, p. 184.
77   Directive to Schweinitz/Vienna, 12 February 1870: GW, Vol. 6b, p. 241.
78   Ed. Stolze, *Preussische Jahrbücher*, July 1924, pp. 3 ff.
79   Busch, *Tagebuchblätter*, Vol. 1, p. 427.
80   Letter of 2 February 1871: M. Doeberl, *Bayern und die Bismarcksche Reichsgründung* (1925), pp. 174 f.
81   Said in conversation at table on 28 September 1870: Busch, *Tagebuchblätter*, Vol. 1, p. 248.
82   GW, Vol. 14, p. 810.
83   Letter of 22 November 1870: GW, Vol. 14, p. 800.
84   Busch, *Tagebuchblätter*, Vol. 1, pp. 465 f.
85   GW, Vol. 14, p. 816.

INDEX OF NAMES